A Long Dark Night

A Long Dark Night

Race in America from Jim Crow to World War II

J. Michael Martinez

ROWMAN & LITTLEFIELD
Lanham • Boulder • New York • London

Published by Rowman & Littlefield
A wholly owned subsidiary of The Rowman & Littlefield Publishing Group, Inc.
4501 Forbes Boulevard, Suite 200, Lanham, Maryland 20706
www.rowman.com

Unit A, Whitacre Mews, 26-34 Stannary Street, London SE11 4AB

British Library Cataloguing in Publication Information Available

Library of Congress Cataloging-in-Publication Data
Names: Martinez, J. Michael (James Michael), author.
Title: A long dark night : race in America from Jim Crow to World War II / J. Michael Martinez.
Description: Lanham : Rowman & Littlefield, 2016. | Includes bibliographical references and index.
Identifiers: LCCN 2015035504| ISBN 9781442259942 (cloth : alk. paper) | ISBN 9781442259966 (electronic)
Subjects: LCSH: United States—Race relations—History. | Southern States—Race relations—History. | African Americans—History—1877-1964. | Racism—United States—History. | Racism—Southern States—History.
Classification: LCC E185.61 .M364 2016 | DDC 305.800973—dc23 LC record available at http://lccn.loc.gov/2015035504

Printed in the United States of America

This book is for my beautiful granddaughter, Emma Kay Lynne Woodson, in hopes that she will live in a nation where she is judged not by the color of her skin, but by the content of her character

I was broken in body, soul, and spirit. My natural elasticity was crushed, my intellect languished, the disposition to read departed; the cheerful spark that lingered about my eye died; the dark night of slavery closed in upon me; and behold a man transformed into a brute!

—Frederick Douglass, *Narrative of the Life of Frederick Douglass, an American Slave*

The people that walked in darkness have seen a great light: they that dwell in the land of the shadow of death, upon them hath the light shined.

—Isaiah 9:2

> He's gone on high to prepare a place
> Trouble done bore me down
> For to prepare a place for me and you
> Trouble done bore me down. . . .
> I've seen some strangers quite unknown
> I'm a child of misery
> I'm sometimes up and sometimes down
> I'm sometimes level with the ground

—"Trouble Done Bore Me Down," Negro Spiritual

Contents

List of Photographs   xi

Introduction and Acknowledgments   1

Prologue: Race in America: "There Is Not a Black America and a White America and Latino America and Asian America"   5

PART I   A Child of Misery

1   The Legacy of Reconstruction   21

2   Jumpin' Jim Crow and Legal Segregation   47

3   Racial Violence and the Plight of the Freedmen   70

PART II   I'm Sometimes Up and Sometimes Down

4   The Rise of the Populist Movement   105

5   Southern Populism   123

6   Washington versus Du Bois   154

PART III   He's Gone on High to Prepare a Place

7   The Great Migration   177

8   A Nadir of Race Relations   194

9   The Rise of a New Black Culture   239

10   Southern Justice, a Depression, and a War   260

     Epilogue: The Postwar American Landscape: "White
     Prejudice and Negro Standards Thus Mutually 'Cause' Each
     Other"   303

Notes   315

References   359

Index   399

About the Author   423

List of Photographs

1.1   A Thomas Nast cartoon of Jefferson Davis as
      Shakespeare's Iago   43
2.1   The iconic black leader Frederick Douglass   49
2.2   An early illustration of the Jim Crow character   52
2.3   Associate Supreme Court Justice John Marshall Harlan   65
3.1   Three Klansmen garbed in Ku Klux Klan regalia   76
3.2   A scene from the Tulsa race riot of 1921   98
3.3   Two lynching victims, Thomas Shipp and Abram Smith,
      1930   101
4.1   Perennial presidential candidate William Jennings Bryan 117
5.1   Georgia politician Tom Watson   130
5.2   Atlanta newspaperman Henry Grady   133
5.3   South Carolina politician "Pitchfork Ben" Tillman   139
5.4   South Carolina politician Coleman Blease   141
5.5   South Carolina Senator "Cotton Ed" Smith   148
6.1   Booker T. Washington, a proponent of
      "accommodationist" race relations   160
6.2   W. E. B. Du Bois, a critic of Washington's
      "accommodationist" views   168
7.1   A famous Jacob Lawrence image of the Great Migration   179
8.1   A scene from the Currier and Ives series *Darktown Comics* 198
8.2   The Gold Dust Twins, "Goldie" and "Dustie," circa 1890 203
8.3   A 1916 magazine supplement advertising Cream of Wheat
      and featuring Rastus   205
8.4   A 1921 image by N. C. Wyeth showing Aunt Jemima   208
8.5   A scene from the film *The Birth of a Nation* showing the Ku
      Klux Klan with the evil Negro Gus   218

8.6   Ku Klux Klan founder William Joseph "Doc" Simmons in
       1921   230
8.7   Ku Klux Klan imperial wizard Hiram Wesley Evans   234
9.1   Langston Hughes, a leading voice of the Harlem
       Renaissance, in 1943   248
9.2   Jamaican entrepreneur and political activist Marcus
       Garvey   257
10.1   President Warren G. Harding   268
10.2   U.S. senators Tom Connally of Texas; Walter F. George of
       Georgia; Richard B. Russell of Georgia; and Claude Pepper
       of Florida shown on January 27, 1938   273
10.3   The Tuskegee Airmen receiving a briefing in March 1945   298
E.1   A black student, George W. McLaurin, attends a
       segregated class at the University of Oklahoma in 1948   310
E.2   President Harry S. Truman after addressing the closing
       session of the 38th annual conference of the NAACP at the
       Lincoln Memorial in Washington, D.C., on June 29, 1947   312

Introduction and Acknowledgments

In 2012, I published a book titled *Coming for to Carry Me Home: Race in America from Abolitionism to Jim Crow*. As I mentioned in the preface to that book, the project started as a reexamination of President Abraham Lincoln's troubled relationship with the Radical Republicans in Congress and evolved into a broader discussion of the politics of race from the 1830s, when the abolitionists rose to prominence, until the 1880s, when southern states enacted segregation statutes following the end of Reconstruction.

As I completed that work, I felt that I had only told part of the story. Much more needed to be said, particularly about that dark period in American history between the advent of the Jim Crow regime in the 1880s and the dawn of the World War II era in the 1940s, a time immediately preceding the rise of the modern civil rights movement during the 1950s and 1960s. This book represents my attempt to finish telling the story. In some ways, therefore, *A Long Dark Night* stands as a sequel to *Coming for to Carry Me Home*. The two books need not be read in tandem, but they do represent my perspective on how the politics and history of race changed in the United States from the 1830s through the 1940s.

Let me acknowledge at the outset that this book is not a groundbreaking work of heretofore undiscovered archival research. While I strongly admire scholars who can dig through previously unknown or neglected records to unearth nuggets of new information, such efforts usually lend themselves to studies focusing on minute aspects of a larger topic. My intent here is to provide a broad overview of many issues that influenced the politics and history of race in the United States across seven decades of history. Rather than exhaustively delving into the details of each subject—a task that would require a fourteen-hundred-plus-page tome in the grand tradition of Gunnar Myrdal's 1944 classic *An American Dilemma*—I provide a synthesis of the crucial activities and events related to race in the United States from the 1880s through the 1940s, painting with a broad brush and recognizing that not every issue can be covered in depth. Setting aside all false modesty, I discovered early in my career a gift (and perhaps I am merely self-deluded here) for digesting large volumes of complex data and distilling the information into an easily understood narrative suitable for advanced college undergraduates and graduate students interested in the topic. If scholars in the field discover useful insight or analysis, so much the better, but they are not the target audience.[1]

Notice that although the book professes to be about race in America, it focuses on blacks and whites. Asians, Native Americans, Latinos, and persons of other races and ethnicities are not discussed at any length. Much has been written about these subjects, and they would be fine topics for a tome on the tortured history of race in the United States. Nonetheless, the publisher and I agreed that this book must be of manageable length and should remain accessible to the general reader. An exhaustive history of race has its place in the literature, but this book was ambitious enough without tackling every aspect of the issue.

In producing a work on the history of the black-white "problem" in the American republic, I am painfully aware of the criticism sometimes leveled at scholars who have not "lived" the reality of racial bias. Myrdal was castigated for adopting a paternalistic tone in his work, suggesting that black people were passive receptors of oppression. Such unconscious prejudice may become an occupational hazard whenever a writer existing apart from a phenomenon describes causes and effects related to the phenomenon. Perhaps an outsider's perspective can provide a much needed measure of objectivity and thereby compensate for any presumed myopia.

One more point deserves mention here. Certain terms appear frequently throughout the text. In the late nineteenth and early twentieth centuries, it was customary to identify dark-skinned Americans as "colored." In time, "Negro" became the preferred term. Beginning in the 1960s, "black" and "African American" became commonplace. This book uses all of these terms as synonyms, generally when discussing the times and places when such terms were used as matters of custom. Yet, even today, these labels are contested because, for some folks, they do not accurately reflect the subjects being described. The term "African American," for example, has become objectionable in some quarters because not all persons of color can directly or indirectly trace their lineage to the continent of Africa. The point is well taken. In short, all descriptions of pigmentation used at different times and in different contexts have been criticized because, in the final analysis, they objectify the subjective persons under discussion, and this objectification of the "other" as alien and undesirable is what ultimately makes many racial characterizations offensive and hurtful.

Ah, if only we lived in a world where race did not matter. I write this pie-in-the-sky abstraction as a white man bearing a Latino surname who is rearing two mixed-race grandchildren ("mulattoes," in the now offensive parlance of an earlier age), a man who fears for their future in a nation where citizens continually insist that race no longer matters despite ugly reminders of racial bias in common discourse and national political life. Alas, because a conversation about race, specifically the history of race, necessitates the use of common terms describing race, labels cannot be avoided, even if they offend sensitive readers. In any event, the most offensive word used to describe persons of color—"nigger"—is never used in these pages unless it is part of a direct quotation and also underscores a point made in the text. Perhaps one day we will not need to use any terms to describe skin color, but that day has not yet dawned.

This book is the product of more than three years of planning, research, and writing, and I would be remiss if I did not thank the many wonderful people who helped me along the way. First and foremost, I appreciate the assistance I received from the kind folks at Rowman & Littlefield, especially Jonathan Sisk, vice president and senior executive editor, Elaine McGarraugh, senior production editor, and Natalie Mandziuk, assistant acquisitions editor.

Several archivists and researchers provided invaluable assistance, most notably Kimberly David at the Library of Congress, Todd Ifft from Photofest, and Sarah Steele, deputy director of the Granger Collection. The interlibrary loan staff at the Horace W. Sturgis Library, Kennesaw State University, proved to be extremely helpful. I also appreciate the marketing assistance I received from Liz Kula of webdesignsbyliz.com. Liz created my website at www.jmichaelmartinez.com and kept it updated. Colleagues at Dart Container Corporation and Kennesaw State University were encouraging and helpful too.

As always, my family and friends have been incredibly supportive. In alphabetical order, I extend thanks to the late Charles DuBose and his wife, Glenda; Shirley Hardrick, housekeeper and babysitter extraordinaire; Wallace and Leila Jordan; Laura Mead and her children; Phil and Carolyn Mead and their children; Martha and Dick Pickett; Gus and Bonnie Poindexter; Dr. William D. Richardson, my mentor who now chairs the political science department at the University of South Dakota; Chuck Redmon, an outstanding friend and colleague; Keith W. Smith, a friend of thirty-plus years extending back to our law school days at Emory University; Barbara Wise and her children and grandchildren; and Bob and Peggy Youngblood. I now have six grandchildren—Brianna Marie Carter, Aswad Elisha "Ellie" Woodson, Christopher Kainan Carter, Skylar Renee Carter, Emma Kay Lynne Woodson, and Nero Blake Carter—and they are always a delight. Thanks also to family members who are fellow writers—Chris Mead (cousin), Loren B. Mead (uncle), Walter Russell Mead (cousin), Robert Sidney Mellette (cousin), William W. Mellette (uncle), and Jim Wise (cousin). They set the bar high.

Needless to say (but I will say it anyway), all errors or omissions in fact or interpretation are my responsibility alone.

Prologue

Race in America: "There Is Not a Black America and a White America and Latino America and Asian America"

Barack Obama's election as the forty-fourth president of the United States was heralded by some pundits as marking a new era in American history, a postracial epoch when individuals would be judged not by the color of their skin but by the content of their character, as Martin Luther King Jr. once dreamed. Obama himself contributed to the rhetoric of a new, more inclusive age when he delivered the keynote address at the Democratic National Convention in Boston, Massachusetts, on July 27, 2004. During a seventeen-minute address that established his reputation as a rising star in the political world, the previously little-known, mixed-race Illinois state legislator exclaimed, "There is not a Black America and a White America and Latino America and Asian America—there's the United States of America."[1]

Obama's comment would have been hopelessly naive throughout most of American history, but the United States at the dawn of the twenty-first century had changed tremendously in a relatively short time. Four decades before Obama arrived so dramatically on the American political scene, Congress passed and President Lyndon B. Johnson signed the Civil Rights Act of 1964, followed a year later by the Voting Rights Act. With these historic laws aimed at reversing the disenfranchisement of people of color—and thanks also to the efforts of black and white civil rights activists and a slew of US Supreme Court opinions, as well as ratification

5

of the Twenty-Fourth Amendment abolishing the poll tax—the Jim Crow regime finally collapsed and died. Black and white citizens' willingness to modify their attitudes about race lagged behind enactment of the two landmark federal statutes and the other remarkable developments in law and policy, but eventually, as new generations replaced their parents and grandparents, change occurred in all avenues of American life.[2]

Unencumbered by the shackles of legal segregation, blacks became visible to white Americans and excelled in all fields of human endeavor. Jackie Robinson integrated American baseball when he moved from the Negro Leagues to play for the Brooklyn Dodgers in 1947. Althea Gibson broke the color line in international tennis during the 1950s. Movie star Sidney Poitier earned an Academy Award as best actor for his work in the 1963 film *Lilies of the Field*. Harry Belafonte, singer, actor, and social activist, received praise for his skills as an entertainer and his willingness to support civil rights. Paul Robeson was another renowned singer, actor, and civil rights activist of the period, albeit far more controversial than Belafonte. James Baldwin won acclaim as one of the most prominent black writers of his generation, and he also became an iconic figure for gays and bisexuals. Cassius Clay, later known as Muhammad Ali, won fame as a legendary boxer and showman. Bill Cosby emerged as a beloved comedian and actor (although later in his career, his reputation suffered when numerous women claimed he had sexually abused them). The list of famous black public figures is long—Lena Horne, Lorraine Hansberry, Richard Pryor, Redd Foxx, Eddie Murphy, Billy Dee Williams, Bessie Smith, Scott Joplin, Mahalia Jackson, Billie Holiday, Nina Simone, Aretha Franklin, Diana Ross, Dionne Warwick, Michael Jackson, Prince, Michael Jordan, Maya Angelou, Toni Morrison, Alice Walker, Tiger Woods—and the names go on and on almost ad infinitum.[3]

In politics, before Barack Obama's triumph, Adam Clayton Powell Jr. represented a congressional district that included Harlem in the US House of Representatives for more than a quarter century, beginning in 1945. Charlie Rangel, Powell's successor, took his seat in the US House of Representatives in 1971 and became one of the longest-serving members of Congress. He also served as chairman of the influential House Ways and Means Committee and cofounded the Congressional Black Caucus. Republican Edward Brooke was elected to the US Senate from Massachusetts in 1966, the only black member of that chamber in the twentieth century until Carol Moseley Braun represented Illinois in 1993. Shirley Chisholm became the first black woman sent to Congress when she won election to the US House of Representatives in 1968. She represented the 12th congressional district of New York from 1969 until 1983. Barbara Jordan was the first black woman from a southern state to serve in the US House, representing the 18th congressional district of Texas from 1973 until her retirement in 1979. Tom Bradley became only the second black mayor of a major US city (after Carl Stokes of Cleveland, Ohio) when he became mayor of Los Angeles in 1973. He served for twenty years. Legendary civil rights activist John Lewis, a veteran Freedom Rider and Student Nonviolent Coordinating Committee leader, became a US congressman from Georgia in 1987 and served with distinction for three decades. Congressman James Clyburn of South Carolina won election to the House in 1992 and served as the majority whip from 2007 until 2011. Colin Powell rose through the ranks of the US military to serve as a four-star general, chairman of the Joint Chiefs of Staff, national security advisor to President Ronald Reagan, and secretary of state during President George W. Bush's first term in office.[4]

It was all so heady and exciting. Less than half a century after the Jim Crow laws were overturned, black men and women occupied an equal place in society beside white Americans. From the perspective of the early twenty-first century, an intensive focus on race was regarded as almost quaint, a reminder that past generations were obsessed with absurd nonsense such as whether a person qualified legally as a mulatto, quadroon, octoroon, or some other strange hereditary mixture.[5]

Yet, for all the eloquent rhetoric and noble ideals, the idea that race was an issue for a bygone era, an antiquated notion—so meaningless, so silly, so twentieth-century—was ridiculous. The cause of civil rights and racial harmony had advanced markedly since the 1960s, but to think that the world had become unrecognizable from days of old was to mistake what happened during the fight for civil rights. Racial politics changed, but the issue did not disappear.

Multiple incidents in the late twentieth and early twenty-first centuries illustrated the continuing relevance of race in American life. The white people involved were not free to go about their business absent legal consequences, indicating that racial attitudes had progressed since the pre–civil rights era when whites harmed blacks with impunity, but the occurrence of violence in the first place suggested that race remained a crucial component in the life of the citizenry. Consider three salient examples.

In Jasper, Texas, on June 7, 1998, three white men kidnapped a black man, James Byrd Jr., chained his ankles to the back of a pickup truck, and dragged him down a country road for three and a half miles until he died after being decapitated. The three perpetrators later were tried and convicted of the crime. The driver of the truck, Shawn Allen Berry, received a life sentence in prison. A second assailant, John William King, was sentenced to death. Lawrence Russell Brewer, the third man, also earned a death sentence. He was executed on September 21, 2011. The day before his execution, Brewer, an avowed white supremacist, told a television news reporter, "As far as any regrets, no, I have no regrets. No, I'd do it all over again, to tell you the truth." The case was a pivotal milestone in the effort to enact state and federal hate crime laws.[6]

In Sanford, Florida, on February 26, 2012, a twenty-eight-year-old Hispanic man, George Zimmerman, shot and killed an unarmed seventeen-year-old black high school student, Trayvon Martin. Zimmerman, a neighborhood watch coordinator in a gated community, claimed he acted in self-defense after he approached the unfamiliar adolescent to question his presence in the neighborhood and Martin attacked him. A jury later acquitted Zimmerman of second-degree murder and manslaughter charges in a case that attracted international attention and polarized the races. A majority of whites supported Zimmerman's self-defense assertions, while a majority of blacks believed Martin had been gunned down because of his race.[7]

In an analogous scenario (except that it involved a law enforcement official), a white patrolman, Darren Wilson, shot and killed an unarmed eighteen-year-old black man, Michael Brown, in Ferguson, Missouri, a St. Louis suburb, on August 9, 2014. Wilson claimed that Brown and his friend Dorian Johnson were walking in the middle of the street. The officer said he drove up in a police car and ordered Brown and Johnson to move onto the sidewalk. At the time he initially spied the men, Wilson did not know they matched the description of two shoplifting suspects. After the officer observed that Brown was sporting a handful of cigars, "that's when it clicked" for Wilson that the men might have been involved in the theft, which had been reported minutes earlier.

Calling for backup and maneuvering his squad car to block the path of the suspects, Wilson resolved to pat down the two young men. When he called out to the men a second time, Brown attacked him through the window of the automobile. The officer raised his service revolver, and the gun discharged. He apparently fired at least one more shot inside the car. The two young black men immediately fled. Wilson pursued Brown and shot him multiple times, killing him. Eyewitnesses disagreed about whether Brown had surrendered before Wilson shot him or had turned and aggressively charged at the policeman.

In the aftermath of the shooting, hundreds of protestors took to the streets to express their anger and frustration at yet another white officer killing an unarmed black teenager. As the protests stretched across multiple nights, looting and vandalism occurred, triggering a police response that some observers believed was necessary to restore order and others believed was an overreaction. Heavily armed policemen using tear gas and riot gear patrolled the streets in a scene reminiscent of military operations in the beleaguered city of a developing nation. Sporadic violence continued in August and September before subsiding. Yet the story did not end there. On November 24, 2014, a grand jury announced its decision not to indict Officer Wilson for his actions during the incident. The decision sparked a new round of protests and violence, not only in Ferguson but across the country.[8]

It was little wonder the black community expressed skepticism concerning the actions of a white law enforcement officer. The list of white police officers who have beaten or shot blacks is disturbingly long, and black citizens argue the incidents typically stem from racial profiling, the idea that law enforcement personnel confront someone not because they possess reasonable suspicion or probable cause that a crime has occurred but because they tend to think that people of color are "up to no good." Even when a suspect may or may not have committed a crime, blacks argue that the police response frequently is violent and disproportionate to the circumstances. Numerous high-profile cases during the late twentieth and early twenty-first centuries support this perspective.[9]

On March 3, 1991, black construction worker Rodney King led Los Angeles police officers on a high-speed automobile chase before they stopped his car. Officers alleged that King was belligerent and charged at them after he stepped from the vehicle. A bystander's video showed police officers striking a prostrate King repeatedly. Four officers eventually were charged with the use of excessive force and assault with a deadly weapon. Their acquittals at trial triggered the Los Angeles riots of April 29 to May 4, 1992, in which fifty-three people died and more than two thousand were injured.[10]

On October 12, 1995, a white police officer stopped Jonny Gammage, a black motorist driving his cousin National Football League player Ray Seals's Jaguar automobile in Allegheny County, Pennsylvania. Gammage was not suspected of committing a crime, but the officer nonetheless thought it was suspicious that Gammage tapped his brakes when he saw the police cruiser parked on the side of the road. Unspoken but implied in the case was the white police officer's curiosity about how a black man came to be driving an expensive sports car unless he had stolen it. After a seven-minute altercation, during which multiple police officers knocked Gammage to the ground and sat on his chest and legs, the motorist lay dead, apparently from asphyxiation due to pressure applied to his chest and neck.[11]

Black men of foreign lineage seemed especially likely to attract unwarranted suspicion. On August 9, 1997, police responded to a call from outside a nightclub in the East Flatbush neighborhood of Brooklyn, New York. An officer claimed that during a confrontation with several individuals, one man, a Haitian immigrant named Abner Louima, assaulted the officer. The police arrested Louima. During the ride to the station, several officials beat the suspect with their fists and nightsticks inside the squad car. Strip-searched and thrown into a cell, Louima was calm and orderly until an officer led him into a precinct bathroom and forcibly sodomized him with a broken broom handle, causing extensive damage to his colon and bladder.[12]

In one of the most infamous cases of the era, four plainclothes New York City police officers shot and killed Amadou Diallo, a twenty-three-year-old black immigrant from Guinea, on February 4, 1999, in the Bronx. The officers had stopped the young man to question him because he matched the physical description of a suspected rapist. When Diallo reached into his pocket and withdrew his wallet to identify himself, the officers mistook the object for a gun and fired forty-one shots, hitting the unarmed man nineteen times and killing him. The incident attracted widespread media attention. Many popular artists referred to the incident, notably American rock singer Bruce Springsteen, whose song "American Skin (41 Shots)" recounts the shooting.[13]

A young Haitian American security guard, Patrick Moses Dorismond, was standing outside a cocktail lounge in midtown Manhattan talking with a friend, Kevin Kaiser, and waiting for a taxicab on March 16, 2000, when an undercover New York City narcotics officer approached and asked where he could purchase marijuana. Dorismond became incensed and loudly insisted that he was not a drug dealer. The officer's partner approached, and a scuffle ensued between the two officers and Dorismond and Kaiser. The officers claimed that Dorismond grabbed a gun from Officer Anthony Vasquez, accidentally causing it to discharge, sending a single bullet into Dorismond's chest. Kaiser claimed he and Dorismond did not know their assailants were police officers and that Vasquez deliberately pulled the trigger. In any case, Dorismond died from his chest wound.[14]

A police officer shot and killed West African immigrant Ousmane Zongo on May 22, 2003, during a raid on a suspected CD/DVD counterfeiting operation inside a warehouse in Manhattan. Zongo was working inside the warehouse at the time, but he was not involved in the counterfeiting scheme. Unable to speak English and confused, Zongo fled from policemen. Officer Bryan Conroy, disguised as a postal worker, pursued the fleeing suspect and shot him four times, twice in the back. Zongo died as a result.[15]

In the early morning hours of November 25, 2006, a twenty-three-year-old black man, Sean Bell, and two friends were holding a bachelor party at a strip club in Queens, New York. Bell was supposed to be married later that day. Joseph Guzman, part of the group, reportedly argued with a man and threatened to retrieve a gun. When Gescard Isnora, a black police officer participating in an undercover prostitution operation, overheard the threat, he informed fellow officers, who approached Bell and his two friends as the three men stepped into Bell's automobile. What happened next was a matter of dispute. The officers claimed they displayed their badges and announced they were policemen. Bell's friends told a different tale. They thought the approaching men were assailants. In any case, Bell drove his car away from the approaching men, struck Isnora, and collided with an unmarked police minivan. Police officers thought they saw Guzman reaching for a gun, so they approached the wrecked car and fired fifty bullets at the three occupants. Sean Bell died. Joseph Guzman was severely injured, as was the other man, Trent Benefield.[16]

Oscar Grant III was twenty-two years old when a Bay Area Rapid Transit (BART) Authority police officer in Oakland, California, shot and killed him early in the morning on New Year's Day 2009. Grant had celebrated New Year's Eve with friends in San Francisco before riding a BART train toward his house. In the meantime, authorities had received reports of a dozen people on the train engaged in a physical altercation. When they investigated, the police ordered a group of people, including Grant, to stand on the platform at the Fruitvale BART Station. According to some accounts, after the police officers pushed Grant to the ground and threatened to use a Taser if he did not extend his hands far enough behind his back to be handcuffed, Grant resisted. BART officer Johannes Sebastian Mehserle believed that Grant was reaching into the waistband of his pants, presumably to draw a gun. Mehserle stood up, pulled his pistol, and shot Grant in the back. The young man, who was unarmed, died in the hospital seven hours later. Bystanders captured parts of the incident on video and circulated the images on the Internet. A January 7, 2009, protest march involving five hundred people erupted into violence, and two hundred policemen were dispatched in response. A 2013 feature film, *Fruitvale Station*, recalls the case but received criticism for altering many facts about Oscar Grant's life.[17]

On July 17, 2014, several police officers stopped a black man who was selling untaxed cigarettes on a city street in Staten Island, New York. The man, Eric Garner, weighed 350 pounds. Garner grew increasingly belligerent as he spoke to the officers. As illustrated by a video of the event, police officers wrestled Garner to the ground, and one officer, Daniel Pantaleo, used a chokehold around the man's neck. The chokehold was a forbidden procedure, but the officers were fearful of the man's strength and large size. As he was pushed onto the sidewalk, Garner repeatedly exclaimed, "I can't breathe; I can't breathe." He died minutes later. New York mayor Bill de Blasio, asked about the incident later, remarked, "Like so many New Yorkers, I was very troubled by the video." The medical examiner determined that Garner died from compression on his chest and neck owing to the chokehold, with his obesity and asthma serving as contributing factors. After a Staten Island grand jury declined to indict Officer Pantaleo on December 3, 2014, protests sprang up across the country. As the decision came only nine days after a grand jury refused to indict Officer Wilson for the shooting death of Michael Brown in Ferguson, Missouri, some Americans questioned whether white police officers could kill unarmed blacks with impunity.[18]

Another 2014 incident involved a black suspect, in this instance a twenty-five-year-old mentally ill man, facing white accusers. Los Angeles police officers stopped Ezell Ford on August 11 in an area of the city known for frequent gang activity and high crime. It was unclear what Ford was doing or why the officers singled him out for additional scrutiny. What happened next became a major point of contention. Two police officers claimed that Ford reached for an officer's handgun. A struggle ensued, and the officers shot Ford multiple times in the back, killing him. Eyewitnesses and Ford's family members disputed the police version of events, arguing that Ford had compiled with the officers' directions, but they shot him in the back while he was stretched out on the ground. Although Ford had a criminal record, his family contended that he was not involved in a gang. Any strange behavior he exhibited was due to his long history of schizophrenia and bipolar disorder.[19]

The incidents continued in 2015. On April 4 of that year, a black motorist named Walter Scott was driving along a public road in North Charleston, South Carolina, when a white police officer, Michael Slager, stopped Scott's car because a taillight was not working. The officer's dashcam recorder showed the two men speaking briefly. As Slager returned to his police cruiser, Scott stepped from his car and ran. The officer chased the man behind a pawnshop. They briefly struggled before Officer Slager used his Taser on Scott. Despite the potentially debilitating blow, Scott once again managed to flee. Officer Slager drew his service revolver and fired eight shots at the unarmed man, hitting him multiple times; a shot in the back claimed Walter Scott's life. An eyewitness, Feidin Santana, used his cell phone to record the altercation on video. Initially, the police officer claimed he fired because Scott had taken his Taser and the officer felt threatened. After reviewing the video, prosecutors charged Slager with murder.[20]

Days later, on April 12, 2015, Baltimore police officers stopped twenty-five-year-old Freddie Gray Jr. near a housing project in a high-crime area. Gray had been arrested for drug crimes and petty offenses in the past, but in this instance his encounter with police became controversial because it was unclear whether the officers possessed probable cause to detain Gray. Eventually arrested for possessing an illegal switchblade knife, the suspect was shoved inside a police van. During the trip to the police station, Gray suffered a severe spinal cord injury and slipped into a coma. He died a week later. Accounts differed as to what happened as well as the timing of the injury. Gray may have been wounded during his arrest or beaten by six officers inside the police van. Initially suspended without pay, the police officers eventually were charged with a variety of crimes ranging from illegal arrest to manslaughter. The incident triggered civil unrest in downtown Baltimore. Following Gray's funeral on April 27, a mob rioted, looting stores and starting fires in the downtown area. The National Guard intervened to stop the violence.[21]

A few months later, one of the worst mass murders in decades occurred, and race appears to have been a motivating factor. A twenty-one-year-old white man, Dylann Roof, entered the Emanuel African Methodist Episcopal Church in Charleston, South Carolina, on June 17, 2015, and opened fire with a .45-caliber handgun during a prayer meeting. He killed nine people in the attack. After he was apprehended by police, Roof revealed that he had hesitated to commit the crime. He had attended the Bible study for an hour, silently observing the discussions before he produced the gun and methodically murdered the parishioners and their minister. Because everyone treated him kindly, Roof briefly entertained second thoughts. Investigators looking into his past discovered that Roof supported white supremacy, although his affiliation with a specific group was murky. Photographs showed the gunman sporting symbols of Apartheid-era South Africa and waving the Confederate battle flag, a controversial symbol that some audiences believe to be a symbol of hatred and bigotry.

Roof's actions renewed calls for the state of South Carolina to remove the Confederate battle flag from the grounds of the statehouse in Columbia. After decades of strife and division over the issue, events moved quickly. In July 2015, less than a month after the murders, the state legislature voted to remove the flag, and Governor Nikki Haley signed the measure into law. In the aftermath of the South Carolina decision, other southern states debated whether they too should remove the battle flag, as well as some Confederate monuments, from public property.[22]

Race was an integral component of the cases cited above, but it also has played a role in instances where, albeit not the predominant factor, it has affected the outcome. When black former football player turned sportscaster and part-time actor O. J. Simpson was indicted for allegedly murdering his estranged white wife and her friend in 1994, his attorneys concocted a defense based on the premise that white racist police officers in Los Angeles had framed an innocent man. Simpson had spent his life and career turning away from his blackness, but when he was on trial for his life, he and his defense team charged authorities with racism. He won an acquittal on the criminal charges, although he was held financially liable for the killings in a subsequent civil trial.[23]

In 1995, a twenty-four-year-old white woman, Susan Smith, claimed that a black man had carjacked her automobile in Union, South Carolina, and fled with her two boys inside—three-year-old Michael and fourteen-month-old Alexander. The seemingly distraught woman took to the television airwaves to plead for their safe return. Nine days later, she confessed to driving her automobile into a nearby lake with the boys strapped inside, drowning them. The tale of a vicious black man absconding with her car was a ruse to throw suspicion onto a fictional, and presumably unsympathetic, suspect. Smith reportedly killed the children because she wanted to pursue a relationship with a man who was not interested in rearing children.[24]

In 1987, Tawana Brawley, a fifteen-year-old black girl in Wappingers Falls, New York, was found lying in a garbage bag, apparently unconscious, with her clothes torn and burned. Her body was smeared with feces, and the words "KKK," "nigger," and "bitch" were drawn on her torso in charcoal. She claimed that a gang of white men had raped her repeatedly over a four-day period. The Reverend Al Sharpton, a controversial civil rights activist with a zeal for intervening in sensational cases, came to Brawley's assistance and transformed the case into a cause célèbre. When medical professionals could find no evidence of sexual assault, a grand jury declined to prosecute anyone. One of the white men who Brawley claimed had raped her, Dutchess County assistant district attorney Steven Pagones, later won a suit for defamation of character against Sharpton and Brawley as well as two of Brawley's attorneys.[25]

Crystal Gail Mangum, a black student at North Carolina Central University in Durham, North Carolina, and a part-time stripper, accused three white members of the Duke University men's lacrosse team of raping her on March 13, 2006, during a party in a house occupied by the two team captains. Authorities acted quickly. The local prosecutor, Mike Nifong, called the matter a hate crime. The three suspects were arrested, the team's coach, Mike Pressler, was forced to resign, and the university cancelled the remainder of the lacrosse season. Later, after investigators could find no evidence of a rape and the victim continually changed her story, prosecutors dismissed the charges. The former defendants filed multiple lawsuits, and prosecutor Nifong was disbarred for prosecutorial misconduct in suppressing exculpatory evidence that should have been disclosed to the defense.[26]

These cases represent only a tiny fraction of the notorious incidents in the United States in which race has been a crucial if not deciding factor in the chain of events. Sometimes whites accuse blacks, and sometimes blacks accuse whites, with supporters of each race lining up to support their cause, often in a rush to judgment on all sides. In the aftermath of such imbroglios, each race becomes more polarized, convinced that the alien "other" is acting in bad faith.

Whenever a race-based story captures headlines, political leaders, scholars, lawyers, and activists publicly lament that "America needs to engage in a racial dialogue to heal old wounds." Such clarion calls for a national conversation on race produce quotable sound bites for the evening news, but they do not provide workable objectives or specific plans for proceeding forward. Who will do the talking, and what will they say? Should a reconciliation commission be established, and what would such a commission be tasked to do? Perhaps reparations should be paid, but from whom to whom? Questions proliferate; answers, if they exist, remain elusive. A dialogue on race may even exacerbate tensions and reopen old wounds.[27]

If the late twentieth and early twenty-first centuries represent an era of postracial American life, not everyone received the memo.

Even if Americans could somehow enter a postracial era, they might resist efforts to dismiss race as a factor in their lives. The old charge of "acting white" or "passing for white" stings black Americans who are proud of an ancient heritage that contributes to an individual's perspective and accomplishments. Who needs or wants to pass for white? At a time when blackness is not a badge of shame, a person of color may prefer to keep in touch with his or her roots and retain a distinct racial or ethnic identity. If identity is at least partially a result of an individual's choice, the person may choose to be identified as black and revel in his or her blackness rather than shy away from it.

In one highly publicized case in 2015, Rachel Dolezal, a National Association for the Advancement of Colored People leader in Spokane, Washington, was criticized for "passing for black" when her family revealed that she was not African American. Pressed to explain why she characterized herself as black when she was Caucasian, Dolezal provided conflicting answers. At one point, she claimed not to understand the question. On another occasion, she argued that she had always felt she was a member of the black race. "I identify as black," she insisted. She also charged that she was unsure of her lineage. "I haven't had a DNA test. There's been no biological proof that Larry and Ruthanne are my biological parents." If race is at least partially a matter of self-selection, Dolezal's claim was not entirely nonsensical, although it suggested that the centuries-old conception of racial identity was woefully misdirected. If racial identity is completely a matter of choice and not an immutable characteristic, as Dolezal intimated, it can be changed exactly as people dye their hair, use contact lenses to alter their eye color, whiten their teeth, or identify as transgender. In years to come, if Dolezal's understanding of race gains traction, racial identity may become an accessory to match one's outfit, shoes, or handbag.[28]

In the meantime, race remains a "hot button" issue for tens of millions of people. Yes, it undeniably has played, and continues to play, a central role in shaping and influencing American history, especially political affairs south of the Mason-Dixon Line. Based on this insight, it behooves Americans of the twenty-first century to understand the long, tortured history of race in the United States. Only by appreciating the passions and interests involved in this controversial topic can students of history hope to continue the slow, steady progress of recent decades.[29]

Historian and political scientist V. O. Key Jr. famously wrote, "In its grand outlines the politics of the South revolves around the position of the Negro. It is at times interpreted as a politics of cotton, as a politics of free trade, as a politics of agrarian poverty, or as a politics of planter and plutocrat. Although such interpretations have a superficial validity, in the last analysis the major peculiarities of southern politics go back to the Negro. Whatever phases of the southern political process one seeks to understand, sooner or later, the trail of inquiry leads to the Negro." Nowhere is this comment better illustrated than in the story of southern society as it evolved from the days of slavery before the 1860s through Reconstruction in the 1860s and 1870s, the rise of segregation at the end of the nineteenth century, and the gradual integration of the races during the latter half of the twentieth century. The insight is not limited to the South, however, for race is a national concern.[30]

American history is partially a story of what might have been. For a brief interval at the end of the Civil War, American political leaders had a chance—a slim one, to be sure—to remake society so that black Americans could realize equal opportunities in civil and political life. It was not to be. With each passing year after the war—especially after Reconstruction ended in the 1870s—American society witnessed the evolution of a new white republic as national leaders abandoned the promise of Reconstruction and justified their racial biases based on political, economic, social, and religious values that supplanted the old North-South/slavery-abolition schism of the antebellum era.[31]

Even before the dawn of the 1880s, the federal government had backed away from commitments made to the recently emancipated slaves, ceding the field to southern whites to carry out their will. As a result, white political leaders developed a system of segregation that disenfranchised people of color for more than eight decades. The legendary civil rights icon of the nineteenth century, Frederick Douglass, was quick to recognize that a full-scale retreat from the promises of Reconstruction was at hand. Referring to the federal government's reluctance to intervene in the affairs of the southern states as they enacted segregation laws, he remarked, "We have been, as a class, grievously wounded, wounded in the house of our friends."[32]

During the years following the war, some national political leaders championed the cause of equal opportunity for the races. By the 1880s, those "radical" men had passed from the scene. The US Supreme Court of the mid- to late twentieth century would protect individual rights and civil liberties for disenfranchised citizens, but until then, the high court closed the door on opportunity and opened the door to segregation. Southern state legislators were only too happy to charge through the door and build a new regime based on white supremacy.[33]

This book tells the story, at least partially, of the long, painful struggle to move away from an exclusive, white supremacist regime toward a more inclusive, tolerant, racially enlightened system. It was and remains an arduous, unfinished journey.

Part I

A CHILD OF MISERY

1

The Legacy of Reconstruction

"Freedom Wasn't No Difference I Knows Of"

Civil war—total, complete, and unrelenting in its blood and fury, its drama and passion, its horror and pathos—had ravaged the American landscape during four exhausting years. Within weeks of Robert E. Lee's surrender at Appomattox Courthouse, Virginia, on April 9, 1865, the costliest conflagration in American history had concluded. Much blood and treasure had been expended. Monumental work would be required to repair a fractured nation, but the military phase ended with the South laid low. The Confederate leadership had sought to secede from the Union and forge a slaveholding republic through force of arms, laying its foundation on the firm bedrock of a racial caste system. With the surrender of southern armies in April 1865, the would-be nation failed to erect a monument to white supremacy on the North American continent.[1]

Or had it? At first blush, through the thick fog of war, the reality of the Southern Confederacy, if not quite its ideals, seemed to have been deposited into the ash bin of history. Embittered by their military repudiation, unreconstructed Confederates groused that the tyrant Abraham Lincoln and his chief lieutenant, the butcher Ulysses S. Grant, had triumphed not because they were virtuous souls—far from it. They had brought the North's superior industrial capacity to bear by evincing a callous disregard for human life. With a larger population of able-bodied males than the South enjoyed, the Union offered up enough cannon fodder eventually to overwhelm and bludgeon the opposition through sheer force of numbers—in men and machines. From the southern perspective, the triumph of the Union rested on a strategy of attrition, sacrifice, and dumb luck.[2]

The battlefield losses stung, but no loss is permanent, no humiliation unending. In the short term, the victors would impose harsh conditions, and the vanquished would chafe under the boot heels of oppression. Yet time dulls all sharp edges. Sooner or later, a war-weary northern public would tire of the burden of operating southern state governments and propping up the freedmen. Until then, southerners would nurse their wounds and await the dawn of a new epoch.

Ex-Confederates were not alone in their grief. Shell-shocked citizens on both sides of the conflict struggled to understand the meaning of the war. Surely the sacrifices had served a higher purpose. Families struggling to cope with the loss of loved ones stolen away longed for an overarching goal and tangible benefits to cite as reasons for absorbing debilitating body blows. Abstract theories of federalism and ideological disputes over property rights were poor substitutes for the lost touch of a husband, son, or brother. What had it all been for, this unprecedented carnage? Had anyone save a handful of Radical Republicans in Congress believed that the war was fundamentally about freeing the bondsmen from centuries of shackles and oppression?[3]

THE PECULIAR INSTITUTION IN THE ANTEBELLUM ERA

Those shackles had been firmly set in place in the American polity for more than two and a half centuries, antedating the US Constitution by generations. Beginning in the seventeenth century, slavery became a way of life for inhabitants of the New World from English-speaking New England to Spanish Florida to French Louisiana. While the history of the institution stretched back to time immemorial, the North American strain was particularly virulent. Whereas a slave in the ancient world was set into bondage for debt or crime and might one day complete his term of service, in the American colonies the institution became a way of life, a rigid social structure that proved remarkably resistant to change. The enslaved masses seldom won their freedom in the New World system.[4]

Ancient slaves could be found among all types of people, but in the English-speaking colonies, enslavement was limited almost exclusively to persons of color. Slavery based on race—the idea that the rights of personhood depend on skin pigmentation—was largely a New World distinction. An African man captured in battle by another tribe and held on the continent might look forward to the day when he earned his freedom. That same captive transported across the Atlantic in the cargo hold of a slave vessel, assuming he survived the arduous passage, could expect to die in captivity. Only in rare cases of insurrection or selective emancipation could he look to the promise of a brighter day. Even if he threw off the shackles of physical confinement, his dark skin doomed him to a life of discrimination and hardship wherever he roamed in the New World. He was a prisoner of diminished expectation and opportunity no matter how well or hard he struggled. For all the subsequent talk of America as a classless society that refused to extend titles of nobility to self-styled aristocrats, persons of color were under no illusions regarding the limitations they faced.[5]

As the seventeenth century gave way to the eighteenth, the disease of slavery metastasized across the American colonies as surely as if it were a contagion spreading throughout the body politic. Affluent planters in the Chesapeake and the Deep South discovered that labor-intensive crops such as tobacco, cotton, indigo, and rice could be cultivated at enormous profit using the sweat of another man's brow. To increase the agricultural yield, increasing numbers of slaves had to be imported to perform the grueling, backbreaking labor. The quest to acquire increased acreage planted with profitable cash crops meant that the so-called peculiar institution of slavery grew so rapidly that the proportion of blacks to whites placed the latter in a numerical minority in some areas. By the middle of the eighteenth century, a sizable plurality of the population of Virginia consisted of slaves. When the first US census was conducted in 1790, the entire population of the colonies numbered some 4 million people, 18 percent of whom were slaves.[6]

With an increase in the number of slaves, the likelihood of an armed revolt grew. Many large plantations housed more black laborers than white overseers; consequently, the possibility of a bloody uprising struck fear into the hearts of masters. Despite the myth of the faithful, contented slave who cherished his white family as his protector, white power brokers realized they must act to forestall a bubbling social revolution in their midst. When a slave revolt was put down, white citizens understood that the numbers portended an ominous fate if they did not take care to tighten an iron grip on the bondsmen.[7]

The institution was characterized as "peculiar" because it rested on contradictory myths. In one version, slaves were amiable, obedient, child-like simpletons that could not be left to their own devices. Their masters were wise, benevolent overlords who provided food, clothing, and shelter in exchange for labor that advanced the interests of everyone living on the premises. Despite the infrequent malcontent who ran off in search of an elusive dream of freedom, most slaves were happy and faithful. If punishments had to be administered to rabble-rousers who would under-mine the discipline and security of the plantation, it was a small price to pay for the maintenance of a fixed social order.[8]

Yet a competing narrative cast slaves as animalistic and wild, easily riled and desirous of engaging in all manner of mischief. If not watched incessantly, the slave would rob his master blind. If not kept in line, he would rise up and slaughter his betters in the dark of night. The slave was a half step removed from a wild beast. No matter how well trained and well treated, he was a vicious, wild creature not to be trusted.[9]

To the white man who would reconcile these competing narratives, the explanation necessarily was convoluted and yet strangely compelling. Slaves who accepted their role in the social order were happy and contented. Those who did not know their place were wild animals that must be broken by force. Beneath the facade of the happy, well-functioning household and plantation business was a threat, sometimes implicit, sometimes explicit. A slave must get in line and fulfill his duties or suffer the ravages of the lash.[10]

Beginning in the eighteenth century, white lawmakers enacted slave codes to ensure that penalties would be severe and unremitting if some charismatic slave took it upon himself to instigate a revolt. An arms race of sorts commenced: The planter elite packed more slaves into the caste system, thereby increasing the possibility of a revolt and stoking fear among whites. Overcrowded, brutal conditions only embittered slaves, leading them to consider escape or revolution as a viable alternative, feeding into the cycle of fear and mistrust between blacks and whites.[11]

For myriad reasons, the institution did not take hold in northern states to the same extent as it did south of the Mason-Dixon Line. Some observers have suggested that northern denizens were not as culturally, emotionally, and economically invested in slave ownership as their southern brethren. Others have argued that northern agriculture did not require the same deep well of labor as did southern crops. Still others have found that the industrialization in New England and the mid-Atlantic states rewarded entrepreneurs who did not wish to compete with slave labor in the marketplace. Whatever the reasons, by the early years of the nineteenth century, northern states had provided for gradual emancipation. The children of slaves found a path forward. After laboring for an owner until adulthood, the fortunate son could look forward to a day when he might exercise a relatively unfettered will.[12]

As the decades passed and the abolitionists grew in power, however, gradualism would come to be vilified as a convenient pretext for sloughing off the issue. If an opportunistic northern politician could argue that the peculiar institution had been set on a course of ultimate extinction, he could move on to less incendiary issues in the quest to win elective office. By the 1830s, a new breed of antislavery man would express his frustration with the gradualist approach. William Lloyd Garrison, in fiery words that established his abolitionist bona fides, declared in no uncertain terms that gradual emancipation was unacceptable. "Tell a man whose house is on fire to give a moderate alarm; tell him to moderately rescue his wife from the hands of the ravisher; tell the mother to gradually extricate her babe from the fire into which it has fallen," he screamed from the pages of his antislavery rag, *The Liberator*, "but urge me not to use moderation in a cause like the present." The well-known "political agitator" Wendell Phillips went even further, declaring the US Constitution "a covenant with death and an agreement with hell" because it permitted slavery in the new nation and frankly admitting, "No abolitionist can consistently take office under it, or swear to support it."[13]

These extreme views did not reflect the mainstream opinion in any region of nineteenth-century America, but they did suggest that attitudes about the continued enslavement of a large group of the underclass were changing. Northerners held a variety of perspectives, sometimes believing that slavery was a necessary evil to ensure the continuation of the nation in perpetuity. In the South, a necessary evil sometimes was transformed into a positive good. Even gradualism was denounced as an assault on the values of white Americans.

The argument extended into the debate over the nation's westward expansion. Predictably, the peculiar institution expanded into the territories—generally south of an agreed-on line—as settlers moved into the old Louisiana Territory and inched ever closer to the Pacific Ocean. Eventually, the institution expanded across Alabama, Mississippi, Louisiana, and Texas, which became the center of a vast cotton empire that ensured the demand for slaves would not abate. Northern founders had entertained mild hopes of slavery's demise when the international slave trade was outlawed after 1808, but by the eve of the Civil War, this naive supposition had been revealed as so much wishful thinking. Too much of the American economy was tied up in the enterprise. More money was invested in slavery than in factories, banks, and railroads in 1860. Absent a major cataclysm, the institution of slavery was not going anywhere.[14]

WAR AND THE DEATH OF THE PECULIAR INSTITUTION

In the long years since fighting erupted between the North and South in 1861, Americans have debated the causes and meanings of the war. More than a century and a half after the event, commentators still cannot agree on the precise reasons for the bloodshed, although they have identified a range of likely explanations. To say that slavery was the sole or paramount cause is to gloss over myriad disputes, real and imagined, concerning the proper relation of citizens in different regions, the expansion of the country westward toward the Pacific, and the nature and extent of government in the states and territories. Yet the opposite is equally true: to contend that slavery was not a root cause is to ignore a crucial factor contributing to sectional hostilities in the early to mid-nineteenth century. In the final analysis, perhaps the best that can be said is that race and slavery were necessary but insufficient conditions leading to civil war. The South sought to establish its independence to preserve the "southern way of life," which featured the institution of slavery as an integral component. The North initially fought to preserve the Union until later in the fighting, when emancipation became an additional goal. Yet, whatever the triggers, the seeds of conflict had been planted much earlier.[15]

Abraham Lincoln eloquently said that the war was about whether a nation conceived in liberty and dedicated to human equality could long endure. In his second inaugural address, he memorably reminded his audience that slavery was somehow the cause of the bloodshed, but he did not precisely explain the role the peculiar institution had played; nor did he expound on the fate of the freedmen after slavery was set on the road to extinction. His soaring rhetoric lived for the ages, but at war's end, the question was whether the words would lead to action. Lincoln intended to honor his promises, but it was not to be. After the sixteenth president died from an assassin's bullet, his successor claimed to follow his policies. Time and circumstances demonstrated that Andrew Johnson was no Abraham Lincoln; nor did he intend to be. He would not champion the cause of the freedmen. The new president's rocky tenure was further exacerbated by an internecine struggle between the executive and the legislature concerning the proper course of reconstruction. It was a murky era, but one fact was clear: if the victorious Union army did not enforce government edicts that slavery was dead and the newly emancipated slaves must be assimilated into society, eloquent phrases would not suffice to secure the blessings of liberty for the black race.[16]

Slaves and persons of color recognized long before Lincoln and the Radicals transformed the war into a battle over emancipation that the unprecedented fighting among whites represented a golden opportunity for freedom. While whites claimed, at least partially, to struggle over esoteric questions of federalism and political power, blacks were determined to use the conflict as a means of escape. "Let the white fight for what they want and we Negroes fight for what we want," one African American commented. Cutting through the tangled morass of complicated theories and nuanced justifications, he clearly and unequivocally expressed the goal of the enslaved. "Liberty must take the day."[17]

Whatever the reasons for the outbreak of war in 1861, as the conflict progressed through the months and years, the peculiar institution inexorably changed. When slaves escaped from their masters and found Federal officers willing to take them in, the so-called contrabands built new lives behind Union lines as laborers. Every escaped slave who entered a contraband camp denied the South his services. Freedom fever spread so

rapidly that the institutional controls that once held the b
in place disintegrated. It was as if southern society had be
foundation of crumbling sandstone. Even before the Arm
Virginia capitulated, the antebellum South had all but disa

Not satisfied to wait for war's end or the supposed benefic
military and political leaders, able-bodied bondsmen fled the   ...s as
soon as the Federals seized control of territory in Virginia, Tennessee, and
Louisiana. The contrabands were persons without legal status. Before the
commencement of hostilities, Federal citizens had been obliged to return
escapees to their rightful owners under the terms of the 1850 Fugitive
Slave Act, no matter how odious such a requirement appeared to good
northern men. After the southern states announced their separation from
the Union in 1861, the law was no longer clear. It would have been ironic,
and more than a bit perverse, if southerners had declared US laws null
and void, only to have their escaped slaves returned to them after they
had repudiated the legal basis for the remedy. The US Congress eventually rectified this anomalous situation by enacting measures governing
the contrabands' wartime role, but at the outset the law failed to keep
pace with circumstances. As for the status of property-turned-escaped-
personage, postbellum plans were left for another day.[19]

Lincoln was the key to unlocking the fate of blacks who desperately
sought a change in status. The president represented the evolving attitude
among whites who viewed slavery negatively but did not count themselves as abolitionists. He famously remarked to newspaperman Horace
Greeley in a public letter in August 1862, "What I do about slavery, and
the colored race, I do because I believe it helps to save the Union; and
what I forbear, I forbear because I don't believe it would help to save the
Union." Lincoln was not insensitive to the needs of the enslaved, but his
constitutional authority, as he saw it, did not extend to wholesale emancipation of all American slaves. Yet the president recognized that the changing nature of the war changed the nature of the peculiar institution as
well. Even as he penned his famous words to Greeley, Lincoln was con-
templating the idea of issuing an emancipation proclamation to free
slaves in the rebellious states. He lacked authority to free all slaves for-
evermore, but during wartime he believed he possessed the necessary
authority to free slaves as an expedient measure in aid of the Union
cause.[20]

Following issuance of the proclamation, as black soldiers enlisted to
fight for the Union army, the nation experienced a transformation. It was
true that black soldiers were treated poorly; they were forced into segregated units, paid lower wages than their white counterparts, and often
ordered to perform menial tasks such as burying corpses or performing
garrison duty. Yet over time, especially after the heroic performance of

e celebrated 54th Massachusetts Volunteer Infantry Regiment in assaulting Fort Wagner in South Carolina in July 1863, black soldiers demonstrably contributed to the national endeavor. If their achievements were not universally heralded, their brave actions demonstrated that Negroes were willing to die for cause and comrade. The experience also transformed the self-assessments of people of color.[21]

Fighting for the Union, even if that Union was not always equitable in its treatment of black soldiers, instilled a measure of dignity in the man who donned a uniform and hoisted a rifle over his shoulder. He was actively participating in life decisions, and that was a welcome change in fortune. Enslavement meant that a man could not control his fate. A slave was expected passively to await his cues from the master or the plantation overseer. The obvious catastrophe of being a slave aside, the institution robbed a person of his or her intentionality. Throughout the Western tradition, at least since the advent of the Enlightenment during the seventeenth century, a central feature of the human identity has been the notion of forming intent and acting upon it. Human laws are constructed on such a foundation: entering into a contract, choosing to marry, acquiring and disposing of property, writing a last will and testament, engaging in prohibited activity and being punished through criminal laws as a result all depend on an assumption that a person possesses free will and acts on that basis. Responsibility can only be assigned to individuals who are free to choose their own course of action absent duress. Robbed of intentionality, the slave was forced to act not on the basis of free will but in reaction to the will of another. Conditions of servitude require passive acceptance of a fate decided by others, and this requirement undermines a person's selfhood. The self-actualized Negro exercising free will posed a threat to the legal and social order and was dangerous because he was no longer a passive vessel. The laws of slavery criminalized activities that promoted social self-worth such as learning to read or congregating in groups.

Blacks who deserted the plantation home as escaped slaves, assisted escapees in finding safe passage from bondage, taught former slaves to read, or enlisted in the Federal army were anathema to slaveholders not only because they endangered the current crop of enslaved masses but because they exposed the lie that masters told themselves as a means of justifying the unjustifiable. Whites had often repeated the homily that people of color were little better than chattel, or personal property. Legally, in fact, slaves were treated as the property of their masters. Slaves were incapable of self-mastery, hence self-governance, because they were a lower order of animal. Keeping such pathetic creatures in bondage therefore was kind, not cruel. Urging a dog owner to emancipate his beagle is not kind to the dog, for the poor creature, lacking the tools necessary to ensure self-sufficiency, will soon perish from starvation, disease, or disorientation in the brave new world of the free. For a certain class of slaveholder, the institution was necessary to meet the needs of master and slave. Without the orderly structure of the plantation home, the bondsman could not forage for himself. Thus was born the myth of the faithful slave and the wise, benevolent master.[22]

The war exposed once and for all the hollow foundations and empty rationales of the peculiar institution—not that it had been a soundly constructed, logical edifice in the first place. Thomas Jefferson provides a suitable illustration of the eternal struggle within the soul of many a slaveholding southerner, although perhaps he is a poor example because his intellect afforded him an especially clear view of causes and effects. In 1789, he observed, "To give liberty to, or rather, to abandon persons whose habits have been formed in slavery is like abandoning children."[23] Yet elsewhere, in *Notes on the State of Virginia*, he famously confessed, "The whole commerce between master and slave is a perpetual exercise of the most boisterous passions, the most unremitting despotism on the one part, and degrading submissions on the other." Whether characterized as a hypocrite or a generally tormented man of goodwill, Jefferson reflects the ambivalence of the more enlightened slaveholder. The institution was a terrible thing, but it was intertwined with so many features of the American character and way of life—northern as well as southern.[24]

Here was the social upheaval unleashed by the self-actualized man of color. If he could fight nobly and well on behalf of his country, if he could read and reproduce the king's English, if he could pull himself up above his sordid station in life through acts undertaken of his own design and free will, what had so much of American history been about? It had been a fraud of the highest caliber, a monument to stupidity and meanness that could not be rehabilitated by any manner of rhetoric or excuse. The man of color who seized his freedom, insisted on the exercise of free will, and embraced intentionality, come what may, threatened the social mores developed over centuries of American and European history. If racial inferiority was a lie, what else of the American character was built on the bedrock of an invidious falsehood?

For all the advances enjoyed by the black race with the death of slavery, the changes wrought by the war were mixed. Some vocal proponents of emigration and colonization reversed their positions. Perhaps the flawed regime could be salvaged. A nation that managed to throw off the shackles of oppression for a group of people held in bondage for centuries might yet reform itself into a society free from the taint of racial bigotry and elite favoritism. Yet that reformation, if it came, was many years in the future. It became clear early in the Reconstruction era that the demise of the peculiar institution did not equal the rise of racial equality. White men might not desire to own their darker-hued brethren, but that did not mean full equality was in the offing.[25]

Among the many challenges facing the United States as the war wound to its conclusion was the question of how to handle the freedmen. Lincoln's decision to issue the Emancipation Proclamation on New Year's Day 1863 and the subsequent ratification in December 1865 of the Thirteenth Amendment prohibiting slavery throughout the country undoubtedly were causes for jubilation, but they were far from the end of the story. The task of providing for a group of people who were alien to the paid labor force and now obliged to fend for themselves in inhospitable environs was almost as daunting as the task of fighting a ruthless civil war.[26]

The transition from slavery to free labor at war's end was challenging but not unprecedented. As Federal forces captured southern territory during the war, victorious troops found former slaves who were anxious to enter the labor force and leave behind a life of bondage. The first major test of the transition occurred in November 1861, when the Union Navy seized the Sea Islands off the South Carolina coast, and white southerners fled their homes to escape the Yankee wrath. In the wake of the mass exodus, ten thousand slaves suddenly found themselves free. With the area under northern control, white civilians set up schools to teach the freedmen to read and write. Despite a measure of paternalism and condescension among the abolitionists and reformers, the former slaves and their children proved to be willing subjects hungry for knowledge. "I never saw children so eager to learn," commented Charlotte Forten, a black antislavery activist and educator from Philadelphia.[27]

For all its successes, the Sea Islands episode also highlighted an ongoing problem involving the labor pool. Northern whites had hoped to step into the shoes of the former plantation owners and turn their fields into cash crops with assistance from former slaves, who would labor in the fields for wages and improved working conditions. Much to their consternation, whites encountered considerable resistance from freedmen who preferred to work as entrepreneurs rather than trade their services to white landowners in exchange for a paycheck. Working for white overseers, whatever the circumstances, resembled slavery too closely for many persons of color.[28]

A more ambitious reconstruction program occurred after Federal forces seized control of New Orleans in 1862 and Vicksburg, Mississippi, a year later. With the liberation of Louisiana and the Mississippi Valley, a much larger population than the former slaves of South Carolina was affected by the presence of the Union army. The experiment quickly turned sour. General Benjamin F. Butler and his successor, General Nathaniel Banks, did not envision wholesale changes to labor relations. Fearful that all the slaves would flee and leave the plantation fields to lie fallow or alienate southern planters who swore a loyalty oath, the Union generals insisted that freedmen sign labor contracts and continue working or face charges of vagrancy. Blacks resented the requirement that they remain on the plantation without the freedom to move as they saw fit, wages or no wages. Whites soon discovered the repercussions of forcing labor on people who had their hearts set on freedom. The freedmen were surly and insubordinate and often refused to work under this new, ignominious system of "compulsory free labor." The experience contained a valuable lesson for postwar reconstruction: simply freeing the slaves and assuming that other conditions would remain unchanged was naive. The transition from bondage to freedom would be onerous for everyone concerned.[29]

Although Lincoln devoted most of his time and energy to prosecuting the war, the president recognized the necessity of planning for the postwar era. He hoped to bring the sections together as seamlessly as possible—an ambitious desire in light of the passions and bloodshed involved. To accomplish his objective, late in 1863 he proposed lenient reconstruction terms to entice reasonable southerners to lay down their arms and thereby create minimal postbellum friction. Under Lincoln's plan, a seceding state could rejoin the Union when a number of citizens equaling 10 percent of the votes cast in the 1860 election affirmed an oath of allegiance to the US Constitution and the laws of the nation, including laws outlawing slavery. The plan was remarkably generous to white southerners, but critics feared it was too lenient. The low threshold for readmission into the United States might be interpreted by unreconstructed rebels as weakness on the part of the victors. In his effort to extend an olive branch to a defeated region, the president might embolden southerners to abuse the freedmen with impunity. For abolitionists who always viewed the war as fundamentally intertwined with the slavery question, Lincoln was turning his back on the men and women who had lived in bondage, dreaming of emancipation, for generations. To provide for a soft peace when they had lived hard lives was unconscionable.[30]

To be fair, Lincoln was not proposing a comprehensive, inviolable plan for reconstructing the Union. Always thinking about methods for speedily conducting the war effort, he sought to motivate moderate southerners who regretted secession to pressure the Confederate leadership to consider laying down arms. The justifications sounded reasonable to moderates who sought a middle course, but the president's rationale infuriated the Radical Republicans, the congressional team that generally championed immediate liberation for the enslaved class. The Radicals had harbored reservations about the man from Illinois since he had first emerged as a presidential contender. The years had not softened their stance. To these men, Lincoln was a hesitant, vacillating leader of uncertain purpose and weak will. Even among the congressmen who viewed their commander in chief as a person of good faith, any national leader who failed to share their zeal was suspect. That is not to say that all Radical Republicans were staunch abolitionists—they still had to keep a watchful eye on the oft-changing desires of fickle constituencies—but they did seek a means for extinguishing the institution of slavery sooner rather than later.

Even among members of the group, the Radicals were not always philosophically consistent, but they did share a desire to resolve the slavery question. For all the divisions within the ranks, the leaders of the faction were vocal supporters of universal emancipation, whether it was a war measure or a principled stance. A bloody civil war, with all of its horrors and decimation, presented a golden, once-in-a-generation opportunity to reset the course of American history and correct the defects found in the original version of the US Constitution, which had allowed slavery to exist. The shackles of subjugation must be loosened now and forever.[31]

In the House of Representatives, Congressman Thaddeus Stevens of Pennsylvania, chairman of the powerful Ways and Means Committee, was among the leaders, as were Congressman Galusha A. Grow of Pennsylvania, who served briefly as Speaker of the House before he was defeated for reelection in 1862; Illinois congressman Owen Lovejoy, brother of murdered abolitionist Elijah Lovejoy; Ohio congressman Joshua Giddings; and Giddings's son-in-law, George W. Julian, an Indiana congressman. Radicals in the US Senate included Charles Sumner of Massachusetts, chairman of the Senate Foreign Relations Committee, and Benjamin Wade of Ohio, president pro tempore of the Senate during the Johnson administration. Senator Henry Wilson of Massachusetts later served as vice president under Ulysses S. Grant for two years beginning in 1873. New Hampshire senator John P. Hale, formerly a presidential candidate from the Free Soil Party, and Senator Zachariah Chandler of Michigan, a fierce, unrelenting critic of the Lincoln administration, counted themselves among the Radicals.[32]

Dissatisfied with Lincoln's lenient wartime reconstruction plans, the Radicals proposed a far more stringent alternative. In July 1864, Senator Wade, working with Maryland congressman Henry Winter Davis, introduced HR 244 requiring at least 50 percent of a state's eligible white males to swear an "ironclad oath" of allegiance. When that number was reached, a state would schedule a constitutional convention. Participants at the convention would have to guarantee equality before the law as a precondition for the state's readmission into the Union. The bill did not require Negro suffrage, but it laid the groundwork for such a measure in the future. High-ranking Confederate military and civilian leaders were ineligible to swear an oath or participate in a state convention, thereby ensuring that prewar elites were not well situated to seize control of southern state governments after the war.[33]

Presented with the bill before Congress adjourned for the summer, Lincoln recognized a congressional rebuke when he saw one. Rather than allow his 10 percent plan time to be implemented, the Radicals were hellbent on seizing control of reconstruction. Declaring that they "have never been friendly to me," Lincoln set the bill aside and allowed it to lapse without his signature. The pocket veto was rarely used at the time, and it infuriated the Radicals. As authors of the bill, Senator Wade and Congressman Davis issued a public "manifesto" expressing their outrage. "The President, by preventing this bill from becoming a law, holds the electoral votes of the Rebel States at the dictation of his personal ambition," they charged. Lincoln's "dictatorial usurpation of power" was unconscionable. In a hyperbolic statement typical of the Radicals, who reveled in employing rhetoric that shed more heat than light on a subject, the two members of Congress wrote that "a more studied outrage on the legislative authority of the people has never been perpetrated."[34]

The break between Lincoln and the Radicals was not permanent. They needed each other if they were to address lingering problems of repairing a divided Union and deciding how former slaves should be treated. Times were changing rapidly, and the peculiar institution was changing as well. If the president and Congress were to lead, they must make sense of the changes sweeping throughout the land, especially in the North. During a national Negro convention in Syracuse, New York, in October 1864, participants passed resolutions calling for immediate abolition of slavery, legal equality without regard to race, and universal manhood suffrage. The group established the National Equal Rights League (NERL) to promote those goals after the convention ended. Three months later, NERL representatives staged a mass meeting in New Orleans calling for black suffrage in Louisiana. Slavery as an institution was forever altered, if not quite dead. As Lincoln had written in 1862, when he urged border state representatives to accept a program of gradual, compensated emancipation, "You can not if you would, be blind to the signs of the times."[35]

One sign of the times was an effort to draft a constitutional amendment permanently outlawing slavery throughout the country. Lincoln had justified his decision to issue the Emancipation Proclamation based on a wartime exigency. Fearful of alienating slaveholders who remained loyal to the Union, the president did not extend the terms of the proclamation to border states or any non-secessionist state. No one knew what to expect when the fighting ceased and the rebellious states rejoined the Union. Would slavery survive the turmoil? If emancipation were allowed to stand, how far would it extend? A constitutional amendment, if properly drafted, would answer the questions unambiguously.

In January 1864, as the war raged on, Missouri senator John B. Henderson, a genuine rarity in that age—namely, a pro-war, Unionist Democrat—offered a congressional resolution urging the required two-thirds of the members of both houses to introduce a constitutional amendment prohibiting slavery in the United States. After a month's debate in the Senate Judiciary Committee, a modified version of Henderson's proposal came to the floor.

For many senators, a major sticking point was whether the amendment should provide for equality before the law in addition to outlawing slavery. Judiciary Committee members ultimately decided it would be difficult enough to shepherd a bill abolishing slavery through Congress without facing the highly contentious matter of equal treatment before the law. Some critics had charged that an amendment encouraging equality was the first step on the road to perdition, which meant intermarriage between the races and a bid for Negro social equality. By limiting the amendment to the slavery question, the Senate authors cleared a path toward ratification. They kept the language short and simple. Section 1 read, "Neither slavery nor involuntary servitude, except as a punishment for crime whereof the party shall have been duly convicted, shall exist within the United States, or any place subject to their jurisdiction." In Section 2, the bill stated, "Congress shall have power to enforce this article by appropriate legislation."

Democrats were expected to oppose the measure, regardless of whether it included a provision on legal equality. In a surprising move, some party members, recognizing the likelihood that the peculiar institution already was doomed, expressed tentative support for an amendment ending slavery. Whether the representatives were sincere or posturing to score political points was never clear. In any case, most Democrats eventually voted against the amendment.

When the Senate put the proposal to a floor vote on April 7, 1864, visitors packed the galleries to mark the historic occasion. As the votes were tallied, forty-four members answered "present," thirty-eight voted yes, and six voted no. With the members who were present not taking part in the tally, supporters needed thirty votes to secure a two-thirds majority. They won. Every Republican senator voted in favor of the proposal, and even a few Democrats joined them.

The amendment moved to the House of Representatives on May 31. On June 15, the representatives voted 93–65 in favor. Yet it failed to garner the necessary supermajority to secure passage. With the 1864 elections

looming before nervous members of Congress, everyone realizec
posed amendment would be tabled until November or later. Ser
charges that he had repeatedly usurped congressional authority,
had been careful to work behind the scenes in the debate. He was disappointed in the outcome, but he was a political pragmatist. If Republicans
won the election, he would be securely planted in the executive's chair
for another term and could work to woo the Congress to provide support.

Despite suffering through a period of low popularity during the summer months, Lincoln handily won reelection in November. With the Democrats' hopes of undermining the Union war effort by defeating Lincoln
through the ballot box now dashed, the president felt empowered to push
the House of Representatives once again to adopt the Thirteenth Amendment and send it to the states for ratification. On January 31, 1865, the
House complied. With 183 members present and 8 casting no vote at all,
110 yes votes were needed. The final tally was 119–56. From there, the
amendment went to the states. In December 1865, eight months after Lincoln was assassinated, Secretary of State William Seward certified that the
amendment had been adopted. Slavery in America was abolished.[36]

Political developments aside, events moved rapidly as the war concluded. Even if a template for assimilating former slaves into society did
not yet exist, the newly freed men and women took matters into their
own hands. As General William T. Sherman marched through Georgia
and the Carolinas in 1864 and 1865, hundreds of black refugees followed
behind. They looked to the Federal army to break their bonds and lead
them to a promised land. Sherman could hardly be called a friend to the
freedmen, but he recognized the need for a short-term solution, if nothing
else. On January 16, 1865, he issued Special Field Order Number 15 setting aside a large swath of land—approximately four hundred thousand
acres in Florida, Georgia, and South Carolina—to be divided into forty-
acre parcels necessary to sustain some eighteen thousand blacks. This act
gave rise to the much touted concept that freedmen were entitled to forty
acres and a mule. President Andrew Johnson later revoked the order,
which meant that it was of limited value to emancipated slaves. As a
symbolic gesture, however, the order planted a seed of hope among people of color that the Reconstruction epoch promised better treatment.[37]

As Sherman continued his march to Bentonville, North Carolina, and
the climax of the war, former slaves celebrated by abandoning their
homesteads in droves. Whereas the institution of slavery had rested on a
brutal but orderly hierarchy, chaos ruled in its absence. Some freedmen
who had dared not speak out of turn suddenly ransacked the houses they
had served only weeks earlier. Where subservience and hesitancy had
been the order of the day, now anger and disobedience reigned supreme,

at least among some former slaves. Other freedmen stayed on the plantation or waited for a more opportune time to skedaddle away from the
homestead. Whatever their long-term significance, Sherman's march and
the collapse of Confederate military forces ensured that the faithful slave,
to the extent he had ever existed, existed no more.[38]

POSTWAR RECONSTRUCTION

With the collapse of the southern independence movement in April 1865,
American history reached a turning point, one of the most traumatic and
dramatic crossroads in the annals of any nation. Slavery had existed in
colonial America for almost two and a half centuries. For many Americans, it represented a way of life—an economic lifeblood, a social arrangement, a civic responsibility. The loss of the institution fundamentally
altered the lives of millions of Americans, especially the 4 million men,
women, and children of the previously enslaved underclass. Forever after,
the life of the nation would be divided between the time when slavery
existed and the time when it was eradicated. The question became how
a new class of leaders would chart a course into heretofore unknown
territory—territory the founding generation had never envisioned or
planned for in designing a republican form of government.[39]

Complicating the transition from bondage to free labor was the long
tradition of mistrust of government. The nation's founders were thoroughgoing classical liberals. Even when they rejected the Articles of Confederation in favor of a constitution that provided for a greater degree of
centralized authority, they remained deeply suspicious of too much political power concentrated in too few hands. Government existed to perform
services the individual could not perform for himself—building roads or
providing for national defense—but institutional legitimacy depended on
the will of the populace, and few citizens supported social welfare policies. American political philosophers had long declaimed that a government is best that governs least. To extend a helping hand to a class of
persons, even those previously oppressed by the iron fist of an obdurate
social system, was anathema to the laissez-faire proponents who populated political office in the pre-Progressive era.[40]

Despite the lack of a consensus for robust government authority,
extraordinary times required extraordinary measures. In the month
before his death, President Lincoln signed a bill establishing a federal
agency known formally as the Bureau of Refugees, Freedmen, and Abandoned Lands. The plan for a Freedmen's Bureau had been in the works
as far back as the spring of 1864. A victory over the southern rebels was
by no means a foregone conclusion in that dark period, but congressmen

and senators recognized the wisdom in contingency planning coupled with wishful thinking. If the institution of slavery was dead, millions of people must be integrated into American society after the war concluded. Government had freed the slaves; assuming emancipation amounted to more than a wartime measure, government must provide for their well-being until they could stand on their own.[41]

For the better part of a year, as the Federal army slowly ground down the rebels' resistance, Congress debated competing versions of a Freedmen's Bureau bill. Persons suspicious of the armed forces objected to the creation of a new organization to be administered by the War Department after the fighting had ended. They feared federal military officials would be reluctant to relinquish power to civilians in an era of peace. Moreover, concerns about the bureau's authority to resolve labor contracts and land-transfer disputes proliferated among classical liberals worried that the organization would exercise judicial power, thereby potentially usurping the courts' constitutionally mandated authority to try civil and criminal cases. The dangers of an insurrectionary force would be quelled, but an overly zealous federal government might overrule the will of the people.

Establishing a Freedmen's Bureau created a powerful precedent that could serve as the basis for future legislation favoring one group over another. The bill applied specifically to freed slaves but not to whites. The distinction generated political controversy because the measure appeared to elevate former slaves above white citizens left impoverished by the war. If former slaves deserved a helping hand to make their way in post-war America, why should poor whites, many of whom had served in uniform, be left behind?

Perhaps the most contentious provisions involved the disposition of land confiscated by the Federal army after southern owners had fled from advancing troops. Authors of the bill had not spent much time grappling with the land-use requirements. The provisions were a last-minute addition to the conference report in response to General Sherman's Special Field Order Number 15. As a consequence, the legislative history was almost completely silent on the legal grounds for seizing property seemingly without due process of law. Detractors could see little method to the madness. The bureau was empowered to allow freedmen to use and enjoy confiscated lands for three years, but beyond that time it was unclear what would happen to the land or its inhabitants.[42]

Ex-Confederates bitterly resented the loss of their real property as well as the heavy-handed manner in which northern troops administered southern lands. If southerners genuinely were full and free citizens and welcome back into the fold, as Lincoln had intimated, treating former Confederate states as conquered territory was a poor means of engendering respect for the law or allegiance to the flag. Many southerners viewed federal government officials, especially bureau representatives, as tyrants who denied them their property in favor of an inferior class of persons.

For their part, northern whites of lowly station believed they had been ignored despite their desperate need for assistance. They had defended their nation, and yet they did not benefit from property disbursements after the fighting ended. The war had been fought to preserve the Union; yet the postwar arrangement favored the Negro over the white man.

Former slaves believed they had been guaranteed land of their own—specifically, land seized from the antebellum planter elite as a penalty for daring to secede and failing in the endeavor. To the victor belong the spoils. Freedmen expected to be awarded clear title to the lands that had prospered by the sweat of their brows prior to emancipation. It was poetic justice that plantations that once had served as monuments to human indignity should become the property of the laborers who had come of age in bondage. Freedmen reveled in the story, probably apocryphal, of a runaway slave who joined the Federal army, fought as a free man, and later returned to occupy his former master's plantation home. Encountering the now down-on-his-luck owner sometime later, the ex-slave reputedly exclaimed, "Hello, massa; bottom rail top dis time."[43]

Freedpeople especially resented the notion that bureau officials were empowered to negotiate labor contracts with white southerners on behalf of former slaves. Aside from the paternalism of the arrangement, black men recoiled at the prospect of serving as wage laborers without possessing landownership rights. A laborer who works at the pleasure of a landowner is only half a step removed from bondage. The laborer, unlike the slave, is free to leave in search of more advantageous work elsewhere, but the freedom is illusory. In an era with few employment opportunities for persons of color, freedom for a black man who owned no land was merely freedom to starve. In later years, a former slave complained about the life of a laborer in the Reconstruction era. "Freedom wasn't no difference I knows of," he lamented. "I work for Marse John just the same."[44]

The Freedmen's Bureau was almost universally excoriated, but no one proposed a clearly preferable system, and so the agency limped along in performing its assigned duties. General Oliver O. Howard became the first commissioner. A pious man of deeply held religious beliefs, the "Christian General" took to the task with alacrity. If anyone could undertake the almost impossible chore and make it work, Howard was the man. He was a career army officer who held degrees from Bowdoin College and the US Military Academy at West Point. More importantly, he understood the necessity of protecting former slaves from opportunistic whites, in both the North and the South. Yet good intentions and formidable administrative skills can only stretch so far when the presidential administration is hostile, Congress is mostly indifferent, and racism is rampant.

General Howard soon realized that Congress had failed to appropriate adequate funds for the bureau's work. He would be forced to improvise. Because he had experience working with military personnel and had no money to hire additional staff, Howard relied heavily on Federal officers scattered throughout the South to assist in establishing schools and negotiating labor contracts with former slave owners. Upon learning of this uneasy predicament, General Sherman told his colleague, "I fear you have Hercules' task."[45]

For critics of Reconstruction, the Freedmen's Bureau represented much of what was wrong with federal Reconstruction policy. Radical Republicans feared the agency did not possess the necessary legal authority and resources to accomplish its goals. Conservative Democrats charged that the bureau was a repository of cronyism, waste, abuse, and fraud. In a sense, both sides were correct. The Freedmen's Bureau was never adequately funded or empowered to assist emancipated slaves in assimilating into society, which meant that General Howard and his staff performed their tasks using makeshift resources and sometimes inferior personnel. The less than stellar results only reinforced the preconceptions of all parties. The Freedmen's Bureau was set up to fail, and it succeeded in achieving that inadvertent objective.

Yet, for all its shortcomings, the bureau could point to some accomplishments. Approximately 22 million freedpeople received rations when they might otherwise have starved. The agency built forty-five hospitals and clinics serving 148,000 former slaves. Some thirty-two thousand Negroes searching for loved ones lost or sold in the wartime years called on the bureau to provide transportation. Under the agency's aegis, ninety-five hundred teachers flocked to the Southland to teach eager pupils how to read and write. Historically black colleges such as Fisk University in Tennessee, Atlanta University in Georgia, and the Hampton Institute in Virginia owed at least part of their existence to bureau efforts. For his part, General Howard eventually founded a black university that bore his name.[46]

At the outset of his tenure, Howard created ten districts from among the former states of the Confederacy to ensure an orderly administration. The experiment was anything but orderly. Aside from lacking resources, bureau representatives became mired in the details of labor disputes between plantation owners and former slaves who believed they were being swindled. Bureau agents often had to depend on local whites to establish schools, but resistance was fierce, and options were limited. When white women, mostly from New England, arrived in the South to teach freedpeople for little pay, they were ostracized by the white community and forced to live with black families, sometimes in fear for their lives. Few people, no matter how dedicated, could live under such appalling conditions for long. Many gifted teachers departed after only a year or two.[47]

Many bureau agents acted in good faith, but even in the best of circumstances, they struggled to make the program work. In cases where the agents lacked training or administrative support, they failed to improve the quality of life for ex-slaves. Sometimes a foolish representative immersed himself in local politics and triggered a white backlash. The occasional corrupt bureau man sought to enrich himself and, as a result, undermined the entire enterprise. Although the mismanagement and abuses were not as rampant as urban legend suggested, the bureau's reputation nonetheless was tarnished in many southern communities already embittered over battlefield defeats and the reality of emancipation. Bureau opponents recalled the observations of Lazarus Powell, a former governor of Kentucky and US senator who criticized emancipation. Powell had argued that Congress should not create an agency to assist former slaves because such an organization would attract only "your broken-down politicians and your dilapidated preachers," men "who are too lazy to work and just a little too honest to steal."[48]

The new president, a thoroughgoing southerner, shared the disdain many citizens felt for the Freedmen's Bureau. He believed the federal government should not assist any group, for any assistance would undermine a free labor ideology and encourage idleness. Andrew Johnson did not share his predecessor's belief that, in Lincoln's words, the "slaves constituted a peculiar and powerful interest" or that "all knew that this interest was somehow the cause of the war." In his view, the conflict amounted to a class struggle wherein the rich white planter elite forced war on the simple white yeoman farmer. Johnson had no use for freedpersons. He wanted to reconstruct the Union as quickly as possible without involving the federal government in the efforts of former slaves to eke out a meager existence.[49]

When congressional Republicans introduced a measure to reauthorize the bureau in February 1866, Johnson vetoed it because, he claimed, the bureau exercised authority as a judicial tribunal; therefore, it violated Article III of the US Constitution, which vested supreme judicial authority in the courts. As Johnson explained, a "system for the support of indigent persons was never contemplated by the authors of the Constitution; nor can any good reason be advanced why, as a permanent establishment, it should be founded for one class or color of our people more than another." Anyone familiar with the original Freedmen's Bureau bill recognized that the agency was never intended to serve "as a permanent establishment," but Johnson feared it would exist in perpetuity despite contrary assurances. In an explanation designed to appear above partisan politics, Johnson contended that the Constitution was not designed to protect "one class or color of our people more than another." The Freedmen's Bureau eventually won reauthorization in Congress and limped on until 1872, but it never lived up to its promise.[50]

The Radical Republicans had hoped Johnson would agree with their Reconstruction plans, but even before he vetoed the reauthorization bill for the Freedmen's Bureau, it was clear a kindred spirit did not occupy the Executive Mansion. When he announced his Reconstruction plan in May 1865, the executive made it clear he intended to be lenient with the South. He agreed to pardon and restore the property rights, except as to slaves, of all southerners save the highest-ranking military and political leaders of the Confederacy. He appointed provisional governors and outlined the conditions necessary for the creation of new state governments that would enjoy full rights in a restored Union. As long as the southern states repudiated secession, abolished slavery, and set aside Confederate debt, their citizens could expect to govern themselves without undue influence from the federal government. It was a remarkably forgiving program in light of the sacrifices made by the northern armies in the war. It is little wonder that the radical faction was so incensed by the president's tepid support for remaking southern society in accordance with northern values.[51]

The subsequent tumult between President Johnson and congressional Republicans over the direction of Reconstruction has been recounted in numerous sources. A ferocious battle between the executive and legislative branches of government for control over federal Reconstruction policy followed Johnson's May 1865 announcement. The dispute ultimately culminated in the first impeachment of a US president. Johnson won an acquittal, but his presidency was mortally wounded. Suffice it to say that the consistency of federal policy, not to mention the fate of the freedpeople, suffered as a result of the dispute.[52]

The story of Reconstruction became the story of what might have been. It might have been a time of healing the nation's wounds and integrating former slaves into national life. It might have been a golden age for living up to the nation's creed as expressed in the Declaration of Independence that all men are created equal. It might have been a period when citizens learned how much they could achieve when they were united as one country and one people. Yet, if these are the criteria by which Reconstruction is judged, the dozen years following the American Civil War represented a failure to live up to the possibilities of remaking the republic.

The late 1860s initially promised better times ahead for the freedmen. Sixteen black men were elected to Congress during Reconstruction, and twenty-two would serve by the end of the century. When local and state positions were tabulated, between fifteen hundred and two thousand people of color held elective office at all levels of government in the United States before the dawn of the twentieth century. They might have been the founders of a new epoch, pioneers in the establishment of a more perfect union where all citizens could aspire to occupy high elective office. It did not happen that way. With few exceptions, black elected officials possessed no real political power. For many southern whites, the elevation of Negroes to positions of political responsibility was galling, a stain on the honor of the South. White people had been taught throughout their lives to regard Negroes as inferior beings. To expect white citizens to accept these humble creatures as their political and social equals was asking too much of a people already humiliated by a lost war and a peace dictated by military officers patrolling their streets and byways.[53]

Historians continue to debate whether federal Reconstruction policy represented an unfinished revolution or the remaking of society after the war was too much to expect of a country that had experienced such turmoil. Proponents of the former interpretation contend that the war and Reconstruction were part and parcel of the same struggle—namely, the transformation of a nation constructed on a cornerstone of slave labor and inequality into a modern country based on equal rights for everyone. By failing to complete the social change from a slave-holding government to a government that refused to tolerate disparate treatment, the generation of leaders who held power in the 1860s and 1870s initiated a revolution they could not or would not finish.

The contrary view suggests that the revolution brought about by the Civil War was separate from a revolution of equal rights. The citizens of that era, no matter how well meaning and enlightened, simply had no stomach for enduring additional cataclysmic change coming so soon on the heels of a civil war. They longed for a peaceful time when they could turn away from the horrors and uncertainties of social upheaval. As a result of this longing for peace, the freedmen paid a steep price. The inattention and unwillingness of white Americans to follow through on promises seemingly made at war's end left former slaves to fend for themselves.

THE AFTERMATH OF RECONSTRUCTION

Beginning in the late 1860s, a "counter-Reconstruction" movement arose. Numerous whites on both sides of the Mason-Dixon Line believed that "radical" Reconstruction had failed. It was time to end federal occupation of the South and return to normal relations. Augustus Summerfield Merrimon, a Democratic US senator from North Carolina, perhaps expressed it best in 1874 when he observed, "Radicalism is dissolving—going to pieces, but what is to take its place, does not clearly appear."[55]

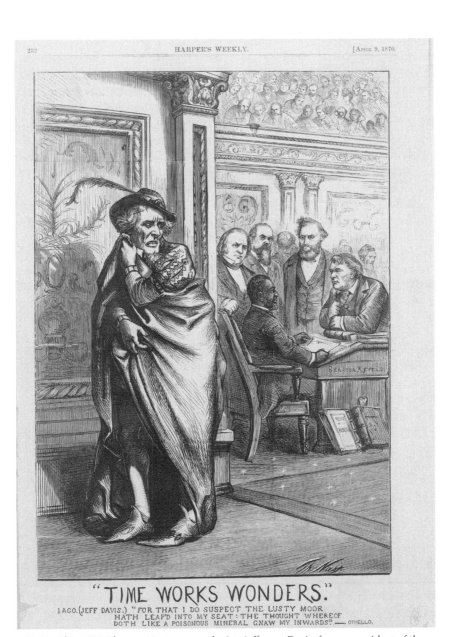

"TIME WORKS WONDERS."

IAGO.(JEFF DAVIS.) "FOR THAT I DO SUSPECT THE LUSTY MOOR
HATH LEAP'D INTO MY SEAT: THE THOUGHT WHEREOF
DOTH LIKE A POISONOUS MINERAL GNAW MY INWARDS." — OTHELLO.

[1.1]   This 1870 Thomas Nast cartoon depicts Jefferson Davis, former president of the Confederate States of America, as the evil Iago, Shakespeare's conniving villain who conspired against Othello, the black Moor leader. Davis was furious because a black man, Hiram Rhodes Revels, had entered the US Senate ("the lusty Moor Hath leap'd into my seat") representing the state of Mississippi. Davis had represented Mississippi in the Senate from 1857 until 1861. Courtesy of the Library of Congress.

When public support for federal Reconstruction policies eroded during President Ulysses S. Grant's second term as president, white southern leaders frequently adopted a facade of reconciliation. If they could assuage the concerns of an anxious northern public by demonstrating that the South was not filled with dangerous miscreants seeking only to return to the glories of the antebellum era, a transition from Reconstruction to a new epoch could be accomplished with minimal sectional strife. Whether the planter elite ever intended to renounce the values of the prewar years seems unlikely, especially in light of subsequent events, but clearly it was in the best interests of southerners who hoped to "win the peace" to persuade their brethren that the region was not replete with unreconstructed Fire-Eaters desirous of revisiting settled public policy. As a demonstration of the new thinking, Lucius Quintus Cincinnatus Lamar, a leading Mississippi politician, took the previously unthinkable step of eulogizing a recently deceased US senator and Radical Republican, Charles Sumner, in the US House of Representatives in April 1874. By the time Lamar deigned it prudent to lionize a former adversary, Reconstruction was dead, if not quite buried. Only South Carolina, Louisiana, and Florida endured "radical" rule until 1877, the year that most historians consider Reconstruction irrevocably over.[56]

As federal officials moved away from reconstructing the nation in the 1870s, promises of equality for the black race were abandoned. Left to their own devices, many southerners went back to the old ways, confident that social relations, except as to slavery, could be restored. A Democrat from North Carolina unabashedly commented, "When the bayonets shall depart, then look out for the reaction. Then the bottom rail will descend from the top of the fence."[57]

A southern state that passed from northern "carpetbagger" control into the hands of southern gentlemen was said to have been "redeemed." The redeemers were sometimes labeled "Bourbons," a not-so-veiled reference to the House of Bourbon, which forgot nothing of the past and learned few lessons from the bloodshed accompanying the French Revolution. The southern Bourbons were determined not to suffer the fate of their namesakes. They would herald the triumph of white supremacy during the 1880s by using the mechanisms of state law and policy to ensure that freedpeople knew their place. The bottom rail must stay at the bottom of the fence, as the Lord intended.

The Redeemers were a strange, eclectic coalition composed of secessionist Democrats and former Whigs, Confederate veterans, proponents of industrialization, the planter elite, and young men who came of age during the ennui of Reconstruction. Whatever their political differences, they sought to remake the South into a land favoring their interests and reversing the gains made by blacks during Reconstruction. "Retrenchment" was the battle cry of those who would clean up state governments by erasing all remnants of the evil carpetbaggers. Lower taxes and less government intrusion into individual lives would allow citizens to escape the yoke of government oppression. "Spend nothing unless absolutely necessary," Florida governor George F. Drew, a Democrat, advised.[58]

Laissez-faire economics and a weak government became crucial components of the southern way of life during the era of Redemption. Minimalist government also provided a convenient rationale for depriving freedmen of government assistance. If the states were stripped of all but "necessary" authority, blacks would be left to sink or swim on their own. That government is best that governs least, the classical liberal mantra, enjoyed a revival.

Retrenchment successfully decimated operations for southern state governments of the 1870s and 1880s. Mississippi cut expenses in half. Other southern states reported similar outcomes. Citizens paid lower property taxes, although the arrangement typically benefited wealthy landowners more than it helped less affluent whites. Poll taxes and licensure fee increases perpetuated the regressive nature of the new taxation system, ensuring that the gulf between the haves and have-nots widened among southerners for generations to come. Public school budgets were slashed so severely that illiteracy became rampant. Whatever else they accomplished during their hour on the stage, the Redeemers ensured that poverty would remain the South's predominant regional feature until well into the next century. It was hardly an uplifting legacy.[59]

Blacks did not immediately lose the gains they achieved during Reconstruction, but as the years passed, white southerners chipped away at the remnants of the hated carpetbagger regime. By 1890, a black elected official was the exception that proved the rule. People of color were no longer slaves, but in some southern locales, the distinction seemed to be without a difference. Wages were low, assuming a black man could find a job in the first place. Rare was the black landowner, at least in the South, and rarer still was the man who could pull himself up by his bootstraps, as the myth of the American dream so often promised.

The steady, sure growth of a new white supremacist regime occurred because the Redeemers did not dismantle Reconstruction policies under the cover of night. They could unapologetically disenfranchise their enemies in broad daylight. If it was necessary to move a polling station with no advance notice in the black community, so be it. If trickery had to be used to ensure social control, it was a small price to pay. In egregious cases, violence would be employed to show uppity freedmen and disgruntled lower-class whites the facts of life, but subterfuge worked most of the time.[60]

The Democratic Party solidified its hold on southern politics, although it hardly enjoyed the hegemonic control of legend. Throughout the 1880s, class resentments festered. Upland whites who had never owned slaves clashed with the planter elite of the low country. The former had hoped to take advantage of the marginalization of blacks to improve their own social position under a white supremacist regime. When poor whites realized that elites had no desire to welcome them into the ranks, they turned to organizations that could look after their interests.[61]

Beginning in the mid-1870s, the National Grange of the Order of Patrons of Husbandry, commonly known as the Grange, emerged in the Southland to encourage poor white farmers to band together and push for policies that benefited the less well-to-do in southern society. Other groups, most of which were informal, pursued a similar goal. The Greenback Party called for monetary policy not backed by bullion, which tended to favor the rich, in favor of "greenbacks," or paper currency, which would increase the amount of money in circulation, trigger an increase in commodity prices, and ease the debt burden on farmers. During the 1870s and 1880s, the Readjuster Party in Virginia sought to reverse the retrenchment cuts in state government services that enriched the planter elite at the expense of less affluent whites.[62]

White Redeemers, with good reason, recognized that a populist backlash could drive them from power. To stave off the threat, they developed the "fusion principle." Never a friend to the freedmen but nonetheless masters of practical politics, Redeemers reached out to blacks, promising to improve their treatment and appoint prominent Negroes to minor political posts in exchange for political support. By fusing white elite and politically astute black interests, the resultant coalition fended off militant populism for a time. The freedmen were not naive. They well understood that they were being used as pawns in a political struggle between different classes of white citizens, but they also understood pragmatism.[63]

For their part, the Bourbons knew they had merely postponed the day when lower-echelon whites would grab control of the mechanisms of government. Theirs was an ironic position. During the 1870s, the white planter elite had seized control from the carpetbaggers as Reconstruction ended. The goal was to recapture antebellum glories to the extent possible with the death of the peculiar institution. Within a decade or less, they had become the thing they had railed against during the carpetbagger era—maintainers of the status quo, protectors of freedmen, and champions of elite values against the will of a white majority. It was an untenable position, as time would demonstrate.[64]

2

Jumpin' Jim Crow and Legal Segregation

"The White Race Deems Itself to Be the Dominant Race"

He was an old man, years past his prime, when he stepped before the Metropolitan A. M. E. Church of Washington, DC, that winter's day in January 1894. Yet even in his dotage he could still find fire in the belly when he needed it, as he needed it now. Although he did not know it at the time, this was to be his last great public address. He must have suspected that the hour was late and his life was almost spent, for it was obvious to all that his hair was graying and his faculties were declining. Undeterred, the elder statesman was determined to serve up a sermon filled with the trademark fire-and-brimstone rhetoric of his youth.

He had accomplished much during his long, active life, and his renowned facility for words was a major reason for his success. Yet he realized the task was far from completed—if it was ever to be completed. As long as the Negro remained a second-class citizen in the land of his birth, battles had to be fought and won, or the long journey had been undertaken in vain. Would a person of color ever find a fulfilling life of equal opportunity in this flawed, unrepentant land? Recognizing that the struggle over public memory of the Civil War, emancipation, and Reconstruction was never-ending, the old man had watched the northern retreat from promises of equal rights and the rise of the southern Lost Cause mythology since the 1870s. If memories of the past were manipulated to serve an exclusionist political cause, what would the future hold for the black man in America? He looked to the horizon for answers, and what he saw there filled him with foreboding.[1]

FREDERICK DOUGLASS AND HIS
VANISHING LEGACY

"No man should come before an audience like the one by whose presence I am now honored, without a noble object and a fixed and earnest purpose," he began, enunciating each word in a deep, rich baritone voice made famous through decades of agitation. "I think that, in whatever else I may be deficient, I have the qualifications indicated, to speak to you this evening." He was being deliberately modest. Frederick Douglass was one of the most famous American men of a century that was rapidly drawing to a close. He had lived at the center of public life ever since he had escaped from chattel slavery almost six decades earlier. If anyone had the qualifications to speak to the plight of the American Negro, it was he.

"I propose to give you a colored man's view of the unhappy relations at present existing between the white and colored people of the Southern States of our union," he said. He did exactly that. For all the gains that black folk had achieved at mid-century, he had looked across the landscape and was not encouraged by the storms he saw brewing. He was worried, he explained, that the "Negro problem" would not be resolved to the satisfaction of either party as long as darker-hued peoples remained the object of unrelenting oppression. "I have waited patiently but anxiously to see the end of the epidemic of mob law and persecution and prevailing at the South," but the wait had been long and torturous. Explaining that "the indications are not hopeful," he lamented the spread of a terrible disease—the disease of prejudice and hatred. "It is no longer local, but national; no longer confined to the South, but has invaded the North," he observed. "The contagion is spreading, extending and over-leaping geographical lines and state boundaries, and if permitted to go on it threatens to destroy all respect for law and order not only in the South, but in all parts of our country—North as well as South."

Although the shackles of slavery had been loosened, and that was no mean achievement, a black man was not fully free. Everywhere across the land, the shadow of racial prejudice fell on him. If a dirty job was required, the Negro would do it. If evidence of a crime was found, the Negro was the first suspect to be interrogated. If a white woman alleged that an insult had been uttered against her virtue, a Negro was the likely culprit, and he would be turned over to the mob for summary justice. Legal niceties were ignored. If a scapegoat was needed, the Negro conve-

[2.1]   The iconic black leader Frederick Douglass feared that whites would not honor promises made to people of color during Reconstruction. His fears proved to be prescient. Courtesy of the National Archives and Records Administration.

niently served in the role. Douglass was appalled that his people might never be afforded gainful employment or an opportunity for advancement. The Negro is not a saint, he told his audience, but surely he is no sinner merely because his skin is dark.

Douglass sadly acknowledged, "The Negro is in some respects, and in some localities, in a worse condition to-day than in the time of slavery" because he was said to be free, but the statement was a thinly veiled lie. In response to persons who would charge that blacks were incapable of self-governance, and therefore that emancipation was a cruel hoax, the old man of abolitionism quickly moved to correct the mistake: "To my mind, the blame for this condition does not rest upon emancipation, but upon slavery. It is not the result of emancipation, but the defeat of emancipation. It is not the work of the spirit of liberty, but the work of the spirit of bondage, and of the determination of slavery to perpetuate itself, if not under one form, then under another. It is due to the folly of endeavoring to retain the new wine of liberty in the old bottles of slavery. I concede the evil but deny the alleged cause."

Douglass worried that powerful forces were arrayed against freedmen. Wherever they turned—in a labor system that kept them impoverished and tied to the land, in an educational system that denied them access to the same opportunities afforded to whites, in a legal system that failed to fulfill promises made when the Civil War amendments were ratified— black citizens found themselves at a distinct disadvantage. "Put away your race prejudice," he concluded. "Banish the idea that one class must rule over another. Recognize the fact that the rights of the humblest citizen are as worthy of protection as are those of the highest, and your problem will be solved." If Americans at the end of the nineteenth century would exhibit the courage to open a new chapter in the nation's history, Douglass admonished, "your Republic will stand and flourish forever."[2]

It was wishful thinking. The legacy of Frederick Douglass was quickly fading, and the grand old man knew it. He had lived long enough to watch the struggle for equal rights wax and wane. When he was born into slavery, the idea that emancipation would occur during his lifetime was absurd. Yet he bore witness to the movement of history toward a fiery war and a push to remake the American republic into a more perfect union. Following the bloodshed, the nation's leaders had ratified the Thirteenth, Fourteenth, and Fifteenth amendments abolishing slavery, providing for due process and equal protection of the law at the state level, and extending the franchise to men regardless of race, respectively. It had all been so promising, but the promises appeared to have been forgotten. Douglass understood that America was retreating from the commitments it supposedly had made through a terrible expenditure of lives and fortunes.[3]

This "retreat" happened with an apparent inevitability as victorious northerners grew weary of policing the recalcitrant South. Rather than reinforce Reconstruction policies into the foreseeable future, northern leaders accepted white southerners' promises that a new day had dawned without making serious inquiries into the veracity of their pledges. The result was hardly surprising to anyone who lived in the South. With the death of Reconstruction, blacks were left to the mercy of their former masters and to the increasingly indifferent populace in the North. Negro leaders such as Frederick Douglass called attention to oaths affirmed and abandoned, but they were marginalized voices crying out against the swift, sure tide of history.[4]

The mechanisms of government employed by federal leaders might have been expected to correct egregious deficiencies, but this was not to be. The 1870s and 1880s witnessed a gradual reversal of the modest civil rights gains that blacks had enjoyed during the 1860s. US Supreme Court opinions from the era provide a case in point. Reviewing the use of literacy tests, grandfather clauses, and poll taxes, the high court held that nothing in the Civil War amendments prohibited such measures if states employed them properly to ensure the accuracy and reliability of voting rolls. In 1883, the court continued dismantling the Reconstruction regime by striking down as unconstitutional the Civil Rights Act of 1875 as well as the anti–Ku Klux Klan laws.[5] By one reckoning, between 1890 and 1910, only 19 of the 528 cases decided by the Supreme Court involving the Fourteenth Amendment applied to Negro rights, and in those cases the outcomes were not favorable. During that same time, 228 of the Fourteenth Amendment cases applied to corporations. Protecting the principles of federalism and the power of corporations, it seems, was more important than ensuring the rights of persons of color.[6]

As the federal government turned away from advancing Negro rights, state governments stepped up and enacted statutes to fill the void. Beginning around 1880, southern states passed a series of segregation measures known as Jim Crow laws. The term originated from a popular character featured in antebellum minstrel shows in which Negroes, stereotyped as buffoons, engaged in all sorts of silly shenanigans. White audiences howled in laughter as these stupid cretins foolishly engulfed themselves in zany situations usually attributable to the backwardness of the participants. T. D. "Daddy" Rice, a performer credited with popularizing the Jim Crow character, toured the country with his antics. The term "Jim Crow" may have referred to a slave named Jim Crow (or Jim Cuff), but eventually it became synonymous with the slow, half-witted creature who could not be expected to govern himself.[7]

The language reflected many, although not all, whites' view of blacks at the end of the nineteenth century. Quasi social scientists and myriad

JIM CROW,

[2.2]   This illustration, dating from the 1835–1845 period, shows a black man wearing tattered clothes as he dances along the riverside. The image is thought to be an early depiction of the "Jim Crow" character. Courtesy of the Library of Congress.

pseudoscientists propagated theories of Negro inferiority. One popular view suggested that dark-skinned peoples represented a missing link between the noble white man and lesser animals. This bastardized Darwinism justified unequal treatment of blacks and became a convenient pretext for practicing disparate legal treatment. Yes, all human beings should expect equal treatment before the law, but the poor, wretched Negro was hardly a full human being in the way a white man was human. Exactly as a dog or horse could not expect the same legal rights as a man, the Negro should understand his place in the existential scheme.

Whether contemplative whites believed the standard mythology or merely mouthed the mantra so they could ignore the consequences of their actions remains an open question. Surely the more philosophical souls on each side of the color line questioned the established order, but reflecting on injustice and correcting it remained vastly different enterprises. As the South moved to institutionalize racial prejudice and the North followed suit, subtleties were lost in the brutal regime that emerged.[8]

With an eye toward meeting the challenges of the future, especially the increase in industrialization and the rise of corporate power, white southerners might have looked to a new crop of leaders to guide them through a difficult period. Such a supposition underestimates the level of anger and frustration that existed with the demise of Reconstruction. Instead of disavowing the values and personnel that sustained the Confederate States of America, embittered southerners defiantly sought out veterans for high office. A former Confederate soldier who otherwise might have been deemed unfit for a political career suddenly found himself jostling with the antebellum elite for a seat at the table of power. In light of the desire for a continuity of purpose, it was little wonder that southern states soundly rejected the politics of Reconstruction in an era of Redemption.[9]

THE TRIUMPH OF THE MISSISSIPPI PLAN

The embrace of the Mississippi Plan epitomized the political machinations of the time. Southern Democrats remained cognizant of the realities of battlefield defeat and emancipation; if they willingly accepted the status quo, they would be marginalized for the foreseeable future. When the victorious Republicans added freedmen to the southern electorate, they secured a reliable voting bloc that could prove costly to white southerners in states such as Mississippi and Louisiana, which boasted high black populations. If white northerners and black southerners formed an ongoing political coalition, Reconstruction policies would continue as before.

The solution was to nullify black voting strength, and the Mississippi Plan proved to be a suitable vehicle. Using voter intimidation as an effective means of disenfranchising the freedmen was hardly innovative, but as former Confederate military leader (and future US senator) James Z. George and influential newspaper editor Ethelbert Barksdale developed the scheme, nothing as gauche as naked violence would be employed. Gone were the days when white southerners would don conical hats and bed sheets, riding under cover of night to instill fear in the hearts of emancipated slaves or administer beatings to uppity Negroes who depended on the good graces of condescending carpetbaggers. The Ku Klux Klan and similar organizations had served their purpose during the late 1860s and early 1870s—crude, but effective, they had sent a message to complacent northern men that a subjugated people would not be oppressed indefinitely—but those groups had been vilified and broken, prosecuted in court, and legislated out of existence.

The times were different, and white southerners needed to respond in a different manner, although the ends were the same: to reinstitute white rule south of the Mason-Dixon Line. With the death of Reconstruction, violence and intimidation could be doled out in a more effective manner than they had been in bygone days. The trick was to act in broad daylight as though state officials were ensuring the orderly administration of government operations. Violence would be used as necessary, but subtle threats would be far more effective in keeping freedmen in line and holding would-be northern interlopers at bay. In short, the Mississippi Plan was erected on a foundation of unadulterated chicanery.[10]

Mindful of the consequences of allowing Republicans to organize a successful electoral coalition, white southerners formed paramilitary organizations that traveled under different names in different states. Mississippi's White Line, Louisiana's White League, Alabama's White Man's Party, and South Carolina's rifle clubs or Red Shirts ostensibly devoted their energies to promoting camaraderie among young men in their communities and ensuring they could protect their communities if the freedmen or other undesirables took up arms. Behind the scenes, the clubs were ominous reminders that Republicans were outnumbered, and possibly outgunned, if they dared to exercise their political rights. If not as fiercely aggressive and violent as the Ku Klux Klan, these successor organizations knew the power of the veiled threat and used it judiciously.[11]

The Red Shirts became one of the most effective paramilitary groups of the time. They first arose around 1875 or perhaps 1876 as white Democrats in several states, including Mississippi, organized their members to implement the Mississippi Plan. The name apparently was a mocking reference to a common practice among northern men—namely, "waving the bloody shirt." Republicans standing for elective office found they could win votes by recalling the traitorous activities of Democrats who had supported the South during the Civil War. Sometimes the candidate literally would display a blood-stained shirt as a physical reminder of the horrors of secession and armed conflict, but more often "waving the bloody shirt" was a coded phrase that subtly equated Democratic support with treason. Governor Oliver P. Morton of Indiana was among the more famous political figures to use this tactic. In a well-known 1866 speech, he figuratively waved the bloody shirt when he claimed that the Democratic Party was "a common sewer and loathsome receptacle, into which is emptied every element of treason, North and South." With their ironic reference to the hated Yankee practice and their promise of political payback, the Red Shirts spread to many southern states, notably South Carolina, where they supported former Confederate general Wade Hampton's successful gubernatorial bid.[12]

With paramilitary groups leading the way, the plan achieved its greatest success in Mississippi as the Reconstruction era wound to a close. During the 1875 state elections, Republicans held rallies to inspire their supporters, including local blacks who could be expected to support the party of emancipation. To disrupt these gatherings, Mississippi officials issued loyalty certificates to Negroes who agreed to support the Democratic cause. The certificate was a guarantee of sorts that the holder and his family would be protected from violence. A black man who found himself without a certificate was presumed to be a Republican, and woe to that man and his loved ones. In addition, state law was amended to require registered voters to disclose their place of employment and their election district. If a Negro realized that Democratic Party appointees were observing his movements and reporting his voting patterns to his employer, he might decline to support the Republicans lest he lose his job and imperil his future economic prospects—to say nothing of his life.

In most places, the threat of violence sufficed to suppress Republican voter support, but bloody skirmishes occasionally broke out between blacks and whites. After armed battles erupted in Clinton and Yazoo City, Governor Adelbert Ames, a carpetbagger whose days in office were numbered, requested military support from the Ulysses S. Grant administration. Fearful that dispatching troops would generate criticism of Republicans as overly militant and hinder political support in other state elections, the president's men demurred. If ever the remaining carpetbagger regimes needed a reminder that their era was passing, the triumph of the plan in Mississippi in 1875 served as a painful political lesson.[13]

The plan was not limited to Mississippi. Other states—South Carolina (1895), Louisiana (1898), North Carolina (1900), Alabama (1901), Virginia (1901), Georgia (1908), and Oklahoma (1910)—followed suit, with each modifying the terms to meet local conditions. Although their tactics differed, the strategy of diluting black political power was the same. In some cases, overt voter intimidation was the key. In other cases, literacy tests, poll taxes, gerrymandering, or state constitutional conventions specifically designed to disenfranchise Negroes accomplished the goal. By the early twentieth century, white supremacy reigned supreme in states of the former Southern Confederacy. If northern states were not as overtly racist as their southern counterparts, no one came to the party with clean hands. A pattern of discrimination existed in northern states as well.[14]

THE FEDERAL GOVERNMENT AND SUPPORT FOR THE WHITE REGIME

Southern state legislatures were not the only organs of government to lend an imprimatur to the Jim Crow regime. At the federal level, members of Congress expressed little support for protecting the freedmen. During the late 1860s and early 1870s, the Radical Republicans had led the charge to assist newly emancipated slaves in moving from bondage into a life of free labor, but that generation of leaders lost influence with the demise of Reconstruction. By the mid-1870s, the Radicals either were dead or out of power. In one last hurrah during the waning days of his political career, Massachusetts senator Charles Sumner pushed through the Civil Rights Act of 1875 to prohibit discrimination in public transportation and accommodation. Yet his last political act would not stand the test of time. A politically conservative US Supreme Court eventually pronounced the law unconstitutional.[15]

The generation of white congressmen and senators who supplanted the Radicals either appeared indifferent to the black man's plight or became overtly hostile. The adherents of indifference were weary of the war and its aftermath. It was time to move forward, especially as the nation industrialized in its march toward the twentieth century. The job of elected officials, many political leaders contended, was to implement policies encouraging laissez-faire economic policies and a full dinner pail. In lieu of waving a bloody shirt, they were content to reject antebellum schisms and clasp hands with their southern brethren. The past should be buried once and for all. Even if southerners seemed reluctant to let bygones be bygones—after all, the Lost Cause mythology suggested that the values of the Old South were noble and enduring—a jaundiced northern public need not be overly concerned with nostalgic longings in the Southland.[16]

Southern members of Congress were as hostile to black interests as ever, but they became adept at a new type of politics. They recognized the need to keep Negroes in line while simultaneously assuring their fellow legislators that nothing was amiss in the former states of the Southern Confederacy. Whereas Fire-Eaters had reveled in uttering defiant, fiery rhetoric during the 1850s and 1860s, a new brand of southern leader uttered sweet nothings in their stead. Lucius Quintus Cincinnatus Lamar, a smooth Mississippi politician, practiced the new craft as well as anyone. He had been an ardent secessionist in 1861, but Lamar was a pragmatic man and understood that he must adapt to his new circumstances. His willingness to praise the late Senator Charles Sumner, the Massachusetts icon and leading Radical Republican, was a new development. Eulogizing a prominent champion of northern values would have been unthinkable a decade earlier, but times had changed, and the olive branch would work wonders where bullets had failed to achieve the desired result. A new strategy of wearing an accommodating, reasonable public face while enforcing white control behind the scenes would carry many a southern politician through a successful legislative career in the ensuing nine decades. If black citizens understood what it was to wear a smiling mask, southern leaders proved that they too could hide their true motives behind a carefully constructed public facade.[17]

The executive branch was no more interested in protecting or advancing the Negro cause than was the Congress. With the old warhorse Ulysses S. Grant retired in the wake of myriad political and financial scandals, his successor, Rutherford B. Hayes, got busy mending fences with ex-Confederates. Hayes already had signaled the federal government's new attitude when he won the office through a series of machinations known as the Wormley Agreements. Following an electoral deadlock during the 1876 presidential contest, Hayes and his people apparently cut a deal. The new administration would withdraw support for carpetbagger governments in unreconstructed states if southern leaders guaranteed "proper protection" for blacks and state Republicans after federal troops had vacated the statehouse grounds. In addition, the Louisiana state legislature would elect a new Democratic US senator after March 10, thereby allowing Hayes time to secure Senate approval for his cabinet nominees without engendering a political firestorm. In one final act of reconciliation, a Hayes administration would appoint a southern Democrat to the cabinet as a good-faith show of support for its new southern allies.[18]

Whether the agreements represented an unconscionably corrupt quid pro quo bargain or a new working coalition in an age of Redemption remains an open question. Perhaps nothing nefarious happened, but it certainly appeared to have. As Hayes affirmed his oath of office in March 1877, however, a changed attitude was indisputable. Shortly thereafter, federal troops stood down, and the last of the southern states were redeemed. The new president insisted the policy was not a wholesale abandonment of the Reconstruction program, although skeptics could be forgiven their suspicions.[19]

Hayes referred to unresolved questions of race in his inaugural address. He understood that the southern states remained mired in poverty and racial divisions, but he was determined that the federal government would improve conditions rather than exacerbate tensions. "The evils which afflict the Southern States can only be removed or remedied by the united and harmonious efforts of both races, actuated by motives of mutual sympathy and regard; and while in duty bound and fully determined to protect the rights of all by every constitutional means at the disposal of my Administration, I am sincerely anxious to use every legitimate influence in favor of honest and efficient local *self*-government as the true resource of those States for the promotion of the contentment and prosperity of their citizens," he wrote. Although initially his words sounded reasonable and sympathetic to blacks and whites, the language was code for a "hands-off" policy that must have warmed the hearts of white southerners anxious to escape federal control.

Hayes was not finished with the platitudes. "In the effort I shall make to accomplish this purpose I ask the cordial cooperation of all who cherish an interest in the welfare of the country, trusting that party ties and the prejudice of race will be freely surrendered in behalf of the great purpose to be accomplished."[20] Whether this was a naively sentimental promise or a not-so-secret pledge to allow the southern states to "guard the interests of both races carefully and equally" as they saw fit—with white supremacy as a core value—can be debated, but the latter seems probable. Unless the new president was blind to two centuries of southern history or cognitively impaired, he must have understood that blacks would be mistreated under southern white rule. In all likelihood, Hayes concluded that a state white supremacist regime implemented at the expense of the freedmen was a price worth paying to bind the wounds of the Civil War.[21]

The president lived up to his word by allowing the South to practice self-governance with little oversight. He also appointed dyed-in-the-wool Democrats to patronage positions, a sure sign of his new southern strategy. During an address to an Atlanta audience in September 1877, Hayes assured black citizens, "I had given that matter some consideration, and now my colored friends, who have thought, or who have been told that I was turning my back upon the men whom I fought for, now listen." Hayes explained that assurances had been made that Negroes would not be left out of the governing structure. "After thinking it over, I believe your rights and interests would be safer if this great mass of intelligent white men were left alone by the General Government," he said.[22]

No one, except possibly President Hayes himself, was fooled. White supremacy was the order of the day. All the assurances in the world would not change the ugly, brutal facts of the Jim Crow regime. With each passing year, it was clear that the institution of slavery, while technically a relic of history, lived on in subtle and not-so-subtle vestiges. When a black man was denied an opportunity to secure a well-paying job because of his skin color, or an educational institution refused to admit his children, or his family could not escape the sharecropping system because the debt was too great to ever repay, the remnants of slavery were reinvigorated. When blacks were sentenced to lengthy prison terms for relatively minor crimes or forced to work on chain gangs, the peculiar institution was alive and well in all but name. When the color line was recognized and its infringements enforced, with all its unwritten rules and taboos in place, the Negro was relegated to the bottom of the heap and reminded daily of his lowly station.[23]

The one branch of government that might have provided a remedy to the inequities of the epoch remained as hostile to blacks as the others. The American Founders had envisioned the judiciary as a mechanism for correcting the abuses that invariably occurred when majority rule was the only guiding principle. By establishing life tenure in the federal courts, the authors of the Constitution believed they had created an institution that would not pander to the masses and would enjoy a level of political autonomy absent from the legislative and executive offices. This institutional independence was especially important because the judiciary would consider cases of individual rights, which would never enjoy the popular support that broad policy questions would engender. A judge or justice who did not fear losing popular support theoretically would be free to render an opinion based on the strict letter of the law and the merits of the case, not the passions of the mob or the tenor of the times.

Yet even in this one undemocratic branch of government, Jim Crow danced his hour upon the stage with impunity. For starters, throughout much of the nineteenth century, the federal courts seldom reviewed state cases. When they did, judges and justices expressed support for a robust system of federalism whereby the federal courts would not intervene in state matters unless a state had clearly violated the US Constitution. The Fourteenth Amendment was one of three Civil War amendments enacted to assist freedmen in throwing off the yoke of slavery and assimilating into the civil life of the remade nation, and initially the amendments appeared to be a means for federal intervention, but the courts narrowly interpreted its language. Section one states, "All persons born or naturalized in the United States and subject to the jurisdiction thereof, are citizens of the United States and of the State wherein they reside. No State shall make or enforce any law which shall abridge the privileges or immunities of citizens of the United States; nor shall any State deprive any person of life, liberty, or property, without due process of law; nor deny to any person within its jurisdiction the equal protection of the laws." Instead of broadly applying the privileges and immunities, due process, and equal protection clauses, the federal courts not only declined to expand the concepts during the late nineteenth century but actively participated in dismantling the Reconstruction regime.[24]

The retreat began in 1873 when the US Supreme Court decided *In Re Slaughterhouse Cases*.[25] Louisiana had enacted a law in 1869 allowing the city of New Orleans to establish a corporation to centralize all slaughterhouse operations. The legislative purpose was to protect public health by prohibiting butchers from tossing rotten animal carcasses into the streets. Incensed that city government would interfere with their livelihoods by creating a legalized monopoly, twenty-five butchers filed a lawsuit to challenge the creation of the corporation. The US Supreme Court agreed to hear five of the cases on appeal. The central question was whether the due process, equal protection, and privileges and immunities clauses of the Fourteenth Amendment applied at the state level. In a narrowly tailored 5–4 decision, the Supreme Court held that the privileges and immunities clause affected only "national citizenship," not state citizenship.[26] The implications were readily apparent: the federal government could not interfere with state rights to protect blacks from racial discrimination at the hands of local and state leaders because principles of federalism required state autonomy whenever possible. In effect, the *Slaughterhouse Cases* severely limited the practical utility of the Fourteenth Amendment, especially the privileges and immunities clause.[27]

The Supreme Court continued its narrow construction of the Civil War amendments throughout the remainder of the nineteenth century. Each decision deferring to state rights dealt another blow to black political rights, inexorably undermining Reconstruction and shoring up the legal bases for de jure segregation. In *United States v. Reese* and *United States v. Cruikshank*, for example, the high court sent an unmistakable message to southerners that white supremacy was compatible with the US Constitution. The former case involved a Kentucky official's refusal to register a black man to vote in a municipal election. Writing for the court, Chief Justice Morrison R. Waite explained that a state possessed authority to regulate its own electoral process without unnecessary federal intervention. The chief justice cleverly explained why the US Constitution would allow states to institute poll taxes and literacy tests. "The Fifteenth Amendment does not confer the right of suffrage upon anyone," he wrote, ignoring the legislative history. "It prevents the states, or the

United States, however, from giving preference, in this particular, to one citizen of the United States over another on account of race, color, or previous condition of servitude." As Waite viewed matters, the federal government was not empowered to interfere with a state's decisions—even if those decisions disenfranchised a large group of citizens.[28]

Cruikshank arose from one of the numerous race riots of the era. On Easter Sunday in 1873, a white mob burned the courthouse in Colfax, Louisiana, after hundreds of blacks took cover inside following a street battle. When the bodies were tallied, scores of blacks lay dead. The numbers ranged from seventy to more than two hundred.[29]

Several white members of the mob were arrested and charged with violating Section 6 the Enforcement Act of 1870, which vested the president of the United States with authority to enforce the first section of the Fifteenth Amendment. Continuing the narrow interpretation of federal constitutional protections that began with the *Slaughterhouse Cases*, the *Cruikshank* court determined that the indictments were invalid because the Enforcement Act was a federal statute, and yet the charges did not involve a denial of federal rights. Writing again for the majority, Chief Justice Waite found that the First Amendment right of assembly and the Second Amendment right to bear arms only protected citizens from federal abuses. Moreover, the due process and equal protection rights referenced in the Fourteenth Amendment applied only to states, not to individuals. Individuals participated in the massacre, the chief justice observed. A state connection was never demonstrated. As for a claim that the mob interfered with the victims' right to vote, the justices were unconvinced. The evidence failed to demonstrate that the defendants had acted on racial grounds.[30]

One after another, the cases came to the high court, and the justices eviscerated the Reconstruction regime. In *Hall v. DeCuir*, an 1878 case, a steamboat operator had refused to serve a black patron. At trial, the patron won a civil judgment under a Louisiana statute prohibiting discrimination. The judgment was upheld on appeal. In his majority opinion, Chief Justice Waite found that the steamboat was engaged in interstate commerce, which was regulated solely by Congress. Because Congress had not provided for integrated facilities, one state (Louisiana) could not force a steamboat engaged in interstate commerce to practice integration.[31]

A dozen years later, in *Louisville, New Orleans, and Texas Railway Company v. Mississippi*, the court determined that a state statute requiring segregation in railroad cars did not violate congressional authority under the commerce clause. In a dissenting opinion, Justice John Marshall Harlan questioned the court's reasoning. Comparing the results in the *Louisville* and *Hall* cases, Harlan could not understand how the court reached markedly different conclusions in factually analogous circumstances:

In its application to passengers on vessels engaged in interstate commerce, the Louisiana enactment forbade the separation of the white and black races while such vessels were within the limits of that state. The Mississippi statute, in its application to passengers on railroad trains employed in interstate commerce, requires such separation of races while those trains are within that state. I am unable to perceive how the former is a regulation of interstate commerce and the other is not. It is difficult to understand how a state enactment requiring the separation of the white and black races on interstate carriers of passengers is a regulation of commerce among the states, while a similar enactment forbidding such separation is not a regulation of that character.[32]

If the two decisions seemed logically inconsistent in their fluid interpretations of the commerce clause—the former case demonstrated that the federal courts would strike down a state law that encroached on interstate commerce with alacrity, while the latter case expressed a grave reluctance to intervene in state affairs—they remained clear in one respect. A law that discriminated on the basis of race would be afforded great deference, while a law that attempted to integrate facilities would face strict judicial scrutiny. Viewed through a prism of racial bias, the opinions suddenly appear remarkably consistent.

As part of the effort to manipulate federalism principles in favor of a desired outcome, the high court turned its attention to Charles Sumner's Civil Rights Act in 1883. The measure had been designed as a means of abolishing the vestiges of slavery, as allowed by Section 2 of the Thirteenth Amendment, which read, "Congress shall have power to enforce this article by appropriate legislation." The *Civil Rights Cases* consisted of five consolidated appeals filed by blacks who had been denied entry into theaters, hotels, and public transportation. The plaintiffs sought to enforce the Civil Rights Act of 1875. To their dismay, the justices of the US Supreme Court held that the first two sections of the statute were unconstitutional because they vested the federal government with too much authority over state rights. Moreover, neither the Thirteenth nor the Fourteenth amendments empowered Congress to enforce public accommodations provisions against private parties. Justice Joseph P. Bradley authored the majority opinion. A conservative jurist who served on the Electoral Commission of 1877, which had thrown the election to Rutherford B. Hayes and helped to bring the Reconstruction era to a close, Bradley was unsympathetic to the plight of the freedmen. His strict interpretation of the Civil War amendments was wholly in keeping with the rise of a postbellum white regime.[33]

If the *Civil Rights Cases* dismantled the Civil Rights Act of 1875, the decision in *Williams v. Mississippi* might be said to have installed the Mississippi Plan in place of the invalidated law. The plan had been enormously successful in empowering white Democratic Party leaders to "persuade" black Republicans to switch parties or refrain from registering to vote. Because jurors were drawn from voter rolls, a decline in registrations resulted in fewer blacks serving on juries. The issue assumed significance when a black man was convicted of murder by an all-white jury in Washington County, Mississippi, in 1896. His defense attorney argued that the exclusion of Negroes from the jury pool, owing to their disfranchisement and the burdensome literacy and poll-tax requirements for blacks (and not whites), had denied the defendant equal protection of the law under the Fourteenth Amendment. It was a logically compelling argument, but logic was not the deciding factor.[34]

By this time, the US Supreme Court was dependably an agent of white supremacy. As if to prove the point, Justice Joseph McKenna's majority opinion in *Williams v. Mississippi* was a monument to obtuseness or chutzpah, depending on how it was read. Justice McKenna contended that blacks were responsible for their low numbers in voter rolls and jury pools. "By reason of its previous condition of servitude and dependencies, this race had acquired or accentuated certain peculiarities of habit, of temperament, and of character which clearly distinguished it as a race from the whites," he explained. Characterizing Negroes as "a patient, docile people, but careless, landless, migratory within narrow limits, without forethought, and its criminal members given to furtive offenses, rather than the robust crimes of the whites," he attributed the likelihood of an all-white jury to a simple matter of numerical odds. Blacks disqualified themselves from consideration owing to their natural habits of lawless behavior. "It cannot be said, therefore, that the denial of the equal protection of the laws arises primarily from the constitution and laws of Mississippi; nor is there any sufficient allegation of an evil and discriminating administration of them."[35]

As odious as the court's opinions of the 1870s and 1880s were for people of color, the landmark case on which the white regime would stand for more than five decades was *Plessy v. Ferguson*, which related to a public accommodations matter arising out of Louisiana. A state statute enacted in 1890 provided for separate accommodations for blacks and whites on railroads if the accommodations were "equal." The law did not define the term "equal." Nonetheless, no one was blind to the cynical meaning of the law, for segregated railroad accommodations were anything but equal in quality. The cars reserved for whites were more luxurious than the squalid, foul-smelling, dilapidated black section of the train.

On June 7, 1892, Homer Adolph Plessy, a light-skinned Creole man who was one-eighth black, boarded a car of the East Louisiana Railroad. He was so fair-skinned that he could have passed for white, but that was not the point. The Citizens' Committee of New Orleans (Comité des

Citoyens) had recruited Plessy to test the state statute. In fact, the committee had alerted the railroad company that Plessy would board the white section of the train that day. Under the law, Plessy was deemed black and required to move to a segregated car.

The script played out precisely as expected. When the conductor approached and ordered him to move, Plessy was defiant, refusing to comply. The company had him removed from the train and arrested for violating state law. When the case came to trial, Plessy argued that the statute had violated his Thirteenth Amendment rights as well as the equal protection clause of the Fourteenth Amendment.

By the time the case reached the US Supreme Court, the justices had already created a line of precedents allowing whites to discriminate against blacks with few legal consequences. They did not intend to change course when those precedents had served the interests of the white community so well. A majority ruled against Plessy, holding that although the Thirteenth Amendment abolished slavery, it did not protect blacks from discriminatory state laws. Justice Henry Billings Brown found that the "separate but equal" doctrine enshrined in many state laws did not violate the US Constitution because the state law was not patently unreasonable. "In determining the question of reasonableness," Brown argued, a state

> is at liberty to act with reference to the established usages, customs, and traditions of the people, and with a view to the promotion of their comfort, and the preservation of the public peace and good order. Gauged by this standard, we cannot say that a law which authorizes or even requires the separation of the two races in public conveyances is unreasonable, or more obnoxious to the Fourteenth Amendment than the acts of Congress requiring separate schools for colored children in the District of Columbia, the constitutionality of which does not seem to have been questioned, or the corresponding acts of state legislatures.[36]

Perhaps the only unusual part of the *Plessy* case was Justice Harlan's vehement dissent. "The white race deems itself to be the dominant race in this country," he reported. "And so it is, in prestige, in achievements, in education, in wealth, and in power. So, I doubt not, it will continue to be for all time, if it remains true to its great heritage, and holds fast to the principles of constitutional liberty."[37]

In one of the most widely quoted parts of his dissent, Harlan penned eloquent words that would be resurrected during the civil rights era long after his death. "Our constitution is color-blind, and neither knows nor tolerates classes among citizens," he argued. "In respect of civil rights, all citizens are equal before the law. The humblest is the peer of the most

[2.3]   Associate Supreme Court Justice John Marshall Harlan penned an eloquent dissent in *Plessy v. Ferguson*, the 1896 court case that upheld the constitutionality of segregation in public accommodations. Courtesy of the Library of Congress.

powerful. The law regards man as man, and takes no account of his surroundings or of his color when his civil rights as guaranteed by the supreme law of the land are involved." He issued a dire prediction that proved to be true. "In my opinion, the judgment this day rendered will, in time, prove to be quite as pernicious as the decision made by this tribunal in the *Dred Scott* Case."[38]

SNATCHING DEFEAT FROM
THE JAWS OF VICTORY

And so, virtually all remnants of the Reconstruction era, with its unfulfilled promises extended to the freedmen, passed into the pages of history. Racial prejudice would also taint subsequent epochs, when generations of whites regarded the Negro as naturally inferior and therefore deserving of his sad, sordid fate. A color line emerged, and with it a new mythology developed containing unwritten rules that blacks ignored at their peril.

As part of the new mythos, white folklore caricatured the Negro as a lesser being. Some fundamentalist preachers in the white churches constructed a theological edifice: the black race was descended from the biblical Ham, Noah's son, who observed his father's nakedness and whose progeny were cursed to serve other races. The less religiously inclined cited evidence produced by legions of pseudoscientists who claimed to have perfected Darwin's theories of evolution to demonstrate that Negroes were not as intellectually or morally advanced as Caucasians. With each new observation, the segregation regime came to appear not only as a convenient model of social relations but as the natural order of things.[39]

Therein lay the problem. Segregation enforced the separation of the races supposedly in the best interests of all parties. Yet socially enforced separation, not the laws of nature, ensured that time and distance would amplify distinctions from the "other." As years passed, and the caste system became a rigid, institutionally protected form of limited social intercourse, few intrepid souls dared to raise questions about its origins or validity. For many Americans, the color line was not an imaginary construct enforced by an entrenched white power structure against a disenfranchised minority. To regard white supremacy as a power relationship whereby one group brutalized another based on a foundational principle of might-makes-right was to expose the hypocrisy that lurked beneath a host of fancy rationalizations and carefully crafted pseudotheories. Whites professed their belief in the legend of the American dream, according to which everyone was free to better himself, to pull himself up by his bootstraps and become a self-made man, successful in his chosen field. They could not bring themselves to examine too closely exceptions that swallowed the rule. Even if somehow they could look past their racial prejudices, the cognitive dissonance would overwhelm their sensibilities. Negroes were inferior beings in accordance with God's plan, and that was as far as an analysis need extend.[40]

Many academics supported the white regime. Consider the position of the social sciences. Scholars and practitioners have always prided themselves on their ability to employ the tools of the "hard" sciences to examine society and the behavior of individuals and draw conclusions based on the data. Ideally, the social scientist develops a research hypothesis, collects information, categorizes the data, and matches observations against the hypothesis to see whether the cases confirm or disprove it. Yet pseudoscientists examining data on race either knowingly reached convenient conclusions or blithely confused cause and effect. Rather than view the depressed state of the black race as the inevitable result of decades of white oppression and control, they concluded that blacks were naturally debased and that white society and governmental institutions were recognizing and reacting to a natural condition. The Negro's general condition was the cause, they said, not the effect, of the actions undertaken by whites.[41]

A Columbia University academic, William Archibald Dunning, became the dean of a new breed of historian sympathetic to southern values and critical of the shortcomings and corruption of northern Reconstruction. Allowing the Negro to vote under the protective hand of northern carpetbaggers was an experiment in social engineering that had backfired horribly, Dunning and his adherents argued. Segregation was a logical response to the empowerment of an inferior race and represented a much needed correction. Although not all historians of the twentieth century were self-proclaimed Dunningites, the Dunning school cast a large shadow over Reconstruction-era history until at least the 1960s.[42]

Of course, exceptions existed, especially in the field of anthropology. Franz Boas, an influential German American anthropologist, refuted pseudoscientific studies about intelligence and the small cranium size of Negroes by demonstrating that health and nutrition, not innate cognitive capacity, influence the size and shape of the human head. From there, he argued that cultural factors affect human behavior to a greater degree than innate biological differences attributable to "inferior" or "superior" races. Boas became a pioneer in the study of folklore, the customs and cultural traditions developed by people to explain phenomena they do not understand. His protégés, Alexander Goldenweiser, Robert H. Lowie, and Alfred L. Kroeber, pioneered work in the field of cultural anthropology, demonstrating that differences among peoples have less to do with preprogrammed biological certainties among races than with cultural distinctions among individuals.[43]

Yet it was all so scholarly and academic. Outside debates within academe, few decision makers took note of genuine, rigorous, scientifically sound advances in biology and anthropology. White opinion leaders dared not question deeply held beliefs and superstitions too closely, lest their "way of life" be threatened. The long dark night of the Negro thus became longer and darker as the nineteenth century limped toward its conclusion.

No one could deny that the segregation regime imposed a heavy burden on dark-skinned Americans. They had been encouraged to pull themselves up from slavery and seek a better, productive life through hard work. If they were to enjoy the fruits of their labors, they must complete an education or learn a skill. Yet the path that had appeared so promising in 1865 had all but disappeared by the 1880s. No matter how skilled or hardworking a black laborer proved to be, he found himself assigned the most menial tasks available for subsistence wages. For many blacks, the only jobs to be had were as domestic servants and agricultural laborers or in the lowest ranks of the textile industry.[44]

A vicious cycle of poverty and crime ravaged generations of black Americans. Unable to exist on the paltry wages they earned laboring at menial tasks, men and women sometimes committed petty crimes. When caught and convicted, black defendants typically received harsh sentences—often harsher than their white counterparts received for the same crimes. In some cases, black men and women were convicted on flimsy or manufactured evidence. In other instances, they were arrested for vague, nebulous offenses such as vagrancy or panhandling. Black males found themselves working on chain gangs on behalf of state governments, which in turn leased their services to corporations and opportunistic entrepreneurs. The system became so oppressive and inequitable that one commentator titled his famous book on the subject *Slavery by Another Name*.[45]

For all the institutionalized racial bias they faced, most blacks refused to be passive victims, no matter how unrelenting the discrimination. Booker T. Washington, a former slave, opened the doors of the Tuskegee Institute in 1881. A black historian, George Washington Williams, published *History of the Negro Race in America from 1619 to 1880* and *A History of the Negro Troops in the War of the Rebellion* in the 1880s, two of the first professionally written histories of Negroes produced during the nineteenth century.[46] In 1889, President Benjamin Harrison appointed Frederick Douglass the Minister Resident of Haiti.[47] Dr. Daniel Hale Williams founded Provident Hospital in Chicago, perhaps the first Negro-owned hospital in the United States. Barred from joining the American Medical Association, twelve Negro physicians formed the National Medical Association during the 1895 Cotton States and International Exposition in Atlanta, Georgia.[48]

Despite these and many other undeniable accomplishments by blacks during the Jim Crow era, whites had firmly established themselves as the dominant race. The color line would not be crossed without dire consequences suffered by anyone audacious enough to make an attempt. To ensure that the American underclass grasped the point, whites frequently employed violence to cement their status. The Ku Klux Klan and the various "White Line" organizations had ceased to exist, but their spirit lived on throughout the South and in other parts of the country as well. Although in a majority of cases the white power structure did not engage in a systematic campaign of violence—most episodes occurred as a result of ad hoc, emotionally charged confrontations—a series of highly visible incidents made it clear that blacks existed at the bottom of the social hierarchy. Most of the time, they could exist peacefully if they knew their place and remained docile. Heaven help the hapless person of color pitted against whites in an armed battle.[49]

3

Racial Violence and the Plight of the Freedmen

"I Say Lynch a Thousand a Week if It Becomes Necessary"

During the last three decades of the nineteenth century, blacks and whites alike faced a world where the social position of the races, so fixed and seemingly permanent in antebellum times, appeared uncertain. Freedmen struggled to assume a place in American society—a society still racially charged and constructed on a firm foundation of racial bias—by acquiring education and pursuing employment, despite limited prospects on both fronts. As former slaves sought to assimilate, many southern whites seethed with bitterness. They had been taught since infancy that Negroes were their social inferiors. Suddenly, following the worst cataclysm in the nation's history, those same white citizens were told to embrace the freedpeople and welcome them into the fold. It was too much to expect a seamless transition.

As a consequence of the angst felt by everyone in the new era, violence was all but inevitable. For most of American history, save for much publicized slave rebellions and the passively aggressive disobedience of bondsmen who surreptitiously sabotaged their masters' efforts in myriad ways, blacks knew their place and stayed within the confines of the peculiar institution. During the years immediately following the war, as northerners assumed control of southern state governments, former slaves rose up from bondage and moved into the middle echelons of economic and political power. Yet the new order could not last. When the Reconstruction era receded into the pages of history, the carpetbaggers' value system largely disappeared. Slavery was dead; its replacement regime lay in tatters. No one knew where he stood in the altered terrain. With the loss of certainty came a clash of races. Periodically violent episodes seemed to presage a dreaded race war sometime in the not-too-distant future.[1]

The pitched battle that occurred in Louisiana on Easter Sunday in 1873 appeared to realize the darkest fears about the possibility of a second civil war. When the fighting ended and the bodies were collected, the Colfax Massacre emerged as one of the bloodiest confrontations of the postwar era. Freedmen were shot as they fled the fighting. In some instances, they were summarily executed after they had laid down their weapons.

Every state of the defunct Southern Confederacy experienced racial tensions during Reconstruction, but the standoffs frequently erupted into violence in Louisiana. New Orleans, the gateway to the Gulf of Mexico at the mouth of the mighty Mississippi River, existed as a cosmopolitan enclave, an amalgamation of races and ethnicities. Yet the worldliness was an illusion. Moreover, the rest of the state was less progressive than the Crescent City. White supremacy, unadulterated and practiced in plain sight, was the order of the day in the bayous and parishes throughout the countryside. Whether enforced by paramilitary groups such as the White League or through the ad hoc predations of loosely organized, grassroots community leaders, white supremacy was a fact of life in the Southland. It had always been that way, and if local opinion leaders had their way, it always would be.

Southerners were not prepared to relinquish social or political control despite the outcome of the Civil War. The Union army had policed the rebellious states in the immediate aftermath of Appomattox, but the years had been long, and northerners were weary of a standing army patrolling streets south of the Mason-Dixon Line. In most southern states, the carpetbagger governments propped up by armed federal soldiers were crumbling or already had been redeemed. It was only a matter of time before the last vestiges of the Reconstruction governments imploded. When an indifferent presidential administration decided that the myriad promises hastily made by a victorious government were too burdensome to honor, the occupation would cease, and the South could get on with the business of restoring state governments to the Union as it was—sans slavery, at least in name.

Despite the fading prospects of Reconstruction, carpetbaggers were not resigned to defeat. In many areas, they strove to create opportunities for freedmen to live, work, vote, and worship as they chose. In Louisiana, Republicans carved out Grant Parish in the north-central part of the state to wrest political control from Democrats who supported a white supremacist local government. Rather than shield Negroes from an oppressive white majority, however, the parish became a battleground where entrenched interests refused to yield.

The Easter Sunday massacre occurred after Republicans and Democrats quarreled about who should police the parish citizenry. William Ward, a black Republican Union veteran and member of the Louisiana State Militia, argued that he represented the law enforcement community by virtue of his position. The idea that a black man could arrest white men horrified unreconstructed southerners. To add insult to injury, Ward declared his candidacy for the state legislature, either oblivious to the effect his announcement would have on the white population or openly defiant of and willfully antagonistic toward traditional mores and customs. Democrat Christopher Columbus Nash, a Confederate veteran, claimed the office of sheriff and, along with his white supporters, refused to recognize Ward's authority. Worried that Nash's men might steal the election, on the evening of March 25, 1873, local Negroes scurried to construct trenches around the courthouse in Colfax, a small settlement in Grant Parish.[2]

Black Republicans hid behind their earthworks for the better part of three weeks, but the calm before the storm could not last indefinitely. Nash and his men finally resolved to remove the offenders and end the stalemate. With assistance from James Hadnot, a well-known white supremacist, they hatched a plan to attack the fortifications and drive the invaders into the street.

On Easter Sunday, Nash assembled a group of approximately three hundred men and directed them to charge the earthworks by force. Acting as a military commander, he marched his troops into the little town and demanded that the defenders surrender or face the consequences. He waited for thirty minutes so that the women and children could depart before the fighting commenced. This was his one concession to southern notions of chivalry and honor.

Each side faced the other with grim determination. The outcome would determine the fate of the parish and perhaps reverberate in the hamlets and cities scattered across the state. Someone would control local politics, and someone would be subservient. Huddled behind their fortifications, the former slaves were under no illusion about their precarious situation. They and their forbears had spent generations toiling in bondage, unable to live their lives free from the oppressive laws of their adopted land. Now, in a supposedly new age of emancipation, they found themselves in an untenable predicament. If they did not arm and protect themselves, they were easy prey for violent acts perpetrated by the white authorities. If they fought back, as they prepared to do on that Easter Sunday of 1873, they faced annihilation by a frantic white population claiming self-defense against Negro miscreants.

As soon as the black defenders saw the white paramilitary group wheel a cannon near the earthworks, they knew their chances for victory, always tenuous, had deteriorated. The barrage commenced within minutes and became increasingly intense throughout the afternoon. Finally, a group of sixty defenders reached a fateful decision: they must get out. When they detected a momentary lull in the firing, they raced from behind the fortifications, apparently intent on disappearing into the nearby woods or jumping into the river. Most of the fleeing defenders never made it. With Nash's troops in hot pursuit on horseback, the desperate men presented easy targets. They were shot in the back before they reached the safety of the levee. Even when the fleeing men stopped to surrender, they were killed in their tracks.

The remaining defenders sought refuge inside the courthouse. The move initially appeared shrewd, for the edifice was well built and would shield the occupants from direct rifle fire. Yet the white paramilitary, its forces augmented by an incensed mob, would not be easily satiated. The crowd now reveled in bloodlust. Whites had killed some of the offending Negroes and were hungry for more.

Someone seized on the idea of forcing the offenders from the building by torching the place. Locals were so intent on victory that they would destroy a symbol of local government rather than withdraw from a confrontation. It was a turning point. When the attackers set fire to the courthouse, the hopelessness of the cause became apparent. As smoke billowed from the roof, at least two men crammed inside the burning structure hoisted white flags of surrender. The shooting ceased long enough for Nash to order the militiamen to step outside.

As the crisis seemed to wane, someone shot James Hadnot, fatally wounding him. Whether the shooting was an accidental incidence of friendly fire from Nash's overzealous men or a final vindictive act of the desperate, embittered Republicans was never clear, although it was unlikely that surrendering men seeking mercy would deliberately provoke a new attack. Whatever the cause, Hadnot's fate ratcheted up the tension.

Outraged white supremacists fired at the black defenders as the surrendering men stepped from the courthouse. Many blacks who had already laid down their weapons were taken prisoner and apparently executed. A lone survivor, Levi Nelson, crawled away without attracting notice.[3]

The state militia eventually arrived to discover the charred remnants of the Colfax courthouse and a slew of corpses strewn across the countryside. The white perpetrators, fearing arrest or reprisals from the black community, had departed well ahead of the authorities' arrival. The number of dead and wounded was never established clearly or completely. Some reports estimated that seventy men had died, but the total might have been double that number. In any event, it was the worst instance of racial violence in the United States during the 1870s.[4]

VIOLENCE DURING RECONSTRUCTION

The Colfax episode occurred at a time when white southerners were struggling with their regional identity. Having survived the rigors of war and social change unlike anything faced by previous generations, they were uncertain of what the future held, but the outlook appeared bleak. As they reflected on their reduced fortunes, white southerners referred to the loss of their "way of life," a general term that had no fixed meaning but suggested that regional customs and traditions dictated socially accepted forms of behavior. The southern way of life included an aristo-cratic culture of honor. For a southern man reared in the upper classes, his good name and community reputation were valuable assets: intangi-ble, to be sure, but nonetheless important. Real or perceived effrontery threatened to undermine his social position. He was expected to defend his honor using whatever means necessary, including violence.

In the eighteenth and early nineteenth centuries, dueling was an accepted practice for men of honor who could not settle their disagree-ments through other channels. By the eve of the Civil War, however, duels were rare. Persons of a similar social position could reach an accommoda-tion through alternative means, including the courts, if necessary. The gradual evolution of attitudes away from dueling did not mean, however, that violence was deemed unacceptable. The use or threat of violence, especially toward one's social inferiors, was a legitimate form of problem resolution. Violence inflicted by a white on a black was not only recog-nized as legitimate but often expected.[5]

The Colfax incident was perhaps the most dramatic example, but vio-lence or the threat of it was always a part of the black experience in North America. During the antebellum epoch, slaves feared violence from their masters, of course, but they typically enjoyed a measure of protection from outside forces. In most instances, a slaveholder possessed an eco-nomic motive for exercising a modicum of restraint. A dead or severely injured slave would produce no income and could prove to be a drain on resources. Violence erupted on the great plantations of the Old South, but it was meted out to ensure social control, not as a means of eradicating the black population.

With the demise of the peculiar institution, emancipated slaves could no longer expect to be shielded from white ruffians hell-bent on acting violently. Freed from the shackles of the old order, former slaves could take control of their lives, at least in theory, but the reality frequently was harsh and unremitting. Embittered whites who had refrained from physically assaulting blacks in the days before slavery was abolished no longer felt constrained by the old customs or the calming influence of self-interest. The freedmen became a convenient target for violence, and with little wonder. Many whites, even those of modest station, reflected on what they had lost during the war. The southern way of life, tinged with nostalgia and therefore all the more cherished in the hearts of the white population, seemed to have slipped away. The social position of the races had been upended. Needing only to look around them to see freedmen, supposedly their inferiors, traipsing around the countryside, white southerners recoiled at the new arrangement. Although a large number of whites begrudgingly accepted the facts of life and struggled to do the best they could under the circumstances, not everyone shared such equanimity about the altered conditions.

During the early postwar years, angry and resentful white southerners donned fanciful disguises and conical hats to disguise their identities as they practiced a ruthless form of vigilantism against the hated freedmen who audaciously flaunted their newfound freedoms. With northern soldiers and carpetbaggers controlling southern state governments during the late 1860s and early 1870s, unreconstructed rebels resolved to fight back in whatever manner they could. Battlefield losses need not be permanent if a fellow fought the status quo in secret. What a white man could not earn in the light of day he could snatch under the cover of night. Thus were white supremacist groups born in the Reconstruction era.[6]

These white supremacist organizations of the postwar South operated under different names and developed various methods for achieving their goals. The most infamous was the Ku Klux Klan (KKK), a shadowy confederacy of like-minded white men that eventually boasted more than half a million members. The figures are at once impressive and suspect. The Klan was never a centralized body of operatives, although early leaders George W. Gordon and Nathan Bedford Forrest attempted to impose a structure on what they hoped would be an underground paramilitary group. In some places, it lived up to their ideals. In other areas, Ku Kluxers engaged in sophomoric mischief similar to the absurd pranks and hazing of immature fraternity boys. Dozens of loosely associated factions claimed to act under the imprimatur of the "true" Ku Klux Klan, but their affiliations were always so tenuous that such claims could not be accepted. Therein lay the strength of the group. The Klan was simultaneously everywhere and nowhere. It represented hundreds of thousands of whites; it represented no one. It was a grassroots movement of angry whites, and it was a small band of malcontents. The fact that no one could find much credible information about the Klan and its mission amplified the group's power and prestige among the white population. It scared the black community as well, which was the organization's purpose.[7]

The Klan unraveled after the federal government investigated the group's origins, organization, and techniques. Major Lewis Merrill of the 7th Cavalry arrived in upstate South Carolina in 1871 with orders to probe the group's actions. Reports received in Washington, DC, alleged that the Klan completely controlled local government and violently repressed the black citizenry. Some federal leaders, especially Democrats,

[3.1]   This drawing of three Klansmen garbed in Ku Klux Klan regalia dates from 1871.
Courtesy of the Library of Congress.

denounced the stories as nothing more than exaggerated, melodramatic fictional accounts drafted to embarrass southerners. During his methodical inquiry, Merrill documented a long train of abuses in the Piedmont region, the first step in a comprehensive investigation of a group that eventually became the "terrorist arm of the Democratic Party." The president and Congress were slow to respond, but when they finally acted, the results led to the demise of the "Invisible Empire." President Ulysses S. Grant suspended the writ of habeas corpus in South Carolina long enough for Major Merrill to round up suspected Klansmen. Attorney General Amos T. Akerman initiated federal court prosecutions. Later, Congress enacted a series of laws providing criminal penalties for persons who employed violence while masking their faces. By the end of the 1870s, the Ku Klux Klan and many similar groups had died out.[8]

Yet Klan ideals lived on long after the formal organization had disbanded. Many white southerners could not accept the social equality of the races and remained committed to the notion that only white men were fit for social, political, and legal control of state and local governments. The paramount consideration was how they could achieve their goals without triggering additional scrutiny from northern forces.

With the end of Reconstruction, an effective strategy became clear. As southerners stepped back into positions of authority, they realized that they need not hide behind sheets and masks to achieve their goals. With the departure of the carpetbagger regimes in state governments, reinvigorated white leaders could use the mechanisms of government to deny blacks equal opportunity. Northern leaders might threaten to reinstitute the federal Reconstruction plan, but as the years passed and the radical elements in Congress faded away, no one in a position of authority had the stomach for additional confrontation. Moreover, constitutional amendments and federal civil rights laws might exist on the books, but if they were never implemented, they remained little more than theoretical constructs. They became paper tigers.[9]

During the 1880s, southerners witnessed the gradual ascension of white supremacy as a way of life. An invisible color line existed, and everyone more or less knew the unwritten code of behavior that enforced racial separation. In most instances, no further reminders were needed. Yet sometimes the line was blurred, or intrepid souls sought to cross over. When these rare events occurred, violence was a crucial component in maintaining the status quo.[10]

GROUND UNDER THE BOOT HEELS
OF JUMPIN' JIM CROW

The Colfax episode in Louisiana was perhaps the most dramatic battle between the races in the aftermath of the Civil War, but it was hardly a singular event. As Reconstruction ended and white southerners assumed the mantle of political power, the struggles in Grant Parish became a template for racial fighting in the states of the former Confederacy. Violence erupted in hundreds and thousands of towns and communities, but the events were isolated and held few consequences for anyone save the parties involved. Most events went unrecorded.[11]

The episodes recounted in the annals of the South reflected many features found in the Colfax fighting: a restless Negro faction struggled to assert its rights against an oppressive white community fearful that blacks threatened the southern way of life. As an example, South Carolina, birthplace of the secessionist movement, witnessed another of the worst outbreaks of racial violence during the 1870s. On July 4, 1876, as the nation celebrated its centennial, a company of South Carolina Negro militia drilling near the small town of Hamburg across the Savannah River from Augusta, Georgia, came upon two white farmers riding in a buggy on Market Street. The whites later filed a complaint in a local court charging that the militiamen had intentionally blocked the road. The soldiers told a different story. They claimed the buggy had deliberately plunged into the crowd of marchers, triggering an unnecessary standoff between blacks and whites. Both sides exchanged heated words, but the brief verbal altercation seemed to end the matter. It appeared to be a run-of-the mill encounter, one of thousands between resentful whites and assertive freedmen.[12]

Yet the Hamburg incident grew into a bitter armed confrontation similar to the Colfax Massacre. Several days after the initial meeting, the white men from the buggy appeared in court. A local trial judge agreed to hold a hearing to determine who should be held responsible. The setting was tailor-made for demagoguery. Matthew Calbraith Butler, a former Confederate brigadier general and lawyer turned politician, appeared on behalf of the farmers and willingly assumed the role of racial instigator. As part of his harangue, Butler insisted that the militia unit disband and hand over its armaments to him. Butler held no position of public trust; nor did he explain why he should receive the militia's armaments. It was a white man's state though. He need not supply a reason. He was supported by a growing crowd of angry whites who arrived to protect the white farmers should the black population turn violent, and that was reason enough.

The Negro militiamen recognized the volatility of the situation. If they surrendered their weapons, they would be left to the mercy of the local white population at a time when the incident was stirring up deep-seated racial animosity. They refused to lay down their guns, reiterating the claim that the incident had occurred through no fault of their own. The two sides had reached an impasse. Had a neutral third party intervened—

assuming a neutral third party could have been found and transported to the scene—the dispute might have been resolved through nonviolent means. As it was, with both sides refusing to yield, the matter quickly spiraled out of control.[13]

Blacks in the postbellum South invariably found themselves in a precarious state. If they submitted to the white power structure, they could expect shoddy treatment and widespread racial discrimination. Always robbed of suitable housing, adequate educational opportunities, and the best jobs, they frequently fell victim to sporadic episodes of violence. Their lives would be wretched, with no hope of advancement beyond a subsistence level, if they did not stand up for their rights. Yet intrepid freedmen who refused to kowtow to white southerners triggered alarm among the citizenry. A black man who did not know his place was a threat to the established order, a problem that must be fixed as rapidly as possible.[14]

The South Carolina militiamen represented a clear menace to the status quo; their refusal to disarm could not go unchallenged. Angry armed white farmers poured into Hamburg by the hundreds. Contrary to rumors circulating that armed Negro marauders roamed the countryside, the group contained only about twenty-five militiamen and perhaps fifteen local black citizens.

Outgunned and outnumbered, the defenders retreated into an armory, alarming the angry white mob. Gunfire erupted as soon as the black men stepped inside the enclosure. In a development eerily reminiscent of the Colfax battle, a white farmer fell dead. It was not clear whether the militiamen deliberately shot him, but the facts no longer mattered. Whites were convinced that a Negro conspiracy was afoot, and something must be done to restore the fixed social positions of the races. The crowd grew restless and finally jubilant when a cannon appeared outside the building. With the arrival of heavy armaments, the result was assured, not that the small band of militiamen had stood a realistic chance of emerging from the confrontation unscathed in the first place.

Fearing wholesale slaughter, most of the militiamen slipped away in the night. One man was shot dead as he tried to escape. Four others were taken prisoner and executed. Once again, as in Louisiana three years earlier, the two races faced each other with raised fists across a chasm of bitterness and resentment, with each side suspicious of the other and certain that no middle ground could be found. Black participants, predictably, fared poorly as they faced a hostile, numerically superior force. A jury indicted ninety-four white men for murder as a result of the incident, but local authorities never prosecuted anyone.[15]

The Colfax and Hamburg incidents revealed the powerlessness of Negroes in newly restored southern state governments, but even when blacks enjoyed a measure of genuine political power, violence occurred. Indeed, Negro empowerment sometimes was precisely the reason that whites felt compelled to engage in violence. Wilmington, North Carolina, at the end of the nineteenth century provides a case in point.[16]

Wilmington is a port city situated where the Cape Fear River meets the Atlantic Ocean. During the war, it had served as a strategic location for Union soldiers and sailors struggling to close off commerce in the Southern Confederacy. In the ensuing three decades, black citizens had developed a thriving middle class, even as whites controlled the North Carolina state government. Although neither race trusted the other, the area had existed peacefully under a fragile truce until the elections of 1894 and 1896, when black Republicans gained a modicum of power.

Accustomed to political impotence in the South, black leaders in the 1870s and 1880s carefully walked a fine line between privately acquiring material goods and a measure of status and publicly displaying the proper obsequiousness to white political leaders. Yet new generations of black denizens were not satisfied with the old arrangement. As the populist movement arose, poor white southerners joined forces with black Republicans to wrench political control in North Carolina away from white Democratic leaders in a shocking blow to the entrenched power structure during the 1894 and 1896 elections. Upset by the fusion of the two interests, white Democrats vowed revenge.

The white Republican governor, Daniel Lindsay Russell Jr., was a Confederate veteran who had accepted the verdict of the war. He no longer adhered to the values of the defunct Confederacy. After winning the gubernatorial election in 1896, he was the first Republican to serve since the end of Reconstruction, and he would be the last until 1973. His political opponents bitterly criticized his administration as the most corrupt in decades, mostly because he was a hated scalawag who owed his election to Negroes. Evidence suggested that his regime was not more corrupt or dysfunctional than its predecessors, but Democrats refused to acknowledge this fact.

As the 1898 elections approached, Democrats realized they could regain lost ground if they demonized the enemy. They took to the task with gusto, freely spewing racial epithets with no compunction. A local party activist candidly explained, "The slogan of the Democratic Party from the mountains to the sea will be but one word . . . Nigger."[17]

Aside from employing heated rhetoric, Democrats revived the Red Shirts, the group that had engineered their electoral victory in the 1876 South Carolina elections and participated in the Hamburg slaughter that same year. Using the techniques an earlier generation had gleaned from the Mississippi Plan, the Red Shirts designed a systematic campaign to intimidate Negroes and keep them from voting in 1898. Three tactics were crucial to the plan: write, speak, and ride. Democrats produced screeds for local newspapers, delivered angry speeches on the dangers of blacks roaming unfettered throughout the countryside, and rode with the Red Shirts to spread the party message and demonstrate strength in numbers to emboldened Republicans.[18]

As if the situation were not already volatile enough, a loquacious Georgia racist named Rebecca Felton exacerbated tensions. Felton's husband was a prominent opinion leader, having been a US congressman and later an influential newspaperman. For her part, Felton penned an occasional column in the *Atlanta Journal* about topics of interest to white rural farmers. During the 1890s, Felton became increasingly worried about the presence of black men in areas where white women were left alone all day while their husbands, brothers, and fathers tended the fields. Echoing fears of miscegenation and the supposedly incorrigible sexual appetite of black men, Felton began to write and speak about the need to control "the black fiend," who desired nothing more than to ravish a white woman. During a speech on Tybee Island, Georgia, in August 1897, Felton famously remarked, "If it takes lynching to protect woman's dearest possession from drunken, ravenous beasts, then I say lynch a thousand a week if it becomes necessary." The speech attracted national media attention and voiced the concerns that many white southerners already harbored about the freedmen.[19]

With the 1898 elections approaching in North Carolina and Felton's speech widely disseminated as part of white Democrats' scheme to retard the black vote, Alex L. Manly, editor of Wilmington's black newspaper, the *Daily Record*, felt compelled to respond. In an editorial published just over a year after Felton's speech, Manly argued that most cases of "rape" involved consensual relations between black men and white women. If southerners wanted to explore questions of rape, perhaps they would be well advised to look back at the relationship between white slave owners and black women held in bondage. "Ms. Felton must begin at the fountain head, if she wishes to purify the stream," he wrote. It was unseemly hypocrisy for whites to bemoan the loss of virtue among white women when they had destroyed the virtue of so many black women. "Don't think ever that your women will remain pure while you are debauching ours," he concluded. "You sow the seed—the harvest will come in good time."[20]

Had the editorial been written in a later age, when the virulent racism of the day had subsided, it might have served as intellectual fodder for dispassionate observers to debate the issue with assistance from the historical record. In 1898, however, exposing such sensitive subjects in newspapers could only lead to greater racial divisions. When Manly's editorial generated additional comment within the black press, it effectively painted a target on his back. The harvest would come, indeed, in short order.

Manly's remarks might have passed with little comment if the Negro community had remained passive and compliant. Yet black voters in 1898 were not as willing to cede the ground to whites as an earlier generation had been. Despite repeated threats and public demonstrations against Republicans, they remained resolute in the face of stiff opposition and promised to defend the electoral gains of 1894 and 1896. Their moxie and valiant efforts, arguably heroic under the circumstances, could not overcome Democratic tactics. When the votes were tallied, Republican allies of Governor Russell suffered a decisive defeat across the state.[21]

In Wilmington, a predominantly black city, the outcome was different. The biracial fusion government clung to power. Recognizing this possibility prior to Election Day, a well-known white supremacist and former congressman, Alfred Moore Waddell, had selected a secret committee to replace victorious blacks. He was anxious to hide his specific plans before the election, but Waddell was not shy about revealing his general goals in public. A local newspaper quoted him as telling white citizens on the eve of the vote, "You are Anglo-Saxons. You are armed and prepared and you will do your duty. Go to the polls tomorrow, and if you find the Negro out voting, tell him to leave the polls and if he refuses, kill him, shoot him down in his tracks. We shall win tomorrow if we have to do it with guns."[22]

When intimidation did not succeed before the election, Waddell and his men engineered a coup d'état against the mayor and aldermen, "persuading" them to resign. With a white mob in control of the city, Waddell had himself installed as mayor. The next order of business was to retaliate against uppity blacks. First on the list was Alex Manly, the newspaperman who had spoken out against Rebecca Felton regarding the lascivious nature of black men.

A group of between four hundred and one thousand angry whites rushed to the offices of the *Daily Record* on November 10, two days after the election, and burned it to the ground. Alex Manly had fled Wilmington before the mob appeared, robbing the crowd of its true desire. The frenzied group rampaged through black neighborhoods, beating and shooting at random. Some Negroes left the city, never to return, so an accurate accounting of the casualties could not be determined. Estimates placed the number of dead at between six and twenty-five, but the actual count may have been in the hundreds.[23]

The Wilmington coup d'état came to hold different meanings, depending on the audience. For white southerners entrenched in racism and hatred, it provided a blueprint for vanquishing political enemies, whatever their color. If ballots could not be rigged through skullduggery, naked violence would do the trick. Nonetheless, to prevent the necessity of employing such ugly, theatrical tactics in the future, the white supremacist government enacted a series of segregation statutes to disenfranchise Negroes. North Carolina had come late to the white supremacy party, but after 1898, the state was committed to dancing a jolly jig with jumpin' Jim Crow.[24]

Blacks learned a valuable lesson too. In the past, they had attributed their plight to their lack of political hegemony. If only they could establish a power base, Negroes might yet enjoy at least a modicum of personal autonomy. They failed to appreciate how threatening a black power enclave would be to the white citizenry. If blacks were to exercise power of any sort south of the Mason-Dixon Line, they could not run afoul of the color line. The consequences, they now knew, could be deadly.[25]

A NEW CENTURY, AN OLD IDEA

It was a lesson that southern blacks repeatedly learned as the nineteenth century gave way to the twentieth. Even in a burgeoning city such as Atlanta, Georgia, a metropolis later described as a "city too busy to hate," racial tension bubbled just below the calm facade of genteel respectability. When the pressures of rapid socioeconomic change combined with white ancestral fears of the black race, as was the case in Wilmington in 1898, violence was never far behind.[26]

By the first decade of the twentieth century, the Civil War was receding into the past. Many civilian and military leaders from that era had already died, and the ranks of the enlisted men diminished with each passing year. The pervasive fears associated with freedmen attempting to assimilate into a culture that had little use for them had dissipated. Yet a new set of worries had taken their place. As southern agriculture declined and industrialization led to the rise of cities, an increasing number of financially destitute persons, white and black, gravitated toward urban areas in search of employment. The close proximity of the races all but ensured conflict.[27]

When black neighborhoods grew in number and importance, alarmed whites looked on with horror at what they perceived as a decadent, hedonistic lifestyle. Decatur Street in the heart of Atlanta was a focal point for frustrated whites who decried the loss of traditional neighborhoods. Situated two blocks away from bustling Peachtree Street, the city's main traffic artery, Decatur Street was the transition point between the elegant stone and brick offices and houses of middle-class neighborhoods and the poorly constructed wooden shanties that characterized the black section of town. With the influx of single, young black males, establishments opened to meet their needs. So-called dime bed dives—saloons, gambling dens, pool halls, pawn shops, and brothels—proliferated. Such degradation was inevitable, whites observed, when blacks infected a city with their loose morals and low-class values.

Matters came to a head during the 1906 gubernatorial election. Two candidates vying for the Democratic nomination, M. Hoke Smith, a former secretary of the interior under President Grover Cleveland and co-owner of the *Atlanta Journal*, and Clark Howell, editor of the *Atlanta Constitution*, recognized that race-baiting was an effective election strategy. Each man sought an advantage by issuing provocative public statements about black debauchery and his plans for rectifying the problem once in office. Smith was especially creative in his denunciations of the brutish Negro, this mythical beast of inferior intellect and uncanny physical prowess, promising to "imitate Wilmington" if elected. He also intimated that black disenfranchisement was best for the Negro race. If not divested of their modest political power, blacks would misuse it, not only harming themselves but encouraging mob violence against black residents. It was in everyone's best interest to keep the Negro oppressed; unfortunately, the lowly creature was too stupid to see the undeniable advantages of being relegated to second-class citizenship. His refusal to lend a hand in his own victimization demonstrated just how wretched the Negro had become.[28]

The campaign moved into the autumn of 1906 as the stories of black misbehavior, already alarming, became increasingly sensational. Tales of drunken Negroes assaulting white women circulated, a direct consequence, it was said, of the bars and brothels that littered Decatur Street. In addition to articles and editorials in Atlanta's two major newspapers, stories about sexual assaults perpetrated by "black brutes" appeared in John Temple Graves's up-and-coming publication, the *Atlanta Georgian*. Everywhere, it seemed, Negroes were destroying the fabric of hardworking, conscientious, Christian, white America.

Tensions reached a crucial juncture between Monday, September 17, and Thursday, September 20, after the press reported on "an intolerable epidemic of rape." Most incidents were complete fabrications or gross exaggerations of minor run-ins between blacks and whites. Still, the hysteria of the times, fanned by the lurid news stories, convinced white citizens that the dens of iniquity stretched out across Decatur Street must be eradicated once and for all.

At around 6 p.m. on September 22, large bands of white men and boys congregated along Peachtree and Decatur Streets, angrily mulling over the decline of the neighborhood and the rash of black sexual assaults on white women. Extra editions of the evening newspapers featuring salacious stories about an imminent Negro uprising had appeared after 5 p.m., further agitating the crowd. As the mob grew, a separate group of Negroes appeared, vehemently denying the press reports.[29]

Name-calling graduated into pushing and shoving. New stories of black men assaulting white women on the streets that night circulated through the crowd, and eventually the tension proved more than anyone could bear. By 9 p.m., Mayor James G. Woodward had instructed police and fire units to assemble and control the throngs of people, estimated at five thousand strong. The mayor also repeatedly begged the crowd to disperse peacefully. Fire Commissioner James W. English addressed the masses standing in front of the Piedmont Hotel, but it was too little, too late. Whites ignored these men, derided as "nigger lovers," and refused to obey.[30]

Matters deteriorated between 9:30 and 11 p.m., when white mobs first brandished weapons. Local police claimed they were on hand to tamp down tensions, but their actions told a different tale. The sheriff of Fulton County supposedly halted gun sales, although he personally authorized hundreds of transactions involving "respectable citizens." When he encountered a rowdy group of two hundred white men, he deputized them. Other law enforcement personnel confiscated weapons from Negroes in the city even as it became clear that white citizens were arming for a violent confrontation.[31]

By 10:30, the mob had taken control of the streets, and the rampage began in earnest. Pouring onto Decatur Street as well as Auburn Avenue, an area sporting Negro businesses generally deemed respectable, the white gangs systematically destroyed property in their path. One prominent gang leader, George W. Blackstock, was heard to exclaim that he and his comrades would "kill every damned nigger in the house."

Most blacks in the vicinity beat a hasty retreat as soon as they recognized the severity of the situation. For some hapless souls, the exits were blocked. One black man picking up his mother from work was shot down for his efforts. The crowd stabbed two Negroes near the Piedmont Hotel and eventually tortured another man to death. His clothes were ripped off his corpse, and his fingers and toes were snipped off as souvenirs. Throughout the city, the story was similar: an outraged, bloodthirsty mob of angry whites roamed the city searching for victims. Although the episode supposedly commenced as a means of controlling low-class blacks who were desecrating the city and the values of its white inhabitants, as the mob grew in size, any Negro was fair game. Some middle-class blacks were beaten or tortured if they happened to be in the wrong place at the wrong time. Nowhere was safe. Blacks who wisely had taken refuge inside their homes to escape the chaos of the streets discovered that white ruffians spoke of protecting the old values, but they exhibited no fear or compunction when it came to trampling on the rights of darker-skinned peoples in the name of mob justice. Walter F. White, future leader of the National Association for the Advancement of Colored People (NAACP), was thirteen years old at the time. He never forgot the carnage of that awful night, when he finally understood his blackness and what it meant in twentieth-century America. "I learned who I was," he later said.[33]

The riot taught many black people who they were. In the city, white political leaders and police officers occasionally intervened to protect a harassed or assaulted black citizen, but mostly the authorities turned a blind eye to the violence. When President Theodore Roosevelt was informed of the incident as it was still in progress, he refused to authorize federal intervention. A president who had entertained Booker T. Washington at the White House almost five years earlier, a president renowned for his fearlessness and political audacity, a president who frequently acted on impulse to champion an unpopular political cause now demonstrated his inability or unwillingness to take up the cause of the black race. As for Booker T. Washington, he long had counseled fellow Negroes to work within the Jim Crow system and play by the white man's rules in the hopes of securing a better life. In the aftermath of the Atlanta blood fest, the old man of accommodation appeared foolish and out of touch with the reality of life for southern blacks.[34]

The figures were never accurately tallied, but perhaps as few as 25 and as many as 40 blacks died during the ordeal, which stretched from September 22 to 24, with another 150 seriously injured and thousands wounded. Untold numbers of Negroes fled the city forever. The incident received national press attention and sent a powerful message about the dangers associated with the races living too close to each other.[35]

For some audiences, high-profile cases of racial violence in the South during those early years of the new century were symptomatic of the sickness that had infected the former states of the Confederacy. Surely the more enlightened areas of the country were immune to racial fever. Alas, this perspective turned out to be delusional. A confrontation in Springfield, Illinois, in 1908 suggested that the disease had spread into the heartland. Famous as the home and final resting place of Abraham Lincoln, Springfield was supposed to be a progressive town far removed from the southern pathology that elevated race above all other considerations. Yet, as Springfield prepared for the hundredth birthday of its most famous resident, an incident occurred that cast an unwelcome spotlight on racial attitudes in this crucial town in the Land of Lincoln.[36]

In retrospect, it should not be surprising that violence erupted in Springfield as blacks migrated north in search of jobs and security. Coupled with increasing rates of foreign immigration, the influx of black workers into neighborhoods that only a few years earlier had been largely white engendered no small measure of hostility among locals. On August 14, 1908, after two black men were incarcerated in the city jail for offenses perpetrated against whites—one man was accused of sexually assaulting a white women, and another allegedly killed a white man who was protecting his daughter's virtue—a crowd formed and demanded that the prisoners be brought to immediate justice. Anticipating this development, local police had whisked the prisoners away in an automobile. The mob learned of the maneuver and became enraged at the trickery. Shocked at the growing wave of lawlessness, the governor activated the state militia, but it was several hours before armed units arrived on the scene. In the interim, the mob, estimated to number somewhere between four and twelve thousand, roamed through the black part of town, looting and burning houses.[37]

One unfortunate soul, a black barber named Scott Burton, found his house surrounded by the throng. He unwisely fired a shotgun, although it was unclear whether he had discharged a warning shot or aimed to kill or wound. No matter. The crowd laid hands on the man and strung him to a tree with clothesline procured from an adjacent yard. His body was so riddled with bullets and knife wounds that it was impossible to determine the exact cause of death.[38]

The state militia eventually arrived and restored a semblance of law and order. Yet the next evening the melee commenced again. An elderly black man, William Donnegan (or Donegan), whose age was listed variously as seventy-six, eighty-four, or somewhere in between, was notorious for having married a white woman thirty years his junior. The rioters dragged him from his home and pounded him with bricks before lynching him from a tree. He died the following day, although his wife slipped away with his infant daughter undetected.[39]

As a result of the violence, forty private homes and twenty-four businesses were destroyed. Two black men and four whites were confirmed dead, with hundreds injured. Blacks, dismayed by the incident, launched a boycott of white businesses in the aftermath. The episode captured national attention because it vividly illustrated the problem of race that extended throughout the country. Southerners noted that whites living in other regions, who frequently condemned racial violence below the Mason-Dixon Line, could no longer look upon their southern brethren with haughty superiority.[40]

A grand jury eventually recorded more than one hundred indictments against members of the mob, although only one defendant, a Jewish merchant named Abraham Raymer, was convicted. He escaped the most serious charge of murder for his participation in the Donnegan killing. Perhaps the most noteworthy long-term effect of the violence occurred hundreds of miles away. A group of white and black citizens assembled

to discuss options for improving race relations. Their discussions led to
the creation of an organization known as the National Association for
the Advancement of Colored People, a civil rights association that would
influence the course of history during the twentieth century.[41]

The NAACP devoted time and resources to investigating racial violence
wherever it occurred. The group was instrumental in focusing attention
on the plight of Negroes who needed legal assistance but could find no
one willing or able to intervene. Individual cases benefited from NAACP
involvement, but some chapters in the sordid annals of racial violence
were simply beyond the means of any single organization to investigate
or ameliorate. The East St. Louis Riots, arguably the worst labor-related
bloodshed in American history, present a case in point.[42]

East St. Louis was a midwestern industrial town known for meatpacking and manufacturing facilities. During the first three decades of the
twentieth century, it also became known as a way station for Negroes
migrating from the Southland to points north. As persons of color moved
into the area, they drove down wages. Employers recognized that blacks
would work for less money, and with an increasing supply of inexpensive
labor, there was no need to pay anyone above the prevailing rate. Friction
between poor whites, upset about new residents streaming into their
neighborhoods, and blacks anxious to find a new place to live, combined
with declining compensation and rumors of black men mixing with white
women at a labor meeting, triggered a series of skirmishes beginning in
1917.[43]

Trouble originated in February when white workers participated in a
labor strike against the Aluminum Ore Company. Instead of negotiating
with laborers over higher wages and improved working conditions, management replaced the strikers with 470 black workers. As this situation
simmered, a crowd of whites estimated at three thousand assembled on
May 28 and began harassing blacks, sometimes yanking them from streetcars, beating them viciously, and destroying black-owned businesses in
the area. The throng was upset about a rumor circulating throughout the
city that an armed black man had attempted to rob a white man. At Governor Frank Lowden's request, the National Guard restored order. After
the Guard unit departed on June 10, residents were uneasy, and rightly
so. The May 28 affair was a prelude to larger riots to come.[44]

Slightly more than a month later, a major outbreak of violence occurred, shattering the peace. The precipitating event was a car cruising
through a black neighborhood during the evening of July 1. White toughs
inside the car reportedly fired shots in the black section of town. Later
that night, someone fired on an unmarked police car patrolling the
streets. Of the four people inside, two men, both police officers, died.
Black homeowners may have fired on the car in the mistaken assumption

that the original vehicle had returned. Such niceties were lost on frantic white citizens. When they learned of the killings, thousands of whites congregated to view the blood-drenched automobile. Afterward, they marched en masse to the black district to exact vengeance for this latest indignity.[45]

On July 2, the bloodletting commenced in earnest. Someone cut the fire hoses, preventing firefighters from responding effectively as white rioters torched black neighborhoods. Roaming thugs lynched several blacks from streetlamps for no reason other than that the unfortunates happened to be in the wrong place as the mob swept through the area. Even children were not immune to reprisals. By the end of the riot, scores of Negroes lay dead. Estimates varied widely, from a low of thirty-nine, as reported by a congressional committee that later investigated, to a high of two hundred, according to the NAACP. More than six thousand blacks were displaced from their homes and places of business.[46]

The black community was quick to condemn the massacre, which, if anything, resembled a European-style pogrom in its ruthless efficiency and comprehensive scope. More than ten thousand people marched in protest in New York City on July 28. Organized by the NAACP and renowned black intellectual W. E. B. Du Bois, the march was designed to publicize the grave injustice perpetrated against East St. Louis Negroes. Marcus Garvey, leader of the Universal Negro Improvement Association and a more confrontational black leader than Du Bois, decried the "crime against the laws of humanity . . . crime against the laws of the nation . . . crime against Nature, and . . . crime against the God of all mankind." Charging that the National Guardsmen dispatched to control the rioters were in fact in cahoots with the rabble-rousers they were supposed to police, Garvey thundered that the "whole thing, my friends, is a bloody farce, and that the police and soldiers did nothing to stem the murder thirst of the mob is a conclusive proof of conspiracy on the part of the civil authorities to condone the acts of the white mob against Negroes."[47]

THE SUMMER OF 1919 AND A CULTURE
OF RACIAL INTOLERANCE

When viewed together, the violent racial episodes that plagued the United States in the late nineteenth and early twentieth centuries appear almost as a contagion, a physical disease passed along from one community to another. Although each event resulted from a unique set of circumstances, each shared a common characteristic. Whites and blacks lived in segregated societies that encouraged, nay required, them to limit their interactions with each other. As the dominant race, whites dictated the terms of when, where, and how interactions occurred, to the extent that they occurred at all. In each interaction, whites insisted on occupying a superior position, justifying the inequality with innumerable self-serving rationales such as the need to preserve the natural order, the desire to craft efficacious social policy, or simply the naked, unadorned concept of might makes right.

As the two races were thrown together through unexpected interactions and the color line became blurred, violence erupted. It was not an unusual reaction. Whenever a person has been taught to avoid the objectified other, to look upon him with distrust and suspicion, to question his motives and intelligence, and to keep him away at all costs, it is little wonder that such a person will employ force to protect the world as he thinks it should exist. White folklore insisted that blacks were inferior beasts that could not be trusted to become full-fledged members of society. When those beasts intruded into a white man's world, the fixed social position of the races was imperiled, and a new world of racial parity could not stand. In the case of Leo Frank, a Jewish factory manager lynched by a mob for supposedly killing a young white girl, white citizens' fears concerning his alien nature, his Yankee ways, and his strange Jewishness propelled them to objectify the man and thereby transform him into a monster who threatened community values. Blacks and Jews were not persons possessing all the virtues and foibles found in white individuals. These nonwhites were not members of the American polity deserving of dignity, respect, and a place in the life of the republic; they were odd, menacing creatures of an altogether different sort. They might not even be fully human.[48]

Many, probably most, episodes were local affairs—minute problems and misunderstandings resulting in small flare-ups that were quickly forgotten, if not quite forgiven. The unexpected interactions that led to sustained, horrific violence frequently sprang from external events removed from the day-to-day intercourse that occurs within any community. The so-called Red Summer of 1919 demonstrates what can happen when external events occur in rapid succession, and violent altercations in one area of the country gather momentum in other places.

It was supposed to be the start of a new era. With the Great War recently ended and President Woodrow Wilson's assurances that future conflicts could be contained or eliminated, the year 1919 dawned with great promise. Black soldiers returning from the killing fields of Europe looked forward to a peaceful coexistence with their white brethren. No one was naive enough to believe that the long-simmering racial tensions that characterized the American experience would dissolve within a fortnight, but hopes were high that the price paid by Negro soldiers would earn them a measure of respect that could translate into racial progress at home. Hopes were soon dashed.[49]

The causes were familiar to anyone cognizant of the record compiled since the end of Reconstruction. In dozens of communities around the country, returning soldiers flooded labor markets, which frequently had too many willing workers for too few available jobs. Change always creates stress, especially when different peoples bump against each other in a fierce competition for scarce resources. Outside race, changes in economics, politics, gender relations, and even fashion ensured that Americans experienced enormous strain during and after the Great War.[50]

For all of the United States' gains as an international power, it was a worrisome time. The carnage in the trenches underscored the fragility of life and the interconnectedness of a world where some people were not sure they wished to be interconnected. The Russian Revolution of 1917 was still fresh in many minds, and onlookers feared a rising tide of bolshevism that would sweep across western Europe and eventually reach American shores. Although the link between Russian communism and blacks struggling to eke out a better life in the nooks and crannies of American cities and towns was tenuous at best and delusional at worst, some Americans worried that race and politics were intermingled. President Wilson, the first southerner to occupy the White House since the Civil War, expressed the fears of many white citizens when he remarked during a private conversation that the "American Negro returning from abroad would be our greatest medium in conveying bolshevism to America."[51]

A fear of emboldened black men bringing newfangled ideas back from Europe was not the only concern. When the war ended and the troops returned home, many Americans were weary of foreign adventures; they embraced presidential candidate Warren G. Harding's promise of a "return to normalcy." Reactionary politics became the order of the day in numerous communities. Any suggestions of change in political or social relations were met with hostility and resentment. Progress in race relations, always incremental to begin with, ground to a halt and suffered reverses during this era.[52]

James Weldon Johnson, a black author and NAACP field secretary, coined the term "Red Summer" to describe the bloodshed that occurred during 1919. So much violence erupted that it was difficult to keep track of it all. More than twenty cities exploded during that long, hot summer. The episode that occurred in Chicago on July 27 was especially horrific. It began when a black swimmer had the audacity to wander into a beach area on Lake Michigan claimed by white bathers. In retaliation, white swimmers pelted the young black man with stones. Other blacks came to his defense. As the two sides bombarded each other, one young black man who was not involved, Eugene Williams, was struck in the head. He collapsed in the water and drowned. After several blacks complained to Daniel Callahan, a white police officer standing nearby, the officer refused to arrest the offenders. Instead, he grabbed one of the complaining blacks and took the fellow into custody. This patently biased response triggered a deadly reaction from gangs of whites and blacks. For thirteen days, the Windy City experienced unprecedented racial strife. When the smoke cleared, authorities discovered that twenty-three blacks and fifteen whites had died, 537 people had suffered injuries, and approximately one thousand black families had been forced from their homes.[53]

In Washington, DC, a young white woman claimed that two black men had pushed her in the street and attempted to snatch her umbrella. It turned out that she was the wife of a naval aviator, which made her fate a matter of honor for uniformed military personnel. As news circulated throughout the capital city, the incident was grossly exaggerated. The police eventually apprehended a suspect but were forced to release him owing to a lack of evidence. This reasonable response upset members of the military. For five days beginning on July 19, white service members viciously attacked a multitude of blacks near Capitol Hill. The mob did not care whether the victims were tied to the original incident. The opportunity to brutalize a Negro was the primary consideration.[54]

In Phillips County, Arkansas, on September 30, a group of blacks congregated in a rural church to discuss organizing a union, the Progressive Farmers and Household Union of America. It was an era when union organizing was popular, although many corporate managers and conservative political leaders smelled a whiff of communism in such endeavors. Phillips County was so sparsely populated and disorganized that the effectiveness of a union was always in doubt, even if V. I. Lenin's Bolshevik conspiracy somehow surreptitiously snaked its way into eastern Arkansas.

In any case, two white police officers and a black trustee from the jail appeared outside the church as the union meeting commenced. Their appearance was never adequately explained. Perhaps their car had broken down, as one version of the tale intimated. Another possible motive, according to some accounts, was that the lawmen were searching for a bootlegger. Negroes guarding the church believed the white officers had conveniently appeared to spy on the gathering and to take down names to retaliate against blacks who dared to organize a union in Phillips County. The two sides exchanged gunfire, and one white officer, Special Agent W. A. Adkins of the Missouri Pacific Railroad, fell dead. Deputy Charles Pratt was badly wounded.[55]

White citizens had grown fearful of local blacks initiating a race war, and this incident suggested that the long-anticipated rebellion was at hand. Anxious to get out in front of the skirmish, the local sheriff issued clear instructions to "hunt Mr. Nigger in his lair." He suffered from no shortage of willing volunteers. To forestall further losses, a white posse descended on the nearby town of Elaine to disarm blacks in a preemptive strike. Emotions ran high, and no one exercised restraint.

Phillips County is situated not far from the Mississippi border, and news of the violence attracted scores of whites from the adjacent state. In the mad dash to join the posse, whites in cars, trains, and trucks eagerly fired their guns at any black face they saw during the journey. It would have been great fun for the white vigilantes had the situation not been so dire.

By the time the bloodletting had concluded, scores of people were dead. Estimates suggested that at least twenty-five blacks and whites had died, but as many as two hundred blacks may have perished. Governor Charles Hillman Brough ordered federal troops into the county to quell the violence. As they policed the most tumultuous areas, the soldiers arrested blacks suspected of killing whites. If a black man could produce a pass authorized by the military and attested to by a reputable white citizen indicating that the holder was not a threat to the community, the potential offender was allowed to leave unmolested by the authorities. Negroes who failed to produce the requisite pass were rounded up and carted off to jail.[56]

The governor appointed a Committee of Seven to investigate the facts and determine whether an insurrection had been in the offing during those turbulent days in late September and early October 1919. Given the whites' antipathy toward blacks, the committee's conclusions were hardly surprising. Shortly after the group initiated its investigations, a committee member told the press that the Elaine riots, as they came to be known, were properly characterized as "a deliberately planned insurrection of the negroes against the whites, directed by an organization known as the 'Progressive Farmers and Household Union of America' established for the purpose of banding negroes together for the killing of white people."[57]

A local grand jury issued indictments for blacks deemed to be ringleaders in the supposed rebellion. Blacks who cooperated by testifying against the ringleaders were allowed to go free. After enduring perfunctory show trials, eleven black men were found guilty of murdering white men and sentenced to death. According to the trial transcript, the defense counsel called no witnesses and produced no evidence in support of his clients. A twelfth black defendant was convicted and sentenced to die several weeks later after the all-white jury deliberated for four minutes. Thirty-six defendants, recognizing that a guilty verdict was a fait accompli, agreed to plead guilty to second-degree murder to avoid a trial. Sixty-seven other defendants pled guilty to lesser offenses. No whites were brought up on charges. Officers of the court, disregarding the circus-like atmosphere of the proceedings, proudly congratulated themselves on the impartiality and fairness of the Arkansas justice system. That no one had been lynched was declared a victory for justice.[58]

Correctly suspecting that the Committee of Seven had rushed to judgment and based its conclusions on racial bias, the NAACP dispatched its assistant secretary, Walter F. White, to conduct his own investigation. White was a rare Negro who could pass for white. With his blonde hair, and blue eyes, he simply did not invite scrutiny as a member of the colored race. Using forged credentials from the *Chicago Daily News*, he traveled to Arkansas as a reporter investigating the hubbub.

As White expected, the arrival of an out-of-town reporter asking potentially embarrassing questions invited suspicion from the locals, but the NAACP had sent the right man for the job. White assuaged their concerns by expressing sympathy for the mob. Soon the intrepid reporter was in the thick of things, eliciting comment from a variety of townspeople. White even finagled an audience with Governor Brough, who expressed approval that a newspaper reporter would come to the state in search of the truth rather than swallow the lies defaming the "good white people of Arkansas" dished up by outside agitators such as the NAACP.

White never spoke directly with the black defendants, but he hatched a plan to do so. Nonetheless, his identity somehow leaked before he could speak to the men. As he walked along West Cherry Street in Elaine on his way to the jail, White encountered a tall, heavy-set Negro who whispered that he had important news. After White followed the man to a secluded area, the fellow told him that the whites in town knew who he was and lay in wait to "fix" him.

Frightened of the consequences, White resolved to leave town as soon as possible. He discovered that a train was departing for Memphis in a few minutes. Hastening to the railroad station, he cautiously boarded the passenger compartment from the opposite side of the platform without a ticket. As the conductor passed through the aisles, White offered to pay cash for a ticket, explaining that he had been unable to purchase one earlier owing to the press of business.

The conductor examined White with frank curiosity. At first, White feared the man had guessed the passenger's identity. After a moment, the conductor remarked, "Why, Mister, you're leaving just when the fun is going to start! There's a damned yellow nigger down here passing for white, and the boys are going to get him."

When White asked what they would do after apprehending the fellow, the conductor gleefully responded, "Well, when they get through with him, he won't pass for white no more."[59]

After this harrowing experience, Walter White returned home and reported what he had learned in the pages of the *Nation*, a progressive publication that had spilled much ink on the race question in the United States. His articles also appeared in the *Chicago Defender* and the *Crisis*, an NAACP publication. When he heard about White's exposé, Governor Brough asked the US Postal Service to prohibit distribution of the *Nation* and the *Crisis*. The governor also attempted to stop delivery of the *Chicago Defender* in local Arkansas communities.[60]

Aside from the public relations recriminations following the Phillips County episode, the defendants' appeal to the US Supreme Court produced a landmark decision in *Moore v. Dempsey*. It was the first major case involving Negro rights of the twentieth century. The high court had not been sympathetic to arguments presented by black defendants in the past. In most cases, the justices had supported the white supremacist regime instituted by state governments determined to circumvent the spirit and letter of the Civil War amendments. In accepting the habeas corpus appeal, the Supreme Court did not decide the question of whether the defendants were guilty or innocent of the alleged crimes. Such factual matters typically are not issues on appeal. Instead, the justices considered whether the mob mentality that prevailed at trial had violated the defendants' due process rights under the Fourteenth Amendment. By a vote of 6–2, the court concluded that the defendants had not received a fair trial.[61]

Justice Oliver Wendell Holmes Jr. penned the majority opinion. He noted that the federal courts should not encroach on the power of the state courts absent serious reservations and compelling circumstances. Holmes explained, "The corrective process supplied by the State may be so adequate that interference by habeas corpus ought not to be allowed." In this case, however, federal intervention regrettably was necessary owing to the state trial court's failure to protect the rights of the criminal defendants. Holmes observed, "If the case is that the whole proceeding is a mask—that counsel, jury and judge were swept to the fatal end by an irresistible wave of public passion, and that the State Courts failed to correct the wrong; neither perfection in the machinery for correction nor the possibility that the trial court and counsel saw no other way of avoiding an immediate outbreak of the mob can prevent this Court from securing to the petitioners their constitutional rights."[62]

The majority opinion was a victory for the Negroes charged with crimes in the Elaine riots, and it marked a new era in Supreme Court jurisprudence, although few observers understood this at the time. The court was more amenable to allowing federal habeas corpus proceedings to supplement state court criminal trials when allegations suggested that a trial violated due process of law under the Fourteenth Amendment. With increased federal court scrutiny of state courts, the seeds of the due process revolution of the Warren Court years were planted in the bitter soil of the Arkansas race riots. It would be a mistake, however, to assume a new day had arrived for race relations, especially in the southeastern United States.[63]

Two years before the decision in *Moore v. Dempsey*, a major race riot occurred in Tulsa, Oklahoma, a city obsessed with race. In 1916, the city council had enacted an ordinance forbidding either blacks or whites from residing on any city block where three-quarters of the inhabitants were members of the other race. The US Supreme Court had struck down this enforced residential segregation law as unconstitutional, but the city had never removed the requirement from the books. Segregation was the practice, whether due to law or custom.[64]

By the 1920s, Tulsa was a booming town following the discovery of oil, attracting all sorts of characters from every walk of life. As Negroes flooded into the area and lived side by side with whites, tensions flared. Two factors especially contributed to the racial confrontation that occurred over a period of sixteen hours on May 31 and June 1, 1921. First, the Greenwood section of the town had developed a reputation as a desirable place for affluent Negroes to live and work, earning it the sobriquet the "Black Wall Street" of America. Such talk stoked the fires of jealousy in the white community.[65] A second factor was that Oklahoma had acquired a well-deserved reputation as a state where lynchings frequently occurred. Between the time Oklahoma joined the Union as a state in 1907 and the Tulsa riots occurred slightly more than thirteen years later, thirty-one people had been lynched; twenty-six of them were black. That figure averages to about one hanging every five months for more than a dozen years. Clearly, Oklahomans were fond of Judge Lynch's expedited system of rough justice.[66]

Tulsa was ripe for racial strife owing to the rise of the black middle class and the tradition of violence against people of color. The presence of the Ku Klux Klan, a Reconstruction-era vigilante group that had died out in the 1870s, added to the volatile mix. In 1915, a new version of the KKK emerged. By the 1920s, the Klan had proliferated into many communities throughout the Deep South and the Midwest. It was not merely a racist group; the Klan was a social organization that allowed white political leaders to fraternize and plan future activities. This was especially true in northeastern Oklahoma. According to one source, Tulsa boasted of a population of seventy-two thousand in 1921—approximately thirty-two hundred of whom were Klansmen.[67]

As with many other violent racial episodes recounted here, an encounter between a black man and a white woman served as the triggering event. A nineteen-year-old black shoeshine worker, Dick Rowland, stepped into an elevator operated by Sarah Page, a seventeen-year-old white girl. He was on his way to the top floor of the Drexel Building in downtown Tulsa to use a restroom provided for Negroes in the highly segregated city. The nature of the encounter has never been clear. Speculation has focused on whether the two were quarreling lovers or the young black man tripped and fell against the white girl. In any event, she screamed after he entered the elevator. Fearing the worst, a white clerk working in the building summoned the police.

Rowland fled to his mother's house in the Greenwood section of town. Flight from the premises might be viewed as a sign of guilt under different circumstances, but it was the only rational course of action at the time. In 1921, a black man accused of assaulting a white woman was considered guilty even before formal charges were filed. Sarah Page declined to prosecute, and the case eventually was dismissed, but in the immediate aftermath of the event, such details were irrelevant. When word circulated that a black man had crossed the color line with a white girl, the community reacted with predictable speed and violence. After Rowland had been apprehended, arrested, and escorted to the courthouse, a mob of some two thousand angry whites formed outside and demanded that the prisoner be turned over to them for swift justice. Another black man, Roy Belton, had been lynched a year earlier, and the newly elected Tulsa sheriff had no wish to suffer the same loss of control that had plagued his predecessor in the Belton case. He refused to comply with the mob's demands, even though he did not command enough deputies to prevent a full-scale riot.[68]

In the meantime, members of the black community in Greenwood assembled not far from the courthouse. Recognizing that young Rowland's life was imperiled, about thirty blacks began arming to attack the whites. A prominent black entrepreneur, O. W. Gurley, attempted to intercede by talking to the sheriff and providing assurances to the black community that a lynching would not occur. The effort was undertaken in vain. Seeing blacks bearing arms, a group of whites resolved to launch a preemptive strike.[69]

It is unclear which side fired the first shots, but a series of roaming gun battles raged through the Tulsa streets during May 31 and June 1. An armed white mob looted local stores in search of ammunition, allowing a brief respite from the violence. It did not last. Even the appearance of the National Guard did not initially quell the disturbance, since the black community was convinced that Guardsmen were aligned with local whites. Such skepticism was well placed in light of reports indicating that uniformed officers rounded up blacks who had not escaped quickly enough to avoid detention.[70]

Around 1 a.m. on June 1, a series of fires erupted in the commercial district adjacent to Greenwood. The Tulsa Fire Department arrived to suppress the blaze, but an armed white gang repulsed firefighters. More than two dozen black businesses perished in the flames. An irate black community responded to what many Negroes concluded were deliberate acts of arson by defending their homes and businesses under force of arms. Other blacks streamed away from Tulsa as thick black smoke billowed across the city skyline.[71]

The dawn brought a renewed attack after a white man fell mortally wounded by a sniper's bullet. The white mob, swollen to numbers far beyond the ability of the Negro community to fight, ventured into the Greenwood district, determined to deliver a fatal blow to black resisters. By this time, outraged whites cared little about guilt or innocence. Any colored skin that came into view was fair game. Some accounts described white men flying World War I biplanes over the city to fire rifles and drop incendiary devices on fleeing Negroes.[72]

Later in the morning, a contingent of Oklahoma National Guardsmen and leaders from nearby localities restored law and order after civil authorities declared martial law. In the wake of the violence, estimates

[3.2]   The Tulsa race riot of 1921 was one of the worst episodes of violence perpetrated against blacks in the United States during the twentieth century. This photograph shows smoke billowing over the city as fires erupt during the melee. Courtesy of the Library of Congress.

varied widely. Some sources figured that twenty-six blacks and ten whites had been killed, but others concluded that as many as sixty-eight blacks and nine whites had perished. The discrepancies in the numbers were never resolved satisfactorily. Some individuals simply vanished. Whether they fled to more hospitable environs or died in the skirmishes was never clear. Even the Tulsa Race Riot Commission, established on the seventy-fifth anniversary of the incident in 1996, could not definitively reach a conclusion. In its 2001 report, the commission recommended payment of reparations to survivors of the riot as well as creation of a memorial to the incident and establishment of an economic development enterprise zone in the historic Greenwood area of Tulsa.[73]

Race riots continued to erupt across the country during the early 1920s. An all-too-familiar incident occurred in Rosewood, Florida, two years after Tulsa. Tensions there had been building. In 1922, a white schoolteacher had been murdered. The Ku Klux Klan was active in northern Florida, and the group was quick to blame the black community for any criminal activity. In this context, a rumor spread on New Year's Day 1923 that Fannie Taylor, a white woman, had been sexually abused by a black man. Local whites were convinced that Jesse Hunter, an escaped convict, was the perpetrator. With approval from the sheriff, a posse formed to search for Hunter, along with his suspected accomplices, Aaron Carrier and Sam Carter, in Rosewood. The posse later imprisoned Carrier and lynched Carter.

The mob also warned Aaron Carrier's cousin, Sylvester, to leave town. When he refused, the white men confronted him at his home. By this time, the sheriff realized he could not control the throng. Despite his attempts to defuse the situation and disband his loosely organized posse, the sheriff was powerless to stop the group.[74]

On January 4, between twenty and thirty whites surrounded Sylvester Carrier's house and shot his dog. When Sylvester's mother, Sarah, stepped onto the porch to investigate, someone shot her in the head. Inside the house, Sylvester realized that he would not survive the encounter if he did not defend himself and his family. Perhaps as many as fifteen to twenty-five people huddled inside, cowering at the large number of armed white men encircling the structure. Sylvester managed to hold off the mob as he exchanged gunfire with the group, eventually killing two men and wounding four before he, too, was killed. Negroes inside the house who survived the gun battle fled into a nearby swamp.[75]

As word of the shootings spread across the state, armed whites streamed into Rosewood, anxious to teach the uppity Negroes a lesson. Sylvester Carrier's house was torched, as was most of the town. A gang of between two and three hundred whites marched through Rosewood, killing animals and burning every structure in sight. Some black citizens escaped with assistance from two train conductors. Others hid in the local general store or in the swamps.[76]

After the melee had ended, six blacks and two whites were reported dead. Every building save the general store and one house had been destroyed. Fearful of future reprisals, the town's black population took up residence elsewhere, including nearby Gainesville. Consequently, Rosewood ceased to exist. In time, the episode faded from the popular memory. Not until 1994—more than seven decades after the riot—did the state legislature vote to provide $150,000 to each of the seven survivors of the episode.[77]

CONCLUSION

The spate of violence perpetrated against Negroes and other nonwhite persons in the United States between the end of the Civil War and the advent of the Great Depression was causally connected to the objectification of "other" persons. Whether racial animus and Jim Crow segregation caused or resulted from the numerous violent episodes remains a controversial issue. Did whites react violently to persons of color and seek separation as a means of self-preservation, as many white supremacists claimed, or did violence stem from the fact that whites rarely interacted with blacks and therefore lacked an empathetic connection, which made it relatively easy to confront the "other" through violent means? Answers are anything but clear.

What is clear from the myriad reports of mass confrontations and small, briefly violent encounters is that American society became sharply divided along a color line. Fears that black men were sexual deviants who preyed on white women triggered many episodes of violence and mass lynchings, but these myths were part of a larger ethic. Pigmentation determined the fate of an individual from the moment of his birth to the instant of his death.[78]

A focus on the most infamous acts of mass racial violence during this time fails to account for the innumerable smaller incidents that have been forgotten by history or never came to light. In particular, the lynching of black Americans, sometimes labeled the "shame of America," typically occurred in small settings in rural areas that attracted little press attention until the NAACP and other groups investigated. According to the best available data, between 1882 and 1968, 3,446 blacks and 1,297 whites were lynched in the United States. Yet even these figures, despite their apparent precision, are open to question since the meaning of the term "lynching" is contested. It derives from Charles Lynch, a justice of the peace in Virginia during the Revolutionary War, who ordered extralegal punishment

[3.3] This infamous photograph shows two black men, Thomas Shipp and Abram Smith, who were lynched in Marion, Indiana, on August 7, 1930. A Jewish schoolteacher from New York, Abel Meeropol, said that the photograph inspired him to write his poem "Strange Fruit" about the horrors of lynching. Courtesy of the Library of Congress.

for American colonists who remained loyal to the British Crown. In a 1922 bill, Congress defined lynching as a practice performed by "an assemblage composed of three or more persons acting in concert for the purpose of depriving any person of his life without authority of law as a punishment for or to prevent the commission of some actual or supposed public offense." Race need not play a part in a lynching, although, in many instances, blacks fell victim to the practice at the hands of riotous white mobs.[79]

Foreign observers might view the American experience with genuine befuddlement at the centrality of race to understanding US history and politics. In other nations, heredity or class was the principal determinant of social position, but in the New World such distinctions were minimized. Yet something in the human animal longs for a shorthand method of categorizing the "worth" of individuals. However much modern men might decry invidious discrimination, history abounds with such distinctions. In the United States, racial bias became a crucial characteristic of American society in the century following the Civil War, and violence often occurred as a result of that bias.[80]

Part II

I'M SOMETIMES UP AND SOMETIMES DOWN

4

The Rise of the
Populist Movement

*"You Shall Not Crucify Mankind
upon a Cross of Gold"*

Populism was always best understood as a loose amalgamation of interests rather than a formal, comprehensive statement of consistent principles. A political party (several iterations, actually) rose and fell under the "Populist" label, but it never found the firm footing of the two major parties because its members could not always agree on means and ends, to say nothing of their failure to articulate an unambiguous platform. In any event, understanding the politics of race in the United States requires an understanding of populism as it was practiced at the end of the nineteenth century and in the early years of the twentieth, for white denizens who scratched out a living in rural areas often competed with freedpeople for scarce resources, and the competition grew bitter and violent. Black populists in the South and West sometimes reluctantly worked with their white brethren, if only for a time, to oppose the moneyed interests from the big cities.[1]

ORIGINS AND DESTINIES

The genesis of the movement dated from the 1870s as American farmers grew increasingly disenchanted with their lot. In the years following the

Civil War, older agrarians fondly recalled the antebellum era, when their livelihoods had seemed far more secure, or so they thought as they sifted through their memories in the soft afterglow of nostalgia. The United States was still a nation populated by small farms where families tilled the soil and depended on local economic conditions and municipal leaders to see them through. The promise of American democracy was that everyone would earn his daily bread and enjoy enough surpluses to ensure at least a small measure of financial prosperity. In the aftermath of that bloody war and the economic panics that ensued, the promise went unfulfilled.[2]

The more intrepid farmers followed the railroads westward in hopes that new scenery would translate into new opportunity. In some cases, it did. All too often, however, farmers who had uprooted their families and left behind all that they knew back east discovered the same powerful commercial forces arrayed against them in the new lands. Hardy souls relied on self-help groups such as the Grange and the Greenback Party to look out for their interests, but in the 1870s these groups were nascent and struggling.[3]

As often happens, people suffering through hard times consoled themselves with the promise of a new day. Yet by the 1880s, it was clear that the plight of the American farmer had not improved. If anything, the 1880s were more financially taxing than the preceding decade. Foreclosures on farm mortgages were on the rise, and the level of personal debt among residents who somehow maintained a tenuous hold on their acreage was one step away from catastrophic. The rich appeared to be getting richer, and the poor were slipping further into a black hole of insolvency. In alarming numbers families were realizing the horror of horrors—becoming landless tenant farmers. No one but the most naive bumpkin could look to the future with optimism.[4]

Great social movements do not spring from despondency alone, but such conditions create momentum. When the forerunner of the National Farmers' Alliance and Industrial Union formed in the 1870s, the impetus was a desperate need among agrarians to oppose commercial enterprises that kept the farmer impoverished. Members received information on the causes and effects of the depressed state of farming, necessary prerequisites to developing an ameliorative strategy. Only after the alliance collapsed did the vestiges of the movement coalesce around a political party based on the power of the people to challenge the interests of corporate America. The People's Party was born in the 1890s from the tatters of the Grange movement that had originated fifteen years earlier.[5]

The two strands of populism that eventually led to the formation of a third party originated in the southern states as well as in the Great Plains. Many southern farmers initially appeared apolitical, but with depressed cotton prices driving so many of them to the brink of desperation, they were amenable to any manner of relief. In the West, the drive for populism seems to have sprung up from uncertain sources. Farmer cooperatives that formed throughout Kansas, Nebraska, Texas, and Missouri during the 1880s created a culture of populist sentiment that first captured national attention in 1890.[6]

The National Farmers' Alliance had been working behind the scenes for much of the 1880s. In January 1887, Charles Macune, head of the Southern Farmers' Alliance, held a conference in Waco, Texas, to discuss methods for alleviating a major agrarian problem—namely, the lack of available credit. So many banks and financial institutions had poured their resources into funding large infrastructure improvements, such as railroad expansion, that little funding was available to assist farmers who needed to invest in feed, seed, and the latest equipment. In Macune's vision of a new emerging economic order, the Farmers' Alliance Exchange could exist as a mammoth cooperative aimed at marketing cotton crops by cutting out middlemen and purchasing in bulk, two actions that would increase the amount of money farmers could collect for their labor.[7]

Despite the favorable economics of Macune's proposal, he faced daunting opposition. In many areas, especially in the politically conservative states of the old Southern Confederacy, even a hint of consolidated power was looked on with deep suspicion. No one who remembered the war could think about collective authority as anything other than invariably oppressive. It is a testament to Macune's considerable powers of persuasion, as well as to the terrible state of agriculture throughout the United States, that attendees at the Waco conference were induced to set aside their well-known aversion to collectivities in favor of creating an agrarian union. Before the year was out, the National Farmers' Alliance and Cooperative Union of America could boast of alliances in ten states. By the time Macune stepped down as the head of the organization at the end of 1889, the alliance listed more than 1 million—perhaps as many as 1.2 million—members.[8]

It was heady stuff, this massive drive to organize farmers, not normally an organizing group, to improve their economic situation. Yet economic cooperatives do not necessarily translate into political power. A change in culture and recognition of politics as an appropriate avenue for reform would be needed. That so many farmers were apolitical and disinterested in the affairs of the major political parties presented a critical obstacle. The cooperatives proved helpful here, too, for although not strictly political entities, they set the stage for a populist revolt in the halls of power. The alliance's dispatch of lecturers in the 1880s to educate rural inhabitants on the need for organized politicking paid dividends in the 1890s.

This is not to suggest that the lecturers met with overnight success. Indeed, their efforts appeared radical to some conservatives, mostly the bankers and financiers who earned good livings ministering to the needs of local farmers (to the extent such needs were met at all). Resistance to change in rural areas is hardly surprising, but even when change was the only means of staving off financial ruin, rural folk were reluctant to step beyond what they had always known. Not until farmers perceived a fundamental flaw in the structure of the financial system, rather than bearing an animus against their friend and neighbor, the local banker, was a genuine agrarian revolt in the offing.[9]

The American banking system in the 1880s was erected on a fixed, seemingly unassailable principle: bank notes must be backed by gold. The gold standard was the bedrock of the eastern financial establishment because it ensured the money supply was tightly controlled and interest rates were high. Yet this conservative fiscal policy, so treasured by the wealthy capitalists of the East Coast, burdened western farmers with a lack of available funds and credit to run their operations. Tight money policy, or money's status as a limited commodity, is always valuable to those who possess it but wreaks havoc on those who do not.

To the impoverished farmer who saw no way out of his dire predicament, the actions of eastern elites, when they could be understood, appeared always to provide advantages to the affluent urban dweller at the expense of the poor, rural workingman. If the average American could not bring himself to enter the budding socialist camp at the end of the nineteenth century, he at least came to appreciate the circumstances that drove many Europeans into left-wing politics.[10]

Mainstream politics in the United States failed to meet the needs of rural citizens in the 1880s and 1890s. The two major political parties had been organized before the war mostly around sectional interests. Despite undeniable changes, such as the destruction of slavery as an institution, voters still clung to party ideologies that existed before the fighting erupted. Southerners mistrusted Republicans as the Party of Lincoln, and northerners viewed Democrats as thinly disguised would-be secessionists. No one, it seemed, was protecting the welfare of the common man. The People's Party would bridge the gap and unite common elements among both parties. The task may have been too gargantuan to accomplish, but in the early days, anything seemed possible. For farmers, any movement, even one that fell short of the ideal, was preferable to the status quo.[11]

THE PEOPLE'S PARTY

If any single event created the conditions for the rise of the People's Party, sometimes labeled the "Populists," it was probably passage of the Mc-Kinley Tariff in 1890, a measure that disadvantaged southern and western farmers because they had to sell their wares in an unprotected market but were forced to purchase manufactured goods at inflated prices. Yet reaction to the tariff was but one link in a larger chain that extended over time. Farmers gradually had come to understand that economic and political power grew out of numbers and organization. Only by banding together could poor white cotton growers from the Southland and struggling wheat farmers from the Midwest force congressional Republicans to pay a political price for championing elitist policies that favored big business conglomerates over the little man.[12]

Two principal groups, the Southern Farmers' Alliance and the Agricultural Wheel, extended overtures to a labor group, the Knights of Labor, in 1889. The Knights' Grand Master Workman, Terence V. Powderly, was not originally a proponent of creating a third party. He was intent on making organized labor a major force in the United States, not on challenging Democrats and Republicans in electoral politics. For all of its triumphs in days to come, the labor movement was in its infancy during the late 1880s. If Powderly and his adherents were to exercise any influence in the 1890s, it would have to be outside the Knights of Labor, which had declined in membership since reaching its peak in the mid-1880s. During a series of conferences he orchestrated between December 1889 and July 1892, Powderly, despite continuing skepticism, realized the advantages of a new party, and the People's Party was born.[13]

A former Minnesota congressman and well-known pseudoscientist, Ignatius L. Donnelly, wrote the preamble to the party platform, which was adopted at a convention in Omaha, Nebraska, on July 4, 1892. Donnelly, a colorful stump politician who loved to use florid language in service of his cause du jour, had recently penned a novel attacking capitalism, *Caesar's Column*, and was seeking a new outlet for his talents when he stumbled into the Populist camp. The fledgling party was tailor-made for a man of Donnelly's tastes and sensibilities. Any would-be demagogue could find material to work with in the anguish suffered by American farmers in the 1890s. He did not disappoint. The preamble, first presented at a meeting in St. Louis five months before the party convention, was filled with fire and brimstone:

> We meet in the midst of a nation brought to the verge of moral, political, and material ruin. Corruption dominates the ballot-box, the Legislatures, the Congress, and touches even the ermine of the bench. The people are demoralized; most of the States have been compelled to isolate the voters at the polling places to prevent universal intimidation and bribery. . . . The fruits of the toil of millions are boldly stolen to build up colossal fortunes for a few, unprecedented in the history of mankind; and the possessors of those, in turn, despise the republic and endanger liberty. From the same prolific womb of governmental injustice we breed the two great classes—tramps and millionaires.[14]

Many Populists would have objected to the characterization of their goals as leftist, perhaps even socialist, but their concerns were consistent with the worldwide movement to improve the lot of the masses. The platform called for reduction of the workday to eight hours; direct election of US senators in lieu of selection by state legislators, as required by Article I, Section 3 of the Constitution; a secret ballot; a graduated federal income tax; civil service reform; and government control of monopolistic industries such as railroads, telegraphs, and telephones. To ensure that money circulated freely, thereby assisting farmers in acquiring capital, the party championed the concept of cheap silver money tied to a rate of sixteen ounces of silver to one ounce of gold.[15]

As the Populists' power grew, the grassroots nature of the movement attracted strange bedfellows. Black Americans were affected by the same issues facing white farmers, and so they too embraced the Populist cause. To say blacks and whites united together in a spirit of brotherhood and harmony under a Populist umbrella would be an exaggeration— segregation and white supremacy were not completely abandoned—but the racism so prominently on display in other areas of life was less prevalent among Populists. Negroes resided near whites; tilled adjacent lands; paid the same exorbitant rates for farm supplies and overplanted, depleted land, as well as regressive taxes; and shouldered heavy responsibilities in a depressed economic era. Recognizing the value of forming organizations to improve their bleak circumstances, blacks formed the Colored Farmers' National Alliance and Cooperative Union, an analogue to the white organization. In some communities, blacks and whites worked cooperatively to achieve common ends, but in most places, especially in the South, the white and black efforts existed side by side without crossing the color line.[16]

Therein lay the problem for the incipient People's Party. When James B. Weaver, a former Iowa congressman and Greenback Party leader, accepted the party's presidential nomination in 1892, he proposed joining forces with colored farmers owing to their common interests. Weaver had run for president on third-party tickets previously. He knew his chances of winning the election, always a long shot at best, would be marginally improved if he could count on Negro support. Hailing as he did from the Midwest, he simply could not fathom how and why farmers in any region would allow racial prejudice to undermine their economic interests. He was not the first person to question the dubious wisdom of segregation as an economic principle if not as a moral question; nor would he be the last.

Weaver's proposal did not sit well with many southerners. Although some white politicians recognized the expediency of joining with blacks in the quest for electoral victory, it would be a mistake to herald the Populist attempt to leverage Negro political support as a biracial movement. Renowned southern historian C. Vann Woodward famously argued that populism was a source of budding, albeit fragile racial harmony in the South, but later historians questioned whether this conclusion was overwrought. Many Populists spoke of whites and blacks working together in service of mutually beneficial goals, but the reality seldom matched the rhetoric. In any case, it is clear that the Populists' uneasy relationship with blacks did not erase the color line or alter political calculations. Although Negroes retained a small measure of political power in some small southern enclaves as late as the 1890s, that anomaly would soon change.[17]

The Populists earned more than 1 million popular votes in the 1892 presidential contest and captured twenty-two electoral votes, winning the states of Colorado, Idaho, Kansas, and Nevada on the strength of their agrarian appeal. Candidate Weaver and his running mate, James G. Field, a former attorney general of Virginia and a major in the Confederate army who had lost a leg at the Battle of Cedar Creek in 1864, made one of the strongest showings of any third-party presidential ticket in American history. When all the votes were tallied, however, Democrat Grover Cleveland had defeated his Republican opponent, Benjamin Harrison, who had driven Cleveland from office four years earlier. Cleveland became the only sitting president ever to lose his bid for a second term only to win reelection four years later. The McKinley Tariff may have been the deciding factor in Harrison's loss.[18]

The People's Party enjoyed its greatest success between 1892 and 1896. An economic depression—the term "panic" was the parlance of the day—in 1893, the worst in twenty years, convinced increasingly desperate Americans that something was dreadfully wrong with the country and reinforced the Populist appeal among a wider array of citizens. The US Treasury was almost completely depleted as crafty speculators took advantage of a complicated scheme whereby silver could be traded for gold. As the Treasury traded away its reserves, the US government was in danger of falling below the levels necessary to ensure that paper currency was backed by gold. President Cleveland eventually pushed through a repeal of the Sherman Silver Purchase Act, the Populist-supported legislation that had exacerbated the currency crisis in the first place. When that measure failed to alleviate the shortfall in the Treasury, the president reached out to wealthy Wall Street financier J. P. Morgan for a loan. Although hardly an altruistic soul, Morgan recognized the possibility of an imminent financial collapse if he sat by idly. The well-known robber baron agreed to pony up $60 million to shore up the US economic system and stave off an unprecedented calamity. Morgan was not a selfless hero in the affair. A syndicate he created with the secretary of the Treasury sold massive gold bond issues that burdened the nation with a crippling national debt and amassed a tidy profit for the bankers who participated in the transaction. Nonetheless, the effort succeeded in propping up the fragile economy.[19]

Average Americans suffered through the Panic of 1893 as never before. People who had lived at least marginally productive lives came to know hunger. Some displaced persons took to the streets and rode the rails as itinerant workers and hobos. In 1894, Ohio businessman Jacob S. Coxey tapped into the despair felt by millions of Americans by organizing some five hundred men to march on Washington, DC, to protest the federal government's policies. "Coxey's Army," as it came to be known, sought to reinstitute "cheap money" policies and provide federal debt-relief programs for rural inhabitants left destitute by the depression. When the marchers reached the US Capitol Building, they were arrested for trespassing. Interest in the march faded rapidly from the public agenda.[20]

Populists were upset by the panic and the federal government's response, including the inglorious end of the Coxey protest. Rather than blaming the Sherman Silver Purchase Act as a partial cause of the crisis because it had encouraged a run on gold, they pointed to multiple conspiracies as the culprits. Once again, wealthy elites were manipulating the economic system to protect and enhance their ill-gotten gains. Anti-Semites recognized a global Jewish cabal as the root cause. Whatever the specific reasons for the depression, the little man was forced to bear a disproportionate share of the financial burden.

With a severe economic downturn causing untold misery across the country and a lack of effective government or private relief efforts, the Populists would have been expected to experience a surge in popularity in future elections. Yet the party never capitalized on the events that occurred between 1892 and 1896. Despite winning labor support following the Panic of 1893 and the Pullman railroad strike of 1894, the Populists saw their electoral chances fade following Republican gains in the 1894 congressional elections.

As the presidential election of 1896 approached, the People's Party suffered a steep decline. The lack of a tight organizational structure, the fissure about whether to allow Negroes to participate fully in the party, and the absence of political savvy among farmers who desired little more than to scratch out a day-to-day living ensured that the third party would have a difficult time competing in national elections. Moreover, leading Democrats realized that a populist appeal would assist candidates in rural areas, and they seized on the appropriate rhetoric. With the Democratic Party threatening to co-opt the Populist message, the party needed something or someone to revitalize the platform and voice the concerns of "the plain people of this country."[21]

WILLIAM JENNINGS BRYAN
AND THE 1896 ELECTION

That someone was a thirty-six-year-old former Nebraska congressman named William Jennings Bryan, a Democrat espousing Populist themes but not a true friend of the People's Party. He cherry-picked the issues he thought would appeal to the electorate. Bryan came late to the cause, but when he arrived, he arrived with a flourish. He was a charismatic, old-style stump orator who knew how to whip a crowd into a frenzy of excitement and Populist anger at the unfair machinations of elites. Early in his career, he had followed the Democratic Party line, championing low tariffs to assist farmers; yet he was not an integral player in the agrarian revolt. As it dawned on the ambitious congressman that he might ride the Populist wave to higher office, Bryan took up the free silver issue. Confessing that he understood only the most basic concepts of monetary policy, Bryan, like any good politician, was undeterred by his lack of expertise. He admitted his motives were purely political, blithely explaining, "The people of Nebraska are for free silver and I am for free silver. I will look up the arguments later."[22]

The Democrats nominated Bryan for president in 1896. In light of their desire to remain independent, People's Party leaders could have chosen someone else as the standard bearer, but in the end the party threw its support behind Bryan when a suitable alternative could not be found.

He appeared "presidential," for whatever it was worth. "Bryan's bearing is graceful; his face is handsome; his utterance is clear and strong, with something of the McKinley sing-song, and his style is free, bold, picturesque, and brilliant," the *New York Times* reported.[23]

Appearances can be deceiving, and not every Populist approved of the choice. Some proponents of establishing a viable third party rightly viewed an alliance with a Democratic candidate, no matter how strongly he supported Populist ideals, as a death knell for the People's Party. Their fears proved to be prescient, for the party declined precipitously after its infatuation with Bryan ended.[24]

Although he was a recent convert, Bryan compensated in enthusiasm for what he lacked in Populist pedigree. This fiery orator earned a name for himself in history when he delivered a memorable oration during the Democratic National Convention in Chicago on July 9, 1896. Known forever after as the "Cross of Gold" speech, the address presented Bryan at his most eloquent, a master thespian playing on the emotions of his audience. "I come to speak to you in defense of a cause as holy as the cause of liberty—the cause of humanity," he told the delegates after opening with a self-deprecating comment about his inability to compete with "the distinguished gentlemen" who preceded him as convention speakers. In an ironic statement, the master self-promoter explained that ideas, not persons, move history. "The individual," he said, "is but an atom; he is born, he acts, he dies; but principles are eternal; and this has been a contest of principle."

The principle, Bryan explained, involved "the money question," which, he believed, "was the paramount issue of the hour." Never a man to traffic in subtlety, he raised the stakes to astronomical heights. "Never before in the history of this country has there been witnessed such a contest as that through which we have passed. Never before in the history of American politics has a great issue been fought out as this issue has been by the voters themselves."

He claimed to be the voice of the little man, the farmer and the laborer who sought to earn an honest, living wage. Given the divisions among the Populists about Bryan's focus on monetary policy as the crucial issue, it was a dubious claim. Still, the message resonated among those who approved of the mythic world that Bryan evoked with his florid language. He refused to castigate East Coast businessmen, he claimed, but he heralded "those hardy pioneers who braved all the dangers of the wilderness, who have made the desert to blossom as the rose—those pioneers away out there, rearing their children near to nature's heart, where they can mingle their voices with the voices of the birds—out there where they have erected schoolhouses for the education of their children and churches where they praise their Creator, and the cemeteries where sleep the ashes of their dead—are as deserving of the consideration of this party as any people in this country."

Echoing the tragedy of the Civil War, which many Americans still remembered, Bryan characterized the contest as internecine: "Brother has been arrayed against brother, and father against son." It was a bit of hyperbole, but it played well to the crowd. Extending his martial metaphor, Bryan admonished his brethren not to take up arms except through their words. "We do not come as aggressors. Our war is not a war of conquest. We are fighting in the defense of our homes, our families, and posterity. We have petitioned, and our petitions have been scorned. We have entreated, and our entreaties have been disregarded. We have begged, and they have mocked when our calamity came."

Referring to President Andrew Jackson's stance against reauthorization of the National Bank of the United States, Bryan suggested, "What we need is an Andrew Jackson to stand as Jackson stood, against the encroachments of aggregated wealth." He denied his critics' claims that the Populists in his camp had modified their positions in the interests of electoral expediency. "They tell us that this platform was made to catch votes. We reply to them that changing conditions make new issues; that the principles upon which rest Democracy are as everlasting as the hills; but that they must be applied to new conditions as they arise."

Bryan argued against a concept supported by some Americans, bimetallism, which would have tied currency to both gold and silver. Republican presidential candidate William McKinley had stated his support for bimetallism by international agreement. "Why, if they tell us that the gold standard is a good thing, we point to their platform and tell them that their platform pledges the party to get rid of a gold standard and substitute bimetallism," Bryan charged. In his view, the issue should be gold or silver, not both. "I want to suggest this truth, that if the gold standard is a good thing we ought to declare in favor of its retention and not in favor of abandoning it; and if the gold standard is a bad thing, why should we wait until some other nations are willing to help us to let it go?"

As for the argument put forth by supporters of the gold standard that industrialization could not tolerate a loose monetary policy, Bryan rejected the idea that cities must be preserved at the expense of farms and rural areas. Such talk was bandied about by elites, but Bryan would have none of it. "You come to us and tell us that the great cities are in favor of the gold standard. I tell you that the great cities rest upon these broad and fertile prairies," he thundered. "Burn down your cities and leave our farms, and your cities will spring up again as if by magic. But destroy our farms and the grass will grow in the streets of every city in the country."

He saved the most memorable rhetoric for the conclusion. As Bryan's voice rose to a crescendo, he issued his famous clarion call to the agrarians to oppose the eastern elites who would impoverish western and southern farmers with their tight money policy. Alluding to Jesus Christ and his struggles on behalf of the poor, Bryan roared, "If they dare to come out in the open field and defend the gold standard as a good thing, we shall fight them to the uttermost, having behind us the producing masses of the nation and the world. Having behind us the commercial interests and the laboring interests and all the toiling masses, we shall answer their demands for a gold standard by saying to them, you shall not press down upon the brow of labor this crown of thorns. You shall not crucify mankind upon a cross of gold."[25]

As Bryan left the stage, the awestruck audience initially remained silent. Within moments, the cheering commenced, and pandemonium reigned over the convention hall. Everyone realized the address was historic. Bryan, always a master showman before a crowd, had outdone himself in delivering such a stirring call to action. Yet dramatic words do not a victory make. Conservatives were frightened by the radicalism, and some Populists felt their major concerns had not been addressed.[26]

In the end, Bryan's appeal was too strong for mainstream Populists to oppose his candidacy and too weak to win him high office. He swept the Democrats and Populists with him to defeat as Republican William McKinley won the presidency with 271 electoral votes to Bryan's 176, a landslide in the electoral college of more than 61 percent. The popular vote was much closer—McKinley prevailed by slightly more than 600,000 votes out of 13.5 million ballots cast—and the Republicans carried twenty-three states compared with twenty-two states for the Democrats. Bryan performed well in the South and in the western states, but he could not overcome the gap in the northeastern states.

The 1896 election was transformative, a watershed in American politics. Republicans solidified control of the US Congress, a trend that continued well into the new century. Businessmen, dismayed by Bryan's radical rhetoric, flocked in massive numbers to the Republicans. They had been drifting toward the Grand Old Party in previous elections, but the McKinley victory sealed their allegiance. A few years later, the Republican president signed into law the Gold Standard Act, which stabilized the value of the dollar by tying it to one ounce of gold. In the process, he dashed the hopes of Populists like Bryan who longed for a silver standard.[27]

William Jennings Bryan went on to run for president again in the new century, but he and the Populists had already experienced their greatest triumphs in electoral politics. The apogee of Bryan's power and influence occurred when he served as Woodrow Wilson's secretary of state from 1913 until 1915. In time, Bryan would be mocked for his presidential bids as well as his defense of Christian fundamentalism during the Scopes Monkey Trial late in his life. To subsequent generations of Americans, he appeared to be a quaint figure. In his own time, he gave hope to millions of rural Americans who found hope in short supply.[28]

Perhaps the most enduring social commentary of this period came from the pen of L. Frank Baum, a conservative Republican, who published *The Wonderful World of Oz* in 1900. According to some commentators, Baum supposedly constructed a fable using symbolic characters to represent key figures in 1890s America. Midwestern farmers (represented by a scarecrow seeking a brain), urban industrial workers (represented by the Tin Woodman who desires a heart), and William Jennings Bryan (the cowardly lion, who roars loudly but lacks bravery and therefore seeks courage) are traveling down a yellow brick road (the gold standard) that leads nowhere. They journey along with naive, innocent Dorothy, who epitomizes the purity of the American people and wears silver shoes to represent free silver. The group sets off for the Emerald City to beseech the Wizard of Oz—"oz." being the symbol for an ounce of gold—for assistance. Just as the People's Party appeared to be all things to all people searching for a utopia, the characters in Baum's tale view the Wizard of Oz through their own rose-colored glasses. They later find that he is not

[4.1] William Jennings Bryan was a perennial presidential candidate in the late nineteenth and early twentieth centuries. Courtesy of the Library of Congress.

a magician who will solve all their problems. He is "a little man with a bald head and a wrinkled face." Although Baum never commented on the political undertones in his story, some subsequent readers interpreted it as a fable about the failures of the Populist movement.[29]

It would be an exaggeration to conclude that Bryan's defeat in 1896 killed off the People's Party, for it limped through several additional election cycles. Yet the party was mortally wounded. In the South, the fusion of Populist and Democratic interests created schisms that simply could not be overcome. Because many southern Democrats were avowedly racist, they resisted the Populist efforts to enlist blacks in the agrarian movement. White supremacy was not the burning issue in the West; therefore, those states were not as divided on the racial issues, but they were furious at Republican and big business control of federal government policy. Disgruntled Populists in the West eventually threw their support behind the Democratic Party as a means of combating the wealthy elites who had flocked to the Republican ranks. Having lost its base, the People's Party lost power and influence before officially dissolving in 1908.[30]

It is difficult to judge dispassionately the historical significance of the Populist movement and the People's Party. Apologists contend that the Populists were liberal reformers seeking social justice for impoverished Americans. They provided a measure of equality for Negroes by agreeing to open their doors and coffers to the Colored Farmers' National Alliance. Their concern for the lower classes, urban and rural, black and white, presaged the civil rights movement and the political cataclysms that occurred in the 1960s, or so the argument goes. Less sympathetic observers view the Populists as a group longing for old times, when farmers could plant and harvest their crops free from outside encumbrances. Their leaders were would-be demagogues who tapped into a source of anger and frustration but ultimately could not unite disparate coalitions behind a coherent cause. Anger at the status quo and fear of the unknown future do not make for efficacious public policy. Any third party that fails to recognize the need for cohesion and organization risks marginalization.[31]

THE PROGRESSIVES

It is tempting to characterize progressivism as a logical extension of populism, a harvest of seeds sown by the agrarians in earlier days. Progressivism was founded on the ideal that progress in technology and scientific inventions, the arts and sciences, and the general enlightenment of the masses can be translated into public policy that will uplift everyone in the regime, even those persons traditionally existing in the lower echelons on the margins of mainstream society. The focus on the plight of the common citizen appears as a major theme in the American brand of populism as well as in the Progressive movement at the turn of the century.

Although Progressives shared the Populist view that the status quo was unacceptable when wealthy elites refused to extend a helping hand to the less fortunate, many Progressives did not support populism, for they did not share the generalized anger and resentment that surged through the People's Party. Progressives preferred to channel their passions into developing policies that would regulate the growth of corporations and address systematic corruption of the country's institutions of government.[32]

For much of American history, the mainstream view was that that government is best which governs least. In contrast, Progressives contended that government is either part of the problem or part of the solution. To be part of the solution, government must intervene to ensure that citizens enjoy a level playing field with elites. When impoverished citizens are hungry, government is obliged to find a means of feeding them. When businesses mistreat workers or foul the environment, government must intervene to ensure a measure of equity. If powerful forces manipulate elections by disenfranchising the poor or stuffing ballot boxes, government should police their behavior and restore confidence in the electoral process.[33]

The Progressive agenda was closely tied to the organized labor movement, which had existed in its infancy during populism's heyday. In particular, Progressives and labor leaders united to oppose brutal working conditions for women and children. Catastrophes in the headlines bolstered the cause. Following the Triangle Shirtwaist Factory fire of March 1911—in which 146 people, mostly girls and young women, died after flames spread through a garment factory and workers could not escape because the exit doors were locked—the Progressives lobbied for government standards policing working conditions.[34]

One of the most celebrated of Progressive endeavors, the settlement house movement, began in England during the 1880s when Victorians, in an effort to lift up the poor and improve their moral lot, developed a means for supplying food, shelter, and clothing. The movement eventually crossed the Atlantic as Progressives established settlement houses in the United States. Settlement house activists supplanted well-meaning amateurs with a new class of professional social workers. Hull House, a settlement house established in Chicago in 1889 by Jane Addams and Ellen Gates Starr, was emblematic of the new social activism of the Progressive era.[35]

Many Progressives became famous. Robert LaFollette Sr., a Wisconsin politician who variously served as a congressman, governor, and senator, opposed railroad trusts, political bosses, and cronyism, as well as US involvement in World War I and participation in the League of Nations. He was a perennial presidential candidate in the 1910s and 1920s. Louis Brandeis, the "people's lawyer," filed lawsuits against railroads, defended child-labor laws, and aggressively represented poor people in court. He later served as an associate justice of the US Supreme Court. John Dewey, a pioneer in experiential education and a tireless supporter of teachers' unions, influenced generations of educators with his innovative ideas. Theodore Roosevelt, the twenty-sixth president of the United States, although nominally a Republican, supported many Progressive causes, especially trust busting and environmental preservation. Muckrakers such as Upton Sinclair, Ida Tarbell, Lincoln Steffens, Jacob Riis, William Allen White, I. F. Stone, and Samuel S. McClure wrote eloquently of the plight of the "other" America—a land where average citizens struggled to survive and eke out a place in the life of the nation.[36]

Although many Progressives were not directly concerned with racial issues, they indirectly touched on race. Because race, class, and poverty frequently are inextricably linked, a campaign to improve one group invariably spills over into efforts to improve another. W. E. B. Du Bois, the black intellectual and activist who cofounded the National Association for the Advancement of Colored People (NAACP), was the exception that proved the rule. As a gifted black man confronting the indignities and stultification of racism and segregation, he spent much of his long career railing against the injustices perpetuated by whites in positions of power.[37]

For all the attention paid to the underclass and the emphasis on enacting social welfare legislation, the Progressive era—that period extending from the 1890s until the United States entered World War I in 1917—was a troubling time for black Americans. With segregation laws firmly in place and no organ of government poised to protect Negro rights, white supremacy reigned supreme, and not only south of the Mason-Dixon Line. Lynching and acts of extreme cruelty against blacks became all too commonplace. One reason that Du Bois and other prominent blacks founded the NAACP was to create an entity to assist blacks under attack by vengeful whites for real or imagined transgressions.[38]

The one pervasive fear that gripped the white imagination more than any other was that black men were brutal rapists with an insatiable appetite for white women. Many lynchings and acts of violence perpetrated against Negroes throughout American history, not only during the Progressive era, originated because a charge had been lodged against a black man for ravishing a white woman or threatening to do so. Although some charges may have been factually accurate, in an overwhelming number of cases the evidence that a crime had occurred was flimsy or nonexistent.

The allegations allowed bitter whites to find a convenient pretext to engage in a frenzy of violence that always lurked below the surface of troubled white-black relations. Even if the charges were true, the American legal system was designed to handle criminal cases in lieu of relying on the vagaries of Judge Lynch.[39]

On the federal level, Congress debated but failed to pass antilynching legislation during the Progressive era. The political will did not exist to assist blacks, and with little wonder. A cruel irony of segregation was that it disenfranchised blacks so that they did not possess the political power to enact the legislation that would have protected them. It became a vicious tautology: to influence the legislative process and ensure they were no longer disenfranchised, blacks had to be enfranchised in the first place.[40]

Race relations reached a low point during this time for many reasons, not the least of which was the way American history had been interpreted since the Civil War. According to the William Archibald Dunning school of historiography, Reconstruction had been a dismal failure because it allowed blacks, carpetbaggers, and scalawags to control southern state governments, when those forces were both inept and corrupt. The resultant misrule nearly destroyed the South and her hallowed traditions. Only after the federal interlopers had departed the scene could true white southern gentlemen resume control and restore the proper social relations between the races. For white supremacists, Reconstruction had been a clear and incontrovertible demonstration that blacks were inferior beings incapable of self-control, much less participation in the political process. They were little better than beasts and could not be trusted.[41]

The culture of the time denigrated blacks in an offhand manner, as though the inferiority of Negroes was an established fact that required no argument or explanation. In advertising, Aunt Jemima and Rastus hawked breakfast foods as part of a culture of paternalism that valued Negroes as long as they willingly accepted their subservient roles in society. *Darktown Comics* and other popular images portrayed blacks as buffoons who were victims of their own ignorant ways. Black children were viciously portrayed as big lipped, larcenous, and lascivious—more bestial than human. Everywhere a person turned, blacks appeared as somehow less than human, as simpletons who lived to serve whites at best and acted as dangerous, sexually perverted brutes at worst. Progressives sought to help the poor, common man, but helping a black man in that time and place was too much. Even the poorest of the poor could hope for a better day if he was white. If his skin was black, his situation was especially dire. Whites of the era essentially viewed the Negro as forever stamped with a badge of inferiority.

In this atmosphere of racial bias, the lack of measures to assist persons of color was regrettable but understandable. White elected leaders had no stomach for protecting an unpopular race at the expense of possible defeat in the next election. The conventional wisdom of the time was that blacks were undeserving of protection. Lone, discordant voices were raised against these shibboleths, but often the voices belonged to black men or crusaders outside mainstream American life and politics.[42]

5

Southern Populism

"Race Antagonism Perpetuates a Monetary System Which Beggars Both"

The standard narrative suggests that the American South during the eighty years following Reconstruction was a solid wall of bigotry and oppression with nary a crack in the facade. During those long years, many whites proudly boasted of their intolerance and hatred of the "other." Their invectives were no idle claims; history records a multitude of egregious sins visited on persons of color in the name of white supremacy as the fundamental organizing principle of southern society. Even in instances when the white ruling class was less than gleeful at the inequities visited on the "other," harsh treatment was rationalized as part of the natural order. With the long train of abuses against Negroes, primarily in the South but elsewhere as well, it is little wonder the standard narrative developed.[1]

Yet human motives and actions seldom conform to a single, simple explanation. The South was not as monolithically racist as is sometimes supposed, and the growth of the Populist movement provides an example of the ambiguity of the regional tradition. Thomas Edward Watson, a politician from Georgia, became a leading public figure calling for black and white coexistence, only later to embrace white supremacy with a vehemence that forever tarnished his legacy. Today his name is synonymous with the most contemptible racial biases of the South, but he did not start his life and career as a symbol of backwardness and intolerance.

The young Watson was a southerner first and a Populist second, but it was a close second. In attempting to bridge the gap between the tradi-

123

tional southern antipathy toward Negroes and the necessity of attracting votes from the few persons of color who still exercised the franchise in the Jim Crow age, he discovered that race, class, and economics were intertwined but not identical. During its brief hour on the stage, populism in some areas sought to fuse the interests of the races into a unified front against powerful forces that benefited from the southern division. Eventually forced to choose between his allegiance to agrarianism and his southern roots, Watson could not betray the land of his birth. The blood in his veins was thicker than the mud on his boots.[2]

TOM WATSON: AGRARIAN RADICAL

Born in rural McDuffie County, Georgia, in the fall of 1856, Tom Watson was old enough to recall the fervor with which so many men in his community marched off to confront the hated Yankees during the war. He also remembered the shame of Confederate defeat and the indignities his family suffered during Reconstruction. He attended Mercer University for a time, but financial hardships forced him to withdraw before he graduated. At that time, the lack of a degree did not prevent him from teaching school or reading the law and sitting for the bar, all of which he did with much success. Watson was nothing if not ambitious, and he won a seat in the state legislature at age twenty-six.

Watson's Populist bent was evident as soon as he took his seat. He won notice for his effort to oppose the mighty railroad. Failing to curb legislative kowtowing to the powerful industry, Watson resigned his seat in disgust and returned to his law practice. He was not finished with politics despite such a graceless or heroic—depending on one's perspective—exit from the public stage. He sat out of politics for most of the 1880s, although he served as a presidential elector for Democratic president Grover Cleveland in 1888 as the incumbent lost his reelection bid. Watson eventually joined the Farmers' Alliance and became an early supporter of the People's Party, founding the Georgia chapter in 1892.

Riding the Populist wave, Watson won a seat in the US House of Representatives in 1890. Abandoning the Democratic caucus, he joined the People's Party and espoused an antielitist view, arguing in favor of Rural Free Delivery of the US mail, abolition of national banks, and public ownership of utility companies. He rose to national prominence when Farmers' Alliance leader Leonidas L. Polk died in June 1892, leaving Watson as the most prominent national Populist spokesman before the rise of William Jennings Bryan in 1896.[3]

Watson faced a tough reelection campaign in 1892. Despite his achievements for the poor people of his congressional district, he needed to make a case for voters to return him to Washington. He viewed the Populist banner as the most promising means of political survival. Yet the Populists were an eclectic lot, and Watson understood he must walk a fine line to unite disparate interests. Tenants, small and larger landowners, blacks, and whites all shared a general sense of unease at the power of big companies and northeastern elites, but they were not favorably disposed to work with each other. "There is a gradation of servitude," Watson remarked. Day laborers, tenant farmers, sharecroppers, and landowners did not suffer to the same extent, and a broad appeal to one group conceivably could alienate the other. He had to convince agricultural workers across the spectrum to set aside their differences and band together to achieve common goals.

In keeping with his Populist message, Watson reached out to black voters, emphasizing commonality within the farming community. He recognized that Negro support could spell the difference between victory and defeat, and Watson was at heart a pragmatist. He scheduled camp meetings and barbecues as well as political events for Negroes in Georgia to assure them of his benign intentions. Of course, Watson had to respect the southern mores of the era. Inviting blacks to attend a political picnic was not tantamount to breaking bread with the freedpeople and their progeny. If he had insisted on full integration at such events, he would have lost more white votes than the number of black votes he would have gained. Nonetheless, the attempt to reach across the color divide, as tepid as it may appear to modern sensibilities, was a novel approach in Georgia during the 1890s.[4]

What Tom Watson said and wrote was almost as important as what he did. A month before the election, he published an extraordinary document on race. Titled "The Negro Question in the South," the manifesto dealt forthrightly with the central issue of southern history. "The Negro Question in the South has been for nearly thirty years a source of danger, discord, and bloodshed," he explained at the outset. "It is an ever-present irritant and menace." Whatever else may be said about the Tom Watson of the 1890s, he must be credited with taking on an issue that affected all southerners but which few deigned to discuss in such frank, honest terms.

Watson traced the source of bitterness between whites and blacks to the challenges created by emancipation and the imperfect promises that northern civil and military leaders had uttered to former slaves. "Several millions of slaves were told that they were the prime cause of the civil war; that their emancipation was the result of the triumph of the North over the South; that the ballot was placed in their hands as a weapon of defence against their former interns; that the war-won political equality of the black man with the white, must be asserted promptly and aggressively, under the leadership of adventurers who had swooped down upon the conquered section in the wake of the Union armies." Southerners did not see the war and its aftermath in the same light. They viewed northerners as carpetbaggers who threw superior armaments and numbers of men into the battle until they bludgeoned the South into submission. Thereafter, they asserted their will on a vanquished land at the end of a bayonet, decimating the economy and subjugating the southern people against their will. It was only after the dastardly interlopers had departed that southern men of good character and reputation had reasserted their will and restored the proper balance and order to social and political relations in the South. Freedpeople, still relying on promises made, if not quite delivered, by their now absent benefactors, chafed at the redemption. "No one, who wishes to be fair, can fail to see that, in such a condition of things, strife between the freedman and his former owner was inevitable," Watson observed with wry understatement.

He was anxious to recast the southern narrative as a struggle between elite forces in the North and the common people who labored on farms for their livelihood, especially in the South. In Watson's interpretation, southern whites and blacks would have recognized their common situation but for the machinations of northern elites who bombarded southern Negroes with messages urging them to mistrust their white counterparts. Northern Democrats and Republicans of all stripes were responsible for nurturing these lingering resentments:

> Now consider: here were two distinct races dwelling together, with political equality established between them by law. They lived in the same section; won their livelihood by the same pursuits; cultivated adjoining fields on the same terms; enjoyed together the bounties of a generous climate; suffered together the rigors of cruelly unjust laws; spoke the same language; bought and sold in the same markets; classified themselves into churches under the same denominational teachings; neither race antagonizing the other in any branch of industry; each absolutely dependent on the other in all the avenues of labor and employment; and yet, instead of being allies, as every dictate of reason and prudence and self-interest and justice said they should be, they were kept apart, in dangerous hostility, that the sordid aims of partisan politics might be served![5]

Under the banner of the People's Party, Watson proposed a merger of interests. Admitting that the "question of social equality does not enter into the calculation at all," he suggested the races could work to mutual advantage even if their relationship did not extend to all forms of intercourse. "Why should the colored man always be taught that the white man of his neighborhood hates him, while a Northern man, who taxes every rag on his back, loves him?" he asked with a rhetorical flourish.

"Why should not my tenant come to regard me as his friend rather than the manufacturer who plunders us both? Why should we perpetuate a policy which drives the black man into the arms of the Northern politician?"[6]

The manifesto was stunning to everyone who regarded the social position of the races as fixed and immutable. Perhaps southern history would have been markedly different had Watson's vision been implemented. It certainly would have thrown blacks and whites into a closer association than they experienced in the decades following his appeal. "They will see a similarity of cause and a similarity of remedy," Watson promised in 1892. "They will recognize that each should help the other in the work of repealing bad laws and enacting good ones. They will become political allies, and neither can injure the other without weakening both. It will be to the interest of both that each should have justice." Would that his plea for justice had been heeded: "And on these broad lines of mutual interest, mutual forbearance, and mutual support the present will be made the stepping-stone to future peace and prosperity."[7]

In the most often quoted section of the statement, Watson set forth his case for a white man and a black man abandoning the major political parties and joining the Populists. "Now the People's Party says to these two men, 'You are kept apart that you may be separately fleeced of your earnings. You are made to hate each other because upon that hatred is rested the keystone of the arch of financial despotism which enslaves you both. You are deceived and blinded that you may not see how this race antagonism perpetuates a monetary system which beggars both.'"[8]

Watson's vision for a radical change in southern politics failed, but his efforts to attract black voters worked, to some extent. Although some Negroes remained suspicious that they were pawns in yet another white man's game, others took the young congressman at his word. For the first time in memory, a white southern political leader was reaching out to Negroes, not in the patronizing or condescending way that some northern do-gooders had exhibited during Reconstruction, when they acted as though they were saving neglected children from damnation, but as a man conversing with his fellow men. H. S. Doyle, a black "preacher of intelligence and courage," delivered more than sixty speeches in favor of Watson's candidacy during the 1892 election cycle. Such an alliance would have been unimaginable in an earlier time, but Watson's message brought hope to many southern blacks who had begun to despair of ever gaining equal rights in the southern states.

He lost his quest for reelection, this strange man straddling the fault line of Old and New South sensibilities, partially because the Populist message in the region simply could not cross the color line. Horrified at the impudent congressman's audacity in proposing a political partnership with blacks, Democrats energized their base by arousing fears of the agrarian radicalism sweeping across the region. They also used violence and intimidation to suppress voter turnout. The Populists would live to fight another day—Marion Butler squeaked out a "fusion" victory in the North Carolina US Senate race in 1894—but ultimately the southern version of populism could never overcome the race issue. In 1910, reflecting on the untenable situation he faced during that election, Watson contrasted his position with William Jennings Bryan's in 1896. "Consider the advantage of position that Bryan had over me," he wrote. "His field of work was the plastic, restless, and growing West: mine was the hidebound, rock-ribbed, Bourbon South. Besides, Bryan had *no everlasting and overshadowing Negro Question to hamper and handicap his progress:* I HAD."[9]

Even in defeat, Tom Watson refused to slink away. He edited a paper, the *People's Party Paper*, devoted to Jeffersonian principles of limited government and a reliance on the citizenry as the final arbiters of national policy. Referring to Alexander Hamilton, Thomas Jefferson's rival for power in the federal government of the late eighteenth and early nineteenth centuries, Watson promised to oppose the "Hamiltonian Doctrines of Class Rule, Moneyed Aristocracy, National Banks, High Tariffs, Standing Armies and formidable Navies—all of which go together as a system of oppressing the people."[10]

Watson remained visible on the national stage, although not always in the manner he desired. A dispute arose during the 1896 presidential election concerning Bryan's running mate. Because he remained the Democratic standard bearer even as he represented the People's Party, the nominee found himself with two separate vice presidential nominees. The Democrats selected Arthur Sewall, a banker from Maine, while the People's Party chose Tom Watson. Because William McKinley won the general election, the dispute did not have to be reconciled, but it was clear from the split that the Populist ranks were divided. Later, Watson was twice a Populist candidate for president, but the People's Party was no longer a potent force in national politics. The Populist hour on the stage had come and gone in the 1890s.[11]

Many blacks had hoped that Watson's early calls for biracialism in the Populist movement were more than empty promises cynically uttered to gain votes. Despite the young politician's apparent sincerity, not every Negro supported his efforts, having grown accustomed to white men's promises that this time things would be different. Young Tom Watson decried lynching and spoke eloquently of issues near and dear to Negro hearts, but the reality did not match the rhetoric. Even if Watson meant what he said, he simply did not possess enough power to effect change in the white supremacist culture of Georgia during the Jim Crow era. Later, the elder Tom Watson, a vocal proponent of lynching and white supremacy, confirmed the doubters' belief that southern politicians were not to be trusted.[12]

HENRY GRADY AND THE NEW SOUTH

If the young Tom Watson sought to marry together the interests of southern farmers, black and white, as a means of possible rapprochement, if not quite complete reconciliation, the young Henry W. Grady sought to extend an olive branch to the northern United States as a means of promoting the concept of a New South. Grady was the son of a Confederate veteran slain in battle, but he was not content to dwell on the primacy of antebellum southern culture or schemes for deconstructing Reconstruction, as were so many of his compatriots. He cherished the history and traditions of his region—up to a point. Times had changed, and the South had better change with them, or the region would forever exist as an impoverished backwater.[13]

A journalist by training and inclination, Grady spent the 1880s as an influential editor of the *Atlanta Constitution,* building the newspaper into a powerful voice for the New South. Using the *Constitution* as his bully pulpit, he repeatedly called for southerners to move away from the days of slavery and agriculture into a bright future of technology and cooperative ventures. He was also a well-known orator, forceful and humorous, always willing to entertain audiences with his ambitious plans for the future.[14]

Grady's most famous oration came in December 1886 when he was invited to speak in New York City before the New England Society. His topic, predictably, was the New South. His speech was hardly original and delivered a bit too enthusiastically for some tastes, but most onlookers and commentators were utterly captivated by this new voice from an old region. Rather than defiantly shake his fist at the triumphant North that had vanquished the aristocratic South, as was the custom among many southern leaders, Grady acknowledged his region's shortcomings and argued that a new and better day was on the horizon. He did not apologize for past transgressions. Instead, he looked to the future.

"The Old South rested everything on slavery and agriculture, unconscious that these could neither give nor maintain healthy growth," he told his rapt New York audience. As a marked contrast, the "New South presents a perfect democracy, the oligarchs leading in the popular movement; a social system compact and closely knitted, less splendid on the surface but stronger at the core—a hundred farms for every plantation, fifty homes for every palace, and a diversified industry that meets the complex needs of this complex age." This was not the land that had been

[5.1] Tom Watson, pictured here late in life, began his career calling for blacks and whites to work together toward a common goal. In his dotage, Watson became a virulent racist and demagogue. Courtesy of the Library of Congress.

conquered slightly more than two decades earlier. "The New South is enamored of her new work. Her soul is stirred with the breath of a new life. The light of a grander day is falling fair on her face. She is thrilling with the consciousness of growing power and prosperity. As she stands upright, full-statured and equal among the people of the earth, breathing the keen air and looking out upon the expanding horizon, she understands that her emancipation came because in the inscrutable wisdom of God her honest purpose was crossed and her brave armies were beaten." They were stirring words, perhaps more wishful thinking than an accurate description of the South in 1886.

Looking to the future did not mean that a southerner turned his back on his roots. Grady revered his dead father even if he did not support the goal of the Confederate States of America to fashion a slaveholding republic on the North American continent. He explained how he could honor a dead soldier without agreeing with the soldier's mission:

> In my native town of Athens is a monument that crowns its central hills—a plain, white shaft. Deep cut into its shining side is a name dear to me above the names of men, that of a brave and simple man who died in brave and simple faith. Not for all the glories of New England—from Plymouth Rock all the way—would I exchange the heritage he left me in his soldier's death. To the foot of that shaft I shall send my children's children to reverence him who ennobled their name with his heroic blood. But, sir, speaking from the shadow of that memory, which I honor as I do nothing else on earth, I say that the cause in which he suffered and for which he gave his life was adjudged by higher and fuller wisdom than his or mine, and I am glad that the omniscient God held the balance of battle in His Almighty hand, and that human slavery was swept forever from American soil—the American Union saved from the wreck of war.[15]

Grady knew that northern men had read horrific tales of the poor relations between blacks and whites in Dixie, and he was eager to assuage their concerns. "No section shows a more prosperous laboring population than the Negroes of the South; none in fuller sympathy with the employing and land-owning class. He shares our school fund, has the fullest protection of our laws and the friendship of our people. Self-interest, as well as honor, demand that he should have this." If not entirely disingenuous, the statement certainly took liberties with the realities of Negro life in the land of cotton. Just as young Tom Watson thought that blacks and whites could find common ground in reaching an accommodation, Henry Grady might have wished that racial inequality was not the central fact of life in the southern states. Yet his unbridled optimism could not rewrite the historical record. He would give it the old college try, though. "The relations of the Southern people with the Negro are close and cordial."[16]

Having dealt with the race issue, albeit in a less than forthright manner, Grady came to the point of his oration. He wanted the North and the South to bury old wounds and unite as a single nation in pursuit of all the bounty the land could provide for the American people:

> Now, what answer has New England to this message? Will she permit the prejudices of war to remain in the hearts of the conquerors, when it has died in the hearts of the conquered? Will she transmit this prejudice to the next generation, that in their hearts, which never felt the generous ardor of conflict, it may perpetuate itself? Will she withhold, save in strained courtesy, the hand which straight from his soldier's heart Grant offered to Lee at Appomattox? Will she make the vision of a restored and happy people, which gathered above the couch of your dying captain, filling his heart with grace, touching his lips with praise and glorifying his path to the grave; will she make this vision on which the last sight of his expiring soul breathed a benediction, a cheat and a delusion?[17]

Other voices would be raised in defense of the New South, but Grady was among the first of his generation to understand the changing nature of American life. The old ways of doing things would no longer suffice. If southerners did not come to terms with the need for crop diversification, increased industrialization, improved race relations, and attraction of capital for infrastructure modernization, the region would fall further behind other areas of the country. The clarion call for a New South mixed idealism with pragmatism in equal measure. Enlightened public policy would yield commercial opportunities.

Henry Grady was ahead of his time. His recommendations reached an enthusiastic audience, especially in the North, but many southerners were not prepared to abandon the old ideas or rhetoric. Conservatives were appalled by his acknowledgment that the war aims of the Southern Confederacy were flawed and rightly defeated. Populists such as Tom Watson feared the *Constitution* editor was too willing to kowtow to northern interests at the expense of southern pride and values. Farmers anxious to cash in on high-yield products such as cotton and tobacco were not convinced that expanding the number of crops would enhance their economic prospects. Even northern men who welcomed a new day in the Old South expressed skepticism about Grady's assurances that Negroes were treated well in Georgia and elsewhere. Most people, it seemed, looked forward to better times for the South, but no one was ready to make the changes necessary to move into a new era. In fact, radical ideas such as populism and the New South ideology ignited a fierce debate that would stretch across many decades of southern history.[18]

[5.2]   Henry Grady, a well-known newspaperman from Atlanta, became a prominent voice of the New South. Courtesy of the Library of Congress.

PITCHFORK BEN AND THE
CONSERVATIVE BACKLASH

One inescapable irony of the nascent biracialism proposed by the Populists in the South was the reaction it triggered among whites fearful of Negro ascendancy. After Reconstruction ended during the 1870s, elite whites had been content to redeem southern state governments and extend an olive branch to the black community. As long as Negroes knew their place and did not challenge the traditional legal strictures and social mores that kept them permanently ensconced at the bottom of the social, political, and economic hierarchy, white leaders could afford to be magnanimous in victory. A form of paternalism developed as "Bourbon" whites seized political and economic power. This "live-and-let-live" approach ensured an orderly control of lower classes, black and white, for much of the 1880s.[19]

When aggrieved farmers organized into alliances aimed at improving their lot, the Bourbons became alarmed. Although the farmers' organizations and the People's Party failed to create a lasting grassroots movement, their attempts to forge alliances with black farmers threatened the established social order. To ensure that lower-class white agrarians did not rise to positions of political power, conservative Bourbon leaders resorted to violence, intimidation, and bribery. In some instances, elite white leaders reached out to blacks, offering all manner of goods and services to dilute political support and prevent a poor man's coalition from forming. The Bourbons siphoned off enough black support from white agrarians to prevent the Populists from promoting a biracial regime as a means of grabbing power. The situation was rich with irony. Blacks had to choose between two groups of whites seeking to exploit them. It was a Hobson's choice. Recognizing that the Bourbons controlled government offices and patronage, most Negroes cast their lot with the powers that be. Exactly as Tom Watson had warned in "The Negro Question in the South," political leaders had driven a wedge between impoverished white and black farmers. Southern politics created strange, awkward bedfellows.[20]

The politics of South Carolina provided a vivid illustration of the schisms found in southern populism. Bourbon support in the Palmetto State was strongest in the low country around Charleston. Before the Civil War, the low country planter elite had amassed enormous fortunes from rice-planting operations along the coast. With the reemergence of these would-be aristocrats after Reconstruction, the plan was to reestablish the white South as it had existed before the war, without the formal institution of slavery, of course. If blacks could be kept in line through informal mechanisms, antebellum society could be restored as much as possible, even if human bondage was not a viable option. Lower-class white farmers were expected to labor as they always had, quietly impoverished and without complaint.

The Bourbons had enjoyed nearly universal control over South Carolina politics in the 1850s, but times had changed. Their influence, while still considerable, gradually waned during the postbellum epoch. Two other areas of the state now contained citizens who were not satisfied to remain compliant. The Piedmont region, a swath of land that gradually gave way to a series of wooded hills known as the upcountry, was situated far inland from the coast. In a bygone era, cotton farmers had earned a good living in the Piedmont, but they had fallen on hard times after the war. Farming practices had improved throughout the country, but southern tenants could not afford to purchase the latest equipment or master best practices. Consequently, they overfarmed the land, depleting the soil of precious nutrients in a vain effort to overcome their inefficient processes. West of the Piedmont, families working small farms and barely able to eke out a living populated the land. Because the soil was less conducive to farming than the area around Charleston, slavery had not been as prevalent in the upcountry. Inhabitants resented the depressed economy following the panics of 1873 and 1893, and they blamed banks, railroads, and Bourbons for their desperate plight.[21]

It was a situation ripe for an opportunistic politician to take advantage of the shifting tide of power. Into this confusion of interests stepped just such an ambitious figure, one Benjamin Ryan Tillman. "Pitchfork Ben"—so named because of his appeal to farmers and because he remarked in 1892 that he would stick a pitchfork into the Democrat "bag of beef" Grover Cleveland—became one of the most colorful, influential, and powerful South Carolina politicians of his epoch. Unlike Tom Watson, who had to ease into white supremacy, Ben Tillman unabashedly embraced the values of the Old South. From his emergence as a political force in 1876 until his death in 1918, Tillman championed the subjugation of blacks at the expense of their white masters. He was largely responsible for changing the South Carolina Constitution in 1895 to add residential and poll-tax requirements, which made it more difficult for Negroes to vote or participate in political affairs, which was precisely the point.[22]

Ben Tillman was born near the present-day town of Trenton in Edgefield County, South Carolina, on August 11, 1847, which made him eligible for service in the Confederate army. As an enthusiastic supporter of the cause, he had intended to serve, but he suffered a calamity before he could enlist. On July 10, 1864, shortly before his seventeenth birthday, Tillman suffered a cranial tumor that almost killed him. A surgeon successfully removed the tumor, but the operation destroyed the young man's eye and left him at death's door. Because he was in no condition to engage in military activities, Ben Tillman spent the balance of the war convalescing, mostly with relatives in Elberton, Georgia. He considered the time a lost period in his life. As he lay prostrate and despondent, his beloved Confederacy also was brought down, a "sad and depressing state of affairs" in Tillman's life.[23]

Tillman became a prime example of the unreconstructed Confederate. He had come of age believing that blacks were inferior beings, and no battlefield losses would alter his thinking. Many white southerners (although by no means everyone) shared his perspective. In the South Carolina upcountry, whites were especially concerned with the relative autonomy of the freedpeople. Vigilante groups appeared on the scene to monitor and control uppity blacks. No vigilante group was more feared than the Ku Klux Klan (KKK), the shadowy paramilitary organization that traveled under cover of darkness to keep politically active blacks in line. Although never formally associated with the KKK, Tillman certainly approved of actions, including violence, that kept Negroes in their proper place.[24]

In 1876, Tillman joined Edgefield County's Sweetwater Sabre Club, a paramilitary organization known as a "rifle club." Rifle clubs served as successors to the Klan. The KKK had been forced to operate as a secret society during Reconstruction for fear that the carpetbaggers in power would resist their efforts to promote white supremacy. Indeed, South Carolina governor Robert K. Scott became so alarmed in 1871 that he contacted President Ulysses S. Grant about the Klan's violent activities. In response, President Grant suspended habeas corpus in the South Carolina upcountry and instructed federal troops to restore law and order. It was an ignominious episode that no one wished to repeat.[25]

Ostensibly, rifle clubs were fraternal organizations of white men who would protect their homes and families if need be. They claimed they were not aggressors devoted to disenfranchising blacks but dispassionate citizens who sought to maintain law and order in their communities. The reality was far different. In most places, the rifle club was a vigilante group pledged to support a white supremacist regime. Just as the Klan had devoted itself to intimidating blacks who exhibited the temerity to vote and take part in the political and civic life of the area, rifle clubs were deployed as a private, substate police force. Members turned up at black political gatherings and outside voting precincts on election day. The message was chilling: any Negro who dared to exercise his constitutional right to vote would pay a severe price for his impudence. Rifle clubs also enjoyed one advantage over the Klan. Members marched and drilled without resorting to disguises or acting at night. Because they frequently reflected the attitudes of the local political leadership—and sometimes drew members from such ranks—the clubs did not fear reprisals from government. The carpetbaggers had either lost their power and influence or long ago departed the scene.

Tillman used his membership in the Sweetwater Sabre Club to good effect. When a confrontation erupted between blacks and whites in the little South Carolina town of Hamburg during the summer of 1876, Tillman claimed to have played an integral part in the violence. Whites from the local area had banded together to slaughter freedmen with little hesitation. Tillman probably exaggerated his role in the Hamburg incident, but it was a testament to the politics of the time that he sought a political advantage by boasting of his participation in multiple murders of black citizens.[26]

With his reputation made, Pitchfork Ben went on to enjoy a long and illustrious career in South Carolina politics. He eventually served as governor and US senator. During his four decades in power, Tillman proved to be an independent politician, following national trends when it suited his purpose and ignoring planks that did not match his needs.[27]

In some cases, he served as a study in inconsistency. A successful politician who was not above using any means necessary to secure reelection, he authored the Tillman Act of 1907, the first federal campaign finance law in American history. (To be fair, the statute's main provision, which prohibited campaign contributions by corporations, reflected Tillman's mistrust of elites in power. Because it did not include an enforcement mechanism and did not apply to primary elections, the law was ineffective.) He ridiculed well-educated southerners as elites and yet promoted the creation of two new schools—an agricultural institution, Clemson, and a school for women, Winthrop College. He championed policies to assist farmers, but he refused to embrace the People's Party, supporting the free silver policy and a graduated federal income tax but rejecting the party's "subtreasury plan," which allowed farmers to borrow money against the value of crops stored in government warehouses while awaiting market price increases. Although he eventually backed off of his position on the subtreasury issue, the wily, one-eyed governor was satisfied to bill himself as the "farmer's friend," even as he opposed efforts to bring white and black farmers together. Time after time, he emphatically opposed attempts to work with blacks. Ben Tillman was no Tom Watson; nor did he wish to be. Moreover, he was not bothered by inconsistent political positions if they consistently advanced the power and influence of Ben Tillman.[28]

Tillman remained steadfast and unyielding on one issue across all the decades of his political career: white supremacy. He endlessly promoted measures that would keep the black race permanently subjugated. Tillman famously supported lynching, explaining that Negroes "must remain subordinate or be exterminated." To ensure that the federal government would not enact laws restricting segregation, he championed state rights and refused to support any bill that would provide assistance to blacks, even if a measure also might benefit whites in his state. When he learned that President Theodore Roosevelt had invited the black leader Booker T. Washington to dine at the White House in 1901, Tillman remarked, "The action of President Roosevelt in entertaining that nigger will necessitate our killing a thousand niggers in the South before they learn their place again."[29]

In the US Senate, he was dubbed the "wild man." In addition to employing incendiary rhetoric, Tillman was not above resorting to physical violence. On one memorable occasion in 1902, the wild man exchanged verbal insults with his Senate colleague from South Carolina, John L. McLaurin, a former ally. When McLaurin responded by calling Tillman a liar, it was too much. Tillman marched across the Senate chamber and punched the offender in the face. McLaurin responded in kind, bloodying Tillman's nose before onlookers separated the two men. The episode eventually resulted in a formal censure for both senators and solidified Tillman's already growing reputation for unseemly behavior.[30]

His impassioned, frequently incoherent tirades occasioned groans and eye rolling among his less demented Senate colleagues, but they tolerated such harangues because employing inflammatory language was the Senate way. Besides, this angry rube was an interesting character. Whatever else could be said of him, Pitchfork Ben could always be counted on to voice the base opinions of the Old South. Traveling into the hinterlands, he sometimes spoke on the lecture circuit about race and the difficulties of dealing with Negroes. In all his years of public life, Tillman demonstrated a remarkable capacity for resisting growth in his intellect. He never found an offensive stereotype he could not make his own. Aside from frequently expressing opinions about the laziness and lasciviousness of blacks, he uttered consistently demeaning views about women. He commented on one occasion that if female citizens could vote, the franchise would "rub the bloom off of the peach."[31]

When he died in 1918, Tillman left behind a rich legacy of racism, demagoguery, and white supremacy that would serve as a monument to the backwardness of the South for generations. He also served as inspiration for future white supremacist leaders who realized that spewing vitriol and denying black citizens their constitutional rights could pay rich dividends in southern politics. Some evidence suggests that Tillman realized his excesses might become the basis for a permanently destructive brand of politics, but he never renounced his views. He worried about the means used but never the ends. Championing white farmers and denigrating the black underclass remained worthy goals in his view.[32]

Yet Tillman lived long enough to witness the consequences of his extreme politics. Toward the end of Tillman's life, a protégé, Coleman Livingston Blease, followed the wild man's footsteps into the governor's mansion. Later, Blease won a US Senate seat, although Tillman had died by that time. Incredibly, Blease was even more reactionary and divisive than his hero had been. No one ever accused Pitchfork Ben of being a deep

[5.3] "Pitchfork Ben" Tillman was a strident proponent of racism and segregation during a lengthy political career in South Carolina. Courtesy of the Library of Congress.

thinker, but he was a towering intellect compared to the ultra-reactionary Blease.[33]

When Blease looked around the world of the early twentieth century, he found much to dislike. He opposed compulsory school attendance, a free press, and carbonated soft drinks, in the latter case denouncing the "the evil of the habitual drinking of Coca-Cola and Pepsi-Cola, and such like mixtures, as I fully believe they are injurious." Drinking Coca-Cola, in Blease's skewed view of the world, qualified as "evil," but murder apparently did not. Early in his political career, Blease had applauded the actions of Jim Tillman, Pitchfork Ben's nephew, when the younger Tillman shot and killed Narciso Gener Gonzales, cofounder of the *State* newspaper, in 1903. At the time of the murder, dubbed the "crime of the century" in South Carolina, Jim Tillman was winding down his term as lieutenant governor of the state. The newspaper had been critical of Ben Tillman's administration as governor in the 1890s and of Jim Tillman's tenure in the second chair. The younger Tillman was acquitted of the crime.[34]

On one issue, Blease stood as firm and inflexible as his mentor had—namely, his intense hatred for persons of color. Blease extolled the virtues of Negro lynching and was said to have buried the finger of a black lynching victim in the garden of the governor's mansion. He was not merely a supporter of lynching but a zealous advocate of vigilantism, observing that when "mobs are no longer possible, liberty will be dead." Blease was said to celebrate tales of lynchings with a "bizarre death dance." South Carolina politics is replete with colorful, sometimes nefarious characters, but even by those standards, Coleman Blease stands apart from the crowd. One commentator called the "convivial, magnetic, dashing" Blease "perhaps the most gifted demagogue in South Carolina history," an astonishing achievement in light of the vast array of charlatans from which to choose.[35]

Blease became so reckless and unstable that even Ben Tillman, never a man known for moderation or sound judgment, questioned the wisdom of promoting this daft character to a position of prominence. The two men eventually had a falling out, as Blease claimed to represent mill workers instead of the farmers who had gravitated to Pitchfork Ben. Tillman also publicly and privately disavowed his former disciple's most outlandish behavior. The old firebrand had not grown soft in his old age; he simply could not accept Blease's brand of buffoonery. Old Ben genuinely thought that he had given a voice to the oppressed farmer, but he came to believe that Blease was only interested in self-aggrandizement. An outsider looking in might be forgiven for seeing a distinction without a difference, but the split between the two men and their supporters was profound.[36]

[5.4] Coleman Blease followed in Ben Tillman's footsteps as a vehement racist and apologist for the Jim Crow regime. Courtesy of the Library of Congress.

Blease's career waxed and waned, but he was unrepentant when it came to his loathing of the Negro. In 1929, after First Lady Lou Hoover invited Jessie DePriest, wife of black congressman Oscar DePriest, to a tea at the White House, Blease stood in the well of the Senate and read a 1901 poem titled "Niggers in the White House." Penned after President Theodore Roosevelt had entertained Booker T. Washington—the event that had so incensed Tillman more than a quarter century earlier—the poem opened with these lines:

> Things at the White House,
> Looking mighty curious;
> Niggers running everything,
> White people furious.[37]

Most of Ben Tillman's political heirs, while not known for enlightened views on race, were not as cartoonish as Blease appeared, and they cast a longer shadow. J. Strom Thurmond, another South Carolinian who later served as a longtime US senator, remembered shaking Tillman's hand as a six-year-old boy. In the ensuing ninety-four years, Thurmond would cite the encounter as a pivotal event in his young life. Tillman had ties to Thurmond's family as well, which no doubt solidified the boy's adoration of this legendary political figure.[38]

In addition to influencing specific political figures, Tillman contributed to the death of the People's Party. By consistently insisting that race superseded class and poverty as the central issue in southern life, he placed southern Populists in an untenable position. A third party faces a daunting task in overcoming the superior name recognition and financial resources of the established political parties. Third-party candidates need to broaden their base as much as possible. Political figures such as Tom Watson recognized the wisdom of mollifying Negroes and enlisting their political support so that the People's Party might effectively compete against the Democrats and the Republicans. When Tillman refused to countenance a rapprochement with Negroes, he all but doomed the People's Party in the South. Defeat probably was inevitable, but Pitchfork Ben hastened the day when the party imploded. He said he wanted to stick a pitchfork into the beefy Democratic president, but in the end he stuck it into the Farmers' Alliance and twisted the tines.[39]

SOUTHERN POPULISM IN LATER YEARS

Southern populism did not die with the collapse of the People's Party, but it changed in myriad ways. In later years, the label "populism" (without a

capital letter) became a generic description of any southern political figure who tapped into the anger of nonelites. To be a "populist" did not
mean that a supporter subscribed to an established party platform, a set
of principles or policies, or a prescribed course of action. A southern populist was a self-proclaimed champion of the people who justified any and
all manner of intemperate language by an appeal to the will of the
masses. How the speaker came to represent the will of the undifferenti-
ated masses was not always clear.[40]

Southern history is filled with populists seeking to capitalize on discontent with the status quo and often, although not always, responding vis-
cerally to a fear of the Negro. James K. Vardaman, a Mississippi politician
who served as governor and later US senator, was one such figure. Vardaman was Tillman's contemporary as well as his match in employing colorful language to disparage blacks. Discussing the education of black
children, he observed that the "only effect of Negro education is to spoil
a good field hand and make an insolent cook." As for a spate of lynchings
throughout the South, the "Great White Chief," as he was nicknamed,
supported the actions of white vigilantes. "If it is necessary, every Negro
in the state will be lynched," he promised. "It will be done to maintain
white supremacy."[41]

Another Mississippi politician, Theodore G. Bilbo, continued the tradition of promoting white supremacy. Serving as governor from 1916 until
1920 and then from 1928 until 1932, he accomplished much for his state,
successfully pushing for compulsory school attendance, increasing physical equipment at state colleges and universities, sponsoring charity hospitals for the poor, and establishing a board of bank examiners. Yet he also
proved to be a vindictive, reactionary partisan. Among other things, he
discharged faculty and staff at state universities to replace them with his
political cronies and so poorly managed state finances in his second term
that the state treasury was empty at the conclusion of his tenure. As a
reward for his work, voters elected him to the US Senate in 1934.
Although he supported many features of the New Deal, Bilbo became
infamous for his race-baiting speeches, including a call to deport Negroes
to Africa as soon as possible, and his defense of the Ku Klux Klan.[42]

As Tillman, Blease, Vardaman, and Bilbo illustrated, white supremacy
remained the central theme of southern politics well into the twentieth
century. For an ambitious candidate seeking to win high office, a firm,
unequivocal statement of "principles" on the race issue was de rigueur.
As the decades passed, more sophisticated political leaders learned to
couch their intentions in suitable euphemisms so as not to alienate a
larger national audience, but no one was fooled by the coded rhetoric.
State rights advocates railed about the Founders' version of federalism
and the desire to check the growth of national authority, but frequently

such exalted speeches were uttered with a wink and a nod. It is difficult to imagine that the down-home constituents, most of whom were not constitutional scholars, would have been especially interested in returning their elected leaders to Washington had the underlying goal been to ensure strict adherence to the Founders' original intent rather than to keep the colored race in its place at the bottom of the social, political, and economic ladder.[43]

Enlightened statesmen looked to each new generation of southern populists with hope that this time things would be different. The promise of a new sensibility was there, but it would be many decades before the reality matched the potential. In the meantime, southern leaders sported new faces but old ideals.

Ellison Durant Smith was one such leader, another South Carolinian who pulled himself up by his bootstraps from obscurity to make a name in the US Senate. During a thirty-five-year career in that august chamber, from 1909 until 1944, he proved to the voters and the world that the Old South was crumbling, but she still had some life left in her. He famously set forth his mantra to "keep the Niggers down and the price of cotton up," a comment that explained his sobriquet, "Cotton Ed." A born showman, Smith was known to drive a cotton wagon, waving a flag in support of white supremacy. Tillman, Vardaman, and Blease departed the scene early in Smith's career, but he kept their spirits alive.[44]

The tragedy of Cotton Ed Smith was that he might have been a different sort of man, but he could not bring himself to abandon the old ways. Born in Lynchburg, South Carolina, in 1864, as the Southern Confederacy gradually succumbed to the greater force of northern arms, he came of age within a reasonably well-to-do clan of prominent Methodist ministers. He once labeled himself the black sheep of the family, joking that he had to do the "cussing for the entire family" because he was among the few Smiths who was not a member of the clergy.

In 1890, the year after Smith graduated from college, Pitchfork Ben caused a stir in statewide politics by winning the gubernatorial race and setting the Bourbon aristocrats back on their heels. As a young man, Smith had been a Bourbon supporter, albeit a tepid one, but he was a farmer at heart, and the agrarian revolt appealed to his rustic sensibilities. He hailed from a family of farmers, and so he knew what it was to resent Wall Street financiers and the urban elite.[45]

Despite his sympathies, Smith never formally became a Populist. In fact, he was mostly apolitical for much of his youth. Only after cotton prices collapsed did he feel compelled to enter the political arena. He soon discovered a natural talent for attracting attention. After attending several agricultural conventions and serving as a field agent for the Southern Cotton Association, he became an effective and popular stump speaker. In time, he decided to run for an open US Senate seat.

The year was 1908. The incumbent senator, Asbury C. Latimer, had died in office. Ben Tillman was sidelined with illness and could not actively promote his favorite son, a former governor named John Gary Evans. Other prominent candidates were weighed down with political baggage. Against all expectations, Cotton Ed Smith captured the prize. He also managed to hang on to it until he died in office in 1944. He lost his Senate seat in his last election, but he expired before his term did.[46]

When he first appeared in Washington in 1909, Smith supported a variety of Progressive causes, including ratification of the Sixteenth Amendment, which provided for a federal income tax, and the Seventeenth Amendment, which allowed citizens, not state legislators, to elect members of the US Senate. He agreed with the creation of the Federal Reserve System as well. Moreover, any federal program supporting agriculture and farmers was sure to warm his heart. Progressive newspapermen noted that Smith could be counted on to cross party lines if he deemed a cause worthy. Despite these liberal sentiments, he was still a southerner, and he towed the line for Dixie. Predictably, Smith promoted racial segregation among federal employees and opposed the women's suffrage movement.[47]

Coleman Blease, the buffoonish ex-governor who broke with Pitchfork Ben, challenged Ed Smith in the 1914 election. The charismatic Blease knew how to work a crowd, but he had met his match. Cotton Ed understood that retail politics is a pageant, and no one threw a pageant as well as the incumbent senator. He scheduled parades to attract crowds and was sure to entertain the throngs with a barn-burning speech in a voice that onlookers swore could be heard a mile away. The cotton parade he held in Anderson, South Carolina, that year featured a brass band, eleven cotton wagons, and 113 participants. His campaign was mostly devoid of the traditional race-baiting antics of previous South Carolina election contests, although, in response to Blease's accusation that he did not support white supremacy, Smith ensured his constituents that white men retained an iron grip on the organs of government and would not relinquish control on his watch. His performances were masterful, and they ensured his reelection.[48]

In the ensuing years, Smith managed to win reelection in 1920, 1926, 1932, and 1938 before suffering a defeat in 1944, although he died before he would have left office in 1945. During his first twenty-four years in the Senate, he was a reliable southerner, but he lacked the enthusiastic oratorical excesses of Tillman, Vardaman, and Blease when it came to demonizing the Negro. By 1933, fresh from his reelection victory, Smith felt his political influence was waning, and he was right. With Franklin

D. Roosevelt in the executive chair, the national government began encroaching on state rights in an unprecedented manner. At first, Smith, as a loyal Democrat, pledged his support for the New Deal, but he had reached his limit by 1934. He simply could not agree with the administration's policies, which in his view undermined southern autonomy. On a personal level, Smith felt that despite his seniority and familiarity with agricultural policy, he was being cut out of national policy making on cotton—his claim to fame. He was also offended by Roosevelt's willingness to appoint Negroes to minor positions of authority in the federal government.[49]

Smith realized he needed to impress the voters back home when he ran for reelection in 1938. A recitation of his legislative successes would not garner votes, for his record of senatorial achievements was paltry by any standard. As many a southern politician before and since his time has understood, nothing ensures success as much as riling up the electorate with tales both of darkies who don't know their station and of the senator's majestic efforts to put them in their place. If he had been hesitant to raise the Negro question in years gone by, Cotton Ed showed no compunction about denigrating blacks in his next-to-last campaign. He had the perfect tale to tell, and tell it he did—again and again.

Known as the "Philadelphia Story," it involved an episode at the 1936 Democratic Convention when Franklin Roosevelt was nominated for a second term as president. Smith had experienced difficulty gaining the necessary credentials to enter the convention floor, and so he arrived just as a black minister was offering the invocation. To the enormous delight of the virtually all-white crowd listening to his stump speeches, Cotton Ed recounted his horror at seeing a "slew-footed, blue-gummed, kinky headed Senegambian" standing on the stage. The southern senator had known what he must do in response to the insult of a Negro speaking to a white man from the rostrum. "And as he started praying . . . I started walking." Smith left the convention in a huff. A handful of incensed colleagues joined him. He had no doubt he had acted in the proper manner. At the conclusion of his tale, the sprightly old man envisioned "old John Calhoun" leaning down "from his mansion in the sky," whispering to the courageous southerner, "You did right, Ed." It was a cornpone anecdote delivered up repeatedly to sympathetic crowds of white supremacists. An appreciative audience typically greeted the tripe with cheers and applause.[50]

Cotton Ed eked out a narrow victory in 1938. It was to be his last. Six years later, he ran his final campaign and lost. He still remained a venerable, well-respected lion of the Senate in the eyes of some southerners, but increasingly, even among many South Carolinians, the old ideas no longer seemed relevant to the rapidly changing world of the 1930s and

1940s. Men and women who fancied themselves progressives were embarrassed by the caricature of the backward, tobacco-juice-spitting politician who spouted clichés and racial epithets without regard for the best interests of the citizenry.[51]

At his death in 1944, Cotton Ed Smith's legacy already was tarnished, for the South of his youth, where white supremacy was an unquestioned value, was teetering on the brink of collapse. Times were changing, but the old man had refused to change with then. One observer assessed the senator's legislative achievements as seriously deficient, for Smith was a man of "words rather than deeds." The "last of the spittoon senators" was dead, his critics gleefully announced. In the *Atlanta Constitution*, editor Ralph McGill commented, "'Cotton Ed' Smith had become so lost in his own anger; so involved with hating the President [Franklin Roosevelt]; so content to stew in his own juice, that he was of no value whatsoever to the state of South Carolina." *Time* magazine perhaps summarized Smith's obsolescence best when it labeled the "walrusy" legislator a "conscientious objector to the twentieth century."[52]

The Tillmans, Bleases, Vardamans, Bilbos, and Smiths, preening and pontificating on political stages large and small, hung onto power longer than history might have expected of such unsubstantial men, but their successes were hardly surprising in an era when white voters rewarded bigoted speech in lieu of legislative accomplishment. In the desperate times of the 1930s, however, expectations began to change, even in the South. Racial harmony did not suddenly become the mantra of the age, but an economic depression forcing almost a third of the nation's workforce onto the unemployment rolls shifted priorities. Action and rhetoric in support of white supremacy remained a staple of politics in most southern states until at least the 1960s, but not every politician made racial appeals a cornerstone of his agenda when so much more could be gained by focusing on class distinctions.[53]

In Louisiana, populist governor and later US senator Huey P. Long captured national attention by arguing that elite forces were destroying the life of the common man. To ensure a more equitable distribution of wealth, Long announced his Share the Wealth program in 1934. Proclaiming "every man a king," the man nicknamed the "Kingfish" delivered a radio address recommending that no one should be able to accumulate a personal net worth exceeding three hundred times the average family fortune. He also sought to cap personal income at $1 million, with inheritances limited to $5 million. All citizens would be entitled to an old-age pension at age sixty. Free education would be provided to all qualified students in colleges and universities.[54]

In rejecting the old bromides on race, Long adapted his demagoguery to questions of class, recognizing that he could forge an effective alliance

[5.5]   Senator "Cotton Ed" Smith, a demagogue in the grand tradition of South Carolina demagogues, famously claimed that his paramount objective was to "keep the Niggers down and the price of cotton up." Courtesy of the Library of Congress.

among Louisiana's poor more effectively than he could demonize the Negro. Denounced as a dangerous socialist, he issued a simple and devastating rejoinder. At the height of the Great Depression, with so many Americans destitute and hungry, Long contended that the wealth had better be redistributed or the have-nots would rebel against their desperate circumstances. Capitalism could only be saved by an enlightened means of improving the lives of the poor. Unlike the southern populists of yesteryear, Long was not merely a poseur bandying about vitriol to stir up political support, although clearly he recognized the political appeal of bashing wealthy elites. He appeared genuinely to empathize with the impoverished, having come from modest means himself. He also was prepared to sponsor legislation to achieve his goals. Because he would back up words with action, Huey Long became one of the most influential southern politicians of the twentieth century.[55]

He lacked the racial animus and hatemongering that characterized the careers of Tillman and his ilk, but the Kingfish kept up the showmanship and outrageous antics that seemed to mix politics with entertainment in the South. His over-the-top behavior became the stuff of legend. Anxious to flout convention, Long sometimes conducted state business wearing pajamas in his hotel room. He was known to engage in fisticuffs when riled up. Newspapermen enjoyed considerable merriment at a widely reported episode when Long attended a charity revue at the exclusive Sands Point Bath Club in Long Island, New York, in August 1933. The inebriated senator insulted almost everyone within earshot by openly flirting with women and muttering boorish comments to one and all. He was heard to address a black musician as "coon" and "shine." He snatched a dinner plate from one woman, reputedly telling her, "I'll eat this for you. You're too fat already." Around midnight, Senator Long stumbled into the men's room, only to reemerge minutes later with a black eye. Conflicting stories circulated about its cause, although in most versions, the senator had urinated on the pants of someone standing next to him, and the enraged patron had punched the offender in the face.[56]

Huey Long would have been one in a long series of southern clowns had he not been so popular among his constituents. He harbored presidential ambitions, and President Roosevelt was said to be concerned that the Kingfish's populist promises might cut into FDR's political base in the 1936 election. As it turned out, the president's legacy was secure. The Kingfish was but a footnote in history—a colorful, enticing footnote, to be sure, but never a serious rival. In any case, an assassin shot Long on September 8, 1935, a month after the senator announced his candidacy for president. He died two days later. It is unlikely he could have secured enough popular support outside the South to snatch the Democratic presidential nomination from President Roosevelt. Nonetheless, the popular acclaim afforded this charismatic politician convinced southern political elites that they must ameliorate the widespread poverty in the region to forestall radical appeals by opportunistic populists in the future.[57]

THE NEO-BOURBONS

The Neo-Bourbons, as they sometimes were called, were outraged at populism run amok. They winced at the popular image of racist southern politicians snapping their suspenders and cackling as tobacco drool slid down their chins and offensive racial epithets spewed from their greasy lips. This group of men dared not challenge conventional wisdom concerning the inferiority of the southern Negro—while a new day was dawning in the region, it was still very early in the morning—but they eschewed violence and were careful not to utter racist sentiments in public. Although they harbored no love for the Negro, their paramount objective was not to denigrate a hapless soul already rendered impotent by a multitude of forces arrayed against him. Instead, this new batch of southern political leaders reached out to businesses with an olive branch. If industrialization was a fait accompli, they sought an advantage in embracing the inevitable.[58]

Few southern politicians were as witty or well-spoken as the Neo-Bourbon John Sharp Williams, a Mississippian born in Memphis, Tennessee, but raised in Yazoo County after his father, a Confederate colonel, died during the Battle of Shiloh in 1862. Williams studied in Europe before earning a law degree at the University of Virginia and forging a career as a cotton planter. A Democrat elected to the US House of Representatives in 1893, he distinguished himself by working with legendary Speaker of the House Uncle Joe Cannon to assign Democrats to committees.

Williams narrowly defeated the race-baiting James K. Vardaman for a US Senate seat in 1907. Vardaman had campaigned by calling for a repeal of the Fifteenth Amendment, which extended the franchise to all male citizens of a certain age, and modification of the Fourteenth Amendment, which applied due process and equal protection of the law requirements to the states. For his part, Williams refused to exploit the plight of the Negro for his own political advancement. The *National Weekly* magazine called Williams "a man of education, wit, and common-sense" who "shared the feelings of his neighbors on the race question" but refused to wallow in the muck because "he had seen enough of other parts of the world to be able to look at that subject in its proper perspective." He went on to support fellow Democrat Woodrow Wilson throughout that man's political career. Demoralized at the collapse of the Wilsonian program,

Williams retired from public life in 1923. "I'd rather be a hound dog and bay at the moon from my Mississippi plantation than remain in the United States Senate," he said upon his retirement. Williams did indeed retire to his plantation, although he did not send word on his nocturnal activities after leaving public office.[59]

Oscar W. Underwood of Alabama was another southern politician who carved out an influential career in the House and Senate without using race as a means of attracting votes from the base elements. Underwood first entered Congress in 1895 and retired in 1927 after spending the last twelve years in the US Senate. Although he opposed Woodrow Wilson for the Democratic nomination in 1912, Underwood eventually supported the Wilson administration. He understood the importance of American leadership in global affairs and greater tolerance in domestic life. Underwood was a well-known opponent of the Ku Klux Klan at a time when the resurrected KKK commanded considerable power throughout the South. He once characterized the group as a "national menace." Underwood barely lost a fight at the 1924 Democratic National Convention to include a statement denouncing the Klan in the party platform.

For all of his modern ideas, Underwood was still a southerner committed to the Jeffersonian ideal of a small federal government with limited constitutional purposes and enumerated powers. He did not believe that government should regulate child labor or extend the vote to women. As a proper Neo-Bourbon, he placed his faith in the sanctity of the private sector to address the needs of society. He would have been aghast at the suggestion that federal powers would be used to improve the Negro's lot; at the same time, he did not believe violence and intimidation were warranted.[60]

Carter Glass was one of the most successful of the new breed of southern politicians. A self-made man who became an influential newspaper editor in his hometown of Lynchburg, Virginia, Glass educated himself on all matters fiscal. He coauthored two major statutes involving financial matters. The Glass-Owen Federal Reserve Act of 1913 created the Federal Reserve System currently in place in the United States. Twenty years later, the US Banking Act of 1933, commonly known as the Glass-Steagall Act, separated the activities of banks and securities firms. The law also created the Federal Deposit Insurance Corporation. Glass served as secretary of the Treasury for slightly more than a year under President Woodrow Wilson.

The man from Lynchburg prided himself on his hard work and intellectual prowess, and those features of his character fit nicely with his fellow Neo-Bourbons. On most issues, he was genuinely progressive and forward thinking. At the same time, Glass did not share Williams's or Underwood's unwillingness to use race as a tool for winning elections. As an influential state senator in 1902, he was asked whether he supported Virginia's 1902 state constitution, which instituted a poll tax and a literacy test. These features discriminated against black citizens and were frequently used to support white supremacy. Glass replied, "Discrimination! Why that is exactly what we propose. To remove every Negro voter who can be gotten rid of, legally, without materially impairing the numerical strength of the white electorate." Whether he expressed what was in his heart or mouthed the requisite platitudes to win votes remains a matter of debate. In any case, Carter Glass, progressive Neo-Bourbon, demonstrated once again the fine line that a southern political figure walked in carving out a path to victory. He might provide national leadership on all manner of vital public issues, but he must still survive the next campaign.[61]

John Nance Garner of Texas was another major politician who sought to break the mold of southern populists. Rising to become the speaker of the US House of Representatives as well as vice president of the United States for almost eight years under Franklin D. Roosevelt, Garner was perhaps the most powerful of the Neo-Bourbons and certainly the most visible. He became the model of a new type of southerner—convivial and skilled at backroom politics but not a fire-eating orator casting aspersions on the elite. In fact, he counted the elite among his most faithful supporters, especially the oil and gasoline industry and the electric power trusts. He was not a profound thinker or a man of grand designs, but he understood arcane parliamentary procedure, and he was not reluctant to strike deals to accomplish his ends. Although race was not a central feature in his politics, he voted in favor of a 1901 poll tax that disenfranchised Negroes and ensured the triumph of Democratic Party politics in Texas for the ensuing six decades.[62]

He and Franklin Roosevelt made for a strange pair. They joined forces early in FDR's tenure to ensure the legislative success of the New Deal, but Garner was at his core a southern conservative. As long as he believed the president's programs aimed for temporary relief from the destructive effects of the Great Depression, the two men could paper over their differences. When Garner finally realized that Roosevelt was a new kind of leader with a new idea of the role of government in the lives of citizens, the vice president led the Democratic revolt against the administration. The rupture was not readily apparent until after Roosevelt's reelection, which meant that Garner remained in the second spot on the ticket in 1936. "Cactus Jack," as Garner was known owing to his support for the prickly pear cactus as the state flower, longed to be the conservative heir apparent to Roosevelt for the 1940 presidential nomination. It was not to be. Aside from his age in 1940—he was over seventy—the prickly pear possessed neither the personal charm nor the political affiliations necessary to win the nomination. When FDR announced his intention to seek a third term, Garner's career on the national stage drew to a close. He retired to his home in Uvalde, Texas, where he survived until 1967. He died fifteen days before his ninety-ninth birthday.[63]

For all of their power and influence, the Neo-Bourbons did not supplant the old race-baiting southern politicians of the late nineteenth and early twentieth centuries. They presented an attractive alternative—the business-friendly, fiscally conservative, intellectually capable southern gentleman who philosophically supported a neo-Jeffersonian view of government as limited and restrained. They had no need of elite-bashing populism, for they were elites or friends of elites. If they occasionally denounced the Negro as an undesirable element, this was the price of electoral success, although the more progressive Neo-Bourbons refrained from employing racial epithets altogether.[64]

Race remained the central focus of many a mainstream southern political leader until the last quarter of the twentieth century. Strom Thurmond, the venerable South Carolina politician who fondly recalled his early meeting with Pitchfork Ben Tillman, led the States' Rights Democratic Party—the so-called Dixiecrats—as it broke from the national Democratic Party in 1948 to promote continued racial segregation. He was a fixture in the South until his retirement from the US Senate in 2003. George Wallace, the powerful governor of Alabama, was a well-known proponent of segregation and articulated the discontent felt by many whites when he ran for president as a third-party candidate in 1968. These men kept alive the fires of sectional hatred and bigotry as long as they could. When blacks eventually earned a measure of political influence, Thurmond, Wallace, and their compatriots discovered the necessity of inclusive politics. Jim Crow eventually collapsed and died, but the old fellow spent many long decades gasping and wallowing on his deathbed.[65]

6

Washington versus Du Bois

"Cast Down Your Bucket Where You Are"

As white American political leaders labored early in the twentieth century to keep Negroes in their place at the bottom of the social, political,
and economic spectrum, black leaders considered their limited options.
They might carve out a niche on one side of the color line and be satisfied
to live out their lives invisible to whites but content with their modest
station within the segregated black community. They might challenge the
status quo and insist on their place in mainstream white society, possibly
undermining, even obliterating, the color line. Such a confrontational
stance likely would trigger a violent response from the entrenched white
majority, but the risk was worth taking if it instilled pride in the Negro
community and improved the lives of average black citizens. A middle
approach appeared impracticable. Either a man lived apart from his fellow man and accepted his lot in life, or he was fully integrated into society and accepted as the full equal of his brethren.[1]

**UP FROM SLAVERY: BOOKER T. WASHINGTON
AND THE ATLANTA COMPROMISE**

Two iconic figures came to represent the deep divide between accepting
the status quo and pushing for change in the black community: Booker T.
Washington and W. E. B. Du Bois. The former was one of the most important black leaders of the late nineteenth and early twentieth centuries; his
rise from obscurity to prominence became the stuff of lore. He came of

154

age under the confines of the peculiar institution, and it shaped everything that followed in his life. His was a familiar story, for he was the offspring of a slave woman and a white master. He never knew the man's name; nor did he harbor resentment at the absence of a father. "I do not find especial fault with him," Washington explained, because the man "was simply another unfortunate victim of the institution" of slavery. It was a remarkably generous attitude since Washington "never heard of his taking the least interest in me or providing in any way for my rearing."[2]

Born in Hale's Ford, Virginia, in 1856, young Booker recalled the jubilation that accompanied the end of the Civil War and the realization that emancipation was at hand. After those heady days when the shackles were lifted from an enslaved people, he understood that with many impediments cleared from his path, he could make his way in the world by the sweat of his brow. He worked diligently to pull himself up by his bootstraps. In that sense, Washington was the embodiment of the American mythos that a fellow could better himself through diligent, honest labor.[3]

The man's optimism appeared boundless. When he reflected back on the peculiar institution in his 1901 autobiography, *Up from Slavery*, he naturally condemned bondage as a tremendous moral lapse by the citizens of a great nation, but it was not an unmitigated calamity or an unforgivable sin. As incredible as it sounds for a former slave to defend the institution, Washington believed that American blacks emerged from enslavement with advantages not afforded to blacks in other countries. "Think about it: We went into slavery pagans; we came out Christians. We went into slavery pieces of property; we came out American citizens. We went into slavery with chains clanking about our wrists; we came out with the American ballot in our hands." His critics were appalled that he could find anything positive to say about the monstrous institution, but Washington refused to wallow in anger and resentment. He was forward-looking, content to let the past be the past. "Notwithstanding the cruelty and moral wrong of slavery," he wrote, "we are in a stronger and more hopeful condition, materially, intellectually, morally, and religiously, than is true of an equal number of black people in any other portion of the globe."[4]

Washington was not a naive fool when he set out to better himself; nor was he just any fellow setting out on a quest of self-improvement in the expectation that America was a land of opportunity. He had only to look at the desperate situation confronting Negroes throughout the nation to appreciate the obstacles that remained after slavery was abolished. Racial discrimination was a fact of life, and anyone with dark skin could not escape that reality.

Former slaves and their children recognized that education was crucial to advancement. In *Up from Slavery*, Washington detailed his early life as well as his determination to obtain an education. His family eventually moved to West Virginia, but the Washingtons were so poor that he had to toil in the salt mines with his stepfather rather than attend school. Nonetheless, he was undeterred. "From the time that I can remember having any thoughts about anything," he reflected, "I recall that I had an intense longing to learn to read." Young Washington rose at 4 a.m. so he could practice his lessons before shuffling off to work in the mines.[5]

He eventually took a job as a houseboy for Viola Ruffner, wife of Lewis Ruffner, the salt mine owner and a former major general in the West Virginia militia during the Civil War. Viola Ruffner had earned a well-deserved reputation as a strict disciplinarian, but she also was a New England–trained schoolteacher. She saw something in this young houseboy—perhaps it was his deep, unquenchable desire to become educated, his keen intelligence, and his essential honesty—that made her eager to encourage his efforts. Washington later called Ruffner the best friend he had ever had. She taught him about the ways of the white world: manners, cleanliness, punctuality, and thrift. He would use these lessons to good effect later in life.

Under Viola Ruffner's tutelage, he continued his studies and displayed an impressive aptitude for hard work. Eventually, at her urging, he applied for and won admission into the Hampton Normal and Agricultural Institute, a school established in Virginia in 1868 to educate freedmen, who were ineligible to enter white universities. He was sixteen years old. Washington was so poor that when he arrived on the campus in October 1872, he had not had a bath for a month, and he desperately needed a haircut. He landed a job as the school janitor to help pay his expenses. A general scholarship paid most of Washington's $70 annual tuition at the institute.[6]

Washington blossomed at Hampton, first as a student and later, after attending Wayland Seminary (now Virginia Union University), as a teacher. The school had adopted a standard industrial curriculum prevalent at the time, and the young man took to his studies with vigor. Students were expected to learn a trade in addition to mastering traditional high school subjects. It was not an academy of philosopher-kings but a vocational school modeled on military academies where drill and repetition were emphasized. Victorian morality was as much a part of the experience as any subject taught in school. Blacks were often thought to be immoral (or, at best, amoral) creatures that would engage in depraved sexual acts at the first opportunity. Hampton students were expected to be a cut above the stereotype. They would demonstrate to each other, and to the outside world, that black men could rise from the muck and become a credit to their race.[7]

Booker T. Washington became an exemplary student in a school filled with exemplary students. While he studied there, he met an educator who would serve as a mentor and friend, Samuel Chapman Armstrong, head of the institute. The son of a missionary, Armstrong was a white Union man who eventually served in the Civil War as a colonel in charge of the 8th US Colored Troops. He joined the Bureau of Refugees, Freedmen, and Abandoned Lands after the war. Armstrong was one of the carpetbaggers so reviled by southerners for their willingness to interfere with the natural order of social relations by lifting up Negroes from their lowly station. To some northerners and blacks, these meddling do-gooders were condescending and smug, so self-congratulatory and paternalistic in their attitude and approach that they were almost as destructive to the black psyche as southern racists. Washington did not see Armstrong this way. He admired his new role model immensely, calling him "the most perfect specimen of man, physically, mentally and spiritually the most Christ-like," as well as "a great man—the noblest, rarest human being that it has ever been my privilege to meet." Armstrong seems to have regarded his young ward with similar affection. He eventually hired this gifted young black man to serve on his faculty.[8]

In 1881, three commissioners from Alabama asked Armstrong to recommend a white principal to head up a new black university modeled on Hampton. Instead of offering up a white candidate, Armstrong recommended the young Washington, calling him a "very competent, capable mulatto" and "the best man we have here." It was a bold choice to send him to the Black Belt. Nonetheless, that same year Washington traveled to the heart of the South and became the new school's first president. He remained in that post until his death in 1915.[9]

In his position as head of a fledgling black college, Washington's skills at negotiation and compromise soon became apparent. His first order of business was to assure local white leaders that the school, named the Tuskegee Normal School for Colored Teachers (later the Tuskegee Normal Industrial Institute and eventually Tuskegee University), was not a threat to the white power structure. He also solicited funding from white philanthropists anxious to appear progressive on race—as long as their efforts were not deemed too radical or destructive of the social order.

Tuskegee's origins were predictably humble. Washington was the only teacher for a time, and he was forced to improvise inside a dilapidated old building. Owing to his unflagging optimism and ability to attract funding, students, and teachers, the new institution flourished. By the time he died twenty-four years later, Washington had built Tuskegee into a university that had educated fifteen hundred students and received contributions from many noted philanthropists, including such luminaries as Andrew Carnegie and George Eastman.[10]

Washington was at heart a conservative man. Modeling his new school on the Hampton Institute, he hoped to train teachers and community leaders to return to their homes and promote vocational education. In speeches and writings that became famous toward the end of the 1880s, he stressed the need for Negroes to be satisfied with their place in society. If they agitated for social equality, they would only anger whites. Far better to build a life on their side of the color line than cross over and inflame dormant prejudices among average white citizens who were not ready to lynch Negroes or join paramilitary organizations. No good could come of pushing too far, too fast. "I fear the Negro race lays too much stress on its grievances and not enough on its opportunities," Washington told an audience at Fisk University, another historically black college, in 1895.[11]

He would return to this theme throughout his career. "The Negro is making progress at the present time as he made progress in slavery times," he observed on another occasion. "There is, however, this difference: In slavery the progress of the Negro was a menace to the white man. The security of the white master depended upon the ignorance of the black slave. In freedom the security and happiness of each race depends, to a very large extent, on the education and the progress of the other." Colored folk under segregation laws could climb the ladder of success— progress that would have been impossible under slavery—but they must take care to reach an accommodation with whites. "The problem of slavery was to keep the Negro down; the problem of freedom is to raise him up. The story of the Negro, in the last analysis, is simply the story of the man who is farthest down; as he raises himself he raises every other man who is above him."[12]

His most famous articulation of his approach occurred in Atlanta, Georgia, on September 18, 1895, in a speech later called the Atlanta Compromise. The occasion was the Cotton States and International Exposition, a large festival held in Piedmont Park from September through December 1895 as a method of garnering attention for one of the most important cities in the South. Washington spoke on the first day to a predominantly white audience that greeted his message with enthusiasm. Critics noted ironically that Washington's speech occurred in 1895, the same year that the legendary black civil rights icon Frederick Douglass died. A new man, a far more conservative man, appeared on the scene at precisely the moment when the old guard had passed and someone needed to pick up the mantle of civil rights.

Washington admonished his fellow Negroes not to look to the North for assistance but to understand "the importance of cultivating friendly relations with the Southern white man, who is their next-door neighbor." Instead of waiting for a new and better day to dawn, he suggested they make the best of the current situation. "I would say: 'Cast down your bucket where you are'—cast it down in making friends in every manly way of the people of all races by whom we are surrounded." With higher-status professions closed to them, blacks should seek advancement in "agriculture, mechanics, in commerce, in domestic service, and in the professions." His critics would deride his willingness to accept his second-class status, but Washington argued that slow, steady advancement was preferable to no advancement or advancement coupled with bloodshed.

> The wisest among my race understand that the agitation of questions of social equality is the extremest folly, and that progress in the enjoyment of all the privileges that will come to us must be the result of severe and constant struggle rather than of artificial forcing. No race that has anything to contribute to the markets of the world is long in any degree ostracized. It is important and right that all privileges of the law be ours, but it is vastly more important that we be prepared for the exercise of these privileges. The opportunity to earn a dollar in a factory just now is worth infinitely more than the opportunity to spend a dollar in an opera-house.[13]

Later generations of black leaders assailed Washington's "accommodationist" thinking, equating his efforts with the Stockholm syndrome, or capture bonding, in which victims of a kidnapping empathize with their captors. By concerning himself with how whites reacted to black advancements rather than worrying about the effect on the disenfranchised, Washington placed the needs of whites before the hopes of his own race. Such insight has a measure of validity, especially when viewed through the prism of a later age, but it also discounts the "Wizard of Tuskegee's" achievements.[14]

His apologists pointed to the realities of the Jim Crow epoch. Urging blacks to take their rightful place alongside whites in mainstream American society in the 1890s would have been tantamount to launching a race war, especially in the South. Washington's task was to allow a black middle class to exist without triggering racial tension and violence. Blacks would continue to work as laborers and domestics in white society. In the meantime, if they rose to become writers, lawyers, or doctors in the black community, it was no business of whites'. Tuskegee would never be Harvard or even the University of Alabama, so whites need not feel threatened if little black boys learned their alphabet in the heart of Old Dixie and earned a university education.

[6.1]   Booker T. Washington, pictured here in the early twentieth century, was a champion of the "accommodationist" school of race relations. Courtesy of the Library of Congress.

His message appealed to whites on multiple levels. For the die-hard racist, Washington suggested that Negro inferiority was acceptable since a prominent black leader encouraged his people to toil away in low-paid, low-status positions. For whites fearful of a race war, Washington was a calming, stabilizing presence. For whites who believed that violence was not the answer and that Negroes deserved some sort of helping hand, Washington intimated that blacks would be willing to accept their charity in a spirit of cheerfulness and perhaps obsequiousness. In all cases, blacks would unflinchingly take on difficult, dirty, demeaning jobs as they always had and, from the white perspective, presumably always would. In this way, an uneasy harmony between the races could exist.[15]

A segregated America would have existed even if Booker T. Washington had not. He was an influential man, but his reach could only extend as far as white paternalism and forbearance would allow. His speeches and writings counseled blacks to accept a situation that already existed. He was a victim looking up at an attacker and saying, "It's all right. I won't raise a fuss."

It was always an uneasy détente. Segregation ensured that two nations coexisted side by side. "Separate but equal" was the catchphrase owing to a US Supreme Court case, *Plessy v. Ferguson*, but the words were spoken with a wink and nod. No one seriously believed that the public accommodations afforded to Negroes in housing, schools, restaurants, hotels, and jobs even approximated the luxuries enjoyed by most whites.

As the nineteenth century departed and the twentieth century took its place, the two races existed in mutually exclusive worlds. When the worlds collided, the explosion almost always proved disadvantageous to persons of color. When a dispute arose over who had caused a traffic accident, failed to honor a labor contract, or neglected to produce the requisite widgets, the black man could expect to bear the burden. When a crime was committed in the white world, a black person frequently was blamed. If the alleged crime involved sex, especially with a white woman, the supposed offender could depend on the swift, sure hand of Judge Lynch. Niceties such as due process of law were seldom permitted.[16]

To his credit, Washington repeatedly told receptive white audiences that the price to be paid for black accommodation was at least a fair process—or fairer than in the past—so that a black man received his day in court. The white farmer must take his hand off the scale when it came time to settle the account at the company store. The sheriff must impartially investigate crimes and allow for the institutions of government to work. Extralegal lynchings must cease. That he was not wholly successful in engineering a more equitable relationship between the races reflects less on Washington than on the tenor of the times and the enormity of his quest, to say nothing of the vagaries of whites who would break the rules simply because they could. In some corners of the world, might makes right no matter how many rules are established.

When the black and white worlds existed separately from each other, blacks enjoyed a measure of freedom to advance. Their activities mostly were invisible to whites. It was their invisibility that made advancement possible. If whites had witnessed the workings of the Negro world, they likely would have denigrated what they saw or would have grown fearful and felt threatened. In either case, blacks would have suffered as a result of the white reaction. By existing unfettered, Negro churches, schools, small businesses, professions, and sports teams could grow and thrive. Every time a black minister preached a powerful sermon of Christian faith, every time a black university produced a graduate who could think and write as well as anyone, every time a black businessman built up his own little entrepreneurial empire, every time a black lawyer or doctor excelled at his profession, and every time a black athlete tossed a baseball, football, or basketball with as much or more skill than his white counterparts, he demonstrated the fundamental lie underlying the Jim Crow regime. Segregation suggested inferiority, but for those who would see, it demonstrated that the inferiority was the product of a warped white imagination.[17]

The Cotton States and International Exposition solidified Booker T. Washington's position as a national figure, equally revered and reviled, depending on one's understanding of race relations. He had come a long way in his life—from an impoverished slave, a "mulatto bastard," in crass terms, to a transformational civil rights icon—and he had done it through his own initiative. He had been fortunate enough to meet inspirational figures along the way, but he was first and foremost a self-made man. He would meet with captains of industry, dine with President Theodore Roosevelt in the White House, and advise a generation of teachers and political leaders on the need to provide a roadmap for success to Negroes living under the dark cloud of segregation.

For all the scorn his successors would heap upon him, Booker T. Washington did something no one else had—not the abolitionists, not Abraham Lincoln, not the Radical Republicans in Congress during Reconstruction, and not the administrators of the Freedmen's Bureau. He had secured space and time for blacks to move from a life of bondage to a life of freedom without fear of white reprisals. To be sure, violent episodes occurred with unsettling regularity across the land—no figure of either race could have prevented such outbreaks of violence in every instance—but Washington had assuaged the concerns of many mainstream whites by arguing that blacks should be able to gain an education and seek employment without endangering whites or triggering an angry backlash. Even if his methods came under intense attack in later years, he must be credited with advancing the cause of Negro civil rights when any progress, no matter how incremental, seemed unlikely, if not impossible.[18]

W. E. B. DU BOIS AND THE TALENTED TENTH

At the dawn of the twentieth century, a new breed of black leaders examined Booker T. Washington's gradualist approach and found it wanting. They took umbrage at the great man's willingness to settle for second-class citizenship. Vocational education had its place, no doubt, but if a Negro could aim no higher than a lowly position working in a factory or laboring in agricultural pursuits, he was only half a step removed from bondage. To dream of a better life is to dream big, and Washington's successors were dismayed that his dreams were so small.[19]

Of all the critics of Washington and the Atlanta Compromise, none were as passionate and eloquent as William Edward Burghardt Du Bois. To a later generation of American Negroes, W. E. B. Du Bois became a role model diametrically opposed to Booker T. Washington. Du Bois was a proud, gifted, unbroken black man—confident, capable, insistent on his rights, and unafraid to challenge white authority. He would never settle for the Atlanta Compromise, or any compromise, when it came to black equality.[20]

His early life differed markedly from Booker T. Washington's. Du Bois had never known slavery; nor had he known the poverty that Washington experienced as a child. Will, as the boy was called, did not hail from a wealthy family, but he grew up relatively sheltered from the harshness of segregation. He was born in Great Barrington, Massachusetts, on February 23, 1868. His father deserted the family when Will was a toddler. His mother reared her son on the edge of poverty, but the boy remained oblivious of their impecunious circumstances until he reached adulthood. As far as he knew, they lived a more or less middle-class lifestyle. He attended Great Barrington High School, an oasis where he never felt inferior to white students. His school principal encouraged him to go on to college, which the young man did after he graduated from high school at the age of sixteen.[21]

He chose to attend Fisk University, a historically black college in Nashville, Tennessee. In later years, after he had studied at Harvard University and in Berlin, Germany, Du Bois recalled Fisk as the place where he was the happiest. "I was at Harvard but not of it," he remarked. "I was a student of Berlin, but still the son of Fisk."[22]

Although he had not experienced bigotry firsthand in his young life, Will Du Bois understood the facts of life. He knew racial bias was an undeniable fact in the Jim Crow era, and it largely defined the quality of a person's life, especially but not exclusively south of the Mason-Dixon Line. If he had forgotten that fact, a small incident served as a vivid reminder. He accidentally bumped into a white woman on a street in

Nashville one day. This was the sort of chance encounter that could esca-
late out of control if a black man did not take care to make amends. Tip-
ping his hat and begging the woman's pardon, Du Bois was not prepared
for her response. Although the woman had not been injured, she was
incensed by his apology. "How dare you speak to me, you impudent
nigger!" she hissed. He was fortunate the angry words were the extent of
the episode, for some black men had been beaten or lynched on far less
provocation.[23]

Du Bois never forgot the episode. Wherever he traveled and whatever
he accomplished in his long, eventful life, he always knew he was a black
man in a world designed by whites for whites. Despite these limitations,
or because of them, he resolved to transform himself into the best specimen of an educated intellectual possible. He succeeded in his quest,
becoming the first black man to earn a doctorate at the prestigious Harvard University. He then moved on to study at the University of Berlin.
His time in Germany taught Du Bois much about America's fixation on
race, for he found far less discrimination in Europe than he had known in
the United States. He realized he had grown suspicious of white people,
assuming they were all bigots. Indeed, he had prejudged whites in much
the same manner as they had prejudged him. In Germany, Du Bois later
wrote, he lost some of his provincial naïveté. "From this uphampered
social intermingling with Europeans of education and manners," he
recalled in his autobiography, "I emerged from the extremes of my racial
provincialism. I became more human; learned the place in life of 'Wine,
Women, and Song'; I ceased to hate or suspect people simply because
they belonged to one race or color; and above all I began to understand
the real meaning of scientific research and the dim outline of methods of
employing its technique and its results in the new social sciences for the
settlement of the Negro problems in America." If Booker T. Washington's
experiences taught him to hunker down and make do under the cruel
weight of segregation, W. E. B. Du Bois learned that a wider world existed
beyond the black-and-white world of the United States. Prejudice was
enforced by man-made institutions, and such institutions could be undermined by the committed iconoclast.[24]

He returned to the United States in 1894 and secured a position at Wilberforce University in Ohio. He had considered a position at the Tuskegee
Institute, and it is interesting to wonder how he and the great Booker T.
Washington would have interacted, but ultimately the Ohio school
seemed a better fit for Will Du Bois than an industrial school in the heart
of the Deep South. He met and married one of his students during his
two-year stint at Wilberforce. Nina Gomer was to remain his wife for
more than half a century, until her death in 1950.

Du Bois moved on to the University of Pennsylvania briefly before teaching sociology and history at Atlanta University from 1898 until 1910. During those years, he became a scholar of the first order, producing many books and articles on slavery and Reconstruction as well as the plight of blacks in America. As he grew in stature, Du Bois was recognized as a brilliant man of letters, if a bit aloof from his colleagues and a strict disciplinarian with his students.[25]

For all of his notable accomplishments, the W. E. B. Du Bois who traveled to Atlanta was a man of the mind, not a man of action. That fact would change in time. His great awakening occurred in 1899. Living and working in the cradle of the old Southern Confederacy again reminded Du Bois of his status in a land where race was a deciding factor in the treatment of one's fellow man. On one occasion, he was denied entry into a Pullman berth on a train because he was a black man. Whatever his achievements or intellect, he must not be allowed to mingle with the white clientele. He met with white colleagues at Atlanta University and throughout the country, but he could not accompany them to a local hotel to discuss the important issues of the day, for Negroes were only permitted to enter such establishments if they were the hired help. Du Bois suffered these indignities, and a thousand other, lesser discourtesies, because he had no choice in the matter. He had come to accept these slights as a part of his life in the southern United States.[26]

An incident involving a Georgia farmer named Sam Hose transformed this modest academic into an activist who would influence American history in myriad ways. As Du Bois later recounted the affair, Hose was accused of murdering his employer, throwing the man's infant son to the floor hard enough to cause brain damage and blindness in one eye, and raping the man's wife. The ugly affair, characterized by Governor Allen D. Candler as "the most diabolical in the annals of crime," occurred in a small farming community, Palmetto, south of Atlanta, on Wednesday, April 12, 1899. After Hose fled the scene, a manhunt ensued.[27]

This was the stuff that southern newspaper editors and demagogues (who were often one and the same) lived for. It had all the elements of "folk pornography," as one commentator described it: a lustful black beast on the loose, a young white couple and their innocent child destroyed by the heinous fiend, and white vigilantes in hot pursuit. Editors gleefully promised that if the "fiend incarnate" were apprehended, he would be lynched—or worse. Georgia law enforcement officers were advised not to interfere with the people's will, for the only justice that existed for such an outrageous offense was to allow the white citizenry to find the "black brute" and make him "suffer the torments of the damned in expiation of the hellish crime."

Two brothers, J. B. and J. L. Jones, knew the suspect might come their way. Sam Hose's mother lived and worked on their farm near Marshall-ville, southwest of Macon, Georgia. After setting a trap, the brothers cap-tured the outlaw and set out on a train to return him to the authorities so that they could collect a large monetary reward. When an angry mob learned that the accused murderer and rapist was aboard the train, the crowd seized the suspect when the train reached Griffin, a small town not far from Atlanta.

The Jones brothers never collected their reward, for to do so, they were required to deliver their prisoner into the hands of the authorities. Instead, the mob administered the rough justice that southern vigilantes frequently employed. Hose probably was guilty of the murder, but he always denied the rape. By the time the mob laid hands on him, however, none of that mattered.

His fate was especially grisly. As white citizens converged on the area, the mob escorted the hapless soul into a place known as the Old Trout-man Field along the Palmetto Road in Newnan, Georgia. The crowd took its time punishing the offender, perhaps as long as half an hour. Someone stepped forward and sliced off Hose's ears. Another man used a knife or perhaps pruning shears to snip off the man's fingers one by one and dis-play them to the adoring crowd of onlookers. Soon thereafter, a man slid a knife between Hose's legs and hacked off his genitals. After several men dumped a can of kerosene over his head, Hose cried out, "Sweet Jesus!" It was too late for Jesus to save him. The vigilantes chained Hose to a tree and set him on fire. As he struggled in agony, his bloodied, beaten, burned body managed briefly to escape from its chains and stagger away from the pyre. Several whites lifted large pieces of wood and pushed the barbecued man back into the flames, where he died.[28]

W. E. B. Du Bois was walking to the offices of the *Atlanta Constitution* to meet with an editor, Joel Chandler Harris, popular author of the Uncle Remus stories. Before he arrived at the newspaper office, Du Bois heard that Hose had been killed and his knuckles were for sale in a grocer's window only a few blocks from where he stood. The news sent Du Bois reeling and "pulled me off my feet." He had not been blind to stories of Judge Lynch or the delight that white mobs took in inflicting pain on the body of black folks, but the Hose case was different in Du Bois's estima-tion. The case was not the act of a small group of coarse whites existing on the fringes of Georgia society. Eleven days of screaming headlines written by supposedly educated white Atlantans, the willingness of the law enforcement community to stand aside and allow a mob to circum-vent due process, and the cavalier manner in which portions of the dead man's body were sold as though he were a side of beef convinced the young scholar that America would never change unless good people took decisive action. Du Bois understood that "one could not be a calm, cool, and detached scientist while Negroes were lynched, murdered and starved."

He never met with Harris that day. Stumbling home to consider the repercussions of the torture, mutilation, and display of a black man accused of a crime and denied due process of law, Du Bois realized he had crossed a personal Rubicon. He could not continue on as before, living a life somewhat insulated from the evils of segregation and racial discrimination. If one black life was forfeited in the interests of white expediency, all black lives lost their value.[29]

For the next six decades, W. E. B. Du Bois dedicated his life to activism on behalf of Negroes. He realized that studying the problem of race, while important, was insufficient. He must act. In 1905, he and William Monroe Trotter initiated the Niagara Movement, an effort dedicated to resisting segregation and Negro disenfranchisement. Through this and other activities, Du Bois became a leading spokesman against Booker T. Washington's "accommodationist" approach to race relations.[30]

Du Bois was disturbed by the "cult" surrounding the Wizard of Tuskegee. Challenging Washington's endeavors risked aggravating the great man's numerous admirers on both sides of the color line; yet Du Bois and his fellow Young Turks believed the time had come to move beyond the gradualism of the Atlanta Compromise. Washington's approach was popular among whites, Du Bois argued, because it kept blacks firmly entrenched in the lower echelon of society. As the Sam Hose case had so vividly illustrated, relations between the races would never improve as long as whites held blacks in low esteem. Segregation ensured that Negroes were objectified as the "other." How could blacks be brutalized in such a nonchalant manner unless they were regarded as inferior beings? In Du Bois's view, systemic change was needed, but it would never occur without active, ongoing, persistent prodding by black leaders who could demonstrate that they were not lesser men. If blacks waited on whites to recognize their worth as human beings, the wait would never end.[31]

Du Bois outlined his opposition to Washington's ideas in many works. One of the most influential and famous was his 1903 book of essays on race, *The Souls of Black Folk*. In that work, Du Bois cautioned blacks not to see themselves through the eyes of whites—a concept he termed "double consciousness"—but to envision a day when they could be reconciled with white America. The problem with segregation was that it constantly delayed the day of reconciliation because it insisted that two worlds exist—a white world of excellence and high expectation and a black world of inferiority and second-class status.[32]

[6.2] W. E. B. Du Bois became a well-known critic of "accommodationist" race relations. Courtesy of the Library of Congress.

Du Bois explained his disagreement with the great man. "Mr. Washington came with a simple definite programme at the psychological moment when the nation was a little ashamed of having bestowed so much sentiment on Negroes and was concentrating its energies on Dollars." In that time and place, Washington may have been correct that small steps were necessary to advance the Negro cause. "His programme of industrial education, conciliation of the South, and submission and silence as to civil and political rights was not wholly original. . . . But Mr. Washington first indissolubly linked these things; he put enthusiasm, unlimited energy, and perfect faith into this programme, and changed it from a by-path into a veritable Way of Life."[33]

Had he characterized industrial education as a first step in a more ambitious program, a temporary respite during a long, difficult journey, Washington might have taken his people with him. But he seemed content to defend the status quo. This willingness to settle for second best led to a schism in the Negro ranks:

> Among his own people, however, Mr. Washington has encountered the strongest and most lasting opposition, amounting at times to bitterness, and even today continuing strong and insistent even though largely silenced in outward expression by the public opinion of the nation. Some of this opposition is, of course, mere envy; the disappointment of displaced demagogues and the spite of narrow minds. But aside from this, there is among educated and thoughtful colored men in all parts of the land a feeling of deep regret, sorrow, and apprehension at the wide currency and ascendancy which some of Mr. Washington's theories have gained.[34]

"I bow to no boss" became the Niagara Movement's mantra, but Du Bois realized that Booker T. Washington, for all of his power and prestige, was but a symbol of a larger problem. After the end of Reconstruction, the standard view was that an experiment in black self-rule had failed owing to corruption and maladministration. Negroes simply were incapable of governing themselves. This conventional wisdom echoed down through the decades and became an accepted proverb of race relations. White citizens, even those who were not rabid white supremacists, no longer questioned the wisdom of such presuppositions. To the extent that Booker T. Washington reinforced the prevailing view of the races, he was seen as an acceptable leader because he was not a threat to the established social order. To challenge Washington was to challenge conventional wisdom, and such challenges presented problems.[35]

Du Bois spoke of the "talented tenth," a term to describe the idea that one in ten black men could become a leader of the race. Such men needed more than the industrial education proposed by Washington and his followers. Du Bois argued that a classical education such as the one he had received would prepare Negroes for important roles in business, the professions, and the arts and sciences. Talented blacks were held back because they lacked not ability but opportunity.[36]

The rise of the Niagara Movement worried the Tuskegee Machine. Washington feared that a new generation of critics pushing for equality would undermine everything he had done to placate whites and carve out a niche for blacks in the face of segregation. If affluent whites perceived a threat to their position, they might cease contributing money to Washington's projects. Without rich, well-connected white benefactors to support his program, Washington's prestige and influence would wane. Whether he opposed Du Bois and the Niagara Movement to preserve his personal perquisites or to counter what he perceived to be a genuine threat to the gains of black Americans depends on one's view of Booker T. Washington.[37]

By 1908, the Niagara Movement had faded into obscurity, partially because of Washington's opposition but also because it lacked sufficient funding and its leaders could not agree on specific goals. Du Bois was undeterred. If anything, he believed a program more ambitious and radical than the Tuskegee plan was desperately required. Sam Hose's 1899 lynching had propelled Du Bois into a life of activism, and the ensuing years had done nothing to change his conviction that blacks needed a new forum for promoting civil rights. The Atlanta race riot of 1906 and the Springfield riots two years later reminded Negroes where they stood in the American regime. Booker T. Washington counseled patience in hopes of soothing the savage beast lurking beneath the facade of white society, but the minute a white citizen raised the possibility of black misbehavior, the facade disappeared, and out came the whips. No person of a darker hue could ever forget his place in the scheme of things. If he did, he would be shown the error of his ways. The organs of government often were bypassed in favor of rough justice. Even if he escaped a lynching, a black man accused of a wicked act learned, when hailed before the courts, that his race influenced the outcome more than the facts of the case.[38]

The spate of lynchings and extralegal behavior scattered across the country during the early 1900s made one fact clear to anyone who dared to see: no one was looking out for the lowly black person who crossed the color line. Prominent civil rights spokesmen could debate the finer philosophical points of whether the Washington scheme for industrial education was superior to Du Bois's plans for greater equality between the races, or vice versa, but such matters affected few people apart from the black intelligentsia. The average Negro toiling day in and day out to scratch out a living and support his family was left helpless and alone, especially if he ran afoul of angry whites who feared and mistrusted him.

The remedy, to the extent that one existed, required an organized group willing and able to stand up for Negro rights when those rights were threatened.

In 1909, four white social reformers, Mary White Ovington, William English Walling, Oswald Garrison Villard, and Henry Moskowitz, met to discuss the creation of a new civil rights organization. From those initial discussions, the National Association for the Advancement of Colored People (NAACP) was born. The association listed the date of its inception as February 12, 1909—Abraham Lincoln's hundredth birthday—although the initial organizational meetings did not occur until some months later. Prominent black activists, including Ida B. Wells-Barnett and Mary Church Terrell, joined the organization, as did Du Bois. The group's charter stated its ambitious agenda: "To promote equality of rights and to eradicate caste or race prejudice among the citizens of the United States; to advance the interest of colored citizens; to secure for them impartial suffrage; and to increase their opportunities for securing justice in the courts, education for the their children, employment according to their ability and complete equality before law."[39]

Except for Du Bois, the NAACP's original leadership ranks were filled with whites, mostly of the Jewish faith. This reality could be viewed positively or negatively. On one hand, by engaging a variety of figures from different races, religions, and beliefs, the association was an inclusive group of men and women dedicated to bettering the lives of all Americans and promoting racial equality. On the other hand, a group that touted itself as the premier civil rights organization in the United States and expressed its intent to advance the interests of colored citizens comprised mostly noncolored citizens. For blacks who believed that their eventual integration into American society required a firm demonstration of their ability to help themselves, an NAACP filled with whites risked perpetuating the benign paternalism that had marred the efforts of social liberals stretching back to the days of Reconstruction. In the end, however, the organization's members realized that all helping hands were needed—white, black, or whatever. The task was too gargantuan and the resources were too strained to refuse any manner of legitimate assistance offered in good faith.[40]

And so the NAACP set off on an ambitious program of grassroots activism. Calling attention to the prevalence of lynching between 1889 and 1919, the group issued a report outlining the problem and calling for national antilynching legislation. Local chapters engaged blacks to push for changes in their neighborhoods, sometimes through incremental means and in other cases through dramatic public awareness campaigns. The NAACP eventually developed a legal defense strategy to challenge Jim Crow laws across the nation. In later years, the group's famous lawyers, Charles Hamilton Houston and Thurgood Marshall, would achieve stunning successes in the courts. Marshall eventually served as lead counsel in a series of famous integration cases, culminating in *Brown v. Board of Education of Topeka*, which struck down separate-but-equal public schools as unconstitutional. Marshall also served as solicitor general of the United States and became the first black associate justice on the US Supreme Court.[41]

For his part, W. E. B. Du Bois used his talents to their best purpose by employing his superior intellect and remarkable facility with the written word to promote the cause. Moving from Atlanta to New York City in 1910, he edited the NAACP's monthly magazine, the *Crisis*, for twenty-four years. More than anything, his work on this publication established his reputation as a thoughtful commentator on race and the state of the Negro in the United States. The *Crisis* also published works by new black literary figures, including Langston Hughes and Countee Cullen of the Harlem Renaissance. Fending off an occasional effort to oust him from his position as editor—and after leaving the publication for a time—Du Bois lent his impassioned voice to the issues of the day, from the time of President William Howard Taft to the advent of the Great Depression and the accession of Franklin D. Roosevelt to the presidency. By the time he ended his tenure with the *Crisis*, Du Bois had moved beyond his earlier conversation with Booker T. Washington.[42]

In a long, distinguished career that saw Du Bois flirt briefly with socialism, publish numerous works on history and race, and investigate the ugly riots of the era, he was seldom far removed from the cause of civil rights. He eventually settled in Ghana, Africa, where he died at the age of ninety-five in 1963. At the time of Du Bois's death, his chief rival, Booker T. Washington, had been in his grave for almost forty-eight years. Time and circumstances had eclipsed the Wizard of Tuskegee, and the Washington–Du Bois conversation had given way to other, more strident debates. Some activists, such as the Jamaican Marcus Garvey, argued that blacks should depart for Africa rather than submit to the indignities of racism. Other black leaders called for radical action, even violence, to overthrow segregation. Du Bois supported many leftist causes and remained a controversial figure until the time he died, but he never fully embraced communism or the most radical policies of the time.[43]

The conversation between Booker T. Washington and W. E. B. Du Bois highlighted the stark choices and limited options available to people of color early in the twentieth century. No matter where blacks turned in the United States, they confronted the harsh reality of race, particularly in the South. In time, some disenchanted souls decided it was time to pull up stakes and head for a more hospitable place. If racial prejudice was rampant in the Deep South, perhaps opportunities in the North would be plentiful and the Jim Crow regime less rigid and brutal. Thus began one of the most important social, economic, political, and geographic movements in American history, an event that became known as the Great Migration.[44]

Part III

HE'S GONE ON HIGH TO PREPARE A PLACE

7

The Great Migration

"I Was Hoping I Would Be Able to Live as a Man"

A sense of place, of family, of tradition has long been part of the southern psyche. To say "My people hail from this county, this town, or this neighborhood" is to express a crucial part of one's identity. Traditionally, residents of Old Dixie considered themselves tied to the land, for agriculture was the primary means by which many folks eked out a living. Yet not everyone felt such pride of place. Whites and blacks together cherished their homeland, but members of the latter group sometimes were forced to qualify their allegiance owing to the degrading circumstances under which they lived and toiled. Colored people felt the terrible burden of existence in the Jim Crow South, and they longed for a better life—even if they must find that life elsewhere.

In folktales and word-of-mouth stories circulated in the backwoods and bayous of the Deep South, they spoke of getting out, heading north by any available means. It seemed that, at one time or another, everyone knew a fellow, or knew a fellow who knew a fellow, who had left the area and flourished in a new and better place. Excitement spread as the tales proliferated. Many Americans longed for a changing vista, the promise of a prosperous future somewhere over the horizon. Negroes naturally shared this wanderlust when they looked around and recognized the diminished choices they faced in their personal and professional lives.

Getting out was an inviting fantasy, but the reality was never a simple affair. A person could set out on foot, but such a journey was almost impossibly perilous. Instead, riding the rails and buses or hitching a ride from someone fortunate enough to own a working automobile was the preferred method. The trek could be expensive, so preparations usually involved months or even years of planning and penny-pinching. Impulsively leaving the community where one had been born, reared, and lived invited heartache and failure. Only a hearty, intrepid person who had meticulously charted a course could expect success.

Not everyone could depart, regardless of the level of planning. Some folks, especially the infirm or aged and those with unusually strong ties to the land, would never leave everything and everyone they knew. Their lives were hard, and their pockets were empty, but they preferred the devil they knew to the one they did not.

It takes a dedicated soul to walk away from the life he knows without a companion to share his trials. Although families were known to leave together, it was difficult for multiple family members to slip out of a community without attracting attention and perhaps inviting recriminations from local whites worried about the loss of a cheap labor source. The expenses could be onerous for an entire family. The logistics of providing for dependents during the days or weeks of the trip would complicate the exodus. Single males who owned little property aside from their meager personal possessions and had few ties to the community were the most promising prospects for migration, but it would be a mistake to conclude that only dispossessed men departed. Similarly, it would be erroneous to infer that impecunious colored folk were the sole travelers. The story of the Great Migration is one of men and women, boys and girls, the old and the young, the relatively affluent and the penniless, who set out, singularly and in pairs, to find a new place—if not quite paradise, at least a location more welcoming and accommodating than the hostile Jim Crow South.[1]

The numbers tell the tale. The total black population of the South increased from 4.2 million in 1860 to 7.9 million in 1900. In 1950, 10 million blacks lived in the region. Yet the 1950 figures, taken out of context, disguise a dramatic increase in the southern white population during that same time that a significant number of blacks left the region. Negroes comprised 34.4 percent of the southern population in 1860 and 32 percent in 1900. In 1900, 90 percent of black Americans lived south of the Mason-Dixon Line. Within seventy years, approximately half of the black population lived outside the region. This great demographic shift has rightly been called the Great Migration. From roughly 1915 until 1970, between 5 and 6 million black citizens departed from the Southland, never to return. If the Negro was not treated fairly in the land of cotton, he would find a place where he might enjoy a life free from the oppressive weight of segregation. Even if the mythical promised land did not exist, sometimes an uncertain future in a faraway land was preferable to one filled with unremitting labor and perpetual humiliation in a familiar place.[2]

CAUSES

Slavery had severely limited black mobility—which, of course, had been a major purpose of the peculiar institution. Keeping a race of people in chains ensured that white masters could rely on a ready source of labor. With the ratification of the Thirteenth Amendment in December 1865, slavery as a formal institution died. Whites employed a series of devices to keep Negroes tied to the land, but nothing was as efficient or effective as the legalized bondage of the antebellum days. Freedom of movement, however limited in practice, encouraged black migration from areas of harsh living to more hospitable environs.[3]

During the early days of Reconstruction, as federal troops patrolled the streets of many southern towns and northern men controlled state governments, black political equality appeared within reach. With the collapse of radical Reconstruction and the erosion of northern political support, the idea that Negroes would one day exercise their rights free

[7.1]   This famous Jacob Lawrence image depicts a scene from the Great Migration. Courtesy of the National Archives and Records Administration.

of intimidation and violence became increasingly unlikely, a dangerous, delusional pipe dream for any person of color who failed to recognize his place at the bottom of the southern hierarchy.[4]

White southerners in the post-Reconstruction era entertained strange notions about blacks, and these notions required the creation of deliberate fictions. Most whites harbored few doubts that their dark-skinned brethren were inferior beings. Sometimes the prejudice stemmed from pseudoscientific theories about race, but more often it was absorbed from friends and family. White citizens assumed that because they had been taught that Negroes were lesser people, it must be so. It appeared to be the natural order of things, and few possessed the critical self-awareness to challenge conventional wisdom. It was a convenient fiction on multiple levels, particularly because it provided a convenient rationale for white supremacy and unequal treatment of blacks. A white man need not mull over the ethics of "might makes right," which ultimately was the foundational principle of white supremacy. He could take comfort that his regime was not based on an odious, flawed theory of authoritarianism. Instead, blacks were treated as lesser human beings because they were, in fact, lesser human beings. According to white supremacist orthodoxy, to afford Negroes equal rights would be tantamount to setting Western civilization on the road to extinction. The consequences of these muddled bromides would affect the course of southern history for many generations.[5]

Naturally, whites who viewed blacks negatively expressed no desire to associate with these inferior creatures socially, culturally, or politically. Segregation thus became both the cause and effect of racism. Whites assumed that blacks were undesirable, so they kept blacks away from white society. By keeping blacks away, they learned little about them, which resulted in a desire to perpetuate segregation as a means of keeping these alien people at bay. The arrangement of southern society created a vicious tautology.

The fiction was that blacks and whites must not—and did not—mix, except in labor relations. The dirty little secret of southern society, of course, was the propensity of white men to have their way with black women under the cover of night, only to disavow any responsibility for the attendant consequences in the light of day. Such trysts had occurred regularly in the slave era, when black women had few options but to submit to the will of their white overlords. After slavery was abolished, white men still found the means to force themselves on black women through threats and intimidation. Many mixed-race children came of age knowing that their white fathers either held them in contempt or simply refused to acknowledge them.[6]

As if this hypocrisy were not galling enough, the great fear of many white southerners was that black men desperately wished to rape white women. This overriding concern drove much of the violence in southern history. As white apologists explained, miscegenation would destroy the purity of the white race. Yet, for all these supposed fears of amalgamation between the races, white men generally did not seem too concerned about the mulatto children spawned by their own sexual escapades across the color line.[7]

Another convenient fiction involved the economic relationship between whites and blacks. For all the antipathy that whites expressed toward blacks, one fact emerged despite whites' protests to the contrary. Southern whites needed southern blacks. The two races were inextricably tied together through mutual economic need. Whites needed laborers for their homes and fields, and blacks needed income. A bigoted white might desperately desire to segregate himself and his family from blacks, but he could never build a wall high enough to sever his dependency. Black men shouldered the most arduous burdens in cotton and tobacco fields—lifting heavy weights under a scorching sun and suffering the illnesses, injuries, and shortened lives that came with such labors. Black women raised white children and ran white households, changing soiled diapers, cooking white families' meals, and cleaning their dirty houses. If Negroes disappeared from the landscape, the most menial, distasteful, backbreaking work would fall on shoulders that were not wide or strong enough to carry the load.[8]

The southern paradox, therefore, was obvious to anyone who dared to look. Whites could not bear to treat blacks with dignity and respect; nor would they afford the Negro an equal standing under law. They looked down on their black neighbors. As a result, whites created barely tolerable, and in some instances intolerable, conditions under which blacks worked and lived. In response, many blacks reached a point where they could no longer exist under such conditions. They did what anyone would do: they cast an eye to the horizon and contemplated, in the words of a well-known book (paraphrasing Richard Wright), the warmth of other suns.[9]

Sometimes they gazed across a vast ocean and considered returning to the land of their ancestors. Many colonization schemes floated about during the nineteenth century. No less a public figure than Abraham Lincoln was known to favor such schemes, at least early in his presidency. Other leaders, even some within the black community, envisioned mass escapes to Liberia, Haiti, or other exotic, and presumably welcoming, locales. With only a few exceptions, these plans usually came to naught. The logistics and expenses associated with moving multitudes across a large body of water aside, colonization was not a panacea, even among blacks who worried that racism might never be eradicated. Many Negroes expressed no desire to uproot their lives and head off to a foreign land.

Their forbears might have lived in those places two, three, or ten generations past, but the current population did not see an advantage in leaving
the land of their birth. If they must abandon the South, they preferred to
head for another town or state within the United States.[10]

Realizing they might lose the source of their labor, whites reacted to
migration schemes with alarm and anger. Sometimes they improved
working conditions in hopes of enticing blacks to stay. The rich irony, of
course, was that whites were forced to upgrade conditions for the inferior
beings they apparently detested. In other cases, whites threatened their
black neighbors with bodily harm if they attempted to flee. Whether they
used the carrot or the stick, whites recognized that no matter how much
they wished to separate their social world from that of the Negro, they
could not extricate their economic well-being from the calculation. This
fundamental bifurcation between whites' desire to be apart from Negroes
and their need to employ Negroes complicated an already complex relationship and imbued southern society with a byzantine set of behavioral
rules.[11]

During the nineteenth century, the black migration away from the
South amounted to little more than a small trickle, hardly the torrent it
would become beginning in the World War I era. Nonetheless, during
the 1870s, some blacks fled the South for the Midwest, notably Kansas.
Freedmen who took to the road believed that the early promises of Reconstruction had not come to fruition. Life in the United States following
the demise of slavery was supposed to be an improvement for the newly
emancipated peoples. They were supposed to assimilate into society and
eventually take a seat at the table of liberty. When it became increasingly
clear that the promises would remain unfulfilled with the collapse of federal Reconstruction policy, some blacks were not content to submit to the
iron fist of white southern political leaders. They searched for a place that
would provide greater opportunities. No area of the United States was
entirely free of racial discrimination, but if an enclave of equal opportunity could be found, some blacks were determined to escape to it.[12]

The 1870s saw the rise of white vigilante groups such as the Ku Klux
Klan, which instituted a reign of terror in many southern states and prevented Negroes from enjoying their newly bestowed political rights. Even
when white mobs did not immediately threaten their safety, blacks typically were employed in backbreaking agricultural work for subsistence
wages that kept them indebted and anchored to the same plantations
where they had worked before emancipation. In some instances, the labor
contracts they were forced to sign provided minuscule improvements
over involuntary servitude. Later in the decade, the departure of federal
troops from southern soil left blacks to fend for themselves against

unscrupulous employers. For many Negroes, life in the South had become unbearable.[13]

Kansas appeared to be a promising prospect for black migration, and it was a logical choice. During the 1850s, the state had been the scene of violent clashes between abolitionists and slaveholders. The messianic abolitionist John Brown had called Kansas home, and many Negroes knew of the "free state" movement he came to symbolize. For lost souls who could no longer tolerate southern injustices, Kansas became a hopeful ideal, a place where black people could live free and exercise their hard-won civil rights.

Although numbers from the era are not always reliable, perhaps as many as fifty thousand blacks left the South in the late 1870s in search of a better life. Known as "Exodusters," these black emigrants joined an exodus out to western states. Some Negroes journeyed to Oklahoma and Colorado, in addition to Kansas. A former slave from Tennessee, Benjamin Singleton, was credited with organizing the effort, although the grass-roots nature of the Exoduster Movement extended beyond the efforts of a single person. Another charismatic former slave, Henry Adams of Louisiana, also encouraged blacks to travel to Kansas. Adams joined the pro-Kansas movement after his plans for establishing a colony in Liberia failed.[14]

As is often the case when people seek greener pastures, not everyone approved of the migration. The great civil rights leader Frederick Douglass denounced the effort. He understood the desires of desperate blacks who wished to build better lives for themselves and their children, but he worried that moving away from the problem would not solve it. If whites discriminated against blacks in one place, they could and would do so in another. Moreover, the journey itself could prove to be calamitous for impoverished families that possessed little money or property in the first place. Douglass was prescient in expressing his concerns. Sometimes the emigrants ran out of money along the way and were forced to settle down in little towns no better than those they had left behind. In some areas, blacks brought diseases with them, infecting townspeople who had no love for Negroes anyway. In St. Louis and other towns, citizens blamed a yellow fever outbreak on migrating Negroes and imposed limitations on who could move into the area.[15]

The US Senate investigated the matter beginning in 1879. In December of that year, the chamber passed a resolution:

Whereas large numbers of negroes from the Southern States are emigrating to the Northern States; and,

   Whereas it is currently alleged that they are induced to do so by the unjust and cruel conduct of their white fellow-citizens towards them in the South, and by the denial or abridgment of their personal and political rights and privileges: Therefore,

Be it resolved, That a committee of five members of this body be appointed by its presiding officer, whose duty it shall be to investigate the causes which have led to the aforesaid emigration, and to report the same to the Senate; and said committee shall have power to send for persons and papers, and to sit at any time.[16]

Three Democrats (Daniel W. Voorhees of Indiana, the chairman, as well as Zebulon B. Vance of North Carolina and George H. Pendleton of Ohio) and two Republicans (William Windom of Minnesota and Henry W. Blair of New Hampshire) served on the committee. Beginning in January 1880, committee members heard testimony from black and white witnesses from the states of North Carolina, Georgia, Alabama, Mississippi, Louisiana, Texas, Missouri, Kansas, and Indiana. When all was said and done, 153 people had testified.[17]

The Senate investigation revealed to some and reminded others that the precarious race relations in the United States were rife with misinformation and error. White southerners who had counted on subservient blacks to know their place and to labor on without complaint were shocked at the level of analysis and organization undertaken by departing Negroes. Well-educated black leaders such as Frederick Douglass, who had been working to secure better treatment for Negroes through the established power structure in the state and federal governments, were stunned that rural, uneducated blacks would take the initiative to move away from their homes en masse without the leadership of an elite black public figure. Many whites and blacks had assumed, rightly or wrongly, that race relations would either continue as they always had or improve, but whatever happened, the outcome would involve a southern solution to a southern problem. The Exoduster Movement, whatever else it accomplished and whatever its failures, demonstrated that blacks would not be content to wait in place for a solution.[18]

As much as the exodus of the late 1870s awakened wanderlust in the hearts of many blacks, another three decades passed before a major black migration occurred. It began around 1910, although some historians date the origins to around 1915, a year after the Great War erupted in Europe. No one planned for a major demographic change. Indeed, no one saw it coming. Yet it became a major event in the history of the United States. One historian labeled it "perhaps the biggest underreported story of the twentieth century."[19]

The question of why they left—and why they left when they did as opposed to at an earlier or later time—has been debated at length. The overall causes have been explained as a series of decisions reached by rational, autonomous agents. Human beings naturally move away from areas where they are treated badly (a push factor) to areas where they believe opportunities will be increased and treatment will improve (a pull factor). Economic factors were crucial components of the migration, but the quest for respect and dignity was also a strong motivator.[20]

The standard narrative suggests that the principal reasons for the migration were intertwined. Aside from running from the backbreaking work, innumerable humiliations, and omnipresent violence found in the South, many blacks gravitated toward attractive opportunities. Industrialization early in the twentieth century led to the creation of numerous factories, railroads, stockyards, and construction firms. Desperate for laborers, these industries raised wages and advertised available positions. Because industries tended to concentrate in cities—a successful manufacturing facility required a convenient transportation hub as well as a reliable base of nearby customers—industrialization evolved hand in hand with urbanization. When recent immigrants and southern Negroes heard stories of the opportunities available in northern industries, they flocked to cities in search of employment. For blacks, Chicago, Detroit, Cleveland, and New York City proved to be especially enticing. West Coast destinations were popular after 1940 as the nation geared up for wartime industrial production.[21]

The timing owed much to the changing world of the early twentieth century. Negroes were "pushed" to depart from the South when episodes of lynchings increased, Jim Crow laws were strictly enforced, and political disenfranchisement showed no signs of abating. As one black man explained his decision, he did not think about being part of a larger movement when he fled from the South. He left, he later recalled, because "I was hoping I would be able to live as a man and express myself in a manly way without the fear of getting lynched at night."[22]

"Pull" factors included the growing number of jobs created in northern factories, enhanced educational opportunities in northern schools, and stories circulating about the rise of a new black culture outside the South. Transportation was available to an extent unknown in the nineteenth century. Many blacks left the region because they had the desire and the means to do so.[23]

The migration may have occurred owing partially to generational change. By 1915, the Civil War had been over for half a century. Many of the men and women who had lived through the war and Reconstruction were dead. Two generations of young Negroes had no living memory of those earlier, turbulent times. They had not known firsthand the terror instilled by masked nightriders threatening to whip or hang uppity Negroes, and so they did not fear what they had never experienced. Older black people, recalling the social control exercised by white vigilantes, may have lost the will to take action apart from trying to survive day to day. Young people knew none of what their elders had experienced, but they knew they were being denied the basic legal, political, social, and economic rights they thought had been promised to their parents and grandparents. They had waited long enough for leaders of both races to fix the obvious inequities in the lives of colored folks. Denied the franchise, which likely would have allowed them to vote responsive political leaders into office, perhaps they realized the best way to vote was with their feet. In the final analysis, however, the migration was not a conscious act of collective civil disobedience or political will as much as a lonely decision made by each individual, eventually joined by hundreds of thousands of like-minded individuals, to get out while the getting was good. If the means existed and the opportunity presented itself, a fellow had better take it.[24]

EFFECTS

The migration did not come without a price. Sometimes entire families moved, but in other cases one or more family members went on ahead to pave the way for others. The time apart could be, and often was, disruptive to family functions. Because no government assistance was provided, blacks either saved their money to finance the move or worked their way across several states by taking a series of menial jobs that sometimes left them stuck in places as undesirable as those they had left behind. As they arrived in new cities and showed up at factory gates, eager for gainful employment, they sometimes discovered that promises made were not promises delivered. Even when they found new jobs, wages sometimes were considerably lower than advertised, or the scope of employment was not nearly as rewarding as the bosses had indicated.[25]

Blacks typically entered the labor pool at the lower end of the market. Their lack of advanced education and inability to negotiate favorable terms ensured that they would perform the most menial and low-paying tasks. Nonetheless, southerners frequently secured gainful employment in higher percentages than northern blacks. Many reasons have been posited for this curious phenomenon, not the least being the eagerness with which new arrivals took to their work and their willingness to complete burdensome tasks that many northern denizens refused to undertake. Another explanation suggests that northern blacks had become accustomed to heavy, repetitive factory labor and realized that they would never advance beyond an entry-level position. Southern blacks may have viewed factory work as a step-up from sharecropping, which would explain their relative zeal for joining the payroll, while northerners had become disillusioned and jaded because they had toiled under disadvantageous factory conditions for a long time.

All hope was not lost. Over time, black factory workers moved up in the ranks, albeit at a glacial pace. They made great strides in the meatpacking, steel, shipbuilding, and automotive industries of the industrial North, nearly doubling the number of workers in heavy industry between 1910 and 1920. In 1910, approximately half a million Negroes labored in those industries. The number grew to over nine hundred thousand by the end of the decade. With the advent of the Great Depression, workers, black and white, in these and other industries banded together to join labor unions. Blacks were drawn to the Congress of Industrial Organizations (CIO) owing to its willingness to protect workers regardless of race. In many cases, the CIO was responsible for ending segregation in employment, a major step in the budding civil rights movement of the twentieth century.[26]

Economic concerns were important, but they were not the sole determinant in a migrant's decision to move to a particular city or area. The choice depended on many factors. If family already resided in the new location, this became an overriding consideration. Having relations in the town or city where one settled would smooth the way, providing housing, job leads, and a welcoming presence, which significantly reduced anxiety for newly arriving citizens. As large numbers of family members arrived and carved out neighborhoods, imbuing them with their identities, different areas became known for the characteristics of their inhabitants. It was common in big cities to identify an area as the black-Mississippian neighborhood, the black-Louisianan neighborhood, or, when the immigrants hailed from foreign shores, the black-Haitian neighborhood, and so forth.[27]

If a newly arriving resident possessed no familial ties, he or she chose a specific city or neighborhood for other reasons. Reports of plentiful jobs unquestionably served as an attractive "pull" feature for a community, but peripatetic southern Negroes also searched for a thriving community of black churches, schools, newspapers, or civil rights organizations, such as the National Association for the Advancement of Colored People or the National Urban League. The presence of one or more of these institutions convinced a new arrival that a given place was a welcoming one in which to start a new life. The importance of churches in the black community was especially crucial and often influenced the decision to an extraordinary degree. In some instances, southern transplants seeking the familiar cadences and rhythms of churches back home started new "southern-style" churches in the North.[28]

Locating clean, affordable housing proved to be challenging, especially in large cities where few accommodations existed. Blacks usually worked and lived in the poorest parts of a city, which meant that housing was dilapidated, dirty, cramped, or nonexistent. Sometimes recent migrants shared a room to hold down expenses and ensure that everyone had a roof over his or her head. Even when they could find a place to call home, southern blacks expressed shock at the higher prices in the North, especially for rent in buildings that were little more than slums. In some large cities, the lack of housing became alarming as increasing numbers of arrivals poured into an area already being transformed into a ghetto.[29]

Nowhere was the continuing discrimination against Negroes as visible as in housing. Southern blacks had fled the unrelenting burdens of the Jim Crow South, but they were under no illusions. The North was not a land of paradise, and equal justice under law remained as elusive as ever. Racial discrimination often occurred owing to fear. White northerners became alarmed as they saw more black faces in their neighborhoods. Worried that changing demographics would drive down property values and perhaps import crime into the area, they pushed community leaders to stem the rising tide of immigrants. In response, white mortgage brokers employed racial covenants to restrict who could buy and sell houses in particular markets. Sometimes the local banker or insurance agent would employ redlining, a process of charging people of color substantially more for their services than they charged whites. The presupposition was that the blacks streaming into northern cities and towns were fleeing a checkered past and would only contaminate the neighborhood with their low-class values and propensity to engage in mischief.[30]

This fear of invading blacks was not unexpected in light of the stereotypes of the day. The typical Negro moving from the Deep South into a northern city was believed to be an impoverished, illiterate sharecropper beaten down by life. He had little stake in the new community because he was a rootless soul, moving from place to place, seeking something that might not exist—a promised land. While this image was not altogether inaccurate, historians have noted that these individuals were a more diverse lot than some early studies suggested. Blacks from cities and towns who worked in nonagricultural jobs also flocked into major metropolises in search of improved opportunities. The demographic characteristics of the migrants varied over time as conditions changed in parts of the South and in the host cities. When word circulated that some areas, especially New York City's Harlem, had become enclaves of black cultural and business activity, ambitious men and women naturally sought to be a part of the scene.[31]

The tide could and would not be stemmed, despite the best efforts of fearful northern whites. For all the injustices and hardships found in the North, they were seldom as brutal and unremitting as the indignities of the Jim Crow South. The promise of improvement, however fleeting and unrealistic, was preferable to the dark reality of life in Dixie, and the absence of a panacea for the racial divide in the United States did not preclude the possibility of finding something better.[32]

And so, as the years passed and the migration continued largely unabated, the large cities of the northern United States grew even larger. Some previously all-white urban areas were transformed within a relatively few years. In 1910, for example, only six thousand blacks lived in Detroit. Within twenty years, the number had ballooned to 120,000. Cleveland, Ohio, saw a rapid influx of Negroes during those years as well. Chicago's demographic shift was especially dramatic. In 1910, the city was home to 44,103 blacks, according to the US Census Bureau. Sixty years later, as the Great Migration ended, 1,102,620 blacks lived in the Windy City—an increase from 2 to 32.7 percent of the city's population.[33]

Tensions invariably mounted as blacks streamed into large cities at the same time that a large wave of immigrants, mostly from Europe, arrived on American shores. Crowded, frequently substandard housing, competition for jobs and wages, and the usual stereotypes about Negroes and foreigners led to violent clashes. Ethnic Irish immigrants especially battled with transplanted southern blacks to the detriment of both groups. Major American cities that had featured virtually all-white populations at the turn of the twentieth century soon became bastions of black and ethnic residents.[34]

The Old South experienced the effects of the migration as well. In many states, the so-called Black Belt was no longer so black anymore. In 1910, around the time that the first wave of the Great Migration began, the populations in Mississippi and South Carolina were more than 50 percent black. In Alabama, Georgia, Louisiana, and Texas, the number was around 40 percent. Sixty years later, only Mississippi's black population approached 30 percent. The mass exodus represented one of the greatest demographic shifts in American history. Although some blacks who decamped for the North eventually returned to Dixie, most escapees did not.[35]

Much of the dirty, physically demanding workload that southern blacks had carried in earlier times now fell to the white population. Whites in the lower echelon often recoiled at the exhausting nature of the work, to say nothing of the low pay and horrific conditions. Although labor unions remained relatively rare in the region, white southerners pushed for improved working conditions and usually managed to engender at least incremental change. Blacks, by contrast, had seldom been able to alter the terms of their labor.[36]

LONG-TERM CONSEQUENCES

Because it was a grassroots movement with no recognizable leaders and no clear political objective, the Great Migration caught many people by surprise. By the time urban planners understood what was happening, the characteristics of major US cities were already changing rapidly. Their infrastructures were strained to capacity.[37]

Two overall trends emerged. Blacks learned, much to their dismay, that many of the prejudices and discriminatory practices so prevalent in the South had followed them from the cotton fields, tobacco farms, and rice fields on their trek to the urban landscape. Jim Crow was a distinctly southern creature, but the factors that led to segregation did not disappear when they left him behind. The arrival of scores of black faces in a neighborhood triggered alarm among Caucasian residents convinced that Negroes brought low values and high crime rates with them. As soon as they could afford to do so, many whites who had lived in inner cities for generations fled to the suburbs. The pace of white flight accelerated after World War II, when the construction of modern highways, the passage of the GI Bill to fund improved education for veterans, and the advent of a new suburban culture provided a means by which middle-class citizens could conveniently alter their lifestyles and change their locales.[38]

As whites fled the city proper, jobs eventually followed them to the outskirts of town. Black citizens who remained inside the city limits soon found the infrastructure crumbling to a greater extent than it had before the white exodus. With a dwindling tax base from which to finance repairs and improvements, and with typical patterns of discrimination hampering the political will to rescue cities, in time the downtown areas of dozens of formerly productive, convivial metropolises resembled war zones in third-world nations. The War on Poverty, President Lyndon B. Johnson's controversial and not altogether successful federal initiative to counter urban blight and reverse the decline of the black middle class (among other things), occurred at the end of the Great Migration. In the meantime, black migrants vividly realized that poverty and racial inequities were not solely the province of the southern states.[39]

The second trend was more positive. Southern blacks who had barely eked out a living on the farms of their youth found a measure of economic prosperity in the North that could not be called luxurious but was certainly a step up from the poverty they had known previously. As wage laborers in northern factories, Negroes enjoyed a freedom of movement and opportunity they had not known before. In the South, a landless worker either scratched out a living as a sharecropper or tenant farmer tied to a specific parcel owned by a white landlord or wandered from farm to farm seeking work as a day laborer at barely subsistence wages.

The options were severely limited, and the mileage between farms could be burdensome for a destitute soul. In large northern cities, numerous factories were easily reached on foot or via public transportation. With high turnover rates and flexible schedules, factories frequently required large numbers of workers to churn out their products. An ambitious young person could earn more money laboring on the factory floor than he ever could back on the farm. Even stuck in menial positions in the lowest economic stratum, he had more options than in southern agricultural pursuits.

Black migrants congregated with other like-minded individuals and discovered similar tastes in food, clothing, and entertainment. In many big cities, black neighborhoods enjoyed a blossoming of cultural activity that would have been unimaginable in a southern farming community. The Harlem Renaissance of the 1920s and 1930s was the most famous flowering of black culture associated with the Great Migration. Black prose writers, poets, artists, and musicians practiced their crafts and established a creative, cultural output of astonishing quality and variety. Best of all from the black perspective, such achievements did not depend upon white society or white permission. Black artists carved out an identity uniquely their own.[40]

Entrepreneurs soon discovered opportunities that would never have existed under the heavy hand of Jim Crow. An urban neighborhood of thriving black workers required goods and services—grocery stores, barber shops, banks, insurance agencies, doctors, lawyers, and so on. The white community often withheld these goods and services or insisted that blacks pay a premium for those offered. With the growth of a black wage class, black businesses could fill the gaps left by recalcitrant white businesses. In time, black neighborhoods recognized the economic and political clout that came with consolidated purchasing power, and they preferred to patronize black-owned businesses. A healthy black middle class—a rarity throughout the land before the Great Migration—arose in big cities such as New York, Chicago, and Detroit.[41]

Aside from engendering a thriving black culture and economy, the Great Migration threw blacks and whites together in large numbers for the first time in generations. Segregation had ensured that interactions between the races were limited in scope and duration, creating an invisible color line where the rules were unwritten but nonetheless strictly enforced. Woe to the hapless soul who tripped across the color line, for he would be severely punished for his unpardonable transgression, especially if he were black. Segregation laws ensured that whites would forever regard a Negro as the alien "other," a shadowy, not quite trustworthy, unquestionably inferior figure.[42]

In the North, blacks and whites did not coexist in an uninhibited manner, but they found themselves engaged in social intercourse in ways that would not have been tolerated in the land of Jim Crow. Although a color line existed in the North and Midwest, generally it was not as fixed and inviolable as in the South. In Harlem, for example, white adolescents and young adults sometimes ventured into black neighborhoods to enjoy music, art, and other cultural activities. Part of the titillating excitement of the experience was the not-quite-proper journey from the white area of town to the black streets and juke joints. Whatever the motivations, a subtle socialization process occurred. Whites and blacks discovered that for all their well-publicized differences, they shared similar cultural tastes. Individuals of another race could not be as alien as advertised if they enjoyed the same art, books, and music as their white counterparts. In some ways, gradually and imperceptibly, the occasional mingling of northern whites and blacks eroded the social position of the races that had so long characterized the American way of life.[43]

The migration slowed during the Great Depression years of the 1930s. Many Americans of all races simply did not have the funds to pull up stakes and move. Even if they somehow scraped together enough money, specific destinations no longer proved as enticing as in earlier years. The factory jobs that had attracted thousands during the 1920s disappeared with the economic downturn.[44]

Historians refer to the Second Great Migration that occurred in the years following World War II, a time when Negroes' willingness and ability to move rebounded. As black soldiers returned home from the war beginning in 1945, they were ready to leave the humble, impoverished backwaters where they had come of age. Having seen parts of the world outside the United States, they understood that race-based segregation need not be a society's paramount organizing principle. Other countries, some considered less developed than the United States, allowed persons of color to come and go as they chose with little or no restriction. Black veterans chafed at a social system that circumscribed their lives. After fighting for their country, they demanded equal treatment as compensation, if nothing else, for sacrifices they and their families had made. Blacks had lost some of their provincial blindness and learned that alternatives existed to the southern way of life. With money more plentiful after years of scarcity and rationing, Americans more than ever were restless and dissatisfied with the status quo. Black Americans shared the desire for change.[45]

By the 1970s, the Second Great Migration had ended. Americans remained mobile, but movement that once had flowed as a torrent slowed to a trickle. Although debate continues over the reasons for the end of the migration, the overriding cause probably was the change in American society and culture. *Brown v. Board of Education of Topeka*, the US Supreme Court case that desegregated public schools, and a host of subsequent opinions changed the legal requirements imposed on major public institutions in the United States. The modern civil rights movement did much to call attention to the plight of the Negro and the inequities faced by citizens of multiple races and ethnicities. Major federal legislation, including the Civil Rights Act of 1964, the Voting Rights Act of 1965, and the Fair Housing Act of 1968, began dismantling the edifice of segregation so methodically constructed in the eighty years following the end of Reconstruction. The Twenty-Fourth Amendment to the US Constitution, ratified in 1964, prohibited poll taxes, a major weapon employed by southern segregationists to deny people of color the franchise.[46]

It is a truism that a society cannot legislate morality; nor can hearts and minds be won through changes to the formal institutions of government. But legislation can set the stage for changing attitudes, and formal mechanisms can push individuals and groups to alter their reactions to government policies. New generations coming of age under new laws and institutions can respond accordingly. A young white child looking across the classroom and seeing a black child looking back will not evince a racist attitude if he has not been taught to hate and kept apart from that black child. The black child will not feel inferior if he has not been shown in a thousand ways that he is inferior to the white child sitting across the room.

The United States remained a nation practicing apartheid until well into the twentieth century. Change was slow in coming, but come it did. As blacks departed from the South in waves, at least a few white Americans recognized that something was terribly wrong with the American system. The modern civil rights movement would accelerate the pace of that recognition and hasten the day of reckoning, but the Great Migration partially initiated the process of change.[47]

8

A Nadir of Race Relations

"It Is Like Writing History with Lightning"

The 1920s are remembered as a respite between two debilitating world wars and an unprecedented global economic depression. At the end of the Great War in 1918, the United States emerged as a global power, while exhausted European nations struggled to recover from the horror of the trenches. Yet for all their newfound prestige and prominence, Americans were weary from the fight and wary of global entanglements. In their view, they had paid a high price in blood and treasure to intervene in European affairs. What had it all been for? The recapture of acres of blood-drenched French and Belgian soil had not been worth more than one hundred thousand lives, and yet that was the human cost of the foreign adventure in 1917 and 1918. As if that price were not high enough, more than six times as many Americans fell victim to the deadly influenza outbreak of 1918 and 1919 than had perished on European battlefields—a consequence, many people believed, of exposing farm-fed young men to overcrowded, infectious conditions among the great unwashed masses of an alien land.[1]

At the dawn of a new decade, no one had the stomach for delving into complex social or political issues, foreign or domestic, especially involving intractable problems such as race relations. A tired population sought to revel in peaceful, happy days. They got their wish for a time. When Republican Warren G. Harding won the 1920 presidential election, his supporters realized their earnest desire for a "return to normalcy." Harding pledged that he would not oversee a vigorous, progressive administration that would tax the pocketbooks or consciences of the American

194

public. With only a few minor exceptions, he seemed as good as his word until his sudden death in 1923 revealed a series of corrupt practices that undermined faith in government for years to come.[2]

Compared with the previous decade, the 1920s are romanticized as a frivolous, carefree, glorious decade highlighted by a laissez-faire attitude toward private-sector economics and the rise of a new popular culture— Vaudeville, motion pictures, and "flappers." Heroes of mass culture emerged, including the suave, debonair movie idol Rudolph Valentino, the death-defying magician and escape artist Harry Houdini, and "Lucky" Lindy, Charles Lindbergh, the unassuming aviation pioneer who completed a dramatic transatlantic airplane crossing despite long odds. Babe Ruth and Lou Gehrig, both in their prime, slugged baseballs over the fence with breathtaking regularity. Resistance to Prohibition's laws forbidding alcohol sales and consumption, as well as a less inhibited view of sexual mores, lent an edge of danger and salaciousness to the era. Even the lawless antics of Al Capone and the gangster class were somehow exciting and entertaining, at least if viewed from a safe distance.[3]

Despite the carefree lives portrayed in popular culture, all was not well, particularly for people of color. While middle-class and affluent white Americans enjoyed a lively era, Negroes were less fortunate. Their ill fortune could be traced back to a time well before the 1920s. The first three decades of the twentieth century arguably represented the nadir of race relations in the United States. Lynchings remained an all-too-frequent occurrence in instances when black men reputedly crossed the color line to harass white women. Education for colored folk was limited to six or seven years of basic instruction in poorly funded, inferior public schools. The few Negroes who graduated and moved on to college typically went to historically black institutions because so few white schools admitted Negroes and those that did provided only a small number of seats under less than ideal conditions. Employment opportunities for colored workers were limited to backbreaking agricultural labor, domestic service, or factory work, performing the dirty, demeaning jobs that no one else wanted.[4]

In the aftermath of the Civil War, although slaves' literal shackles fell away, figurative shackles remained firmly in place. The dominant white culture continued to treat Negroes as inferior beings. These attitudes were reflected in myriad ways, sometimes overtly, sometimes subtly. A pervasive culture of debasement ensured that the context of race relations would begin and end with one self-evident truth: in the words of Alexander Stephens, vice president of the Southern Confederacy, "the negro is not equal to the white man." For all the talk of equality in the Declaration of Independence and the subsequent efforts to ensure a measure of equal treatment under law through mechanisms such as the Emancipation Proclamation, the Civil War amendments to the US Constitution, and various legislative enactments, colored people, even when not physically attacked or denied their political rights, were dismissed as lesser creatures unworthy of full citizenship or consideration.[5]

When Reconstruction died and white supremacy became a civil religion in the South, the public image of black citizens was open to interpretation and therefore endlessly malleable. For whites who knew of Negroes only as inferiors—former slaves, field hands, day laborers, domestic servants, imprisoned convicts—the popular depiction of a black person as the "other," a being somehow alien and existing apart from white culture and society, was not challenged. The Jim Crow regime ensured that blacks would always stand apart: whites would never mingle with the strange, enigmatic Negro or count him as a neighbor and friend, but the only way to know a person of color as such would be to mingle with him. "Separate but equal" guaranteed disparate, inferior treatment of the "other."[6]

Throughout the years from Reconstruction until well into the next century, popular culture in the United States treated non-Caucasians as strange creatures. This way of thinking did not happen overnight or as part of a coordinated campaign. It was a subtle, gradual process that usually moved quietly but inexorably. At approximately the same time that southern state legislatures passed segregation statutes in the 1880s and 1890s, mass-circulation newspapers became popular throughout the United States. Newspapers had served as an important source of news and political opinion since the earliest days of the republic, but technological advances and lowered costs resulted in wider circulation. They were no longer strictly the province of well-educated opinion leaders, for numerous rags were inexpensive and readily available. The masses could, and frequently did, gain access to publications as one century drew to a close and another beckoned. Owners and editors anxious to boost sales catered to the needs and desires of their readership, which meant that hard news stories about state and nation, while important, were not the only features to attract subscribers. Newspapers increasingly included sections that proved to be popular among all classes of readers—cartoons and advertisements.[7]

IMAGES OF BLACKS IN CARTOONS

Cartoons had existed for years, but they became ubiquitous with the advent of a popular, inexpensive press. Thomas Nast made a name for himself as the foremost political cartoonist of his day during the 1860s and 1870s, drawing popular images such as the Republican elephant, the Democratic donkey, Santa Claus, and a familiar symbol of the United

States, Uncle Sam. By the 1890s, however, Nast's cartooning style was in decline. Comic strips featuring recurring characters that told a story over several frames became the rage. It wasn't long before Negroes appeared in the strips, and their images both reflected and perpetuated demeaning stereotypes.[8]

Thomas Worth's *Darktown Comics* was among the earliest and most popular series of sketches depicting Negroes in the 1880s and 1890s. Published by Currier and Ives as inexpensive hand-colored prints, each segment in the series proved to be a best seller. Typically, each comic showed a before-and-after scene highlighting the buffoonery of Negroes. The first panel showed blacks engaged in some common activity—playing sports, arguing politics, driving a team of horses, attending a party, and so forth. The supposed humor sprang from the second panel. The sporting event collapsed into anarchy, the political discussion degenerated into fisticuffs, the team of horses was derailed, or the party became a disastrous brouhaha. The central message was clear: Negroes were incapable of performing even the simplest of common tasks or engaging in ordinary social intercourse without lapsing into idiocy or violence. Judging by their willingness to snap up the latest lithographs, whites found these images hilarious, or at least well worth the modest purchase price.[9]

Another sign of things to come occurred in 1893. The World's Columbian Exposition, held in Chicago from May through October to celebrate America's emergence as an industrial powerhouse, agreed to schedule a "Colored People's Day" on August 25. Many blacks expressed reluctance to attend for fear they would be laughed and jeered at as spectacles themselves. Their fears were realized when the popular weekly periodical *Puck*, renowned for its biting wit, published cartoonist Frederick Opper's drawing titled "Darkies' Day at the Fair." The cartoon included many insulting images associated with Negroes. A "Grand Parade of the Sons of Ham" showed a procession of blacks dressed as spear-carrying jungle natives adorned in grass skirts, as well as ornately dressed "coons" and ridiculously attired military men. The motley assortment of coloreds lined up to buy watermelons, an appropriate activity since the fair organizers had ordered twenty-five hundred melons to feed the expected crowd of Negro attendees that day. Each caricature sported thick lips, coal-dark skin, and a mischievous grin, except for Major Moon, the "saddened coon" who had hoped to sell his melons, but "he got no pay."[10]

More cartoon strips depicting black characters followed. An Ohio artist, Richard F. Outcault, drew a number of popular comic strips from the 1890s until the 1920s. He became well known for creating a character called the "Yellow Kid" in the series *Hogan's Alley*, a strip he started in 1895. In *Here's the New Bully*, a cartoon that appeared in the *New York World*, Outcault depicted a dangerous Negro street tough based on popu-

A LITERARY DEBATE IN THE DARKTOWN CLUB.
The Question Settled.

[8.1] *Darktown Comics*, a popular series of prints produced by Currier and Ives during the 1880s and 1890s, depicted scenes of black Americans engaged in mischief. This illustration, circa 1885, shows the results of a debate between two Negroes who have settled the question through violence. Two pictures on the wall, "A. Linkum" and "U. S. Grant," "honor" the men who led the northern effort to defeat the South in the Civil War. Above the picture of Grant, the slogan for his 1868 presidential campaign, "Let Us Have Peace," has been obliterated. A sign featuring "G. Washington" has been used to clobber one of the men. Courtesy of the Library of Congress.

lar notions of blacks as brutes. Abandoning that strip, Outcault went on to create the popular Buster Brown character. Buster Brown enjoyed a long, storied career, including a stint as the symbol for an eponymous brand of shoes.

Between drawing *Hogan's Alley* and *Buster Brown*, Outcault created a black character, Pore Lil Mose. Mose initially appeared in the *New York Herald* in January 1901 and was the first major black figure to serve as the central character in a comic strip. The stories featured two diverse settings. In Cottonville, Georgia (nicknamed "Coon Town"), the black residents were indolent, irresponsible, and larcenous. They constantly stole watermelons, ran from ghosts, and engaged in shenanigans expected of southern Negroes. In the face of this stereotypical behavior, Mose and his animal buddies cavorted about innocently in his small-town environment. When Outcault had Mose and his critters visit New York City, the artist delighted in highlighting the humor that resulted from country blacks blundering their way through unfamiliar terrain, including scenes with well-known northern landmarks such as Coney Island, streetcars, and department stores. Outcault was never progressive on race, but for his time, and despite the offensive stereotypes of most characters, his portrayal of this young colored child was sweet and marginally sympathetic.[11]

In some ways, the *Pore Lil Mose* strip was reminiscent of the Uncle Remus stories first published by white author Joel Chandler Harris in the 1870s. A newspaperman by trade, Harris also collected folklore. He was interested in the black oral tradition and sought to preserve the animal stories and songs he had heard. The tales resembled Aesop's fables. Colorful animal characters, most notably Br'er Rabbit, taught valuable moral lessons to readers by showing the folly of some actions and the wisdom of others. Uncle Remus was a kindly old former slave who spoke in a traditional Negro dialect to children gathered around to hear his tales. The stories were first compiled into a book late in 1880 and were enormously popular. They would remain a staple of children's literature for more than eighty years, until some critics pointed to the depiction of the "uncle" character and his broken English as demeaning to blacks. Nonetheless, compared with many other images of colored folk, Pore Lil Mose and Uncle Remus, while undoubtedly paternalistic and one-dimensional, were relatively benign.[12]

Sambo was perhaps the most enduring black character to emerge from American folklore. In 1899, a Scottish author, Helen Bannerman, published *The Story of Little Black Sambo*. The original edition's illustrations showed a child of mixed-race heritage, which was in keeping with the text. Sambo was a South Indian boy who lived with his parents, Black Jumbo and Black Mumbo. Bannerman apparently did not intend to tap into the "darky iconography"—the formal, scholarly designation for drawings of blacks with big lips, frizzy hair, and bulbous eyes—but she was playing off the word "Sambo." The term originated sometime during the eighteenth century and derives from the Spanish word *zambo*, which refers to a person with Native American and African blood.[13]

Until the early twentieth century, "Sambo" usually was not considered a derogatory term. English novelist William Makepeace Thackeray's celebrated novel from the 1840s, *Vanity Fair*, referred to a dark-skinned Indian servant named Sambo. In 1852, Harriet Beecher Stowe featured an overseer named Sambo in *Uncle Tom's Cabin*. During the nineteenth century, "Sambo" was used as a stereotypical name for people of color, often when they were "mulatto," or of mixed-race origins. It became a common description in the Spanish and Portuguese cultures as well as in parts of

Latin America. The term evolved into a commonly used racial epithet in the early 1900s.[14]

William Marriner popularized the American Negro version of the character in his strip *Sambo and His Funny Noises* between 1905 and 1914. The exaggerated features were all there—Sambo's bulbous eyes, protruding lips, tortured dialect, and seeming inability to reason his way out of even the simplest and most inane situations. The humor, such as it was, arose from Sambo's backwardness and ignorance of the ways of the world. The strip frequently ended with Sambo taking a knock on his hard head or otherwise being defeated by his white antagonists. On the rare occasions when Sambo emerged triumphant, he did so accidentally, as when he tripped and avoided a blow from a tormentor or escaped the clutches of an evildoer through happenstance.[15]

Even after Marriner no longer penned his strip, "Sambo" or "little black Sambo" remained a well-known stereotype, an encapsulation of white peoples' standard view of Negroes, especially children, as somehow innocent, naive, simplistic, and stupid. The images occasionally were sympathetic, but far more often they were paternalistic and insulting. Sambo became the best known of the perennially popular pickaninny stereotypes.[16]

Depictions of pickaninnies differed slightly over time, but mostly they were caricatures—cartoons or photographs—of black children with coal-dark skin, large, often blood-red, grotesquely protruding lips, and wild, nappy hair. Attired in tattered, ill-fitting clothing, the little ragamuffins frequently engaged in offensive or outrageous behavior owing to their innate stupidity. One often reproduced scene shows a pickaninny sucking on a straw dipped into an inkwell sporting the caption "mother's milk" or "nigger milk." The implication was that coal-black skin came from ingesting ink. Other scenes showed pickaninnies shoveling watermelon or fried chicken into their large, greedy mouths. Still other scenes depicted ravenous alligators preparing to devour "gator bait" black children, or pigs encountering pickaninnies and asking, "Whose baby is 'oo?"[17]

In 1957, Sam Battistone Sr. and Newell Bohnett opened a restaurant that eventually became a chain. Little did they realize in 1957 that they would insert themselves into a nasty racial controversy. For the restaurant's name, they combined Battistone's first name with the first two letters of Bohnett's last name: it became Sambo's. As a marketing gimmick, the founders decorated the walls with characters and scenes from *The Story of Little Black Sambo*. By 1979, the chain had spread to forty-seven states, with more than eleven hundred restaurants. When public anger about the name grew during the 1970s, however, Sambo's operators realized that times had changed and they had better change too. After experimenting with different names and management concepts, the company filed for bankruptcy protection in 1981 and wound down operations. As of this writing, the only remaining restaurant from the original chain was Sambo's on the Beach in Santa Barbara, California. The restaurant's tag line was "Keep calm; eat pancakes."[18]

Even when not originally intended to be demeaning, Sambo and similar characters perpetuated myths and stereotypes that had existed for decades. Such images were not limited to children, either, although cartoons showing full-grown Negroes did not always portray adults as benign creatures. Adult caricatures ranged from the kindly mammy—traditionally a fat old black domestic servant wearing a rag wrapped around her head and calling the "chil'ren" in for supper—to the dangerous black brute loose on the prowl, anxious to snare a white woman and defile her to satisfy his deviant sexual appetite. Black adults sometimes were happy-go-lucky simpletons, dancing about, flapping their arms, and bumbling around comically. They could be cunning, menacing, mischievous, and randy, but they were never three-dimensional human beings. Illustrations of colored people were drawn from the perspective of whites who, thanks to segregation, had only limited contact with blacks and never knew, or cared to know, their hearts and minds. Whites knew only the mask "that grins and lies," that "hides our cheeks and shades our eyes," in the words of poet Paul Laurence Dunbar.[19]

STEREOTYPES OF BLACKS IN ADVERTISEMENTS

With no understanding of the black psyche and no genuine interest in discovering it, whites usually greeted the popular images with approval. As the stereotypes solidified, they appeared in advertisements for products that whites were likely to purchase. Among the earliest of the commercial depictions of stock black characters occurred in the 1880s, just as many southern states were enacting segregation statutes. The N. K. Fairbank Company of Chicago offered a product known as Gold Dust washing powder, a reference to its color and fine, granular, powdery form. A company executive had seen a cartoon in the British humor magazine *Punch* showing two black children washing each other in a tub. "Warranted to wash clean and not fade," the caption claimed. This "joke" struck the executive as so funny that he decided it would be a clever advertisement for Gold Dust washing powder.

By 1887, artist E. W. Kembel had produced a series of drawings of the fictional Gold Dust Twins. They morphed over time into two black figures with all the usual physical characteristics of pickaninnies. During a Chicago trade convention in 1902, two real-life black children were selected to portray the twins, although the use of live models did not last for long. The images, however, remained popular, and "Goldie" and "Dustie" could be spotted frequently on billboards, posters, buttons, tin containers, calendars, trade cards, and other promotional items, many of which became expensive collectibles. The product slogan, "Let the Gold Dust Twins do your work," became almost as well known as the images themselves.[20]

Another popular advertisement of the era featured ol' Rastus, a grinning black chef who became associated with the Cream of Wheat brand of breakfast porridge. It came about without much advance planning. Three businessmen from Grand Forks, North Dakota—George Bull, Emery Mapes, and George Clifford—bought the Diamond Milling Company in 1890 and churned out flour. Their Scottish-born head miller, Thomas Amidon, prevailed on the owners to offer his "middling" breakfast porridge for sale. In the meantime, Mapes stumbled upon an old woodcut of a smiling Negro chef carved onto a skillet. The skillet became a mold for the image that adorned packages of the "middling" product he called Cream of Wheat. Mapes referred to the Negro chef as Rastus, a reference to a happy-go-lucky stock Negro character who cavorted about in minstrel shows of the time.

Cream of Wheat was popular almost as soon as it appeared. In fact, it proved to be so popular that the Diamond Milling Company stopped producing flour, changed its name, and offered up Cream of Wheat exclusively. The woodcut served as a trademark until 1925, when Mapes happened to be dining in a Chicago restaurant and noticed the broad, smiling face of his black waiter. He persuaded the good-natured man to pose in a chef's hat for $5, and a new mascot was born. The new smiling-chef image replaced the older symbol and became iconic. The model for the 1920s version of Rastus never received additional compensation for the use of his image, and his subsequent whereabouts are unknown.

The Cream of Wheat advertisements varied, but typically they showed Rastus wearing a smock and a chef's hat, sometimes discussing the virtues of the product in a tortured Negro dialect with one or more of his relatives. When Rastus interacted with other Negroes, his pals always appeared as stereotypical pickaninnies or adult domestic workers. Other advertisements showed Rastus working in the fields to harvest the good old Cream of Wheat. He could be seen on occasion spooning up the breakfast food for happy, smiling white children, who were secure in the knowledge that this servile, asexual black man meant no harm and could be counted on to dish out some mighty good victuals. In one noteworthy advertisement, recalling a popular nursery rhyme, Rastus served Cream of Wheat to a little white girl dressed in fancy clothes. The caption read, "Little Miss Muffett, Sat on a Tuffet, Winsome, Charming and Sweet, Our

[8.2]   The Gold Dust Twins—"Goldie" and "Dustie"—depicted as two adorable pickaninnies sharing a washtub, became a popular symbol of the N. K. Fairbank Company's Gold Dust washing powder. This image, printed on a trade card, dates from about 1890. Later drawings showed fewer details in the boys' faces, in effect dehumanizing the twins. Around 1900, advertisements featured them with coal-dark skin and bulbous lips, wearing tutus displaying the words "Gold" and "Dust." Frequently, the figures danced, skated, played the piano, bused dishes, embraced a large globe, or happily cavorted with each other in a variety of scenes and contexts. The company's motto, "Let the Twins Do Your Work," became one of the best-known slogans in advertising history, and Gold Dust washing powder was among the earliest instantly recognizable product brands.
Courtesy of Corbis.

Fat Darkey Spied Her, and Put Down Beside Her, a Luncheon of Good CREAM OF WHEAT." When Rastus addressed the audience directly, he offered a message in the uneducated, phonetic spelling of the Negro vernacular guaranteed to appeal to white biases. In one memorable layout, Rastus held up a large bowl of porridge and assured his audience, "Bigges' I Could get, Sah! Mo' wheh Dis Comed Fum, Yas Sah, Cream of Wheat." In another circular he displayed a small chalkboard with a simple message. "Maybe Cream of Wheat aint got no vitamines, I don't know what them things is. If they's bugs they aint none in Cream of Wheat but she's sho' good to eat and cheap. Costs 'bout 1¢ fo' a great big dish. Rastus."[21]

Aunt Jemima was another popular advertising stereotype, perhaps Rastus's obese cousin. She became arguably the most recognizable and enduring of all the stock black characters in American advertising during the nineteenth and twentieth centuries. The figure was always shown as portly and asexual, decked out in a red headdress and wearing a smock or apron as well as some type of kitchen dress suitable for a cook or domestic servant. "Auntie" hearkened back to the old black mammy who reared the white children and proved her worth in the kitchen, a popular symbol of the colored women who had sacrificed so much of their own family lives in the antebellum era to serve their white masters with devotion and something approximating love, at least in the eyes of whites.

Like Rastus, Aunt Jemima originated with a milling company. In 1888, *St. Joseph Gazette* reporter Chris L. Rutt teamed up with mill owner Charles G. Underwood to purchase the Pearl Milling Company. After searching for a product to make, they settled on pancakes as their signature offering. Self-rising pancake mix was not known at the time, and so Rutt and Underwood were excited when they produced a batch that seemed unique in the marketplace. Their early sales, in paper bags labeled "Self-Rising Pancake Flour," were promising, but they needed an advertising strategy if they hoped to succeed in the long term.

Legend has it that Rutt attended a minstrel show one evening in 1889 in St. Joseph, Missouri. Two whites wearing blackface, Baker and Farrell, performed several musical numbers, including a familiar song called "Old Aunt Jemima." The song, composed by a well-known minstrel performer named Bill Kersands, dated back to about 1870 and had been popular in minstrel shows for two decades. Minstrel shows were popular among whites because they portrayed stereotypical Negroes as bumbling simpletons. Rutt was thrilled with the performance and realized he had found a familiar symbol for the company's pancake recipe.

Rutt and Underwood might have made a go of it if their money had held out, but for all their work in creating a tasty product and preparing

"A COLORED SUPPLEMENT"

[8.3]   This 1916 magazine advertisement—"A Colored Supplement"—for Cream of Wheat shows Rastus with a pickaninny (holding a Cream of Wheat box) and an elderly Negro woman depicted as a domestic servant. Courtesy of the Granger Collection.

a marketing campaign, they simply could not finance the venture. In 1890, they sold out to the Randolph Truett Davis Milling Company of St. Joseph, Missouri. R. T. Davis had been in business for fifty years and possessed the resources and distribution channels necessary to manufacture and market the pancake mix. The company immediately set to work. In addition to changing parts of the pancake recipe, Davis promoted the Aunt Jemima brand vigorously. Alas, the mill suffered a series of setbacks, filing for bankruptcy reorganization in 1903. In 1914, the company became the Aunt Jemima Mills Company. Quaker Oats Company purchased the enterprise in 1926.

After acquiring the pancake mix from Rutt and Underwood, R. T. Davis hired an actress to portray Aunt Jemima. The company found Nancy Green, a former slave born in Montgomery County, Kentucky, in 1834. She later moved to Chicago and worked as a cook for a judge and his family. When she signed on to her new role, Green became the face of Aunt Jemima pancakes. She staffed a promotional exhibition at the World's Columbian Exposition in Chicago in 1893 next to the "world's tallest flour barrel." In keeping with her new persona, Green cooked pancakes, sang songs, and told stories about the land of cotton where old times were not forgotten. As part of the act, she spoke with a thick southern accent and a folksy, exaggerated tone of voice peppered with the expected Negro colloquialisms. From the perspective of her employers, Nancy Green was a resounding success. She toured the country promoting the brand and selling untold numbers of pancakes. She would retain the role until she was struck and killed by an automobile in Chicago on September 23, 1923.

No one portrayed the character in the years immediately following Green's death. Eventually, a series of actresses inhabited the role. Therese "Tess" Gardella was perhaps the best-known actress to assume the Aunt Jemima persona in the 1920s and 1930s. She adopted the stage name "Aunt Jemima" when she appeared in Vaudeville productions. A star of stage and screen, the hefty Italian American Gardella appeared wearing blackface and lumbering about in accord with the usual stereotypes of large black women who supposedly waddled when they walked. Her most famous role, in the 1927 musical *Show Boat*, featured "Aunt Jemima" Gardella as the character Queenie belting out the classic tune "Can't Help Lovin' Dat Man."

By the 1950s, multiple Aunt Jemimas appeared in the marketplace. The icon turned up at trade shows, supermarket openings, and even amusement parks such as Disneyland. The role, more than a single actress could handle, became a franchise for any woman of ample proportion and servile disposition. Race was an optional feature because a white actress could wear blackface. Even an actor could slip into the role if he were willing to dress as a matronly woman. In fact, a white man wearing black-face and woman's clothing sometimes was preferred because the obvious race and gender differences further demeaned the Jemima character and added to the hilarity of the stereotype.

As Aunt Jemima became a ubiquitous presence in American retail, merchandising opportunities proliferated. An Aunt Jemima ragdoll became popular early in the twentieth century. Numerous Aunt Jemima dolls appeared in subsequent years. Aunt Jemima also appeared on syrup pitchers, sugar bowls, creamers, salt and pepper shakers, cookie jars, spice sets, and assorted paraphernalia. Sometimes the image clearly depicted Aunt Jemima. Sometimes it showed a hefty black woman with a rag on her head and might have been Aunt Jemima or a generic black mammy. The assorted products became collector's items, especially in the years after new items were no longer produced.

As times changed, so did the reaction the figure triggered among viewers. In the early years of the twentieth century, blacks did not complain. Jim Crow laws were still in place and raising objections to a paternalistic stereotype in an age when people of color were fired from their jobs, driven from their homes, beaten with whips, or lynched from trees for slight infractions was unwise. As the modern civil rights movement brought changing sensibilities, people of color objected to the Aunt Jemima character. Portraying blacks and women in such stereotypical ways ensured that they would remain caricatures in the white imagination. Moreover, far from a term of endearment, "aunt" recalled the days of slavery when elderly Negroes were either "aunt" or "uncle" and never "missus" or "mister." A hefty black woman wearing a headdress smacked of the old plantation where whites pretended to feel affection toward the old lady who cleaned up their messes. When the mask was stripped away, the mammy character was not a lovable adjunct family member but an aging woman forced to bend to a more powerful force. Whatever else can be said about such an asymmetric relationship, it is not always, if ever, based on bonds of genuine affection. Genuine, healthy relationships require mutual dignity, respect, and freedom of choice.

Quaker Oats recognized the company's public relations problem. The brand changed throughout the years to make Aunt Jemima slightly less portly and matronly, but the revisions were marginal, and the voices of critics grew louder with each passing year. During the 1960s, an artist's rendition replaced the portrait or photograph of an actual person; however, the image remained recognizably Aunt Jemima, queen of the black mammies. Advertisements gradually ceased using black dialect in any promotional copy or on the packaging, but the outdated image was an increasingly worrisome problem for the company.

[8.4]   This image, part of an advertisement for the Randolph Truett Davis Milling Company's pancake mix, features the familiar "mammy" figure of Aunt Jemima offering up pancakes to white patrons at the World's Columbian Exposition in Chicago in 1893. In the bottom scene, auntie acts as a faithful cook and domestic servant. Nancy Green, the actress who portrayed Aunt Jemima from 1890 until 1923, worked a pancake-cooking display at the exposition, often appearing next to the "world's largest flour barrel." N. C. Wyeth, a well-known American artist, produced this artwork in 1921.
Courtesy of the Granger Collection.

In 1989, Quaker Oats unveiled a new image. Jemima remained a smiling, friendly, familiar visage, but the headdress was gone, she wore a regular dress instead of an apron, and she sported a small pearl earring. The goal was to retain the positive features of the image—a familiar, warm, welcoming, smiling face that encouraged consumers to purchase pancake mix—while removing the offensive, racially tinged features such as the headdress. The new Aunt Jemima could be any black woman—a modern homemaker, a mother, a professional, or a combination of identities. The change satisfied some critics, although others contended that the image would always be offensive and should be abandoned altogether. Modern black artists produced sarcastic drawings of an angry, defiant Aunt Jemima shaking a clenched fist with a scowl plastered on her face—a new, bold symbol of militancy and black power.[22]

Other advertisements persisted in featuring the old familiar image of Negroes—Uncle Ben's Rice from the 1940s is the most obvious example—but changing times brought changing sensibilities and different images. After the 1960s, black images in advertising were less demeaning and, in many cases, reflected positive portrayals. Black icons such as Michael Jackson, Michael Jordan, Bill Cosby, and Tiger Woods enjoyed lucrative relationships with Madison Avenue advertisers. During the first decades of the 1900s, however, the image of colored persons reached a low point in terms of bigotry, although the exact year when race relations reached their nadir remains a point of debate.[23]

CARICATURES OF BLACKS IN
EARLY AMERICAN FILMS

It was only natural that if demeaning stereotypes of blacks existed in cartoons and advertising, they would carry over into motion pictures. Film is a powerful medium; it can create indelible images that stay with the viewer long after the performance has ended. As Hollywood directors and producers developed the rules of the trade, they elevated the drama of the story above all else, including factual accuracy. This emphasis on producing an entertaining film at the expense of almost everything else ensured that the treatment of Negroes in films would mirror their treatment in other areas of popular culture. In black-and-white silent films of the early twentieth century, white actors wearing blackface appeared on screen impersonating Negroes—not as these people existed but as the white imagination stereotyped them.[24]

When the plot required a black character, he belonged to a particular archetype. A series of stock characters evolved, and it was rare to see a person of color transcend these categories. One scholar has classified blacks in early Hollywood films into five broad types: Toms, coons, tragic mulattoes, mammies, and bucks. Each category features several subcategories, but blacks in early American films always fell into one of the five broad groupings.[25]

The "Tom" category referred to the lead character in Harriet Beecher Stowe's classic 1852 novel *Uncle Tom's Cabin*. An Uncle Tom was a kindly, selfless Negro—often an older, avuncular, asexual character—who knew his place and did not step out of line. So loyal was he to his white patrons that he willingly sacrificed his interests to preserve theirs. Two early films,

Confederate Spy (1910) and *For Massa's Sake* (1911), prominently depicted the Uncle Tom stereotype. In the former film, as the title implies, a Negro spies on Union forces because he cannot bear for the Yankees to capture his white family and destroy the lifestyle they cherish. Even as he is executed by a northern firing squad, the character is satisfied to know he has done everything possible to protect his slave masters. In *For Massa's Sake*, the Uncle Tom character is so distraught by his master's impecunious circumstances that he voluntarily sells himself back into slavery to provide financial relief.[26]

The coon was another popular stock character—in this instance the bumbling, stupid, naive buffoon so beloved in the minstrel shows of the nineteenth century. A coon child was a pickaninny well known from cartoons and advertisements. On film, however, the image could be exploited to even greater heights. The pickaninny's eyes would bulge, his hair would stand on end, and his mouth would form an oval of surprise, accentuating his huge lips. He was a harmless enough character, sometimes described as an "inky kid," a "smoky kid," a "black lamb," or a "cute ebony." The coon child could be seen in the earliest of film reels. As Thomas Edison experimented with motion pictures in 1893, he photographed blacks dancing a jig. In 1904, his short film *Ten Pickaninnies* showed Negro children jumping about in excitement. Pickaninnies were among the most durable of the coons, appearing in a variety of films, including *Uncle Tom's Cabin* (1927), *Topsy and Eva* (1927), referring to the character Topsy from *Uncle Tom's Cabin*, and Hal Roach's *Our Gang* series in the 1920s and 1930s, whose lovable pickaninny characters Farina and Buckwheat became audience favorites.[27]

The grown coon, while less cuddly than a "cute ebony" pickaninny, proved to be just as entertaining to whites who reveled in the antics of zany black caricatures. *The Wooing and Wedding of a Coon* (circa 1905) shows a black couple on their honeymoon tripping through one misadventure after another. In *How Rastus Got His Turkey* and *Rastus in Zululand*, both dating from around 1910, a crazy Negro simpleton steals a turkey for his Thanksgiving dinner and dreams of moving to Zululand in Africa, respectively. The popular radio show *Amos 'n' Andy*, later transferred to television, became one of the most successful of the adult coon entertainment series. Listening to or watching ignorant, unsophisticated Negro stereotypes bumble through a series of absurd situations was hilarious stuff to whites of a certain disposition.[28]

By appearing in a series of films as the same stock character, Rastus was a forerunner of the most famous coon of them all, Stepin Fetchit. The stage name of a black actor, Lincoln Theodore Monroe Andrew Perry, the alter ego Stepin Fetchit appeared in fifty-four films between 1925 and 1976, with the apex of his career coming in the 1930s. The bumbling, stuttering, kowtowing coon proved to be an enduring character and one of the most effective means of perpetuating a demeaning stereotype in cinematic history.[29]

The Uncle Remus character was the last of the coon variety. In some ways, he resembled an Uncle Tom except that Remus embodied a measure of humor missing from Uncle Tom, who was often a tragic, long-suffering figure. Uncle Remus was a comic philosopher, regaling audiences with his folksy homilies. In some films, he used the name Remus, but other films gave the stereotype a different sobriquet. Remus could be seen most notably in *The Green Pastures* (1936) and *The Song of the South* (1946).[30]

The third type of black character in early films was the tragic mulatto. As the child of a black-white union, this unfortunate figure was bound for heartache and disappointment, at best, and perhaps for something far worse. Recalling the fears of miscegenation that so dominated the nineteenth century, the moral of the story of a mulatto onscreen was that blacks and whites should not mix, or the results would be undesirable. In a 1912 silent picture, *The Debt*, star-crossed young lovers who have grown up together discover they cannot marry because the father of the white boy is also the father of a black girl, born of the white father's mistress. A frequent theme involved the mulatto attempting to pass for white and being discovered at the last minute. In *The Octoroon*, a kindly white father grants freedom to a mulatto slave girl sometime around 1850, but later the film's villain sells the girl into slavery. Recalling the notion that even a single drop of black blood—the so-called one-drop rule—was enough to classify an individual as a Negro, early films demonstrated the problems associated with race mixing. Sometimes the contamination that comes from carrying black blood in a person's veins is too much to bear. In the film *In Humanity's Cause*, a white soldier receives a blood transfusion from a black man and becomes deranged as a result. The film *In Slavery Days* presents a tale in which a slave girl's mulatto baby is switched at birth with the white master's baby. The mulatto girl grows up acting white even though her lineage is forever tainted by her black blood. She eventually sells the white girl (mistakenly thought to be a mulatto) into slavery. White audiences found this tragedy of errors horrific, but had the genuine mulatto been sold into slavery, presumably the sale would have been acceptable. The unstated irony, of course, is that if the mulatto could "pass for white," how much "damage" could black blood cause? Stated another way, if one cannot distinguish the corrupted version from the real thing, is this a distinction without a difference? Early films never directly addressed such disturbing questions.[31]

The fourth stock character was the mammy. Aunt Jemima was the quintessential mammy, but many beloved mammies populated stage and screen throughout history. Mammy was a big, fat, aproned black woman who ruled over the kitchen and cared for the white "chil'ren." She tended to be sweet tempered and deeply religious, but mammy could become ferocious if provoked by the film's villain. She would not allow harm to come to children under her care; nor would she tolerate indignities against her white patrons. Hattie McDaniel's Mammy in the classic 1939 film *Gone with the Wind* remains probably the best-known portrayal of this type of character. McDaniel earned an Academy Award for Best Supporting Actress for the role, the first time a Negro had been honored with an Oscar.[32]

The last type of character was the brutal black buck. He was a strong, frenzied, lascivious black man on the prowl, always anxious to rape white women and steal anyone's property. This image of the lustful, animalistic, out-of-control black male has been the source of untold mischief throughout American history. Many of the beatings and lynchings that occurred in the late nineteenth and early twentieth centuries can be tied to this image. Even an unsubstantiated allegation of black insubordination or sexual misbehavior could lead to violence if a young black man could be found anywhere nearby to stand in for the brutal buck character. For whites harboring an intense hatred of blacks, it did not matter much if the brutal buck they punished was guilty of the particular charge. If the buck was not the culprit here, he undoubtedly was responsible for some heretofore unreported heinous crime. Ridding the world of one more Negro buck was a cause for mirth and celebration.[33]

The Gus character in D. W. Griffith's seminal film *The Birth of a Nation* is a vivid example of the brutal black buck. The film proved to be so controversial that the buck disappeared from American cinema for decades, emerging again in the late 1960s and early 1970s as black exploitation (or blaxploitation) films became popular. In those instances, however, the brutal black buck was used as an ironic figure or as a satirical symbol. Films such as *Bone*, *Last of the Mobile Hot Shots*, and *Good Luck, Miss Wyckoff* (also known as *Secret Yearnings*) depict brutal black bucks whose sexual advances sometimes are reciprocated. In *Bone*, the lead black character rips at the clothing of a white woman while he screams, "I'm just a big black buck doing what's expected of me."[34]

The portrayal of blacks in American culture could be said to hinge on white expectations. The belief that blacks were lazy, stupid, immoral, lusty, and somehow less deserving than whites permeated virtually every aspect of popular culture during the years between Reconstruction and the advent of the civil rights movement in the 1950s and 1960s. This culture of debasement appeared to reach an apogee of sorts during the 1920s.[35]

Despite the onslaught of images in cartoons, advertisements, and films, black people did not passively accept this sometimes not-so-subtle denigration. They developed a rich, vibrant culture all their own. Yet their achievements frequently were invisible to whites.[36]

Many white Americans in the 1920s were not motivated by racial animus, or they were casual bigots not called to action against Negroes. They had jobs to go to, families to feed, and lives to lead. To the extent that blacks suffered from cultural attacks, whites either failed to recognize that any attacks had occurred, or they shrugged and murmured, "What are you going to do?" Persons of color had been devalued for so long throughout the history of the republic that a continuation of the status quo did not alarm any but the most conscientious or politically liberal white people.[37]

A small percentage of white Americans moved beyond casual bigotry in reaction to the barrage of negative black images. These zealous racists felt threatened by changes in American society—changes brought on by urbanization, industrialization, and immigration, among other things—and resolved to strike out at forces they believed were eroding their way of life. Because popular culture and their own familial traditions told them blacks were a drain on white culture, they used violence to keep blacks in line. Some whites acted on an ad hoc basis, while others banded together to join like-minded individuals in seeking to root out the blight of an inferior people. One of the most infamous of the groups to arise in the period around World War I was a new organization with an old name: the Ku Klux Klan (KKK).[38]

THE RESURGENCE OF THE KU KLUX KLAN

The original Klan was a Reconstruction-era terrorist group created in late 1865 or early 1866. Although some disagreement exists regarding why six young ex-Confederate soldiers fashioned an organization encouraging its members to parade around wearing masks, it is undisputed that by 1867 the KKK had evolved into an extralegal paramilitary group dedicated to policing the Negro community and preventing freedmen from exercising their political rights. Investigations by federal military forces, the enactment of congressional statutes outlawing Klan activities, and the redemption of southern state governments by white supremacists at the end of Reconstruction killed the Klan. The federal punishment for "Kluxing" was harsh, and southerners realized they need not attack freedmen when they could keep the coloreds in line using state government as a blunt instrument. Before the end of the 1870s, the KKK had ceased to exist as an active faction.[39]

For some southerners, the idea of the Klan as a grassroots organization unencumbered by legal technicalities and devoted to protecting white Christian values remained appealing long after the original group had died out. As the nineteenth century ended, unreconstructed southerners, upset at the outcome of the Civil War and bitter about the continued economic backwardness of the South, mythologized the KKK as noble, righteous, and heroic. They saw the Klan not as a group of dangerous terrorists circumventing the US Constitution to create a rigid, race-based caste system but as a community league created to correct the injustices and mismanagement of the Reconstruction regime.[40]

The Klan might have remained buried in the pages of history but for a series of events that occurred early in the new century. The first involved a southern-born Baptist minister with a gift for racist demagoguery. If anyone could boast of serving as the father of a new era of Klan activity, the title of paterfamilias belonged to Thomas Dixon Jr. No backwoods rube spouting mindless epithets, Dixon was a well-educated lawyer turned preacher. Born in Shelby, North Carolina, in 1864, he distinguished himself as a student at Wake Forest College before matriculating to the new graduate school at Johns Hopkins University. While pursuing his graduate studies, he befriended a studious young man named Thomas Woodrow Wilson, another southerner who shared Dixon's views on race. Their association would pay dividends later in Dixon's career.[41]

Over Wilson's strenuous objections, the young North Carolinian left Johns Hopkins without earning a degree to pursue a career as a stage actor. When that effort failed, Dixon came home to North Carolina. He eventually returned to school, acquired a law degree, and set forth on a career in politics.[42]

Although elected to the North Carolina General Assembly before he could even vote, Dixon soon found politics distasteful and resolved to enter the ministry. In October 1886, he was ordained as a Baptist minister. A self-important, dramatic figure, Dixon discovered a flair for exciting his congregation from the pulpit. He moved on from churches in Goldsboro, North Carolina, to Boston and ultimately New York City. Everywhere he went, he excited crowds with fiery sermons that covered all manner of subjects, not simply Christian or spiritual themes. Wealthy businessman John D. Rockefeller was so smitten with this charismatic figure that he offered to construct a gargantuan tabernacle for Dixon to use as he spouted his unique brand of the gospel.[43]

Dixon's favorite subject was race. Immersed in the culture of debasement he saw all around him, the young minister was alarmed at the "creeping negroidism" spreading through early-twentieth-century America. As the years passed, his sermons evolved into lengthy harangues on the dangers miscegenation posed for white Americans, a subject he believed to be worthy of a man of God spreading the teachings of Christ. He came to realize that much of his time as a minister was spent on church issues and not enough was devoted to lectures on race. Mired in the mundane issues of running a church, Dixon grew disenchanted with the ministry and concentrated on carving out a literary career. He thought he could circulate his message through popular fiction, and he found he was correct.[44]

Dixon discovered his true calling in 1901 after he saw a stage play of Harriet Beecher Stowe's antebellum novel *Uncle Tom's Cabin*. Furious at what he considered historical inaccuracies as well as grievous, slanderous insults to southerners, he churned out a trilogy of novels with one clear purpose: "My object is to teach the North, the young North, what it has never known—the awful suffering of the white man during the dreadful Reconstruction period." In his 1902 diatribe *The Leopard's Spots: A Romance of the White Man's Burden, 1865–1900*, Dixon proved true to his word.[45]

The Leopard's Spots was hardly great literature, but it tapped into the sour mood among many southerners who shared Dixon's views on race. The mawkish plot involved former Confederate soldiers returning home from the war only to discover nefarious schemes aimed at denigrating the South and undermining her cherished traditions. In the novel, an evil white man and a bestial black man intend to redistribute the wealth of white southerners to blacks. The novel's name comes from one character's observation on being told that freedmen should be educated in agricultural and mechanical subjects. Fearful that an educated Negro is a dangerous, restless Negro, the character argues that former slaves have no place in white society and would be better served by colonization. "Even you are still labouring under the delusions of 'Reconstruction,'" he argues. Uplifting such a debased creature is not possible. "The Ethiopian can not change his skin, or the leopard his spots. Those who think it possible will always tell you that the place to work this miracle is in the South. Exactly. If a man really believes in equality, let him prove it by giving his daughter to a negro in marriage."[46]

The Leopard's Spots became an instant success among white audiences, but the second book of the trilogy, *The Clansman*, became Dixon's best-known work. In it, he is unrelenting in his characterization of "a thick-lipped, flat nosed, spindle-shanked Negro, exuding his nauseous animal odour." Throughout the book, Dixon relies on such stereotypical descriptions of blacks. In another scene, he describes a Negro trooper as possessing "the short, heavy-set neck of the lower order of animals." The man's "skin was coal black, his lips so thick they curled both ways up and down." Elsewhere, he describes the soldier's facial features: "His nose was flat," and he had "sinister beady eyes" that were "set wide apart and gleamed ape-like." According to this revisionist historical fiction, the creation of a noble, patriotic organization, the Ku Klux Klan, had saved the white citizens of the South during Reconstruction. *The Clansman* glorified the KKK as a much needed corrective to the debauchery of the postwar era when northern carpetbaggers and treacherous southern turncoats (scalawags) had conspired to elevate the Negro beyond his natural station in life. Dixon did not create this mythical interpretation of Klan history, but he popularized it for an approving white public that was all too willing to believe that Negroes were beasts.[47]

Dixon's written work alone probably would not have revitalized the Klan, but he was at heart a dramatist. Just as *Uncle Tom's Cabin*, the antislavery novel that had so upset him, was adapted for the theater, Dixon saw an opportunity to translate the written word from the page to the stage. The former preacher took his show on the road for a live audience, casting himself as the lead in several theatrical productions. The book had been a spectacular success, but the complicated tale, with a cast of many dozens, was not well suited to the stage. Even reliably racist critics and theatergoers found much of the fare insipid and objectionable. Despite its limitations as quality theater, the drama played to sold-out, enthusiastic crowds across the South. Audiences willingly overlooked the play's hackneyed elements because they found the central message of white supremacy and Negro degradation so uplifting and inspirational.[48]

Around the same time the stage version of *The Clansman* appeared, Hollywood, the land that would eventually become synonymous with moviemaking, was emerging as a mythical place of hopes and dreams. Dixon dreamed of raising money to film his stage play of *The Clansman* and treat a larger circle of white patrons to his special brand of bigotry. He did not possess the funds or wherewithal to make that happen, but he found a fellow who did.

Enter David Wark Griffith, the son of an unreconstructed Confederate veteran. D. W. Griffith, as he came to be known, had once worked as an actor in a Dixon theatrical production. Yet he longed for more ambitious projects to showcase his talents. He fancied himself a Hollywood director, and he had handled a few small projects as he yearned for his big break. He just needed exactly the right property—a story that was intensely visual in its approach and epic in its scope. When he learned that the rights to *The Clansman* were available, he was enthusiastic. Griffith knew of one previous unsuccessful effort to film the book, but he was unconcerned. Like all great visual artists to follow him, he possessed an intuitive understanding of a story's cinematic appeal. He realized this could be exactly the project to propel him into the front ranks of filmmakers. Yet he was apprehensive that Dixon would reject him out of hand when the author realized that a former actor in his play would direct the film. He need not have worried. When Dixon learned that Griffith would be at the helm, he responded approvingly. "Oh, yes," he exclaimed. "I've heard a lot about him—he used to work for me."[49]

The rest, as they say, is history. Griffith became the first of many directors to surprise and delight audiences with his mastery of the new medium. Throughout the filming, he took liberties with the text of *The Clansman*, which itself had taken liberties with the historical record. Whatever was needed to capture exciting scenes that heightened dramatic tension, Griffith was willing to do, the budget be damned. Consequently, he depleted his funding before principal photography had ended. Desperate to stay in business, he reached out to virtually everyone he knew and even a few people he didn't. He also persuaded cast and crew to work without pay. In the end, Griffith finished the film, eventually titled *The Birth of a Nation*, in time for a release early in 1915, the fiftieth anniversary of the end of the Civil War. The film required twelve reels and clocked in at more than three hours running time. It cost $110,000—almost $2.6 million when adjusted for inflation one hundred years later—an astronomical sum at the time.[50]

The plot loosely follows the revisionist history popularized in *The Clansman*, but it emphasizes the depravity of the black characters and exaggerates the dastardly actions of the evil carpetbaggers in a dramatic manner only a film can bring to life. Abraham Lincoln appears early in the story as a well-meaning simpleton, a stooge too weak and kindly to lead a nation at war, but at least he is not intent on punishing the South. After Lincoln's assassination, the Radical Republicans in Congress seize power and impose their will on the prostrated region. Now the federal government will exact vengeance. The dark days of Reconstruction descend on the nation as the Republicans hatch a scheme to install former slaves in positions of authority in southern state governments to the detriment of the white population.

The second half of the story shows marauding Negroes taking advantage of good-hearted, kindly Christian whites during the postwar epoch. When all hope appears lost, a hero emerges to save the day in the sentimental style that would soon become standard Hollywood fare. Here Griffith, following Dixon's lead, remade history from whole cloth.

In the pivotal scene of the second half, a sexually depraved freedman, Gus—the classic brutal buck archetype—threatens lovely, innocent, virginal Flora Cameron, the daughter of a pure, Christian, southern white family fighting against the oppressive carpetbagger regime. Rather than be ravished by the sex-hungry black beast and sacrifice her virtue, Flora throws herself from a cliff to her death when the black buck Gus menaces her. Ben Cameron, Flora's brother, is distraught. He swears that her death will be avenged by all that is holy and righteous.

The heroic Cameron family cannot rely on the civil authorities to bring Gus to justice, for the government is controlled by lawless carpetbaggers and power-hungry scalawags, assisted by the barbaric freedmen. Despondent, Cameron spies a group of white children hiding beneath sheets and pretending to be ghosts. In a burst of inspiration, Cameron realizes how he can avenge his sister's death. With truth, justice, and Christian virtue on his side, he bands together with other noble southern white men to form the Ku Klux Klan, a group that will protect the white citizenry from the machinations of the thugs seeking to destroy the South and its people.

After they dress in full Klan regalia and mount their horses, the masked forces of goodness and virtue track down the unholy black man, Gus, and hold a vigilante-style trial. The Negro is undoubtedly guilty; the Klan need not waste time with too many procedural niceties. They lynch the foul creature and dump his body on the doorstep of the leading carpetbagger, Silas Lynch, a greedy, disgusting Radical Republican loosely

[8.5]   In this image from *The Birth of a Nation*, the chivalric Ku Klux Klan prepares to punish the evil black buck Gus for menacing a defenseless white woman. A white actor wearing blackface, Walter Long, portrayed Gus. Courtesy of Photofest.

modeled on former Pennsylvania congressman and Radical Republican Thaddeus Stevens. The audience realizes that Lynch is evil because he chases his Negro servant around in a lascivious manner, an allusion to Stevens's real-life sexual relationship with his black housekeeper. The idea that anyone from a different race would openly engage in a sexual relationship with a person of another race was simply too horrible to contemplate unless both persons were depraved beyond all hope of redemption. (What occurred in private, after dark, was another matter altogether.)

Later in the film, in the climactic scene when the vicious carpetbaggers and crazed freedmen are poised to conquer the noble white family, the Klan arrives to save the day. The villains are vanquished, the Camerons are triumphant, and the illegitimate Reconstruction government of the corrupt Silas Lynch is driven into exile. As the film draws to a conclusion, Jesus Christ gazes down from heaven, smiling, satisfied that thanks to the Klan, justice has been served.[51]

It was powerful, dramatic storytelling, the most effective pro-KKK propaganda imaginable. White southerners sitting inside a movie theater watching the heroic group onscreen rescue friends and neighbors from evil blacks and insidious white northerners felt proud. The South had lost the war, but with the help of the Klan, it could win the peace. The historical record could be shaped into a pro-southern polemic.[52]

In addition to glorifying the Ku Klux Klan, *The Birth of a Nation* capitalized on the stereotype of Negroes as animalistic, brutal, and essentially beasts of burden. It was a popular image in the 1920s. From gator bait to Rastus to Aunt Jemima to Stepin Fetchit, blacks were characterized either as barbarians or simpletons. In a final insult to persons of color, white actors wearing blackface played Gus and other black characters in the film. Except in scenes where blacks appeared as extras in the background, Griffith refused to allow Negroes to appear as Negroes, presumably because he did not trust them to portray members of their race in a convincing manner.[53]

Griffith was anxious to garner as many positive testimonials as he could arrange before the film's release. Tom Dixon's contacts proved to be invaluable in this effort. In January 1915, Dixon wrote to his old friend from his youth at Johns Hopkins, Woodrow Wilson. Wilson had experienced a meteoric rise in the years since he and Dixon had studied together. As Dixon prepared his new film for widespread distribution, Wilson was entering his third year as president of the United States. Wilson received the letter from his former classmate, but he initially expressed reservations, fearing yet another job seeker was intent on cashing in on old ties. Despite his misgivings, the president warily welcomed Dixon to the Executive Mansion on February 3, 1915. As their conversation began, President Wilson was relieved to learn that his old college friend only wished to show a motion picture to the president and a small group of intimates. Wilson happily assented. On February 18, 1915, Dixon, D. W. Griffith, and members of the crew arrived in the East Room of the White House and set up a projector. President Wilson, his daughters, and several cabinet officers sat quietly as the story unfolded. It was the first time a motion picture had been screened in the White House.

After the film ended and the lights came up, the filmmakers anxiously awaited the verdict. Obviously moved, the president vigorously shook hands with the author, director, and members of the crew. In a possibly apocryphal comment that would become famous, Wilson gushed that the film's impact was monumental. "It is like writing history with lightning," he said, "and my only regret is that it is all so terribly true." Wilson's enthusiastic reaction delighted Dixon and Griffith beyond anything they had expected.[54]

The comment was not as astonishing as it might seem more than a century later. The first southerner elected president since Reconstruction, Wilson, a Virginian by birth, had grown up in a world where white supremacy was a self-evident reality. He did not question the inferiority of the black race. He had been taught since birth in thousands of subtle and not-so-subtle ways that whites were, and should be, the dominant race. During his presidency, he accepted southern leaders' arguments that issues of race were properly the province of state governments and the federal government should not be involved. Even worse for black Americans, Wilson curtailed the already modest number of black appointees to federal government positions and instituted the odious southern practice of racially segregating federal offices and restrooms. For all of his celebrated progressivism in public policy and idealism in advocating the creation of a League of Nations at the end of the Great War, Wilson embraced the romanticized southern view of Negroes as good servants during antebellum times and buffoons incapable of self-governance or even self-control during Reconstruction.[55]

Ecstatic at his old classmate's reaction, Dixon could have stopped there and his public relations campaign would have been an unqualified success. Yet he had one more prominent endorsement to collect. Another friend in government, Secretary of the Navy Josephus Daniels, arranged for a meeting between Dixon and Edward D. White, chief justice of the US Supreme Court. White was a renowned curmudgeon and septuagenarian known for his old-fashioned views and fierce resistance to change. After Dixon had been shown into the jurist's home library and explained that he wanted the old man to see a film, the chief justice snarled, "Moving picture! It's absurd, sir. I never saw one in my life and I haven't the slightest curiosity to see one. I'm very busy. I'll have to ask you to excuse me."

It appeared that the meeting would end badly, but Dixon knew his man well. White had been born and raised in Louisiana, and his father had served as governor before the son's birth. White was related through his mother to the famous Lee family of Virginia, which included the southern icon Robert E. Lee. As a young man, White had served in the Confederate army during the war, although the nature of his service was a point of controversy. As an associate justice, he had voted with the majority to uphold segregation in the landmark US Supreme Court case *Plessy v. Ferguson*. (Later in 1915, White would author the unanimous opinion striking down grandfather causes for state literacy tests, *Guinn v. United States*, but one case in favor of the disenfranchised did not a civil libertarian make. The statutes in *Guinn* were so egregious they bore no rational relationship to a legitimate state interest.)[56] In short, White's pro-southern proclivities were no secret.

Hoping to pique the justice's interest, Dixon explained that the purpose of the film was to set the record straight about the Civil War and Reconstruction. Dixon also said the heroic KKK was featured prominently in the story. The storyteller had made exactly the right pitch. Moments earlier, White had been prepared to show his visitor the door. With this revelation, the chief justice warmed to the author.

"I was a member of the Klan, sir," White confessed as he slipped the eyeglasses from his face, leaned back in his swivel chair, and reflected on his youth. "Through many a dark night, I walked my sentinel's beat through the ugliest streets of New Orleans with a rifle on my shoulder." The chief considered the petitioner with a wary eye. "You've told the true story of that uprising of outraged manhood?"

Dixon assured him that justice had been done to the facts of Reconstruction. "In a way I'm sure you'll approve."

"I'll be there!" Justice White exclaimed.[57]

Word that two of the most important men in the federal government had enthusiastically bestowed their blessing on the film circulated widely, in no small measure because Dixon and Griffith spread the message at every opportunity. The architects of the motion picture had feared their time and efforts would not be rewarded, but Wilson's and White's purported reactions were typical of most white audiences. Almost everywhere the film was shown, especially in the South, it received fulsome praise. Even at $2 per person, far beyond what most tickets cost in that era, moviegoers flocked to the theater to enjoy the lavish spectacle.[58]

Its story line aside, *The Birth of a Nation* was a technically stunning film. With Griffith's tight editing of scenes, his close-ups to capture characters' facial expressions, the innovative camera work that drew the audience into the action, and the lush orchestral arrangement, *The Birth of a Nation* ushered in a new era of professional filmmaking. Everything that came before it was bland, unoriginal, and uninspiring by comparison. Critics pronounced it an instant classic. In the end, the project paid off handsomely for Griffith and Dixon. The film raked in almost $18 million at the box office.[59]

When they learned of the film and its subject, National Association for the Advancement of Colored People (NAACP) members feared it was yet another in a long line of artistic works depicting Negroes in a harsh, inaccurate manner. They were right to be worried. *The Birth of a Nation* broadcast a powerful image of blacks either as happy idiots content in their native inferiority or dangerous, sexually warped brutes. When pressed to defend these offensive stereotypes as well as the supposed accuracy of events depicted in the film, Dixon and Griffith insisted the work faithfully reflected the historical record.

The story could not stand unchallenged. Through an aggressive, sustained lobbying campaign before the National Board of Censorship and in a series of public protests, NAACP representatives called on all races to avoid viewing such anti-Negro propaganda. Association members were arrested at several screenings when they attempted to enter the "whites only" section of theaters showing the film. Boston mayor James Curley initially agreed with the NAACP, but eventually he allowed the movie to be shown in the city after the filmmakers deleted several offensive scenes. A similar protest required additional revisions before the film could be screened in New York. The state of Kansas prohibited theaters from playing the film until 1923.[60]

As powerful as it was, *The Birth of a Nation* alone was not enough to revitalize the Ku Klux Klan. Two other developments were necessary to open a new chapter for the group. The first arose when somebody strangled poor little Mary Phagan and left her corpse lying in a pile of sawdust in the basement of the pencil factory where she worked in Atlanta, Georgia. The dastardly crime occurred on April 26, 1913—Confederate Memorial Day in Georgia—a day that lived in the heart of many a southerner who longed for old times when the South and her cherished traditions had existed unmolested by the federal government. Mary was only thirteen years old, a forgotten urchin who had been discarded and ignored during her brief life. She counted for little as a living, breathing being. In death, she became a revered child of the South, a delicate creature whose killing had to be avenged with dispatch. Mary Phagan the symbol was far more important to southerners than Mary Phagan the flesh-and-blood child had been.[61]

The offender must have been someone connected with the pencil factory, for the criminal knew just where to leave the body so it would go unnoticed. Only after a night watchman happened upon the grim discovery was the alarm raised. In an era before fingerprints and forensic evidence were used routinely to identify a suspect, Georgia authorities swarmed to the site and contaminated the scene in their zeal to apprehend the assailant. They had few leads to pursue at the outset. After initially suspecting the watchman, investigators stumbled onto a fortuitous clue. Bloodstains "identified positively as the dead girl's" were found in a workroom near the office of the girl's employer, Leo M. Frank.

By itself, the bloodstain evidence was circumstantial, requiring an explanation as to how it had materialized in the workroom, but it was not damning. Yet this Frank fellow struck the police as suspicious. He was a Jew from New York with a college degree from Cornell University. Those factors certainly made him an unusual character but perhaps not dangerous. Aside from his foreign ways and strange heritage, he was an odd man—thin, almost girlish in appearance, standoffish, a gentleman with a vaguely condescending air. Something about his manner struck onlookers as effete. In a factory staffed by impecunious waifs, Frank was well-to-do, a manager earning a portion of the profits from the sweat and toil of his employees, many of whom were children. In addition, he was the last person to be seen with Mary Phagan. Laid off from her job several days before the murder, she had returned to retrieve her pay. People saw her talking with Frank—a man who reportedly had flirted with her in the past—and hours later, she was dead, possibly raped. The pencil factory manager became a prime suspect—as much for his personality as for his supposed crime.[62]

One nagging loose end involved a black factory janitor named Jim Conley. Someone saw him not long after the murder as he scrubbed a dirty blue shirt that might have been bloody. Although testing revealed no blood on the shirt, the police caught Conley in multiple lies when they questioned him about the episode. He contradicted himself repeatedly. Despite his unreliability as a witness, the authorities listened intently when Conley finally implicated Frank and claimed to have helped the manager hide Phagan's body in the basement. It was a rare occasion when white authorities did not immediately accuse a Negro of the crime. Ironically, the one time a Negro escaped suspicion for destroying a young white girl, he may have been the culprit. Reviewing the case decades later, modern commentators were convinced that Conley was the perpetrator.[63]

Based largely on Conley's testimony, Leo Frank was arrested and charged with the crime. A trial of sorts ensued, but it did little to expose the facts of the case. Instead, the prosecutor deliberately stoked the fires of xenophobia, portraying the northern Jew as predisposed to committing atrocities. Southerners' hatred of Negroes was well documented, but the Leo Frank case revealed a previously dormant undercurrent of southern anti-Semitism. In the festive, carnival-like atmosphere of the trial, Frank was convicted and sentenced to die.[64]

When the cause appeared lost, help came from an unexpected source: retiring Georgia governor John Slaton commuted the sentence to life imprisonment. Slaton harbored genuine doubts about the fairness of the proceedings and acted on his conscience. It may have been one of the few acts of political courage by a southern white leader to emerge from the era of lynching. The governor's actions were almost uniformly denounced by a hysterical public anxious to mete out harsh punishment for a sensational crime.[65]

The case might have ended there. The defendant had been tried, convicted, sentenced, and dispatched to prison, presumably to rot away behind bars for the rest of his natural life. Leave it to a talented demagogue to exploit the crime for his own benefit.

Tom Watson, once labeled an "agrarian rebel," was one of those public figures the South occasionally offers up as a paean to the virtues of majoritarian democracy. During the populist era of his youth, Watson had been relatively moderate on questions of race (see chapter 5), but that version of his public persona was dead and buried by 1913. A publicity-seeking newspaper editor and former US congressman in the waning phase of a long career, Watson delighted in stirring up the masses to rebel against real or perceived threats to the power of the people. The "reactionary populist" was the intellectual heir of numerous unreconstructed Confederates who mourned the death of the Confederacy, championed the ideology of white supremacy, and cast aspersions on anyone who dared to violate the sensibilities of the common man.

During the trial, Watson used the pages of his two widely disseminated publications, *Watson's Magazine* and the *Jeffersonian*, to denounce the "Jewpervert" who had brutalized an innocent white girl and defiled all of southern womanhood. After the execution had been delayed repeatedly, his harangues, already noteworthy for their lack of measured restraint or thoughtful reflection, became increasingly shrill. "How much longer is the innocent blood of little Mary Phagan to cry in vain to Heaven for vengeance?" he asked.

Watson viewed Governor Slaton's commutation of the sentence for what it was: a public relations gift presented to anyone with the foresight to traffic in histrionic prose. "Our grand old Empire State HAS BEEN RAPED," he screamed in the *Jeffersonian*. "We have been betrayed! The breath of some leprous monster has passed over us, and we feel like crying out, in horror and despair, 'Unclean! UNCLEAN!'" On and on it went, with each issue of the newspaper struggling to top the hyperbole of the previous edition. Watson had no doubt of Frank's guilt, for Jews were known to have "a ravenous appetite for the forbidden fruit." Perhaps Watson, so blinded by racism that he could not temper his views, considered his tirades a public service, or perhaps he was motivated by less noble sentiments. In any case, sensationalism was good for business. Circulation of the *Jeffersonian* stood at twenty-five thousand before Watson became Mary Phagan's guardian angel. Within a few months, he was moving eighty-seven thousand copies a week. Outrage, then as now, sells newspapers.[66]

This kind of intemperate prose was designed to move men to action, and so it did. A mob hailing from Mary Phagan's hometown of Marietta resolved to avenge her murder. On August 16, 1915, a group of twenty-five men drove to the prison farm in Milledgeville, Georgia, where inmate Frank resided, and kidnapped him from his cell under cover of darkness. By all accounts, the jailers were none too upset or surprised by the sudden appearance of vigilantes.

Calling themselves the Knights of Mary Phagan, the kidnappers transported their prisoner 175 miles to Marietta. Although some of the men grew squeamish and left before the deed was done, most of the group remained on hand. They escorted him into a field near a grove of trees, affixed a hangman's noose around Frank's neck, handcuffed his wrists, and draped a hood over his head. Leo Frank died an excruciating death. After the executioners hoisted him from the ground and kicked a table from beneath his legs, his neck did not snap immediately. Frank flailed about for at least half an hour before he choked. Leaders of the death squad had justified their actions as necessary to preserve the honor of the South, but their grand words proved to be hollow. As the sun rose, each of the fellows, fearful of capture and potential prosecution, scampered away from the site. Presumably, if they had acted in the advancement of a genuinely noble cause, as they claimed, the executioners would have waited around for the inevitable congratulations forthcoming from a grateful citizenry.[67]

Some Georgians were pleased with the outcome. Word spread that the notorious Jewish criminal was dangling from a rope on the outskirts of Marietta, and cars packed with curious spectators converged on the grove. At least one person brought a camera to memorialize the auspicious event. The resultant photographs showed gawking men and boys, some gazing in awe at the figure hanging above their heads. Others scowled at the camera as though challenging onlookers to disapprove of their presence. Examined in sequence, the photographs reveal a ghastly fact. Leo Frank's clothing grew progressively scanty with each successive shot. Souvenir hunters ripped off swatches from his garments to preserve mementos of the lynching. The grisly photographs as well as authenticated pieces of rope later turned up for sale in the streets of Atlanta.[68]

The reaction to *The Birth of a Nation* and the Leo Frank murder case revealed an undercurrent of hate and fear present in the United States during the era of the Great War. Immigration was on the rise. An unprecedented, worldwide conflagration raged in Europe. The automobile and new advances in technology were decreasing the size of the globe, threatening to undermine traditional kinship relationships that had long defined the lives of Americans. The confluence of these troubling events convinced a thirty-five-year-old former Methodist minister, William Joseph "Doc" Simmons, that the time was right to form a new organization based on an old idea. He was the final contributor to the rise of a new Ku Klux Klan.[69]

Simmons was born in Harpersville, Alabama, in 1880. A self-made man in the sense that he could boast of few genuine achievements, he was not one to permit facts to interfere with his enormously healthy self-esteem. Despite evidence to the contrary, he was convinced that he was destined for greatness. His father was a country doctor, and young Simmons later said he was too. Although he claimed to have graduated from Johns Hopkins Medical School, no record of his attendance could be located.

A Spanish-American War veteran, Simmons experienced a religious conversion during a revival meeting after the war. He soon became a Methodist minister and rode the circuit in Alabama and Florida. Unfortunately for the ambitious young man, he could not make the ministry pay despite his abundant oratorical gifts. He was a gifted rabble-rouser, to be sure, but his inability to keep up with the administrative requirements of the church doomed his prospects. In 1912, the Alabama Conference denied him a pulpit owing to his general inefficiency as well as his "moral impairment." The latter may have been a veiled reference to Simmons's frequent overindulgence in his favorite liquid refreshment, Kentucky bourbon.

After moping about in a Birmingham boardinghouse operated by his relatives for a few years, Simmons fell into his life's work. "I am a fraternalist," he exclaimed when people inquired about his profession. It was a time when new organizations were springing up all over the country. Simmons noticed this phenomenon as he roamed around "teaching history" to anyone who would listen to his tall tales. He joined numerous fraternal clubs so that he could make friends and learn what made people tick. His greatest success before 1915 was as the Atlanta-area organizer for the Woodmen of the World, a fraternal society stressing patriotism, civic pride, volunteerism, and financial solvency. Throughout his travels, he searched for a suitable outlet for his restless energy.

Early in 1915, a car skidded around a corner and slammed into Simmons as he stood on a street in downtown Atlanta. During his long recuperation, he came across a copy of Tom Dixon's popular book *The Clansman*, as well as the original Reconstruction-era Ku Klux Klan prescript from 1867. As he thumbed through these materials, Simmons realized the fabulous new motion picture that everyone was talking about, *The Birth of a Nation*, was based on Dixon's novel. The prescript, essentially the original KKK's bylaws and mission statement, suggested to Simmons that the Dixon/Griffith stories were factually accurate. In the meantime, the newspapers were filled with screaming headlines about the Leo Frank case. Simmons was thrilled to learn that the vigilantes calling themselves the Knights of Mary Phagan had delivered justice to the wretched villain when the government had failed to act with the appropriate severity. To the messianic ex-preacher, the confluence of events was no accident. They all led to one place—the resurgence of that great old fraternal group of yesteryear, the Ku Klux Klan. He had found his place in history, for he, William Joseph Simmons, would be the founding father of a new order based on a classic idea.[70]

Now that he knew what providence had in store for him, Simmons planned for the revitalized KKK meticulously. In keeping with the modus operandi of the Reconstruction-era Klan, he insisted on secrecy for his group. He created a shorthand language to prevent outsiders from discovering his plans. He attached the prefix "kl" to words—for instance, he anticipated having a "klonversation" with fellow Klansmen. They would swear allegiance to a holy book known, strangely enough, as the "Kloran." Simmons also developed mysterious acronyms. "AYAK" stood for "Are you a Klansman"? The appropriate response was "AKIA," short for "A Klansman I am."[71]

It all sounded so jejune, and perhaps in the early days of 1915 it was, but Simmons was determined to restore the KKK to its rightful place as a savior of southern society. On October 26 of that year, having joined forces with several Knights of Mary Phagan, Simmons filed an application with the state of Georgia to create a "purely benevolent and eleemosynary" fraternal order. He listed himself as the imperial wizard. The Knights of the Ku Klux Klan officially existed again in the Southland.[72]

He needed a flashy, exciting, dramatic event to launch the new group, and the opportunity arose on Thanksgiving night. He gathered twenty or so men (the number varies, depending on the source) at Atlanta's Piedmont Hotel for inaugural festivities. Two original Reconstruction era Klansmen were among the select invitees. When the founders assembled, Simmons unveiled a surprise. He intended to hold the ceremony atop Stone Mountain, an enormous granite slab sixteen miles outside Atlanta. Several gentlemen, fearing the cold November chill, declined to participate, but sixteen others, including Simmons, traveled by bus to the site. They picked their way through the dark night using flashlights and assembled around a makeshift, sixteen-foot wooden cross erected on the mountaintop. Standing under an American flag, they read passages from the twelfth chapter of Romans in the Bible and swore allegiance to the Invisible Empire, the Knights of the Ku Klux Klan. In a dramatic gesture, the budding Klansmen set fire to the cross. As Simmons later explained,

"Thus on the mountain top that night at the midnight hour while men braved the surging blasts of wild wintry mountain winds and endured a temperature far below freezing, bathed in the sacred glow of the fiery cross, the Invisible Empire was called from its slumber of half a century to take up a new task and fulfill a new mission for humanity's good."[73]

As usual, Simmons recalled the event with more than a touch of melodrama. The temperature was somewhere in the forties that night. Moreover, while careful to follow many rituals used by the Reconstruction-era Klan, he also understood the need to transform the modern Klan into a functional and relevant entity designed to meet twentieth-century needs. The new organization would not confine itself to keeping colored people in line, as the original KKK had done. Any racial or ethnic group or "foreigner" threatening the status quo eventually became a Klan target.[74]

During the Atlanta premiere of *The Birth of a Nation*, Colonel W. J. Simmons, founder and imperial wizard of the Klan, ran advertisements for his group in the Atlanta newspapers—a strange practice for an organization claiming to cherish its secrecy—and instructed his followers to don bed sheets and ride on horseback down Peachtree Street close to crowds assembled outside the theater waiting to watch the film. The stunts were effective promotional tools. Enraptured moviegoers could see actual Klansmen parading about before they shuffled inside to watch the film, or patrons could emerge from the theater to spy replicas of the masked men extolled moments earlier in celluloid. An impressionable young fellow might find himself drawn to the image of white southern chivalry so gallantly depicted in *The Birth of a Nation*. Within a few weeks, Simmons's fledgling group could boast of ninety-two members.[75]

W. J. Simmons discovered, however, that forming a group and increasing its membership over time required skills that he did not possess in abundance. Aside from its members' vague dissatisfaction with the state of the world, especially the rise in immigration and the seeming proliferation of vagrants and immoral women, the Klan was adrift, a patriotic organization in search of a cause. America's entry into World War I provided a bit of guidance, but the KKK desperately needed a leader to give it purpose and direction. Within five years of its rebirth, the Klan's membership plateaued at a few thousand.

Simmons realized he needed to look outside for assistance. In 1920, he struck a deal with Edward Young Clarke and Mary Elizabeth Tyler, partners in a group called the Southern Publicity Association. The pair had become adept at generating marketing and publicity for groups such as the Red Cross, the Anti-saloon League, the Theodore Roosevelt Memorial Fund, and the Salvation Army. The Southern Publicity Association was the sort of issues-management/public relations firm that would become famous during the era of interest group politics later in the twentieth century. In the 1920s, such groups were novel.[76]

Clarke and Tyler agreed to recruit members for a hefty 80 percent of whatever membership fees they collected. With a financial incentive in place, the pair audaciously sent out press releases, often tying their media outreach to publicity associated with *The Birth of a Nation*. Tyler later reflected that the original plan was to reach out to white supremacists and disaffected southerners along the lines of the original Klan, but the duo soon realized that a larger untapped membership pool existed. They marketed the newly formed KKK as a nativist organization designed to protect all things American in a world where those values appeared to be imperiled. During a visit to New York, Tyler surmised that Jews would be upset with the updated mission because the Klan "teaches the wisdom of spending American money on American men," and Jews somehow were alien and un-American. No comment was too offensive or off-putting if it parlayed vague feelings of resentment and hate into a dues-paying membership.[77]

Although scapegoating Negroes remained a tried-and-true recruitment tool, the new KKK also targeted Jews, Catholics, Asians, and anyone else who was foreign and less than "one-hundred-percent-American." The group promoted strong Christian values in keeping with the image of Jesus Christ in *The Birth of a Nation* as well as Doc Simmons's ties to the church. The nativist message and Christian appeals paid off. Within only a few months, the Southern Publicity Association had pushed membership to one hundred thousand members. The following year, as the *New York World* investigated alleged Klan abuses and triggered a congressional inquiry, Tyler brilliantly used the negative press attention as a tool to attract yet more members. She argued that elites in the press and Congress worried that the KKK was empowering white citizens and speaking the truth about undesirables that undermined the American dream. In 1921, membership supposedly topped 1 million.[78]

Because Klan organizers depended on local grassroots networks to implement the vision, membership numbers and the types of activities varied from place to place. In some communities, the group existed as a fraternal organization that encouraged patrons to congregate and discuss important local issues—a sort of civic club akin to a chamber of commerce. In other areas, it was an extralegal quasi-police force that patrolled the streets in search of people loitering, gambling, selling illicit substances, or engaging in prostitution. In still other communities, Klansmen were paramilitary officers who used violence to keep the coloreds and undesirable characters in line. For southern communities that strictly controlled people of color through a rigid caste system, KKK members took it upon themselves to administer beatings and whippings. Riding the roads by night with the benefit of a disguise allowed zealous Klansmen to justify any mischief, no matter how wantonly cruel, as necessary to maintain order within the community.[79]

Congress launched an investigation after the Klan's activities came to light in a series of *New York World* articles. Summoned before the House of Representatives Rules Committee in October 1921, Simmons insisted that the group was dedicated to promoting Christian values and was not a racist or terrorist organization. By this time, the colonel was on his way out. His attempts to grow the membership now appeared crude and ineffective. He was being shunted to the side as Tyler and Clarke led the KKK to greater glory. In any case, Simmons's testimony before the House, while hardly a virtuoso performance, was not the calamity some Klan supporters feared it would be.[80]

As a last hurrah, Simmons supposedly took part in a secret ceremony in the Green Room of the White House at which President Warren G.

[8.6]   William Joseph "Doc" Simmons is pictured in October 1921 during a break in his testimony before the US House of Representatives Rules Committee. Although Simmons was the founding father of a revitalized Ku Klux Klan, by 1921 he had lost control of the group. Courtesy of the Library of Congress.

Harding was sworn into the Klan. Whether such a meeting occurred remains a point of no small controversy. Harding always publicly denied his involvement with the group, although some sources characterized him as a "close ally," if not quite a formal member. Harding apologists point to his well-known public statements condemning lynching as evidence that he was never a Klan member or supporter. In later years, many influential political figures joined the KKK, so it is not implausible to suggest that the president of the United States was a Klansman, but the sources claiming to have been present at the Harding initiation were hardly unimpeachable. The issue cannot be resolved to anyone's satisfaction.[81]

It is undeniable, however, that the group became politically powerful during the 1920s under the leadership of a new imperial wizard. A dentist from Dallas, Texas, Hiram Wesley Evans, assumed the helm shortly before engineering Simmons's ouster in 1924. At least Colonel Simmons managed to finagle a $145,000 cash payment in return for ceding control to Evans. Tyler saw the handwriting on the wall and left to marry a wealthy Atlanta businessman before she could be shown the door. Edward Young Clarke was not as fortunate; he too soon found himself banished from the organization he had done so much to promote.[82]

No longer satisfied with expressing vague discontent with the power of elites and undesirable ethnicities, Evans brought the group an even higher profile than ever before when he pushed to increase the KKK's political power. It was not enough to rile up a crowd, as Simmons had done. Rabble-rousing did not pay off in the long run. The most effective means of promoting the Klan's agenda was by infiltrating the halls of power at all levels of government. Watching developments from his position in exile, Edward Young Clarke complained that the original purpose of the revitalized KKK was not political; rather it had been "designed to build-up and develop spiritually, morally and physically the Protestant white men of America." Clarke did not specify how the Protestant ascent would occur, but it no longer mattered. *He* no longer mattered. Evans had a vision and a plan for promoting it.

First, he would provide a measure of consistency and control over local groups, or klaverns, which had increased in number willy-nilly in recent years. Order and discipline were crucial to achieving the group's objectives. After all, Nathan Bedford Forrest, leader of the Reconstruction-era Klan, had ordered the group to disband when he could no longer oversee local Kluxers who did not understand the need for consistent, coherent, coordinated KKK control. After distributing pamphlets outlining strategies for making the Klan a "civic asset" in the community, Evans promoted educational topics such as the history of Protestantism and the origins of white supremacy. He deemphasized Simmons's blatantly religious appeal. Although the Klan remained an organization devoted to white Christian values, its crucial features were militant nativism and political activism. Evans believed he could attract new members and political clout by promising and delivering specific, concrete action on specific, concrete goals.[83]

In his quest to legitimize the political power of the KKK, Evans faced an enormous obstacle at the outset. Violence perpetrated by members of the klaverns became a problem. Whereas Simmons simply denied such incidents had ever occurred, Evans could not ignore multiple press reports of beatings and lynchings at the hands of Kluxers everywhere. He also understood that some whites joined the Klan so that they could experience fellowship with their neighbors while violently attacking blacks and other nonwhites with impunity. The crude, pedestrian methods of white-sheeted toughs torturing hapless minorities because "might makes right" in a town composed mostly of white citizens were exactly the features that attracted some lower-class Caucasians.

Evans had no empathy for the coloreds, Jews, and Catholics on the receiving end of the stick, but he understood that public outrage over reports of mob violence undermined his long-term political objectives. He walked a fine line between reining in his more violence-prone, less refined rank-and-file membership and broadening the Klan's appeal among middle- and upper-class whites who shared the ends of white supremacy even as they winced at the means employed by lower-class Klansmen. To combat press reports about the violent episodes, Evans instructed local Klan leaders to retain tight control over uniforms and members. He explained that it was more effective to support law enforcement officers and lobby elected leaders than to take the law into one's own hands. If the Klan could be seen as part of the solution and not part of the problem, the group could control its enemies more effectively by working inside the political system. Since so many white men in positions of authority already agreed with the Klan's pro-American, pro-Caucasian policy, why risk alienating people who could serve as natural allies?[84]

It was a shrewd strategy, and it paid handsome dividends. Klan violence declined during Evans's tenure, while the organization's political clout increased. Exceptions existed, of course, but overall the Klan became a lobbying organization in many parts of the country. Throughout the 1920s, the KKK shared credit or blame, as the case may be, for electing a bevy of city councilmen, mayors, state legislators, and governors. An untold number of congressmen owed their seat in the US House of Representatives to Klan support. Perhaps as many as sixteen US senators, not only in the South, won elections with KKK assistance. Evans and his operatives were not limited to one party. Like all great opportunists, they aligned themselves with whichever party was in power or seemed most likely to triumph in the next election. By the end of the decade, Klan membership was the sine qua non of a political career in many places.[85]

Many famous American politicians of the age became proud Klansmen in the 1920s and found themselves apologizing for their membership as old men. Hugo Black, the long-serving associate justice of the US Supreme Court who became famous as a civil libertarian, joined the Klan in Birmingham, Alabama, when he was a young lawyer. He later explained that he joined because the group was dedicated to fighting against the "moneyed interests" and also because he believed it was necessary to be a Kluxer if he hoped to sustain a life in public service in Alabama during the 1920s. Whatever his reason, Black resigned his Klan membership after only a few years. He was not alone in using the group as a stepping-stone to loftier heights in American politics.[86]

The Klan reached its apex in the Midwest, especially in Indiana. The state was well known for intolerance, particularly where Catholics were concerned, and the KKK was a natural vehicle for expressing fear over the infiltration of foreign elements into the Hoosier State. The largest Klan gathering ever recorded occurred in Kokomo, Indiana, at a Fourth of July celebration in 1923. More than two hundred thousand men, women, and children congregated on that day to show their allegiance to all things American and "pure."[87]

In 1924, the Klan intruded into national politics by urging candidates at both the Republican and Democratic national conventions not to criticize the Invisible Empire. Evans appeared on the cover of *Time* magazine, attesting to his importance as a national political figure. The Republicans refrained from tackling the KKK at their convention, but Democrats engaged in an internecine struggle that helped to divide the party. A plank denouncing the Klan lost by less than a single vote, thanks to the way different states divided their party delegations.[88]

With its national prominence, the Klan became a lightning rod for criticism. Anti-Klan factions sprang up throughout the land beginning in the mid-1920s. Even as the KKK organized a march on Washington, DC, of between thirty and fifty thousand people on August 8, 1925, the group was facing hard times. As it turned out, a prominent Klansman from the Indiana stronghold became embroiled in a scandal that would strip away the mask of nobility that Kluxers claimed to wear and hasten a day of reckoning.[89]

His name was David Curtis Stephenson, but he went by "Steve." He was an ambitious fellow of uncertain origins. Refusing to shed light on his background, Steve Stephenson once told a reporter, "It's no one's business where I was born or who my folks were." No wonder he was less than forthcoming about his roots. Stephenson was born in Houston, Texas, in 1891 and apparently dropped out of elementary school. After-

[8.7]   A Texas dentist, Hiram Wesley Evans, served as imperial wizard of the Ku Klux Klan from 1922 until 1939. He is shown here dressed in full regalia, sans mask, for a KKK parade in Washington, DC, during the mid-1920s. Courtesy of the Library of Congress.

ward, he demonstrated an aptitude for military life and womanizing, not necessarily in that order. He just missed fighting in World War I, emerging from the service as a second lieutenant, although later stories elevated his rank to major. During the postwar years, Stephenson experimented with socialism and seemed destined for a less than lucrative career as a ne'er-do-well until he stumbled into the burgeoning Klan movement.

A natural salesman with a charismatic personality and messianic tendencies, Stephenson made his home in Evansville, Indiana, and proved remarkably adept at bringing new KKK members into the fold. He was said to have married and abandoned two wives by the time he set up shop in the heartland. He and Hiram Evans later became enemies, but during those early years the two men forged an alliance that helped to oust Doc Simmons from the Klan leadership. Stephenson was well rewarded for playing his part in the palace coup. Not only did he control the Indiana Klan, but Evans asked him informally to oversee developments in many other northern and Midwestern states. Over time, however, Evans recognized the young upstart as an overly ambitious, dangerous rival.[90]

Stephenson controlled every aspect of the growing organizational empire. He created a state newspaper devoted to Klan issues, the *Fiery Cross*. He surrounded himself with sycophants who fancied themselves military elites. He also activated a group known as the Horse Thief Detective Association. A nineteenth-century Indiana statute allowed a group of men to apply to the county commissioner for permission to pursue horse thieves under color of law. The quasi-legal posse system had not been used in decades, but the law was still on the books in 1922. Always an opportunist, Steve Stephenson proposed using the Horse Thief Detective Association as a paramilitary adjunct to the KKK. He also organized the Queens of the Golden Mask, a women's group that provided a flood of new members and funds to the Indiana Klan.[91]

Having established a private fiefdom and attracted national media attention for his organizational skills and personal charisma, Stephenson proposed a bold new program. He was going to purchase a small institution of higher education, Valparaiso College, that was struggling with massive debt. Nothing would shore up the group's legitimacy quite as much as bringing a small but respected college into the Klan family. Much of the purchase was to be financed with funds sent from the Atlanta office. When the financing fell through, an incensed Stephenson blamed Evans and resolved to take an even bolder step. He would split the Indiana Klan from the national organization.[92]

On September 27, 1923, Steve Stephenson resigned from his offices in the national KKK. It was time, he said, to form a rival group using the Klan name. The national Klan under Evans was being "prostituted and cheated in a manner which to a fourth-grade school boy would seem either dishonest or silly and incompetent." Although he and Evans agreed to keep the schism under wraps until after the 1924 primary elections, the stage was set for a major change in the direction of the Klan.[93]

For all their later differences, Stephenson shared Evans's view that the group could most effectively achieve its goals by capturing political office. From his base in Indiana, Stephenson hoped to win a US Senate seat as a Republican in 1926 and perhaps to parlay that success into a successful GOP presidential nomination in 1928. His Klan organization might even propel him into the White House. If that happened, the new president would be well positioned to increase Klan membership virtually ad infinitum. Hiram Evans realized that while this scenario would promote KKK goals, it would embolden the Stephenson faction and destroy the national Klan.[94]

The ambitious plans never came to fruition. Stephenson simply could not or would not control his base impulses. At the height of his influence, the power seemed to go to his head. Famously declaring, "I am the law in Indiana," Steve concluded that he need not obey the rules. When he met a young woman named Madge Oberholtzer early in 1925, he decided he would have her, and the consequences be damned.

It started innocently enough. Stephenson was smitten with the twenty-eight-year-old woman, who still lived with her parents. Introduced to her at an inaugural ball for Governor Edward Jackson, he asked her for a date. She initially declined, but he repeatedly requested the pleasure of her company. She eventually agreed. Steve was attracted to a bright young lady who was far more educated and polished than the usual sort of floozy he dated, and she was flattered by the attentions of such a powerful, charming man.

On the appointed night, Steve dispatched his bodyguard to pick up his date. When young Madge did not return home afterward, her frantic mother and father alerted the police. Their daughter turned up two days later in a horrible condition, physically and emotionally. As the details emerged, it was clear that Steve Stephenson was not the morally upright public servant he claimed to be. He had forced a reluctant Oberholtzer to drink alcohol and accompany him on a train trip. "You're going to Chicago with me," he insisted. "I love you more than any woman I've ever known." In a sleeper car on the train, he violently removed her clothes and shoved her into a lower berth over her vehement protests. As Oberholtzer later recalled, Stephenson "chewed me all over my body, bit my neck and face, chewed my tongue, chewed my breasts until they bled, my back, my legs, my ankles, and mutilated me all over my body." He also raped her.

It was a time when a young woman of virtue was expected to remain pure or at least be discreet about her sexual escapades. To lose one's virtue and good name, at least for some young ladies, was to lose everything. When she awoke the next morning in Hammond, Indiana, Oberholtzer was distraught. Having been compromised and violently assaulted, she did not wish to live. She begged her tormentor to kill her, and Stephenson pointed a pistol at her ribs. When he did not pull the trigger, she resolved to kill herself. Forced to spend another night with the beast, she managed to buy a box of mercuric chloride tablets. When she was alone, she swallowed six pills.

Vomiting blood and obviously in distress, Oberholtzer required immediate medical attention. Stephenson said he would transport her to a hospital if she posed as his wife. When she refused, he forced her to spend the night at his house. By the time one of Stephenson's men carried her home, her condition was so severe that doctors held out little hope for her survival. She died on April 14, 1925, a month following the initial assault, after she suffered a staph infection that combined with kidney failure to end her life.[95]

Despite his assertion that he was the law in Indiana, Steve Stephenson was arrested on assault and kidnapping charges. When Madge Oberholtzer died, the charge was upgraded to second-degree murder. Unrepentant, the cocksure defendant assured reporters, "I've been framed before and this is another frame-up."[96]

The story made national news. The KKK always claimed to protect women and their virtue, and yet here was one of the most influential Klan leaders in the country charged with second-degree murder. The lurid details outraged Americans. Klan supporters were appalled that Stephenson, supposed to be a new breed of Klansman, had acted so recklessly and irresponsibly when he knew that as a high-profile representative of the group, his actions would harm the organization. Klan opponents argued that the sordid episode was exactly what should be expected of brutal racists who carried out violent, illegal acts in the name of chivalry.[97]

At trial, Stephenson's defense attorney contended that because Oberholtzer had voluntarily consumed the mercuric chloride tablets, his client could not be charged with murder. The intervening act of the victim obviated any murder charge. In a less emotionally laden atmosphere, the defense might have succeeded, but the tide of public opinion had turned. Stephenson was everyone's darling before he garnered negative press attention, but the salacious circumstances tarnished his image as well as the Klan's public profile. He was convicted of second-degree murder and sentenced to life in prison, although he won parole thirty years later.[98]

More than anything else, Steve Stephenson's ignominious fall from grace sealed the fate of the Ku Klux Klan in the 1920s. The group could no longer hide in the shadows and pretend to uphold American values when its leaders were exposed as miscreants and thugs. The numbers told the story vividly. From its phenomenal high of 350,000 members, the Indiana Klan fell to only 15,000 members within a year of the Stephenson trial. Nationally, Klan membership was estimated at approximately 6 million in 1924, but by 1930 it had declined to 30,000. The entire decline could not be laid at Stephenson's feet—newspaper reports of other Klan outrages and changing sensibilities among the citizenry contributed as well—but his well-publicized misdeeds stole the headlines during the 1920s. The KKK experienced a revival around the time the civil rights movement was born in the 1950s and 1960s, but it never again experienced the surge of popular support among large segments of the American population that it did from its second coming in 1915 through the decade of the Roaring Twenties.[99]

9

The Rise of a
New Black Culture

"We Are Descendants of a Suffering People"

Whites produced much of the literature about blacks early in the twentieth century, and their works predictably reflected the tired, old stereotypes frequently found in cartoons, advertisements, and early films. The characters and sagas tended to fall into one of two camps. The more benign artistic works depicted blacks as harmless uncles, aunties, and mammies who good-naturedly cared for whites and willingly prostrated themselves before their social superiors. Uncle Remus from Joel Chandler Harris's stories portrayed the quintessential "good Negro" who knew his place and never appeared threatening or sexually lascivious.[1]

The second type of work featured noble whites triumphing over evil, brutish blacks who did not know their place. Thomas Dixon's enormously popular trilogy—*The Leopard's Spots*, *The Clansman*, and *The Traitor*—was perhaps the best-known example of this type of literature. Thomas Nelson Page was another popular writer in this vein. The scion of two prominent families—both considered among the first families of Virginia—and a well-connected lawyer, Page served as President Woodrow Wilson's ambassador to Italy during World War I. Beginning in the 1880s, he also penned a series of stories and books embracing the Lost Cause mythology. According to Page, the Old South was a noble, chivalrous land where "good old darkies" stayed on the plantation, as God intended, unlike the Reconstruction-era "new issue," who were "lazy, thriftless, intemperate, insolent, dishonest, and without the most rudimentary elements of morality." To the delight of many southerners, Page defended lynching as a necessary means to keep rowdy blacks in line.²

If whites insisted on perpetuating demeaning stories about black folk, it was only natural that black folk sought to set the record straight in their own stories, poems, and books.

Negroes were objects of scorn and derision for many white Americans at the beginning of the twentieth century, but the moral blindness of the majority did not wholly define the life and culture of the minority. Men and women living across the color line, mostly invisible to whites, developed their own brand of literature, art, and music that existed in stark contrast to the demeaning stereotypes of Negroes portrayed in white society's cartoons, advertisements, and mainstream films. The exclusivity of the black culture that arose during the first four decades of the twentieth century contained one advantage: it provided an opportunity for people of color to develop their talents mostly free from white interference.

For much of the twentieth century, black writers, artists, and musicians dealt with race as an overriding theme. Living in a country where they were reminded daily of their differences and their presumed inferiority, blacks explored the causes of discrimination through artistic expression. Especially compelling were plots in which a protagonist navigated the tricky, deceptive world of white rules to build a satisfying life. Some works, notably Richard Wright's *Native Son*, tackled controversial issues such as the reasons colored people reflected popular stereotypes, acting out whites' version of blacks as criminals and social deviants. Other works, such as Ralph Ellison's *Invisible Man*, straightforwardly addressed the humiliation of living in a world where a black person was treated as less than a white person, judged "inferior" or rendered "invisible."³

EARLY WRITINGS BY BLACK
AMERICAN AUTHORS

Persons of color did not enjoy the same access to schools and publishers as their white counterparts—two requirements often, but not always, associated with artistic endeavors—but this did not stop them from producing creative works even before the death of the peculiar institution. Phillis Wheatley, an eighteenth-century black woman seized in West Africa and sold in Boston, became one of the earliest black poets in the English-speaking colonies of North America. George Moses Horton, a slave who lived long enough to enjoy his freedom, was another early black poet. He gained fame as the "Colored Bard of North Carolina" for sonnets and other poems depicting a life of servitude and, later, the pleasures of pastoral scenes. Wheatley's ambiguous role as a protest poet has been fiercely debated, but Horton's willingness to express his unhappiness with his social status was well known. In the aptly named "The Slave's Complaint," he muses, "Must I dwell in Slavery's night, / And all pleasure take its flight, / Far beyond my feeble sight, / Forever?" In this work, among others, he laid a foundation for the vast body of black protest works to follow.[4]

Some black poets used a classical style of writing, while others employed Negro dialect and experimental forms of verse. The poet Albery Allson Whitman is a prime example of the former. Born as a slave in Kentucky 1851, he tried his hand at several jobs following emancipation. He eventually became a financial agent for Wilberforce University, a historically black college in Ohio, as well as a pastor in the African Methodist Church of Springfield, Ohio. Between 1879 and 1883, Whitman moved to Georgia, Kansas, and Texas to establish new churches. Even as he worked as a pastor, he fashioned a career as a traditionalist poet, emulating the European Romantic poets. In works such as *Not a Man, and Yet a Man* (1877) and *The Rape of Florida* (1884), Whitman established his reputation as the "Poet Laureate of the Negro Race."[5]

Frances Ellen Watkins Harper, one of the earliest black American women to put pen to paper, was born in Baltimore, Maryland, in 1825 to free black parents. Educated at a time when Negroes and women seldom received formal instruction of any kind, she carved out a career as a poet and writer. Her best-known work, *Poems of Miscellaneous Subjects*, was celebrated by northern audiences for its antislavery messages after it was published in 1854. Thirty-eight years later, her novel *Iola Leroy, or Shadows Uplifted*, penned when Harper was sixty-seven years old, was thought to be the first novel by a black American writer, although earlier works have since been found. This pioneering literary figure gave the lie to the myth that Negroes in the nineteenth century were incapable of producing works of lasting artistic merit.[6]

Another influential black American woman, Pauline E. Hopkins, won fame for her writings at the turn of the century. Born in Portland, Maine, in 1859, she hailed from a family that made up the Hopkins Colored Troubadours, a group of touring performers renowned for their public performances of plays and musicals. Under her family's influence, in 1880 the twenty-year-old young woman wrote a musical play, *Slaves' Escape; or, The Underground Railroad*, later presented in a revised version under the title *Peculiar Sam; or, The Underground Railroad*. She is best remembered for a series of short stories and four novels she published between 1900 and 1903, including the groundbreaking *Contending Forces: A Romance Illustrative of Negro Life North and South* (1900), a detailed and realistic portrayal of Negro life in the years before the Great War. Her novels sometimes are compared with the work of Charles W. Chesnutt because both writers explored the themes of interracial romance and the problems of racial identity for children of mixed blood.[7]

For his part, Chesnutt wrote one of the earliest novels focusing specifically on race and identity. Titled *The Marrow of Tradition*, his 1901 book chronicled a race riot in the fictional town of Wellington, an allusion to the 1898 riots in Wilmington, North Carolina. Born to two "free persons of color" living in Fayetteville, North Carolina, Chesnutt had a complexion so fair that he could have "passed for white" had he been so inclined. Instead, he moved to Cleveland, Ohio, and devoted much of his life to grappling with what it meant to be black. Was it a choice, in his case, or a fixed identity? Although he earned his primary income from a court-reporting business, he was active in the National Association for the Advancement of Colored People (NAACP) and published short stories and novels exploring emotional issues such as the challenges facing mixed-race citizens living in a segregated society. He was never able to support himself as a writer, but Chesnutt was recognized as one of the first black writers to achieve national acclaim.[8]

Sutton E. Griggs, born in 1872 and reared in Texas, began his career as a Baptist minister, following in his father's footsteps. He became a prolific author, eventually writing more than thirty books and pamphlets, many of which he pedaled door-to-door. He also sold his works at revival meetings. Griggs gained a reputation as a militant social critic calling for a separation from whites in the same vein as Marcus Garvey, the well-known Jamaican separatist. During his life and career, however, Griggs appeared to be an integrationist. A fan of the leading black intellectual W. E. B. Du Bois, Griggs considered himself a supporter of the Niagara Movement and a fervent NAACP supporter.

His reputation for having a militant outlook no doubt originated with his first novel, *Imperium in Imperio: A Study of the Negro Race Problem*, published in 1899. The book relies on a well-worn plot device: the binding together of two people, separated by time and circumstance, through common characteristics, in this instance, race. The novel, sometimes characterized as the first Black Nationalist work, follows the lives of two childhood friends separated at an early age. Light-skinned militant Bernard Belgrave becomes the leader of a shadow government based in Waco, Texas, while his friend, Belton Piedmont, a dark-skinned Negro, argues for cooperation with whites and an integrationist approach. Belgrave orders his old friend executed as a traitor to the cause when Piedmont refuses to support an effort to overthrow the Texas state government. Griggs's later works—including *The Hindered Hand*, a 1905 novel written to contradict Thomas Dixon's white supremacist tract *The Leopard's*

Spots—proved to be popular among Negroes but never achieved the success of his first work.[9]

Chesnutt and Griggs enjoyed success as prose authors, while Paul Laurence Dunbar won an unprecedented level of acclaim, at least for a black author, for his poems written in the late nineteenth and early twentieth centuries. Dunbar wrote several works in standard English, while others featured the Negro dialect so popular among white readers. The child of former slaves from Kentucky, he was born in the decade following the Civil War and grew up in Ohio. Although not immune to the humiliating effects of racial prejudice, Dunbar did not live under the suffocating shroud of segregation. His career was brief, but he was prolific, churning out numerous poems and short stories, as well as several novels, before he died of tuberculosis at the age of thirty-three. He left an enduring legacy, especially with his poetry.[10]

THE HARLEM RENAISSANCE

By the 1920s, a cultural movement was under way. Although initially invisible to whites, an artistic revolution occurred across the color line, especially in black Harlem, New York, during the years that US race relations reached a low point. Harlem, a large neighborhood situated in upper Manhattan, became a destination of choice for many Negroes who fled the South during the Great Migration. In the nineteenth century, Harlem had been a prestigious white neighborhood featuring stately homes and cultural centers such as the Harlem Opera House and the Polo Grounds, three stadiums used for sporting events from the 1880s until the 1960s. With large numbers of immigrants flooding into the area at the end of the nineteenth century, the demographics changed. Whites moved away from Harlem, and non-Caucasians took up residence. As foreign immigration slowed to a trickle in the era of the Great War and blacks departed the South in droves, Harlem became increasingly black.

From the end of the Great War until the mid-1930s, Harlem was the center of a cultural movement among black writers, artists, and musicians. Despite the demeaning portrayal of colored people in the white world, or perhaps because of it, Negro artists flourished during this era. The artistic output was so voluminous and accomplished that it became known as the Harlem Renaissance, part of the New Negro Movement, the rise of a new, vital black culture—or perhaps the continuation, in full flower, of an older tradition. Cultural contributions came from many places throughout the country and even as far away as France, but Harlem was the epicenter of the rebirth.[11]

No specific social, political, religious, or cultural event precipitated the renaissance. It sprang up owing to a mixture of historical changes. As the Great Migration intensified, larger numbers of people crowded into ever smaller houses and neighborhoods. With an influx of new people came the desire to develop a unique culture in this celebrated black oasis surrounded by a desert of racial prejudice. Religion played a role, too, as many black Protestant churches embraced the social gospel movement, which called for social progress as a means of realizing Christianity. With the white world so intent on lynching Negroes in the South and denigrating black folk around the country, persons of color yearned to give voice to their pain and anger at the injustices confronting them in their homeland.[12]

Hubert H. Harrison, a socialist writer sometimes called the father of Harlem radicalism, argued that the notion of a renaissance was a myth, yet another creation of whites who wanted to explain an event they did not understand or appreciate. Harrison contended that a rebirth was unnecessary because the artistic output attributed to Harlem during the 1920s simply continued an unbroken tradition that extended far back into the nineteenth century. Black culture had never died, so it did not need to be reborn. As a founder of the Liberty League, an organization dedicated to promoting a "New Negro" who refused to bow down to Jim Crow indignities, and founder of the organization's newspaper, the *Voice*, Harrison became one of the leading black intellectuals of his day. The West Indian–born social activist remained influential until his death at the age of forty-four, but he could not derail the notion of a Harlem Renaissance.[13]

Assuming Harrison's view is discounted, the renaissance probably originated around 1917. Arguably it began when three one-act plays written by white playwright Ridgely Torrence, a former editor of *Cosmopolitan* magazine, premiered on Broadway. The one-act plays—*The Rider of Dreams, Simon, the Cyrenian,* and *Granny Maumee*—presented black characters as fully realized human beings with problems and concerns every bit as nuanced and genuine as those faced by whites. The stage plays were a far cry from the caricatures presented in minstrel shows or in mainstream American films. No black characters bumbled about spouting broken English or kowtowed to their white superiors in a Torrence drama. James Weldon Johnson, the NAACP secretary, civil rights activist, and celebrated poet, hailed the production, perhaps with only a hint of exaggeration, as "the most important single event in the entire history of the Negro in the American Theater."[14]

Johnson himself was a key figure in the Harlem Renaissance. He was a renaissance man in the broad sense of the term. After graduating from college at Atlanta University, he taught public school in Jacksonville, Florida, eventually becoming a principal in a segregated school. He studied law and became the first Negro to pass the Florida bar examination since Reconstruction more than two decades earlier. Later, he served as an NAACP field secretary and rose to become the first black executive secretary of the organization. Johnson was credited with coining the term "Red Summer" to describe the horrific acts of violence against people of color in the United States during the race riots of 1919.

Aside from serving as an educator, lawyer, and civil rights activist, Johnson proved to be a talented writer of poems, song lyrics, essays, and books. His poem "Lift Ev'ry Voice and Sing," set to music by his brother Rosamond, became so popular that it was known as the Negro national anthem. He also published several books of poems and a well-received novel, *The Autobiography of an Ex-Colored Man*, about a black man who "passes for white" after he undergoes a series of horrifying experiences, such as witnessing a lynching.[15]

Other black writers and artists flourished as the 1920s dawned. Jamaican-born writer and poet Claude McKay became another key figure in the renaissance. Following the explosive race riots during the Red Summer of 1919, McKay penned a strident plea for his fellow Negroes to stand up to their oppressors. Although he did not mention specific episodes or races, McKay urged members of an unnamed audience to defend themselves. "Though far outnumbered let us show us brave," he wrote in "If We Must Die." "Like men we'll face the murderous, cowardly pack, / Pressed to the wall, dying, but fighting back!"[16]

New York–born Countee Cullen arguably was the most representative of the many renaissance figures in the 1920s. Cullen earned a college degree from New York University and a master's degree from Harvard. He began writing poetry as a young man and published his work in the NAACP's magazine, the *Crisis*, as well as in the National Urban League's publication, *Opportunity*. His work appeared in the mainstream white press too, including *Harper's*, *Century Magazine*, and *Poetry*. Unlike many of his peers, Cullen did not focus exclusively on racial issues. He had been raised in a white community, and although he sometimes commented on race, he explored other subjects as well.[17]

As the renaissance gained momentum throughout the 1920s, the output was staggering and impressive in terms of both quantity and quality. Most works explored the centrality of blackness in American life. Two major figures especially confronted the issue of skin color, albeit in different contexts. Jean Toomer, a light-skinned man of mixed white and Negro ancestry, published books and essays about the dilemma in choosing one's identity and race. Because he was so light-skinned that he appeared to be "racially indeterminate," Toomer lived in both black and white society throughout his life. *Cane*, his 1923 book, presents a series of vignettes about racial identity. Partially because it does not follow the traditional structure of a novel, it was a strange book for most readers. *Cane* was not influential at the time of publication, but in later years critics hailed it as a brilliant addition to the literature of the Harlem Renaissance.[18]

As a contrast to Toomer, novelist Wallace Thurman explored colorism, the idea that lighter-skinned Negroes discriminate against darker-skinned Negroes. Thurman himself was dark-skinned, and he believed he had met with discrimination not only from whites but from lighter-skinned Negroes who unconsciously mimicked whites' disdain for dark pigmentation. Thurman's 1929 book *The Blacker the Berry: A Novel of Negro Life* follows the tribulations of a young black woman forced to come to terms with her dark skin.[19]

Zora Neale Hurston, a black woman who wrote four novels and more than fifty plays, essays, and short stories, made her name with a 1937 novel, *Their Eyes Were Watching God*. A tangled tale about the trials and tribulations of a young black woman coming of age in central Florida early in the twentieth century, the novel was not well received on publication, but later generations recognized it as a masterpiece. In 2005, *Time* magazine identified *Their Eyes Were Watching God* as one of the one hundred best English-language novels published since 1923.[20]

Although the lion's share of his work appeared after the mid-1930s, when the Harlem Renaissance was thought to be in decline, Frank Marshall Davis became another successful black writer of the period. Davis moved to Chicago in 1927 and began publishing short stories in magazines and newspapers. In 1930, he moved to Atlanta and published the *Atlanta Daily World*, the first ongoing black newspaper in the United States. He later returned to Chicago as managing editor for the Associated Negro Press. Davis's *Black Man's Verse* and *I Am the American Negro* became well known for their use of jazz rhythms and free verse to attack segregation. His most famous book, *47th Street*, first published in 1948, presents a picture of life among various races and ethnicities on Chicago's South Side.[21]

Dorothy West was the youngest of the writers associated with the Harlem Renaissance. Her initial contribution was to establish the *Challenge*, a journal devoted to creative writing and political activism. Her 1948 novel, *The Living Is Easy*, follows the lives of an affluent black family. She remained enormously productive until shortly before her death in 1998, having outlived every other writer of her era.[22]

Poet, playwright, and short story writer Langston Hughes became the acknowledged dean of the Harlem Renaissance. Born in Joplin, Missouri, in 1902, Hughes hailed from a racially mixed family. His paternal great-grandmothers were black but his paternal great-grandfathers were white slave owners from Kentucky. When he was a child, Hughes's family moved to a succession of small towns. He lived with his maternal grand-mother in Lawrence, Kansas, a well-known abolitionist stronghold during the Civil War, after his father deserted the family and his mother was forced to travel in search of employment. He later credited his grand-mother with instilling in him a fierce sense of pride in his race. Around the same time, he developed his lifelong love of literature and books. After his grandmother died, he lived with family friends before he and his mother settled in Cleveland, Ohio.

Hughes studied at Columbia University briefly and worked a series of odd jobs, including a stint laboring aboard a ship that took him to West Africa and Europe. He eventually became a protégé of poet Vachel Lind-say and earned a degree from Lincoln University, a historically black col-lege in Chester County, Pennsylvania.

Hughes's first poem appeared in print in 1921. Titled "The Negro Speaks of Rivers," the short verse, written when he was not yet eighteen years old, shows his extraordinary depth of feeling and sensitivity about race in America. It was no accident that the NAACP's the *Crisis* featured the work in its pages. The poem later appeared in Hughes's first collec-tion, *The Weary Blues*, in 1926.

Hughes developed a distinctive voice in the works that followed. For more than four decades, he used drama, prose, and poems to articulate the sensibilities of black Americans. During the 1920s and 1930s, his work featured jazz rhythms and dialect. Later in life, he became a popular lec-turer and traveled internationally. Hughes was a prolific writer until his death in 1967.[23]

Although poets and prose writers were usually hailed for the works created during the Harlem Renaissance, artists and musicians also con-tributed their talents. Aaron Douglas, a graphic artist and painter, arrived in Harlem in 1925 as a young man in his mid-twenties. He had loved art as a child watching his mother paint watercolors. As a student at the University of Nebraska, he developed his gift. After moving to Harlem, Douglas submitted work to the *Crisis* and *Opportunity* and established his reputation by illustrating Alain LeRoy Locke's influential book *The New Negro*. Douglas collaborated with many important figures from the renaissance. He and Wallace Thurman, Zora Neale Hurston, Countee Cullen, and Langston Hughes, among others, produced a black literary magazine called *Fire!!* After the magazine's offices ironically burned fol-lowing the appearance of the inaugural issue, they did not publish subse-quent editions.

Douglas's modernist portrayal of scenes of American Negro life in a variety of books, including James Weldon Johnson's poetry collection *God's Trombone* and Paul Morand's short story collection *Black Magic*, attracted so much attention and praise that soon Douglas was called the

[9.1]   Langston Hughes, pictured here in 1943, became a leading voice in the Harlem Renaissance. Courtesy of the Library of Congress.

father of African American arts. A humble man embarrassed by the appellation, Douglas asked that he not be given such an exalted title. He was driven by inspiration to create his works of art.[24]

Loïs Mailou Jones was one of the few black women painters to achieve national and international fame during the renaissance. Trained at the School of the Museum of Fine Arts in Boston, she became a virtuoso, demonstrating an uncanny ability to master many styles, from traditional landscape to abstract. She enjoyed a long career, painting into her nineties, long after the Harlem Renaissance had ended. She looked forward to a day when black artists would not have to wear labels identifying their race. In the meantime, she relished the idea that she was a role model, "proof of the talent of black artists." Her work was exhibited in many famous museums, including the Metropolitan Museum of Art, the National Portrait Gallery, and the Hirshhorn Museum and Sculpture Garden.[25]

Jacob Lawrence is sometimes associated with the Harlem Renaissance although his breakthrough work, *Migration Series*, a group of paintings based on the Great Migration, appeared after the generally acknowledged end of the period. Lawrence referred to his style as "dynamic cubism." His prodigious output and distinctive, colorful scenes of black life made him one of the most famous artists of his generation.[26]

Musical creations became as important as literary and artistic achievements during the era. Of all the lasting contributions from the Harlem Renaissance, jazz music sometimes is cited as the most accessible. Developed from Negro music and heavily dependent on syncopation and improvisation, jazz was difficult to define, but it was instantly popular among Negroes in the 1920s. The crucial element was the manner in which jazz flouted traditional musical arrangements. No two performances were the same, and the energy of the performers often mirrored that of the audience.

The names of jazz singers during the 1920s became legendary. A Creole from Louisiana, Ferdinand Joseph LaMothe—known professionally as Jelly Roll Morton—became a well-known jazz pianist and arranger, performing in minstrel shows around the turn of the century. He reputedly adopted the name "Jelly Roll" from a slang term for female genitalia around the time he played piano in a brothel. Jelly Roll Morton became one of the earliest jazz artists to popularize the new style of music. He claimed to have invented jazz, although no one took his claim seriously.[27]

Cab Calloway, a jazz bandleader famous for his "scat" singing, became a frequent performer in a Harlem nightclub, the Cotton Club. His band featured many famous players, including trumpeter John Birks "Dizzy" Gillespie. Calloway remained an active performer until his death at the age of eighty-six in 1994. Jazz orchestra leader and composer Duke Ellington also appeared in Harlem at the height of the renaissance in the mid-1920s, and he too became a frequent fixture at the Cotton Club.[28]

Toward the end of the renaissance in the 1930s, Billie Holiday emerged as one of the leading vocalists in jazz. Her powerful, sultry voice and passionate delivery, coupled with brilliant phrasing, transformed her into an icon before her untimely death at the age of forty-four in 1959. Holiday's 1956 autobiography, *Lady Sings the Blues*, and the 1972 film version starring Diana Ross depict a troubled life that included heroin addiction.[29]

Owing to his continued presence in popular culture, Louis Armstrong, a trumpeter, coronet player, and singer, may be the most renowned musician to emerge from the Harlem Renaissance. He became an important jazz artist by emphasizing solo performances. Armstrong's distinctive, gravelly voice and charismatic stage presence made him a star. He "crossed over," playing not only for black audiences but for whites as well. At the time of his death in 1971, "Satchmo," as he was nicknamed, remained one of the few black performers to have transcended color, although many more artists would follow in his footsteps in the closing decades of the twentieth century.[30]

MARCUS GARVEY AND BLACK NATIONALISM

For all the successes of the Harlem Renaissance, black cultural expressions in the 1920s and 1930s were not limited to artistic output. One of the strongest cultural movements in the first quarter of the twentieth century revolved around Black Nationalism. It was no wonder that Negroes began to express nationalistic fervor beginning in the era of the Great War.[31]

Black soldiers had borne sacrifices during the war, exactly as their white brethren had. Over 1 million Negro men answered the draft call beginning in 1917. Of that number, almost four hundred thousand were inducted into the US Army. As they marched off to war, black recruits hoped their sacrifices would convince whites that men of color should enjoy equal treatment and respect. Blacks had fought in every armed conflict since the American Revolution, and they believed their bravery should be acknowledged and rewarded as evidence of their manhood and dignity. If they demonstrated their national pride by agreeing to serve in the ranks, and if their blood could be spilled as easily as a white man's blood, surely their comrades would recognize their worth as human beings. As Shakespeare noted in the famous St. Crispin's Day speech in *Henry V*,

> We few, we happy few, we band of brothers;
> For he to-day that sheds his blood with me
> Shall be my brother; be he ne'er so vile,
> This day shall gentle his condition.[32]

Unfortunately, the stain of racial prejudice would not be overcome, despite Negroes' exemplary military service. The army assigned blacks to segregated units, most of which performed menial tasks. White military leaders believed that blacks were incapable of undertaking combat functions and instead should perform services such as kitchen and garbage duty. To add insult to injury, segregated units often were assigned to army installations in the southern United States where the men endured the countless daily humiliations associated with Jim Crow.[33]

On August 23, 1917, a group of 156 black soldiers in the 3rd Battalion, 24th Infantry, stationed at Camp Logan, Texas, decided that they had suffered enough abuse at the hands of white citizens, especially the police, in Houston. The soldiers marched through the city for two hours, retaliating against the white community. Twelve white civilians and four law enforcement officers were killed and four blacks died in the melee. In the aftermath, three courts-martial convicted 110 soldiers, with 63 men receiving life sentences and 13 being sent to the gallows. The episode held the distinction of being the only race riot in American history in which more whites than blacks died in the fighting. White segregationists cited the incident as proof that Negroes could not be trusted to serve in uniform or to bear arms.[34]

In addition to harboring fears engendered by the Camp Logan mutiny, whites worried that blacks who served in the military had been spoiled by the experience. Demands by returning soldiers for equality and a loosening of the bonds of Jim Crow suggested that black citizens were "uppity" and no longer knew their place. In conjunction with soldiers returning from war in 1918, the advent of the Great Migration meant that almost 1 million people of color moved from rural areas to cities during the war years. Crowded into urban areas, often in close proximity, citizens of all races were forced to coexist and compete for scarce jobs, housing, and food. It was an untenable situation. Blacks were not welcomed with open arms wherever they went, but it was unrealistic to expect them to return to prewar conditions. In the words of a popular ditty from the era,

> How ya gonna keep 'em down on the farm
> After they've seen Paree'?
> How ya gonna keep 'em away from Broadway
> Jazzin around and paintin' the town?
> How ya gonna keep 'em away from harm, that's a mystery
> They'll never want to see a rake or plow
> And who the deuce can parley-vous a cow?
> How ya gonna keep 'em down on the farm
> After they've seen Paree'?[35]

The answer was that they would not be kept down on the farm. In his essay "Returning soldiers," W. E. B. Du Bois captured the mood of former military men who had grown impatient with the status quo. He urged them to take up the struggle of civil rights and improve the nation by insisting that whites recognize the worth of black citizens. "This is the country to which we Soldiers of Democracy return," Du Bois wrote. "This is the fatherland for which we fought! But it is *our* fatherland. It was right for us to fight. The faults of *our* country are *our* faults. Under similar circumstances, we would fight, again. But by the God of Heaven, we are cowards and jackasses if now that that war is over, we do not marshal every ounce of our brain and brawn to fight a sterner, longer, more unbending battle against the forces of hell in our own land."[36]

For many black Americans, Du Bois's clarion call for an end to Jim Crow and the integration of blacks into white society struck precisely the right chord. It was time for Negroes to take their rightful place at the table alongside whites, to enjoy the same rights and privileges guaranteed by the US Constitution to all Americans. Yet the war and its aftermath, along with the Great Migration, had radicalized some factions. For some young black men and women, W. E. B. Du Bois, once a Young Turk who had so audaciously challenged the Wizard of Tuskegee, had become an ancient, revered figure himself. In displacing Booker T. Washington, Du Bois had become the very thing he had challenged: an icon of the status quo ante. The times were changing, and the integrationist approach to race relations had to change as well. Radical blacks charged that the old man had relied too much on whites to create and operate the NAACP. In the parlance of a subsequent age, he had sold out. Du Bois reclaimed his status as a change agent toward the end of his life, but subsequent civil rights leaders opted for new approaches aside from working through the NAACP. In the meantime, Du Bois remained suspicious and wary of discordant elements. Radical methods in service of a noble cause he could support, but outlandish schemes that threatened to undermine gains in civil rights were to be avoided at all costs.[37]

And outlandish schemes proliferated during the post–World War I era. One schemer and dreamer in particular attracted enormous attention in the black community. Enter a Jamaican immigrant named Marcus Mosiah Garvey Jr. He seemed an unlikely figure to play an important role in American history. Born in a small town, St. Ann's Bay, on the northern coast of Jamaica in 1887, Garvey received only a limited formal education. As he grew to adulthood, he worked a variety of odd jobs in several countries, including Nicaragua, Honduras, Colombia, Venezuela, and Ecuador. A 1912 visit to London brought him into contact with blacks who had emigrated from Africa. He realized that racial discrimination was widespread across the globe and that "white men did not regard the lives of black men as equal to those of white men." In Garvey's estimation, whites did not intend to protect blacks and would never offer "a square deal." Two years later, as he returned to Jamaica, the ambitious young man, now in his mid-twenties, was determined to unite "all the Negro peoples of the world into one."[38]

Unlike many conventional Negro leaders, including Booker T. Washington and W. E. B. Du Bois, Garvey was convinced that blacks and whites could never live side by side. Their differences were too vast, and whites were so deeply invested in segregating themselves from colored people that such prejudice could never be overcome. Garvey also was dismayed by the indifference that many Jamaicans displayed when he founded the Universal Negro Improvement Association (UNIA). The UNIA languished because, according to Garvey, "the colored gentry" in his own island nation would not get behind the organization. He believed the only practical method for realizing his goals was to solicit support from Negro leaders in the United States who might be willing to lend a hand.[39]

Garvey wrote letters to Booker T. Washington in 1914 and 1915 seeking support. The young Jamaican had read Washington's autobiography *Up from Slavery* and was moved by the man's efforts to pull himself up by his bootstraps, despite the systemic discrimination he faced during his early life. Looking back at the two men, it is difficult to imagine a pair of black leaders more diametrically opposed to each other, but they shared a belief that good people of color were in need of a helping hand. It was their methods that differed radically. Whereas Washington thought sympathetic whites could be counted on to help improve the Negro condition, Garvey came to distrust the motives of the dominant race.[40]

The old Wizard of Tuskegee was in the twilight of a long and illustrious career, but he still responded to the younger man's entreaties. He assured Garvey that he would receive a polite, if not exactly warm, welcome if he visited the Tuskegee Institute. "I hope that when you come to America you will come to Tuskegee and see for yourself what we are striving to do for the colored young man and woman of the South," Washington wrote to Garvey in September 1914. "I thank you for the printed matter which you sent. I shall give it a careful reading at the earliest convenience. I regret, however, that I am not able now to make a contribution toward your work."[41] By the time Garvey ventured to the United States in 1916, however, Washington was already in his grave. In light of their different perspectives and personalities, the possibility of a face-to-face meeting of these two distinct figures is intriguing, in any case.[42]

After spending time in Harlem, young Garvey branched out on a tour of America that eventually took him to thirty-eight states. He was already more radical than prominent Negro leaders of the time, but his journey further convinced him that any attempts to forge black-white integration were doomed to failure. An appeal to whites to do the right thing and afford blacks the rights guaranteed in the US Constitution had not resulted in any significant improvements and never would. Garvey argued for black self-reliance rather than reliance on white beneficence. "Race first" became his mantra.[43]

In his quest to uplift the black race, Garvey argued for a reinterpretation of history. The earliest civilizations, he suggested, sprang out of the Middle East where the residents were colored. Many of the great leaders of the ancient world were black, and their achievements far surpassed those of later white civilizations, which frequently stole ideas and treasures from black cultures. Garvey also argued that the historical Jesus was black. When his critics scoffed at this heretical view, Garvey said that God does not think in terms of color, but since color is so important in the world of white men, blacks should consider the logical consequences: "If man was made in the image and likeness of God, then black men should depict a God in their own image and likeness, which would inevitably be black."[44]

Garvey also appreciated the role that symbols played in appealing to the masses. As part of his campaign to uplift Negroes, he designed a new flag with red, black, and green colors to represent Africa. On a trip to Harlem, he announced the formation of a Black Congress. He urged "the 400,000,000 Negroes to claim Africa for themselves" rather than continue to submit to the will and military might of colonial European powers. In 1917, he established the UNIA headquarters in Harlem and called for all blacks to embrace a nationalist message that, among other things, would lead to an eventual return to Africa. If Booker T. Washington had counseled people of color to cast down their buckets where they were and work diligently to improve their lives, Marcus Garvey argued that the bucket must be cast farther away in miles and sensibility—to Africa, the land where it all began. Only after the entire continent became a vast Negro nation-state would blacks truly be able to experience lives filled with meaning and purpose.[45]

Although not well educated, Garvey intuitively understood the psychology of mass appeal. He loved ostentatious displays of Negro pride as a means of attracting UNIA members. During the years after the Great War ended and well into the 1920s, he developed a cult following of "Garveyites" who gravitated to his offices in Harlem. The great man himself sometimes led parades through the streets adorned in a military-style uniform featuring bright purple, green, and black colors. Proclaiming himself the "provisional president of Africa" and sporting a large hat decorated with white plumes, Garvey rode in a large Packard automobile and held court while surrounded by his admirers.[46]

Anticipating that membership in the UNIA would blossom, in 1918 he created a newspaper, *Negro World*, to serve as a forum for spreading the gospel of Marcus Garvey and his philosophy of separatism. Within two years, he claimed a large circulation, sometimes placing the number at fifty thousand readers and on other occasions boasting of two hundred thousand. In 1919, he purchased an auditorium in Harlem, calling it Liberty Hall and using it as his base of operations. On many nights, he held mass meetings for thousands of people as he preached his radical new message. At the beginning of the 1920s, the rotund Jamaican, who only a few years earlier had been an obscure, marginal figure, had emerged as a prominent black leader, an inspiration to untold thousands of Negroes.[47]

During the UNIA's first annual convention, held in Harlem in August 1920, Garvey put on a dazzling show that was not soon forgotten by onlookers. One high point of the convention was a stirring speech before a crowd estimated at between twenty and twenty-five thousand in Madison Square Garden. "We are descendants of a suffering people," he thundered, but the race would no longer be kept subjugated by the oppressor. "We shall now organize the 400,000,000 negroes of the world into a vast organization to plant the banner of freedom on the great continent of Africa."[48]

Convention attendees adopted the Declaration of Rights of the Negro Peoples of the World, a statement of principles that directly confronted the lowly status of colored folk in the United States and around the globe. The declaration observed, "Nowhere in the world, with few exceptions, are black men accorded equal treatment with white men, although in the same situation and circumstances, but, on the contrary, are discriminated against and denied the common rights due to human beings for no other reason than their race and color." Echoing sentiments found in the US Declaration of Independence, the statement insisted that all people are created equal, and no exceptions should be observed. In recognition of this fact, the document enumerated fifty-four rights that should be provided to blacks, including the right to equal accommodations in employment, housing, and travel. As a first enumerated right, the declaration stated, "Be it known to all men that whereas, all men are created equal and entitled to the rights of life, liberty and the pursuit of happiness, and because of this we, the duly elected representatives of the Negro peoples of the world, invoking the aid of the just and Almighty God, do declare all men, women and children of our blood throughout the world free citizens, and do claim them as free citizens of Africa, the Motherland of all Negroes." The statement concluded, "These rights we believe to be justly ours and proper for the protection of the Negro race at large, and because of this belief we, on behalf of the four hundred million Negroes of the world, do pledge herein the sacred blood of the race in defense, and we hereby subscribe our names as a guarantee of the truthfulness and faithfulness hereof in the presence of Almighty God, on the 13th day of August, in the year of our Lord one thousand nine hundred and twenty."[49]

Despite his frequent public promises to reclaim Africa and create a paradise for the 400 million Negroes of the world, Garvey never developed a specific plan to implement his vision. He thought about settling a small group of pioneers in Liberia as an initial step, but conditions there were so poor that he realized the current government would have to be overthrown before Garveyites could establish a new regime. When the Liberian government learned of the scheme, officials seized and deported Garvey's followers from the country, ultimately prohibiting any "person or persons leaving the United States under the auspices of the Garvey movement" from entering Liberia.[50]

The remainder of his program was a mixture of the practical and the fantastical. As an example of the former, Garvey recognized that blacks would never enjoy political power until they gained economic power. Rather than depend on white merchants to supply their clothes and food, he urged his brethren to develop new black businesses as well as to patronize already existing black businesses. This element of his plan was an incremental approach that could yield tangible results. Subsequent black leaders would champion the concept with great success.[51]

In a fantastical vein, Garvey hatched a scheme to promote all-black shipping. He purchased a former coal ship, the *Yarmouth*, for $168,500 and renamed it the *Frederick Douglass*, after the great nineteenth-century civil rights leader. The vessel was to be the first ship in a new Garvey company called the Black Star Line, an all-black steamship enterprise he created in 1919. Its name was an allusion to the famous White Star Line, a venerable English shipping company that became infamous for the dramatic loss of its most celebrated ship, the RMS *Titanic*, when the vessel struck an iceberg and sank in the Atlantic Ocean in April 1912. With the help of investors, large and small, Garvey purchased two additional ships and planned to acquire a fourth, but the company suffered one major setback after another. The *Frederick Douglass* attracted considerable attention from blacks curious to see whether Garvey could compete in the cutthroat world of international shipping. Thousands of people lined the docks in Harlem as the ship prepared to depart on its maiden voyage in 1919. It had moved only a short distance, however, before being halted by authorities because the company had failed to obtain the proper insurance. After that matter was cleared up, the *Frederick Douglass* departed for Cuba. During the journey, it suffered a problem with its boilers. Later trips proved equally calamitous. The Black Star Line eventually sold the ship for $1,625—less than one-hundredth of the original price. The other ships fared no better. In 1922, after only three years in existence, the Black Star

[9.2] During the 1920s, the Jamaican entrepreneur and political activist Marcus Garvey became a vocal proponent of Black Nationalism and Pan-Africanism.
Courtesy of the Library of Congress.

Line declared bankruptcy, and the investors lost everything they had contributed to the venture.[52]

Reactions to Marcus Garvey and his Black Nationalist movement varied. Some observers saw him as a clownish figure. In *Black No More: Being an Account of the Strange and Wonderful Workings of Science in the Land of the Free, AD 1933–1940*, black conservative author George Samuel Schuyler satirized a number of prominent Negro leaders, including Garvey. The novel takes as its premise that a black scientist has discovered a method for erasing racial distinctions so that black people become white. The humor derives from the reactions of various people and groups to this radically altered terrain. Describing Santop Licorice, the thinly veiled Garvey caricature, Schuyler is devastatingly witty:

> Mr. Licorice for some fifteen years had been very profitable advocating the emigration of all the American Negroes to Africa. He had not, of course, gone there himself and had not the slightest intention of going so far from the fleshpots, but he told the other Negroes to go. Naturally the first step in their going was to join his society by paying five dollars a year membership, ten dollars for a gold, green and purple robe and silver-colored helmet that together cost two dollars and a half, contributing five dollars to the Santop Licorice Defense Fund (there was a perpetual defense fund because Licorice was perpetually in the courts for fraud of some kind) and buying shares at five dollars each in the Royal Black Steamship Company, for obviously one could not get to Africa without a ship and Negroes ought to travel on Negro-owned and operated ships. The ships were Santop's especial pride. True, they had never been to Africa, had never had but one cargo and that, being gin, was half consumed by the unpaid and thirsty crew before the vessel was saved by the coast guard, but they had cost more than anything else the Back-to-Africa Society had purchased even though they were worthless except as scrap iron. Mr. Licorice, who was known by his followers as Provisional President of Africa, Admiral of the African Navy, Field Marshal of the African Army and Knight Commander of the Nile, had a genius for being stuck with junk by crafty salesmen. White men only needed to tell him that he was shrewder than white men and he would immediately reach for a check book.[53]

Not everyone viewed Garvey as a comical figure. W. E. B. Du Bois recognized the Jamaican as a powerful orator and a stirring role model for some Negroes and praised the Black Star Line as "original and promising," but he questioned Garvey's separatist sentiments and his strident nationalism. In the pages of the *Crisis*, Du Bois famously remarked, "Marcus Garvey is, without doubt, the most dangerous enemy of the Negro race in America and in the world. He is either a lunatic or a traitor." The US government worried that Garvey was the latter and would incite racial unrest and trigger violence. An investigation by the Bureau of Investigation (later known as the Federal Bureau of Investigation) and the US Postal Service led to charges of mail fraud filed against Garvey for selling stock in the Black Star Line when the company did not own the ship pictured in the brochure mailed to investors.[54]

Garvey and three associates were tried in court, but only Garvey was convicted. He was sentenced to five years in prison. Beginning in 1925, he served his time in the federal prison in Atlanta, Georgia. Throughout the entire ordeal, Garvey argued that the charges were politically motivated and the trial was a sham. He was probably correct, to some extent. The Black Star Line was poorly run, and the company cut many corners, but the charges were extreme, and the harsh sentence was unusual under such circumstances.[55]

President Calvin Coolidge commuted the sentence, allowing Garvey to be released from prison in November 1927. Because he was not a US citizen and had been convicted of a felony, Garvey was characterized as an undesirable alien. The US government deported him back to Jamaica. He lived another dozen years and continued to travel widely in search of followers and financial support, but Marcus Garvey never again set foot in the United States.[56]

His legacy is difficult to assess. On one hand, he was a proud, prominent black leader who dared to articulate a standard of equality for all people of color. He was a radical preacher of a powerful message amid a sea of relatively conformist black leaders in the 1920s. Thousands of black people the world over found him to be an inspirational public figure, a shining example of unbowed, unrepentant Negro manhood existing in a world of dangerous, humiliating white supremacy.

On the other hand, he was a bombastic, opportunistic, self-aggrandizing demagogue who spoke about all sorts of grandiose plans but failed to deliver on his overly ambitious, unrealistic agenda. He was not difficult to marginalize because he appeared so buffoonish, a caricature parading about in a feathered hat and spouting nonsense about being the president of Africa. Garvey scared whites who felt sympathy for the cause of civil rights but feared violent confrontations with militant blacks.

Whatever else he did, Marcus Garvey demonstrated that many Negroes were no longer content to stand by and allow whites to dictate the terms of their lives. As the 1930s dawned, it was clear that changes were coming soon. The looming questions concerned the nature, extent, and timing of the changes.[57]

10

Southern Justice, a Depression, and a War

"I Am Deeply Troubled about the Whole Situation"

On April 12, 1921, President Warren G. Harding stepped before a joint session of Congress to deliver a speech, generally considered his finest, on the problems facing the United States in the aftermath of the Great War. He had served as the nation's chief executive for just thirty-nine days, but already Harding was prepared to outline a plan for returning the country to "normalcy" and getting back to business. During the course of his talk, he turned his attention to the issue of race, an extraordinary topic in light of the federal government's relative indifference to such matters in the years since the end of Reconstruction.[1]

Violence inflicted on people of color had captured national attention in recent years, and the president acknowledged the problem as well as the federal government's responsibility to explore potential solutions. "Congress ought to wipe the stain of barbaric lynching from the banners of a free and orderly, representative democracy," he said. The race problem might be "ameliorated by a humane and enlightened consideration of it, a study of its many aspects, and an effort to formulate, if not a policy, at least a national attitude of mind calculated to bring about the most satisfactory possible adjustment of relations between the races, and of each race to the national life." The president argued it was in everyone's best interests to tackle the sensitive issue. "I am convinced that in mutual tolerance, understanding, charity, recognition of the interdependence of the races, and the maintenance of the rights of citizenship lies the road to righteous adjustment."[2]

If Harding had said no more about the matter, he would still have been a trailblazer, one of the few officials of the federal government to comment in a forthright manner on a pressing domestic issue. Yet the president followed up, first by writing a letter to James Weldon Johnson of the National Association for the Advancement of Colored People (NAACP) agreeing that "a commission embracing representatives of both races" would "bring about the most satisfactory adjustment of relations between the races." He had met with Johnson repeatedly to discuss the sordid state of race relations in the country. Harding and his successor, Calvin Coolidge, supported the formation of a commission, but the plan never advanced beyond the proposal stage.[3]

Harding's second effort was genuinely extraordinary when viewed in the context of the times. In October 1921, the president visited Birmingham, Alabama, a bastion of white supremacy. During an October 26 address commemorating the city's fiftieth anniversary, Harding faced a crowd estimated at somewhere between thirty and one hundred thousand, a third of whom were black. Most onlookers expected the usual political speech filled with platitudes and self-serving observations designed to pander to the audience. In fact, much of the address consisted of exactly those types of bromides. Suddenly, however, Harding's remarks took an unexpected turn. The president condemned lynching and urged his audience to allow blacks an opportunity to improve their lot in life. In a statement that shocked his white audience, Harding expressed hope that "we shall find an adjustment of relations between the two races, in which both can enjoy full citizenship, the full measure of usefulness to the country and of opportunity for themselves, and in which recognition and reward shall at last be distributed in proportion to individual deserts, regardless of race or color." He was careful to point out that he did not advocate full social equality—such a sentiment would have been unthinkable in the Deep South—but he believed that blacks, recognizing their distinctive culture and traditions, should not be automatically relegated to the bottom of the social ladder: "I would say let the black man vote when he is fit to vote: prohibit the white man from voting when he is unfit to vote. Especially would I appeal to the self-respect of the colored race. I would inculcate in it the wish to improve itself as a distinct race, with a heredity, a set of traditions, an array of aspirations all its own. Out of such racial ambitions and pride will come natural segregations, without narrowing any rights, such as are proceeding in both rural and urban communities now in Southern States, satisfying natural inclinations and adding notably to happiness and contentment."[4]

Harding's comments were not radical prescriptions for refashioning the republic. In fact, his thesis essentially was a restatement of Booker T. Washington's 1895 Atlanta Compromise. But coming from an American president addressing a mostly white crowd in a segregated southern city, the sentiments were electrifying. Appalled white southerners condemned the speech, while some blacks and liberal whites hailed it as a break-through statement on the race problem in twentieth-century America.[5]

It is difficult to believe that the Warren G. Harding who spoke out against lynching and called for a commission to discuss race in America was the same man whom history recorded as a disastrous president, a leader whose administration was so rife with corruption that it was pro-claimed a historic failure. Some accounts even suggest that Harding later was sworn into the Ku Klux Klan, although the event is shrouded in mys-tery and highly contested. It appears to have been a story circulated by Harding's political enemies to tarnish his reputation in retaliation for his support of antilynching legislation. In any case, the president of the United States was on record as opposing Judge Lynch's rule. It was an auspicious chapter in a long, tortuous political debate over antilynching legislation, but it was not the first time agents of the federal government had considered the matter.[6]

ANTILYNCHING INITIATIVES

The national campaign against lynching, a major objective of the NAACP, found a champion in Congress even before President Harding uttered his famous remarks in 1921. The history of such efforts could be traced back to the 1880s and 1890s, even before the NAACP existed, a time when lynchings increased in the wake of numerous state laws passed to segre-gate blacks and whites. The legendary muckraker Ida B. Wells-Barnett, a black female civil rights activist, penned pamphlets condemning Judge Lynch at the end of the nineteenth century. She sought to raise national awareness of the mobs that immediately killed blacks suspected of crimes without providing for due process of law. In some instances, law enforce-ment officers handed over detainees to mobs of incensed whites clamor-ing for a hanging even if the responsible parties could not be identified or even if a crime had not occurred. In later years, W. E. B. Du Bois and the NAACP took up the issue and urged the national government to intervene.[7]

The question was whether lynchings were properly the subject of fed-eral legislation. Under the American system of federalism, some issues are the province of the states, including most criminal laws. To propo-nents of dual federalism, the federal government has limited constitutional purposes and is restricted to its enumerated powers. Under such a narrow interpretation, legislation to curb lynch mobs is best handled at the state level. The problem was that many southern states were governed by the same men who participated in mob violence or by their relatives.[8]

Referring to lynchings during his annual message to Congress in December 1892, President Benjamin Harrison remarked, "Such acts are a reproach to the community where they occur, and so far as they can be made the subject of federal jurisdiction the strongest repressive legislation is demanded." The president had identified the problem, but he could offer no solutions owing to the possibility that federal power was limited. In June 1899, responding to the well-publicized lynching of a black man, Sam Hose, in Newnan, Georgia, US Attorney General John W. Griggs answered Harrison's implicit query about the limits of federal jurisdiction regarding lynchings. In Griggs's opinion, "the case had no Federal aspect, and therefore the Government would take no action whatever in regard to it."[9]

Despite this narrow interpretation of federal jurisdiction, members of Congress discussed the possibility of enacting antilynching legislation from time to time. The earliest effort occurred on January 20, 1900, when Congressman George Henry White of North Carolina, one of the few black members of Congress to hold political office in the post-Reconstruction era, introduced an antilynching measure. He enjoyed virtually no political support, but White knew it was important to call attention to a problem that was becoming a national disgrace. As expected, the bill died in committee. Still angry about the defeat, White referred to his proposal a month later during a debate over territorial expansion as an instrument of American foreign policy. "Should not a nation be just to all her citizens, protect them alike in all their rights, on every foot of her soil, in a word, show herself capable of governing all within her domain before she undertakes to exercise sovereign authority over those of a foreign land—with foreign notions and habits not at all in harmony with our American system of government?" It was a powerful rhetorical question that no one dared tackle in 1900.[10]

The next effort occurred a little less than two years later. By that time, North Carolina had retired George White, making him the last black US congressman of the Jim Crow era. Senator George Frisbee Hoar of Massachusetts introduced an antilynching bill into the upper chamber. That Hoar should be the architect of the measure was understandable. He had built a reputation as an advocate for the rights of women and ethnic minorities. His father, Samuel Hoar, had been expelled from South Carolina in 1844 after he was sent to investigate whether free black citizens of Massachusetts had been illegally seized and impressed into service as sailors. George Hoar kept the family's tradition of liberal activism alive with his introduction of the Federal Elections Bill in 1890. If enacted, the bill would have protected black voting rights in the South by allowing representatives of the federal government to supervise federal elections. The Republican-controlled House of Representatives passed the measure, but the Democrats in the Senate filibustered, thereby killing it. Hoar could derive little comfort from the knowledge that his initiative enjoyed majority support from both houses of Congress as well as from President Benjamin Harrison. It was the first major bill in US history to be defeated by a Senate filibuster despite support within the legislative and executive branches of government.[11]

Hoar was temporarily defeated, but he remained devoted to the cause of protecting black rights. After Massachusetts attorney general Albert E. Pillsbury drafted an antilynching measure in 1901, Hoar introduced the language as Senate Bill 1171 on December 9, 1901. It was referred to the Senate Judiciary Committee for consideration. Congressman William H. Moody of Massachusetts introduced the companion measure, House Bill 4572, into the House of Representatives. The Hoar Bill, as it was known colloquially, was designed to "protect citizens of the United States against lynching in default of protection by the States." It also allowed members of a lynch mob to be tried for murder in a federal court exercising appropriate jurisdiction.[12]

Prospects for securing a favorable committee report appeared bright. Hoar served as chairman of the Senate Judiciary Committee, where the bill would be heard, which meant he could control the terms and conditions of debate. Despite his powerful position as committee chairman, however, Hoar did not persuade a majority of the committee members to vote with him. A strict state rights interpretation of the US Constitution distinguished between federal and state authority, deferring to the states in the area of criminal law. Senators on the committee could not overcome their reluctance to involve the federal government in matters traditionally deemed state affairs, even if they agreed that lynching was despicable. For all of his passionate commitment and political power, George Hoar failed.[13]

Seventeen years later, another member of Congress, Leonidas Carstarphen Dyer, resolved to pass an antilynching measure. A lawyer from Missouri who first won election to the US House of Representatives in 1910, Dyer served with distinction, with one small break in service, for more than two decades. His St. Louis district was a point of destination for many blacks during the Great Migration. Soon blacks made up a majority of his constituents. The congressman was concerned about the racial violence that swept the nation in the era of the Great War, especially the East St. Louis riots in 1917.

Dyer desperately wanted Congress to pass an antilynching law, but he was not a naive liberal do-gooder. He knew of previous attempts to enact legislation, and the outlook was not promising. As he contemplated introducing a bill in the House, he was familiar with Senator Hoar's defeat. Much time had passed, however, and the need for federal legislation was greater than ever. The Progressives had sponsored legislation against child labor, and a variety of social reforms had been debated in the years since Hoar's bill had faltered in committee. Surely, if other social legislation could be considered, the time was ripe to introduce a measure protecting the lives of citizens who had never been convicted of a crime.[14]

Dyer introduced the bill, HR 11279, in the House on April 18, 1918. It was soon mired down in the Judiciary Committee. After the congressman eventually introduced a modified version in 1921, President Harding announced his support for the measure during his Birmingham speech in October of that year. The possibility of securing some sort of legislation improved. "If this bill is enacted into law," Dyer explained in a last-ditch effort to garner votes, "it will help to save the lives of human beings and to protect communities from mobs and these lynchings that have come to disgrace our Republic."[15]

Leonidas Dyer had momentum on his side, and he achieved a milestone that had been denied to George Hoar: the Dyer bill received a favorable report from the Judiciary Committee. From there, it advanced to the floor of the House of Representatives. Southern representatives attempted to flee the chamber to deny the majority a voting quorum, but supporters were prepared. They had the doors locked and issued warrants to round up their absentee colleagues and compel their return. Despite these machinations, final debate was postponed until after the holiday recess.[16]

When the House put the proposal to a floor vote in January 1922, the debate grew ugly as representatives from both sides traded epithets. Perhaps the most vitriolic exchange occurred between Mississippi's Thomas Sisson and Wisconsin's Henry Allen Cooper. Sisson dramatically declared, "We of the South are fighting the battles of the white man. You who support this bill are traitors to the white race. We are fighting to prevent the destruction of our white civilization. You who vote for this bill are destroying our white civilization."[17]

It was all too much for Cooper. He rose to his feet and traded insults with his fellow legislator in a back-and-forth worthy of petulant children arguing on any playground in America. The *Congressional Record* captured the low level of discourse verbatim.

"It is the first time that I have heard mob law openly advocated in the Congress of the United States," Cooper said.

"I never advocated mob law," Sisson insisted. "Does the gentleman advocate rape?"

Cooper was incredulous. "Oh, this is simply silly."

"The gentleman is just as idiotic as any man I know."

"Oh, that is pretty cheap," Cooper answered.

Sisson had to have the last word. "Of course, you are always cheap."[18]

When the debate, such as it was, ended and the matter came to a vote, the bill passed the House 231–119, with 4 members voting "present" and 74 not casting a vote at all. Of the total, only 8 of 131 Democrats favored the bill, and they were from northern urban areas with relatively large black populations. In the meantime, only 17 of the 301 Republicans voted against the bill, and those members represented rural areas, mostly in the western and border states.[19]

Predictably, southerners condemned the initiative as another example of federal government encroachment on the powers of the states. From Raleigh, North Carolina, the *News and Observer* went further, denouncing the bill as "Negro coddling." In contrast, the NAACP hailed the Dyer Bill as a triumph. Although he realized that no legislation would automatically prevent lynch mobs from forming, James Weldon Johnson viewed the measure as a crucial first step. Demonstrating his penchant for exaggeration, he proclaimed the bill the greatest concerted action the Negro people had ever undertaken.[20]

Despite a victory in the House, the measure still had to pass the Senate, and that would be a tougher fight. No one had forgotten how the Senate filibuster had killed the Hoar Bill all those years before. Before it came to a floor vote, however, it had to survive in the Judiciary Subcommittee chaired by Senator William E. Borah of Idaho. Borah, nicknamed the "Big Potato," was a powerful senator known to champion liberal causes on occasion, but he was regarded also as something of a prickly fellow who fell back on his conservative roots. Sure enough, the senator let it be known that while he certainly did not support the practice of illegal lynchings, he did not believe the matter was properly handled at the federal level owing to constitutional limitations on congressional authority. If Borah could not be counted on to support the proposal, the likelihood of passage appeared remote.

Although Borah did not favor the legislation, he was not a vehement opponent either. The bill narrowly passed out of the Judiciary Committee on July 28, 1922, by a vote of 8–6. Borah voted against it on the grounds that he did not believe it would survive a constitutional challenge in the courts.[21]

Pleased with the victory in committee, Dyer and his supporters recognized that the bill faced enormous challenges on the floor of the Senate. Several Republicans were rumored to be against the bill, and southern Democrats could be counted on to oppose the measure using every tactic they could employ. The sponsors hoped that Harding would lend his prestige to the effort in light of his previous statements condemning the barbaric practice of lynching. For a brief instant, the president appeared to lend his support. A group of Negro women visited with him at the White House on August 14, 1922. When they discussed the Senate legislation, Harding agreed that he would urge Congress to take up the bill after several other matters cleared the calendar. The delegation departed in high spirits, mistakenly convinced the president would champion the bill.[22]

Dyer and his supporters had misjudged their man. They failed to consider how indifferent Harding was to the bill or how passively he occupied the executive chair. He had been elected as an antidote to the adventurous idealism of the Woodrow Wilson administration, which had vigorously supported a host of measures, including participation in a world war, that left the American populace weary and apathetic. The last thing Harding desired was to become embroiled in a controversy over legislation that probably would not pass the Senate. Even if it somehow managed to win the requisite votes and Harding signed the new law, he believed, as did many federal leaders, the law would be challenged in court and deemed unconstitutional by the US Supreme Court. Thus, when Warren G. Harding condemned lynching, his public statements were mere admonishments against behavior he found distasteful. He did not mean that he would use the power of his office to combat such behavior. Similarly, his promise to urge congressional approval of Dyer's antilynching bill did not mean that the president would throw himself into the thick of the fight. He would sign a bill if one emerged from Congress, but he would acquiesce in the meantime, convinced the Supreme Court would have the last word even if the bill cleared Congress.[23]

Senator Henry Cabot Lodge, an ostensible supporter of the Senate bill, allowed a junior senator, Samuel Shortridge of California, to shepherd the measure to the floor for consideration on September 21, shortly before adjournment. When southern senators learned that the bill might be considered, they immediately maneuvered to delay the vote until the Senate adjourned. For supporters, Lodge's willingness to allow a junior senator to control the measure on the floor demonstrated his tepid support.[24]

When the Senate reconsidered the matter in November 1922, southern partisans were prepared with an array of parliamentary procedures, long-winded speeches, and delaying tactics. Senator Oscar W. Underwood, a Democrat from Alabama, informed the Republicans that he and his colleagues would filibuster until the antilynching bill was withdrawn from the floor. James Weldon Johnson, lobbying on behalf of the NAACP, urged Senator Lodge and his supporters to fight the southern delegation, but to no avail. Bill supporters realized that they were beaten and withdrew

[10.1] Warren G. Harding called for improved race relations early in his tenure as president. Alas, Harding's actions did not match his rhetoric.
Courtesy of the Library of Congress.

support. The bill failed. For all of its support at the outset, the Dyer proposal joined its predecessors as a dead letter.[25]

In January 1934, a little over a decade after the Dyer bill failed, Senator Edward P. Costigan, a Democrat from Colorado, and Senator Robert F. Wagner, a Democrat from New York, introduced an antilynching bill that attempted to address concerns about the federal government interfering with state rights. The bill prohibited mob (defined as three or more persons) behavior leading to a lynching with the collusion of state or local law enforcement officials. A police officer found guilty of conspiring with a mob to orchestrate a lynching in his jurisdiction could be subject to between five and twenty-five years in prison and a fine of between $2,000 and $10,000, which would be earmarked for the victim's family. The sponsors argued that this measure was an improvement over the Dyer Bill because it did not interpose the federal government into state criminal affairs directly. Instead of making lynching a federal crime, the bill proposed to hold state and local officials accountable for collusion and to allow thirty days for a local investigation into a lynching before the federal government could intervene. By allowing state action prior to federal involvement, Costigan and Wagner hoped to assuage the southern fears that had doomed the Dyer Bill.[26]

Critics charged that lynching might occur without the knowledge or participation of law enforcement officials. The concern was legitimate. In later years, many lynchings would occur in secret without direct law enforcement approval. Nonetheless, the measure was designed to curtail the large public lynchings that seemed to take place with alarming frequency in all parts of the country, not only in the South.

Even as the bill was winding its way through Congress, an incident occurred illustrating precisely the set of circumstances the sponsors hoped to prevent. A black man named Rubin Stacy appeared at the door of a white woman in Fort Lauderdale, Florida, one day in July 1935. The woman who lived there, Marion Jones, claimed he viciously attacked her before he ran off. Authorities arrested Stacy, a day laborer, three days later. Jones identified him as her assailant, at which point the police escorted the suspect to the local jail. Upon hearing that a black man had attacked a white woman, an angry mob formed outside the jail. Deputy Sheriff Bob Clark decided the prisoner should be moved, and a judge ordered him to be transported to Miami for "safekeeping." Whether Clark was complicit or merely overwhelmed by a superior force became a matter of dispute; in any case, the mob intercepted the prisoner and lynched him from a tree. According to some accounts, Clark passed around his handgun so onlookers could shoot at the dying man. Grisly photographs of the scene show a corpse swinging from a tree, surrounded by a crowd of gleeful whites, some of them grinning children.[27]

Outraged supporters of the Costigan-Wagner legislation cited the Stacy murder as yet another shameful episode, exactly the type of incident the bill would prevent beforehand or punish afterward. They lobbied President Franklin D. Roosevelt to intervene and offer public support for the bill. In what had become a familiar refrain, Roosevelt, who had condemned lynching in public, worried about the political costs and refused to lend his support. Southern Democrats were enormously powerful in Congress, and the president feared his legislative agenda would suffer if he alienated such a crucial voting bloc by publicly praising the legislation. As his wife, Eleanor, who supported the bill, later explained in a letter to Walter White of the NAACP, "The President feels that lynching is a question of education in the states, rallying good citizens, and creating public opinion so that the localities themselves will wipe it out. However, if it were done by a Northerner, it will have an antagonistic effect." At the same time, the First Lady was sympathetic. "I am deeply troubled about the whole situation as it seems to be a terrible thing to stand by and let it continue and feel that one cannot speak out as to his feeling. I think your next step would be to talk to the more prominent members of the Senate." Walter White and the NAACP certainly reached out to other senators, but they could not drum up the necessary votes. As so often happened with antilynching bills, the proposal died in the Senate.[28]

Once again, however, Congress took up the effort. In 1937, Congressman Joseph A. Gavagan of New York introduced an antilynching measure in the House of Representatives. The bill passed the House and moved into the Senate Judiciary Committee, where it joined a Senate bill sponsored by Senator Wagner and Senator Frederick Van Nuys of Indiana. The Wagner–Van Nuys bill was similar to the Costigan-Wagner bill. It provided for a prison term of up to five years as well as a $5,000 fine for a state official who did not protect a prisoner from a lynch mob. The earlier legislation had defined a "mob" as at least three persons, but the Wagner–Van Nuys bill lowered the minimum number to two. The county where the lynching occurred could be liable for as much as $10,000 to a victim's family under the Wagner–Van Nuys plan. Illinois senator William Dieterich slipped in a rider that exempted mobster and labor-related murders because he thought the definition of the crimes covered in the bill was too broad. On June 22, 1937, the Senate Judiciary Committee reported favorably on the twin bills, although committee members stated their preference for the Senate version.[29]

In mid-August 1937, the legislation came before the full Senate. The southern bloc knew the bill was advancing to the floor, and the members came equipped with the usual constitutional arguments. They also were organized and prepared for a long fight. Texas senator Thomas Connally, a week shy of his sixtieth birthday, was the nominal leader of the group.

Smart, experienced, and thoroughly versed in old-style southern oratory, he was also a smooth character, having recognized that the vitriolic rhetoric of avowed racists such as South Carolina's "Cotton Ed" Smith or Mississippi's Theodore Bilbo was not a recipe for success with senators from outside the South or with much of the public everywhere.[30]

Rather than fall back on the tired old cliché of protecting southern women from sexually lascivious black men, Connally grounded his opposition to antilynching legislation in a constitutional principle. On August 11 and 12, he explained his views in a dramatic oration demonstrating a level of sophistication absent from many state rights addresses. Northern legislators, he said, were pushing antilynching legislation in a cynical attempt to attract political support from black voters in urban areas of the North, a tacit acknowledgment of the ramifications of the Great Migration. Southerners, being faithful constitutional stewards, could not allow such self-serving misuse of the Fourteenth Amendment. In addition, the problem of lynching, he continued, was mostly settled. The South had handled the issue, and there was no need to pervert the Constitution to address a nonissue. "In the matter of lynching," he assured his colleagues, "we are opposed to lynchings. I am opposed to lynchings, and over the years the problem has been largely solved."[31]

The speech galled the bill's supporters, but they had few options but to watch as the initiative wound its way through the Senate with the glacial speed so characteristic of the body. It sat on the calendar for another three months while the Senate handled other matters, including a farm bill. When he heard criticism of the Senate's willingness to delay consideration of the antilynching bill, Connally, known for his acerbic wit, tartly replied, "The President wants the Congress to address itself first to farm legislation," while Wagner "wants to go on a vote-catching expedition in Harlem." As for the bill, Connally appealed to his fellow southerners by contending that Wagner and Van Nuys were hell-bent on tarnishing the South's reputation. "This is a bill to brand us as barbarians. This is a bill to brand us as backwards. This is a bill to cover all of us with odium, without keeping any on their hands if they can help it."[32]

When Wagner–Van Nuys finally came up for consideration at the end of the year, one southerner after another stood in the well of the Senate and thundered against the bill. Although some senators understood the new constitutional arguments and used them skillfully, others—generally the old-timers who did not bother to study up on the legal niceties or temper their remarks—spouted the usual white supremacist rhetoric that had served them well with their constituents. Even statements designed to be minimally abrasive were filled with paternalistic language indicating the second-class citizenship extended to Negroes. Senator Charles O. Andrews of Florida uttered the quintessential statement of southern orthodoxy as he waxed eloquent about the wonderful state of race relations south of the Mason-Dixon Line. Recalling how black women customarily had cared for white children in the Old South, he wistfully commented, "There is nothing more beautiful in history than the relation which then existed, and to a large extent now exists, between the old black mammy and her charges."[33]

The year 1937 ran out, but the Senate had yet to vote on the measure. The leadership agreed to take up the antilynching bill as the first order of business in January 1938. Initially, the southern bloc feared that the bill supporters had gathered enough votes to invoke cloture, a Senate rule allowing debate to be halted if at least two-thirds of the senators agreed to cut off discussion. (The Senate changed the requirement to a three-fifths vote in 1975.) Nonetheless, despite the risks, the southern men knew they had to fight passage of the bill, using the filibuster, if possible. As Senator Richard B. Russell of Georgia remarked to a constituent around this same time, "If we are finally exhausted and permit the passage of the anti-lynch bill, it would be followed by legislation to break down segregation of the races in schools, hospitals, churches, restaurants, hotels, bath houses, and all other public places, as well as by bills giving the ballot to every negro, and striking down State statutes preventing intermarriage of the races." In short, allowing any legislation undermining the southern way of life to emerge from the Senate would begin the long process of dismantling the racial caste system painstakingly constructed by white southerners in the decades since the end of Reconstruction.[34]

As they had done late in 1937, southern senators rose on the Senate floor one after another and held court for hours. When the expected cloture motion came to a vote on January 27, 1938, they were delighted to find that the majority could not muster the two-thirds needed to close debate. In fact, Wagner–Van Nuys supporters could not scrape together even a majority to vote on their behalf. The bill did not pass, and the Senate had other business to transact. On February 21, 1938, Alben W. Barkley, the Senate majority leader, moved to end the filibuster by setting aside the Wagner–Van Nuys bill, effectively killing the measure.[35]

Uncertain whether they won on the merits or because their fellow senators refused to vote for cloture (fearing retaliation in other legislation), southerners nevertheless declared victory in defeating the antilynching bill. As Connally told his southern colleagues at the time, however, the Senate bloc would have to remain eternally vigilant. He doubted whether northern members of Congress would be satisfied with the status quo for long.[36]

He was correct. Additional antilynching measures followed the death of Wagner–Van Nuys, but they met the same fate as their predecessors. A 1940 bill, for example, languished in committee, mirroring the Hoar Bill

[10.2]   A group of US senators led a filibuster against passage of antilynching legislation. Several southern senators—from left to right, Tom Connally of Texas, Walter F. George of Georgia, Richard B. Russell of Georgia, and Claude Pepper of Florida—are shown here on January 27, 1938, the day they survived a cloture vote to cut off debate and end the filibuster. Courtesy of the Library of Congress.

from early in the century. Following yet another legislative defeat, civil rights crusaders realized it was time to shift their strategy, or they might never overcome the southern bloc's power in the Senate. They focused on attacking poll taxes, literacy tests, and other cornerstones in the house that Jim Crow built. During the 1950s and 1960s, their efforts would ignite a national civil rights movement that would topple the segregation regime that had stood for close to a century. As the 1930s dawned, however, those successes were decades in the future. A more immediate concern for most Americans was an unprecedented economic depression and, later, a global war that would transform the United States in myriad ways.[37]

It was evident the federal government was unwilling or unable to come to the aid of black Americans throughout the 1920s and 1930s. For southerners, it was a matter of white supremacy. Blacks simply were inferior to whites, and it was not the business of naive, politically liberal, northern do-gooders to interfere in matters that did not concern them. If those senators and congressmen who always seemed intent on policing southern affairs wanted to take up racial matters, they should look closer to home. The North was hardly a sanctuary for blacks moving up from the South. Racism, high unemployment, and occasional violence were present there as well, to say nothing of the dismal working conditions waiting for Negroes in northern factories.

And so the lynchings continued without federal intervention. In some years, the numbers decreased, only to spike the following year. It was true that the overall numbers were far lower in the 1920s and 1930s than they had been during the 1890s, when lynching seemed to be a favorite southern pastime, but the raw data failed to capture the total political, social, and economic control that white southerners exercised over a majority of the black population.[38]

THE SCOTTSBORO BOYS

Aside from lynching, perhaps nothing illustrated the rampant racism and white domination of Negroes in the southern United States during the era better than a court case that became a cause célèbre, the Scottsboro Boys affair. Nine black defendants charged with raping two white women in Alabama escaped lynching—a victory of sorts—and were afforded numerous trials and appeals, which convinced many whites that the cause of justice had been served. A dispassionate observer could not help but recoil at the lack of fairness in the trials, but whites of the era believed they had demonstrated an admirable level of restraint by preventing Judge Lynch from interceding in the matter.[39]

The episode began in Stevenson, Alabama, on March 25, 1931, when a stationmaster in the railroad depot looked up to see a group of hobos standing before him. Although stowing away in boxcars was illegal, more than two hundred thousand Americans across the country had taken to the rails out of desperation during the Great Depression. Many so-called hobos were homeless, hungry, and in search of work and food. They could not afford to buy a ticket, so they hopped aboard and rode for free. On this day, the hobos standing before the stationmaster were white.[40]

Normally, stowaways avoided contact with railroad employees at all costs, but in this instance one fellow, bleeding from the head, complained that a "bunch of Negroes" had thrown him and several white companions from a freight train of the Southern Railway line traveling out of Chattanooga, Tennessee. The whites insisted they wanted to press charges. With black thugs on the loose, the stationmaster quickly overlooked the white hobos' transgressions. He telephoned ahead and discovered that the train was approaching the small town of Paint Rock, located in Jackson County, Alabama.[41]

Jackson County sheriff M. L. Wann learned of the incident and immediately called his deputy, Charlie Latham, on the telephone. Sheriff Wann was not on the scene in Paint Rock. In his absence, he instructed Deputy Latham to deputize as many local citizens as needed to "capture every Negro on the train and bring them to Scottsboro." Latham complied by assembling a posse of men to greet the freight train at the Paint Rock depot. Anxious to avoid a bloody incident, he instructed the men to hold their fire unless their safety demanded an armed response.

The newly minted deputies searched all forty-two boxcars and discovered nine black men and boys as well as one white man and, surprisingly, two white women dressed in overalls. The young black men—Charley Weems, Ozie Powell, Clarence Norris, Olen Montgomery, Willie Roberson, Haywood Patterson, Andrew (Andy) Wright, Leroy (Roy) Wright, and Eugene Williams—were not traveling together except for the brothers Wright. They were typical hobos—poor, more or less homeless, and frightened when rousted from the boxcars.[42]

Although black men accused of a crime against whites in Depression-era Alabama could expect to receive harsh treatment, the matter might have ended with little more than a minor brouhaha had the two women not been present. Black and white stowaways fighting on a train was a crime, to be sure, but it wasn't the sort of encounter that usually led to a lynching. Yet the episode took an unexpected turn when the two women told an astonishing tale. Ruby Bates and Victoria Price informed Deputy Sheriff Latham that the nine black men and boys had gang-raped them on the train.[43]

The idea that nine black men would rape two white women on a slow-moving train traveling through the South and wait around to be apprehended was preposterous, but the charge fit neatly with the supposed propensity of black men to rape white women at any opportunity. Bates and Price were the kind of low-class white women excoriated in the South—they were known to trade sex for money and food with both black and white men—but their rape charge allowed white authorities to ignore the unsavory character of the women and focus on the sordid nature of the crime.[44]

Deputy Latham and his posse immediately arrested the nine black suspects and herded them into the Scottsboro jail. As word spread of the dastardly deed, an angry crowd assembled outside the building. With each telling, the stories grew ever more vivid and brutal. One version portrayed the "black brutes" as having "chewed off" one of Ruby Bates's breasts. Outraged, the mob chanted, "Let those niggers out!" "Give 'em to us." This was precisely the type of situation in which a frenzied crowd might overpower law enforcement officers, barge into the jail, drag the prisoners from the building, and take them to a tree.[45]

Sheriff Wann arrived at the jailhouse and immediately understood the gravity of the situation. However much he despised the crime, he was determined not to allow Judge Lynch to hold court in his county. Afraid of imminent mob violence, the sheriff telephoned Governor Benjamin Meeks Miller for assistance. The governor was no friend of Negroes, but he was a law-and-order, anti-Klan official. Realizing that he would have a riot on his hands if he did not take immediate, decisive action, Miller dispatched the National Guard to protect the prisoners. By 11 p.m., Major Joseph Starnes was on his way to Scottsboro from Guntersville, twenty miles away, with twenty-five armed Guardsmen under his command. There would be no lynchings on Governor Miller's watch.[46]

Scottsboro was barely a dot on the map in 1931. Only thirty-five hundred people lived there, and they were unaccustomed to attention from the state or the nation. Yet on the morning after the arrests, mobs of reporters, law enforcement personnel, National Guardsmen, and curiosity seekers from neighboring communities suddenly descended on the town. The Scottsboro episode was shaping up to be a national, and eventually an international, story.[47]

H. G. Bailey, the circuit solicitor, announced that a grand jury would be convened forthwith to determine whether the nine defendants would be indicted for rape. He also said that he would seek the death penalty. Judge Alfred E. Hawkins informed the press that the trials would be fair and impartial—as if these features were rarities in an Alabama courtroom. He agreed to appoint defense counsel from among the seven members of the Scottsboro bar association. Eventually, the judge had to look elsewhere when all seven members explained they could not assist in the defense. Milo C. Moody, an impecunious sixty-nine-year-old lawyer described as a "doddering, extremely unreliable, senile individual," who needed the modest fee offered for the case, stepped forward to offer his services. Family members from among several of the Scottsboro defendants also scraped together enough money to retain an alcoholic real estate attorney from Chattanooga, Stephen Roddy, to appear as codefense counsel. The judge appointed the pair to represent all nine suspects.[48]

The defense attorneys sought a change of venue in light of the clamorous mood of the throngs of people milling around outside the courthouse, but the judge denied the motion. He also agreed to allow the defendants to be tried together in groups of two or three. First up were Clarence Norris and Charley Weems.[49]

The prosecution's strongest witness, feisty Victoria Price, took the stand and testified about a vicious gang rape initiated by black brutes wielding guns and knives. The defense lawyers tried to impeach her character by depicting her as a woman of "easy virtue," in euphemistic terms, and given to indiscriminate sexual escapades, but Judge Hawkins, an old southern gentleman who refused to entertain the idea of a lascivious white woman, would have none of it. He refused to allow Moody and Roddy to pursue such an insulting line of questioning. Rebuffed by the judge, the inexperienced defense attorneys should have shifted their attention to the flimsy medical evidence, the weakest part of the state's case. Had they done so, they could have hammered home the point that the physician who examined Victoria Price and Ruby Bates discovered "nonmotile" semen, indicating the women had engaged in sexual intercourse much earlier than the time of the alleged attack. If the women had been raped by nine males only hours before the examination, the physical evidence would have included live semen.[50]

Given the widespread racial prejudice that existed in Alabama at the time, the defense never had much of a chance at securing an acquittal, but whatever marginal hopes it had died when Clarence Norris took the stand. The defense attorneys repeatedly argued that no rape had ever taken place. Their theory of the case was that Victoria Price had fabricated the story and bullied the more pliant Ruby Bates into corroborating her account so they could avoid being prosecuted for vagrancy after they were pulled from the freight train. Norris, however, contradicted the defense theory. He claimed that a rape had occurred but that he had taken no part. As a black man living in the South in 1931, Norris believed the jury would conclude a rape had occurred regardless of the physical evidence. After all, if a white woman claimed it had happened, she had to be taken at her word. His only hope was to confirm that a crime had occurred but to deny that he was a perpetrator. It was a disastrous choice. By admitting a rape had taken place, Norris supported the prosecution's theory of the case.[51]

The all-white jury departed from the courtroom to deliberate. Immediately afterward, the second trial, featuring Haywood Patterson as the sole defendant, began inside the same courtroom. The case followed the same pattern as the first. Victoria Price was the lead witness. If anything, she was more polished and persuasive the second time around, having learned from the dress rehearsal in the first trial how to sharpen her testimony and eliminate inconsistencies in her tale. Ruby Bates followed, and she remained the same terrible witness from the first trial who could not recall the sequence of events or specific details. She was fortunate that the verdict was a foregone conclusion. A neutral observer listening to her testimony would have noticed the flaws and contradictions. She simply was not a credible witness.[52]

No sooner had Ruby Bates left the stand than jurors from the first trial announced that they had reached a verdict. They found Norris and Weems guilty and recommended the death penalty. When word of the result reached the crowd amassed outside the courthouse, the roar of approval was unmistakable. Men and women laughed and hollered in jubilation.

The message was clear: black males would be marked for death if a white woman accused them of a sex crime, regardless of the evidence. Whether through slavery, segregation, peonage, medical experimentation, forced sterilization, lynching, or jury trials on trumped-up charges, the South always had exercised control over darker-hued peoples and always would, or so it seemed. The message was repeated in the trials that followed: eight of the nine Scottsboro defendants were convicted and sentenced to death. Only twelve-year-old Roy Wright received a slightly different outcome. His case ended in a mistrial because the jurors were divided over the means for punishing a child. The date for execution of the other defendants in the electric chair was set for July 10, 1931.[53]

The NAACP had been following the case closely in the media and was debating whether its lawyers should intervene in the matter. One overriding consideration was the defendants' guilt or innocence. The association carefully guarded its reputation and did not want to commit resources to the case if the defendants were guilty. With the NAACP absent from Scottsboro, the International Labor Defense (ILD), the legal arm of the American Communist Party, offered to assist the defendants in an appeal. Fearing the negative publicity for Negroes if a group with Communist ties appeared in Alabama, the NAACP later sought to wrest control of the case from ILD representatives, but it was too late.[54]

To no one's surprise, the Alabama Supreme Court upheld the convictions on appeal by a vote of 6–1. In an odd bit of reasoning, the justices refused to condemn the hasty trial for infringing on the defendants' constitutional rights. Instead, they decided the trial court's quick action instilled respect for the law and prevented the mob from taking matters into its own hands. Similarly, the high court did not comment on the tense atmosphere caused by a mob of angry whites encircling the courthouse during the trials. To the Alabama justices, the National Guard on the scene had ensured that law and order prevailed. The court also was unfazed by the appointment of defense counsel on the morning of the trial, finding that nothing that happened in Scottsboro that day deprived the defendants of their Sixth Amendment right to effective assistance of counsel.[55]

Now fully committed to the case, the ILD handled an appeal from the Alabama Supreme Court to the US Supreme Court. The appeal presented three constitutional arguments. First, the lawyers argued the presence of a mob outside the courthouse violated the Fourteenth Amendment due process clause. The absence of blacks from the jury pool also denied the defendants equal protection of the law and due process of law. Finally, the defendants were denied effective assistance of counsel. The US Supreme Court granted certiorari and heard oral arguments on October 10, 1932.[56]

The high court announced its decision in *Powell v. Alabama* on November 7, 1932, with Justice George Sutherland writing for a majority of seven. The court agreed with the ILD that the defendants' right to competent legal counsel under the Sixth Amendment as well as their Fourteenth Amendment due process rights had been denied. "In the light of the facts outlined in the forepart of this opinion—the ignorance and illiteracy of the defendants, their youth, the circumstances of public hostility, the imprisonment and the close surveillance of the defendants by the military forces, the fact that their friends and families were all in other states and communication with them necessarily difficult, and, above all, that they stood in deadly peril of their lives—we think the failure of the trial court to give them reasonable time and opportunity to secure counsel was a clear denial of due process," Sutherland wrote. The law requires that criminal defendants be afforded adequate protection so that their guilt or innocence can be ascertained without prejudice. The Scottsboro trials were prime examples of a rush to judgment. The trial judge dredged up an old lawyer who was not an expert in criminal law, and his cocounsel was an out-of-state real estate attorney. Sutherland explained, "In a capital case, where the defendant is unable to employ counsel and is incapable adequately of making his own defense because of ignorance, feeble mindedness, illiteracy, or the like, it is the duty of the court, whether requested or not, to assign counsel for him as a necessary requisite of due process of law, and that duty is not discharged by an assignment at such a time or under such circumstances as to preclude the giving of effective aid in the preparation and trial of the case." At the conclusion of his majority opinion, Justice Sutherland granted the defendants a new trial.[57]

To ensure the defendants were well represented during the retrials, the ILD engaged Romanian-born Samuel S. Leibowitz, a legendary trial lawyer from New York known for his brilliant mind and courtroom prowess. Initially, he seemed to be an ideal choice, the best lawyer money could buy. As time would demonstrate, Leibowitz was not an ideal advocate to try a case in the wilds of Alabama. Although he was not a Communist Party member, his ILD connection, Jewish surname, and "Yankee ways" transformed him into an outsider who seemed to hold southerners in contempt. Leibowitz also insisted on attacking the credibility of the two women, Victoria Price and Ruby Bates, which struck white citizens as an attack on southern womanhood by a foreign man who sought to besmirch the traditions of the South.[58]

As the first order of business, the state of Alabama retried Haywood Patterson at the end of March 1933. This time, the court allowed a change of venue to the town of Decatur, sixty-five miles away from Scottsboro. Standing before the judge and jury, Leibowitz was well prepared and devastating in his questioning. He exposed numerous inconsistencies in eyewitness testimony offered by the prosecution. Ruby Bates even recanted her earlier testimony. A neutral consideration of the facts suggested that the defendant would be acquitted. Yet for all his legal acumen, Leibowitz failed to appreciate southern mores. White jurors in Alabama would not accept the word of a black man over the testimony of a white woman. If Victoria Price said that Haywood Patterson had raped her, no other testimony or physical evidence was necessary to convict the defendant. As in the first trial, the jury immediately found Patterson guilty and sentenced him to death.[59]

That verdict might have been the end of the story—another shameful example of southern "justice" meted out to a poor, black defendant—had it not been for Judge James Edward Horton Jr., an Alabama trial judge presiding in Decatur and celebrated for his "unusually equable nature, great legal ability and fairness." When the case commenced, Judge Horton believed that the defendants probably were guilty, but the evidence changed his mind. Listening intently in court as Leibowitz presented his case, Judge Horton recognized the inconsistencies in Victoria Price's testimony, the flawed physical evidence, and the improbability of a gang rape. A jury verdict convicting the defendant was all but assured, but what happened next in Judge Horton's courtroom shocked white people across the South.[60]

Horton faced a courtroom packed to overflowing on June 22, 1933. Reading his opinion aloud, he expressed skepticism that a crime had occurred in the first place. "How can the physical condition of Price be reconciled with the gang rape she claimed to have suffered? Why did the jagged chert not bruise her back? Why did the pistol lick on her head not leave a visible wound? Why was no semen found in her pubic hair? Why was the spermatozoa in her vagina non-motile? Why was her respiration and pulse normal less than two hours after the rapes? Why was she not hysterical or crying?" The only reasonable explanation was the obvious one: the women had not been raped. The defendants had been falsely accused.[61]

In remarks that demonstrated the judge's willingness to risk an assault on southern womanhood, he commented on the character of the accusers.

> History, sacred and profane, and the common experience of mankind teach us that women of the character shown in this case are prone for selfish rea-

sons to make false accusations both of rape and of insult upon the slightest provocation for ulterior purposes. These women are shown, by the great weight of the evidence, on this very day before leaving Chattanooga, to have falsely accused two Negroes of insulting them, and of almost precipitating a fight between one of the white boys they were in company with and these two Negroes. This tendency on the part of the women shows that they are predisposed to make false accusations upon any occasion whereby their selfish ends may be gained.

In a stunning conclusion, Judge Horton summarized his position:

The Court will not pursue the evidence any further. As heretofore stated, the law declares that a defendant should not be convicted without corroboration where the testimony of the prosecutrix bears on its face indications of improbability or unreliability and particularly when it is contradicted by other evidence. The testimony of the prosecutrix in this case is not only uncorroborated, but it also bears on its face indications of improbability and is contradicted by other evidence, and in addition thereto the evidence greatly preponderates in favor of the defendant. It therefore becomes the duty of the Court under the law to grant the motion [to override the jury] made in this case.[62]

He set aside the jury's guilty verdict, ordered a new trial for Haywood Patterson, and delayed the retrial of the other Scottsboro defendants. In announcing the ruling, Judge Horton knew he was risking his position within the white community and might face reprisals. Nonetheless, he believed he had a duty to uphold the law.[63]

The state of Alabama could have declined to retry the Scottsboro defendants, but the politically ambitious state attorney general, Thomas G. Knight Jr., knew he could enhance his stature among voters by prosecuting the cases. Perhaps he could use the publicity to launch a viable candidacy for the governor's mansion. Knight was upset that Judge Horton had interfered with his carefully laid plans. To ensure that no such results occurred again, Knight searched for a judge who understood the importance of white supremacy in the South and would not perform his judicial duties by neutrally examining the evidence.[64]

Knight found exactly the judicial temperament he needed in William Washington Callahan, a racist septuagenarian with no patience for black men daring to exercise the constitutional rights enjoyed by whites. Knight surreptitiously called in favors to have Callahan installed as the judge for the next round of proceedings. It was a brilliant maneuver, reinforcing the old cliché that a good lawyer knows the law, but a great lawyer knows the judge. Knight knew the character of his judge. Callahan despised Negroes so much that he would always rule in favor of the prosecution.

The defendants' black skin had convicted them before the retrials commenced in Judge Callahan's courtroom.[65]

The next round began in November 1933, and it was clear that a new judge was at the helm. Judge Horton had permitted black citizens to observe the proceedings, but Callahan would have none of that. A transparent legal process would not serve the prosecution's or the judge's purposes. The fewer bystanders present in the courtroom, the better for southern justice. As in the first trial, a motion for change of venue was denied, and defense counsel was prohibited from exploring Victoria Price's sexual history. To no one's surprise, Haywood Patterson and Clarence Norris were convicted and once again sentenced to death.[66]

Samuel Leibowitz appealed to the Alabama Supreme Court, but, as anticipated, the high court upheld the convictions. Afterward, Leibowitz appealed to the US Supreme Court. For a second time in a case involving the Scottsboro defendants, the highest court in the land granted certiorari to review the convictions. In *Norris v. Alabama* and its companion case, *Patterson v. Alabama*, the Supreme Court justices determined that deliberately excluding black jurors from a black defendant's jury constitutes a denial of equal protection of the laws under the Fourteenth Amendment to the US Constitution.[67]

An unusual event occurred during the oral argument before the Supreme Court on February 15, 1935. Samuel Leibowitz told the justices that someone had doctored the records in Jackson County to add black voters' names to the roll of eligible jurors, presumably to counter a charge that Negroes were excluded from jury service. Leibowitz argued that such a deliberate act constituted fraud "not only against the defendants but against this very court itself." Chief Justice Charles Evans Hughes was incredulous; he could not believe that Alabama officials would employ such patently fraudulent tactics. The chief justice challenged Leibowitz to prove the allegation. It is rare for US Supreme Court justices to delve into the details of trial proceedings apart from reviewing the written record, but in this instance they decided to do so. Leibowitz had expected such a challenge, and he was prepared. As soon as Chief Justice Hughes issued his challenge, Leibowitz produced the Alabama jury rolls as well as a magnifying glass. At Leibowitz's invitation, each justice took a turn hunching over the list and peering at the forged names. Most names in the rolls were arranged neatly in alphabetical order, but the names of the eligible Negro jurors were appended at the end of the list in the same color ink, indicating they had been scribbled there in a deliberate act of fraud. One by one, the justices expressed their astonishment. The US Supreme Court had never before allowed such an exhibit to be placed before the bench during oral argument.[68]

When the court issued its opinion six weeks later, the chief justice wrote, "Exclusion of all negroes from a grand jury by which a negro is indicted, or from the petit jury by which he is tried for the offense, resulting from systematic and arbitrary exclusion of negroes from the jury lists solely because of their race or color, is a denial of the equal protection of the laws guaranteed to him by the Fourteenth Amendment." The court reversed the defendants' convictions and, citing dicta from *Neal v. Delaware*, an 1881 case, agreed to infer intentional discrimination when blacks were absent from jury service. The holding was a significant milestone in expanding the Supreme Court's willingness to scrutinize state court proceedings to ensure fundamental fairness in criminal proceedings.[69]

Having the convictions reversed was a crucial victory, but it did not mean that the defendants were free men. Alabama prosecutors once again presented information on the crime to a grand jury. On November 13, 1935, the grand jury returned yet another indictment against the nine suspects. Judge Callahan, apparently unfazed by a rebuke from the US Supreme Court, set the new trial date for January 20, 1936.[70]

The most noticeable change during the new retrial was at the defense table. Samuel Leibowitz was still celebrated as a skilled trial lawyer, especially adept at marshaling evidence and presenting compelling arguments. He realized, however, that he could not win a jury trial for black defendants in the state of Alabama. The juries he had encountered were less interested in reviewing the evidence than in judging the race of the defendants and the Yankee ways, Jewish surname, and aggressive tactics of their attorney. Reluctantly acknowledging the realities south of the Mason-Dixon Line, Leibowitz stepped aside as Haywood Patterson's lead attorney. Local counsel Clarence Watts from Huntsville, Alabama, took charge of the defense.[71]

Although the change would marginally improve Patterson's chances in an Alabama courtroom, no one could forget that a black man still faced a legal system heavily biased against him. As if to illustrate the point, Judge Callahan made no attempt to hide his prejudices. During the new trial, he constantly uttered comments sympathetic to the prosecution, repeating a remark he had made during the previous trial that a strong legal presumption existed that a white woman, no matter how lowly, would never yield voluntarily to intercourse with a Negro.[72]

The testimony and evidence presented in the new trials were mind-numbingly familiar. The same witnesses were paraded forward, the same arguments were voiced, and the same conclusions were reached—with one minor exception. Haywood Patterson no longer faced the death penalty after he was convicted. The jury sentenced him to serve seventy-five years in prison. It was not a victory, but it was as close to justice and mercy as an Alabama jury could provide during the 1930s.[73]

The general consensus was that no one wanted to pursue these cases anymore. At the same time, no one could let them go. Alabama prosecutors could not allow black men to escape harsh punishment for a reputed rape, regardless of the lack of evidence. The defense could not allow innocent men and boys to remain imprisoned without seeking legal redress through all available avenues. And so the cases dragged on. Following his inevitable conviction, Clarence Norris was sentenced to death a third time. Andy Wright and Charley Weems, convicted once again, drew sentences of ninety-nine and seventy-five years, respectively.[74]

The pattern finally changed on July 25, 1937. In a startling development, four defendants won their freedom. The prosecution concluded that insufficient evidence existed to convict the nearly blind Olen Montgomery. Willie Roberson, seriously ill with venereal disease at the time of the alleged attack and therefore physically incapable of raping anyone, was not prosecuted again. Roy Wright and Eugene Williams were juveniles when the alleged rape occurred in 1931. They were not tried again. It was not the exoneration sought by innocent men, but it was a victory for four of the nine defendants.[75]

The four recently released Scottsboro Boys appeared at a series of public events in the North. For a brief time, they were in high demand. Outrage over the episode reached a fever pitch once again, but outrage can only last for a short time. The young men soon found their audience had disappeared. In the meantime, Leibowitz and his defense team worked to win the release of the five men still behind bars in Alabama. As public attention waned, Leibowitz feared that the defendants would languish in prison for decades. They might not be executed, but they could become forgotten property of the state.[76]

Clarence Norris's next appeal landed in the Alabama Supreme Court in June 1938, and again the court affirmed his conviction. The court also upheld convictions for Andy Wright and Charley Weems. Alabama governor Bibb Graves later commuted Norris's sentence to life in prison, ensuring that none of the defendants would die in the state's electric chair. Leibowitz had hoped the governor would pardon the men, but Graves declined to do so.[77]

With their appeals exhausted and media attention all but nonexistent, it appeared that the remaining defendants would never be released. Eventually, though, with the passing years, each defendant left prison. The state paroled Charley Weems on November 17, 1943. Ozie Powell secured his release in 1946 but was forever scarred by his experiences: On January 24, 1936, Powell had slashed a guard's throat while prisoners were being transferred between prisons. Another guard stepped forward and shot Powell in the face, causing permanent brain damage.[78]

Tired of waiting for a release that might never come, Clarence Norris jumped parole in 1946 and headed north. Alabama governor George Wallace formally pardoned Norris thirty years later. Three years after that, Norris published his autobiography, *The Last of the Scottsboro Boys*. He died on January 23, 1989. As he indicated by the title of his book, Norris had been the last surviving Scottsboro defendant.[79]

Haywood Patterson escaped from prison in 1948. Two years later, he published a book about the episode, *The Scottsboro Boy*. When Alabama authorities discovered that he was hiding in Michigan, they asked the state's governor, G. Mennen Williams, to extradite Patterson, but the governor refused. Never able to escape his violent past, Patterson later stabbed a man in a bar fight and was sent to prison again. He died of cancer behind bars in 1952 after serving only a year of his new sentence.[80]

Andy Wright was the last of the defendants to leave prison. He had been discharged previously but was forced back into custody after he violated the terms of his parole. He was finally released in 1950 and moved to New York.[81]

Long after all the principal players had died, the legacy of the Scottsboro cases lingered. Black citizens in the Jim Crow era knew that if accused of a crime, especially, although not exclusively, in the South, they could expect brutal treatment. If they somehow managed to escape a lynch mob, they could be assured of a trial in a venue that was openly, sometimes proudly, hostile to their interests. For all their pronouncements on the constitutional due process requirements for a fair trial, the US Supreme Court had neither the time nor the inclination to accept appeals of every state court proceeding in which deficiencies had allegedly occurred.

Closing a long, tortured chapter in southern history, on November 21, 2013, the Alabama Board of Pardons and Paroles posthumously pardoned Charley Weems, Andy Wright, and Haywood Patterson. They were the last of the Scottsboro defendants who had not had their convictions overturned or received a pardon. The judgment of the courts, of the Alabama Board of Pardons and Paroles, and of history is that the lives of nine young men were ruined by the vagaries of a justice system that could not, or would not, weigh the interests of black defendants without bias. Sadly, while the Scottsboro cases were dramatic and grabbed headlines, they were not unique in the annals of southern courts.[82]

LABOR, WAGES, AND THE GREAT DEPRESSION

As undeniably tragic as lynchings and trumped-up criminal charges were for black Americans in the first three or four decades of the twentieth century, such horrific episodes did not directly affect every family. The fear of a sudden eruption of white violence against blacks was an omnipresent concern, but it existed in the background, the white noise of Negro life in a nation constructed on a foundation of racial apartheid. The state of the economy—and, more importantly, the effect of macroeconomics on Negro labor and wages—was a more immediate worry for people of color during those years. The lives of impoverished Negroes had always been miserable, but the advent of the Great Depression only increased the level of misery. With the establishment of federal policies designed to assist poor farmers and industrial workers, the Depression also demonstrated the difficulty of implementing government programs to ameliorate the desperate situation for black Americans.[83]

Economic downturns were thought to be cyclical, but the reversal of the 1930s was unlike anything Americans had ever experienced. It caught everyone by surprise as it deepened with each passing month and year. Herbert Hoover, commerce secretary under Presidents Harding and Coolidge, entered the White House in 1929, less than a year before the stock market crash that triggered the worldwide economic downturn. For all of his considerable skills as a master bureaucrat, Hoover was ill-suited to the role of chief executive during a global crisis. Franklin D. Roosevelt, his successor, would lead the charge from a bully pulpit vastly different from Hoover's. Roosevelt understood that the economic calamity facing the nation during the 1930s was unprecedented in its scope and destructive effect. Business cycles always rise and fall, but the Great Depression was something altogether different. If the suffering of millions of Americans was to be lessened, FDR believed that the government must respond in new and creative ways to stimulate the economy.[84]

Roosevelt's early years as president were devoted to finding a fix for economic and social concerns—rampant unemployment, hunger, the lack of a suitable infrastructure, and social security for the elderly and disabled, among other issues. Although the economic policies of Roosevelt's first term (and part of his second)—the package of reforms he labeled the New Deal—did not resolve every problem for which they were designed, the new administration demonstrated a willingness to use the engine of government in flexible, innovative ways. The federal executive branch would not sit on the sidelines and passively watch the business community limp through the worst financial crisis in the nation's history. A new approach was needed. As popularized by the British economist John Maynard Keynes, one theory held that government should respond energetically by freely spending money to create jobs so that individual citizens would have more money in their pockets. Increasing consumer confidence and providing more readily available cash theoretically would lead to more private-sector spending and thereby boost aggregate demand. Armed with Keynesian justifications, the administration moved forward aggressively. No issue was too small to escape the scrutiny of the newly revitalized, undeniably robust federal authority.[85]

Agriculture was especially affected, and the early 1930s saw the position of the American farmer worsen precipitously. Industrial businesses could restrict production and at least partially influence price fluctuations, but most farmers barely eked out a living. They could ill afford to decrease output. Consequently, many commodities flooded the market, creating surpluses that drove down prices. The US Department of Agriculture noted that farm production in 1933 was only 6 percent below 1929 levels; yet prices had decreased by more than 60 percent. Farmers found themselves in desperate straits. Because the prices they could charge for their products had fallen drastically, but the prices they paid for industrial goods and raw materials remained relatively flat, thousands of small family farmers were driven to bankruptcy as the Great Depression continued to sweep across the land. Around the same time, a series of droughts and dust storms in the plains states destroyed the topsoil that farmers depended on to sustain their crops, creating a new generation of migrant workers who abandoned many thousands of family farms and headed west in search of better lives.[86]

The economic collapse hit black Americans particularly hard. Because people of color usually were employed in low-paying, low-skill jobs, often in agriculture, their economic fortunes frequently were tied to the land. The 1930 census found that 56 percent of Negroes in the United States resided in rural areas, with about 40 percent employed in agricultural pursuits. Approximately 97 percent of blacks identified as "farmers" lived in the South, but only 20 percent owned their land. Mostly they were tenant farmers, sharecroppers, or wage laborers hired seasonally to plant or harvest crops. As farmwork disappeared, blacks laboring at the most menial jobs took the heaviest blow.[87]

By 1932, when FDR was elected president, fully half of all blacks were unemployed compared with slightly less than a third of the overall workforce. Racial violence rose as increasingly desperate people undertook increasingly desperate measures to protect a vanishing way of life. Lynchings in 1932 had declined to eight, but they skyrocketed to twenty-eight the following year. Although the number of violent episodes could not be tied solely to sour economic conditions, observers noticed a correlation between a populace fearful of starvation and homelessness and an increase in the number of violent racial incidents.[88]

Assuming that any New Deal programs could be counted on to alleviate black unemployment, the question arose as to how the programs should be constructed for maximum effect. Recognizing that many agricultural laborers did not own their land, the NAACP urged the federal government to help those agricultural workers who needed it most without regard to race. "The natural desire of the Negro citizenry of this country is that the New Deal administration shape its course in such a way as to bring relief to those elements of the national population which have suffered most," an NAACP missive explained. "They hope that the slogans of the new administration will have meaning for black farmers as well as for white farmers."[89]

As part of the New Deal, the Roosevelt administration developed the Agricultural Adjustment Administration (AAA), an alphabet soup agency within the US Department of Agriculture, to pay farmers not to produce. The goal was to curtail production of cotton, field corn, hogs, milk, rice, tobacco, and wheat products to prevent surpluses from driving down prices for these basic commodities. In 1934 and 1935, the AAA added barley, cattle, flax, grain rye, peanuts, potatoes, sorghums, sugar beets, and sugarcane to the list.[90]

The NAACP had urged the administration and sympathetic legislators to consider the disparate impact that any farming legislation would have on agricultural workers who did not own their land, but Congress passed the AAA bill with little attention paid to tenant farmers, sharecroppers, and wage laborers. Paying landowners to allow their fields to lie fallow might put more money in their pockets, but it had the opposite effect on non-landowners. Farmers who had depended on crops for their sustenance or who needed agricultural work to earn wages realized that they had no work, hence no money. In time, the AAA was refined to allow tenant farmers to receive a percentage of the federal benefits sent to landowners, but usually tenant farmers received less than they had during the pre-Depression years. The administration also changed the requirement so that farmers could plant some crops but leave 40 percent of their acreage unplanted.[91]

When NAACP representatives pointed out that the program hurt tenant farmers, some of the poorest workers in the country, during a time of unparalleled economic hardship, they were assured that everyone would benefit if the entire economy improved, and the AAA would ensure that commodity prices increased over time. The adage "A rising tide lifts all boats" would be used for decades to justify a disproportionate impact on one party or the other in American economic policy. Administration proponents also contended that sharecroppers, for example, not only would receive a government benefit but could plant 60 percent of the crop and sell off the surplus after fulfilling their duties to landowners. This argument assumed that sharecroppers could find a market for their surplus crops and that landowners would deal with them honestly, neither of which was likely.

From the perspective of black farmers, the AAA program could, and frequently did, lead to tragic consequences. Some white landowners determined that the most efficient means of cutting 40 percent of their farming acreage was to discharge tenant farmers altogether. In a well-meaning but naive effort to ensure fair dealing, AAA administrators investigated charges of tenant displacement, requiring farmers to affirm they had not released tenants and sharecroppers to meet the requirement. It was a simple matter to doctor records so that an investigation would show a tenant had been released for cause, had left of his own accord, or had never existed at all.[92]

The question of how many non-landowning farmers were displaced owing to the AAA program was never answered to everyone's satisfaction, but the 1940 census indicated that there were 192,000 fewer Negro tenants and 150,000 fewer white tenants than had existed ten years earlier. Undoubtedly, some of these people died, moved elsewhere, chose another line of work, or were discharged as a result of improvements in mechanized agricultural equipment, but others were forced off the land by thrifty landowners seeking to maximize their income by whatever means they could devise. The great American theologian Reinhold Niebuhr commented on the unintended consequences in 1936: "There is no more striking irony in modern politics than the fact that the provisions of the Agricultural Adjustment Administration, designed to alleviate the condition of the American farmer, should have aggravated the lot of the poorest of our farmers, the southern sharecroppers."[93]

While NAACP representatives understood the Roosevelt administration was committed to providing assistance to all citizens—a distinct improvement over the previous administration—they also knew the realities of politics. The situation for black agricultural workers would never improve unless organized groups applied pressure to force federal officials to remedy the inequities. In speeches and resolutions, NAACP officers complained about the "oppression suffered by the Negro—America's real 'forgotten man'—under the New Deal." The constant tirade against the AAA's policies never convinced the agency or the administration to postpone paying benefits to landowners suspected of cheating the system, but it did awaken a few politically conscious whites, mostly northern liberals who were predisposed to be sympathetic in the first place.[94]

As the Great Depression stretched across the years of the 1930s, the Roosevelt administration changed its tactics based on reports about which programs appeared to work and which did not. The AAA was criticized for many reasons, including the lack of equity in distributing benefits. Eventually, the administration searched for new ways of improving farmers' plight. One program, the Farm Security Administration (FSA), authorized by Congress in July 1937, provided low-interest loans for citizens to purchase farms so that the number of tenant farmers could be reduced. Fearing discrimination in the real estate market, NAACP representatives lobbied Congress to create a civil service commission to ensure that black federal administrators would be hired to assist would-be landowners of color who sought to buy farms. Powerful southern members of Congress prevented such a proposal from passing into law.[95]

Critics of the administration observed that New Deal programs for farmers were underfunded and not especially mindful of the problems that Negroes faced in buying property. Aside from confronting systemic racial discrimination, often they were the least qualified borrowers when applying for a mortgage. Even if they could somehow finagle a purchase, they still needed to buy the necessary accouterments: animals, plows, tools, feed, and seed. Recognizing this difficulty, the FSA implementing legislation included a rehabilitation program that provided funding for the supporting equipment and materials required to get a farm up and running. Perhaps it was too little, too late, as detractors charged, but it was preferable to nothing.[96]

Looking back, Franklin Roosevelt's record on assisting black farmers was mixed. The AAA undoubtedly provided relief for ailing farmers, but the disparities in benefit distribution were difficult to ignore. The five hundred thousand most affluent farmers received 40 percent of the AAA benefits even though they comprised only 8 percent of eligible recipients, while the bottom 50 percent of the farming population, many of whom were Negroes, received a scant 15 percent. More than 3 million farmers received less than $1,000 a year. After 1935, the administration attempted to correct these allocation deficiencies, but their efforts did not compare with the scope of the original AAA program. The FSA, in particular, strove to lend a helping hand to black farmers, but the agency provided fewer than two thousand tenant purchase loans to people of color and resettled only fourteen hundred Negro families.[97]

The administration also struggled to rescue the industrial sector and provide for black workers. It was clear that industry was almost as desperate for assistance as the agricultural sector; therefore, New Dealers proposed a similar policy to provide relief—namely, federal financial assistance. Economic data for 1933, Roosevelt's first year in office, showed that manufacturing production had decreased to less than half the level of four years earlier. Gross national product was down by 30 percent. More than 12 million industrial workers were unemployed when the new president was sworn in, in March 1933.[98]

Administration officials viewed the problem of a sluggish economy as a lack of consumer stimulation. Production volumes and high unemployment could be alleviated by establishing government standards for the manufacture of specific products and requiring that higher wages be paid for companies that met the standards. The advantage in government regulation, administration officials argued, was that a consistent, across-the-board standard would eliminate ruthless competition among companies that pushed a particular sector into an internecine price war and drove down production and wages. If the federal government developed clear, consistent standards, it could also push companies to pay higher wages, which would jump-start economic recovery because workers with higher wages would enjoy increased purchasing power.

The plan depended on several crucial factors. First, the administration had to propose exemptions from antitrust laws that prohibited specific industries from agreeing to production levels and pricing in specified markets. Moreover, government officials would need to reduce the number of hours that each worker could labor in a week so that companies would hire unemployed workers to meet rising demand. Production costs probably would increase as a result of taking on more workers, but administration officials believed the costs could be passed on to consumers by increasing the price of the goods being manufactured. If consumers brought in more income because of an economic recovery, they would be willing and able to pay the increased costs. The theory was that government intervention into the market could arrest the downward spiral of the Depression by artificially manipulating the marketplace through a series of prearranged supply-and-demand signals.[99]

Congress enacted a key component of the New Deal, the National Industrial Recovery Act, in June 1933. President Roosevelt used his new authority under the law to create the National Recovery Administration (NRA), an agency tasked with an ambitious agenda. According to Section 1 of the statute, the NRA was designed to

> provide for the general welfare by promoting the organization of industry for the purpose of cooperative action among trade groups, to induce and maintain united action of labor and management under adequate governmental sanctions and supervision, to eliminate unfair competitive practices, to promote the fullest possible utilization of the present protective capacity of industries, to avoid undue restriction of production (except as may be temporarily required), to increase the consumption of industrial and agricultural products by increasing purchasing power, to reduce and relieve unemployment, to improve standards of labor, and otherwise to rehabilitate industry and to conserve natural resources.[100]

A legion of critics characterized the law as a step toward socialism because it authorized the United States to control major components of the economy. By "encouraging" trade associations to develop codes of competition with government approval, the statute ensured that the fed-

eral government would be an integral part of the national economy. Senator Robert F. Wagner of New York, a sponsor of the legislation, defended
the law as a means of repairing a capitalist economy, not subverting it.
"The bill does not abolish competition," the senator explained. "It purifies
and strengthens it." The difference was that the law strengthened "competition on a high standard of efficiency rather than on a low standard of
exploitation of labor."[101]

If any group of industrial workers needed relief from labor exploitation, it was the black underclass. Data from October 1933 revealed that
17.8 percent of the Negro population received some kind of government
relief compared with 9.5 percent of the non-Negro population. The question was whether the NRA was a suitable program to alleviate the problem. "The elimination of inequalities and class distinctions are the
underlying principles of the National Recovery Administration," President Roosevelt said in a public statement, but this proved to be far easier
said than done. With racial discrimination widespread throughout the
United States, blacks often were the last hired and first fired in the manufacturing sector. In many areas, not only in the South, Negroes were
viewed as a source of cheap labor, and they typically received a lower
wage for the same work performed by whites.[102]

Section 7a of the law provided for collective bargaining, although a
dispute arose about the meaning of that section. The laboring class
argued that the NRA encouraged the development of independent labor
unions, while management believed it allowed for company-led unions
to organize. In any case, Negroes were seldom involved with organized
labor, which meant that however Section 7a was interpreted, blacks
received few benefits. Black leaders hoped the administration would take
action to compel labor unions to increase opportunities for people of
color, but they were disappointed when the promises fell short of
reality.[103]

Another provision within the NRA, Section 2, established the Public
Works Administration (PWA), a program that authorized the federal government to spend $3.3 billion to construct "a comprehensive program of
public works." Road construction accounted for 11,428, or one-third, of
the PWA projects undertaken between July 1933 and March 1939. School
construction was the second most common project, accounting for 14 percent of spending. Other construction projects included hospitals, airports,
electricity-producing dams, bridges, and warships for the US Navy. The
money was distributed by allocating funds to appropriate federal agencies already in existence, providing grants and loans to state agencies
and other public offices, and lending money to a private entity such as a
railroad.[104]

More than other New Deal programs, the PWA seemed well positioned to assist blacks in economic recovery. Because the money was earmarked to pay for labor to build large-scale public works projects, it would benefit laborers more directly than other government programs did. In addition, because some of the projects included public housing, even if blacks were not employed on a specific work site, the new building would provide a benefit to the community. The housing projects were segregated, which was more than a little vexing to Negroes anxious to break out of their second-class citizenship, but a new segregated housing project was preferable, at least in theory, to no housing project at all.

The difficulty with the PWA, as with many government programs created during the Great Depression, was that federal goals to provide assistance regardless of race changed when money and jobs flowed through other hands. Unless federal guidelines specifically required the use of Negro labor as a precondition to being awarded federal funding for a construction project, white supervisors simply refused to hire black Americans. Responding to complaints that several construction sites employed no one of color, Harold Ickes, secretary of the interior and administrator of the PWA, ordered that PWA projects henceforth evince "no discrimination exercised against any person because of color or religious affiliation." Even this express order did not eliminate racial discrimination in PWA projects. Companies would hire a token black person or two and consider their duty done. Eventually, PWA administrators developed a formula that assumed racial discrimination existed if contractors failed to pay a portion of the total payroll to blacks equal to one-half their percentage of the total labor force based on data gleaned from the occupational census of 1930. The agency later changed the percentage requirement.[105]

In May 1935, President Roosevelt issued an executive order transferring some functions from the PWA and the Federal Emergency Relief Administration (FERA) to the Works Progress Administration (WPA), later renamed the Work Projects Administration. Established by the Emergency Relief Appropriation Act of 1935, the WPA was designed to extend the work of the FERA program. Harry Hopkins, one of Roosevelt's closest advisers, headed the WPA. Aware of the discrimination faced by black workers, Hopkins eventually issued an order similar to Ickes's at the PWA prohibiting discrimination against Negroes.[106]

The WPA record in meeting the needs of black Americans was mixed. On one hand, the agency offered higher wages than were available to blacks in private employment, especially in the South. As a result, Negroes enjoyed a higher standard of living than they would have if working for private companies in their communities. On the other hand, the agency sometimes kowtowed to southern politicians who insisted that black workers be released when it was time to plant or harvest crops, lest the region suffer a labor shortage in agriculture that would further harm the South economically. Blacks came to resent the cavalier way they were treated when southern whites pressured the WPA to change its employment policies to reflect the realities of the Jim Crow regime.[107]

By the end of the 1930s, all but the most myopic observers had to conclude that Franklin Roosevelt was not the president blacks had hoped he would be. Too often he turned a blind eye to the special problems faced by people of color, or he acquiesced in the face of political pressure when a firm, fair champion was needed. Yet for all of his deficiencies as an advocate of civil rights, Roosevelt made an effort, however limited and riddled with exceptions and problems, to forge a coalition of the disenfranchised. More than any other leader of the era, he offered hope to the poor, as well as ethnic minorities and people of color, that the United States could become a more inclusive nation with help from the federal government.[108]

A new voting pattern emerged with the birth of the New Deal. Most blacks of that time voted for the Republican Party because it had been the party of Lincoln, but the electorate shifted with FDR's appearance on the national stage. Roosevelt allowed black visitors at the White House and even appointed a few black advisers. This was not enough to placate leaders of black organizations such as the NAACP and the National Urban League, but average black citizens generally appreciated Roosevelt's efforts, however limited. Throughout the 1930s, people of color flocked to the Democratic Party to support this new man who appeared to be at least marginally sympathetic to their plight.[109]

While some black leaders found Roosevelt too plodding and unresponsive in his approach to civil rights, some whites feared that he was moving too fast. The president was always mindful of the powerful southern bloc in the US Congress, and he was careful to compromise when he believed it would improve his political position. Any recognition that black Americans deserved a helping hand upset southern whites. White supremacists were so incensed by this change in the "natural order of things" that Roosevelt and his leftist wife, Eleanor, met with a decidedly hostile reception from reactionary white southerners. One racist cartoon making the rounds during the 1940s depicted the couple conversing above this unforgettable caption: "You kiss the niggers, I'll kiss the Jews. We'll stay in the White House as long as we choose."[110]

THE GREAT WAR, PART II

The deprivations of the Great Depression eventually disappeared with the coming of World War II. While the New Deal ostensibly lessened the effects of a stagnant economy on a nation of impoverished souls, the undeniable engine of economic prosperity arrived in the guise of warfare, especially the business of warfare. Mobilizing to defeat Nazi Germany and the Empire of Japan required millions of Americans to fight overseas and millions more to work in factories building the planes, tanks, guns, and bombs necessary to support the soldiers.[111]

War changes people and nations forever. That observation was certainly true for black Americans during World War II. More than 1 million blacks served in uniform—with 125,000 sent overseas—during the conflict. As had been the case in previous American wars, they served in segregated units. In most cases, they served in noncombat roles.[112]

Negroes had served with distinction in all of the nation's wars, but somehow when the bloodshed ceased and peacetime returned, white Americans suffered from collective amnesia. It happened after every conflict. Victorious whites forgot about or conveniently downplayed black Americans' contributions to the war effort. To acknowledge that Negroes had played a part in the victory would be a step toward acknowledging people of color as productive, autonomous citizens deserving of dignity and respect. The American system of racial discrimination could not allow such recognition to occur. During the late nineteenth and early twentieth centuries, the Jim Crow regime could withstand numerous assaults, but it could not survive a true accounting of the dignity and worth of people who had fought and sometimes died for their country. Segregation required whites in power to maintain the fiction that white people were superior to coloreds.[113]

The inability or unwillingness to honor the debt the nation owed to its black soldiers was notable after the Great War concluded in 1918. With the end of the battles in Europe, the US Army developed a policy of excluding Negroes from serving in combat units because mixing blacks and whites together was an impermissible breach of the social contract. Even by the standards of the day, the Army Air Corps policy appeared draconian, declaring, "Applications from colored men for this branch of service cannot be considered." An Army War College report from 1925 unreflectively embraced the South's values, characterizing black soldiers as unfit for military duty because they were physically unqualified, too subservient, and too susceptible to "crowd psychology." These supposedly innate features rendered blacks unable to control themselves during times of danger and stress. In keeping with official army protocol, the few blacks who served in the military between the two world wars were assigned menial tasks in service or maintenance units. A black man could scrub a toilet or empty a trash bin, but he could not be trusted to fire a rifle in defense of his country.[114]

Outraged at the denigration of the Negro character and the lack of opportunity in the military, black leaders lobbied the service branches to allow people of color to join and advance through the ranks based on merit. The black press, the NAACP, and the National Urban League joined forces during World War II to launch a program known as the Double V initiative, a campaign to declare victory over fascism overseas and Jim Crow at home. The goals of the initiative were intertwined, but a frustrating tautology arose, as the Double V revealed. Blacks sought an opportunity to serve in combat and thereby demonstrate their worthiness to become full citizens, but people lacking full citizenship had a difficult time convincing the military powers that be to allow them to serve in combat. Achieving a double victory first required a single victory on at least one front. Therein lay the root of the problem.[115]

Initially reluctant to upset white southern political leaders, the Roosevelt administration appeared unresponsive to the plight of black soldiers. Franklin Roosevelt was supposed to be a new kind of leader, a man dissatisfied with the old way of doing things. He had courted the black vote during his 1932 campaign, but after he stepped into the presidency, he became cautious on matters of race. It was the same old story: a candidate calling for change before he won the election became reluctant to institute widespread change after he assumed the burdens of office. Change came during Roosevelt's tenure, but it was slow and not always consistent.

After Congress passed the Civil Aeronautics Act at the end of 1938, blacks were permitted to obtain civilian pilot licenses, albeit in segregated training programs, a move that represented incremental progress toward allowing black airmen to fight in combat. War had not yet erupted, but the administration was taking steps to ensure that the nation would be somewhat prepared should hostilities engulf the United States. It was a piecemeal effort, but an important one. Prior to World War II, only nine black Americans held commercial pilot licenses. The Civilian Pilot Training Program would increase that paltry figure.[116]

Continuing to exert pressure on a reluctant administration, black leaders met with President Roosevelt late in September 1940 to discuss the role of Negroes in the armed forces as well as their support for the defense industry. They encountered a wary president who was anxious to garner black support but also feared taking any action that might harm his standing with southern political leaders. On October 9, as a result of the meeting, the administration released a statement reaffirming its preference for black participation in military service in numbers reflecting the percentage of blacks in the US population. Although the statement was encouraging, blacks noticed that administration support did not include a provision desegregating military units.[117]

That same year, Congress enacted and the president signed the Selective Training and Service Act, the first peacetime conscription statute in American history. Under the law, Negroes could serve in segregated combat units. At the time, only six black units existed in the US military, comprising 4,450 soldiers. More than 2.5 million Negroes registered for the draft after the law was enacted.[118]

Although black leaders continually called for desegregation in the military, administration officials and military personnel argued that units separated by race were the only effective means for ensuring unit cohesion and high morale among the troops. Two leaders, the NAACP's Walter White and labor activist A. Philip Randolph, led efforts to compel the administration to integrate the armed forces, and they disputed this self-serving rationale. They viewed the statute as a bittersweet victory. Blacks could prove their mettle in combat, but they would be forced to do so in all-black units that might be held back from meaningful service or, alternatively, dispatched to carry out suicide missions.[119]

Now committed to developing units for colored soldiers, the War Department located a suitable place to train Negro pilots in Tuskegee, Alabama. Home to the legendary black institution of higher learning, the Tuskegee Institute, a legacy of the renowned black leader Booker T. Washington, the town would further add to its luster as cadets began training at the Tuskegee Army Air Field in July 1941. The inaugural group of cadets eventually joined the 99th Pursuit Squadron, the first all-black aircraft fighter squadron in US history.

The white officers initially assigned to train the Tuskegee cadets shared many of their generation's attitudes toward black cadets. They either viewed the trainees as incapable of mastering the skills necessary to fight in combat or deliberately antagonized the men based on deep reservoirs of hatred toward colored people. Often the commanders prohibited white training officers from fraternizing with black enlisted men, a move that appeared to undermine unit cohesion and morale more than any other practice in the armed services. In time, the War Department corrected this mistake, appointing officers more sympathetic to the goals of the program and the dignity of the men.[120]

Black leaders were pleased with their progress, but it was not time to rest on their laurels. A. Philip Randolph and Walter White met with President Roosevelt as well as Assistant Secretary of War Robert P. Patterson and other administration officials on June 18, 1941, to protest continued segregation in the defense industries. They alerted the administration to plans for a national march on Washington during the summer of 1941 to call attention to the disparate treatment of Negroes in the war effort. Randolph confidently predicted that tens of thousands of people would participate.[121]

[10.3] The Tuskegee Airmen were renowned for their bravery during World War II. Here, members of the unit attend a briefing in Ramitelli, Italy, in March 1945.
Courtesy of the Library of Congress.

After the meeting, the president met with his advisers and agreed to accede to some of the group's demands. On June 25, 1941, Roosevelt issued Executive Order 8802 banning discrimination in defense industries receiving government contracts. The order stated, in part, "I do hereby reaffirm the policy of the United States that there shall be no discrimination in the employment of workers in defense industries or government because of race, creed, color, or national origin, and I do hereby declare that it is the duty of employers and of labor organizations, in furtherance of said policy and of this Order, to provide for the full and equitable participation of all workers in defense industries, without discrimination because of race, creed, color, or national origin." The order established the Fair Employment Practices Committee (FEPC), a federal agency designed to ensure compliance with the new law. Although the FEPC was continually understaffed and underfunded, the new policy represented a major shift in federal practice.[122]

A year before the president issued the executive order, William H. Hastie, a distinguished black lawyer and jurist, joined the administration as an assistant to Secretary of War Henry Stimson. In his position, Hastie was tasked with advising administration officials on methods for desegregating the armed forces. Frustrated at the inertia he encountered as well as continuing segregation at military training facilities, Hastie was convinced the administration would not take decisive action before the war ended. He resigned his position on January 15, 1943, to protest the lack of progress.[123]

Even in the face of ongoing discrimination, blacks distinguished themselves repeatedly during the war. In noncombat roles, Negroes drove convoy trucks in the Red Ball Express, which transported half a million tons of supplies to armies marching through Europe after the D-day invasion in 1944. During the invasion, approximately seventeen hundred black men served on Omaha and Utah beaches, some in supporting roles and others as soldiers. The 761st Tank Battalion spent 183 days in combat as part of General George S. Patton's Third Army. The battalion assisted in capturing thirty towns in France, Belgium, and Germany. When German troops launched a final offensive in December 1944 known as the Battle of the Bulge, all-white divisions in the US Army compensated for personnel shortages by bringing up black soldiers from noncombat units to supplement their strength. When the crisis ended, black soldiers were reassigned to their segregated units.[124]

Individual black soldiers distinguished themselves time and again. Doris "Dorie" Miller, a cook in the US Navy, rendered heroic service during the Japanese attack on Pearl Harbor on December 7, 1941, by caring for wounded men and eventually firing a Browning .50-caliber antiaircraft gun from the deck of the USS *West Virginia* until he exhausted his ammunition. Miller earned the Navy Cross, the third-highest award for gallantry at the time, for his actions that day. The Davis family, a father-son combination, also answered the call of duty in exemplary fashion. Benjamin O. Davis Sr. became the first black general officer in US history when he was promoted to brigadier general in 1940. His son, Benjamin O. Davis Jr., commanded the 99th and later the 332nd fighter groups of the US Army Air Forces, commonly known as the Tuskegee Airmen (along with the 477th Bombardment Group, which bore that same appellation). In 1944, the "Golden Thirteen," a group of black enlisted men, became the first commissioned and warrant officers in the US Navy. Eight months later, in November 1944, Samuel L. Gravely Jr. was commissioned as an ensign in the US Navy. He became the first black man to serve on a navy fighting ship as an officer and later the first black man to command a navy ship, the first black fleet commander, and the first black flag officer.[125]

Although the United States did not award the Medal of Honor to any blacks during World War II, the US Army decided to investigate the matter in 1993 by commissioning a study from Shaw University in Raleigh, North Carolina, "to determine if there was a racial disparity in the way Medal of Honor recipients were selected." The study determined that race played a role in whether to award or withhold the medal and recommended that ten soldiers be considered for a belated award. The US government eventually awarded the Medal of Honor to seven black men who had served in World War II. Congress enacted appropriate legislation, and President Bill Clinton presented the awards in a ceremony on January 13, 1997, offering six medals posthumously. Vernon Baker received the seventh award for his actions at Viareggio, Italy, on April 5 and 6, 1945. President Clinton personally presented the medal to the retired soldier. According to the medal citation,

> When his company was stopped by the concentration of fire from several machine gun emplacements, he crawled to one position and destroyed it, killing three Germans. Continuing forward, he attacked an enemy observation post and killed two occupants. With the aid of one of his men, Lieutenant Baker attacked two more machine gun nests, killing or wounding the four enemy soldiers occupying these positions. He then covered the evacuation of the wounded personnel of his company by occupying an exposed position and drawing the enemy's fire. On the following night Lieutenant Baker voluntarily led a battalion advance through enemy mine fields and heavy fire toward the division objective.[126]

Black soldiers undoubtedly contributed to the American victory in World War II, yet remained ensconced in segregated units, with some notable exceptions. They also remained more likely than their white counterparts to receive a "blue discharge," an administrative removal from the service that was not classified as either "honorable" or "dishonorable," although frequently it was interpreted as the latter. A recipient of a blue discharge found it difficult to secure postwar employment and usually did not qualify for benefits under the Servicemen's Readjustment Act of 1944, known popularly as the GI Bill. The US Army issued 48,603 blue discharges between December 1, 1941, and June 30, 1945. Of that total, 22.23 percent, or 10,806, went to black soldiers even though they comprised only 6.5 percent of army personnel. Racial discrimination most likely played a crucial role in the high proportion of such discharges among blacks.[127]

During the last year of the war, the NAACP's Walter White traveled through England, Italy, North Africa, and the South Pacific to investigate allegations of mistreatment of black soldiers. At General Dwight D. Eisenhower's request, White sent a fourteen-point memorandum to the War Department, along with recommendations for improving conditions. His book *A Rising Wind* detailed his findings and won widespread praise for its evenhanded approach. President Harry S. Truman later relied on the work when he issued his executive order abolishing racial discrimination in the US armed forces.[128]

By the end of the war, black Americans could point with pride to their achievements. They had stepped up to fill the ranks in service of a country that seldom welcomed them with open arms. In the face of continuing discrimination and countless humiliations, large and small, they had persevered, offering their time, talents, and sometimes their limbs and lives to fight foreign aggressors threatening the homeland. Yet the homeland sometimes was a land as alien and hostile as any place on earth.[129]

Black servicemen returned to a country that had compiled a sordid, sorry record of racial discrimination extending many generations into the past. Yet the 1940s opened up new possibilities. Unlike in earlier epochs, genuine hope and change were on the horizon. The distinctive service of black Americans in World War II helped to prompt, among other things, President Truman's issuance of Executive Order 9981 in July 1948 ordering all US armed forces to abolish racial discrimination in their ranks "as rapidly as possible," provided the goal could be accomplished "without impairing efficiency or morale." With this monumental change, the institutional forces of segregation in American life began to crack and crumble as never before. To paraphrase Winston Churchill from another context, it was not the beginning of the end, but perhaps it was the end of the beginning of the Jim Crow regime in the United States.[130]

Epilogue

The Postwar American Landscape: "White Prejudice and Negro Standards Thus Mutually 'Cause' Each Other"

In 1944, distinguished Swedish economist and sociologist Gunnar Myrdal published a groundbreaking tome titled *An American Dilemma: The Negro Problem and Modern Democracy*. The Carnegie Foundation for the Advancement of Teaching commissioned the study and chose a non-American to oversee the research in hopes that the work would benefit from a relatively unbiased perspective. During the early phases of the project, Myrdal relied on the well-known Howard University black political scientist Ralph Bunche as his major researcher and assistant.

Myrdal traveled throughout the United States collecting information and data beginning in 1938, although it was not his first visit to the country. He eventually wrote the book during a ten-month period in 1941 and 1942, at precisely the time when the United States entered World War II. Unlike anything written previously, *An American Dilemma* forthrightly addressed the second-class treatment afforded to people of color.[1]

GUNNAR MYRDAL AND
AN AMERICAN DILEMMA

Although appalled by the racial discrimination he witnessed during his travels throughout the American South, Myrdal was an optimist. He believed that the nation's creed that all men are created equal and entitled to rights guaranteed by the US Constitution eventually would lead white citizens to understand that treating blacks as inferior beings was hypocritical and violated basic American values. Myrdal was careful not to criticize whites as evil or vicious. They simply needed instruction on a better way to live out the national creed.

An American Dilemma characterized the "Negro problem" as a problem for whites. "If we forget about the means, for the moment, and consider only the quantitative goal for Negro population policy, there is no doubt that the overwhelming majority of white Americans desire that there be as few Negroes as possible in America," he observed. "If the Negroes could be eliminated from America or greatly decreased in numbers, this would meet the whites' approval—provided that it could be accomplished by means which are also approved. Correspondingly, an increase of the proportion of Negroes in the American population is commonly looked upon as undesirable."[2]

Myrdal described a cycle of oppression in which whites mistreated blacks by denying them equal opportunities in housing, education, and jobs, forcing Negroes to settle for inferior positions in society. Afterward, whites pointed to Negroes' lack of advancement as proof that the race deserved inferior treatment. "White prejudice and discrimination keep the Negro low in standards of living, health, education, manners and morals," he wrote in a famous passage. "This, in its turn, gives support to white prejudice. White prejudice and Negro standards thus mutually 'cause' each other." As far as Myrdal was concerned, the lives of black folks would never improve until whites ceased their unrelenting campaign of oppression or lifted up blacks enough so that people who had been treated as second-class citizens could catch up with the achievements of whites.[3]

When Myrdal's work first appeared in print, many appreciative readers hailed the book as a classic, the first systematic examination of race since the all-but-forgotten black historian George Washington Williams published *History of the Negro Race in America from 1619 to 1880*. W. E. B. Du Bois called it a "monumental and unrivaled study." Eminent black American sociologist E. Franklin Frazier remarked that the book "contains a lot of dynamite" and urged every American to read it. Chief Justice Earl Warren cited *An American Dilemma* in the famous 1954 Supreme Court case *Brown v. Board of Education of Topeka*, which desegregated public schools in the United States. Without a doubt, it was a landmark work filled with sociological, economic, and political insight.[4]

For all of its celebrated perspicacity, the study did not satisfy everyone. Critics subsequently assailed the book for its unfounded presuppositions.

Ever the eternal optimist, Myrdal placed his faith in an eventual awakening and acknowledgment among whites, especially in the South, that racism and adherence to American values could not coexist. He failed to understand how people can reconcile and justify diametrically opposed values and concepts. Yet American history is replete with such manifest rationalizations among people who should know better. The Declaration of Independence claimed that "all men are created equal," and yet many American Founders, including the author of those words, owned slaves. The would-be secessionists of the Confederate States of America resolved to establish a slaveholding republic without irony, for they did not consider the interests of black men and women to be worthy of consideration. Generations of whites claimed to fear the rapacious sexual appetite of black men even as the evidence existed that white men were far more likely to force themselves on black women than black men were to force themselves on white women. Myrdal was naive in his belief that human beings depend on reason as a means of progressing toward the light of knowledge and wisdom. People can exist indefinitely in a state of self-delusion and denial, as American history has demonstrated repeatedly.[5]

Myrdal also treated blacks paternalistically, as passive receptors of white oppression or benevolence, depending on the circumstances. If resolving the Negro problem required whites either to change their behavior toward blacks or to bestow their largesse on the impoverished, subjugated little brown peoples whom whites crushed under their boot heels, no role existed for blacks to help themselves. Myrdal infantilized the subject of his study, as did so many white liberals throughout American history, whether they were abolitionists, Radical Republicans in Congress during the 1860s, carpetbaggers headed to the South to teach the freedpeople how to read and write during Reconstruction, or white civil rights activists of the twentieth century. It was perhaps a benign, well-intentioned form of paternalism, but it nonetheless failed to acknowledge the role that people of color played, and should play, in their own advancement. At a time when blacks were struggling to convince American political and military leaders that Negroes should serve in combat positions within the US military, Gunnar Myrdal was urging whites to reform their ways and help out the lowly wretches who had been held down for so long.[6]

Myrdal believed that the 1940s could be a time of change in America, a precursor to a more enlightened era of racial progress. In some ways, he was correct. Yet the decade was the best of times and the worst of times for race relations. For every step forward, the social position of black people often took a step backward. Moreover, most of the time, for better or worse, black citizens were far from passive in their original actions and in their reactions to white racism, despite Myrdal's characterization.[7]

VIOLENCE DURING THE 1940s

As whites living in the era of World War II sought to keep the social relations between the races in the same fixed position they had been in since the end of Reconstruction, blacks proved increasingly reluctant to accept their lowly status. Violence erupted frequently during the 1940s, as it had earlier in the twentieth century. On January 10, 1942, an argument between white policemen and black soldiers over the arrest of a black soldier in an area of Alexandria, Louisiana, populated with bars and nightclubs led to a melee in which twenty-nine blacks suffered injuries. A similar altercation between black soldiers and white military police with southern roots occurred at Fort Dix, New Jersey, in April 1943. Three people were killed in a fifteen-minute eruption of violence.[8]

In fact, the incidents of racial violence that occurred during 1943 were among the most severe since riots erupted at the end of World War I. They were remarkable because, in many instances, the fighting occurred outside the South, although disturbances were reported in Mobile, Alabama, on May 25 and in Beaumont, Texas, on June 16. Some of the most widely reported episodes demonstrated that blacks and other ethnic minorities would not settle for long-established patterns of white dominance. The Zoot Suit Riots of 1943 in Los Angeles involved multiple confrontations between white soldiers and Latinos living in the area. Similar outbreaks of violence between whites and Latinos occurred in Evansville, Indiana, as well as San Diego, Oakland, Chicago, Detroit, Philadelphia, and New York City.[9]

The Detroit riots of June 20, 1943—perhaps the worst of a riotous decade—were the culmination of demographic changes that brought blacks and whites together. Black workers who arrived in Michigan during the Great Migration found themselves laboring side by side with southern whites who moved north to find work in the war industry. As racial animosity simmered, a white sailor claimed that a black man had insulted the sailor's girlfriend. Fighting broke out and spread across the city on the strength of rumors that a group of whites had thrown a black woman and her baby into the Detroit River. Another rumor intimated that a black man had raped and murdered a white woman. At the end of a three-day rampage, after federal troops arrived to restore law and order, thirty-four people—twenty-five of them Negroes—were dead, and more than seven hundred had been injured. Seventeen of the dead Negroes were killed by white policemen. Estimates placed the property damage at $2 million.[10]

In Harlem, New York, on August 1 and 2, 1943, black residents became incensed when a white police officer shot a black soldier. The police officer claimed that the soldier had physically assaulted him, but because the soldier was shot as he fled the scene, the residents did not believe the report. A crowd of three thousand gathered. False rumors circulated that the soldier had been killed, prompting the mob to engage in indiscriminate looting. Six people died, nearly six hundred were arrested, and the community suffered hundreds of thousands of dollars' worth of property damage.[11]

By the end of the war, people of color did not enjoy equal treatment in the American polity. Black servicemen returned home to live under the same stultifying Jim Crow regime they thought they had left behind. As they enrolled in schools and universities to take advantage of the Servicemen's Readjustment Act of 1944 (the GI Bill), they received inferior treatment compared with their white colleagues. In addition, black veterans and their families continued to labor under appalling conditions of racial discrimination. They were forced to use separate facilities for schools, hospitals, hotels, restaurants, and other public accommodations.[12]

GOVERNMENT AS AN AGENT OF CHANGE

Too much had happened during the war years for blacks to accept the status quo placidly. During the civil rights movement of the 1950s and 1960s, black leaders would depend on grassroots participation from ordinary citizens who marched in the streets in numerous acts of civil disobedience, but efforts in the 1940s relied on the mechanisms of government to achieve results. Consequently, W. E. B. Du Bois, after a decade's absence, returned to the National Association for the Advancement of Colored People (NAACP) to lead an effort before the United Nations, the newly created international organization dedicated to promoting cooperation among nations of the world. Acting as the NAACP's director of special research, Du Bois led a group of influential lawyers and scholars in preparing a book-length petition for equal rights for African Americans living in the United States. Titled *An Appeal to the World: A Statement of Denial of Human Rights to Minorities in the Case of Citizens of Negro Descent in the United States of America and an Appeal to the United Nations for Redress*, the petition presented a devastating critique of the history of race relations in the United States. Du Bois and his coauthors sent the petition to the United Nations in October 1947. The petition charged,

A nation which boldly declared "All men equal," proceeded to build its economy on chattel slavery; masters who declared race-mixture impossible, sold their own children into slavery and left a mulatto progeny which neither law nor science can today disentangle; churches which excused slavery as calling the heathen to God, refused to recognize the freedom of converts or admit them to equal communion. Sectional strife over the vast profits of slave labor and conscientious revolt against making human beings real estate led to bloody civil war, and to a partial emancipation of slaves which neverthe-less even to this day is not complete. Poverty, ignorance, disease, and crime have been forced on these unfortunate victims of greed to an extent far beyond any social necessity; and a great nation, which today ought to be in the forefront of the march toward peace and democracy, finds itself continu-ously making common cause with race hate, prejudiced exploitation and oppression of the common man. Its high and noble words are tuned against it, because they are contradicted in every syllable by the treatment of the American Negro for three hundred and twenty-seven years.[13]

At the conclusion of the petition, Du Bois placed the case before the world tribunal, stating, "We American Negroes appeal to you; our treatment in America is not merely an internal question of the United States. It is a basic problem of humanity; of democracy; of discrimination because of race and color; and as such it demands your attention and action. No nation is so great that the world can afford to let it continue to be deliber-ately unjust, cruel and unfair toward its own citizens."[14]

Closer to home, federal courts in the United States inched away from the legacy of *Plessy v. Ferguson*, the 1896 US Supreme Court case that upheld the constitutionality of segregation based on race. The courts were not prepared to outlaw segregation in one broad opinion in the 1940s, but through a series of incremental steps, it became clear that Jim Crow no longer jumped with the same vim and vigor he had evinced earlier in the century. Typically, the cases relied on the federal government's broad interstate commerce authority or a spirited interpretation of the newly reinvigorated Fourteenth Amendment.[15]

After a black woman named Irene Morgan refused to move from her seat to the back of a Greyhound bus traveling from Gloucester County, Virginia, to Baltimore, Maryland, on July 16, 1944, she was arrested for violating a Virginia state statute requiring racial segregation in public vehicles. Convicted in the lower courts, Morgan appealed to the US Supreme Court. Two prominent black lawyers, William H. Hastie and Thurgood Marshall, handled the appeal. In a 6–1 opinion announced on June 3, 1946, the high court held that a state statute requiring segregated seating on interstate motor carriers impermissibly hindered commerce and therefore was invalid. It was not the resounding death knell for segre-gation that blacks might have hoped for, but *Morgan v. Virginia* nonethe-less was a victory for black citizens. In an ironic twist, the court cited *Hall v. DeCuir* as a precedent. *Hall* was an 1878 case holding that a state could not force a common carrier engaged in interstate commerce to practice integration. The *Hall* court determined that integration was a burden on interstate commerce, while *Morgan* decided that segregation represented the burden. Informed of the result, Irene Morgan remarked, "If something happens to you which is wrong, the best thing to do is have it corrected in the best way you can. The best thing for me to do was to go to the Supreme Court."[16]

Several additional court cases during the 1940s eroded the legal bases for segregation. In *Smith v. Allwright*, the US Supreme Court held that a Texas state law authorizing the Democratic Party to establish a white primary was unconstitutional because it violated the Fourteenth and Fifteenth amendments, which provide, respectively, for equal protection of the laws and the right to vote regardless of race.[17] *Sweatt v. Painter*, a 1950 case, chipped away at the constitutionality of separate-but-equal facilities in education. A black man named Heman Marion Sweatt applied for admission to the University of Texas Law School in 1946. He was denied admission owing to his race. Sweatt filed a civil suit that eventually landed in the US Supreme Court. The justices unanimously decided that "separate but equal" was a fiction because a Negro law school that was supposed to have opened in 1947 would not have provided the same caliber of legal education provided by the University of Texas Law School. "We hold that the Equal Protection Clause of the Fourteenth Amendment requires that petitioner be admitted to the University of Texas Law School," Chief Justice Frederick Moore Vinson wrote. Although the opinion was narrowly tailored and the court declined to rule on the "petitioner's contention that *Plessy v. Ferguson* should be reexamined in the light of contemporary knowledge respecting the purposes of the Fourteenth Amendment and the effects of racial segregation," the *Sweatt* case represented an important step in dismantling the Jim Crow regime in public education. It would serve as a precedent when the high court reexamined *Plessy v. Ferguson* four years later.[18]

In *McLaurin v. Oklahoma State Regents*, another education case from 1950, the court held that treating students enrolled in publicly funded institutions of higher education solely on the basis of race violated the equal protection clause of the Fourteenth Amendment. The plaintiff, George W. McLaurin, had been admitted to the University of Oklahoma in 1948, but the university required him to use separate facilities such as a special table in the dining hall and a specified desk in the library. He was allowed to listen in on classes from a desk positioned outside the classroom door, but he was never allowed to participate fully in his education.[19]

Cases involving racially restrictive covenants also arrived in the Supreme Court during this era. In 1917, the US Supreme Court held in *Buchanan v. Warley* that municipally mandated racial segregation was unconstitutional. Thus, if government-sanctioned racial discrimination

[E.1] Although educational opportunities increased for people of color following World War II, the Jim Crow regime remained entrenched in American society. In this photograph, a black student, George W. McLaurin, attends a segregated class at the University of Oklahoma in 1948. McLaurin later sued the Oklahoma State Regents for Higher Education. In a unanimous opinion, the US Supreme Court held that disparate treatment of students in public institutions of higher education solely on the basis of race violates the Equal Protection Clause of the Fourteenth Amendment. Courtesy of the Library of Congress.

was not available to ensure residential segregation in certain neighborhoods, southerners developed private, legally enforceable covenants in real estate contracts restricting the sale of property to whites only. The typical language in a contract stated, "Hereafter no part of said property or any portion thereof shall be occupied by any person not of the Caucasian race, it being intended hereby to restrict the use of said property against occupancy as owners or tenants of any portion of said property for resident or other purposes by people of the Negro or Mongolian race."[20]

The NAACP had challenged racial covenants on numerous occasions in the 1920s and 1930s, but with little success. Finally, a case arrived in the US Supreme Court in 1948 that invalidated racially restrictive covenants. J. D. Shelley, a black man, purchased a house in St. Louis, Missouri, in 1945. He was unaware that a restrictive covenant had been placed on the property in 1911. As the Shelley family was preparing to move into the house, a white property owner, Louis Kraemer, sued to enjoin the new black owners from occupying the house. The Supreme Court of Missouri held that the covenant was enforceable because it was a private agreement between parties and "ran with the land." As a result, the court could not invalidate the covenant because it was not directed specifically at a person protected by the Fourteenth Amendment. The Shelleys appealed to the US Supreme Court. The court granted certiorari to hear *Shelley v. Kraemer* as well as a companion case from Detroit, Michigan, *McGhee v. Sipes*, which presented factually analogous issues.

On May 3, 1948, the court announced an opinion cleverly circumventing the notion that a restrictive covenant is part of a private real estate contract and therefore not subject to Fourteenth Amendment requirements. The court decided that "racially-based restrictive covenants are not, on their face, invalid under the Fourteenth Amendment," but any attempt to enforce them in court would involve state action. State action cannot violate the equal protection clause of the Fourteenth Amendment. In other words, the court could not prevent parties from including racially restrictive covenants in real property contracts, but it could prevent a government entity from enforcing them. In effect, such covenants were legally unenforceable, hence invalid.[21]

Chief Justice Vinson wrote the majority opinion. In his conclusion, he reminded readers of the American creed that Gunnar Myrdal had lauded in *An American Dilemma* earlier in the decade:

> The historical context in which the Fourteenth Amendment became a part of the Constitution should not be forgotten. Whatever else the framers sought to achieve, it is clear that the matter of primary concern was the establishment of equality in the enjoyment of basic civil and political rights and the preservation of those rights from discriminatory action on the part of the States based on considerations of race or color. Seventy-five years ago this Court announced that the provisions of the Amendment are to be construed with this fundamental purpose in mind. Upon full consideration, we have concluded that in these cases the States have acted to deny petitioners the equal protection of the laws guaranteed by the Fourteenth Amendment.[22]

While much of the dismantling of the Jim Crow laws occurred in the judicial branch through court cases, the executive branch also played a role. President Harry S. Truman proved to be a key figure. In a highly symbolic gesture, the president stood on the steps of the Lincoln Memorial and addressed the NAACP's thirty-eighth annual convention on June 29, 1947.[23]

"It is my deep conviction that we have reached a turning point in the long history of our country's efforts to guarantee freedom and equality to all our citizens," he said at the outset. Some ten thousand people listened as Truman spoke eloquently about the racial problems confronting the United States. "Many of our people still suffer the indignity of insult, the harrowing fear of intimidation, and, I regret to say, the threat of physical injury and mob violence," he lamented. "The prejudice and intolerance in which these evils are rooted still exist. The conscience of our nation, and the legal machinery which enforces it, have not yet secured to each citizen full freedom from fear."[24]

It was time for government to rectify past abuses, the president insisted. He had already acted. On December 5, 1946, Truman had issued Executive Order 9808, establishing the President's Committee on Civil

[E.2]   In this photograph, President Harry S. Truman has finished addressing the closing session of the thirty-eighth annual conference of the National Association for the Advancement of Colored People at the Lincoln Memorial in Washington, DC, on June 29, 1947. The president is leaving the platform, accompanied by NAACP president Walter White (walking at the left, scratching his face) and US Supreme Court chief justice Fred Vinson (walking slightly behind and between White and Truman). Courtesy of the National Archives and Records Administration.

Rights (PCCR). Charles E. Wilson, head of the venerable General Electric Company, served as chair.[25]

Truman referred to the PCCR near the end of his address to the NAACP: "This is a difficult and complex undertaking. Federal laws and administrative machineries must be improved and expanded. We must provide the government with better tools to do the job. As a first step, I appointed an Advisory Committee on Civil Rights last December. Its members, fifteen distinguished private citizens, have been surveying our civil rights difficulties and needs for several months. I am confident that the product of their work will be a sensible and vigorous program for action by all of us."[26]

The committee announced its findings, *To Secure These Rights: The Report of the President's Committee on Civil Rights*, on October 29, 1947. After reviewing problems associated with race, the committee recommended that the federal government create a permanent civil rights commission, a joint congressional committee on civil rights, and a civil rights division within the US Department of Justice. The PCCR also called for passage, finally, of an antilynching law, abolition of the poll tax, a permanent Fair Employment Practices Committee, desegregation of the US military, and laws designed to enforce fair housing, education, health care, and employment.[27]

Several recommendations required that action be undertaken by other federal and state entities, but President Truman decided to act unilaterally on two matters under his immediate control. On July 26, 1948, he signed executive orders 9980 and 9981. The former implemented fair employment practices within the federal executive branch by ordering desegregation of all civilian federal executive branch agencies. The latter ordered the armed forces to desegregate. "It is hereby declared to be the policy of the President that there shall be equality of treatment and opportunity for all persons in the armed services without regard to race, color, religion or national origin," Executive Order 9981 stated. Truman established the President's Committee on Equality of Treatment and Opportunity in the Armed Services to ensure the order was implemented effectively. Solicitor General Charles H. Fahy was designated as the chair of the seven-member committee. Historians have applauded Truman's groundbreaking work, but at the time his civil rights activism infuriated the southern wing of the Democratic Party and imperiled his reelection.[28]

By the dawn of the 1950s, American society was changing. Segregationists were not yet ready to concede defeat, but their days of unchallenged white supremacy were numbered. People of color had endured an arduous journey from the death of Reconstruction to the beginning of a twentieth-century civil rights movement. They had suffered untold indignities and deprivations during that time, and they had been forced into an American version of apartheid. Generations of black men and women reflected on the Declaration of Independence's insistence that "all men are created equal" and bitterly understood that the reality fell far short of the promise. If they did not yet enjoy the full rights of citizenship guaranteed by the US Constitution, however, their time would come. They had to keep the faith that a new day was somehow, somewhere out there just beyond the horizon.[29]

Notes

INTRODUCTION AND ACKNOWLEDGMENTS

1. Myrdal, *An American Dilemma*.

PROLOGUE

1. Quoted in Remnick, *The Bridge*, 399. See also Remnick, *The Bridge*, 396–402; Wolffe, *Renegade*, 38.

2. See, for example, Litwack, *Trouble in Mind*; Packard, *American Nightmare*; Woodward, *The Strange Career of Jim Crow*.

3. Information on these public figures and many others can be found in a four-volume work: Smith, *Encyclopedia of African-American Popular Culture*. For more information on the Cosby scandal, see, for example, Siegemund-Broka, "How the Bill Cosby Story Snowballed," 10.

4. For information on blacks elected to public office in the United States, see, for example, Carey, *African-American Political Leaders (A to Z of African Americans)*. See also Gillespie, *The New Black Politician*; Gillespie, "Red, White, and Black," 64–66; King, *African American Politics*.

5. Grant-Thomas and Orfield, *Twenty-First Century Color Lines*; Smith, "Ackerman's Civil Rights Revolution and Modern American Racial Politics," 2906–40; ya Azibo, "Teaching the Mulatto Hypothesis to Combat African-U.S. Colorism," 88–100. According to one celebrated historian, "race" is in fact a myth, a socially constructed rationale used by the powerful to exploit the powerless. Jones, *A Dreadful Deceit*.

6. Burka, "James Byrd Jr.," 126; Graczyk, "Supremacist Executed in Texas," A52; Hennessy-Fiske, "Texas Executes Participant in Black Man's Dragging Death," AA2.

315

7. Amber, "The Danger Outside," 102–7; Cashill, *"If I Had a Son"*; Ford, "Reflections in Real-Time," 58–61; Jonsson, "Trayvon Martin's Mom," 10. Zimmerman's acquittal in 2013 triggered a movement known as "Black Lives Matter," an initiative that calls attention to the worth and dignity of all people, regardless of race. See, for example, Blow, "Beyond 'Black Lives Matter,'" A17; Paulson, "King Events Punctuated by Protests over Deaths of Black Men," A10.

8. Altman and Miller, "No. 2," 110–14; Loury, "Ferguson Won't Change Anything," 14–30; Rothman, "Taking Sides in Ferguson," 18–22.

9. Allen and Parker, "Police Officers and Their Perceived Relationship with Urban Communities," 82–95; Amber, "The Danger Outside," 102–7; Ford, "Reflections in Real-Time," 58–61.

10. Cannon, "Rodney King Remembered," 22, 24–25; Maurantonio, "Remembering Rodney King," 740–55; Monroe, "South Central," 132–40.

11. Boyd, "Louima and Gammage," 4; "Parents of Jonny Gammage Awarded $1.5 Million in Wrongful Death Suit," 50; Reynolds, "Our Sons under Siege," 139–40, 206–12.

12. Boyd, "Louima and Gammage," 4; Ioanide, "The Story of Abner Louima," 4–26; Van Thompson, *Eating the Black Body*, 145–65.

13. Diallo, with Wolff, *My Heart Will Cross This Ocean*; Puddington, "The War on the War on Crime," 25–30; Roy, *41 Shots*. Information on the Bruce Springsteen song "American Skin (41 Shots)" can be found in Carlin, *Bruce*, 401–6; Roy, *41 Shots*, 70.

14. "Excerpt from Report on Shooting of Unarmed Man," B6; "The Patrick Dorismond Case," A22; Rosen, "Excessive Force," 24.

15. Boyd, "African Craftsman Slain by Police," 3; Graves, "When Will Police Stop Murdering Unarmed Black Men?," 8; Salaam, "Prayer, Anger, and Sorrow for Zongo," 4.

16. Gray, "Moms on a Mission," 102–5; Hicks "33. Unreasonable Force," 345–54; McGrath, "Fifty Shots," 38–40.

17. Antony and Thomas, "'This Is Citizen Journalism at Its Finest,'" 1280–96; Haun, *"Fruitvale Station,"* 10–12; Johnson, "Ryan Coogler's Gripping Film, *Fruitvale Station*, Traces the Last Day of Oscar Grant's Young Life," 56; Martinot, "On the Epidemic of Police Killings," 52–75; Taylor, "'We Are All Oscar Grant,'" 187–97.

18. De Blasio is quoted in Goldstein and Schweber, "Man's Death after Chokehold Raises Old Issue for Police," A1. See also "A Search for Justice in the Garner Case," A30; Siegel, "The Lonesome Death of Eric Garner," A30; "The Unnecessary Death of Eric Garner," 14.

19. Knoll, "Hundreds Rally for Black Man Killed by Police," AA1; Lovett, "3 Shots from Police Killed Los Angeles Man," A12; Medina, "Man Is Shot and Killed by the Police in California," A16.

20. Miah, "How Far Backward?," 2–3; Von Drehle, "In the Line of Fire," 24–28.

21. Conley, "'Delayed, Not Destroyed,'" 28; Gilmore, "Freddie Gray, the Day after the Night," 42; Von Drehle, "The Roots of a Riot," 34–39.

22. Costa, Horwitz, and Wan, "Man Arrested in Charleston Killings," A1; Fausset, "Steeped in Racial History," A12; Fausset and Blinder, "Era Ends as

South Carolina Lowers Confederate Flag," A9; Tanfani and Serrano, "Charleston Church Shooting," A1.

23. Fairchild and Cowan, "The O.J. Simpson Trial," 583–91; Foley, "Serializing Racial Suspects," 69–88; Toobin, *The Run of His Life*.

24. Hasian and Flores, "Mass Mediated Representations of the Susan Smith Trial," 163–78; Mayo, *American Murder*, 327–30; Williams, *Gendered Politics in the Modern South*.

25. Jones, "Brawley and Others," 376–78; Maddox, "Setting the Record Straight in the Brawley Case," 13; Tucker, "The Tawana Brawley Case," 19–20, 22.

26. Cohan, *The Price of Silence*; Dezenhall, *Glass Jaw*, 9, 159; Hassett-Walker, "Race, Social Class, Communication, and Accusations," 267–94; Hemmens, "American Skin," 297–306; Len-Rios, "Image Repair Strategies, Local News Portrayals and Crisis Stage," 267–87.

27. Coates, "The Case for Reparations," 54–71; Holder, "We Should Have an Open Dialogue on Race," 164–66; Kilgore, "Reparations," 1–14; Manglitz, Guy, and Meriweather, "Knowledge and Emotions in Cross-Racial Dialogues," 111–18; Sue, "Race Talk," 663–72.

28. Perez-Peña, "Black or White?," A1; Susman and Pearce, "The Nation," A5.

29. Dreisinger, *Near Black*; Papish, "Promoting Black (Social) Identity," 1–25; Winant, "The Dark Matter," 600–607.

30. Quoted in Glaser, *Race, Campaign Politics, and the Realignment in the South*, 2. See also Martinez, *Coming for to Carry Me Home*, 12–13; Simkins and Roland, *A History of the South*, 493.

31. Blum, *Reforging the White Republic*, 3–4, 10–13; Budiansky, "How a War of Terror Kept Blacks Oppressed Long after the Civil War Had Ended," 30–37; Grimsley, "Wars for the American South," 6–36.

32. Douglass, *The Life and Times of Frederick Douglass*, 396. See also Lears, *Rebirth of a Nation*, 24–25.

33. Foner, *Forever Free*, 207–11; Foner, *Reconstruction*, 602–12; Klarman, *From Jim Crow to Civil Rights*, 10–14; Lears, *Rebirth of a Nation*, 22–23; Logan, *The Betrayal of the Negro*, 12–13, 83; Simkins and Roland, *A History of the South*, 352; Valelly, *The Two Reconstructions*, 117–18.

CHAPTER 1: THE LEGACY OF RECONSTRUCTION

1. Catton, *The American Heritage New History of the Civil War*, 576; McPherson, *Battle Cry of Freedom*, 848–51.

2. Brands, *The Man Who Saved the Union*, 588; Keegan, *The American Civil War*, 329–30. For an extended discussion of General Grant's military reputation, see, for example, Bonekemper, *A Victor, Not a Butcher*; Marshall-Cornwall, *Grant as a Military Commander*.

3. The literature on the causes and meaning of the Civil War is voluminous. See, for example, Blight, *Race and Reunion*; McPherson, *What They Fought For, 1861–1865*.

4. Ira Berlin has performed extensive research into the origins of slavery in the English-speaking colonies of North America. See, for example, his works *Many Thousands Gone* and "Time, Space, and the Evolution of Afro-American Slavery on British Mainland North America."

5. See, for example, Foner, *Forever Free*, 8–16; Horton and Horton, *Slavery and the Making of America*.

6. Fogel and Engerman, *Time on the Cross*, 44–49; Sobel, *The World They Made Together*.

7. The Marxist historian Herbert Aptheker has done the most famous work in this field. See, for example, his article and book of the same name: *American Negro Slave Revolts*. See also Genovese, *From Rebellion to Revolution*; Wish, "American Slave Insurrections before 1861."

8. The myth of the simpleton slave is typified in the work of Professor Ulrich B. Phillips, a proponent of the Dunning School of historiography, which criticized Reconstruction as detrimental to the South. According to Phillips, the development of American slavery was not surprising in light of "the nature of the typical negroes themselves." In Phillips' view, American Negroes were well suited for slavery owing to their character as a race. "Impulsive and inconstant, social and amorous, voluble, dilatory, and negligent, but robust, amiable, obedient and contented, they have been the world's premium slaves." Phillips, *American Negro Slavery*, 8. For a criticism of Phillips' view, see, among others, Genovese, *Roll, Jordan, Roll*, 587–88; Stampp, *The Peculiar Institution*, 8–9. For more on the Dunning School and its adherents, see also Smith and Lowery, *The Dunning School*.

9. Foner, *Forever Free*, 22–24, 37–40; Litwack, *Been in the Storm So Long*, 46–48.

10. Foster, *Witnessing Slavery*, 127–41; Litwack, *Been in the Storm So Long*, 10–11.

11. Foner, *Forever Free*, 8–10; Taylor, "Eighteenth Century Black Slave Codes," in *From Timbuktu to Katrina*, 17–19.

12. Bonner, "Roundhead Cavaliers?," 34–59; McPherson, *Battle Cry of Freedom*, 7–8; Rothman, "Slavery and National Expansion in the United States," 23–29.

13. Garrison is quoted in Martinez, *Coming for to Carry Me Home*, 2–3. Phillips is quoted in Austin, *The Life and Times of Wendell Phillips*, 119. See also Mayer, *All on Fire*; Newman, *The Transformation of American Abolitionism*; Polgar, "'To Raise Them to an Equal Participation'"; Stewart, *Abolitionist Politics and the Coming of the Civil War*.

14. Bonner, *Mastering America*; Guelzo, *Fateful Lightning*, 513–17; Hammond, *Slavery, Freedom and Expansion in the Early American West*; Hammond, "'They Are Very Much Interested in Obtaining an Unlimited Slavery'"; Saraydar, "A Note on the Profitability of Ante Bellum Slavery"; Zambelli, "Looking at History through an Economic Lens," 55–59.

15. Daly, *When Slavery Was Called Freedom*; Keegan, *The American Civil War*, 356–57; Manning, *What This Cruel War Was Over*; Mason, *Slavery and Politics in the Early American Republic*; McPherson, *Battle Cry of Freedom*, 311–12; McPherson, *What They Fought For, 1861–1865*.

16. Jayne, *Lincoln and the American Manifesto*, 227–70; White, *The Eloquent President*, 277–303; White, *Lincoln's Greatest Speech*; Swanson, *Manhunt*; Sefton, *The United States Army and Reconstruction*, 42–62.

17. Quoted in Foner, *Forever Free*, 42. See also Foner, *Forever Free*, 42–43; Foner, *Reconstruction*, 4–7; Litwack, *Been in the Storm So Long*, 17–18.

18. Litwack, *Been in the Storm So Long*, 149–63; McPherson, *Battle Cry of Freedom*, 355–57; Quarles, *The Negro in the Civil War*, 60–65.

19. Foner, *Forever Free*, 22–23; McPherson, *Battle Cry of Freedom*, 497–98.

20. Quoted in "AL to Horace Greeley," in Gates, *Lincoln on Race and Slavery*, 243–44. See also Cox, *Lincoln and Black Freedom*, x, 183; Foner, *The Fiery Trial*, 228; Green, *Freedom, Union, and Power*, 153; White, *A. Lincoln*, 504; Yoo, *Crisis and Command*, 219–20.

21. Emilio, *A Brave Black Regiment*; McPherson, *Battle Cry of Freedom*, 500, 564–66; Quarles, *The Negro in the Civil War*.

22. Fischer, *Liberty and Freedom*, 339–40; Foner, *Forever Free*, 80–84; Litwack, *Been in the Storm So Long*, 1–63.

23. Quoted in Padover, *Thomas Jefferson on Democracy*, 158. See also Gordon-Reed, *The Hemingses of Monticello*, 536–39.

24. Jefferson, *Notes on the State of Virginia*, 162. See also Davis and Mintz, *The Boisterous Sea of Liberty*, 356; Miller, *The Wolf by the Ears*, 2–3; Onuf, "'To Declare Them a Free and Independent People,'" 1–46; Wilentz, "Jeffersonian Democracy and the Origins of Political Antislavery in the United States," 375–401.

25. Blight, *Race and Reunion*, 55, 294–95; Litwack, *Been in the Storm So Long*, 261–74.

26. Abraham Lincoln, Tuesday, July 22, 1862 (Preliminary Draft of the Emancipation Proclamation) in Abraham Lincoln, *Abraham Lincoln Papers at the Library of Congress* (Washington, DC: Library of Congress, Manuscript Division, American Memory Project, 1959), http://memory.loc.gov/ammem/alhtml/malhome .html: http://memory.loc.gov/ammem/alhtml/almss/dep001.html (accessed November 2013) (hereafter ALPLC). See also Brands, "Hesitant Emancipator," 58–59; Donald, *Lincoln*, 365–66; Goodwin, *Team of Rivals*, 464–65; Guelzo, *Lincoln's Emancipation Proclamation*, 4–5, 126; Holzer, *Lincoln*, 155–74; Holzer, "A Promise Fulfilled," 32; Livingstone, "The Emancipation Proclamation, the Declaration of Independence, and the Presidency," 206–7; McPherson, *Battle Cry of Freedom*, 840–42.

27. Quoted in Foner, *Forever Free*, 59.

28. Foner, *Forever Free*, 59–61; Foner, *Reconstruction*, 53–55; Williamson, *After Slavery*, 54–58.

29. Cox, *Lincoln and Black Freedom*, 59–69; Foner, *Reconstruction*, 46–50; Litwack, *Been in the Storm So Long*, 68; McPherson, *Battle Cry of Freedom*, 355; Rankin, "The Impact of the Civil War on the Free Colored Community of New Orleans," 380–83.

30. Abraham Lincoln, Tuesday, December 8, 1863 (Proclamation of Amnesty and Reconstruction), ALPLC. See also Goodwin, *Team of Rivals*, 589–90; Hesseltine, *Lincoln's Plan of Reconstruction*, 35–50; Trefousse, *The Radical Republicans*, 283–86; White, *A. Lincoln*, 613–14; Williams, *Lincoln and the Radicals*, 301–3.

31. Bogue, "Historians and the Radical Republicans," 8–9; Carwardine, *Lincoln*, 137–45; Donald, *Lincoln*, 331–33; Donald, *Lincoln Reconsidered*, 105–9; Trefousse, *The Radical Republicans*, 4–20; Williams, *Lincoln and the Radicals*, 5–9; Williams, "Lincoln and the Radicals," 43–44.

32. Bogue, "Historians and the Radical Republicans," 9–10; Bogue, "The Radical Voting Dimension in the U.S. Senate during the Civil War," 460–61; Foner, *The Fiery Trial*, 218; Harris, *Public Life of Zachariah Chandler*, 54; Magdol, *Owen Lovejoy*, 320–21; Tap, "Chandler, Zachariah (1813–1879)," 398–99; Trefousse, *The Radical Republicans*, 5–15; Williams, *Lincoln and the Radicals*, 5–17; Williams, "Lincoln and the Radicals," 44–45.

33. Carwardine, *Lincoln*, 240; Donald, *Lincoln*, 511; Goodwin, *Team of Rivals*, 639–40.

34. Quoted in Donald, *Lincoln*, 511. The manifesto is quoted in Trefousse, *The Radical Republicans*, 289–94. See also Carwardine, *Lincoln*, 239–40; Harris, *With Charity for All*, 189–90; Williams, *Lincoln and the Radicals*, 324–27.

35. Quoted in Masur, *Lincoln's Hundred Days*, 57. See also Carwardine, *Lincoln*, 290–94; Flood, *1864*, 130–44, 362–70; Foner, *Reconstruction*, 27–28; Waugh, *Re-electing Lincoln*, 36–41, 271–72; White, *A. Lincoln*, 632–45; Williams, "Lincoln and the Radicals," 56–57.

36. The dramatic story of the enactment of the Thirteenth Amendment can be found in many sources. See, for example, Foner, *Forever Free*, 62–63; Foner, *Reconstruction*, 66–68; Flood, *1864*, 362–70; Holzer, *Lincoln*, 155–74; McPherson, *Battle Cry of Freedom*, 712–13, 838–40; Oakes, *Freedom National*, 430–88; Vorenberg, *Final Freedom*, 53–60; Waugh, *Re-electing Lincoln*, 271–72.

37. Cox, "The Promise of Land for the Freedmen," 413–40; Du Bois, *The Souls of Black Folk*, 22; Harrison, "New Representations of a 'Misrepresented Bureau,'" 216.

38. Foner, *Reconstruction*, 3–34; Litwack, *Been in the Storm So Long*, 132–33; Oakes, *Freedom National*, 373–76.

39. Horton and Horton, *Slavery and the Making of America*, 13–46; Oakes, *Freedom National*, x–xi, 2–3; Waldstreicher, *Slavery's Constitution*, 3–19.

40. Donovan, *Mr. Madison's Constitution*, 6; Ellis, *The Quartet*, 5–28; Jensen, *The Articles of Confederation*, 244; Rothman, "Slavery and National Expansion in the United States," 23–29.

41. Foner, *Reconstruction*, 68–70; Henry, *The Story of Reconstruction*, 59–61; Simkins and Roland, *A History of the South*, 261–62; Winik, *April 1865*, 210–11.

42. Belz, "The Freedmen's Bureau Act of 1865," 197–217; Foner, *Reconstruction*, 68–70; Harrison, "New Representations of a 'Misrepresented Bureau,'" 206; Newell and Shrader, "The U.S. Army's Transition to Peace, 1865–66," 884–86.

43. Quoted in Litwack, *Been in the Storm So Long*, 102. See also Foner, *Forever Free*, 80–84; Foner, *Reconstruction*, 151–53; McPherson, *Battle Cry of Freedom*, 862.

44. Quoted in Murphy, *The Nation Reunited*, 44. See also Foner, *Reconstruction*, 409; Saville, *The Work of Reconstruction*, 138.

45. Quoted in Foner, *Reconstruction*, 143. See also Foner, *Forever Free*, 76–77; Langguth, *After Lincoln*, 275–77; Simkins and Roland, *A History of the South*, 261–62.

46. Foner, *Forever Free*, 97–99; Harrison, "New Representations of a 'Misrepresented Bureau,'" 219; Henry, *The Story of Reconstruction*, 58–61; Langguth, *After Lincoln*, 276–77; Newell and Shrader, "The U.S. Army's Transition to Peace, 1865–66," 885–86; Simkins and Roland, *A History of the South*, 261–62.

47. Foner, *Reconstruction*, 153–55; Harrison, "New Representations of a 'Misrepresented Bureau,'" 219; Henry, *The Story of Reconstruction*, 59–60; Simkins and Roland, *A History of the South*, 262.

48. Quoted in Henry, *The Story of Reconstruction*, 61. See also Foner, *Reconstruction*, 144–47; Harrison, "New Representations of a 'Misrepresented Bureau,'" 218–19; Henry, *The Story of Reconstruction*, 60–62; Newell and Shrader, "The U.S. Army's Transition to Peace, 1865–66," 886; Simkins and Roland, *A History of the South*, 262; Stampp, *The Era of Reconstruction*, 134–35.

49. Foner, *Reconstruction*, 144–47; Harrison, "New Representations of a 'Misrepresented Bureau,'" 218–19; Simpson, *The Reconstruction Presidents*, 92–94.

50. Quoted in Foner, *Reconstruction*, 248. See also Calabresi and Yoo, "The Unitary Executive during the Second Half-Century," 741–42; Currie, "The Reconstruction Congress," 392–93; Foner, *Reconstruction*, 246–49; Milton, *The Age of Hate*, 287–89; Simkins and Roland, *A History of the South*, 262–63; Trefousse, *The Radical Republicans*, 330–31.

51. Calabresi and Yoo, "The Unitary Executive during the Second Half-Century," 739–41; Foner, *Reconstruction*, 183–84; Henry, *The Story of Reconstruction*, 46–48; Hyman, *The Radical Republicans and Reconstruction*, 246–47; Means, *The Avenger Takes His Place*, 201–16; Simkins and Roland, *A History of the South*, 256–58.

52. Calabresi and Yoo, "The Unitary Executive during the Second Half-Century," 755–58; Currie, "The Reconstruction Congress," 449–52; DeWitt, *The Impeachment and Trial of Andrew Johnson*, 597–629; Foner, *Reconstruction*, 333–37; Genovese, *The Power of the American Presidency*, 93; Henry, *The Story of Reconstruction*, 308–9; Mantell, *Johnson, Grant, and the Politics of Reconstruction*, 90–96; Stewart, *Impeached*, 284–304.

53. Dray, *Capitol Men*, ix–x, 380.

54. See, for example, Baker, *What Reconstruction Meant*; Foner, "Panel II," 1585–606; Foner, *Reconstruction*, 603–12; Foner, "Reconstruction Revisited," 82–100; Huston, "Reconstruction as It Should Have Been," 358–63.

55. Quoted in Foner, *Reconstruction*, 528. See also Franklin, *Reconstruction after the Civil War*, 197–207; Lemann, *Redemption*, 27–29.

56. Foner, *Forever Free*, 197–98; Foner, *Reconstruction*, 524–29; Franklin, *Reconstruction after the Civil War*, 197–207; Rable, *But There Was No Peace*, 151; Trefousse, *The Radical Republicans*, 465–70.

57. Quoted in Foner, *Reconstruction*, 588; Gould, *Grand Old Party*, 75. See also Franklin, *Reconstruction after the Civil War*, 222–23; Gould, *Grand Old Party*, 75–76; Simpson, *The Reconstruction Presidents*, 199–200.

58. Quoted in Foner, *Forever Free*, 201. See also Lemann, *Redemption*, 65; Perman, *The Road to Redemption*, 178–80; Simkins and Roland, *A History of the South*, 304–7; Woodward, *Origins of the New South*, 14–15.

59. Perman, *The Road to Redemption*, 143; Simkins and Roland, *A History of the South*, 315–18; Williams, *Beyond Redemption*, 111–12, 146; Woodward, *Origins of the New South*, 58–62.

60. Foner, *Reconstruction*, 592–93; Lemann, *Redemption*, 184–85; Simkins and Roland, *A History of the South*, 341; Woodward, *Origins of the New South*, 55–58, 81; Woodward, *The Strange Career of Jim Crow*, 53–54, 82–86.

61. Hild, *Greenbackers, Knights of Labor, and Populists*, 31–32; Simkins and Roland, *A History of the South*, 342–43; Woodward, *Origins of the New South*, 76–82.

62. Ayers, *The Promise of the New South*, 214–16; Foner, *Reconstruction*, 548–49; Hild, *Greenbackers, Knights of Labor, and Populists*, 12–13; Lears, *Rebirth of a Nation*, 150–57; Lewinson, *Race, Class, and Party*, 69–71; Simkins and Roland, *A History of the South*, 341–43; Woodward, *Origins of the New South*, 82–83; Woodward, *The Strange Career of Jim Crow*, 56–59.

63. Hild, *Greenbackers, Knights of Labor, and Populists*, 80–81; Simkins and Roland, *A History of the South*, 341; Woodward, *Origins of the New South*, 103–6; Woodward, *The Strange Career of Jim Crow*, 57–59.

64. Ayers, *The Promise of the New South*, 34–35; Lewinson, *Race, Class, and Party*, 54–55; Simkins and Roland, *A History of the South*, 318–19; Woodward, *Origins of the New South*, 78–86.

CHAPTER 2: JUMPIN' JIM CROW
AND LEGAL SEGREGATION

1. Logan, "Introduction," xi–xii. See also Blight, "'For Something beyond the Battlefield,'" 1165–69.

2. The full text of Douglass's 1894 speech can be found, among other places, on the Library of Congress American Memory website. See "Address by Hon. Frederick Douglass, Delivered in the Metropolitan A. M. E. Church, Washington, D.C., Tuesday, January 9th, 1894," Library of Congress American Memory, http:// lcweb2.loc.gov/rbc/lcrbmrp/t21/t2110.sgm_old (accessed March 2014). See also Logan, "Introduction," xi–xii.

3. Blight, *Frederick Douglass' Civil War*, 224–29; Foner, *Reconstruction*, 590–96.

4. Blum, *Reforging the White Republic*, 7; Lears, *Rebirth of a Nation*, 21; Simkins and Roland, *A History of the South*, 304–12.

5. *Civil Rights Cases*, 109 U.S. 3 (1883).

6. Logan, *The Betrayal of the Negro*, 100. See also Simkins and Roland, *A History of the South*, 310, 352–53, 492–93.

7. Foner, *Forever Free*, 37–38, 208; Langguth, *After Lincoln*, 362–62; Woodward, *Origins of the New South*, 211–12, 353–54; Woodward, *The Strange Career of Jim Crow*, 7–8.

8. Blum, *Reforging the White Republic*, 102, 223; Foner, *Forever Free*, 192–93; Simkins and Roland, *A History of the South*, 494–95.

9. Foner, *Forever Free*, 137–39; Foner, *Reconstruction*, 527–29; Franklin, *Reconstruction after the Civil War*, 199–200; Fredrickson, "Masters and Mudsills," 43–45; Henry, *The Story of Reconstruction*, 496–97.

10. Dray, *Capitol Men*, 180, 336; Foner, *Reconstruction*, 558–63; Henry, *The Story of Reconstruction*, 544–45; Lemann, *Redemption*, 170–209; Lewinson, *Race, Class, and Party*, 85–86; Simkins and Roland, *A History of the South*, 284–86.

11. Foner, *Forever Free*, 195–97; Franklin, *Reconstruction after the Civil War*, 155–57; Lemann, *Redemption*, 80–82; Simkins and Roland, *A History of the South*, 284–85.

12. Quoted in Gould, *Grand Old Party*, 57. See also Drago, *Hurrah for Hampton!*; Longacre, *Gentleman and Soldier*, 262–63; Simkins and Roland, *A History of the South*, 284–85; Williams, *Hampton and His Red Shirts*.

13. Foner, *Reconstruction*, 558–62; Lemann, *Redemption*, 121–24, 136–37, 144–46; Simkins and Roland, *A History of the South*, 285.

14. Foner, *Reconstruction*, 558–63; Henry, *The Story of Reconstruction*, 544–53; Lemann, *Redemption*, 170–71; Simkins and Roland, *A History of the South*, 285–88.

15. Blight, "'For Something beyond the Battlefield,'" 1159; *Civil Rights Cases*, 109 U.S. 3 (1883); Dray, *Capitol Men*, 326–32; Klarman, *From Jim Crow to Civil Rights*, 19–20, 49–50; Litwack, *Trouble in Mind*, 392; Woodward, *Origins of the New South*, 216; Woodward, *The Strange Career of Jim Crow*, 71.

16. Foner, *Reconstruction*, 337–39; Slap, *The Doom of Reconstruction*, 223–24; Trefousse, *The Radical Republicans*, 402–4. For an excellent discussion of the transformation of political and economic attitudes during the Gilded Age, see, especially, Calhoun, *From Bloody Shirt to Full Dinner Pail*.

17. Foner, *Forever Free*, 197–98; Foner, *Reconstruction*, 524–29; Franklin, *Reconstruction after the Civil War*, 197–207; Langguth, *After Lincoln*, 362–63; Rable, *But There Was No Peace*, 151; Trefousse, *The Radical Republicans*, 465–70.

18. Bilhartz and Elliott, *Currents in American History*, 121–23; Foner, *Reconstruction*, 580–82; Franklin, *Reconstruction after the Civil War*, 214; Hoogenboom, *The Presidency of Rutherford B. Hayes*, 46–47; Witcover, *Party of the People*, 249–50; Woodward, *Origins of the New South*, 44–45.

19. Blair, "The Use of Military Force to Protect the Gains of Reconstruction," 388, 396; Foner, *Reconstruction*, 582; Gould, *Grand Old Party*, 75–76; Henry, *The Story of Reconstruction*, 591–92; Lewinson, *Race, Class, and Party*, 55–57; Stampp, *The Era of Reconstruction*, 186; Witcover, *Party of the People*, 251–52; Young, "The Year They Stole the White House," 1461.

20. Quoted in Joint Congressional Committee on Inaugural Ceremonies, *Inaugural Addresses of the Presidents of the United States*, 155–56.

21. Fitzgerald, *Splendid Failure*, 209; Foner, *Reconstruction*, 582–83; Franklin, *Reconstruction after the Civil War*, 214–15; Simpson, *The Reconstruction Presidents*, 213–14; Woodward, *Origins of the New South*, 41–42.

22. Quoted in Simpson, *The Reconstruction Presidents*, 213. See also Fitzgerald, *Splendid Failure*, 209; Foner, *Reconstruction*, 582–83; Franklin, *Reconstruction after the Civil War*, 214–15; Simpson, *The Reconstruction Presidents*, 213–14; Woodward, *Origins of the New South*, 41–42.

23. Franklin, *Reconstruction after the Civil War*, 216–17; Langguth, *After Lincoln*, 359; Simpson, *The Reconstruction Presidents*, 213–14; Woodward, *Origins of the New South*, 46–47. For a cogent discussion of the issue of "slavery by another name," see Blackmon, *Slavery by Another Name*.

24. Baum, *The Supreme Court*, 22–24; O'Brien, *Storm Center*, 42–43.

25. 83 U.S. 36 (1872).

26. 83 U.S. 36, 72, 74.

27. Aynes, "Constricting the Law of Freedom," 632–37; Franklin, *Reconstruction after the Civil War*, 206–7; O'Connor, "Time out of Mind," 700–705; Woodward, *The Strange Career of Jim Crow*, 70–72.

28. *States v. Reese*, 92 U.S. 214, 217 (1875). See also Goldman, *Reconstruction and Black Suffrage*, 87; Logan, *The Betrayal of the Negro*, 101; Martinez, *Carpetbaggers, Cavalry, and the Ku Klux Klan*, 201; Woodward, *The Strange Career of Jim Crow*, 71.

29. Keith, *The Colfax Massacre*, xi–xviii; Lemann, *Redemption*, 12–20, 173; Logan, *The Betrayal of the Negro*, 108–10; Rable, *But There Was No Peace*, 127–29.

30. *United States v. Cruikshank*, 92 U.S. 542 (1876). See also Beatty, *Age of Betrayal*, 136–40; Goldman, *Reconstruction and Black Suffrage*, 76; Halbrook, *Freedmen, the Fourteenth Amendment, and the Right to Bear Arms*, 169; Kaczorowski, *The Politics of Judicial Interpretation*, 180–91; Keith, *The Colfax Massacre*, 132–52; Lemann, *Redemption*, 22–23, 163; Woodward, *The Strange Career of Jim Crow*, 71.

31. *Hall v. DeCuir*, 95 U.S. 485, 488–89, 490 (1878).

32. *Louisville, New Orleans, and Texas Railway Company v. Mississippi*, 133 U.S. 587, 594 (1890).

33. *The Civil Rights Cases*, 109 U.S. 3 (1883). See also Blight, "'For Something beyond the Battlefield,'" 1159; Dray, *Capitol Men*, 326–32; Klarman, *From Jim Crow to Civil Rights*, 19–20, 49–50; Litwack, *Trouble in Mind*, 392; Woodward, *Origins of the New South*, 216; Woodward, *The Strange Career of Jim Crow*, 71.

34. *Williams v. Mississippi*, 170 U.S. 213 (1898). See also Ayers, *The Promise of the New South*, 304; Dray, *Capitol Men*, 343; Lemann, *Redemption*, 170–71; Richardson, *West from Appomattox*, 176–77; Woodward, *The Strange Career of Jim Crow*, 71.

35. *Williams v. Mississippi*, 170 U.S. 213, 222 (1898).

36. *Plessy v. Ferguson*, 163 U.S. 537, 550–51 (1896). See also Cooper, "President's Message," 8; Harris, "Symposium," 889–901; Klarman, *From Jim Crow to Civil Rights*, 4; Lears, *Rebirth of a Nation*, 191; Logan, *The Betrayal of the Negro*, 83–84; Woodward, *The Strange Career of Jim Crow*, 54, 71.

37. 163 U.S. 537, 559.

38. 163 U.S. 537, 559.

39. Foner, *Forever Free*, 192–93; Simkins and Roland, *A History of the South*, 493–95.

40. Foner, *Forever Free*, 207–11; Woodward, *Origins of the New South*, 354–56.

41. Foner, *Forever Free*, 207–11; Hovenkamp, "Social Science and Segregation before *Brown*," 624–72; Simkins and Roland, *A History of the South*, 516–18.

42. See, for example, Dunning, *Reconstruction, Political and Economic*. See also Foner, *Reconstruction*, 236–39; Foner, "Reconstruction Revisited," 82; Lemann, *Redemption*, 194; Simkins and Roland, *A History of the South*, 257–58; Smith and Lowery, *The Dunning School*.

43. See, for example, Boas, *Race, Language, and Culture*; Goldenweiser, "The Principle of Limited Possibilities in the Development of Culture," 259–90; Kroeber, *The Nature of Culture*; Lowie, *The History of Ethnological Theory*; Simkins and Roland, *A History of the South*, 494.

44. Alston and Kauffman, "Up, down, and off the Agricultural Ladder," 266; Dill, *Across the Boundaries of Race and Class*; Harley, "For the Good of Family and Race," 336–49; Ransom and Sutch, *One Kind of Freedom*, 95; Simkins and Roland, *A History of the South*, 495–96; Woodman, "Post–Civil War Southern Agriculture and the Law," 324; Wright, "The Economic Revolution in the American South," 161–78.

45. Blackmon, *Slavery by Another Name*. See also Adamson, "Punishment after Slavery," 555–69; Cohen, "Negro Involuntary Servitude in the South, 1865–1940," 31–60.

46. Williams, *History of the Negro Race in America from 1619 to 1880*; Williams, *A History of the Negro Troops in the War of the Rebellion*.

47. See, for example, Dayan, "A Few Stories about Haiti, or, Stigma Revisited," 157–72; Sears, "Frederick Douglass and the Mission to Haiti, 1889–1891," 222–38.

48. Buckner, *Daniel Hale Williams*; Olivier, "In Proper Perspective," 96–97; Patterson, *Sure Hands, Strong Heart*.

49. Clarke, "Without Fear or Shame," 269–89; Lemann, *Redemption*, 71–75, 84–91; Woodward, *Origins of the New South*, 158–60.

CHAPTER 3: RACIAL VIOLENCE AND THE PLIGHT OF THE FREEDMEN

1. See, for example, Foner, *Reconstruction*, 442–44; Shapiro, *White Violence and Black Response*, xi–xvi.

2. The episode is discussed in many sources. See, for example, Dray, *Capitol Men*, 142–43; Keith, *The Colfax Massacre*, 37–38, 86–88; Lemann, *Redemption*, 12; Rable, *But There Was No Peace*, 142.

3. Dray, *Capitol Men*, 146; Keith, *The Colfax Massacre*, 103; Lemann, *Redemption*, 18–19.

4. Keith, *The Colfax Massacre*, 111–12; Rable, *But There Was No Peace*, 127–28.

5. Genovese, *Roll, Jordan, Roll*, 37–40; Hartman, *Scenes of Subjection*, 3–36; Wells, "The End of the Affair," 1805–47.

6. Foner, *Reconstruction*, 442–43; Litwack, *Trouble in Mind*, 86–88.

7. Fry, *Night Riders in Black Folk History*, 122–25; Horn, *Invisible Empire*, 58–66; Mr. and Mrs. Romine, *A Story of the Original Ku Klux Klan*, 15; Rose, *The Ku Klux Klan*, 43–47; Tourgee, *The Invisible Empire*, 131, 419–23; Trelease, *White Terror*, 18–19, 53–54; Wade, *The Fiery Cross*, 59–60.

8. Amos T. Akerman to William W. Belknap, January 8, 1872, in Merrill Military Files, M.103.C.B.1863; Holt, *Black over White*, 30–35; Kaczorowski, "Federal Enforcement of Civil Rights during the First Reconstruction," 164–65; Sefton, *The United States Army and Reconstruction*, 226; Shapiro, "The Ku Klux Klan during Reconstruction," 46; Singletary, "The Negro Militia during Radical Reconstruction," 181–86; Taylor, *The Negro in South Carolina during Reconstruction*, 202–3; Williams, *The Great South Carolina Ku Klux Klan Trials*, 49–50.

9. Foner, *Reconstruction*, 587–601; Lemann, *Redemption*, x–x; Perman, *The Road to Redemption*, 173–74.

10. Ayers, *The Promise of the New South*, 3–8; Blum, *Reforging the White Republic*, 7; Lears, *Rebirth of a Nation*, 21.

11. Emberton, *Beyond Redemption*, 6–10; Shapiro, *White Violence and Black Response*, 8–16.

12. Budiansky, *The Bloody Shirt*, 226–27; Budiansky, "How a War of Terror Kept Blacks Oppressed Long after the Civil War Had Ended," 35; Foner, *Reconstruction*, 570–72; Shapiro, "Afro-American Responses to Violence during Reconstruction," 158–70.

13. Budiansky, *The Bloody Shirt*, 228–32; Budiansky, "How a War of Terror Kept Blacks Oppressed Long after the Civil War Had Ended," 35–37; Zuczek, *State of Rebellion*, 163.

14. Foner, *Reconstruction*, 119–23; Henry, *The Story of Reconstruction*, 237–38.

15. Budiansky, *The Bloody Shirt*, 232–37; Budiansky, "How a War of Terror Kept Blacks Oppressed Long after the Civil War Had Ended," 35–37; Foner, *Reconstruction*, 570–72; Shapiro, "Afro-American Responses to Violence during Reconstruction," 158–70; Zuczek, *State of Rebellion*, 163–64.

16. Budiansky, *The Bloody Shirt*, 270–72; Foner, *Reconstruction*, 590–91; Smith, *How Race Is Made*, 68–72.

17. Quoted in Wormser, *The Rise and Fall of Jim Crow*, 84. See also Hossfeld, *Narrative, Political Unconscious, and Racial Violence in Wilmington, North Carolina*, 4–6; "North Carolina Politics," 2; "North Carolina's Race Feud," 4; Wormser, *The Rise and Fall of Jim Crow*, 80–85.

18. Budiansky, *The Bloody Shirt*, 6; Drago, *Hurrah for Hampton!*, 1–12; Zuczek, *State of Rebellion*, 170, 206, 210.

19. Quoted in Dray, *At the Hands of Persons Unknown*, 125. See also Prather, "We Have Taken a City," 23; Hossfeld, *Narrative, Political Unconscious, and Racial Violence in Wilmington, North Carolina*, 5.

20. Quoted in Dray, *At the Hands of Persons Unknown*, 125–26. See also Whites, "Love, Hate, Rape, Lynching," 158–59; Crow and Durden, *Maverick Republican in the Old North State*, 129; McKoy, *When Whites Riot*, 34–35.

21. Prather, "We Have Taken a City," 19–20; Crow and Durden, *Maverick Republican in the Old North State*, 117–37.

22. Quoted in Schultz and Schultz, *The Price of Dissent*, 123.

23. "Nineteen Negroes Shot to Death," 1; "The Wilmington Riots," 1. See also Dray, *At the Hands of Persons Unknown*, 126–27; Tyson and Cecelski, "Introduction," 4–5; McKoy, *When Whites Riot*, 34–35.

24. Edmonds, *The Negro and Fusion Politics in North Carolina*, 158–74; Foner, *Reconstruction*, 592–93; Tyson and Cecelski, "Introduction," 6.

25. Mitchell, *Righteous Propagation*, 57; Painter, *Southern History across the Color Line*, 120–23.

26. For more on the origins of modern Atlanta as a "city too busy to hate," see Kruse, *White Flight*, 14, 19–20.

27. Simkins and Roland, *A History of the South*, 503–4; Wright, *Black History and Black Identity*, 200–201.

28. Bauerlein, *Negrophobia*, 7–8; Burns, *Rage in the Gate City*, 4–5; Collins, *All Hell Broke Loose*, 48; Godshalk, *Veiled Visions*, 48–52.

29. "Atlanta Mobs Kill Ten Negroes," 1. See also Bauerlein, *Negrophobia*, 62–63, 102, 135–38; Burns, *Rage in the Gate City*, 43–44, 153, 175–76; Godshalk, *Veiled Visions*, 123–24.

30. Bauerlein, *Negrophobia*, 149–53; Burns, *Rage in the Gate City*, 124, 130, 141; Collins, *All Hell Broke Loose*, 50–51; Godshalk, *Veiled Visions*, 88.

31. "The Atlanta Riots," 8; Collins, *All Hell Broke Loose*, 52.

32. Quoted in Bauerlein, *Negrophobia*, 244. See also Burns, *Rage in the Gate City*, 126, 127, 159; Godshalk, *Veiled Visions*, 95, 148.

33. Quoted in Weinstein and Gatell, *The Segregation Era*, 126. See also Bauerlein, *Negrophobia*, 146–48, 150–51; Burns, *Rage in the Gate City*, 176.

34. Bauerlein, *Negrophobia*, 50, 254–57; Godshalk, *Veiled Visions*, 133.

35. Burns, *Rage in the Gate City*, 4–8; Collins, *All Hell Broke Loose*, 53–54; Mixon, *The Atlanta Riot*, 117; "Paper Blamed for Riots," 1.

36. Crouthamel, "The Springfield Race Riot of 1908," 164; Dray, *At the Hands of Persons Unknown*, 167; Moon, "Springfield, Illinois, Riot," 70; Senechal de la Roche, *In Lincoln's Shadow*, 1.

37. Crouthamel, "The Springfield Race Riot of 1908," 166–70; Moon, "Springfield, Illinois, Riot," 70; Senechal de la Roche, *In Lincoln's Shadow*, 1–2.

38. Crouthamel, "The Springfield Race Riot of 1908," 173; Dray, *At the Hands of Persons Unknown*, 167–68; Senechal de la Roche, *In Lincoln's Shadow*, 35–37.

39. "'Intolerable,' Says Deneen," 3; "Rioters Hang Another Negro," 1, 3; "The Savages of Springfield," 6; "Troops Check Riots, Sixth Victim Dies," 1, 2. See also Crouthamel, "The Springfield Race Riot of 1908," 173–74; Dray, *At the Hands of Persons Unknown*, 168; Senechal de la Roche, *In Lincoln's Shadow*, 44–46.

40. "Springfield Riots End," 14; "20 Race War Indictments," 6. See also Crouthamel, "The Springfield Race Riot of 1908," 177–81; Dray, *At the Hands of Persons Unknown*, 168–69; Moon, "Springfield, Illinois, Riot," 70; Senechal de la Roche, *In Lincoln's Shadow*, 190–95.

41. Crouthamel, "The Springfield Race Riot of 1908," 176–77; Kirk, "The Long Road to Equality," 53; Senechal de la Roche, *In Lincoln's Shadow*, 1–2, 170–72.

42. Collins, *All Hell Broke Loose*, 56; Dray, *At the Hands of Persons Unknown*, 234–35.

43. Collins, *All Hell Broke Loose*, 56; Lumpkins, *American Pogrom*, 1–2, 19.

44. "Mob of 3,000 Rules in East St. Louis," 3; "Race Riots Continue in East St. Louis," 6. See also Collins, *All Hell Broke Loose*, 56–57; Lumpkins, *American Pogrom*, 56–58, 93–101.

45. Collins, *All Hell Broke Loose*, 58; Dray, *At the Hands of Persons Unknown*, 234–35; Lumpkins, *American Pogrom*, 110–12.

46. "Army Begins Inquiry into Race Rioting," 9; "Race Rioters Fire East St. Louis and Shoot or Hang Many Negroes," 1, 6; "Troops Blamed for Riots Spread," 5. See also Collins, *All Hell Broke Loose*, 58–59; Lumpkins, *American Pogrom*, 58–59.

47. Collins, *All Hell Broke Loose*, 59–61; Lumpkins, *American Pogrom*, 59–61. Garvey is quoted in "Gateway Album," 41. See also Hill, *The Marcus Garvey Universal Negro Improvement Association Papers*, 1:217.

48. Chalmers, *Hooded Americanism*, 71; Dinnerstein, *The Leo Frank Case*, 139–47; MacLean, *Behind the Mask of Chivalry*, 12; Oney, *And the Dead Shall Rise*, 561–72; Wade, *The Fiery Cross*, 144.

49. Coffman, *The War to End All Wars*, 69–73; McWhirter, *Red Summer*, 12–13.

50. Barbeau and Henri, *The Unknown Soldiers*, 177–78; McWhirter, *Red Summer*, 12–13.

51. Quoted in Foley, *Spectres of 1919*, 13.

52. Barbeau and Henri, *The Unknown Soldiers*, 173–76; Coffman, *The War to End All Wars*, 319–22; Foley, *Spectres of 1919*, 137–41.

53. "Order in Chicago," 8; "28 Dead, 500 Hurt in Three-Day Race Riots in Chicago," 1, 3; "Troopers Restore Order in Chicago," 10. See also Barbeau and

Henri, *The Unknown Soldiers*, 182; Foley, *Spectres of 1919*, 12–13; McWhirter, *Red Summer*, 127–48.

54. "4 Dead, 5 Dying, 70 Hurt in New Race Riots in Washington," 1; "Race War in Washington," 8. See also Dray, *At the Hands of Persons Unknown*, 254–55; McWhirter, *Red Summer*, 96–113.

55. "Nine Killed in Fight with Arkansas Posse," 4; "Six More Are Killed in Arkansas Riots," 6.

56. "Six More Are Killed in Arkansas Riots," 6. See also Biegert, "Legacy of Resistance," 84–88.

57. Quoted in Stockley, *Blood in Their Eyes*, 87. See also "Planned Massacre of Whites Today," 1; "Trace Plot to Stir Negroes to Rise," 7.

58. The episode is recounted in detail in McWhirter, *Red Summer*, 209–32. See also Biegert, "Legacy of Resistance," 84–88; Dray, *At the Hands of Persons Unknown*, 237–45; Gordon, *Caste and Class*, 3–4, 130–37; Stockley, *Blood in Their Eyes*, xviii, 3–6, 29, 46, 72, 76–77, 131.

59. The incident is recalled in several sources. See, for example, Dray, *At the Hands of Persons Unknown*, 237–45; Janken, *Walter White*, 50–53; Leiter, *In the Shadow of the Black Beast*, 62.

60. Dray, *At the Hands of Persons Unknown*, 243; Stockley, *Blood in Their Eyes*, 44–45.

61. *Moore v. Dempsey*, 261 U.S. 86 (1923).

62. 261 U.S. 86, 91.

63. Karst, "*Moore v. Dempsey*, 261 U.S. 86 (1923)," 1757–58.

64. Hirsch, *Riot and Remembrance*, 41.

65. Brophy, *Reconstructing the Dreamland*, 22–23; Ellsworth, *Death in a Promised Land*, 16; Hirsch, *Riot and Remembrance*, 30–31; Madigan, *The Burning*, 2–3, 8–9, 18–19.

66. Brophy, *Reconstructing the Dreamland*, 9–12, 18–19, 74–78; Ellsworth, *Death in a Promised Land*, 17–18; Hirsch, *Riot and Remembrance*, 32–38; Madigan, *The Burning*, 24, 46, 68, 70.

67. Brophy, *Reconstructing the Dreamland*, 5–6; Ellsworth, *Death in a Promised Land*, 98–103; Hirsch, *Riot and Remembrance*, 57–59; Madigan, *The Burning*, 31–32, 37, 64–67.

68. Brophy, *Reconstructing the Dreamland*, 20–26; Ellsworth, *Death in a Promised Land*, xvi, 40–42, 45–49; Hirsch, *Riot and Remembrance*, 66–67, 78–79; Madigan, *The Burning*, 39–40.

69. Hirsch, *Riot and Remembrance*, 30, 136, 151–52; Madigan, *The Burning*, 18–19, 135–38, 170–74.

70. "85 Whites and Negroes Die in Tulsa Riots as 3,000 Armed Men Battle in Streets," 1; "Series of Fierce Combats," 1. See also Ellsworth, *Death in a Promised Land*, 51–54; Hirsch, *Riot and Remembrance*, 92–103.

71. Brophy, *Reconstructing the Dreamland*, 93–95; Ellsworth, *Death in a Promised Land*, 55; Hirsch, *Riot and Remembrance*, 103; Madigan, *The Burning*, 120–21.

72. Hirsch, *Riot and Remembrance*, 106; Madigan, *The Burning*, 131.

73. Brophy, *Reconstructing the Dreamland*, 103–5; Ellsworth, *Death in a Promised Land*, 84–92; Hirsch, *Riot and Remembrance*, 242, 268–71, 312–13; Madigan, *The*

Burning, 256–68; "Military Control Is Ended at Tulsa," 1; "Thirty Whites Held for Tulsa Rioting," 21.

74. "Florida Race Riot Has Seventh Victim," S5; "Kill Six in Florida," 1. See also D'Orso, *Like Judgment Day*, 2–5; Dye, "Rosewood, Florida," 611–15; Johnson, *Negroes and the Gun*, 190.

75. "Last Negro Homes Razed in Rosewood," 4. See also D'Orso, *Like Judgment Day*, 9, 48–53; Dye, "Rosewood, Florida," 615–16.

76. "Kill Six in Florida," 1. See also D'Orso, *Like Judgment Day*, 56–57; Dye, "Rosewood, Florida," 615–22; Johnson, *Negroes and the Gun*, 190–92.

77. Collins, *All Hell Broke Loose*, 123–24; D'Orso, *Like Judgment Day*, 264–73, 295; Dye, "Rosewood, Florida," 605.

78. Dray, *At the Hands of Persons Unknown*, 66–69, 162; Johnson, *Negroes and the Gun*, 113–14; Leiter, *In the Shadow of the Black Beast*, 1–6.

79. Dray, *At the Hands of Persons Unknown*, xvii, 21; Shuler, *The Thirteenth Turn*, 163–66.

80. Budiansky, *The Bloody Shirt*, 1–2; Emberton, *Beyond Redemption*, 2–10; Lemann, *Redemption*, x–xi; Simkins and Roland, *A History of the South*, 279–80.

CHAPTER 4: THE RISE OF
THE POPULIST MOVEMENT

1. Goodwyn, *The Populist Movement*, viii–vviv; Witcover, *Party of the People*, 270–71.

2. Goodwyn, *The Populist Movement*, 9–19; Hild, *Greenbackers, Knights of Labor, and Populists*, 3–4.

3. Hild, *Greenbackers, Knights of Labor, and Populists*, 9–40; McCabe, *History of the Grange Movement*, 409–18; Wilson, *The Greenbackers and Their Doctrines*, 5–6.

4. Cochrane, *The Development of American Agriculture*, 95; Goodwyn, *The Populist Movement*, 72–73; Rome, "Farmers as Entrepreneurs," 45–49.

5. Goodwyn, *The Populist Movement*, 25–32; McCabe, *History of the Grange Movement*, 409–18; Witcover, *Party of the People*, 270–71.

6. Goodwyn, *The Populist Movement*, 63–69; McMath, *American Populism*, 50–53, 147–48.

7. Goodwyn, *Democratic Promise*, xx, 237–42; Goodwyn, *The Populist Movement*, 74–90; Macune, "The Wellsprings of a Populist," 140, 155–56; McMath, *American Populism*, 87–88; Saloutos, *Farmer Movements in the South*, 90–91; Smith, "'Macuneism,' or the Farmers of Texas in Business," 224–25.

8. McMath, *American Populism*, 97, 102–3; McMath, *Populist Vanguard*, 145; Saloutos, *Farmer Movements in the South*, 137; Smith, "'Macuneism,' or the Farmers of Texas in Business," 242–44.

9. Goodwyn, *The Populist Movement*, 57–60; McMath, *American Populism*, 143–45, 151.

10. Gramm and Gramm, "The Free Silver Movement in America," 1108–20; McMath, *American Populism*, 200, 202; Goodwyn, *The Populist Movement*, 9–10, 312; Witcover, *Party of the People*, 270–76.

11. Goodwyn, *The Populist Movement*, 293–96; Gould, *Grand Old Party*, 109; Witcover, *Party of the People*, 270–71.

12. Goodwyn, *The Populist Movement*, 293–310; Gould, *Grand Old Party*, 109; Witcover, *Party of the People*, 270–71.

13. Goodwyn, *The Populist Movement*, 107–8; Phelan, *Grand Master Workman*, 250–51.

14. Quoted in Piven, *Challenging Authority*, 15. See also Goodwyn, *The Populist Movement*, 165–67; Ridge, *Ignatius Donnelly*, 300–303; Zinn, *A People's History of the United States*, 282–83.

15. Goodwyn, *The Populist Movement*, 55, 86–87; Hicks, *Populist Revolt*, 343–49.

16. Goodwyn, *The Populist Movement*, 118–23; Hicks, *Populist Revolt*, 114–15; McMath, *American Populism*, 94–94, 98–99.

17. See, for example, Woodward, *The Strange Career of Jim Crow*, 80. See also Goodwyn, *The Populist Movement*, 118–23, 172; Hicks, *Populist Revolt*, 229–36; Kazin, *A Godly Hero*, 36–37; Zinn, *A People's History of the United States*, 283–85.

18. Gould, *Grand Old Party*, 112; Kane, *Facts about the Presidents*, 253–54; Witcover, *Party of the People*, 271, 274; Zinn, *A People's History of the United States*, 283.

19. Brands, *American Colossus*, 594–98; Hicks, *Populist Revolt*, 321; Kazin, *A Godly Hero*, 40–41; Strouse, *Morgan*, 339–52.

20. Brands, *American Colossus*, 530–34; Hicks, *Populist Revolt*, 308–10; Strouse, *Morgan*, 318–24.

21. Goodwyn, *The Populist Movement*, 306–10; Witcover, *Party of the People*, 279–85.

22. Quoted in Hofstadter, *The American Political Tradition and the Men Who Made It*, 245. See also Goodwyn, *The Populist Movement*, 216–17; McMath, *American Populism*, 200–201.

23. "Bryan, Free Silver, and Repudiation," 1.

24. Goodwyn, *The Populist Movement*, 254–55; Kane, *Facts about the Presidents*, 260–61; Zinn, *A People's History of the United States*, 288–89.

25. The speech is reprinted in many sources. See, for example, Safire, *Lend Me Your Ears*, 923–26; Bryan, *The Cross of Gold*. For an analysis, see Hofstadter, *The American Political Tradition and the Men Who Made It*, 241–43; Kazin, *A Godly Hero*, 59–61.

26. "Bryan the Demagogue," 3; "Bryan, Free Silver, and Repudiation," 1; Gould, *Grand Old Party*, 124; Kazin, *A Godly Hero*, 61–63.

27. Goodwyn, *The Populist Movement*, 282–86; Kane, *Facts about the Presidents*, 262; Kazin, *A Godly Hero*, 76–79, 84; Williams, *Realigning America*, 149–50.

28. Gould, *Grand Old Party*, 126–27; Kane, *Facts about the Presidents*, 264–65; Kazin, *A Godly Hero*, 94–107, 213–42; Witcover, *Party of the People*, 287–92; Zinn, *A People's History of the United States*, 289.

29. The question of whether Baum's story was a political fable about populism or merely an entertaining children's story has been debated at length. See, for example, Hansen, "The Fable of the Allegory," 254–64; Littlefield, "The Wizard of Oz," 47–58.

30. Goodwyn, *The Populist Movement*, 307–10; McMath, *American Populism*, 206–7; Williams, *Realigning America*, 164–65.

31. Goodwyn, *The Populist Movement*, 302–22; Hofstadter, *The Age of Reform*, 4–5, 8–9; McMath, *American Populism*, 209–11.

32. Goodwin, *The Bully Pulpit*, xi–xii; Gould, *Grand Old Party*, 153–54; Piott, *American Reformers*, 158–60; Witcover, *Party of the People*, 297–98.

33. Amstutz, "Nebraska's Live Stock Sanitary Commission and the Rise of Progressivism," 259–60; Eisenach, "Progressivism as a National Narrative in Biblical-Hegelian Times," 61–64.

34. Barrett, "The Struggles of Women Industrial Workers to Improve Work Conditions in the Progressive Era," 43–48; Burt, "Working Women and the Triangle Fire," 189–99; Murdach, "Does American Social Work Have a Progressive Tradition?," 82–86.

35. Elshtain, "A Return to Hull House," 105–13.

36. On Progressives and their agenda, see Goodwin, *The Bully Pulpit*, especially xiii–xii, 655–57, 670. Goodwin discusses Theodore Roosevelt at length. See also Unger, *Fighting Bob La Follette*; Urofsky, *Louis D. Brandeis*; Westbrook, *John Dewey and American Democracy*.

37. Hahn, *A Nation under Our Feet*, 460; Logan, *The Betrayal of the Negro*, 344–45; Simkins and Roland, *A History of the South*, 507; Woodward, *Origins of the New South*, 367–68.

38. Ayers, *The Promise of the New South*, 325–27; Dray, *At the Hands of Persons Unknown*, viii, 167, 170–72; Lacy, *Cheer the Lonesome Traveler*, 43–45; Lears, *Rebirth of a Nation*, 129–30; Logan, *The Betrayal of the Negro*, 313, 331–32; Woodward, *Origins of the New South*, 367–68.

39. Dray, *At the Hands of Persons Unknown*, x; McKoy, *When Whites Riot*, 34–35; Simkins and Roland, *A History of the South*, 497.

40. Dray, *At the Hands of Persons Unknown*, 258–72; Shuler, *The Thirteenth Turn*, 183–88.

41. Foner, *Reconstruction*, 236–39; Foner, "Reconstruction Revisited," 82; Lemann, *Redemption*, 194; Simkins and Roland, *A History of the South*, 257–58.

42. Foner, *Forever Free*, 214–22. See also Bogle, *Toms, Coons, Mulattoes, Mammies, and Bucks*, 3–9; Kern-Foxworth, *Aunt Jemima, Uncle Ben, and Rastus*, xvii–xx.

CHAPTER 5: SOUTHERN POPULISM

1. Foner, *Forever Free*, 189–238; Simkins and Roland, *A History of the South*, 492–522.

2. Goodwyn, *The Populist Movement*, 160–61, 188–90, 325; Woodward, *Tom Watson*, 225–26, 330–33, 399.

3. Watson's young life is recalled in several sources. See, for example, Bartley, *The Creation of Modern Georgia*, 87–92; Bryan, *Henry Grady or Tom Watson?*, 34–37; Woodward, *Tom Watson*, 14–243.

4. Fingerhut, "Tom Watson, Blacks, and Southern Reform," 326–30; Woodward, *Tom Watson*, 219–22.

5. Quoted in Kennedy and Bailey, *The American Spirit*, 52. See also Cooper and Terrill, *The American South*, 2:437–43; Watson, "The Negro Question in the South," 118–28.

6. Quoted in Krugman, *The Conscience of a Liberal*, 29.

7. Quoted in Krugman, *The Conscience of a Liberal*, 29.

8. Quoted in Kennedy and Bailey, *The American Spirit*, 53.

9. Quoted in Woodward, *Tom Watson*, 220. Emphasis in the original.

10. Quoted in Moltke-Hansen, "Turn Signals," 185–86. See also Goodwyn, *The Populist Movement*, 164, 206, 250; Woodward, *Tom Watson*, 181–84.

11. Kane, *Facts about the Presidents*, 262; Kazin, *A Godly Hero*, 65; Witcover, *Party of the People*, 285, 296–97.

12. Goodwyn, *The Populist Movement*, 325; Woodward, *Origins of the New South*, 393; Woodward, *Tom Watson*, 370–72.

13. Davis, *Henry Grady's New South*, 29–31; Gaston, *The New South Creed*, 101–5; Simkins and Roland, *A History of the South*, 312.

14. Davis, *Henry Grady's New South*, 36–43, 66–71; Gaston, *The New South Creed*, 68.

15. Quoted in Collins, *Speeches That Changed the World*, 360–61.

16. Quoted in Reed, *Modern Eloquence*, 585. See also Gaston, *The New South Creed*, 102–4; Simkins and Roland, *A History of the South*, 312–13.

17. Quoted in Reed, *Modern Eloquence*, 588.

18. Gaston, *The New South Creed*, 37; Simkins and Roland, *A History of the South*, 322, 345.

19. Kantrowitz, "Ben Tillman and Hendrix McLane, Agrarian Rebels," 518–23; Kantrowitz, *Ben Tillman and the Reconstruction of White Supremacy*, 5–6; Simkins and Roland, *A History of the South*, 304–19.

20. Kantrowitz, *Ben Tillman and the Reconstruction of White Supremacy*, 110–14; Simkins and Roland, *A History of the South*, 340–42; Woodward, *Tom Watson*, 56, 66.

21. Kantrowitz, "Ben Tillman and Hendrix McLane, Agrarian Rebels," 512–15; Kantrowitz, *Ben Tillman and the Reconstruction of White Supremacy*, 22, 118–20; Simkins and Roland, *A History of the South*, 304–19.

22. Kantrowitz, *Ben Tillman and the Reconstruction of White Supremacy*, 6–9; Simkins, "Ben Tillman's View of the Negro," 161–62; Simkins and Roland, *A History of the South*, 346; Woodward, *Tom Watson*, 371.

23. Kantrowitz, *Ben Tillman and the Reconstruction of White Supremacy*, 10–39; Simkins, *Pitchfork Ben Tillman*, xviii, 23; Simkins and Roland, *A History of the South*, 346–48.

24. Kantrowitz, *Ben Tillman and the Reconstruction of White Supremacy*, 53–64; Shapiro, "The Ku Klux Klan during Reconstruction," 34–55; Stagg, "The Problem of Klan Violence," 303–18; Zuczek, *State of Rebellion*, 55–134.

25. Kantrowitz, "Ben Tillman and Hendrix McLane, Agrarian Rebels," 509; Kantrowitz, *Ben Tillman and the Reconstruction of White Supremacy*, 60–67; Shapiro, "The Ku Klux Klan during Reconstruction," 34–55; Simkins, *Pitchfork Ben Tillman*, 58–61, 66, 67; Simkins and Roland, *A History of the South*, 284, 286, 287; Zuczek, *State of Rebellion*, 55–134.

26. Budiansky, *The Bloody Shirt*, 232–37; Budiansky, "How a War of Terror Kept Blacks Oppressed Long after the Civil War Had Ended," 35–37; Foner, *Reconstruction*, 570–72; Kantrowitz, *Ben Tillman and the Reconstruction of White Supremacy*, 64–71; Shapiro, "Afro-American Responses to Violence during Recon-

struction," 158–70; Simkins, *Pitchfork Ben Tillman*, 61–64; Simkins and Roland, *A History of the South*, 284, 286, 287; Zuczek, *State of Rebellion*, 163–64.

27. Kantrowitz, *Ben Tillman and the Reconstruction of White Supremacy*, 1–9; Simkins and Roland, *A History of the South*, 346–49.

28. Grier and Munger, "The Impact of Legislator Attributes on Interest-Group Campaign Contributions," 350; Kantrowitz, "Ben Tillman and Hendrix McLane, Agrarian Rebels," 522–23; Kantrowitz, *Ben Tillman and the Reconstruction of White Supremacy*, 127–28, 147–51, 230, 232; Simkins, *Pitchfork Ben Tillman*, 179–81; Sitkoff, "Politics and the Business of Corruption," 30.

29. Quoted in Brown and Webb, *Race in the American South*, 216. See also Davis, *Guest of Honor*, 254–55; Kantrowitz, *Ben Tillman and the Reconstruction of White Supremacy*, 259; Kennedy, *Nigger*, 8; Simkins, *Pitchfork Ben Tillman*, 400.

30. Kantrowitz, *Ben Tillman and the Reconstruction of White Supremacy*, 254–56; Simkins, *Pitchfork Ben Tillman*, 1–6, 8–12, 385–90.

31. Quoted in Kantrowitz, *Ben Tillman and the Reconstruction of White Supremacy*, 232. See also Kantrowitz, "Ben Tillman and Hendrix McLane, Agrarian Rebels," 498, 524; Simkins, "Ben Tillman's View of the Negro," 172.

32. Kantrowitz, *Ben Tillman and the Reconstruction of White Supremacy*, 1–9, 306–9; Simkins, "Ben Tillman's View of the Negro," 172–74; Simkins, *Pitchfork Ben Tillman*, xxv–xxviii.

33. Ayers, *The Promise of the New South*, 413; Hollis, "Coleman Blease," 16; Simkins, *Pitchfork Ben Tillman*, 487–90; Simon, "The Appeal of Coleman Blease of South Carolina," 63–64; Simkins and Roland, *A History of the South*, 529–30; Woodward, *Origins of the New South*, 393–94.

34. Quoted in South Carolina General Assembly, *Journal of the Senate of the General Assembly of the State of South Carolina*, 85. See also Kantrowitz, *Ben Tillman and the Reconstruction of White Supremacy*, 255–56; Simon, "The Appeal of Coleman Blease of South Carolina," 64.

35. Blease's comment on lynching is quoted in Hollis, "Coleman Blease," 6. The characterization of Blease is found in Hollis, "'Cotton Ed Smith,'" 242. See also Simon, "The Appeal of Coleman Blease of South Carolina," 82–84; Woodward, *Origins of the New South*, 393–94.

36. Hollis, "Coleman Blease," 3, 16; Kantrowitz, *Ben Tillman and the Reconstruction of White Supremacy*, 296–99.

37. "Niggers in the White House," 6. See also Day, "Herbert Hoover and Racial Politics," 13; "White House Tea Starts Senate Stir," 38.

38. The incident when the six-year-old Thurmond shook hands with Tillman has been recounted in many sources. See, for example, Bass and Thompson, *Ol' Strom*, 25; Cohodas, *Strom Thurmond and the Politics of Southern Change*, 29; Crespino, *Strom Thurmond's America*, 18.

39. Goodwyn, *The Populist Movement*, 197–98; Kantrowitz, *Ben Tillman and the Reconstruction of White Supremacy*, 8, 128, 246, 265.

40. Olsen, "Populism, American Style," 6–20; Savage, "Populist Elements in Contemporary American Political Discourse," 178–79; Winter, "The Evolution of Politics in the Deep South," 93–105.

41. Quoted in Wilkerson, *The Warmth of Other Suns*, 39. See also Morgan, "Of Gentlemen and SOBs," 52–56; Simkins and Roland, *A History of the South*, 529; White, "Mississippi's Great White Chief," 442–46.

42. Fitzgerald, "'We Have Found a Moses,'" 293–320; Morgan, "Of Gentlemen and SOBs," 52–64; Simkins and Roland, *A History of the South*, 529–30; Woodward, *Origins of the New South*, 394–95.

43. Simkins and Roland, *A History of the South*, 531; Winter, "The Evolution of Politics in the Deep South," 93–105; Woodward, *Origins of the New South*, 392–95.

44. Hollis, "'Cotton Ed Smith,'" 235–37; Simon, *A Fabric of Defeat*, 191–93; "Sen. Smith, 'Cotton Ed,' Dies at 80," 1, 2.

45. Hollis, "'Cotton Ed Smith,'" 236–37; Simkins, *Pitchfork Ben Tillman*, 70–168.

46. Hollis, "'Cotton Ed Smith,'" 239; McGill, "The Lesson of 'Cotton Ed' Smith," 4; "Sen. Smith, 'Cotton Ed,' Dies at 80," 1, 2.

47. Hollis, "'Cotton Ed Smith,'" 240–41; Yarbrough, *A Passion for Justice*, 16–17.

48. Hollis, "Coleman Blease," 2–3; Hollis, "'Cotton Ed Smith,'" 242–43.

49. Hollis, "'Cotton Ed Smith,'" 245–56; McGill, "The Lesson of 'Cotton Ed' Smith," 4; "Sen. Smith, 'Cotton Ed,' Dies at 80," 1, 2; Yarbrough, *A Passion for Justice*, 16.

50. Hollis, "'Cotton Ed Smith,'" 249, 251; Yarbrough, *A Passion for Justice*, 16.

51. Hollis, "'Cotton Ed Smith,'" 250–55; McGill, "The Lesson of 'Cotton Ed' Smith," 4; Stokes, "A Tradition Passed with 'Cotton Ed' Smith," 7; Yarbrough, *A Passion for Justice*, 16–17.

52. Hollis, "'Cotton Ed Smith,'" 256; McGill, "The Lesson of 'Cotton Ed' Smith," 4; Stokes, "A Tradition Passed with 'Cotton Ed' Smith," 7. The phrase "conscientious objector to the twentieth century" is quoted in Hollis, "'Cotton Ed Smith,'" 256.

53. Simkins and Roland, *A History of the South*, 527–31; Winter, "The Evolution of Politics in the Deep South," 97–99.

54. Jeansonne, "Challenge to the New Deal," 332–34; White, *Kingfish*, 144.

55. Simkins and Roland, *A History of the South*, 531–32; White, *Kingfish*, 244. For a discussion of whether Long was genuinely committed to assisting the poor or simply a political opportunist, see Jeansonne, "Challenge to the New Deal," 331–39. For a discussion of Long's views on race, see Jeansonne, "Huey Long and Racism," 265–82.

56. Hair, *The Kingfish and His Realm*, 258–59; White, *Kingfish*, 92, 185–87.

57. Hair, *The Kingfish and His Realm*, 274, 320–25; White, *Kingfish*, 259–64, 267–68.

58. Feldman, *The Irony of the Solid South*, 127–29; Simkins and Roland, *A History of the South*, 533–34.

59. Quoted in Simkins and Roland, *A History of the South*, 537. See also Morgan, "Of Gentlemen and SOBs," 51–55.

60. Pruitt, *Taming Alabama*, 91–92, 107; Simkins and Roland, *A History of the South*, 536–37; Witcover, *Party of the People*, 299, 305, 307, 340, 341; Woodward, *Origins of the New South*, 475–78, 481.

61. Quoted in Woodward, *Origins of the New South*, 333. See also Broz, *The International Origins of the Federal Reserve System*, 195–97; Simkins and Roland, *A History of the South*, 535–36.

62. Dewhirst, *Encyclopedia of the United States Congress*, 238–30; Simkins and Roland, *A History of the South*, 534–35.

63. Dewhirst, *Encyclopedia of the United States Congress*, 228–30; Simkins and Roland, *A History of the South*, 353; Witcover, *Party of the People*, 354, 378.

64. Feldman, *The Irony of the Solid South*, 121, 171–74; Simkins and Roland, *A History of the South*, 533–34, 536–44.

65. Bass and Thompson, *Ol' Strom*, 2–3, 18, 97–117; Carter, *The Politics of Rage*, 12–14, 368–96; Cohodas, *Strom Thurmond and the Politics of Southern Change*, 2–3, 185–88, 190–92; Crespino, *Strom Thurmond's America*, 66–71, 74–88; Lesher, *George Wallace*, xii–xvi, 387–427; Perlstein, *Nixonland*, 340–45, 347–49.

CHAPTER 6: WASHINGTON VERSUS DU BOIS

1. Foner, *Forever Free*, 214–17; McPherson, *The Abolitionist Legacy*, 300–301; Simkins and Roland, *A History of the South*, 508–13; Woodward, *Origins of the New South*, 366–68.

2. Washington, *Up from Slavery*, 2. See also McPherson, *The Abolitionist Legacy*, 354–57; Richardson, *West from Appomattox*, 202–4.

3. Johnson and Watson, "The W. E. B. Du Bois and Booker T. Washington Debate," 66; Norrell, *Up from History*, 17–18; West, *The Education of Booker T. Washington*, 69.

4. Washington, *Up from Slavery*, 9, 10. See also Norrell, *Up from History*, 217–23.

5. Washington, *Up from Slavery*, 13. See also Harlan, *Booker T. Washington in Perspective*, 25–47; Norrell, *Up from History*, 17; West, *The Education of Booker T. Washington*, 111–16.

6. Harlan, *Booker T. Washington in Perspective*, 14, 35–41; Norrell, *Up from History*, 25–30; West, *The Education of Booker T. Washington*, 121–30; Wolters, *Du Bois and His Rivals*, 42–46.

7. Norrell, *Up from History*, 38; West, *The Education of Booker T. Washington*, 197.

8. Washington, *Up from Slavery*, 32. See also Harlan, *Booker T. Washington in Perspective*, 12, 13, 21, 22; Norrell, *Up from History*, 31–39; West, *The Education of Booker T. Washington*, 21, 116–17; Wolters, *Du Bois and His Rivals*, 43–48.

9. Norrell, *Up from History*, 40; West, *The Education of Booker T. Washington*, 40, 210–11; Wolters, *Du Bois and His Rivals*, 47–49.

10. Harlan, *Booker T. Washington in Perspective*, 94–95; Johnson and Watson, "The W. E. B. Du Bois and Booker T. Washington Debate," 67–68; Norrell, *Up from History*, 8–14, 40–50; West, *The Education of Booker T. Washington*, 70.

11. Quoted in Woodward, *Origins of the New South*, 359. See also McPherson, *The Abolitionist Legacy*, 354–57; Richardson, *West from Appomattox*, 202–4.

12. Washington, *The Story of the Negro*, 399.

13. Washington, "The 1895 Atlanta Compromise Speech," 583–87. See also Blackmon, *Slavery by Another Name*, 161; Harlan, *Booker T. Washington in Perspective*,

83–84, 110–11; Johnson and Watson, "The W. E. B. Du Bois and Booker T. Washington Debate," 68; Lears, *Rebirth of a Nation*, 131–32; Norrell, *Up from History*, 277–78, 432–34; West, *The Education of Booker T. Washington*, 11–13, 26, 51; Wolters, *Du Bois and His Rivals*, 51–53.

14. Johnson and Watson, "The W. E. B. Du Bois and Booker T. Washington Debate," 66–67; Logan, *The Betrayal of the Negro*, 313; Simkins and Roland, *A History of the South*, 506–7; Woodward, *Origins of the New South*, 367. One scholar suggests that Washington secretly longed for acceptance as an intellectual on par with Du Bois. Gibson, "The Envy of Erudition," 52–54.

15. Ayers, *The Promise of the New South*, 325–26; Foner, *Forever Free*, 211–12; Simkins and Roland, *A History of the South*, 505–6; Woodward, *Origins of the New South*, 357–61.

16. *Plessy v. Ferguson*, 163 U.S. 537 (1896). For more on Judge Lynch, see Dray, *At the Hands of Persons Unknown*, ix, 177.

17. Simkins and Roland, *A History of the South*, 521–22; Woodward, *Origins of the New South*, 354–57; Woodward, *The Strange Career of Jim Crow*, 97–102.

18. Foner, *Forever Free*, xxv–xxvi; Logan, *The Betrayal of the Negro*, 344–49; Simkins and Roland, *A History of the South*, 508–13; Woodward, *Origins of the New South*, 366–68.

19. Logan, *The Betrayal of the Negro*, 313; Simkins and Roland, *A History of the South*, 506–7; Woodward, *Origins of the New South*, 367.

20. Ayers, *The Promise of the New South*, 325–27; Lacy, *Cheer the Lonesome Traveler*, 43–45; Martinez, *Coming for to Carry Me Home*, 239.

21. Egerton, *The Wars of Reconstruction*, 321–22; Horne, *W. E. B. Du Bois*, xii; Johnson and Watson, "The W. E. B. Du Bois and Booker T. Washington Debate," 68; Lewis, *W. E. B. Du Bois*, 11–12, 29–31; Marable, *W. E. B. Du Bois*, 2; Wolters, *Du Bois and His Rivals*, 5–11.

22. Quoted in Wolters, *Du Bois and His Rivals*, 12. See also Egerton, *The Wars of Reconstruction*, 322; Horne, *W. E. B. Du Bois*, 4, 7–9; Johnson and Watson, "The W. E. B. Du Bois and Booker T. Washington Debate," 68; Lewis, *W. E. B. Du Bois*, 45; Marable, *W. E. B. Du Bois*, 3–4.

23. Quoted in Egerton, *The Wars of Reconstruction*, 322. See also Wolters, *Du Bois and His Rivals*, 11–12.

24. Quoted in Etuk, *From David Walker to Barack Obama*, 40. See also Egerton, *The Wars of Reconstruction*, 322; Horne, *W. E. B. Du Bois*, 13–15; Marable, *W. E. B. Du Bois*, 16–18; Wolters, *Du Bois and His Rivals*, 20–23.

25. Horne, *W. E. B. Du Bois*, 18–22; Lewis, *W. E. B. Du Bois*, 111–21.

26. Egerton, *The Wars of Reconstruction*, 322–23; Lewis, *W. E. B. Du Bois*, 173–74.

27. "Capture of Sam Hose Seems to Be a Matter of Only a Few Hours," 1; "Circle of Vengeance Slowly Closing on Fleeing Sam Hose," 1; "Sam Hose Still Eagerly Pursued," 3. See also Dray, *At the Hands of Persons Unknown*, 4–5.

28. "*Constitution* Paid $500 to Capturer of Sam Hose," A7. See also Dray, *At the Hands of Persons Unknown*, 9–14; Horne, *W. E. B. Du Bois*, 28; Lewis, *W. E. B. Du Bois*, 162–63.

29. Quoted in Lewis, *W. E. B. Du Bois*, 163. See also Dray, *At the Hands of Persons Unknown*, 3, 14–15; Horne, *W. E. B. Du Bois*, 28; Wolters, *Du Bois and His Rivals*, 74.

30. Egerton, *The Wars of Reconstruction*, 324; Horne, *W. E. B. Du Bois*, 50–55; Lewis, *W. E. B. Du Bois*, 216–21; Wolters, *Du Bois and His Rivals*, 66–72.

31. Ayers, *The Promise of the New South*, 325–27; Lacy, *Cheer the Lonesome Traveler*, 43–45; Lears, *Rebirth of a Nation*, 129–30; Logan, *The Betrayal of the Negro*, 313, 331–32; Woodward, *Origins of the New South*, 367–68.

32. Horne, *W. E. B. Du Bois*, 25, 29, 39–41; Martinez, *Coming for to Carry Me Home*, 239–41; Wolters, *Du Bois and His Rivals*, 61, 64.

33. Du Bois, *The Souls of Black Folk*, 41–42.

34. Du Bois, *The Souls of Black Folk*, 45. See also Woodward, *Origins of the New South*, 367–68.

35. Egerton, *The Wars of Reconstruction*, 320–25; Gibson, "The Envy of Erudition," 62–63; Johnson and Watson, "The W. E. B. Du Bois and Booker T. Washington Debate," 8–69; Lewis, *W. E. B. Du Bois*, 215–22, 228–30.

36. Hahn, *A Nation under Our Feet*, 460; Lewis, *W. E. B. Du Bois*, 119, 182; Logan, *The Betrayal of the Negro*, 344–45; Wolters, *Du Bois and His Rivals*, 67–68, 72.

37. Lewis, *W. E. B. Du Bois*, 215–22, 228–30; Norrell, *Up from History*, 321, 337–38.

38. Dray, *At the Hands of Persons Unknown*, 138–43, 166–67; Norrell, *Up from History*, 345–46, 386. Even Washington himself barely escaped an angry mob in 1911. Dray, *At the Hands of Persons Unknown*, 187–89.

39. Quoted in Hasday, *The Civil Rights Act of 1964*, 9. See also Egerton, *The Wars of Reconstruction*, 324; Lewis, *W. E. B. Du Bois*, 252–66, 280–86; Wolters, *Du Bois and His Rivals*, 72.

40. Dray, *At the Hands of Persons Unknown*, 171–72, 186; Horne, *W. E. B. Du Bois*, 61–62; Lewis, *W. E. B. Du Bois*, 531–40.

41. *Brown v. Board of Education of Topeka*, 347 U.S. 483 (1954); Gormley, "Justice Thurgood Marshall," 63–66; Lewis, *W. E. B. Du Bois*, 572, 647, 699; McNeil, *Groundwork*, 3–4, 200–201, 347.

42. Dray, *At the Hands of Persons Unknown*, 185–86; Lewis, *W. E. B. Du Bois*, 252–53, 265–80; Wolters, *Du Bois and His Rivals*, 78–93, 211–14, 220, 224–25, 232–34, 272, 298.

43. Lewis, *W. E. B. Du Bois*, 416–34; Marable, *W. E. B. Du Bois*, 213; Wolters, *Du Bois and His Rivals*, 240–53.

44. Johnson and Watson, "The W. E. B. Du Bois and Booker T. Washington Debate," 68–69; Lemann, *The Promised Land*, 14–21; Lewis, *W. E. B. Du Bois*, 125, 141–42, 145, 165–79, 265, 267; Wilkerson, *The Warmth of Other Suns*, 12–13.

CHAPTER 7: THE GREAT MIGRATION

1. Simkins and Roland, *A History of the South*, 503; Tolnay, "The African American 'Great Migration' and Beyond," 211–16; Wilkerson, *The Warmth of Other Suns*, 8–11.

2. Boustan, "Was Postwar Suburbanization 'White Flight'?," 417–18; Collins and Wanamaker, "Selection and Economic Gains in the Great Migration of African Americans," 220–21; Tolnay, "The African American 'Great Migration' and Beyond," 210.

3. Collins and Wanamaker, "Selection and Economic Gains in the Great Migration of African Americans," 223; Sernett, *Bound for the Promised Land*, 59; Simkins and Roland, *A History of the South*, 503.

4. Collins and Wanamaker, "Selection and Economic Gains in the Great Migration of African Americans," 223; Foner, *Forever Free*, 63–64; Foner, *Reconstruction*, 114–16, 602–12.

5. Dattel, "King Cotton," 16–21; Foner, *Forever Free*, 192–93; Valiunas, "And the War Came," 36–38.

6. Genovese, *Roll, Jordan, Roll*, 414–23; Talty, *Mulatto America*, 20–22, 63–64.

7. Genovese, *Roll, Jordan, Roll*, 414–31; Pascoe, *What Comes Naturally*, 27–33, 86–87; Simkins and Roland, *A History of the South*, 144–45.

8. Dattel, "King Cotton," 16–21; Genovese, *Roll, Jordan, Roll*, 5–6, 363–71.

9. Paraphrased in Wilkerson, *The Warmth of Other Suns*, vii. See also Simkins and Roland, *A History of the South*, 503; Tolnay, "The African American 'Great Migration' and Beyond," 211–16; Wilkerson, *The Warmth of Other Suns*, 8–11.

10. Foner, *Forever Free*, 25–26, 189–90; Foner, *Reconstruction*, 598–600; Simkins and Roland, *A History of the South*, 501–2; Sonneborn, *The Great Black Migrations*, 21–22; Valiunas, "And the War Came," 37.

11. Sernett, *Bound for the Promised Land*, 59; Simkins and Roland, *A History of the South*, 503.

12. LeForge, "Alabama's Colored Conventions and the Exodus Movement," 3–4, 24; Mathieu, "The African American Great Migration Reconsidered," 20; Painter, "Millenarian Aspects of the Exodus to Kansas of 1879," 331. See also Sernett, *Bound for the Promised Land*, 14, 26, 80; Simkins and Roland, *A History of the South*, 503.

13. Foner, *Forever Free*, 171–77; LeForge, "Alabama's Colored Conventions and the Exodus Movement," 12; Sernett, *Bound for the Promised Land*, 12; Tolnay, "The African American 'Great Migration' and Beyond," 331–32.

14. LeForge, "Alabama's Colored Conventions and the Exodus Movement," 26–27; Painter, "Millenarian Aspects of the Exodus to Kansas of 1879," 331, 334; Sernett, *Bound for the Promised Land*, 14, 26, 80; Simkins and Roland, *A History of the South*, 503; Van Deusen, "The Exodus of 1879," 112–19.

15. Foner, *Reconstruction*, 600–601; Painter, *Exodusters*, 165–66; Simkins and Roland, *A History of the South*, 503–4; Stauffer, "Frederick Douglass and the Aesthetics of Freedom," 133–34; Van Deusen, "The Exodus of 1879," 123, 125.

16. United States Government Printing Office, *Journal of the Senate of the United States of America*, 79.

17. Painter, *Exodusters*, 252–55, 267; Van Deusen, "The Exodus of 1879," 111.

18. Painter, *Exodusters*, 260–61; Van Deusen, "The Exodus of 1879," 128–29; Wilkerson, *The Warmth of Other Suns*, 161.

19. Wilkerson, *The Warmth of Other Suns*, 9. See also Sernett, *Bound for the Promised Land*, 3, 37; Simkins and Roland, *A History of the South*, 503; Tolnay, "The African American 'Great Migration' and Beyond," 217.

20. Tolnay, "The African American 'Great Migration' and Beyond," 214; Wilkerson, *The Warmth of Other Suns*, 9–10.

21. Sernett, *Bound for the Promised Land*, 3, 37; Simkins and Roland, *A History of the South*, 503; Tolnay, "The African American 'Great Migration' and Beyond," 217.

22. Quoted in Wilkerson, *The Warmth of Other Suns*, 229.

23. Sernett, *Bound for the Promised Land*, 37; Tolnay, "The African American 'Great Migration' and Beyond," 217.

24. Sernett, *Bound for the Promised Land*, 37, 157; Simkins and Roland, *A History of the South*, 503; Tolnay, "The African American 'Great Migration' and Beyond," 216–17.

25. Simkins and Roland, *A History of the South*, 503–4; Tolnay, "The African American 'Great Migration' and Beyond," 218–19.

26. Harris, *The Harder We Run*, 61, 111–12.

27. Mathieu, "The African American Great Migration Reconsidered," 19–20; Tolnay, "The African American 'Great Migration' and Beyond," 217.

28. Boyd, "The Storefront Church Ministry in African American Communities of the Urban North during the Great Migration," 319–32; Mathieu, "The African American Great Migration Reconsidered," 20; Tolnay, "The African American 'Great Migration' and Beyond," 217, 223.

29. Grossman, *Land of Hope*, 127–28; Tolnay, "The African American 'Great Migration' and Beyond," 219.

30. Mathieu, "The African American Great Migration Reconsidered," 21; Sonneborn, *The Great Black Migrations*, 75–79; Tolnay, "The African American 'Great Migration' and Beyond," 221.

31. Mathieu, "The African American Great Migration Reconsidered," 21–22; Tolnay, "The African American 'Great Migration' and Beyond," 213–14.

32. Tolnay, "The African American 'Great Migration' and Beyond," 220.

33. Boustan, "Was Postwar Suburbanization 'White Flight'?," 424–26; Grossman, *Land of Hope*, 4, 124–26; Mathieu, "The African American Great Migration Reconsidered," 20–21; Sonneborn, *The Great Black Migrations*, 74; Tolnay, "The African American 'Great Migration' and Beyond," 220–22.

34. Grossman, *Land of Hope*, 176–78; Tolnay, "The African American 'Great Migration' and Beyond," 221.

35. Blaustein, *The American Promise*, 36–38; Gregory, *The Southern Diaspora*, xii, 4, 17–22; Simkins and Roland, *A History of the South*, 582–83.

36. Grossman, *Land of Hope*, 128; Simkins and Roland, *A History of the South*, 503–4; Sonneborn, *The Great Black Migrations*, 79–80.

37. Gregory, *The Southern Diaspora*, xii–xiii.

38. Boustan, "Was Postwar Suburbanization 'White Flight'?," 417–18; DuBose, "World War II," 436–37; Grossman, *Land of Hope*, 168.

39. DuBose, "World War II," 436–37; Gregory, *The Southern Diaspora*, 238.

40. Gregory, *The Southern Diaspora*, 131–35; Sonneborn, *The Great Black Migrations*, 5, 50–51, 107.

41. Gregory, *The Southern Diaspora*, 120–23; Sernett, *Bound for the Promised Land*, 143; Sonneborn, *The Great Black Migrations*, 41, 49.

42. Gregory, *The Southern Diaspora*, 120–23; Sonneborn, *The Great Black Migrations*, 21–22.

43. Gregory, *The Southern Diaspora*, 118–21.

44. Mathieu, "The African American Great Migration Reconsidered," 21–22; Sonneborn, *The Great Black Migrations*, 8, 107.

45. Boustan, "Was Postwar Suburbanization 'White Flight'?," 417–18; DuBose, "World War II," 437–38; Sonneborn, *The Great Black Migrations*, 72–75.

46. Lemann, *The Promised Land*, 309–10; Sonneborn, *The Great Black Migrations*, 72–75; Tolnay, "The African American 'Great Migration' and Beyond," 219.

47. Sonneborn, *The Great Black Migrations*, 97; Tolnay, "The African American 'Great Migration' and Beyond," 222–23.

CHAPTER 8: A NADIR OF RACE RELATIONS

1. Currell, *American Culture in the 1920s*; Hogan, "Head and Heart," 1036–38; Murphy, *The New Era*. On the 1918–1919 influenza outbreak, see Barry, *The Great Influenza*.

2. McCartney, *The Teapot Dome Scandal*; Wilson, "Harding's Rhetoric of Normalcy," 406–11.

3. Bryson, *One Summer*, 64–65, 70–74, 107–10, 109–10, 405–7, 410–12; Currell, *American Culture in the 1920s*, 77, 192, 193; Kalush and Sloman, *The Secret Life of Houdini*; Murphy, *The New Era*, 7, 213.

4. Chapman, *Prove It on Me*, 27–28, 31; Dray, *At the Hands of Persons Unknown*, 299–300; Simkins and Roland, *A History of the South*, 513–15.

5. Quoted in Cameron, *The Abolitionist Movement*, 221. See also Blum, *Reforging the White Republic*, 39, 43–44; Foner, *Forever Free*, 128–29; Foner, *Reconstruction*, 31–32.

6. Cooper, "President's Message," 8; Dray, *Capitol Men*, 314–27; Foner, *Forever Free*, 207–11.

7. See, for example, Lawrence, Bates, and Cervenka, "Politics Drawn in Black and White," 139–43; Schudson, *Discovering the News*, 80–81, 98, 106.

8. Halloran, *Thomas Nast*; Jarman, "The Graphic Art of Thomas Nast," 156–89; Lawrence, Bates, and Cervenka, "Politics Drawn in Black and White," 139–43; Webb, "Thomas Nast," 42–43.

9. Cronin, "Currier and Ives," 326, 327–28; Foner, *Forever Free*, 182–83; Le Beau, "African Americans in Currier and Ives's America," 71–83; Sheluk, "An American Lithographic Legacy," 36.

10. Foner, *Forever Free*, 216. See also Brown, *Lamb's Biographical Dictionary of the United States*, 6:72–73.

11. Foner, *Forever Free*, 219–20; Havig, "Richard F. Outcault's 'Poor Lil' Mose,'" 33–41; Outcault, *The Yellow Kid*.

12. Harris, *The Works of Joel Chandler Harris*; Peterson, "Slavery's Bestiary," 30–47; Ritterhouse, "Reading, Intimacy, and the Role of Uncle Remus in White Southern Social Memory," 585–622.

13. Bannerman, *The Story of Little Black Sambo*. See also Lester, "Can a 'Last Comic Standing' Finally Rescue Little Black Sambo from the Jungle?," 60–97; Martin, "Jungle Visions," 40–52.

14. Foner, *Forever Free*, 220–21; Lester, "Can a 'Last Comic Standing' Finally Rescue Little Black Sambo from the Jungle?," 60–97; Yuill, "Little Black Sambo," 72–73.

15. Foner, *Forever Free*, 220–21; Lehman, *The Colored Cartoon*, 9–10; Smith, *Encyclopedia of African-American Popular Culture*, 256–57.

16. Kern-Foxworth, *Aunt Jemima, Uncle Ben, and Rastus*, 31; Lehman, *The Colored Cartoon*, 48–50; Smith, *Encyclopedia of African-American Popular Culture*, 328.

17. Kern-Foxworth, *Aunt Jemima, Uncle Ben, and Rastus*, 30–32; Lehman, *The Colored Cartoon*, 48–50. A good source of information on pickaninny stereotypes can be found in the Ferris State Museum of Racist Memorabilia (http://www .ferris.edu/jimcrow/picaninny).

18. Kern-Foxworth, *Aunt Jemima, Uncle Ben, and Rastus*, 44, 98; "A New Name," 69; Carlino, "75 Years," 11–28.

19. Goings, "Aunt Jemima and Uncle Mose Travel the USA," 133–39; Kern-Foxworth, *Aunt Jemima, Uncle Ben, and Rastus*, 30–33. Dunbar's poem "The Mask" can be found in Dunbar, *The Collected Poetry of Paul Laurence Dunbar*, 71.

20. Kern-Foxworth, *Aunt Jemima, Uncle Ben, and Rastus*, 46–48; Morgan, *Symbols of America*, 52; Sacharow, *Symbols of Trade*, 57.

21. "Little Miss Muffet" and "Bigges' I could get, Sah!" quoted in DuRocher, *Raising Racists*, 65. "Maybe Cream of Wheat aint got no vitamines" quoted in Foner, *Forever Free*, 222. See also Cox, *Dreaming of Dixie*, 38; Kern-Foxworth, *Aunt Jemima, Uncle Ben, and Rastus*, 45–46; Sacharow, *Symbols of Trade*, 66; Watkins, *The 100 Greatest Advertisements*, 21.

22. The story of Aunt Jemima can be found in many sources. See, for example, Decker, *Show Boat*, 114–17; DuRocher, *Raising Racists*, 77–78; Goings, "Aunt Jemima and Uncle Mose Travel the USA," 133, 139, 140; Griffin, "Aunt Jemima," 75–77; Kern-Foxworth, *Aunt Jemima, Uncle Ben, and Rastus*, 61–108; Manring, *Slave in a Box*, 59–78; Roberts, *The Myth of Aunt Jemima*, 1–3, 165.

23. Kern-Foxworth, *Aunt Jemima, Uncle Ben, and Rastus*, 48–54; Pieterse, *White on Black*, 188–236; Smith, *Encyclopedia of African-American Popular Culture*.

24. Bogle, *Toms, Coons, Mulattoes, Mammies, and Bucks*, 4, 11; Cole and Davis, "Routes of Blackface," 7–12.

25. Bogle, *Toms, Coons, Mulattoes, Mammies, and Bucks*, 3–18. See also Croteau, Hoynes, and Milan, *Media/Society*, 194.

26. Bogle, *Toms, Coons, Mulattoes, Mammies, and Bucks*, 4, 6–7; Croteau, Hoynes, and Milan, *Media/Society*, 194; Hamilton, "The Strange Career of Uncle Tom," 22–27.

27. Bogle, *Toms, Coons, Mulattoes, Mammies, and Bucks*, 7–8; Croteau, Hoynes, and Milan, *Media/Society*, 194.

28. Bogle, *Toms, Coons, Mulattoes, Mammies, and Bucks*, 8; Ely, *The Adventures of Amos 'n' Andy*; Hilmes, "Invisible Men," 301–21; Holtzman and Sharpe, *Media Messages*, 360.

29. Bogle, *Toms, Coons, Mulattoes, Mammies, and Bucks*, 38–44; Holtzman and Sharpe, *Media Messages*, 361.

30. Bogle, *Toms, Coons, Mulattoes, Mammies, and Bucks*, 67–69, 135–36; Inge, "Walt Disney's *Song of the South* and the Politics of Animation," 219–30; Peterson, "Slavery's Bestiary," 30–47.

31. Bogle, *Toms, Coons, Mulattoes, Mammies, and Bucks*, 8. See also Regester, *African American Actresses*, 320–22; Sollors, *Neither Black nor White yet Both*, 234–45.

32. Bogle, *Toms, Coons, Mulattoes, Mammies, and Bucks*, 9, 82–86; Croteau, Hoynes, and Milan, *Media/Society*, 190, 194; Holtzman and Sharpe, *Media Messages*, 99–100; Regester, *African American Actresses*, 11–13, 75–76.

33. Bogle, *Toms, Coons, Mulattoes, Mammies, and Bucks*, 10–18; Croteau, Hoynes, and Milan, *Media/Society*, 194.

34. Quoted in Haggard, "The Birth of the Black Rapist," 90–91. See also Christian, "Can You Dig It?," 116–21, 134; Wright, "Black Outlaws and the Struggle for Empowerment in Blaxploitation Cinema," 63–86.

35. Drowne and Huber, *The 1920s*, 12–13; Goldfield, *Black, White, and Southern*, 1–4, 7–8.

36. Dattel, "King Cotton," 18–21; Kern-Foxworth, *Aunt Jemima, Uncle Ben, and Rastus*, 131–63.

37. Drowne and Huber, *The 1920s*, 12–13; O'Neal, *America in the 1920s*, 30, 34, 43–52.

38. Blee and McDowell, "The Duality of Spectacle and Secrecy," 249–50; Jackson, *The Ku Klux Klan in the City*, 3–4.

39. Chalmers, *Hooded Americanism*, 8–21; Dray, *At the Hands of Persons Unknown*, 39–47; Martinez, *Coming for to Carry Me Home*, 191–96; Simkins and Roland, *A History of the South*, 278–82; Wade, *The Fiery Cross*, 31–111.

40. Chalmers, *Hooded Americanism*, 21, 22–23; Martinez, *Carpetbaggers, Cavalry, and the Ku Klux Klan*, 241–42; Wade, *The Fiery Cross*, 119–39.

41. Chalmers, *Hooded Americanism*, 23–24; Slide, *American Racist*, 19; Wade, *The Fiery Cross*, 122–23.

42. Chalmers, *Hooded Americanism*, 23–24; Gillespie and Hall, "Introduction," 4–5; Slide, *American Racist*, 20; Wade, *The Fiery Cross*, 122–23.

43. Chalmers, *Hooded Americanism*, 23–24; Gillespie and Hall, "Introduction," 6; Slide, *American Racist*, 20.

44. Chalmers, *Hooded Americanism*, 24; Gillespie and Hall, "Introduction," 6; Martinez, *Carpetbaggers, Cavalry, and the Ku Klux Klan*, 242; Slide, *American Racist*, 19–20; Wade, *The Fiery Cross*, 123.

45. Quoted in Martinez, *Carpetbaggers, Cavalry, and the Ku Klux Klan*, 242. See also Chalmers, *Hooded Americanism*, 24; Gillespie and Hall, "Introduction," 7; Ruiz-Velasco, "Order Out of Chaos," 152; Slide, *American Racist*, 3; Wade, *The Fiery Cross*, 123.

46. Dixon, *The Leopard's Spots*, 463–64. See also Chalmers, *Hooded Americanism*, 24; Gillespie and Hall, "Introduction," 7; Ruiz-Velasco, "Order Out of Chaos," 150–57; Slide, *American Racist*, 3; Wade, *The Fiery Cross*, 123.

47. Dixon, *The Clansman*, 290, 216. See also Gillespie and Hall, "Introduction," 7–8; Langguth, *After Lincoln*, 234–35; Slide, *American Racist*, 8; Wade, *The Fiery Cross*, 123.

48. Chalmers, *Hooded Americanism*, 25; Dray, *At the Hands of Persons Unknown*, 191; Gillespie and Hall, "Introduction," 10; Slide, *American Racist*, 53–65; Wade, *The Fiery Cross*, 124.

49. Quoted in Wade, *The Fiery Cross*, 122. See also Gillespie and Hall, "Introduction," 11; Slide, *American Racist*, 3, 7–8.

50. Chalmers, *Hooded Americanism*, 24–26; Dessommes, "Hollywood in Hoods," 16; Gillespie and Hall, "Introduction," 11–13; Niderost, "The Birth of a Nation," 64; Wade, *The Fiery Cross*, 124–25.

51. Chalmers, *Hooded Americanism*, 24–26; Dessommes, "Hollywood in Hoods," 16; Langguth, *After Lincoln*, 234–35; MacLean, *Behind the Mask of Chivalry*, 12–13; McVeigh, "Structural Incentives for Conservative Mobilization," 1464; Niderost, "The Birth of a Nation," 62; Wade, *The Fiery Cross*, 123–25; West, *The Reconstruction Ku Klux Klan in York County, South Carolina*, app. 3, 130.

52. Dessommes, "Hollywood in Hoods," 16; Gillespie and Hall, "Introduction," 12–13; McVeigh, "Structural Incentives for Conservative Mobilization," 1464; Niderost, "The Birth of a Nation," 64; Wade, *The Fiery Cross*, 124–25.

53. Bogle, *Toms, Coons, Mulattoes, Mammies, and Bucks*, 10–15; Dessommes, "Hollywood in Hoods," 16; Slide, *American Racist*, 53; Wade, *The Fiery Cross*, 125.

54. Quoted in Wade, *The Fiery Cross*, 126. See also Chalmers, *Hooded Americanism*, 26–27; Dray, *At the Hands of Persons Unknown*, 197–98; Jackson, *The Ku Klux Klan in the City*, 3–4; Gillespie and Hall, "Introduction," 11–12; Niderost, "The Birth of a Nation," 66; Ruiz-Velasco, "Order Out of Chaos," 150; Wade, *The Fiery Cross*, 125–26.

55. Martinez, *Carpetbaggers, Cavalry, and the Ku Klux Klan*, 246; Niderost, "The Birth of a Nation," 66; Slide, *American Racist*, 83–84.

56. *Guinn v. United States*, 238 U.S. 347 (1915).

57. Chalmers, *Hooded Americanism*, 27; Slide, *American Racist*, 84; Wade, *The Fiery Cross*, 126–27. After seeing the film, Justice White disavowed his association with the project. If he never quite became a reliable friend to Negroes, he refused to embrace the most extreme tenets of white supremacy. Langguth, *After Lincoln*, 363.

58. Chalmers, *Hooded Americanism*, 27; Martinez, *Carpetbaggers, Cavalry, and the Ku Klux Klan*, 246; Slide, *American Racist*, 84–86; Wade, *The Fiery Cross*, 127–28.

59. Bogle, *Toms, Coons, Mulattoes, Mammies, and Bucks*, 10; Dray, *At the Hands of Persons Unknown*, 190–91; Gillespie and Hall, "Introduction," 13; Niderost, "The Birth of a Nation," 66; Wade, *The Fiery Cross*, 128–32.

60. Bogle, *Toms, Coons, Mulattoes, Mammies, and Bucks*, 15–17; Gillespie and Hall, "Introduction," 12–13; McVeigh, "Structural Incentives for Conservative Mobilization," 1465; Slide, *American Racist*, 84–85; Wade, *The Fiery Cross*, 133–39.

61. Dinnerstein, *The Leo Frank Case*, 1–9, 19–28, 55–57; MacLean, *Behind the Mask of Chivalry*, 12; MacLean, "The Leo Frank Case Reconsidered," 917–18; McVeigh, "Structural Incentives for Conservative Mobilization," 1464–65; Oney, *And the Dead Shall Rise*, 18–33, 61–70; Slide, *American Racist*, 85–86; Wade, *The Fiery Cross*, 143–44.

62. Dray, *At the Hands of Persons Unknown*, 207–8; "Graduates of Cornell Will Aid Leo M. Frank in Fight for Life," 2; "Mary Phagan: The Victim," 3; Oney, *And the Dead Shall Rise*, 10, 80; Oney, "The People v. Leo Frank," 35–36; "Will Defense Put Character of Leo Frank before Jury?," 3.

63. Dinnerstein, *The Leo Frank Case*, 1–9, 19–28, 55–57; Oney, *And the Dead Shall Rise*, 61–70, 644–49; Oney, "The People v. Leo Frank," 34–35; Slide, *American Racist*, 85–86.

64. Britt, "Leo Frank's Trial Is Attracting Universal Interest in Georgia," 2; "Leo Frank's Fate Up to Gov. Salton as Final Arbiter," 1; Oney, *And the Dead Shall Rise*, 340–43; Oney, "The People v. Leo Frank," 33.

65. "Leo Frank's Fate Up to Gov. Salton as Final Arbiter," 1; Oney, *And the Dead Shall Rise*, 540–43; Oney, "The People v. Leo Frank," 34.

66. Quoted in Woodward, *Tom Watson*, 441. See also Dray, *At the Hands of Persons Unknown*, 209–10; Oney, *And the Dead Shall Rise*, 540–43; Oney, "The People v. Leo Frank," 34; Wade, *The Fiery Cross*, 143–44.

67. Dray, *At the Hands of Persons Unknown*, 213–14; "Lynching of Leo Frank Denounced by Daniels," 3; Oney, *And the Dead Shall Rise*, 561–66; Oney, "The People v. Leo Frank," 34; "Posses [*sic*] Chase Frank Mob," 1.

68. Chalmers, *Hooded Americanism*, 71; Dinnerstein, *The Leo Frank Case*, 139–47; MacLean, *Behind the Mask of Chivalry*, 12; MacLean, "The Leo Frank Case Reconsidered," 938, 940; Oney, *And the Dead Shall Rise*, 561–72; Wade, *The Fiery Cross*, 144.

69. Alexander, "Kleagles and Cash," 349–50; Chalmers, *Hooded Americanism*, 28–38, 225; Feldman, *Politics, Society, and the Klan in Alabama*, 12–13; Jackson, "William J. Simmons," 351–53; MacLean, *Behind the Mask of Chivalry*, 4–6, 12; McVeigh, "Structural Incentives for Conservative Mobilization," 1464; Niderost, "The Birth of a Nation," 80; Ridgeway, *Blood in the Face*, 52; Simmons, *America's Menace*, 60–65; Wade, *The Fiery Cross*, 140–48.

70. Chalmers, *Hooded Americanism*, 28–38, 225; Dray, *At the Hands of Persons Unknown*, 214; Feldman, *Politics, Society, and the Klan in Alabama*, 12–13; Jackson, "William J. Simmons," 351–53; Langguth, *After Lincoln*, 364; MacLean, *Behind the Mask of Chivalry*, 4–6, 12; Simcovitch, "The Impact of Griffith's *Birth of a Nation* on the Modern Ku Klux Klan," 45–54.

71. Chalmers, *Hooded Americanism*, 29–31, 117–18; Jackson, "William J. Simmons," 351–53; MacLean, *Behind the Mask of Chivalry*, 4–5; Ridgeway, *Blood in the Face*, 52; Simmons, *America's Menace*, 63–65; Wade, *The Fiery Cross*, 142–44.

72. Chalmers, *Hooded Americanism*, 30; Jackson, "William J. Simmons," 353; Langguth, *After Lincoln*, 364; Wade, *The Fiery Cross*, 146.

73. Quoted in Wade, *The Fiery Cross*, app. B, 249. See also Chalmers, *Hooded Americanism*, 30; Dray, *At the Hands of Persons Unknown*, 214; Jackson, "William J. Simmons," 353; MacLean, *Behind the Mask of Chivalry*, 5; Martinez, *Carpetbaggers, Cavalry, and the Ku Klux Klan*, 251.

74. Chalmers, *Hooded Americanism*, 33; Jackson, "William J. Simmons," 353–54; MacLean, *Behind the Mask of Chivalry*, 5–6; Wade, *The Fiery Cross*, 147–48.

75. Chalmers, *Hooded Americanism*, 31; Jackson, "William J. Simmons," 355–56; MacLean, *Behind the Mask of Chivalry*, 5; Simcovitch, "The Impact of Griffith's *Birth of a Nation* on the Modern Ku Klux Klan," 45–54; Wade, *The Fiery Cross*, 146–47.

76. Chalmers, *Hooded Americanism*, 31; Corry, "The Klan Hearings of 1921," 90–91; Jackson, "William J. Simmons," 355–59; MacLean, *Behind the Mask of Chivalry*, 5–6; Wade, *The Fiery Cross*, 148–55.

77. Quoted in Newton, *The Ku Klux Klan*, 99. See also Chalmers, *Hooded Americanism*, 32–35; Jackson, "William J. Simmons," 359–60; MacLean, *Behind the Mask of Chivalry*, 5–8; Wade, *The Fiery Cross*, 154–59.

78. Chalmers, *Hooded Americanism*, 34–38; Jackson, "William J. Simmons," 358–60; Langguth, *After Lincoln*, 366; McVeigh, *The Rise of the Ku Klux Klan*, 23; Wade, *The Fiery Cross*, 150–66.

79. Blee and McDowell, "The Duality of Spectacle and Secrecy," 249–54; Chalmers, *Hooded Americanism*, 40–43; MacLean, *Behind the Mask of Chivalry*, 19–22; McVeigh, *The Rise of the Ku Klux Klan*, 143–44.

80. Chalmers, *Hooded Americanism*, 35–36; Corry, "The Klan Hearings of 1921," 91–105; Jackson, *The Ku Klux Klan in the City*, 11–13; Langguth, *After Lincoln*, 366; MacLean, *Behind the Mask of Chivalry*, 5; McVeigh, *The Rise of the Ku Klux Klan*, 21–23; Wade, *The Fiery Cross*, 160–62.

81. Corry, "The Klan Hearings of 1921," 89–90; Fryer and Levitt, "Hatred and Profits," 1884; Langguth, *After Lincoln*, 365; MacLean, *Behind the Mask of Chivalry*, 7; Newton, *The Ku Klux Klan*, 17; Wade, *The Fiery Cross*, 165.

82. Chalmers, *Hooded Americanism*, 104–5; Jackson, *The Ku Klux Klan in the City*, 16; Jackson, "William J. Simmons," 360–63; McVeigh, *The Rise of the Ku Klux Klan*, 24–25; Wade, *The Fiery Cross*, 186–92.

83. Jackson, *The Ku Klux Klan in the City*, 16–18; MacLean, *Behind the Mask of Chivalry*, 20–22; McVeigh, *The Rise of the Ku Klux Klan*, 24–25; Newton, *The Ku Klux Klan*, 15; Wade, *The Fiery Cross*, 192–93.

84. Chalmers, *Hooded Americanism*, 109–14; MacLean, *Behind the Mask of Chivalry*, 20–22, 49–51; McVeigh, *The Rise of the Ku Klux Klan*, 25; Newton, *The Ku Klux Klan*, 15–16; Wade, *The Fiery Cross*, 193–97.

85. Blee and McDowell, "The Duality of Spectacle and Secrecy," 253–54, 258–62; McVeigh, *The Rise of the Ku Klux Klan*, 7–9, 25–28; Newton, *The Ku Klux Klan*, 15–16; Wade, *The Fiery Cross*, 196–97.

86. Chalmers, *Hooded Americanism*, 314–16; Jackson, *The Ku Klux Klan in the City*, 82; Newton, *The Ku Klux Klan*, 17; Wade, *The Fiery Cross*, 197.

87. Chalmers, *Hooded Americanism*, 164–65; Dray, *At the Hands of Persons Unknown*, 278–79; McVeigh, *The Rise of the Ku Klux Klan*, 1–4; Wade, *The Fiery Cross*, 215–18.

88. Chalmers, *Hooded Americanism*, 203–12; Dray, *At the Hands of Persons Unknown*, 279; Jackson, *The Ku Klux Klan in the City*, 248–49; MacLean, *Behind the Mask of Chivalry*, 50; McVeigh, *The Rise of the Ku Klux Klan*, 185–87; Wade, *The Fiery Cross*, 197–99; Witcover, *Party of the People*, 338–41.

89. "Klan's Big Rally Ends with Oratory," 26; "40,000 Klansmen Parade in Washington," 1. See also Chalmers, *Hooded Americanism*, 286–88; Newton, *The Ku Klux Klan*, 17–18; Wade, *The Fiery Cross*, 249–50.

90. Chalmers, *Hooded Americanism*, 167–68; Jackson, *The Ku Klux Klan in the City*, 144–46; McVeigh, *The Rise of the Ku Klux Klan*, 27; Newton, *The Ku Klux Klan*, 17–18; Wade, *The Fiery Cross*, 221.

91. Chalmers, *Hooded Americanism*, 166; Jackson, *The Ku Klux Klan in the City*, 145; McVeigh, *The Rise of the Ku Klux Klan*, 135; Newton, *The Ku Klux Klan*, 51, 85; Wade, *The Fiery Cross*, 224–25, 230.

92. Chalmers, *Hooded Americanism*, 167–70; Jackson, *The Ku Klux Klan in the City*, 154–56; Newton, *The Ku Klux Klan*, 50; Wade, *The Fiery Cross*, 233–35.

93. Chalmers, *Hooded Americanism*, 167–70; Jackson, *The Ku Klux Klan in the City*, 154–56; Newton, *The Ku Klux Klan*, 50; Wade, *The Fiery Cross*, 233–35.

94. McVeigh, *The Rise of the Ku Klux Klan*, 27; Newton, *The Ku Klux Klan*, 18; Wade, *The Fiery Cross*, 233–38.

95. Chalmers, *Hooded Americanism*, 171–72; Jackson, *The Ku Klux Klan in the City*, 157; McVeigh, *The Rise of the Ku Klux Klan*, 191–92; Newton, *The Ku Klux Klan*, 18; Wade, *The Fiery Cross*, 239–47.

96. Quoted in Wade, *The Fiery Cross*, 244. See also Chalmers, *Hooded Americanism*, 172; "Alleged Victim of Ex-Dragon Dies," 11; "Ex-Dragon Must Face Girl's Serious Charge," B7; "Klan's Ex-Dragon Held for Murder," 15.

97. "Alleged Victim of Ex-Dragon Dies," 11; Chalmers, *Hooded Americanism*, 172; "Stephenson Held for Death of Girl," 3; Wade, *The Fiery Cross*, 244–45.

98. Chalmers, *Hooded Americanism*, 172, 174; "Ex-Chief of Klan Free," 32; "Finds Ex-Klan Head Murdered Woman," 1, 23; "Klan Figure Free in a 1925 Murder," 10; McVeigh, *The Rise of the Ku Klux Klan*, 192; Newton, *The Ku Klux Klan*, 18; "Stephenson Receives Sentence for Life," 10; Wade, *The Fiery Cross*, 245–47.

99. Blee and McDowell, "The Duality of Spectacle and Secrecy," 249–50, 260–62; McVeigh, *The Rise of the Ku Klux Klan*, 192–94; Newton, *The Ku Klux Klan*, 17–19; Wade, *The Fiery Cross*, 248–49.

CHAPTER 9: THE RISE OF
A NEW BLACK CULTURE

1. Bogle, *Toms, Coons, Mulattoes, Mammies, and Bucks*, 67–69, 135–36; Inge, "Walt Disney's *Song of the South* and the Politics of Animation," 219–30; Kern-Foxworth, *Aunt Jemima, Uncle Ben, and Rastus*, 61.

2. Quoted in Page, *The Negro*, 80. See also Dray, *At the Hands of Persons Unknown*, 70–71, 145; Hagood, "'Prodjickin,' or Mekin' a Present to Yo' Fam'ly,'" 423–39; Martin, "The Two-Faced New South," 19–20; Slide, *American Racist*, 3; Wade, *The Fiery Cross*, 123; Watson, "Mary Church Terrell v. Thomas Nelson Page," 72–75.

3. Hayes, "The Paradox of the Ethical Criminal in Richard Wright's Novel *The Outsider*," 162–71; Jarenski, "Invisibility Embraced," 85–109; Matthews, "Black Boy No More?," 276–97.

4. "The Slave's Complaint" is quoted in Van Deburg, *Slavery and Race in American Popular Culture*, 59. See also Jackson, "George Moses Horton, North Carolinian," 140–47; Shields, *Phillis Wheatley's Poetics of Liberation*.

5. Sollors, "The Celtic Nations and the African Americas," 318; Wilson, "Introduction," 1–17.

6. Ammons, "Frances Ellen Watkins Harper (1825–1911)," 61–66; Hubbard, "Frances Ellen Watkins Harper," 68–75; Petrino, "'We Are Rising as a People,'" 133–53.

7. Much has been written about Hopkins. See, for example, Wallinger, *Pauline E. Hopkins*; Dworkin, *Daughter of the Revolution*.

8. For biographical information, see Andrews, *The Literary Career of Charles W. Chesnutt*. See also Hubbs, "Goophering Jim Crow," 12–26; Wilson, "Reading *The Human Stain* through Charles W. Chesnutt," 138–50; Worden, "Birth in the Briar Patch," 1–20.

9. Coleman, *Sutton E. Griggs and the Struggle against White Supremacy*; Fabi, "Desegregating the Future," 113–32; Levander, "Sutton Griggs and the Borderlands of Empire," 57–84.

10. Harrell, *We Wear the Mask*; Mullen, "'When He Is Least Himself,'" 277–82; Robinson and Robinson, "Paul Laurence Dunbar," 215–25.

11. Delgado-Tall, "The New Negro Movement and the African Heritage in a Pan-Africanist Perspective," 288–310; Gill, *Harlem*; Robertson, White, and Garton, "Harlem in Black and White," 864–80.

12. Bynum, "'An Equal Chance in the Race for Life,'" 1–20; Gregory, *The Southern Diaspora*, 131–35; Sonneborn, *The Great Black Migrations*, 5, 50–51, 107.

13. Gill, *Harlem*, 208; Perry, *Hubert Harrison*.

14. Johnson is quoted in Peterson, *The African American Theatre Directory*, 87. See also Gill, *Harlem*, 238; Hart, "Black-White Literary Relations in the Harlem Renaissance," 613–14; Huggins, *Harlem Renaissance*, 293–94, 295.

15. Gill, *Harlem*, 172–73, 188, 213–14, 254; Huggins, *Harlem Renaissance*, 17–19, 21; Nowlin, "Race Literature, Modernism, and Normal Literature," 503–18.

16. Quoted in Maxwell, *New Negro, Old Left*, 64. See also Gill, *Harlem*, 223–24; Huggins, *Harlem Renaissance*, 24, 29, 118, 121; Ruff, "The World That War Made," 15.

17. Anderson, "The Too-Brief Career of Countee Cullen," 24–27; Gill, *Harlem*, 257; Huggins, *Harlem Renaissance*, 161, 206–8.

18. Foley, "The Color of Blood," 237–53; Gill, *Harlem*, 257; Huggins, *Harlem Renaissance*, 179–87; Nowlin, "The Strange Literary Career of Jean Toomer," 207–35.

19. Gill, *Harlem*, 262–63; Huggins, *Harlem Renaissance*, 191–95, 239–43; Rottenberg, "Wallace Thurman's *The Blacker the Berry* and the Question of the Emancipatory City," 59–74.

20. "All-TIME 100 Novels"; Frydman, "Zora Neale Hurston, Biographical Criticism, and African Diasporic Vernacular Culture," 99–118; Gill, *Harlem*, 260, 280, 281; Huggins, *Harlem Renaissance*, 74–75, 129–33.

21. Takara, "Frank Marshall Davis," 215–27; Tidwell, *Writings of Frank Marshall Davis*.

22. Gill, *Harlem*, 315; Huggins, *Harlem Renaissance*, xxviii; Sherrard-Johnson, *Dorothy West's Paradise*.

23. Dworkin, "'Near the Congo,'" 631–57; Ferris, "'My Idol Was Langston Hughes,'" 53–71; Gill, *Harlem*, 262–64; Huggins, *Harlem Renaissance*, 65–69, 153–54, 133–36; Nielson, "A 'High Tension' in Langston Hughes's Musical Verse," 165–85; Sundquist, "Who Was Langston Hughes?," 55–59.

24. Gill, *Harlem*, 263; Huggins, *Harlem Renaissance*, 168–72; Maine, "Inside the Harlem Renaissance," 154–57.

25. Finley, "Loïs Mailou Jones," 80–93; Johnson, "Loïs Mailou Jones," 20–22; Robinson-English, "Celebrating Loïs Mailou Jones," 124–28.

26. Capozzola, "Jacob Lawrence," 291–95; Gill, *Harlem*, 312; Huggins, *Harlem Renaissance*, 166; Lorensen, "Between Image and Word, Color, and Time," 571–86; Valentine, "Real Life, True Color," 55; Wheat, *Jacob Lawrence*.

27. Gill, *Harlem*, 195; Gioia, *The History of Jazz*, 6, 20, 38–41; Huggins, *Harlem Renaissance*, 64, 198.

28. Gill, *Harlem*, 346, 370; Gioia, *The History of Jazz*, 90, 193, 237; Teachout, "The Case for Cab Calloway," 66–70.

29. Daubney, "Songbird or Subversive?," 17–28; Gill, *Harlem*, 268, 439; Gioia, *The History of Jazz*, 167–68; Storhoff, "'Strange Fruit,'" 105–13.

30. Gill, *Harlem*, 265, 268; Gioia, *The History of Jazz*, 65–66, 67; Huggins, *Harlem Renaissance*, 197–98.

31. Robinson, *Black Nationalism in American Politics and Thought*, 1, 8, 54; Ruff, "The World That War Made," 9–15.

32. Ruff, "The World That War Made," 13. The quote can be found in Shakespeare, *Henry V*, IV.iii.165.

33. Barbeau and Henri, *The Unknown Soldiers*, 5–6, 7, 100; Ruff, "The World That War Made," 13.

34. Barbeau and Henri, *The Unknown Soldiers*, xiii, 75–76; Ruff, "The World That War Made," 12; Shapiro, *White Violence and Black Response*, 107–9; Williams, *Torchbearers of Democracy*, 32–39. For a detailed analysis of the riot, see Haynes, *A Night of Violence*.

35. Quoted in Williams, *Torchbearers of Democracy*, 328. See also Davis, "Not Only War Is Hell," 477; Ruff, "The World That War Made," 13–14; Williams, *Torchbearers of Democracy*, 20.

36. Quoted in Taylor, *From Timbuktu to Katrina*, 2:26.

37. Mackie, *The Great Marcus Garvey*, 91–96; Radcliff, "The Radical Evolution of Du Bosian Pan-Africanism," 151–70; Wintz, *African American Political Thought*, 126–31.

38. Quoted in Hill, *The Marcus Garvey Universal Negro Improvement Association Papers*, 1:5. See also Cronon, *Black Moses*, 15; Grant, *Negro with a Hat*, 34–37; Stein, *The World of Marcus Garvey*, 28.

39. Cronon, *Black Moses*, 18–19; Dagnini, "Marcus Garvey," 199; Eburne, "Garveyism and Its Involutions," 1–4; Grant, *Negro with a Hat*, 53–54; Martin, *Race First*, 6, 22; Stein, *The World of Marcus Garvey*, 1.

40. Cronon, *Black Moses*, 19; Stein, *The World of Marcus Garvey*, 34–35.

41. "Letter To: Marcus Mosiah Garvey, Tuskegee, Alabama—September 17, 1914," Booker T. Washington Society, http://www.btwsociety.org/library/letters/7.php.

42. Cronon, *Black Moses*, 20; Dagnini, "Marcus Garvey," 200; Grant, *Negro with a Hat*, 68; Stein, *The World of Marcus Garvey*, 35.

43. Martin, *Race First*, 23–24; Satter, "Marcus Garvey, Father Divine and the Gender Politics of Race Difference and Race Neutrality," 44; Stein, *The World of Marcus Garvey*, 43–48.

44. Quoted in Martin, *Race First*, 69. See also Grant, *Negro with a Hat*, 389; Satter, "Marcus Garvey, Father Divine and the Gender Politics of Race Difference and Race Neutrality," 45.

45. Quoted in Cronon, *Black Moses*, 65. See also Grant, *Negro with a Hat*, 53, 105–9, 163–64.

46. Cronon, *Black Moses*, 133, 185; Dagnini, "Marcus Garvey," 200; Eburne, "Garveyism and Its Involutions," 4; Grant, *Negro with a Hat*, 243–44, 262–66, 272, 278–80; Stein, *The World of Marcus Garvey*, 86.

47. Cronon, *Black Moses*, 49–50; Grant, *Negro with a Hat*, 197–98; Satter, "Marcus Garvey, Father Divine and the Gender Politics of Race Difference and Race Neutrality," 49, 50; Stein, *The World of Marcus Garvey*, 53, 61–63.

48. Quoted in Cronon, *Black Moses*, 64. See also Grant, *Negro with a Hat*, 247–49; Stein, *The World of Marcus Garvey*, 86.

49. Quoted in Wintz, *African American Political Thought*, 208–15.

50. Grant, *Negro with a Hat*, 265–93; Martin, *Race First*, 125–28.

51. Cronon, *Black Moses*, 124–32; Grant, *Negro with a Hat*, 381–89; Stein, *The World of Marcus Garvey*, 114–27, 208–21.

52. Cronon, *Black Moses*, 51–60, 71–104, 114–21, 126; Dagnini, "Marcus Garvey," 198–200; Eburne, "Garveyism and Its Involutions," 11–12, 14–15; Grant, *Negro with a Hat*, 183–215, 219–34; Stein, *The World of Marcus Garvey*, 68, 78–99, 104, 114–15, 133–36.

53. Schuyler, Black No More, 101–2.

54. Du Bois is quoted in Wintz, *African American Political Thought*, 129. See also Cronon, *Black Moses*, 40, 110, 120, 126, 133–34, 140; Grant, *Negro with a Hat*, 360, 367–71; Stein, *The World of Marcus Garvey*, 137, 164, 186.

55. Cronon, *Black Moses*, xiv, 135–41; Grant, *Negro with a Hat*, 391–94; Stein, *The World of Marcus Garvey*, 207–8.

56. Cronon, *Black Moses*, 142; Grant, *Negro with a Hat*, 409–11; Stein, *The World of Marcus Garvey*, 1, 207.

57. Cronon, *Black Moses*, xii, 201; Grant, *Negro with a Hat*, 453–55; Stein, *The World of Marcus Garvey*, 248–75.

CHAPTER 10: SOUTHERN JUSTICE, A DEPRESSION, AND A WAR

1. Akers, *Flames after Midnight*, 153; Dray, *At the Hands of Persons Unknown*, 259; Francis, *Civil Rights and the Making of the Modern American State*, 86; Holloman, "Rejecting League, Harding Pleads for Treaty," 1, 9; Schneider, *"We Return Fighting,"* 175.

2. Quoted in "President's Address to Congress on Domestic and Foreign Policies," 7. See also Brown, "Advocates in the Age of Jazz," 388; Dean, *Warren G. Harding*, 100–101; Francis, *Civil Rights and the Making of the Modern American State*, 83–86.

3. Dean, *Warren G. Harding*, 123–24; Francis, *Civil Rights and the Making of the Modern American State*, 79, 86–89; Payne, *Dead Last*, 119, 125.

4. Quoted in Podell and Anzovin, *Speeches of the American Presidents*, 481. See also Warren G. Harding, *Address of the President of the United States of America at the Celebration of the Semicentennial of the Founding of the City of Birmingham, Alabama, October 26, 1921*, 3–12; Dean, *Warren G. Harding*, 125–26; Payne, *Dead Last*, 120–24; Walker, *Presidents and Civil Liberties from Wilson to Obama*, 59.

5. Holloman, "Rejecting League, Harding Pleads for Treaty," 1, 9; Payne, *Dead Last*, 123–25.

6. Byas, "Libel," 34; Fryer and Levitt, "Hatred and Profits," 1884; Langguth, *After Lincoln*, 365; Newton, *The Ku Klux Klan*, 17; Wade, *The Fiery Cross*, 165.

7. Brown, "Advocates in the Age of Jazz," 378, 380; Burns, "Without Due Process," 234; Dray, *At the Hands of Persons Unknown*, 53–65; Holloway, *Getting Away with Murder*, 38; Waldrep, *The Many Faces of Judge Lynch*, 4–5.

8. Brown, "Advocates in the Age of Jazz," 385; Dray, *At the Hands of Persons Unknown*, 56–57; Holloway, *Getting Away with Murder*, v–vii, 2–5. For a detailed analysis of federalism principles and constitutional questions in federal antilynching legislation, see, for example, Harvey, "Constitutional Law," 369–77.

9. President Harrison is quoted in Richardson, *Messages and Papers of the Presidents*, 332. Griggs is quoted in Goldstone, *Inherently Unequal*, 8. See also Burns, "Without Due Process," 235; Dray, *At the Hands of Persons Unknown*, 113.

10. Quoted in White, *The Writings, Speeches, and Letters of George Henry White*, 167. See also Burns, "Without Due Process," 235; Dray, *At the Hands of Persons Unknown*, 260–61; Francis, *Civil Rights and the Making of the Modern American State*, 100; Schneider, *"We Return Fighting,"* 262.

11. Berg, *Popular Justice*, 153–54; Burns, "Without Due Process," 235–36; Francis, *Civil Rights and the Making of the Modern American State*, 100; Holloway, *Getting Away with Murder*, 30; Schneider, *"We Return Fighting,"* 180.

12. Berg, *Popular Justice*, 154; Burns, "Without Due Process," 233–34, 237; Holloway, *Getting Away with Murder*, 4; Schneider, *"We Return Fighting,"* 173.

13. Berg, *Popular Justice*, 154; Burns, "Without Due Process," 238–41.

14. Berg, *Popular Justice*, 154; Burns, "Without Due Process," 241–43; Dray, *At the Hands of Persons Unknown*, 260–64; Finley, *Delaying the Dream*, 16; Holloway, *Getting Away with Murder*, 59–60; Schneider, *"We Return Fighting,"* 172–73.

15. Quoted in Holloway, *Getting Away with Murder*, 28. See also Burns, "Without Due Process," 243–44; Schneider, *"We Return Fighting,"* 173; Waldrep, *The Many Faces of Judge Lynch*, 135.

16. Burns, "Without Due Process," 245; Dray, *At the Hands of Persons Unknown*, 261–66.

17. *Congressional Record*, January 25, 1922, 1718.

18. *Congressional Record*, January 25, 1922, 1721. See also Francis, *Civil Rights and the Making of the Modern American State*, 116–17.

19. *Congressional Record*, January 25, 1922, 1795. See also Brown, "Advocates in the Age of Jazz," 391; Burns, "Without Due Process," 245; Dray, *At the Hands of Persons Unknown*, 266; Finley, *Delaying the Dream*, 16; Rable, "The South and the Politics of Antilynching Legislation," 206.

20. Quoted in Goldstein, "The Dyer Anti-lynching Bill," 79. See also Dray, *At the Hands of Persons Unknown*, 266–68.

21. Dray, *At the Hands of Persons Unknown*, 267–68; Francis, *Civil Rights and the Making of the Modern American State*, 120–21; Rable, "The South and the Politics of Antilynching Legislation," 218.

22. "Negro Women See Harding," 10. See also Goldstein, "The Dyer Antilynching Bill," 92.

23. Brown, "Advocates in the Age of Jazz," 389; Goldstein, "The Dyer Antilynching Bill," 92–94; Payne, *Dead Last*, 124–25.

24. Dray, *At the Hands of Persons Unknown*, 266–67, 271–72; Goldstein, "The Dyer Anti-lynching Bill," 92–96; Rable, "The South and the Politics of Anti-lynching Legislation," 206.

25. Berg, *Popular Justice*, 154; Burns, "Without Due Process," 245–46; Dray, *At the Hands of Persons Unknown*, 270–72; Rable, "The South and the Politics of Antilynching Legislation," 206; Schneider, *"We Return Fighting,"* 190.

26. Dray, *At the Hands of Persons Unknown*, 341–42; Finley, *Delaying the Dream*, 16–17; Holloway, *Getting Away with Murder*, 60; Janken, *Walter White*, 202–3; Rable, "The South and the Politics of Antilynching Legislation," 209.

27. Apel, *Imagery of Lynching*, 40–42; Dray, *At the Hands of Persons Unknown*, 338; Finley, *Delaying the Dream*, 19.

28. Eleanor Roosevelt in quoted in Harrell et al., *Unto a Good Land*, 942. See also Dray, *At the Hands of Persons Unknown*, 340–44; Finley, *Delaying the Dream*, 17; Leuchtenburg, *The White House Looks South*, 57–59; Rable, "The South and the Politics of Antilynching Legislation," 208–9.

29. Finley, *Delaying the Dream*, 20–25; Janken, *Walter White*, 225; Rable, "The South and the Politics of Antilynching Legislation," 219.

30. "Legislation Tied Up," 1, 4. See also Dray, *At the Hands of Persons Unknown*, 359; Finley, *Delaying the Dream*, 26–27.

31. Quoted in Finley, *Delaying the Dream*, 28. See also Dray, *At the Hands of Persons Unknown*, 356; "Lynch Bill Is Set for Action in 1938," 6.

32. Quoted in Finley, *Delaying the Dream*, 29. See also "Legislation Tied Up," 1, 4.

33. Finley, *Delaying the Dream*, 31–32. The quote appears on p. 31.

34. "Filibuster Waits on Barkley Move," 3; Finley, *Delaying the Dream*, 41–44. The Russell quote appears on p. 43 of Finley.

35. Dray, *At the Hands of Persons Unknown*, 356–57; "Filibuster Ended as Senate Shelves Anti-lynch Bill," 1, 5; "Filibuster Waits on Barkley Move," 3; Finley, *Delaying the Dream*, 49; "Lynching in the North," 123; Rable, "The South and the Politics of Antilynching Legislation," 215–16.

36. Dray, *At the Hands of Persons Unknown*, 361–62; Finley, *Delaying the Dream*, 49–53; Rable, "The South and the Politics of Antilynching Legislation," 209–12.

37. Finley, *Delaying the Dream*, 57–59; Rable, "The South and the Politics of Antilynching Legislation," 215, 219–20.

38. Dray, *At the Hands of Persons Unknown*, 362; Finley, *Delaying the Dream*, 30, 39.

39. Broussard, "The Worst of Times," 119–20; Curriden, "The Saga of the Scottsboro Boys Begins," 72; Dray, *At the Hands of Persons Unknown*, 307–15; Simkins and Roland, *A History of the South*, 505.

40. Dray, *At the Hands of Persons Unknown*, 307; Gildersleeve, "The Struggle for Justice," 90; Rapley, *Witch Hunts*, 142.

41. Carter, *Scottsboro*, 4; Klarman, "Scottsboro," 380.

42. Carter, *Scottsboro*, 5; Dray, *At the Hands of Persons Unknown*, 307; Gildersleeve, "The Struggle for Justice," 90–91.

43. Dray, *At the Hands of Persons Unknown*, 307; Gildersleeve, "The Struggle for Justice," 90–91; Rapley, *Witch Hunts*, 143.

44. Klarman, "Scottsboro," 381; Miller, *Remembering Scottsboro*, 10; Miller, Pennybacker, and Rosenhaft, "Mother Ada Wright and the International Campaign to Free the Scottsboro Boys," 387–88.

45. Quoted in Carter, *Scottsboro*, 7.

46. Carter, *Scottsboro*, 9; Goodman, *Stories of Scottsboro*, 17; Klarman, "Scottsboro," 381.

47. Carter, *Scottsboro*, 6–7, 11–13; Gildersleeve, "The Struggle for Justice," 90–91.

48. Carter, *Scottsboro*, 17–18; Gildersleeve, "The Struggle for Justice," 91–92; Goodman, *Stories of Scottsboro*, 13; Klarman, "Scottsboro," 381.

49. Carter, *Scottsboro*, 24; Klarman, "Scottsboro," 383–84.

50. Carter, *Scottsboro*, 25–27; Gildersleeve, "The Struggle for Justice," 92; Klarman, "Scottsboro," 383–84.

51. Carter, *Scottsboro*, 32–34; Klarman, "Scottsboro," 384.

52. Carter, *Scottsboro*, 35–43; Gildersleeve, "The Struggle for Justice," 92.

53. *Powell v. Alabama*, 287 U.S. 45, 50 (1932). See also Gildersleeve, "The Struggle for Justice," 93; Klarman, "Scottsboro," 384–85; Rapley, *Witch Hunts*, 146.

54. Carter, *Scottsboro*, 51–103; Gildersleeve, "The Struggle for Justice," 95–99; Goodman, *Stories of Scottsboro*, 101; Klarman, "Scottsboro," 385–90; Miller, *Remembering Scottsboro*, 10; Miller, Pennybacker, and Rosenhaft, "Mother Ada Wright and the International Campaign to Free the Scottsboro Boys," 390–92; Norris and Washington, *The Last of the Scottsboro Boys*, 58–59.

55. *Powell v. Alabama*, 287 U.S. 45, 50 (1932). See also Carter, *Scottsboro*, 51–103; Gildersleeve, "The Struggle for Justice," 99–100; Klarman, "Scottsboro," 390–93. The *Montgomery Advertiser* quote appears on p. 392 of Klarman.

56. *Powell v. Alabama*, 287 U.S. 45, 50–51 (1932). See also Klarman, "Scottsboro," 393–98.

57. *Powell v. Alabama*, 287 U.S. 45, 71 (1932).

58. Carter, *Scottsboro*, 210, 241–42; Klarman, "Scottsboro," 400–402; Rapley, *Witch Hunts*, 147.

59. Leibovitz is quoted in Klarman, "Scottsboro," 402. See also Carter, *Scottsboro*, 238–42.

60. Carter, *Scottsboro*, 184, 193–239; Gildersleeve, "The Struggle for Justice," 100–101; Klarman, "Scottsboro," 399; Norris and Washington, *The Last of the Scottsboro Boys*, 64.

61. Quoted in Rapley, *Witch Hunts*, 160.

62. Quoted in Healey, *When I Was Not My Brother's Keeper*, 38.

63. Carter, *Scottsboro*, 268–69; Klarman, "Scottsboro," 403; Rapley, *Witch Hunts*, 160–62.

64. Carter, *Scottsboro*, 270–73; Klarman, "Scottsboro," 403–4.

65. Carter, *Scottsboro*, 274–76; Goodman, *Stories of Scottsboro*, 212, 217; Gildersleeve, "The Struggle for Justice," 102; Klarman, "Scottsboro," 404.

66. Gildersleeve, "The Struggle for Justice," 103; Klarman, "Scottsboro," 405–6.

67. Carter, *Scottsboro*, 322–23; Klarman, "Scottsboro," 407–8.

68. *Patterson v. Alabama*, 294 U.S. 600 (1935). See also Carter, *Scottsboro*, 319, 324; Klarman, "Scottsboro," 407.

69. *Norris v. Alabama*, 294 U.S. 587, 589 (1935). See also Baker, "Trials of the Century," 45; Carter, *Scottsboro*, 322–24; Curriden, "The Saga of the Scottsboro Boys Begins," 72; Gildersleeve, "The Struggle for Justice," 103; Klarman, "Scottsboro," 407–8; *Neal v. Delaware*, 103 U.S. 370, 397 (1881); Simkins and Roland, *A History of the South*, 505.

70. Carter, *Scottsboro*, 338–41; Gildersleeve, "The Struggle for Justice," 103.

71. Carter, *Scottsboro*, 340–43; Klarman, "Scottsboro," 410–11.

72. Carter, *Scottsboro*, 272–308, 325–80; Dray, *At the Hands of Persons Unknown*, 314–15; Klarman, "Scottsboro," 404–6.

73. Carter, *Scottsboro*, 342–45; Gildersleeve, "The Struggle for Justice," 103; Goodman, *Stories of Scottsboro*, 256, 303; "Scottsboro Hero," 45–47.

74. Carter, *Scottsboro*, 373–75; Rapley, *Witch Hunts*, 163.

75. Curriden, "The Saga of the Scottsboro Boys Begins," 72; "Scottsboro Hero," 45–47.

76. Carter, *Scottsboro*, 375–77, 384–86; Gildersleeve, "The Struggle for Justice," 103–5.

77. Carter, *Scottsboro*, 366–67, 389–96; Klarman, "Scottsboro," 413.

78. Carter, *Scottsboro*, 349, 411; Klarman, "Scottsboro," 412–13; Rapley, *Witch Hunts*, 164.

79. Carter, *Scottsboro*, 425–27; Dray, *At the Hands of Persons Unknown*, 315; Rapley, *Witch Hunts*, 165.

80. Carter, *Scottsboro*, 412–13; Rapley, *Witch Hunts*, 164–65.

81. Carter, *Scottsboro*, 411–15; Miller, *Remembering Scottsboro*, 4; Norris and Washington, *The Last of the Scottsboro Boys*, 243, 253.

82. Blinder, "Pardons for the Last 'Scottsboro Boys,'" A14.

83. Cushman, *African-Americans and the Quest for Civil Rights*, 47–48; Greenberg, *To Ask for an Equal Chance*, 9; Wolters, *Negroes and the Great Depression*, 7–8.

84. Broussard, "The Worst of Times," 125; Fleming, *In the Shadow of Selma*, 70; Greenberg, *To Ask for an Equal Chance*, 45; Harvey, "Learning from the New Deal," 89–90; Vieru, "Failure of Capitalism?," 190.

85. Fleming, *In the Shadow of Selma*, 70–71; Greenberg, *To Ask for an Equal Chance*, 45–46; Harvey, "Learning from the New Deal," 90–91, 103.

86. Hornbeck, "The Enduring Impact of the American Dust Bowl," 1477–507; Wolters, *Negroes and the Great Depression*, 3–4.

87. Broussard, "The Worst of Times," 105–6; Sitkoff, *A New Deal for Blacks*, 35; Wolters, *Negroes and the Great Depression*, 7–8.

88. Cushman, *African-Americans and the Quest for Civil Rights*, 48–49; Dray, *At the Hands of Persons Unknown*, 303–4; Wolters, *Negroes and the Great Depression*, 116–17.

89. Quoted in Fleming, *In the Shadow of Selma*, 72. See also Wolters, *Negroes and the Great Depression*, 8.

90. Broussard, "The Worst of Times," 113; Fleming, *In the Shadow of Selma*, 70–71; Greenberg, *To Ask for an Equal Chance*, 50; Novak, Pease, and Sanders, *Agricultural Policy in the United States*, 77; Sklaroff, *Black Culture and the New Deal*, 17.

91. Broussard, "The Worst of Times," 113; Fleming, *In the Shadow of Selma*, 71–72; Wolters, *Negroes and the Great Depression*, 10–13.

92. Broussard, "The Worst of Times," 113; Fleming, *In the Shadow of Selma*, 72; Sitkoff, *A New Deal for Blacks*, 53; Wolters, *Negroes and the Great Depression*, 26–32.

93. Quoted in Wolters, *Negroes and the Great Depression*, 79. See also Broussard, "The Worst of Times," 113.

94. Quoted in Wolters, *Negroes and the Great Depression*, 44. See also Greenberg, *To Ask for an Equal Chance*, 48; Sitkoff, *A New Deal for Blacks*, 49.

95. Broussard, "The Worst of Times," 114–15; Fleming, *In the Shadow of Selma*, 72–73; Greenberg, *To Ask for an Equal Chance*, 60–61; King, "The Farm Security Administration and Its Attack on Rural Poverty," 155–61; Wolters, *Negroes and the Great Depression*, 65–73.

96. Broussard, "The Worst of Times," 115; Fleming, *In the Shadow of Selma*, xvii; Wolters, *Negroes and the Great Depression*, 67–73.

97. Cushman, *African-Americans and the Quest for Civil Rights*, 50–51; Wolters, *Negroes and the Great Depression*, 78–79.

98. Sitkoff, *A New Deal for Blacks*, 47–48; Wolters, *Negroes and the Great Depression*, 83–84.

99. Harvey, "Learning from the New Deal," 88; Vieru, "Failure of Capitalism?," 190–92, 200.

100. Quoted in National Archives and Records Administration, *Our Documents*, 160. See also Cushman, *African-Americans and the Quest for Civil Rights*, 50; Wolters, *Negroes and the Great Depression*, 88–90.

101. Wagner is quoted in Wolters, *Negroes and the Great Depression*, 90.

102. Roosevelt is quoted in Wolters, *The Negro and the New Deal Economic Recovery Program*, 140. See also Wolters, *Negroes and the Great Depression*, 90–91.

103. Sitkoff, *A New Deal for Blacks*, 175; Wolters, *Negroes and the Great Depression*, 169–87.

104. Broussard, "The Worst of Times," 115; Sitkoff, *A New Deal for Blacks*, 66–68; Wolters, *Negroes and the Great Depression*, 193–203.

105. Broussard, "The Worst of Times," 115–16; Greenberg, *To Ask for an Equal Chance*, 50; Harvey, "Learning from the New Deal," 93; Wolters, *Negroes and the Great Depression*, 196–98.

106. Broussard, "The Worst of Times," 115; Greenberg, *To Ask for an Equal Chance*, 48–49; Harvey, "Learning from the New Deal," 91–93; Sitkoff, *A New Deal for Blacks*, 49; Wolters, *Negroes and the Great Depression*, 196–203.

107. Greenberg, *To Ask for an Equal Chance*, 28, 30, 50; Harvey, "Learning from the New Deal," 100; Wolters, *Negroes and the Great Depression*, 203–9.

108. Witcover, *Party of the People*, 374; Wolters, *Negroes and the Great Depression*, 145–46.

109. Broussard, "The Worst of Times," 108; Sklaroff, *Black Culture and the New Deal*, 16–17; Witcover, *Party of the People*, 372–76.

110. The ditty is quoted in Leuchtenburg, *The White House Looks South*, 459n36. See also Broussard, "The Worst of Times," 117, 125; Leuchtenburg, *The White House Looks South*, 58; Sklaroff, *Black Culture and the New Deal*, 1.

111. See, for example, Baime, *The Arsenal of Democracy*.

112. Moore, *Fighting for America*, 29; Wynn, *The African American Experience during World War II*, 45.

113. Moore, *Fighting for America*, 3–18; Wynn, *The African American Experience during World War II*, 1–9.

114. Moore, *Fighting for America*, 17–18; Newby, "The Fight for the Right to Fight and the Forgotten Negro Protest Movement," 86–88; Wynn, *The African American Experience during World War II*, 7–8.

115. Knauer, *Let Us Fight as Free Men*, 6, 32; Moore, *Fighting for America*, 30; Wynn, *The African American Experience during World War II*, 41–42, 66, 98.

116. Caver, Ennels, and Haulman, *The Tuskegee Airmen*, 27; Homan and Reilly, *Black Knights*, 18–19; Moye, *Freedom Flyers*, 23–24.

117. Walker, *Presidents and Civil Liberties from Wilson to Obama*, 106–7; Wynn, *The African American Experience during World War II*, 27–29.

118. Knauer, *Let Us Fight as Free Men*, 18; Newby, "The Fight for the Right to Fight and the Forgotten Negro Protest Movement," 87–88; Wynn, *The African American Experience during World War II*, 26–28.

119. Homan and Reilly, *Black Knights*, 9, 27–28; Moore, *Fighting for America*, 135–39, 162–63; Moye, *Freedom Flyers*, 49, 57–59; Reef, *African Americans in the Military*, xiv–xv; Wynn, *The African American Experience during World War II*, 44–45.

120. Caver, Ennels, and Haulman, *The Tuskegee Airmen*, 53; Homan and Reilly, *Black Knights*, 71, 76–78; Moye, *Freedom Flyers*, 57–61.

121. Moore, *Fighting for America*, 27–28; Wynn, *The African American Experience during World War II*, 34.

122. Quoted in Davis, *Race Relations in the United States*, 22. See also Knauer, *Let Us Fight as Free Men*, 15; Moore, *Fighting for America*, 28; Newby, "The Fight for the Right to Fight and the Forgotten Negro Protest Movement," 85–86; Wynn, *The African American Experience during World War II*, 34–35.

123. Davis, *Race Relations in the United States*, 29; Moore, *Fighting for America*, 125; Reef, *African Americans in the Military*, xv; Wynn, *The African American Experience during World War II*, 45–46.

124. Moore, *Fighting for America*, 189–93; Wynn, *The African American Experience during World War II*, 53–54.

125. Caver, Ennels, and Haulman, *The Tuskegee Airmen*, 21, 23, 73, 103; Moore, *Fighting for America*, 29, 31–33; Moye, *Freedom Flyers*, 58–60; Reef, *African Americans in the Military*, xv, 80–85, 123–25, 166–67; Wynn, *The African American Experience during World War II*, xi–xii, 29.

126. Quoted in Moore, *Fighting for America*, 270. See also Moore, *Fighting for America*, 141; Reef, *African Americans in the Military*, xvi, 24–25.

127. Jones, "The Gravity of Administrative Discharges," 2–3; Knauer, *Let Us Fight as Free Men*, 44–45.

128. Janken, *Walter White*, 281, 282, 298; White, *A Rising Wind*.

129. Moore, *Fighting for America*, 320–21; Wynn, *The African American Experience during World War II*, 81–83.

130. Knauer, *Let Us Fight as Free Men*, 4, 112–21; Newby, "The Fight for the Right to Fight and the Forgotten Negro Protest Movement," 83–110; Warber, "Public Outreach, Executive Orders, and the Unilateral Presidency," 272; Wynn, *The African American Experience during World War II*, 92–95.

EPILOGUE

1. Barber, *Gunnar Myrdal*, xii, 64–65, 75; Etzemüller, *Alva and Gunnar Myrdal*, 252; Jackson, *Gunnar Myrdal and America's Conscience*, xiv–xvii; Thernstrom and Thernstrom, "The Prescience of Myrdal," 37.

2. Myrdal, *An American Dilemma*, 1:167. See also Barber, *Gunnar Myrdal*, xii; Etzemüller, *Alva and Gunnar Myrdal*, 253–55; Jackson, *Gunnar Myrdal and America's Conscience*, 219; Lyman, "Gunnar Myrdal's *An American Dilemma* after a Half Century," 328; Thernstrom and Thernstrom, "The Prescience of Myrdal," 39.

3. Myrdal, *An American Dilemma*, 1:75. See also Barber, *Gunnar Myrdal*, 74–75; Darity, "The Undesirables, America's Underclass in the Managerial Age," 146–47; Etzemüller, *Alva and Gunnar Myrdal*, 253; Jackson, *Gunnar Myrdal and America's Conscience*, 197; Thernstrom and Thernstrom, "The Prescience of Myrdal," 39.

4. Du Bois is quoted in Jackson, *Gunnar Myrdal and America's Conscience*, 245. Frazier is quoted in Jackson, *Gunnar Myrdal and America's Conscience*, 170. Chief Justice Warren cited *An American Dilemma* in *Brown v. Board of Education of Topeka*, 347 U.S. 483, 495n11 (1954). See also Barber, *Gunnar Myrdal*, xii, 76–77; Jackson, *Gunnar Myrdal and America's Conscience*, 241–49; Thernstrom and Thernstrom, "The Prescience of Myrdal," 39, 40.

5. Barber, *Gunnar Myrdal*, 77–78; Darity, "The Undesirables, America's Underclass in the Managerial Age," 148–49; Etzemüller, *Alva and Gunnar Myrdal*, 261–62; Jackson, *Gunnar Myrdal and America's Conscience*, 261; Lyman, "Gunnar Myrdal's *An American Dilemma* after a Half Century," 331–34.

6. Etzemüller, *Alva and Gunnar Myrdal*, 255–61; Jackson, *Gunnar Myrdal and America's Conscience*, 219–20.

7. Jackson, *Gunnar Myrdal and America's Conscience*, 301; Thernstrom and Thernstrom, "The Prescience of Myrdal," 38, 40, 41–42.

8. Dailey, "The Sexual Politics of Race in World War II America," 154; Simpson, "A Tale Untold?," 133–49.

9. Bruns, *Zoot Suit Riots*; Shapiro, *White Violence and Black Response*, 330–32, 338.

10. "Army Patrols End Detroit Rioting," 1; "Detroit Watchful in 'Mop Up' of Riots," 23; Sitkoff, "The Detroit Race Riot 1943," 183–206. This account does not touch on violence that erupted late in the 1940s, through the 1950s, and into the 1960s. Additional volumes would have to be written (and have been written) to address these episodes adequately—from the 1946 maiming and blinding of a black veteran, Isaac Woodard, to the lynching of two black couples in Walton County, Georgia, in 1946, to the 1955 murder of fourteen-year-old Emmett Till, and on and on. See, for example, Dray, *At the Hands of Persons Unknown*, 36–370, 377–83, 422–32; King, *Devil in the Grove*, 120–23; Wexler, *Fire in a Canebrake*; Whitfield, *A Death in the Delta*; Wynn, *The African American Experience during World War II*, 87–88.

11. "Harlem Is Orderly with Heavy Guard Ready for Trouble," 1, 10; "Harlem's Tragedy," 18; Janken, *Walter White*, 275–77.

12. Turner and Bound, "Closing the Gap or Widening the Divide," 145–46, 170–72; Wynn, *The African American Experience during World War II*, 61, 83. For a detailed discussion, see Parker, *Fighting for Democracy*.

13. Du Bois, "An Appeal to the World." See also Taylor, *Freedom to Serve*, 81; Wolters, *Du Bois and His Rivals*, 247.

14. Du Bois, "An Appeal to the World." See also Mitoma, *Human Rights and the Negotiation of American Power*, 142.

15. See, for example, Klarman, *From Jim Crow to Civil Rights*, 403–21; O'Brien, *Storm Center*, 276–78, 318.

16. Morgan is quoted in Setegn, "Irene Morgan," E1. See also *Hall v. DeCuir*, 95 U.S. 485 (1878); *Morgan v. Virginia*, 328 U.S. 373 (1946).

17. *Smith v. Allwright*, 321 U.S. 649 (1944).

18. *Sweatt v. Painter*, 339 U.S. 629, 636 (1950).

19. *McLaurin v. Oklahoma State Regents*, 339 U.S. 637 (1950). See also Kirk, "The Long Road to Equality," 56.

20. Quoted in *Shelley v. Kraemer*, 334 U.S. 1, 4–5 (1948). See also *Buchanan v. Warley*, 245 U.S. 60 (1917).

21. Prior to *Shelley v. Kraemer*, cases involving home ownership by blacks in white neighborhoods usually resulted in a loss for the black property owner whether or not a racially restrictive covenant was involved. One exception that proved the rule dated from the 1920s. In 1925, a black physician from Detroit, Michigan, Ossian Sweet, was tried for murder when he and his friends tried to defend his home and family from a white mob furious that a black man had purchased a home in a white neighborhood. Gunshots were fired from the Sweet home, hitting two white men, one of whom was killed. Dr. Sweet and his codefendants won an acquittal from an all-white jury in the so-called Sweet Trials. It helped to have one of the greatest trial lawyers in American history, Clarence Darrow, serve as lead defense counsel. Dray, *At the Hands of Persons Unknown*, 283–92; Fleming, "The Murder Trial of Dr. Ossian Sweet," 106–8, 110–12, 114. For a detailed discussion, see Boyle, *The Arc of Justice*.

22. *Shelley v. Kraemer*, 334 U.S. 1, 23 (1948).

23. Dray, *At the Hands of Persons Unknown*, 384; Leuchtenburg, *The White House Looks South*, 171–72; McCullough, *Truman*, 569–70; Walker, *Presidents and Civil Liberties from Wilson to Obama*, 141.

24. Quoted in Taylor, *Freedom to Serve*, 78–79.

25. McCullough, *Truman*, 570; Taylor, *Freedom to Serve*, 76, 135.

26. Quoted in Taylor, *Freedom to Serve*, 79.

27. Dray, *At the Hands of Persons Unknown*, 384–85; Leuchtenburg, *The White House Looks South*, 172–73; McCullough, *Truman*, 588; Simkins and Roland, *A History of the South*, 589; Taylor, *Freedom to Serve*, 82–86.

28. Dray, *At the Hands of Persons Unknown*, 385; Taylor, *Freedom to Serve*, 2–3, 99.

29. Klarman, *From Jim Crow to Civil Rights*, 443–50; Simkins and Roland, *A History of the South*, 588–617.

References

"4 Dead, 5 Dying, 70 Hurt in New Race Riots in Washington." *New York Times*, July 22, 1919, 1.

"20 Race War Indictments." *New York Times*, August 23, 1908, 6.

"28 Dead, 500 Hurt in Three-Day Race Riots in Chicago." *New York Times*, July 30, 1919, 1, 3.

"85 Whites and Negroes Die in Tulsa Riots as 3,000 Armed Men Battle in Streets; 30 Blocks Burned, Military Rule in City." *New York Times*, June 2, 1921, 1.

"40,000 Klansmen Parade in Washington as 200,000 Spectators Look on Quietly; Called Order's Biggest Demonstration; Sight Astonishes Capital." *New York Times*, August 9, 1925, 1.

"A New Name." *Time* 118, no. 7 (August 17, 1981): 69.

"A Search for Justice in the Garner Case." *New York Times*, December 4, 2014, A30.

Adamson, Christopher R. "Punishment after Slavery: Southern State Penal Systems, 1865–1890." In "Private and Public Justice," *Social Problems* 30, no. 5 (June 1983): 555–69.

"Address by Hon. Frederick Douglass, Delivered in the Metropolitan A. M. E. Church, Washington, D.C., Tuesday, January 9th, 1894." Library of Congress, American Memory, http://lcweb2.loc.gov/rbc/lcrbmrp/t21/t2110.sgm_old (accessed March 2014).

Akers, Monte. *Flames after Midnight: Murder, Vengeance, and the Desolation of a Texas Community*. Austin: University of Texas Press, 2011.

Alexander, Charles C. "Kleagles and Cash: The Ku Klux Klan as a Business Organization, 1915–1930." *Business History Review* 39, no. 3 (autumn 1965): 348–67.

"All-TIME 100 Novels." *Time*, October 16, 2005, http://entertainment.time.com/2005/10/16/all-time-100-novels (accessed February 2015).

"Alleged Victim of Ex-Dragon Dies." *Atlanta Constitution*, April 15, 1925, 11.

Allen, Terrence T., and M. Michaux Parker. "Police Officers and Their Perceived Relationship with Urban Communities: Does Living in the Community Influence Police Decisions?," *Social Development Issues* 35, no. 3 (fall 2013): 82–95.

Alston, Lee J., and Kyle D. Kauffman. "Up, down, and off the Agricultural Ladder: New Evidence and Implications of Agricultural Mobility for Blacks in the Post-bellum South." *Agricultural History* 72, no. 2 (spring 1998): 263–79.

Altman, Alex, and Zeke J. Miller. "No. 2: The Activists Ferguson Protesters." *Time* 184, nos. 24/25 (December 22, 2014): 110–14.

Amber, Jeannine. "The Danger Outside." *Essence* 43, no. 2 (June 2012): 102–7.

Ammons, Elizabeth. "Frances Ellen Watkins Harper (1825–1911)." *Legacy* 2, no. 2 (fall 1985): 61–66.

Amstutz, David Lee. "Nebraska's Live Stock Sanitary Commission and the Rise of Progressivism." *Great Plains Quarterly* 28, no. 4 (fall 2008): 259–75.

Anderson, Michael. "The Too-Brief Career of Countee Cullen." *New Criterion* 31, no. 8 (April 2013): 24–27.

Andrews, William L. *The Literary Career of Charles W. Chesnutt*. Baton Rouge: Louisiana State University Press, 1980.

Antony, Mary Grace, and Ryan J. Thomas. "'This Is Citizen Journalism at Its Finest': YouTube and the Public Sphere in the Oscar Grant Shooting Incident." *New Media & Society* 12, no. 8 (December 2010): 1280–96.

Apel, Dora. *Imagery of Lynching: Black Men, White Women, and the Mob*. New Brunswick, NJ: Rutgers University Press, 2004.

Aptheker, Herbert. "American Negro Slave Revolts." *Science & Society* 1, no. 4 (summer 1937): 512–38.

———. *American Negro Slave Revolts*. New York: International Publishers Company, 1983 [1943].

"Army Begins Inquiry into Race Rioting." *New York Times*, July 5, 1917, 9.

"Army Patrols End Detroit Rioting; Death Toll at 29." *New York Times*, June 23, 1943, 1.

"Atlanta Mobs Kill Ten Negroes." *New York Times*, September 23, 1906, 1.

"The Atlanta Riots." *New York Times*, September 25, 1906, 8.

Austin, George Lowell. *The Life and Times of Wendell Phillips*. Boston: B. B. Russell & Company, 1884.

Ayers, Edward L. *The Promise of the New South: Life after Reconstruction*. 15th anniv. ed. New York: Oxford University Press, 2007.

Aynes, Richard L. "Constricting the Law of Freedom: Justice Miller, the Fourteenth Amendment, and the Slaughter-House Cases." *Chicago-Kent Law Review* 70, no. 2 (1994): 627–88.

Baime, A. J. *The Arsenal of Democracy: FDR, Detroit, and an Epic Quest to Arm an America at War*. New York: Houghton Mifflin Harcourt, 2014.

Baker, Bruce E. *What Reconstruction Meant: Historical Memory in the American South*. Charlottesville: University of Virginia Press, 2007.

Baker, Debra. "Trials of the Century." *ABA Journal* 85, no. 1 (January 1999): 42–49.

Bannerman, Helen. *The Story of Little Black Sambo*. Cutchogue, NY: Buccaneer Books, 1976 [1899].

Barbeau, Arthur E., and Florette Henri. *The Unknown Soldiers: African-American Troops in World War I*. Cambridge, MA: Da Capo Press, 1996 [1974].

Barber, William J. *Gunnar Myrdal: An Intellectual Biography*. New York: Palgrave MacMillan, 2008.

Barrett, Nancy J. "The Struggles of Women Industrial Workers to Improve Work Conditions in the Progressive Era." *OAH Magazine of History* 13, no. 3 (spring 1999): 43–49.

Barry, John M. *The Great Influenza: The Story of the Deadliest Pandemic in History.* New York: Viking Penguin, 2005.

Bartley, Numan V. *The Creation of Modern Georgia.* 2nd ed. Athens: University of Georgia Press, 1990.

Bass, Jack, and Marilyn W. Thompson. *Ol' Strom: An Unauthorized Biography of Strom Thurmond.* Marietta, GA: Longstreet Press, 1998.

Bauerlein, Mark. *Negrophobia: A Race Riot in Atlanta, 1906.* San Francisco: Encounter Books, 2001.

Baum, Lawrence. *The Supreme Court.* 3rd ed. Washington, DC: Congressional Quarterly Press, 1989.

Beatty, Jack. *Age of Betrayal: The Triumph of Money in America, 1865–1900.* New York: Alfred A. Knopf, 2007.

Belz, Herman. "The Freedmen's Bureau Act of 1865 and the Principle of No Discrimination According to Color." *Civil War History* 21, no. 3 (September 1975): 197–217.

Berg, Manfred. *Popular Justice: A History of Lynching in America.* Lanham, MD: Ivan R. Dee, 2011.

Berlin, Ira. *Many Thousands Gone: The First Two Centuries of Slavery in North America.* Cambridge, MA: Harvard University Press, 1998.

———. "Time, Space, and the Evolution of Afro-American Slavery on British Mainland North America." *American Historical Review* 85, no. 1 (February 1980): 44–78.

Biegert, M. Langley. "Legacy of Resistance: Uncovering the History of Collective Action by Black Agricultural Workers in Central East Arkansas from the 1860s to the 1930s." *Journal of Social History* 32, no. 1 (autumn 1998): 73–99.

Bilhartz, Terry D., and Alan C. Elliott. *Currents in American History: A Brief History of the United States.* Vol. 2: *From 1861.* Armonk, NY: M. E. Sharpe, 2007.

Blackmon, Douglas A. *Slavery by Another Name: The Re-enslavement of Black Americans from the Civil War to World War II.* New York: Doubleday, 2008.

Blair, William Alan. "The Use of Military Force to Protect the Gains of Reconstruction." *Civil War History* 51, no. 4 (December 2005): 388–402.

Blaustein, Arthur I., ed. *The American Promise: Equal Justice and Economic Opportunity.* New Brunswick, NJ: Transaction Publishers, 2009.

Blee, Kathleen, and Amy McDowell. "The Duality of Spectacle and Secrecy: A Case Study of Fraternalism in the 1920s U.S. Ku Klux Klan." *Ethnic and Racial Studies* 36, no. 2 (February 2013): 249–65.

Blight, David W. "'For Something beyond the Battlefield': Frederick Douglass and the Struggle for the Memory of the Civil War." *Journal of American History* 75, no. 4 (March 1989): 1156–78.

———. *Frederick Douglass' Civil War: Keeping Faith in Jubilee.* Baton Rouge: Louisiana State University Press, 1989.

———. *Race and Reunion: The Civil War in American Memory.* Cambridge, MA: Harvard University Press, 2009.

Blinder, Alan. "Pardons for the Last 'Scottsboro Boys.'" *New York Times*, November 22, 2013, A14.

Blow, Charles M. "Beyond 'Black Lives Matter': Commentary." *New York Times*, February 9, 2015, A17.

Blum, Edward J. *Reforging the White Republic: Race, Religion, and American Nationalism, 1865–1898*. Baton Rouge: Louisiana State University Press, 2005.

Boas, Franz. *Race, Language, and Culture*. Chicago: University of Chicago Press, 1982 [1940].

Bogle, Donald. *Toms, Coons, Mulattoes, Mammies, and Bucks: An Interpretative History of Blacks in American Films*. 4th ed. New York: Continuum Books, 2002.

Bogue, Allan G. "Historians and Radical Republicans: A Meaning for Today." *Journal of American History* 70, no. 1 (June 1983): 7–34.

———. "The Radical Voting Dimension in the U.S. Senate during the Civil War." *Journal of Interdisciplinary History* 3, no. 3 (winter 1973): 449–74.

Bonekemper, Edward H., III. *A Victor, Not a Butcher: Ulysses S. Grant's Overlooked Military Genius*. Washington, DC: Regnery, 2004.

Bonner, Robert B. *Mastering America: Southern Slaveholders and the Crisis of American Nationhood*. Cambridge: Cambridge University Press, 2009.

———. "Roundhead Cavaliers? The Context and Limits of a Confederate Racial Project." *Civil War History* 48, no. 1 (March 2002): 34–59.

Boustan, Leah Platt. "Was Postwar Suburbanization 'White Flight'? Evidence from the Black Migration." *Quarterly Journal of Economics* 125, no. 1 (February 2010): 417–43.

Boyd, Herb. "African Craftsman Slain by Police." *New York Amsterdam News* 94, no. 22 (May 29, 2003): 3.

———. "Louima and Gammage: Two Names Linked to Police Brutality." *New York Amsterdam News* 88, no. 42 (October 16, 1997): 4.

Boyd, Robert L. "The Storefront Church Ministry in African American Communities of the Urban North during the Great Migration." *Social Science Journal* 35, no. 3 (July 1998): 319–22.

Boyle, Kevin. *The Arc of Justice: A Saga of Race, Civil Rights, and Murder in the Jazz Age*. New York: Henry Holt, 2004.

Brands, H. W. *American Colossus: The Triumph of American Capitalism, 1865–1900*. New York: Anchor Books, 2011.

———. "Hesitant Emancipator: Abraham Lincoln Endured Hours of Personal Anguish before He Unveiled the Proclamation That Ended Slavery." *American History* 44, no. 2 (June 2009): 54–59.

———. *The Man Who Saved the Union: Ulysses S. Grant in War and Peace*. New York: Knopf, 2013.

Braxton, Joanne M., ed., *The Collected Poetry of Paul Laurence Dunbar*. Charlottesville: University of Virginia Press, 1993.

Britt, Craig. "Leo Frank's Trial Is Attracting Universal Interest in Georgia." *Atlanta Constitution*, August 4, 1913, 2.

Brophy, Alfred L. *Reconstructing the Dreamland: The Tulsa Race Riot of 1921: Race, Reparations, and Reconciliation*. New York: Oxford University Press, 2003.

Broussard, Albert S. "The Worst of Times: African-Americans in the Great Depression." In *The Great Depression: People and Perspectives*, edited by Hamilton Cravens and Peter C. Mancall, 105–26. Santa Barbara, CA: ABC-CLIO, 2009.

Brown, David, and Clive Webb. *Race in the American South: From Slavery to Civil Rights*. Edinburgh: Edinburgh University Press, 2007.

Brown, John Howard, ed. *Lamb's Biographical Dictionary of the United States*. Vol. 6. Boston: James H. Lamb Company, 1903.

Brown, Mary Jane. "Advocates in the Age of Jazz: Women and the Campaign for the Dyer Anti-lynching Bill." *Peace and Change* 28, no. 3 (July 2003): 378–419.

Brown v. Board of Education, 347 U.S. 483 (1954).

Broz, J. Lawrence. *The International Origins of the Federal Reserve System*. Ithaca, NY: Cornell University Press, 1997.

Bruns, Roger. *Zoot Suit Riots*. Santa Barbara, CA: ABC-CLIO, 2014.

"Bryan the Demagogue." *New York Times*, July 11, 1896, 3.

Bryan, Ferald J. *Henry Grady or Tom Watson? The Rhetorical Struggle for the New South, 1880–1890*. Macon, GA: Mercer University Press, 1994.

"Bryan, Free Silver, and Repudiation." *New York Times*, July 11, 1896, 1.

Bryan, William Jennings. *The Cross of Gold: Speech Delivered before the National Democratic Convention at Chicago, July 9, 1896*. Lincoln: University of Nebraska Press, 1996.

Bryson, Bill. *One Summer: America, 1927*. New York: Doubleday, 2013.

Buchanan v. Warley, 245 U.S. 60 (1917).

Buckner, Helen. *Daniel Hale Williams: Negro Surgeon*. Lanham, MD: Pitman Publishing, 1968.

Budiansky, Stephen. *The Bloody Shirt: Terror after the Civil War*. New York: Plume Books, 2008.

———. "How a War of Terror Kept Blacks Oppressed Long after the Civil War Had Ended: A Massacre in Hamburg, S.C., Epitomized the Violence That Eviscerated Reconstruction." *American History* 43, no. 1 (April 2008): 30–37.

Burka, Paul. "James Byrd Jr." *Texas Monthly* 27, no. 9 (September 1999): 126.

Burns, Adam. "Without Due Process: Albert E. Pillsbury and the Hoar Anti-lynching Bill." *American Nineteenth Century History* 11, no. 2 (June 2010): 233–52.

Burns, Rebecca. *Rage in the Gate City: The Story of the 1906 Atlanta Race Riot*. Rev. ed. Athens: University of Georgia Press, 2009.

Burt, Elizabeth V. "Working Women and the Triangle Fire: Press Coverage of a Tragedy." *Journalism History* 30, no. 4 (winter 2005): 189–99.

Byas, Steve. "Libel: Warren Harding Was Our Worst President." *New American* 31, no. 2 (January 19, 2015): 33–39.

Bynum, Cornelius L. "'An Equal Chance in the Race for Life': Reverdy C. Ransom, Socialism, and the Social Gospel Movement, 1890–1920." *Journal of African American History* 93, no. 1 (winter 2008): 1–20.

Calabresi, Steven G., and Christopher S. Yoo. "The Unitary Executive during the Second Half-Century." *Harvard Journal of Law & Public Policy* 26, no. 3 (summer 2003): 667–801.

Calhoun, Charles W. *From Bloody Shirt to Full Dinner Pail: The Transformation of Politics and Governance in the Gilded Age*. New York: Hill and Wang, 2010.

Cameron, Christopher. *The Abolitionist Movement: Documents Decoded*. Santa Barbara, CA: ABC-CLIO, 2014.

Cannon, Lou. "Rodney King Remembered: Three Myths about the Beating That Changed the World." *National Review* 64, no. 13 (July 9, 2012): 22, 24–25.

Capozzola, Christopher. "Jacob Lawrence: Historian." *Rethinking History* 10, no. 2 (June 2006): 291–95.

"Capture of Sam Hose Seems to Be a Matter of Only a Few Hours: Latest Report Says He Is Surrounded at Moreland, Near Newnan by a Determined Mob." *Atlanta Constitution*, April 15, 1899, 1.

Carey, Charles W. *African-American Political Leaders (A to Z of African Americans)*. New York: Facts on File, 2003.

Carlin, Peter Ames. *Bruce*. New York: Touchstone Books, 2012.

Carlino, Bill. "75 Years: The Odyssey of Eating Out." *Nation's Restaurant News* 28, no. 1 (January 1994): 11–28.

Carter, Dan T. *The Politics of Rage: George Wallace, the Origins of the New Conservatism, and the Transformation of American Politics*. New York: Simon & Schuster, 2000.

———. *Scottsboro: A Tragedy of the American South*. Rev. ed. Baton Rouge: Louisiana State University Press, 2007.

Carwardine, Richard. *Lincoln: A Life of Purpose and Power*. New York: Knopf, 2003.

Cashill, Jack. *"If I Had a Son": Race, Guns, and the Railroading of George Zimmerman*. Birmingham, AL: Notable Trials Library, 2013.

Catton, Bruce. *The American Heritage New History of the Civil War*. Edited by James M. McPherson. New York: Viking Penguin, 1996.

Caver, Joseph, Jerome Ennels, and Daniel Haulman. *The Tuskegee Airmen: An Illustrated History: 1939–1949, with a Comprehensive Chronology of Missions and Events*. Montgomery, AL: NewSouth Books, 2011.

Chalmers, David M. *Hooded Americanism: The History of the Ku Klux Klan*. 3rd ed. Durham, NC: Duke University Press, 1987.

Chapman, Erin D. *Prove It on Me: New Negroes, Sex, and Popular Culture in the 1920s*. New York: Oxford University Press, 2012.

Christian, Margena A. "Can You Dig It?," *Ebony* 69, no. 6 (April 2014): 116–21, 134.

"Circle of Vengeance Slowly Closing on Fleeing Sam Hose: Hundreds of Armed Men Are Beating the County for the Murderer of Alfred Cranford." *Atlanta Constitution*, April 18, 1899, 1.

Civil Rights Cases, 109 U.S. 3 (1883).

Clarke, James W. "Without Fear or Shame: Lynching, Capital Punishment and the Subculture of Violence in the American South." *British Journal of Political Science* 28, no. 2 (April 1998): 269–89.

Coates, Ta-Nehisi. "The Case for Reparations." *Atlantic* 313, no. 5 (June 2014): 54–71.

Cochrane, Willard W. *The Development of American Agriculture: A Historical Analysis*. Minneapolis: University of Minnesota Press, 1993.

Coffman, Edward M. *The War to End All Wars: The American Military Experience in World War I*. Lexington: University Press of Kentucky, 1968.

Cohan, William D. *The Price of Silence: The Duke Lacrosse Scandal, the Power of the Elite, and the Corruption of Our Great Universities*. New York: Scribner, 2014.

Cohen, William. "Negro Involuntary Servitude in the South, 1865–1940: A Preliminary Analysis." *Journal of Southern History* 42, no. 1 (February 1976): 31–60.

Cohodas, Nadine. *Strom Thurmond and the Politics of Southern Change*. Macon, GA: Mercer University Press, 1995 [1993].

Cole, Catherine M., and Tracy C. Davis. "Routes of Blackface." *TDR: The Drama Review* 57, no. 2 (summer 2013): 7–12.

Coleman, Finnie D. *Sutton E. Griggs and the Struggle against White Supremacy*. Knoxville: University of Tennessee Press, 2007.

Collins, Ann V. *All Hell Broke Loose: American Race Riots from the Progressive Era through World War II*. Santa Barbara, CA: ABC-CLIO, 2012.

Collins, Owen, Compiler. *Speeches That Changed the World*. Louisville, KY: Westminster John Knox Press, 1999.

Collins, William J., and Marianne H. Wanamaker. "Selection and Economic Gains in the Great Migration of African Americans: New Evidence from Linked Census Data." *American Economic Journal: Applied Economics* 6, no. 1 (January 2014): 220–52.

Congressional Record, January 25, 1922, 1718–21, 1795.

Conley, John J. "'Delayed, Not Destroyed." *America* 212, no. 19 (June 8, 2015): 28.

"*Constitution* Paid $500 to Capturer of Sam Hose." *Atlanta Constitution*, June 5, 1904, A7.

Cooper, N. Lee. "President's Message—the Harlan Standard: Former Associate Justice Can Teach Us the Value of Reasoned Dissent." *ABA Journal* 83, no. 1 (June 1997): 8.

Cooper, William J., and Thomas E. Terrill. *The American South: A History*. Vol. 2. Lanham, MD: Rowman & Littlefield, 2009.

Corry, Constance. "The Klan Hearings of 1921: A Triumph of One Interpretation of Americanism." *Melbourne Historical Journal* 15, no. 1 (1983): 86–107.

Costa, Robert, Sari Horwitz, and William Wan. "Man Arrested in Charleston Killings." *Washington Post*, June 19, 2015, A1.

Cox, Karen L. *Dreaming of Dixie: How the South Was Created in American Popular Culture*. Chapel Hill: University of North Carolina Press, 2011.

Cox, LaWanda Fenlason. *Lincoln and Black Freedom: A Study in Presidential Leadership*. Columbia: University of South Carolina, 1994 [1981].

———. "The Promise of Land for the Freedmen." *Mississippi Valley Historical Review* 45, no. 3 (December 1958): 413–40.

Crespino, Joseph. *Strom Thurmond's America*. New York: Hill and Wang, 2012.

Cronin, Morton. "Currier and Ives: A Content Analysis." *American Quarterly* 4, no. 4 (winter 1952): 317–30.

Cronon, E. David. *Black Moses: The Story of Marcus Garvey and the Universal Negro Improvement Association*. Madison: University of Wisconsin Press, 1969 [1955].

Croteau, David R., William D. Hoynes, and Stefania Milan. *Media/Society: Industries, Images, and Audiences*. 4th ed. Thousand Oaks, CA: Sage Publications, 2012.

Crouthamel, James L. "The Springfield Race Riot of 1908." *Journal of Negro History* 45, no. 3 (July 1960): 160–81.

Crow, Jeffrey J., and Robert Franklin Durden. *Maverick Republican in the Old North State: A Political Biography of Daniel L. Russell*. Baton Rouge: Louisiana State University Press, 1977.

Currell, Susan. *American Culture in the 1920s*. Edinburgh: Edinburgh University Press, 2009.

Curriden, Mark. "The Saga of the Scottsboro Boys Begins—March 25, 1931." *ABA Journal* 99, no. 3 (March 2013): 72.

Currie, David P. "The Reconstruction Congress." *University of Chicago Law Review* 75, no. 1 (2008): 383–495.

Cushman, Sean Dennis. *African-Americans and the Quest for Civil Rights, 1900–1990.* New York: New York University Press, 1991.

D'Orso, Michael. *Like Judgment Day: The Ruin and Redemption of a Town Called Rosewood.* New York: Putnam, 1996.

Dagnini, Jérémie Kroubo. "Marcus Garvey: A Controversial Figure in the History of Pan-Africanism." *Journal of Pan African Studies* 2, no. 3 (March 2008): 198–208.

Dailey, Jane. "The Sexual Politics of Race in World War II America." In *The Fog of War: The Second World War and the Civil Rights Movement,* edited by Kevin M. Kruse and Stephen Tuck, 145–70. New York: Oxford University Press, 2012.

Daly, John Patrick. *When Slavery Was Called Freedom: Evangelism, Proslavery, and the Causes of the Civil War.* Lexington: University Press of Kentucky, 2002.

Darity, William, Jr. "The Undesirables, America's Underclass in the Managerial Age: Beyond the Myrdal Theory of Racial Inequality." *Daedalus* 124, no. 1 (winter 1995): 145–65.

Dattel, Gene. "King Cotton." *New Criterion* 33, no. 2 (October 2014): 16–21.

Daubney, Kate. "Songbird or Subversive? Instrumental Vocalisation Technique in the Songs of Billie Holiday." *Journal of Gender Studies* 11, no. 1 (March 2002): 17–28.

Davis, David. "Not Only War Is Hell: World War I and African American Lynching Narratives." *African American Review* 42, no. 3 (fall/winter 2008): 477–91.

Davis, David Brion, and Steven Mintz. *The Boisterous Sea of Liberty: A Documentary History of America from Discovery through the Civil War.* New York: Oxford University Press, 1998.

Davis, Deborah. *Guest of Honor: Booker T. Washington, Theodore Roosevelt, and the White House Dinner That Shocked a Nation.* New York: Atria Books, 2012.

Davis, Harold E. *Henry Grady's New South: Atlanta, a Brave and Beautiful City.* Tuscaloosa: University of Alabama Press, 1990.

Davis, Thomas J. *Race Relations in the United States, 1940–1960.* Westport, CT: Greenwood Press, 2008.

Day, David S. "Herbert Hoover and Racial Politics: The DePriest Incident." *Journal of Negro History* 65, no. 1 (winter 1980): 6–17.

Dayan, Joan. "A Few Stories about Haiti, or, Stigma Revisited." *Research in African Literatures* 35, no. 2 (summer 2004): 157–72.

Dean, John W. *Warren G. Harding: The American Presidents Series: The 29th President, 1921–1923.* New York: Times Books, 2004.

Decker, Todd. *Show Boat: Performing Race in an American Musical.* New York: Oxford University Press, 2013.

Delgado-Tall, Sonia. "The New Negro Movement and the African Heritage in a Pan-Africanist Perspective." *Journal of Black Studies* 31, no. 3 (January 2001): 288–310.

Dessommes, Nancy Bishop. "Hollywood in Hoods: The Portrayal of the Ku Klux Klan in Popular Film." *Journal of Popular Culture* 32, no. 4 (spring 1999): 13–22.

"Detroit Watchful in 'Mop Up' of Riots." *New York Times*, June 28, 1943, 23.

Dewhirst, Robert E. *Encyclopedia of the United States Congress*. New York: Facts on File, 2006.

DeWitt, David Miller. *The Impeachment and Trial of Andrew Johnson, Seventeenth President of the United States: A History*. New York: MacMillan Company, 1903.

Dezenhall, Eric. *Glass Jaw: A Manifesto for Defending Fragile Reputations in an Age of Instant Scandal*. New York: Twelve Books, 2014.

Diallo, Kadiatou, with Craig Wolff. *My Heart Will Cross This Ocean: My Story, My Son, Amadou*. New York: One World/Ballantine, 2003.

Dill, Bonnie Thornton. *Across the Boundaries of Race and Class: An Exploration of Work and Family among Black Female Domestic Servants*. New York: Garland, 1994.

Dinnerstein, Leonard. *The Leo Frank Case*. Birmingham, AL: Notable Trials Library, 1991.

Dixon, Thomas, Jr. *The Clansman: An Historical Romance of the Ku Klux Klan*. New York: A. Wessels Company, 1907.

———. *The Leopard's Spots: A Romance of the White Man's Burden, 1865–1900*. New York: A. Wessels Company, 1906.

Donald, David Herbert. *Lincoln*. New York: Simon & Schuster, 1995.

———. *Lincoln Reconsidered: Essays on the Civil War Era*. 3rd ed. New York: Vintage Books, 2001.

Donovan, Frank. *Mr. Madison's Constitution: The Story behind the Constitutional Convention*. New York: Dodd Mead & Company, 1965.

Douglass, Frederick. *The Life and Times of Frederick Douglass, Written by Himself: His Early Life as a Slave, His Escape from Bondage, and His Complete History*. New York: Cosimo Classics, 2008 [1892].

———. *Narrative of the Life of Frederick Douglass, an American Slave*. Mineola, NY: Dover Publications, 1995 [1845].

Drago, Edmund L. *Hurrah for Hampton! Black Red Shirts in South Carolina during Reconstruction*. Fayetteville: University of Arkansas Press, 1998.

Dray, Philip. *At the Hands of Persons Unknown: The Lynching of Black America*. New York: Modern Library, 2003.

———. *Capitol Men: The Epic Story of Reconstruction through the Lives of the First Black Congressmen*. Boston: Houghton Mifflin, 2008.

Dreisinger, Baz. *Near Black: White-to-Black Passing in American Culture*. Amherst: University of Massachusetts Press, 2008.

Drowne, Kathleen, and Patrick Huber. *The 1920s: American Popular Culture through History*. Westport, CT: Greenwood Press, 2004.

Du Bois, W. E. B. "An Appeal to the World: A Statement of Denial of Human Rights to Minorities in the Case of Citizens of Negro Descent in the United States of America and an Appeal to the United Nations for Redress," BlackPast .org, October 1947, http://www.blackpast.org/1947-w-e-b-dubois-appeal -world-statement-denial-human-rights-minorities-case-citizens-n (accessed February 2015).

———. *The Souls of Black Folk: Essays and Sketches*. 8th ed. Chicago: A. C. Mc- Clurg & Company, 1909.

DuBose, Carla J. "World War II." In *Jim Crow: A Historical Encyclopedia of the American Mosaic*, edited by Nikki M. Brown and Barry M. Stentiford, 436–45. Santa Barbara, CA: ABC-CLIO, 2014.

Dunning, William Archibald. *Reconstruction, Political and Economic, 1865–1877.* The American Nation: A History 22. New York: Harper & Row, 1962 [1907].

DuRocher, Kristina. *Raising Racists: The Socialization of White Children in the Jim Crow South.* Lexington: University Press of Kentucky, 2011.

Dworkin, Ira, ed. *Daughter of the Revolution: The Major Nonfiction Works of Pauline E. Hopkins.* New Brunswick, NJ: Rutgers University Press, 2007.

———. "'Near the Congo': Langston Hughes and the Geopolitics of Internationalist Poetry." *American Literary History* 24, no. 4 (winter 2012): 631–57.

Dye, R. Thomas. "Rosewood, Florida: The Destruction of an African American Community." *Historian* 58, no. 3 (March 1996): 605–22.

Eburne, Jonathan P. "Garveyism and Its Involutions." *African American Review* 47, no. 1 (spring 2014): 1–19.

Edmonds, Helen G. *The Negro and Fusion Politics in North Carolina, 1894–1901.* Chapel Hill: University of North Carolina Press, 2003.

Egerton, Douglas R. *The Wars of Reconstruction: The Brief, Violent History of America's Most Progressive Era.* New York: Bloomsbury, 2014.

Eisenach, Eldon J. "Progressivism as a National Narrative in Biblical-Hegelian Times." *Social Philosophy & Policy* 24, no. 1 (January 2007): 55–83.

Ellis, Joseph J. *The Quartet: Orchestrating the Second American Revolution, 1783–1789.* New York: Knopf, 2015.

Ellsworth, Scott. *Death in a Promised Land: The Tulsa Race Riot of 1921.* Baton Rouge: Louisiana State University Press, 1992.

Elshtain, Jean Bethke. "A Return to Hull House: Reflections on Jane Addams." *Feminist Issues* 15, nos. 1–2 (March 1997): 105–13.

Ely, Melvin Patrick. *The Adventures of Amos 'n' Andy: A Social History of an American Phenomenon.* Charlottesville: University of Virginia Press, 2001.

Emberton, Carole. *Beyond Redemption: Race, Violence, and the American South after the Civil War.* Chicago: University of Chicago Press, 2013.

Emilio, Luis F. *A Brave Black Regiment: The History of the 54th Massachusetts, 1863–1865.* Cambridge, MA: Da Capo, 1995.

Etuk, Emma S., PhD. *From David Walker to Barack Obama: Ethiopianists as Keepers of the African Dream.* Bloomington, IN: iUniverse, 2011.

Etzemüller, Thomas. *Alva and Gunnar Myrdal: Social Engineering in the Modern World.* Lanham, MD: Lexington Books, 2014.

"Ex-Chief of Klan Free; 'I Am the Law' Stephenson Paroled after 30 Years." *New York Times*, December 23, 1956, 32.

"Ex-Dragon Must Face Girl's Serious Charge." *Atlanta Constitution*, April 12, 1925, B7.

"Excerpt from Report on Shooting of Unarmed Man." *New York Times*, July 28, 2000, B6.

Fabi, M. Giulia. "Desegregating the Future: Sutton E. Griggs' Pointing the Way and American Utopian Fiction in the Age of Jim Crow." *American Literary Realism* 44, no. 2 (winter 2012): 113–32.

Fairchild, Halford H., and Gloria Cowan. "The O.J. Simpson Trial: Challenges to Science and Society." *Journal of Social Issues* 53, no. 3 (fall 1997): 583–91.

Fausset, Richard. "Steeped in Racial History, Charleston Ponders Future after Massacre." *New York Times*, June 20, 2015, A12.

Fausset, Richard, and Alan Blinder. "Era Ends as South Carolina Lowers Confederate Flag." *New York Times*, July 11, 2015, A9.

Feldman, Glenn. *The Irony of the Solid South: Democrats, Republicans, and Race*. Tuscaloosa: University of Alabama Press, 2013.

———. *Politics, Society, and the Klan in Alabama, 1915–1949*. Tuscaloosa: University of Alabama Press, 1999.

Ferris, William R. "'My Idol Was Langston Hughes': The Poet, the Renaissance, and Their Enduring Influence." *Southern Cultures* 16, no. 2 (summer 2010): 53–71.

Ferris State Museum of Racist Memorabilia, "The Pickaninny Stereotype." Ferris State University, http://www.ferris.edu/jimcrow/picaninny (accessed February 2015).

"Filibuster Ended as Senate Shelves Anti-lynch Bill; Vote of 58 to 22 to Lay Measure Aside for Relief Bill Taken on Motion by Barkley." *New York Times*, February 22, 1938, 1, 5.

"Filibuster Waits on Barkley Move; Southern Group Hopes Senate Leader Will Ask Majority to Quit Contest." *New York Times*, January 30, 1938, 3.

"Finds Ex-Klan Head Murdered Woman; Indiana Jury Convicts Stephenson in Second Degree—Penalty Is 20 Years." *New York Times*, November 15, 1925, 1, 23.

Fingerhut, Eugene R. "Tom Watson, Blacks, and Southern Reform." *Georgia Historical Quarterly* 60, no. 4 (winter 1976): 324–43.

Finley, Cheryl. "Loïs Mailou Jones: Impressions of the South." *Southern Quarterly* 49, no. 1 (fall 2011): 80–93.

Finley, Keith M. *Delaying the Dream: Southern Senators and the Fight against Civil Rights, 1938–1965*. Baton Rouge: Louisiana State University Press, 2008.

Fischer, David Hackett. *Liberty and Freedom: A Visual History of America's Founding Ideas*. New York: Oxford University Press, 2005.

Fitzgerald, Michael W. *Splendid Failure: Postwar Reconstruction in the American South*. Chicago: Ivan R. Dee, 2008.

———. "'We Have Found a Moses': Theodore Bilbo, Black Nationalism, and the Greater Liberia Bill of 1939." *Journal of Southern History* 63, no. 2 (May 1997): 293–320.

Fleming, Cynthia Griggs. *In the Shadow of Selma: The Continuing Struggle for Civil Rights in the Rural South*. Lanham, MD: Rowman & Littlefield, 2004.

Fleming, Thomas J. "The Murder Trial of Dr. Ossian Sweet." *Ebony* 25, no. 12 (October 1970): 106–8, 110–12, 114.

Flood, Charles Bracelen. *1864: Lincoln at the Gates of History*. New York: Simon & Schuster, 2009.

"Florida Race Riot Has Seventh Victim." *New York Times*, January 7, 1923, S5.

Fogel, Robert William, and Stanley L. Engerman. *Time on the Cross: The Economics of American Negro Slavery*. New York: Little, Brown and Company, 1974.

Foley, Barbara. "The Color of Blood: John Brown, Jean Toomer, and the New Negro Movement." *African American Review* 46, nos. 2/3 (summer/fall 2013): 237–53.

———. *Spectres of 1919: Class and Nation in the Making of the New Negro*. Urbana: University of Illinois Press, 2003.

Foley, Megan. "Serializing Racial Suspects: The Stagnation and Suspense of the O.J. Simpson Saga." *Quarterly Journal of Speech* 96, no. 1 (February 2010): 69–88.

Foner, Eric. *The Fiery Trial: Abraham Lincoln and American Slavery*. New York: W. W. Norton, 2010.

———. *Forever Free: The Story of Emancipation and Reconstruction*. Illus. ed., with a commentary by Joshua Brown. New York: Knopf, 2005.

———. "Panel II: Reconstruction Revisited." *Columbia Law Review* 112, no. 7 (November 2012): 1585–606.

———. *Reconstruction: America's Unfinished Revolution: 1863–1877*. Francis Parkman Prize ed. New York: History Book Club, 2005 [1988].

———. "Reconstruction Revisited." *Reviews in American History* 10, no. 4 (December 1982): 82–100.

Ford, Wallace. "Reflections in Real-Time—the Sad Saga of Trayvon Martin and the Lessons from the Trial of George Zimmerman." *Black Renaissance/Renaissance Noire* 13, nos. 2/3 (fall 2013): 58–61.

Foster, Frances Smith. *Witnessing Slavery: The Development of Ante-Bellum Slave Narratives*. Madison: University of Wisconsin Press, 1979.

Francis, Megan Ming. *Civil Rights and the Making of the Modern American State*. Cambridge: Cambridge University Press, 2014.

Franklin, John Hope. *Reconstruction after the Civil War*. Chicago: University of Chicago Press, 1961.

Frederickson, George M. "Masters and Mudsills: The Role of Race in the Planter Ideology of South Carolina." *South Atlantic Urban Studies* 2, no. 1 (1978): 34–48.

Fry, Gladys-Marie. *Night Riders in Black Folk History*. Knoxville: University of Tennessee Press, 1975.

Frydman, Jason. "Zora Neale Hurston, Biographical Criticism, and African Diasporic Vernacular Culture." *MELUS* 34, no. 4 (winter 2009): 99–118.

Fryer, Roland G., Jr., and Steven D. Levitt. "Hatred and Profits: Under the Hood of the Ku Klux Klan." *Quarterly Journal of Economics* 127, no. 4 (November 2012): 1883–925.

Gaston, Paul M. *The New South Creed: A Study in Southern Mythmaking*. Montgomery, AL: New South Books, 2012 [1970].

Gates, Henry Louis, Jr., ed. *Lincoln on Race and Slavery*. Princeton, NJ: Princeton University Press, 2009.

"Gateway Album: Marcus Garvey's 'Conspiracy of the East St. Louis Riots.'" *Gateway Heritage: The Magazine of the Missouri Historical Society* 19, no. 1 (summer 1998): 40–45.

Genovese, Eugene D. *From Rebellion to Revolution: Afro-American Slave Revolts in the Making of the Modern World*. Baton Rouge: Louisiana State University Press, 1992 [1979].

———. *Roll, Jordan, Roll: The World the Slaves Made*. New York: Vintage Books, 1976.

Genovese, Michael A. *The Power of the American Presidency, 1789–2000*. New York: Oxford University Press, 2001.

Gibson, Ernest L., III. "The Envy of Erudition: Booker T. Washington and the Desire for a Du Boisian Intellectuality." *Black Scholar* 43, no. 1/2 (spring 2013): 52–68.

Gildersleeve, Shanna. "The Struggle for Justice: How the Media Convicted and Freed the 'Scottsboro Boys,' 1931–1937." *Atlanta Review of Journalism History* 8, no. 1 (September 2009): 90–113.

Gill, Jonathan. *Harlem: The Four Hundred Year History from Dutch Village to Capital of Black America.* New York: Grove Press, 2011.

Gillespie, Andra. *The New Black Politician: Cory Booker, Newark, and Post-racial America.* New York: New York University Press, 2012.

———. "Red, White, and Black: Three Generations of African American Politicians." *Washington Monthly* 45, nos. 1/2 (January/February 2013): 64–66.

Gillespie, Michele K., and Randall L. Hall. "Introduction." In *Thomas Dixon Jr. and the Birth of Modern America,* edited by Michele K. Gillespie and Randall L. Hall, 1–22. Baton Rouge: Louisiana State University Press, 2006.

Gilmore, Scott. "Freddie Gray, the Day after the Night." *Maclean's* 128, no. 18 (May 11, 2015): 42.

Gioia, Ted. *The History of Jazz.* New York: Oxford University Press, 2011.

Glaser, James M. *Race, Campaign Politics, and the Realignment in the South.* New Haven, CT: Yale University Press, 1996.

Godshalk, David Fort. *Veiled Visions: The 1906 Atlanta Race Riot and the Reshaping of American Race Relations.* Chapel Hill: University of North Carolina Press, 2005.

Goings, Kenneth. "Aunt Jemima and Uncle Mose Travel the USA: The Marketing of Memory through Tourist Souvenirs." *International Journal of Hospitality & Tourism Administration* 2, nos. 3/4 (2001): 131–61.

Goldenweiser, A. A. "The Principle of Limited Possibilities in the Development of Culture." *Journal of American Folklore* 26, no. 101 (July/September 1913): 259–90.

Goldfield, David R. *Black, White, and Southern: Race Relations and Southern Culture, 1940 to the Present.* Baton Rouge: Louisiana State University Press, 1990.

Goldman, Robert M. *Reconstruction and Black Suffrage: Losing the Vote in Reese and Cruikshank.* Lawrence: University Press of Kansas, 2001.

Goldstein, Joseph, and Nate Schweber. "Man's Death after Chokehold Raises Old Issue for Police." *New York Times,* July 19, 2014, A1.

Goldstein, Robert Paul. "The Dyer Anti-lynching Bill: Movement for Federal Control of Lynching, 1900–1922." MA thesis, University of Wisconsin, 1966.

Goldstone, Lawrence. *Inherently Unequal: The Betrayal of Equal Rights by the Supreme Court, 1865–1903.* New York: Walker Publishing Company, 2011.

Goodman, James. *Stories of Scottsboro.* New York: Doubleday, 1995.

Goodwin, Doris Kearns. *The Bully Pulpit: Theodore Roosevelt, William Howard Taft, and the Golden Age of Journalism.* New York: Simon & Schuster, 2013.

———. *Team of Rivals: The Political Genius of Abraham Lincoln.* New York: Simon & Schuster, 2005.

Goodwyn, Lawrence. *Democratic Promise: The Populist Movement in America.* New York: Oxford University Press, 1976.

———. *The Populist Movement: A Short History of the Agrarian Revolt in America.* New York: Oxford University Press, 1978.

Gordon-Reed, Annette. *The Hemingses of Monticello.* New York: W. W. Norton, 2008.

Gordon, Fon Louise. *Caste and Class: The Black Experience in Arkansas, 1880–1920.* Athens: University of Georgia Press, 2007.

Gormley, Ken. "Justice Thurgood Marshall." *ABA Journal* 78, no. 1 (June 1992): 62–66.

Gould, Lewis L. *Grand Old Party: A History of the Republicans*. New York: Random House, 2003.

Graczyk, Michael. "Supremacist Executed in Texas." *Newsday*, September 22, 2011, A52.

"Graduates of Cornell Will Aid Leo M. Frank in Fight for Life." *Atlanta Constitution*, August 31, 1913, 2.

Gramm, Marshall, and Phil Gramm. "The Free Silver Movement in America: A Reinterpretation." *Journal of Economic History* 64, no. 4 (December 2004): 1108–29.

Grant, Colin. *Negro with a Hat: The Rise and Fall of Marcus Garvey and His Dream of Mother Africa*. New York: Oxford University Press, 2008.

Grant-Thomas, Andrew, and Gary Orfield, eds. *Twenty-First Century Color Lines: Multiracial Change in Contemporary America*. Philadelphia: Temple University Press, 2009.

Graves, Earl G., Jr. "When Will Police Stop Murdering Unarmed Black Men?," *Black Enterprise* 45, no. 2 (September 2014): 8.

Gray, Katti. "Moms on a Mission." *Essence* 45, no. 8 (December 2014): 102–5.

Green, Michael S. *Freedom, Union, and Power: Lincoln and His Party during the Civil War*. New York: Fordham University Press, 2004.

Greenberg, Cheryl Lynn. *To Ask for an Equal Chance: African Americans in the Great Depression*. Lanham, MD: Rowman & Littlefield, 2009.

Gregory, James N. *The Southern Diaspora: How the Great Migrations of Black and White Southerners Transformed America*. Chapel Hill: University of North Carolina Press, 2005.

Grier, Kevin B., and Michael C. Munger. "The Impact of Legislator Attributes on Interest-Group Campaign Contributions." *Journal of Labor Research* 7, no. 4 (fall 1986): 349–61.

Griffin, Johnnie. "Aunt Jemima: Another Image, Another Viewpoint." *Journal of Religious Thought* 54/55, nos. 1/2 (spring/fall 1998): 75–77.

Grimsley, Mark. "Wars for the American South: The First and Second Reconstructions Considered as Insurgencies." *Civil War History* 58, no. 1 (March 2012): 6–36.

Grossman, James R. *Land of Hope: Chicago, Black Southerners, and the Great Migration*. Chicago: University of Chicago Press, 1989.

Guelzo, Allen C. *Fateful Lightning: A New History of the Civil War and Reconstruction*. New York: Oxford University Press, 2012.

———. *Lincoln's Emancipation Proclamation: The End of Slavery in America*. New York: Simon & Schuster, 2006.

Guinn v. United States, 238 U.S. 347 (1915).

Haggard, Nicole A. "The Birth of the Black Rapist: The 'Brutal Black Buck' in American Culture." In *A History of Evil in Popular Culture: What Hannibal Lecter, Stephen King, and Vampires Reveal about America*, edited by Sharon Packer and Jody Pennington, 1:83–94. Santa Barbara, CA: ABC-CLIO, 2014.

Hagood, Taylor. "'Prodjickin,' or Mekin' a Present to Yo' Fam'ly': Rereading Empowerment in Thomas Nelson Page's Frame Narratives." *Mississippi Quarterly* 57, no. 3 (summer 2004): 423–39.

Hahn, Steven. *A Nation under Our Feet: Black Political Struggles in the Rural South from Slavery to the Great Migration*. Cambridge, MA: Belknap Press of Harvard University Press, 2005.

Hair, William Ivy. *The Kingfish and His Realm: The Life and Times of Huey P. Long*. Baton Rouge: Louisiana State University Press, 1991.

Halbrook, Stephen P. *Freedmen, the Fourteenth Amendment, and the Right to Bear Arms, 1866–1876*. Westport, CT: Praeger, 1998.

Hall v. DeCuir, 95 U.S. 485 (1878).

Halloran, Fiona Deans. *Thomas Nast: The Father of Modern Political Cartoons*. Chapel Hill: University of North Carolina Press, 2012.

Hamilton, Kendra. "The Strange Career of Uncle Tom." *Black Issues in Higher Education* 19, no. 8 (June 6, 2002): 22–27.

Hammond, John Craig. *Slavery, Freedom and Expansion in the Early American West*. Charlottesville: University of Virginia Press, 2007.

———. "'They Are Very Much Interested in Obtaining an Unlimited Slavery': Rethinking the Expansion of Slavery in the Louisiana Territories, 1803–1805." *Journal of the Early Republic* 23, no. 3 (fall 2003): 353–80.

Hansen, Bradley A. "The Fable of the Allegory: The Wizard of Oz in Economics." *Journal of Economic Education* 33, no. 3 (summer 2002): 254–64.

Harding, Warren G. *Address of the President of the United States of America at the Celebration of the Semicentennial of the Founding of the City of Birmingham, Alabama, October 26, 1921*. Washington, DC: Government Printing Office, 1921.

Harlan, Louis R. *Booker T. Washington in Perspective: Essays of Louis R. Harlan*. Edited by Raymond W. Smock. Jackson: University Press of Mississippi, 1988.

"Harlem Is Orderly with Heavy Guard Ready for Trouble." *New York Times*, August 3, 1943, 1, 10.

"Harlem's Tragedy." *New York Times*, August 3, 1943, 18.

Harley, Sharon. "For the Good of Family and Race: Gender, Work, and Domestic Roles in the Black Community, 1880–1930." *Signs* 15, no. 2 (winter 1990): 336–49.

Harrell, David Edwin, Edwin S. Gaustad, John B. Boles, Sally Foreman Griffith, Randall M. Miller, and Randall B. Woods. *Unto a Good Land: A History of the American People*. Vol. 1. Cambridge, UK: William B. Eerdmans Publishing Company, 2005.

Harrell, Willie J., Jr., ed. *We Wear the Mask: Paul Laurence Dunbar and the Politics of Representative Reality*. Kent, OH: Kent State University Press, 2010.

Harris, Cheryl I. "Symposium: Race Jurisprudence and the Supreme Court: Where Do We Go from Here? In the Shadow of *Plessy*." *University of Pennsylvania Journal of Constitutional Law* 7, no. 3 (February 2005): 867–901.

Harris, Joel Chandler. *The Works of Joel Chandler Harris: Uncle Remus*. New York: McKinlay, Stone & Mackenzie, 1908.

Harris, William C. *With Charity for All: Lincoln and the Restoration of the Union*. Lexington: University Press of Kentucky, 1999.

Harris, William H. *The Harder We Run: Black Workers since the Civil War*. New York: Oxford University Press, 1982.

Harris, Wilmer Carlyle. *Public Life of Zachariah Chandler, 1851–1875*. Lansing: Michigan Historical Commission, 1917.

Harrison, Robert. "New Representations of a 'Misrepresented Bureau': Reflections on Recent Scholarship on the Freedmen's Bureau." *American Nineteenth Century History* 8, no. 2 (June 2007): 205–29.

Hart, Robert C. "Black-White Literary Relations in the Harlem Renaissance." *American Literature* 44, no. 4 (January 1973): 612–28.

Hartman, Saidiya V. *Scenes of Subjection: Terror, Slavery, and Self-Making in Nineteenth-Century America*. New York: Oxford University Press, 1997.

Harvey, Philip. "Learning from the New Deal." *Review of Black Political Economy* 39, no. 1 (March 2012): 87–105.

Harvey, William Burnett. "Constitutional Law: Anti-lynching Legislation." *Michigan Law Review* 47, no. 3 (January 1949): 369–77.

Hasday, Judy L. *The Civil Rights Act of 1964: An End to Racial Segregation*. New York: Chelsea House, 2007.

Hasian, Marouf, Jr., and Lisa A. Flores. "Mass Mediated Representations of the Susan Smith Trial." *Howard Journal of Communications* 11, no. 3 (July/September 2000): 163–78.

Hassett-Walker, Connie. "Race, Social Class, Communication, and Accusations: The Duke University Lacrosse Team Party." *Journal of Ethnicity in Criminal Justice* 10, no. 4 (October/December 2012): 267–94.

Haun, Harry. "*Fruitvale Station*: Date with Destiny." *Film Journal International* 116, no. 8 (August 2013): 10–12.

Havig, Alan. "Richard F. Outcault's 'Poor Lil' Mose': Variations on the Black Stereotype in American Comic Art." *Journal of American Culture* 11, no. 1 (spring 1988): 33–41.

Hayes, Floyd W., III. "The Paradox of the Ethical Criminal in Richard Wright's Novel *The Outsider*: A Philosophical Investigation." *Black Renaissance/Renaissance Noire* 13, no. 1 (spring/summer 2013): 162–71.

Haynes, Robert V. *A Night of Violence: The Houston Riot of 1917*. Baton Rouge: Louisiana State University Press, 1976.

Healey, James Sean. *When I Was Not My Brother's Keeper: When Fear, Hate and Prejudice Administer the Law*. Charleston, SC: BookSurge Publishing, 2007.

Hemmens, Craig. "American Skin: The Duke LaCrosse Rape Scandal and the Intersection of Race, Class, Gender, and Injustice." *American Journal of Criminal Justice* 33, no. 2 (October 2008): 297–306.

Hennessy-Fiske, Molly. "Texas Executes Participant in Black Man's Dragging Death; the Racist 1998 Killing of James Byrd Jr. Helped Inspire Federal Hate-Crime Legislation." *Los Angeles Times*, September 22, 2011, AA2.

Henry, Robert Selph. *The Story of Reconstruction*. New York: Konecky & Konecky, 1999.

Hesseltine, William B. *Lincoln's Plan of Reconstruction*. Chicago: Quadrangle Books, 1967.

Hicks, Darrin. "33. Unreasonable Force: Image Schemas in the *New York Times* Coverage of the Sean Bell Shooting." In *Conference Proceedings—National Communication Association/American Forensic Association (Alta Conference on Argumentation)*, Alta, Utah, 2007, 346–54.

Hicks, John D. *Populist Revolt: A History of the Farmers' Alliance and the People's Party*. Minneapolis: University of Minnesota Press, 1931.

Hild, Matthew. *Greenbackers, Knights of Labor, and Populists: Farmer-Labor Insurgency in the Late-Nineteenth-Century South.* Athens: University of Georgia Press, 2007.

Hill, Robert A., ed. *The Marcus Garvey Universal Negro Improvement Association Papers.* Vol. 1: *1826–August 1919.* Berkeley: University of California Press, 1983.

Hilmes, Michelle. "Invisible Men: *Amos 'n' Andy* and the Roots of Broadcast Discourse." *Critical Studies in Mass Communication* 10, no. 4 (December 1993): 301–21.

Hirsch, James S. *Riot and Remembrance: America's Worst Race Riot and Its Legacy.* Boston: Houghton Mifflin, 2002.

Hofstadter, Richard. *The Age of Reform: From Bryan to F.D.R.* New York: Vintage Books, 1955.

———. *The American Political Tradition and the Men Who Made It.* New York: Vintage Books, 1989 [1948].

Hogan, David W., Jr. "Head and Heart: The Dilemmas of American Attitudes toward War." *Journal of Military History* 75, no. 4 (October 2011): 1021–54.

Holder, Eric. "We Should Have an Open Dialogue on Race: Concerning Race We Have Always Been a Nation of Cowards." *Vital Speeches of the Day* 75, no. 4 (April 2009): 164–66.

Hollis, Daniel W. "Coleman Blease: The Years between the Governorship and the Senate, 1915–1925." *South Carolina Historical Magazine* 80, no. 1 (January 1979): 1–17.

———. "'Cotton Ed Smith': Showman or Statesman?," *South Carolina Historical Magazine* 71, no. 4 (October 1970): 235–56.

Holloman, James A. "Rejecting League, Harding Pleads for Treaty; 'Irreconcilables' Are Disappointed in First Message." *Atlanta Constitution*, April 13, 1921, 1, 9.

Holloway, Vanessa A. *Getting Away with Murder: The Twentieth-Century Struggle for Civil Rights in the U.S. Senate.* Lanham, MD: University Press of America, 2015.

Holt, Thomas. *Black over White: Negro Political Leadership in South Carolina during Reconstruction.* Urbana: University of Illinois Press, 1977.

Holtzman, Linda, and Leon Sharpe. *Media Messages: What Film, Television, and Popular Music Teach Us about Race, Class, Gender, and Sexual Orientation.* London: Routledge, 2015.

Holzer, Harold. "A Promise Fulfilled." *Civil War Times* 48, no. 6 (December 2009): 28–35.

———. *Lincoln: How Abraham Lincoln Ended Slavery in America.* New York: Newmarket Press, 2012.

Homan, Lynn M., and Thomas Reilly. *Black Knights: The Story of the Tuskegee Airmen.* Gretna, LA: Pelican Publishing Company, 2001.

Hoogenboom, Ari. *The Presidency of Rutherford B. Hayes.* Lawrence: University Press of Kansas, 1988.

Horn, Stanley F. *Invisible Empire: The Story of the Ku Klux Klan, 1866–1871.* Montclair, NJ: Patterson Smith, 1969.

Hornbeck, Richard. "The Enduring Impact of the American Dust Bowl: Short- and Long-Run Adjustments to Environmental Catastrophe." *American Environmental Review* 102, no. 4 (June 2012): 1477–507.

Horne, Gerald. *W. E. B. Du Bois: A Biography*. Santa Barbara, CA: Greenwood Press, 2010.

Horton, James Oliver, and Lois E. Horton. *Slavery and the Making of America*. New York: Oxford University Press, 2005.

Hossfeld, Leslie H. *Narrative, Political Unconscious, and Racial Violence in Wilmington, North Carolina*. London: Routledge, 2004.

Hovenkamp, Herbert. "Social Science and Segregation before *Brown*." *Duke Law Journal* 1985, nos. 3/4 (June/September 1985): 624–72.

Hubbard, LaRese. "Frances Ellen Watkins Harper: Proto-Africana Womanist." *Western Journal of Black Studies* 36, no. 1 (winter 2012): 68–75.

Hubbs, Jolene. "Goophering Jim Crow: Charles Chesnutt's 1890s America." *American Literary Realism* 46, no. 1 (fall 2013): 12–26.

Huggins, Nathan Irvin. *Harlem Renaissance*. New York: Oxford University Press, 2007 [1971].

Huston, James L. "Reconstruction as It Should Have Been: An Exercise in Counterfactual History." *Civil War History* 51, no. 4 (December 2005): 358–63.

Hyman, Harold M. *The Radical Republicans and Reconstruction, 1861–1870*. Indianapolis: Bobbs-Merrill, 1967.

In Re Slaughterhouse Cases, 83 U.S. 36 (1872).

Inge, M. Thomas. "Walt Disney's *Song of the South* and the Politics of Animation." *Journal of American Culture* 35, no. 3 (September 2012): 219–30.

"'Intolerable,' Says Deneen: Governor Says He Will Protect Every Citizen and His Property." *New York Times*, August 16, 1908, 3.

Ioanide, Paula. "The Story of Abner Louima: Cultural Fantasies, Gendered Racial Violence, and the Ethical Witness." *Journal of Haitian Studies* 13, no. 1 (spring 2007): 4–26.

Jackson, Blyden. "George Moses Horton, North Carolinian." *North Carolina Historical Review* 53, no. 2 (April 1976): 140–47.

Jackson, Charles O. "William J. Simmons: A Career in Ku Kluxism." *Georgia Historical Quarterly* 50, no. 4 (December 1966): 351–65.

Jackson, Kenneth T. *The Ku Klux Klan in the City, 1915–1930*. Chicago: Ivan R. Dee, 1967.

Jackson, Walter A. *Gunnar Myrdal and America's Conscience: Social Engineering and Racial Liberalism, 1938–1987*. Chapel Hill: University of North Carolina Press, 1994.

Janken, Kenneth Robert. *Walter White: Mr. NAACP*. Chapel Hill: University of North Carolina Press, 2006.

Jarenski, Shelly. "Invisibility Embraced: The Abject as a Site of Agency in Ellison's *Invisible Man*." *MELUS* 35, no. 4 (winter 2010): 85–109.

Jarman, Baird. "The Graphic Art of Thomas Nast: Politics and Prosperity in Postbellum Publishing." *American Periodicals: A Journal of History, Criticism, and Bibliography* 20, no. 2 (2010): 156–89.

Jayne, Allen. *Lincoln and the American Manifesto*. Amherst, NY: Prometheus Books, 2007.

Jeansonne, Glen. "Challenge to the New Deal: Huey P. Long and the Redistribution of National Wealth." *Louisiana History* 21, no. 4 (autumn 1980): 331–39.

———. "Huey Long and Racism." *Louisiana History* 33, no. 3 (summer 1992): 265–82.

Jefferson, Thomas. *Notes on the State of Virginia*. Edited by William Peden. Chapel Hill: University of North Carolina Press, 1954.

Jensen, Merrill. *The Articles of Confederation: An Interpretation of the Social-Constitutional History of the American Revolution, 1774–1781*. Madison: University of Wisconsin Press, 1963.

Johnson, Brett. "Ryan Coogler's Gripping Film, *Fruitvale Station*, Traces the Last Day of Oscar Grant's Young Life." *Essence* 44, no. 4 (August 2013): 56.

Johnson, Keith V., and Elwood Watson. "The W. E. B. Du Bois and Booker T. Washington Debate: Effects upon African American Roles in Engineering and Engineering Technology." *Journal of Technology Studies* 30, no. 4 (fall 2004): 65–70.

Johnson, Mark M. "Loïs Mailou Jones: A Life in Vibrant Color." *Art & Activities* 150, no. 2 (October 2011): 20–22.

Johnson, Nicholas. *Negroes and the Gun: The Black Tradition of Arms*. Amherst, NY: Prometheus Books, 2014.

Joint Congressional Committee on Inaugural Ceremonies. *Inaugural Addresses of the Presidents of the United States*. New York: Cosimo Classics, 2008.

Jones, Bradley K. "The Gravity of Administrative Discharges: A Legal and Empirical Evaluation." *Military Law Review* 59, no. 1 (winter 1973): 1–26.

Jones, Jacqueline. *A Dreadful Deceit: The Myth of Race from the Colonial Era to Obama's America*. New York: Basic Books, 2015.

Jones, Jeff. "Brawley and Others: Justice in the Hudson Valley." *Nation* 246, no. 11 (March 19, 1988): 376–78.

Jonsson, Patrik. "Trayvon Martin's Mom: It Was My Son Screaming." *Christian Science Monitor*, July 5, 2013, 10.

"Jury Convicts Three New York City Cops in Abner Louima Torture Case." *Jet* 97, no. 15 (March 20, 2000): 52.

Kaczorowski, Robert J. "Federal Enforcement of Civil Rights during the First Reconstruction." *Fordham Urban Law Journal* 23 (fall 1995): 155–86.

———. *The Politics of Judicial Interpretation, the Federal Courts, Department of Justice and Civil Rights, 1866–1876*. Dobbs Ferry, NY: Ocean Publications, 1985.

Kalush, William, and Larry Sloman. *The Secret Life of Houdini: The Making of America's First Superhero*. New York: Atria Books, 2006.

Kane, Joseph Nathan. *Facts about the Presidents: A Compilation of Biographical and Historical Data*. New York: Ace Books, 1976.

Kantrowitz, Stephen. "Ben Tillman and Hendrix McLane, Agrarian Rebels: White Manhood, 'The Farmers,' and the Limits of Southern Populism." *Journal of Southern History* 66, no. 3 (August 2000): 497–524.

———. *Ben Tillman and the Reconstruction of White Supremacy*. Chapel Hill: University of North Carolina Press, 2000.

Karst, Kenneth L. "*Moore v. Demsey*, 261 U.S. 86 (1923)." In *Encyclopedia of the American Constitution*, edited by Leonard W. Levy and Kenneth L. Karst, 4: 1757–58. Detroit: MacMillan Reference USA, 2000.

Kazin, Michael. *A Godly Hero: The Life of William Jennings Bryan*. New York: Knopf, 2006.

Keegan, John. *The American Civil War: A Military History*. New York: Knopf, 2009.

Keith, LeAnna. *The Colfax Massacre: The Untold Story of Black Power, White Terror, and the Death of Reconstruction*. New York: Oxford University Press, 2008.

Kennedy, David M., and Thomas A. Bailey. *The American Spirit: United States History as Seen by Contemporaries*. 13th ed. Boston: Cengage, 2016.

Kennedy, Randall. *Nigger: The Strange Career of a Troublesome Word*. New York: Pantheon Books, 2002.

Kern-Foxworth, Marilyn. *Aunt Jemima, Uncle Ben, and Rastus: Blacks in Advertising, Yesterday, Today, and Tomorrow*. Westport, CT: Greenwood Press, 1994.

Kilgore, John. "Reparations: Don't Go There." *Vocabula Review* 16, no. 7 (July 2014): 1–14.

"Kill Six in Florida; Burn Negro Houses." *New York Times*, January 6, 1923, 1.

King, Gilbert. *Devil in the Grove: Thurgood Marshall, the Groveland Boys, and the Dawn of a New America*. New York: HarperCollins, 2012.

King, Joe J. "The Farm Security Administration and Its Attack on Rural Poverty." *Rural Sociology* 7, no. 2 (June 1942): 155–61.

King, Kendra A. *African American Politics*. Malden, MA: Polity Press, 2010.

Kirk, John. "The Long Road to Equality." *History Today* 59, no. 2 (February 2009): 52–58.

"Klan Figure Free in a 1925 Murder; Was Serving Life Sentence—Once Boasted He Was 'the Law in Indiana.'" *New York Times*, December 22, 1956, 10.

"Klan's Big Rally Ends with Oratory: Speakers Denounce Jews, Scientists, Bootleggers and Newspapers." *New York Times*, August 10, 1925, 26.

"Klan's Ex-Dragon Held for Murder." *New York Times*, April 19, 1925, 15.

Klarman, Michael J. *From Jim Crow to Civil Rights: The Supreme Court and the Struggle for Equality*. New York: Oxford University Press, 2004.

———. "Scottsboro." *Marquette Law Review* 93, no. 2 (winter 2009): 379–432.

Knauer, Christine. *Let Us Fight as Free Men: Black Soldiers and Civil Rights*. Philadelphia: University of Pennsylvania Press, 2014.

Knoll, Corina. "Hundreds Rally for Black Man Killed by Police; They March through Downtown L.A. to Protest the Fatal Shooting of Ezell Ford." *Los Angeles Times*, August 18, 2014, AA1.

Kroeber, A. L. *The Nature of Culture*. Chicago: University of Chicago Press, 1952.

Krugman, Paul. *The Conscience of a Liberal*. New York: W. W. Norton, 2009.

Kruse, Kevin M. *White Flight: Atlanta and the Making of Modern Conservatism*. Princeton, NJ: Princeton University Press, 2013.

Lacy, Leslie Alexander. *Cheer the Lonesome Traveler: The Life of W. E. B. Du Bois*. New York: Dial Press, 1970.

Langguth, A. J. *After Lincoln: How the North Won the Civil War and Lost the Peace*. New York: Simon & Schuster, 2014.

"Last Negro Homes Razed in Rosewood." *New York Times*, January 8, 1923, 4.

Lawrence, Wendy Y., Benjamin Bates, and Mark Cervenka. "Politics Drawn in Black and White." *Journalism History* 40, no. 3 (fall 2014): 138–47.

Le Beau, Bryan F. "African Americans in Currier and Ives's America: The Darktown Series." *Journal of American & Comparative Cultures* 23, no. 1 (spring 2000): 71–83.

Lears, Jackson. *Rebirth of a Nation: The Making of Modern America, 1877–1920.* New York: HarperCollins, 2009.

LeForge, Judy Bussell. "Alabama's Colored Conventions and the Exodus Movement, 1871–1879." *Alabama Review* 63, no. 1 (January 2010): 32–46.

"Legislation Tied Up: Wagner's Sudden Move to Act on Anti-lynch Bill Stirs Tempest." *New York Times,* August 12, 1937, 1, 4.

Lehman, Christopher P. *The Colored Cartoon: Black Representation in American Animated Short Films, 1907–1954.* Amherst: University of Massachusetts Press, 2008.

Leiter, Andrew B. *In the Shadow of the Black Beast: African American Masculinity in the Harlem and Southern Renaissances.* Baton Rouge: Louisiana State University Press, 2010.

Lemann, Nicholas. *The Promised Land: The Great Migration and How It Changed America.* New York: Knopf, 1991.

———. *Redemption: The Last Battle of the Civil War.* New York: Farrar, Straus & Giroux, 2006.

Len-Rios, Maria E. "Image Repair Strategies, Local News Portrayals and Crisis Stage: A Case Study of Duke University's Lacrosse Team Crisis." *International Journal of Strategic Communication* 4, no. 2 (September 2010): 267–87.

"Leo Frank's Fate Up to Gov. Slaton as Final Arbiter." *Atlanta Constitution,* May 11, 1915, 1.

Lesher, Stephan. *George Wallace: American Populist.* Cambridge, MA: Da Capo, 1995.

Lester, Neal A. "Can a 'Last Comic Standing' Finally Rescue Little Black Sambo from the Jungle?," *Valley Voices: A Literary Review* 10, no. 2 (fall 2010): 60–97.

Leuchtenburg, William E. *The White House Looks South: Franklin D. Roosevelt, Harry S. Truman, and Lyndon B. Johnson.* Baton Rouge: Louisiana State University Press, 2005.

Levander, Caroline Field. "Sutton Griggs and the Borderlands of Empire." *American Literary History* 22, no. 1 (spring 2010): 57–84.

Lewinson, Paul. *Race, Class, and Party: A History of Negro Suffrage and White Politics in the South.* New York: Grosset & Dunlap, 1965.

Lewis, David Levering. *W. E. B. Du Bois: A Biography, 1868–1963.* New York: Henry Holt, 2009.

Lincoln, Abraham. *Abraham Lincoln Papers at the Library of Congress.* Washington, DC: Library of Congress, Manuscript Division, American Memory Project, 1959. Available at http://memory.loc.gov/ammem/alhtml/malhome.html (accessed November 2013).

Littlefield, Henry M. "The Wizard of Oz: Parable on Populism." *American Quarterly* 16, no. 1 (spring 1964): 47–58.

Litwack, Leon F. *Been in the Storm So Long: The Aftermath of Slavery.* New York: Vintage Books, 1979.

———. *Trouble in Mind: Black Southerners in the Age of Jim Crow.* New York: Knopf, 1998.

Livingstone, David. "The Emancipation Proclamation, the Declaration of Independence, and the Presidency: Lincoln's Model of Statesmanship." *Perspectives on Political Science* 28, no. 4 (fall 1999): 203–10.

Logan, Rayford W. *The Betrayal of the Negro: From Rutherford B. Hayes to Woodrow Wilson.* Cambridge, MA: Da Capo Press, 1997 [1965].

———. "Introduction." In *The Life and Times of Frederick Douglass* by Frederick Douglass, v–xii. Mineola, NY: Dover Publications, 2003.

Longacre, Edward G. *Gentleman and Soldier: A Biography of Wade Hampton III.* Lincoln: Bison Books, University of Nebraska Press, 2009.

Lorensen, Jutta. "Between Image and Word, Color, and Time: Jacob Lawrence's *The Migration Series.*" *African American Review* 40, no. 3 (fall 2006): 571–86.

Louisville, New Orleans, and Texas Railway Company v. Mississippi, 133 U.S. 587 (1890).

Loury, Glenn C. "Ferguson Won't Change Anything. What Will?," *Boston Review* 40, no. 1 (January/February 2015): 14–30.

Lovett, Ian. "3 Shots from Police Killed Los Angeles Man, Autopsy Finds." *New York Times,* December 30, 2014, A12.

Lowie, Robert H. *The History of Ethnological Theory.* New York: Holt, Rinehart and Winston, 1937.

Lumpkins, Charles L. *American Pogrom: The East St. Louis Race Riot and Black Politics.* Athens: Ohio University Press, 2008.

Lyman, Stanford M. "Gunnar Myrdal's *An American Dilemma* after a Half Century: Critics and Anticritics." *International Journal of Politics, Culture and Society* 12, no. 2 (winter 1998): 327–89.

"Lynch Bill Is Set for Action in 1938: Wagner Agrees to Delay as Filibuster Threat Imperils Administration Program." *New York Times,* August 13, 1937, 6.

"Lynching in the North." *America* 53, no. 6 (May 18, 1935): 123.

"Lynching of Leo Frank Denounced by Daniels." *Atlanta Constitution,* August 18, 1915, 3.

Mackie, Liz. *The Great Marcus Garvey.* Hertford, UK: Hansib Publications, 2008.

MacLean, Nancy. *Behind the Mask of Chivalry: The Making of the Second Ku Klux Klan.* New York: Oxford University Press, 1994.

———. "The Leo Frank Case Reconsidered: Gender and Sexual Politics in the Making of Reactionary Populism." *Journal of American History* 78, no. 3 (December 1991): 917–48.

Macune, Charles W., Jr. "The Wellsprings of a Populist: Dr. C. W. Macune before 1886." *Southwestern Historical Quarterly* 90, no. 2 (October 1986): 139–58.

Maddox, Alton H., Jr. "Setting the Record Straight in the Brawley Case." *New York Amsterdam News* 92, no. 15 (April 12–18, 2001): 13.

Madigan, Tim. *The Burning: Massacre, Destruction, and the Tulsa Race Riot of 1921.* New York: Thomas Dunne Books, 2001.

Magdol, Edward. *Owen Lovejoy: Abolitionist in Congress.* New Brunswick, NJ: Rutgers University Press, 1967.

Maine, Stephen. "Inside the Harlem Renaissance: A Leading Illustrator for the New Negro Movement in the 1920s, Aaron Douglas Is the Focus of a Traveling Exhibition Now at New York's Schomburg Center." *Art in America* 96, no. 9 (October 2008): 154–57.

Manglitz, Elaine, PhD, Talmadge C. Guy, EdD, and Lisa R. Meriweather. "Knowledge and Emotions in Cross-Racial Dialogues: Challenges and Opportunities for Adult Educators Committed to Racial Justice in Educational Settings." *Adult Learning* 25, no. 3 (August 2014): 111–18.

Manning, Chandra. *What This Cruel War Was Over: Soldiers, Slavery, and the Civil War*. New York: Knopf, 2007.

Manring, Maurice M. *Slave in a Box: The Strange Career of Aunt Jemima*. Charlottesville: University of Virginia Press, 1998.

Mantell, Martin E. *Johnson, Grant, and the Politics of Reconstruction*. New York: Columbia University Press, 1973.

Marable, Manning. *W. E. B. Du Bois: Radical Black Democrat*. Rev. ed. Boulder, CO: Paradigm Publishers, 2005.

Marshall-Cornwall, James. *Grant as a Military Commander*. New York: Barnes & Noble Books, 1970.

Martin, Matthew R. "The Two-Faced New South: The Plantation Tales of Thomas Nelson Page and Charles W. Chesnutt." *Southern Literary Journal* 30, no. 2 (spring 1998): 17–36.

Martin, Michelle H. "Jungle Visions: Sambo, Sambo, and Sambo Again." *Sankofa* 6, no. 1 (2007): 40–52.

Martin, Tony. *Race First: The Ideological and Organizational Struggles of Marcus Garvey and the Universal Negro Improvement Association*. Westport, CT: Greenwood Press, 1976.

Martinez, J. Michael. *Carpetbaggers, Cavalry, and the Ku Klux Klan: Exposing the Invisible Empire during Reconstruction*. Lanham, MD: Rowman & Littlefield, 2007.

———. *Coming for to Carry Me Home: Race in America from Abolitionism to Jim Crow*. Lanham, MD: Rowman & Littlefield, 2012.

Martinot, Steve. "On the Epidemic of Police Killings." *Social Justice* 39, no. 4 (winter 2012): 52–75.

"Mary Phagan: The Victim." *Atlanta Constitution*, August 26, 1913, 3.

Mason, Matthew. *Slavery and Politics in the Early American Republic*. Chapel Hill: University of North Carolina Press, 2006.

Masur, Louis P. *Lincoln's Hundred Days: The Emancipation Proclamation and the War for the Union*. Cambridge, MA: Belknap Press of Harvard University Press, 2012.

Mathieu, Sarah-Jane (Saje). "The African American Great Migration Reconsidered." *OAH Magazine of History* 23, no. 4 (October 2009): 19–23.

Matthews, Kadeshia L. "Black Boy No More? Violence and the Flight from Blackness in Richard Wright's *Native Son*." *Modern Fiction Studies* 60, no. 2 (summer 2014): 276–97.

Maurantonio, Nicole. "Remembering Rodney King: Myth, Racial Reconciliation, and Civil Rights History." *Journalism & Mass Communication Quarterly* 91, no. 4 (December 2014): 740–55.

Maxwell, William J. *New Negro, Old Left: African-American Writing and Communism between the Wars*. New York: Columbia University Press, 1999.

Mayer, Henry. *All on Fire: William Lloyd Garrison and the Abolition of Slavery*. New York: St. Martin's Press, 1998.

Mayo, Mike. *American Murder: Criminals, Crime, and the Media*. Canton, MI: Visible Ink Press, 2008.

McCabe, James Dabney [originally published under the pseudonym Edward Winslow Martin]. *History of the Grange Movement: or, The Farmer's War against Monopolies: Being a Full and Authentic Account of the Struggles of the American Farmers against the Extortions of the Railroad Companies. With a History of the Rise and Progress of the Order of Patrons of Husbandry, Its Objects, Present Condition and Prospects. To Which Is Added Sketches of the Leading Grangers.* Chicago: National Publishing Company, 1874.

McCartney, Laton. *The Teapot Dome Scandal: How Big Oil Bought the Harding White House and Tried to Steal the Country.* New York: Random House, 2008.

McCullough, David. *Truman.* New York: Simon & Schuster, 1992.

McGill, Ralph. "The Lesson of 'Cotton Ed' Smith." *Atlanta Constitution,* July 29, 1944, 4.

McGrath, Ben. "Fifty Shots." *New Yorker* 82, no. 41 (December 11, 2006): 38–40.

McKoy, Sheila Smith. *When Whites Riot: Writing Race and Violence in American and South African Culture.* Madison: University of Wisconsin Press, 2001.

McLaurin v. Oklahoma State Regents, 339 U.S. 637 (1950).

McMath, Robert C., Jr. *American Populism: A Social History, 1877–1898.* New York: Hill and Wang, 1993.

———. *Populist Vanguard: A History of the Southern Farmers' Alliance.* Chapel Hill: University of North Carolina Press, 1975.

McNeil, Genna Rae. *Groundwork: Charles Hamilton Houston and the Struggle for Civil Rights.* Philadelphia: University of Pennsylvania Press, 1983.

McPherson, James M. *The Abolitionist Legacy: From Reconstruction to the NAACP.* Princeton, NJ: Princeton University Press, 1976.

———. *Battle Cry of Freedom: The Civil War Era.* New York: Ballantine Books, 1988.

———. *What They Fought For, 1861–1865.* Baton Rouge: Louisiana State University Press, 1994.

McVeigh, Rory. *The Rise of the Ku Klux Klan: Right-Wing Movements and National Politics.* Minneapolis: University of Minnesota Press, 2009.

———. "Structural Incentives for Conservative Mobilization: Power Devaluation and the Rise of the Ku Klux Klan, 1915–1925." *Social Forces* 77, no. 4 (June 1999): 1461–96.

McWhirter, Cameron. *Red Summer: The Summer of 1919 and the Awakening of Black America.* New York: Henry Holt & Company, 2011.

Means, Howard. *The Avenger Takes His Place: Andrew Johnson and the 45 Days That Changed the Nation.* New York: Harcourt, 2006.

Medina, Jennifer. "Man Is Shot and Killed by the Police in California." *New York Times,* August 14, 2014, A16.

Merrill Military Files, M.103.C.B.1863. Record Group 94, National Archives and Records Administration.

Miah, Malik. "How Far Backward? The Murder of Walter Scott." *Against the Current* 30, no. 2 (May/June 2015): 2–3.

"Military Control Is Ended at Tulsa." *New York Times,* June 4, 1921, 1.

Miller, James A. *Remembering Scottsboro: The Legacy of an Infamous Trial.* Princeton, NJ: Princeton University Press, 2009.

Miller, James A., Susan D. Pennybacker, and Eve Rosenhaft. "Mother Ada Wright and the International Campaign to Free the Scottsboro Boys, 1931–1934." *American Historical Review* 106, no. 2 (April 2001): 387–430.

Miller, John Chester. *The Wolf by the Ears: Thomas Jefferson and Slavery*. New York: Free Press, 1977.

Milton, George Fort. *The Age of Hate: Andrew Johnson and the Radicals*. New York: Coward-McCann, 1930.

Mitchell, Michele. *Righteous Propagation: African Americans and the Politics of Racial Destiny after Reconstruction*. Chapel Hill: University of North Carolina Press, 2004.

Mitoma, Glenn. *Human Rights and the Negotiation of American Power*. Philadelphia: University of Pennsylvania Press, 2014.

Mixon, Gregory. *The Atlanta Riot: Race, Class, and Violence in a New South City*. Gainesville: University Press of Florida, 2005.

"Mob of 3,000 Rules in East St. Louis." *New York Times*, May 29, 1917, 3.

Moltke-Hansen, David. "Turn Signals: Shifts in Values in Southern Life Writing." In *Dixie Redux: Essays in Honor of Sheldon Hackney*, edited by Raymond Arsenault and Orville Vernon Burton, 166–99. Montgomery, AL: New South Books, 2013.

Monroe, Sylvester. "South Central: 20 Years since . . ." *Ebony* 67, no. 7 (May 2012): 132–40.

Moon, Fletcher F. "Springfield, Illinois, Riot (1908)." In *Freedom Facts and Firsts: 400 Years of the African American Civil Rights Experience*, edited by Jessie Carney Smith and Linda T. Wynn, 70. Canton, MI: Visible Ink Press, 2009.

Moore, Christopher Paul. *Fighting for America: Black Soldiers—the Unsung Heroes of World War II*. New York: Presidio Press, 2005.

Moore v. Dempsey, 261 U.S. 86 (1923).

Morgan, Chester M. "Of Gentlemen and SOBs: The Great War and Progressivism in Mississippi." *Southern Quarterly* 51, no. 3 (spring 2014): 51–65.

Morgan, Hal. *Symbols of America*. New York: Viking Penguin, 1987.

Morgan v. Virginia, 328 U.S. 373 (1946).

Moye, J. Todd. *Freedom Flyers: The Tuskegee Airmen of World War II*. New York: Oxford University Press, 2010.

Mullen, Harryette. "'When He Is Least Himself': Dunbar and Double Consciousness in African American Poetry." *African American Review* 41, no. 2 (summer 2007): 277–82.

Murdach, Allison D. "Does American Social Work Have a Progressive Tradition?," *Social Work* 55, no. 1 (January 2010): 82–89.

Murphy, Paul Vincent. *The New Era: American Thought and Culture in the 1920s*. Lanham, MD: Rowman & Littlefield, 2011.

Murphy, Richard W. *The Nation Reunited: War's Aftermath*. Alexandria, VA: Time-Life Books, 1987.

Myrdal, Gunnar. *An American Dilemma: The Negro Problem and Modern Democracy*. Vols. 1–2. New York: Harper & Brothers, 1944.

National Archives and Records Administration. *Our Documents: 100 Milestone Documents from the National Archives*. New York: Oxford University Press, 2003.

Neal v. Delaware, 103 U.S. 370 (1881).

"Negro Women See Harding." *New York Times*, August 15, 1922, 10.

Newby, John L., II. "The Fight for the Right to Fight and the Forgotten Negro Protest Movement: The History of Executive Order 9981 and Its Effect upon

Brown v. Board of Education and Beyond." *Texas Journal of Civil Liberties & Civil Rights* 10, no. 1 (winter 2004): 83–110.

Newell, Clayton R., and Charles R. Shrader. "The U.S. Army's Transition to Peace, 1865–66." *Journal of Military History* 77, no. 3 (July 2013): 867–94.

Newman, Richard S. *The Transformation of American Abolitionism: Fighting Slavery in the Early Republic.* Chapel Hill: University of North Carolina Press, 2002.

Newton, Michael. *The Ku Klux Klan: History, Organization, Language, Influence and Activities of America's Most Notorious Secret Organization.* Jefferson, NC: McFarland & Company, 2006.

Niderost, Eric. "The Birth of a Nation." *American History* 40, no. 4 (October 2005): 60–80.

Nielson, Erik. "A 'High Tension' in Langston Hughes's Musical Verse." *MELUS* 37, no. 4 (winter 2012): 165–85.

"Niggers in the White House." *Kentucky News Era,* March 13, 1903, 6.

"Nine Killed in Fight with Arkansas Posse." *New York Times,* October 2, 1919, 4.

"Nineteen Negroes Shot to Death: Fatal Race Riots in North and South Carolina." *New York Times,* November 11, 1898, 1.

Norrell, Robert J. *Up from History: The Life of Booker T. Washington.* Cambridge, MA: Belknap Press of Harvard University Press, 2009.

Norris, Clarence, and Sybil D. Washington. *The Last of the Scottsboro Boys.* New York: Putnam, 1979.

Norris v. Alabama, 294 U.S. 587 (1935).

"North Carolina Politics: The Combination of the White Voters to Resist the Possibility of Negro Domination." *New York Times,* November 5, 1898, 2.

"North Carolina's Race Feud: Steps Taken by Wilmington Citizens 'to Assert the Supremacy of the White Man.'" *New York Times,* November 10, 1898, 4.

Novak, James L., James Pease, and Larry Sanders. *Agricultural Policy in the United States: Evolution and Economics.* London: Routledge, 2015.

Nowlin, Michael. "The Strange Literary Career of Jean Toomer." *Texas Studies in Literature and Language* 53, no. 2 (summer 2011): 207–35.

Nowlin, Michael Everett. "Race Literature, Modernism, and Normal Literature: James Weldon Johnson's Groundwork for an African American Literary Renaissance." *Modernism/Modernity* 20, no. 3 (2013): 503–18.

O'Brien, David M. *Storm Center: The Supreme Court in American Politics.* New York: W. W. Norton, 1986.

O'Connor, Michael P. "Time out of Mind: Our Collective Amnesia about the History of the Privileges or Immunities Clause." *Kentucky Law Journal* 93, no. 3 (2004/2005): 659–735.

O'Neal, Michael J. *America in the 1920s.* New York: Stonesong Press, 2006.

Oakes, James. *Freedom National: The Destruction of Slavery in the United States, 1861–1865.* New York: W. W. Norton, 2013.

Olivier, Albert F., MD. "In Proper Perspective: Daniel Hale Williams, M.D." *Annals of Thoracic Surgery* 37, no. 1 (January 1984): 96–97.

Olsen, Henry. "Populism, American Style." *National Affairs* 4, no. 1 (summer 2010): 3–20.

Oney, Steve. *And the Dead Shall Rise: The Murder of Mary Phagan and the Lynching of Leo Frank.* New York: Vintage Books, 2004.

―――. "The People v. Leo Frank." *Atlanta* 53, no. 5 (September 2013): 32–36.

Onuf, Peter S. "'To Declare Them a Free and Independent People': Race, Slavery, and National Identity in Jefferson's Thought." *Journal of the Early Republic* 18, no. 1 (spring 1998): 1–46.

"Order in Chicago." *New York Times*, July 31, 1919, 8.

Outcault, Richard F. *The Yellow Kid: A Centennial Celebration of the Kid Who Started the Comics*. Northampton, MA: Kitchen Sink Press, 1995.

Packard, Jerrold M. *American Nightmare: The History of Jim Crow*. New York: St. Martin's Griffin, 2003.

Padover, Saul K., ed. *Thomas Jefferson on Democracy*. New York: New American Library, 1939.

Page, Thomas Nelson. *The Negro: The Southerner's Problem*. New York: Charles Scribner's Sons, 1904.

Painter, Nell Irvin. *Exodusters: Black Migration to Kansas after Reconstruction*. New York: W. W. Norton, 1992 [1976].

―――. "Millenarian Aspects of the Exodus to Kansas of 1879." *Journal of Social History* 9, no. 3 (spring 1976): 331–38.

―――. *Southern History across the Color Line*. Chapel Hill: University of North Carolina Press, 2002.

"Paper Blamed for Riots: Grand Jury Accuses *Atlanta News* of Stirring Up Race Feeling." *New York Times*, September 28, 1906, 1.

Papish, Laura. "Promoting Black (Social) Identity." *Social Theory & Practice* 41, no. 1 (January 2015): 1–25.

"Parents of Jonny Gammage Awarded $1.5 Million in Wrongful Death Suit." *Jet* 94, no. 5 (June 29, 1998): 50.

Parker, Christopher S. *Fighting for Democracy: Black Veterans and the Struggle against White Supremacy in the Postwar South*. Princeton, NJ: Princeton University Press, 2009.

Pascoe, Peggy. *What Comes Naturally: Miscegenation Laws and the Making of Race in America*. New York: Oxford University Press, 2009.

"The Patrick Dorismond Case." *New York Times*, March 21, 2000, A22.

Patterson, Lillie. *Sure Hands, Strong Heart: The Life of Daniel Hale Williams*. Nashville, TN: Abington Press, 1981.

Patterson v. Alabama, 294 U.S. 600 (1935).

Paulson, Michael. "King Events Punctuated by Protests over Deaths of Black Men." *New York Times*, January 20, 2015, A10.

Payne, Phillip A. *Dead Last: The Public Memory of Warren G. Harding's Scandalous Legacy*. Athens: Ohio University Press, 2009.

Perez-Peña, Richard. "Black or White? Woman's Story Stirs Up Furor." *New York Times*, June 13, 2015, A1.

Perlstein, Rick. *Nixonland: The Rise of a President and the Fracturing of America*. New York: Scribner, 2008.

Perman, Michael. *The Road to Redemption: Southern Politics, 1869–1879*. Chapel Hill: University of North Carolina Press, 1984.

Perry, Jeffrey B. *Hubert Harrison: The Voice of Harlem Radicalism, 1883–1918*. New York: Columbia University Press, 2009.

Peterson, Bernard L., Jr. *The African American Theatre Directory, 1816–1960: A Comprehensive Guide to Early Black Theatre Organizations, Companies, Theatres, and Performing Groups*. Westport, CT: Greenwood Press, 1997.

Peterson, Christopher. "Slavery's Bestiary: Joel Chandler Harris's *Uncle Remus* Tales." *Paragraph* 34, no. 1 (March 2011): 30–47.

Petrino, Elizabeth A. "'We Are Rising as a People': Frances Harper's Radical Views on Class and Racial Equality in *Sketches of a Southern Life*." *ATQ: American Transcendental Quarterly* 19, no. 2 (June 2005): 133–53.

Phelan, Craig. *Grand Master Workman: Terence Powderly and the Knights of Labor*. Westport, CT: Praeger, 1998.

Phillips, Ulrich Bonnell. *American Negro Slavery: A Survey of the Supply, Employment and Control of Negro Labor as Determined by the Plantation Regime*. New York: D. Appleton, 1929.

Pieterse, Jan Nederveen. *White on Black: Images of Africa and Blacks in Western Popular Culture*. New Haven, CT: Yale University Press, 1995.

Piott, Stephen L. *American Reformers, 1870–1920: Progressives in Word and Deed*. Lanham, MD: Rowman & Littlefield, 2006.

Piven, Frances Fox. *Challenging Authority: How Ordinary People Change America*. Lanham, MD: Rowman & Littlefield, 2006.

"Planned Massacre of Whites Today." *New York Times*, October 6, 1919, 1, 3.

Plessy v. Ferguson, 163 U.S. 537 (1896).

Podell, Janet, and Steven Anzovin, eds. *Speeches of the American Presidents*. 2nd ed. Bronx, NY: H. W. Wilson Company, 2001.

Polgar, Paul J. "'To Raise Them to an Equal Participation': Early National Abolitionism, Gradual Emancipation, and the Promise of African American Citizenship." *Journal of the Early Republic* 31, no. 2 (summer 2011): 229–58.

"Posses [*sic*] Chase Frank Mob: Prisoner Rushed from State Farm in an Automobile." *Atlanta Constitution*, August 17, 1915, 1.

Powell v. Alabama, 287 U.S. 45 (1932).

Prather, H. Leon, Sr. "We Have Taken a City: A Centennial Essay." In *Democracy Betrayed: The Wilmington Race Riot of 1898*, edited by David S. Cecelski and Timothy B. Tyson, 15–41. Chapel Hill: University of North Carolina Press, 1998.

"President's Address to Congress on Domestic and Foreign Policies." *New York Times*, April 13, 1921, 7.

Pruitt, Paul M., Jr. *Taming Alabama: Lawyers and Reformers, 1804–1929*. Tuscaloosa: University of Alabama Press, 2010.

Puddington, Arch. "The War on the War on Crime." *Commentary* 107, no. 5 (May 1999): 25–30.

Quarles, Benjamin. *The Negro in the Civil War*. Cambridge, MA: Da Capo, 1988 [1953].

Rable, George C. *But There Was No Peace: The Role of Violence in the Politics of Reconstruction*. Athens: University of Georgia Press, 1984.

———. "The South and the Politics of Antilynching Legislation, 1920–1940." *Journal of Southern History* 51, no. 2 (May 1985): 201–20.

"Race Rioters Fire East St. Louis and Shoot or Hang Many Negroes; Dead Estimated at from 20 to 76." *New York Times*, July 3, 1917, 1, 6.

"Race Riots Continue in East St. Louis." *New York Times*, May 30, 1917, 6.

"Race War in Washington." *New York Times*, July 23, 1919, 8.

Radcliff, Anthony J. "The Radical Evolution of Du Bosian Pan-Africanism." *Journal of Pan African Studies* 5, no. 9 (March 2013): 151–70.

Rankin, David C. "The Impact of the Civil War on the Free Colored Community of New Orleans." *Perspectives in American History* 11, no. 1 (1977–1978): 377–416.

Ransom, Roger L., and Richard L. Sutch. *One Kind of Freedom: The Economic Consequences of Emancipation*. 2nd ed. Cambridge: Cambridge University Press, 2001.

Rapley, Robert. *Witch Hunts: From Salem to Guantánamo Bay*. Quebec: McGill-Queens University Press, 2007.

Reed, Thomas B., ed. *Modern Eloquence: Library of After-Dinner Speeches, Lectures, and Occasional Addresses*. Vol. 13. Philadelphia: J. D. Morris and Company, 1900.

Reef, Catherine. *African Americans in the Military*. New York: Facts on File, 2010.

Regester, Charlene. *African American Actresses: The Struggle for Visibility, 1900–1960*. Bloomington: Indiana University Press, 2010.

Remnick, David. *The Bridge: The Life and Rise of Barack Obama*. New York: Knopf, 2010.

Reynolds, Barbara. "Our Sons under Siege." *Essence* 30, no. 7 (November 1999): 139–40, 206–12.

Richardson, Heather Cox. *West from Appomattox: The Reconstruction of America after the Civil War*. New Haven, CT: Yale University Press, 2007.

Richardson, James D. *Messages and Papers of the Presidents, 1789–1907*. Washington, DC: Bureau of National Literature and Art, 1908.

Ridge, Martin. *Ignatius Donnelly: The Portrait of a Politician*. St. Paul: Borealis Books, 1991.

Ridgeway, James. *Blood in the Face: The Ku Klux Klan, Aryan Nations, Nazi Skinheads, and the Rise of a New White Culture*. 2nd ed. New York: Thunder's Mouth Press, 1995.

"Rioters Hang Another Negro." *New York Times*, August 16, 1908, 1, 3.

Ritterhouse, Jennifer. "Reading, Intimacy, and the Role of Uncle Remus in White Southern Social Memory." *Journal of Southern History* 69, no. 3 (August 2003): 585–622.

Roberts, Diane. *The Myth of Aunt Jemima: Representations of Race and Region*. London: Routledge, 1994.

Robertson, Stephen, Shane White, and Stephen Garton. "Harlem in Black and White: Mapping Race and Place in the 1920s." *Journal of Urban History* 39, no. 5 (September 2013): 864–80.

Robinson, Dean E. *Black Nationalism in American Politics and Thought*. Cambridge: Cambridge University Press, 2001.

Robinson, Lillian S., and Greg Robinson. "Paul Laurence Dunbar: A Credit to His Race?," *African American Review* 41, no. 2 (summer 2007): 215–25.

Robinson-English, Tracey. "Celebrating Loïs Mailou Jones." *Ebony* 61, no. 2 (December 2005): 124–28.

Rome, Adam Ward. "Farmers as Entrepreneurs, 1870–1900." *Agricultural History* 56, no. 1 (January 1982): 37–49.

Romine, Mr. and Mrs. W. B. *A Story of the Original Ku Klux Klan*. Pulaski, TN: Pulaski Citizen, 1934.

Rose, Mrs. S. E. F. *The Ku Klux Klan or Invisible Empire*. New Orleans, LA: L. Graham Company, 1914.

Rosen, Jeffrey. "Excessive Force—Why Patrick Dorismond Didn't Have to Die." *New Republic*, April 10, 2000: 24.

Rothman, Adam. "Slavery and National Expansion in the United States." *Magazine of History* 23, no. 2 (April 2009): 23–29.

Rothman, Noah C. "Taking Sides in Ferguson: The Media's Shameful Performance." *Commentary* 138, no. 3 (October 2014): 18–22.

Rottenberg, Catherine. "Wallace Thurman's *The Blacker the Berry* and the Question of the Emancipatory City." *Mosaic: A Journal for the Interdisciplinary Study of Literature* 46, no. 4 (December 2013): 59–74.

Roy, Beth. *41 Shots . . . and Counting: What Amadou Diallo's Story Teaches Us about Policing, Race, and Justice*. Syracuse, NY: Syracuse University Press, 2009.

Ruff, Allen. "The World That War Made: Shaping 20th-Century Black America." *Against the Current* 174, no. 1 (January/February 2015): 9–15.

Ruiz-Velasco, Chris. "Order Out of Chaos: Whiteness, White Supremacy, and Thomas Dixon Jr." *College Literature* 34, no. 4 (fall 2007): 148–65.

Sacharow, Stanley. *Symbols of Trade: Your Favorite Trademarks and the Companies They Represent*. New York: Art Direction Company, 1982.

Safire, William, ed. *Lend Me Your Ears: Great Speeches in History*. New York: W. W. Norton, 2004.

Salaam, Yusef. "Prayer, Anger, and Sorrow for Zongo." *New York Amsterdam News* 94, no. 24 (June 12, 2003): 4.

Saloutos, Theodore. *Farmer Movements in the South, 1865–1933*. Berkeley: University of California Press, 1960.

"Sam Hose Still Eagerly Pursued: There Is No Thought of Giving Up the Chase." *Atlanta Constitution*, April 19, 1899, 3.

Saraydar, Edward. "A Note on the Profitability of Ante Bellum Slavery." *Southern Economic Journal* 40, no. 4 (April 1964): 325–32.

Satter, Beryl. "Marcus Garvey, Father Divine and the Gender Politics of Race Difference and Race Neutrality." *American Quarterly* 48, no. 1 (March 1996): 43–76.

Savage, Ritchie. "Populist Elements in Contemporary American Political Discourse." *Sociological Review Monograph* 58, no. 1 (December 2010): 167–88.

"The Savages of Springfield." *New York Times*, August 18, 1908, 6.

Saville, Julie. *The Work of Reconstruction: From Slave to Wage Laborer in South Carolina, 1860–1870*. Cambridge: Cambridge University Press, 1994.

Schneider, Mark Robert. *"We Return Fighting": The Civil Rights Movement in the Jazz Age*. Lebanon, NH: Northeastern University Press, 2002.

Schudson, Michael. *Discovering the News: A Social History of American History*. New York: Basic Books, 1978.

Schultz, Bud, and Ruth Schultz. *The Price of Dissent: Testimonies to Political Repression in America*. Berkeley: University of California Press, 2001.

Schuyler, George Samuel. *Black No More: Being an Account of the Strange and Wonderful Workings of Science in the Land of the Free, AD 1933–1940*. Lebanon, NH: Northeastern University Press, 1989 [1931].

"Scottsboro Hero." *Time* 30, no. 5 (August 2, 1937): 45–47.

Sears, Louis Martin. "Frederick Douglass and the Mission to Haiti, 1889–1891." *Hispanic American Historical Review* 21, no. 2 (May 1941): 222–38.

Sefton, James E. *The United States Army and Reconstruction, 1865–1877.* Westport, CT: Greenwood Press, 1967.

"Sen. Smith, 'Cotton Ed,' Dies at 80: South Carolina Solon Held Record for Long Service." *Atlanta Constitution,* November 18, 1944, 1, 2.

Senechal de la Roche, Roberta. *In Lincoln's Shadow: The 1908 Race Riot in Springfield, Illinois.* Carbondale: Southern Illinois University Press, 2008.

"Series of Fierce Combats." *New York Times,* June 2, 1921, 1.

Sernett, Milton C. *Bound for the Promised Land: African American Religion and the Great Migration.* Durham, NC: Duke University Press, 1997.

Setegn, Lea. "Irene Morgan." *Richmond Times-Dispatch,* February 13, 2002, E1.

Shakespeare, William. *Henry V.* New York: Washington Square Press, 1995 [1599].

Shapiro, Herbert. "Afro-American Responses to Violence during Reconstruction." *Science & Society* 36, no. 2 (summer 1972): 158–70.

———. "The Ku Klux Klan during Reconstruction: The South Carolina Episode." *Journal of Negro History* 49, no. 1 (January 1964): 34–55.

———. *White Violence and Black Response: From Reconstruction to Montgomery.* Amherst: University of Massachusetts Press, 1988.

Shelley v. Kraemer, 334 U.S. 1 (1948).

Sheluk, Judy Penz. "An American Lithographic Legacy: Currier & Ives Continue to Charm 21st Century Collectors." *Antiques & Collecting Magazine* 112, no. 9 (November 2007): 34–39.

Sherrard-Johnson, Cherene M. *Dorothy West's Paradise: A Biography of Class and Color.* New Brunswick, NJ: Rutgers University Press, 2012.

Shields, John C. *Phillis Wheatley's Poetics of Liberation: Backgrounds and Contexts.* Knoxville: University of Tennessee Press, 2010.

Shuler, Jack. *The Thirteenth Turn: A History of the Noose.* New York: Public Affairs, 2014.

Siegel, Harry. "The Lonesome Death of Eric Garner." *New York Daily News,* December 4, 2014, 25.

Siegemund-Broka, Austin. "How the Bill Cosby Story Snowballed: It Took a New Book, a Stand-Up's Scorn and Plenty of Social Media to Reignite Years-Old Claims of Sexual Abuse and Derail the 77-Year-Old Legend's Career." *Hollywood Reporter* 420, no. 42 (December 5, 2014): 10.

Simcovitch, Maxim. "The Impact of Griffith's *Birth of a Nation* on the Modern Ku Klux Klan." *Journal of Popular Film* 1, no. 1 (winter 1972): 45–54.

Simkins, Francis Butler. "Ben Tillman's View of the Negro." *Journal of Southern History* 3, no. 2 (May 1937): 161–74.

———. *Pitchfork Ben Tillman: South Carolinian.* Columbia: University of South Carolina Press, 2002 [1944].

Simkins, Francis Butler, and Charles Pierce Roland. *A History of the South.* 4th ed. New York: Knopf, 1972.

Simmons, William Joseph. *America's Menace, or the Enemy Within.* Atlanta: Patriotic Books, 1926.

Simon, Bryant. *A Fabric of Defeat: The Politics of South Carolina Millhands, 1910–1948.* Chapel Hill: University of North Carolina Press, 1998.

———. "The Appeal of Coleman Blease of South Carolina: Race, Class, and Sex in the New South." *Journal of Southern History* 62, no. 1 (February 1996): 57–86.

Simpson, Brooks D. *The Reconstruction Presidents*. Lawrence: University Press of Kansas, 1998.

Simpson, William M. "A Tale Untold? The Alexandria, Louisiana, Lee Street Riot (January 10, 1942)." *Louisiana History: The Journal of the Louisiana Historical Association* 35, no. 2 (spring 1994): 133–49.

Singletary, Otis A. "The Negro Militia during Radical Reconstruction." *Military Affairs* 19, no. 4 (winter 1955): 177–86.

Sitkoff, Harvard. *A New Deal for Blacks: The Emergence of Civil Rights as a National Issue: The Depression Decade*. New York: Oxford University Press, 1978.

———. "The Detroit Race Riot 1943." *Michigan History* 53, no. 3 (May 1969): 183–206.

Sitkoff, Robert H. "Politics and the Business of Corruption." *Regulation* 26, no. 1 (winter 2003–2004): 30–36.

"Six More Are Killed in Arkansas Riots." *New York Times*, October 3, 1919, 6.

Sklaroff, Laura Rebecca. *Black Culture and the New Deal: The Quest for Civil Rights in the Roosevelt Era*. Chapel Hill: University of North Carolina Press, 2009.

Slap, Andrew L. *The Doom of Reconstruction: The Liberal Republicans in the Civil War Era*. Bronx, NY: Fordham University Press, 2006.

Slide, Anthony. *American Racist: The Life and Films of Thomas Dixon*. Lexington: University Press of Kentucky, 2004.

Smith, Jessie Carney, ed. *Encyclopedia of African-American Popular Culture*. Santa Barbara, CA: ABC-CLIO, 2010.

Smith, John David, and J. Vincent Lowery, eds. *The Dunning School: Historians, Race, and the Meaning of Reconstruction*. Lexington: University Press of Kentucky, 2013.

Smith, Mark M. *How Race Is Made: Slavery, Segregation, and the Senses*. Chapel Hill: University of North Carolina Press, 2006.

Smith, Ralph A. "'Macuneism,' or the Farmers of Texas in Business." *Journal of Southern History* 13, no. 2 (May 1947): 220–44.

Smith, Rogers M. "Ackerman's Civil Rights Revolution and Modern American Racial Politics." *Yale Law Journal* 123, no. 8 (June 2014): 2906–40.

Smith v. Allwright, 321 U.S. 649 (1944).

Sobel, Mechal. *The World They Made Together: Black and White Values in Eighteenth-Century Virginia*. Princeton, NJ: Princeton University Press, 1987.

Sollors, Werner. "The Celtic Nations and the African Americas." *Comparative American Studies* 8, no. 4 (December 2010): 316–22.

———. *Neither Black nor White yet Both: Thematic Explorations of Interracial Literature*. Cambridge, MA: Harvard University Press, 1997.

Sonneborn, Liz. *The Great Black Migrations: From the Rural South to the Urban North*. New York: Chelsea House, 2010.

South Carolina General Assembly. *Journal of the Senate of the General Assembly of the State of South Carolina, Being the Regular Session Beginning Tuesday, January 10, 1911*. Columbia: Gonzales and Bryan, State Printers, 1910–1911.

"Springfield Riots End." *New York Times*, August 20, 1908, 14.

Stagg, J. C. A. "The Problem of Klan Violence: The South Carolina Up-Country, 1868–1871." *Journal of American Studies* 8, no. 3 (December 1974): 303–18.

Stampp, Kenneth M. *The Era of Reconstruction, 1865–1877*. New York: Alfred A. Knopf, 1965.

———. *The Peculiar Institution: Slavery in the Ante-bellum South*. New York: Vintage Books, 1989 [1956].

Stauffer, John. "Frederick Douglass and the Aesthetics of Freedom." *Raritan* 25, no. 1 (summer 2005): 114–36.

Stein, Judith. *The World of Marcus Garvey: Race and Class in Modern Society*. Baton Rouge: Louisiana State University Press, 1986.

"Stephenson Held for Death of Girl; Indiana Officials Accuse Ex–Ku Klux Dragon and Two Others of Attack on Her." *New York Times*, April 21, 1925, 3.

"Stephenson Receives Sentence for Life; Ex-Klan Leader in Dramatic Speech Denies Having Slain Miss Oberholtzer." *New York Times*, November 17, 1925, 10.

Stewart, David O. *Impeached: The Trial of President Andrew Johnson and the Fight for Lincoln's Legacy*. New York: Simon & Schuster, 2009.

Stewart, James Brewer. *Abolitionist Politics and the Coming of the Civil War*. Amherst: University of Massachusetts Press, 2008.

Stockley, Grif. *Blood in Their Eyes: The Elaine Race Massacres of 1919*. Fayetteville: University of Arkansas Press, 2004.

Stokes, Thomas L. "A Tradition Passed with 'Cotton Ed' Smith." *Atlanta Constitution*, November 20, 1944, 7.

Storhoff, Gary. "'Strange Fruit': *Lady Sings the Blues* as Crossover Film." *Journal of Popular Film and Television* 30, no. 2 (summer 2002): 105–13.

Strouse, Jean. *Morgan: American Financier*. New York: Random House, 1999.

Sue, Derald Wing. "Race Talk: The Psychology of Racial Dialogues." *American Psychologist* 68, no. 8 (November 2013): 663–72.

Sundquist, Eric J. "Who Was Langston Hughes?," *Commentary* 102, no. 6 (December 1996): 55–59.

Susman, Tina, and Matt Pearce. "The Nation: Ex-NAACP Leader Answers Critics; Rachel Dolezal Says, 'I Identify as Black,' and Claims She's Unsure Who Her Parents Are." *Los Angeles Times*, June 17, 2015, A5.

Swanson, James L. *Manhunt: The 12-Day Chase for Lincoln's Killer*. New York: William Morrow, 2006.

Sweatt v. Painter, 339 U.S. 629 (1950).

Takara, Kathryn Waddell. "Frank Marshall Davis: A Forgotten Voice in the Chicago Black Renaissance." *Western Journal of Black Studies* 26, no. 4 (winter 2012): 215–27.

Talty, Stephan. *Mulatto America: At the Crossroads of Black and White Culture: A Social History*. New York: Harper Paperbacks, 2004.

Tanfani, Joseph, and Richard A. Serrano. "Charleston Church Shootings; Families Tell of Anguish, Forgiveness; Charleston Relatives Face Killer in Court." *Los Angeles Times*, June 20, 2015, A1.

Tap, Bruce. "Chandler, Zachariah (1813–1879)." In *Encyclopedia of the American Civil War: A Political, Social, and Military History*, edited by David Stephen Heidler and Jeanne T. Heidler, 398–99. New York: W. W. Norton, 2002.

Taylor, Alrutheus Ambush. *The Negro in South Carolina during Reconstruction*. Washington, DC: Association for the Study of Negro Life and History, 1924.

Taylor, Jack. "'We Are All Oscar Grant': Police Brutality, Death, and the Work of Mourning." *Transforming Anthropology* 21, no. 2 (October 2013): 187–97.

Taylor, Jon E. *Freedom to Serve: Truman, Civil Rights, and Executive Order 9981*. London: Routledge, 2013.

Taylor, Quintard, Jr. *From Timbuktu to Katrina: Readings in African American History*. Vols. 1–2. Boston: Wadsworth Thomson Higher Education, 2008.

Teachout, Terry. "The Case for Cab Calloway." *Commentary* 31, no. 1 (January 2011): 66–70.

Thernstrom, Abigail, and Stephan Thernstrom. "The Prescience of Myrdal." *Public Interest* 128 (summer 1997): 36, 54.

"Thirty Whites Held for Tulsa Rioting." *New York Times*, June 5, 1921, 21.

Tidwell, John Edgar, ed. *Writings of Frank Marshall Davis: A Voice of the Black Press*. Jackson: University Press of Mississippi, 2007.

Tolnay, Stewart E. "The African American 'Great Migration' and Beyond." *Annual Review of Sociology* 29, no. 1 (August 2003): 209–32.

Toobin, Jeffrey. *The Run of His Life: The People v. O.J. Simpson*. New York: Random House, 1996.

Tourgee, Albion W. *The Invisible Empire: Part I—a New, Illustrated, and Enlarged Edition of a Fool's Errand, by One of the Fools; the Famous Historical Romance of Life in the South since the War; Part II—a Concise Review of Recent Events, Showing the Elements on Which the Tale Is Based, with Many Thrilling Personal Narratives and Other Startling Facts and Considerations, Including an Account of the Rise, Extent, Purpose, Methods, and Deeds of the Mysterious Ku-Klux Klan; All Fully Authenticated*. New York: Fords, Howard & Hulbert, 1879.

"Trace Plot to Stir Negroes to Rise." *New York Times*, October 4, 1919, 7.

Trefousse, Hans L. *The Radical Republicans: Lincoln's Vanguard for Racial Justice*. New York: Knopf, 1969.

Trelease, Allen W. *White Terror: The Ku Klux Klan Conspiracy and Southern Reconstruction*. Baton Rouge: Louisiana State University Press, 1971.

"Troopers Restore Order in Chicago." *New York Times*, August 2, 1919, 10.

"Troops Blamed for Riots Spread." *New York Times*, July 4, 1917, 5.

"Troops Check Riots, Sixth Victim Dies." *New York Times*, August 17, 1908, 1, 2.

Tucker, William. "The Tawana Brawley Case: The Mystery of Wappingers Falls." *New Republic* 198, no. 12 (March 21, 1988): 19–20, 22.

Turner, Sarah, and John Bound. "Closing the Gap or Widening the Divide: The Effects of the G.I. Bill and World War II on the Educational Outcomes of Black Americans." *Journal of Economic History* 63, no. 1 (March 2003): 145–77.

Tyson, Timothy B., and David S. Cecelski. "Introduction." In *Democracy Betrayed: The Wilmington Race Riot of 1898*, edited by David S. Cecelski and Timothy B. Tyson, 3–13. Chapel Hill: University of North Carolina Press, 1998.

Unger, Nancy C. *Fighting Bob La Follette: The Righteous Reformer*. Madison: Wisconsin Historical Society Press, 2008.

United States Government Printing Office. *Journal of the Senate of the United States of America, Being the Second Session of the Forty-Sixth Congress Begun and Held at the City of Washington, December 1, 1879, in the One Hundred and Fourth Year of the Independence of the United States*. Washington, DC: United States Government Printing Office, 1879.

United States v. Cruikshank, 92 U.S. 542 (1876).

United States v. Reese, 92 U.S. 214 (1875).

"The Unnecessary Death of Eric Garner." *National Review* 66, no. 24 (December 31, 2014): 14.

Urofsky, Melvin I. *Louis D. Brandeis: A Life*. New York: Schocken Books, 2009.

Valelly, Richard M. *The Two Reconstructions: The Struggle for Black Enfranchisement*. Chicago: University of Chicago Press, 2004.

Valentine, Victoria. "Real Life, True Color: The Art of Jacob Lawrence." *New Crisis* 108, no. 4 (July/August 2001): 55–58.

Valiunas, Algis. "And the War Came: And It Was about Slavery and Nothing Else." *Commentary* 132, no. 1 (July/August 2011): 35–39.

Van Deburg, William L. *Slavery and Race in American Popular Culture*. Madison: University of Wisconsin Press, 1984.

Van Deusen, John G. "The Exodus of 1879." *Journal of Negro History* 21, no. 2 (April 1936): 111–29.

Van Thompson, Carlyle. *Eating the Black Body: Miscegenation as Sexual Consumption in African American Literature and Culture*. New York: Peter Lang, 2006.

Vieru, Elena Bianca. "Failure of Capitalism? The Fairy Tale Known as the New Deal." *Virgil Madgearu Review of Economic Studies and Research* 6, no. 1 (June 2013): 187–211.

Von Drehle, David. "In the Line of Fire." *Time* 185, no. 14 (April 20, 2015): 24–28.

———. "The Roots of a Riot." *Time* 185, no. 17 (May 11, 2015): 34–39.

Vorenberg, Michael. *Final Freedom: The Civil War, the Abolition of Slavery, and the Thirteenth Amendment*. Cambridge: Cambridge University Press, 2001.

Wade, Wyn Craig. *The Fiery Cross: The Ku Klux Klan in America*. New York: Oxford University Press, 1987.

Waldrep, Christopher. *The Many Faces of Judge Lynch: Extralegal Violence and Punishment in America*. New York: Palgrave MacMillan, 2002.

Waldstreicher, David. *Slavery's Constitution: From Revolution to Ratification*. New York: Hill and Wang, 2009.

Walker, Samuel. *Presidents and Civil Liberties from Wilson to Obama: A Story of Poor Custodians*. Cambridge: Cambridge University Press, 2012.

Wallinger, Hanna. *Pauline E. Hopkins: A Literary Biography*. Athens: University of Georgia Press, 2005.

Warber, Adam L. "Public Outreach, Executive Orders, and the Unilateral Presidency." *Congress & the Presidency* 41, no. 3 (2014): 269–88.

Washington, Booker T. "The 1895 Atlanta Compromise Speech." In *The Booker T. Washington Papers*, edited by Louis R. Harlan, 3:583–87. Urbana: University of Illinois Press, 1974.

———. "Letter to: Marcus Mosiah Garvey, Tuskegee, Alabama—September 17, 1914," Booker T. Washington Society, http://www.btwsociety.org/library/letters/7.php (accessed October 2014).

———. *The Story of the Negro: The Rise of the Race from Slavery*. Vol. 2. London: Forgotten Books, 2013 [1909].

———. *Up from Slavery*. New York: Doubleday, Page, and Company, 1901.

Watkins, Julian Lewis. *The 100 Greatest Advertisements, 1852–1958: Who Wrote Them and What They Did*. 2nd ed. Mineola, NY: Dover Publications, 2012 [1949].

Watson, Martha Solomon. "Mary Church Terrell v. Thomas Nelson Page: Gender, Race, and Class in Anti-lynching Rhetoric." *Rhetoric & Public Affairs* 12, no. 1 (spring 2009): 65–90.

Watson, Thomas E. "The Negro Question in the South." In *A Populist Reader: Selections from the Works of American Populist Leaders*, edited by George Brown Tindall, 118–28. New York: Harper & Row, 1966.

Waugh, John C. *Re-electing Lincoln: The Battle for the 1864 Presidency*. New York: Crown Books, 1997.

Webb, Jodi. "Thomas Nast: King of Political Cartoons." *History Magazine* 10, no. 3 (February/March 2009): 42–43.

Weinstein, Allen, and Frank Otto Gatell. *The Segregation Era, 1863 to 1954: A Modern Reader*. Oxford: Oxford University Press, 1970.

Wells, C. A. Harwell. "The End of the Affair: Anti-dueling Laws and Social Norms in Antebellum America." *Vanderbilt Law Review* 54 (May 2001): 1805–47.

West, Jerry L. *The Reconstruction Ku Klux Klan in York County, South Carolina, 1865–1877*. Jefferson, NC: McFarland & Company, 2002.

West, Michael Rudolph. *The Education of Booker T. Washington: American Democracy and the Idea of Race Relations*. New York: Columbia University Press, 2006.

Westbrook, Robert B. *John Dewey and American Democracy*. Ithaca, NY: Cornell University Press, 1991.

Wexler, Laura. *Fire in a Canebrake: The Last Mass Lynching in America*. New York: Scribner, 2003.

Wheat, Ellen Harkins. *Jacob Lawrence: American Painter*. Seattle: University of Washington Press, 1990.

White, Eugene E. "Mississippi's Great White Chief: The Speaking of James K. Vardaman in the Mississippi Gubernatorial Campaign of 1903." *Quarterly Journal of Speech* 32, no. 4 (December 1946): 442–46.

White, George Henry. *The Writings, Speeches, and Letters of George Henry White*. Edited by Benjamin R. Justesen. Lincoln, NE: iUniverse, 2004.

White, Richard D., Jr. *Kingfish: The Reign of Huey P. Long*. New York: Random House, 2006.

White, Ronald C., Jr. *A. Lincoln: A Biography*. New York: Random House, 2009.

———. *The Eloquent President: A Portrait of Lincoln through His Words*. New York: Random House, 2005.

———. *Lincoln's Greatest Speech: The Second Inaugural*. New York: Simon & Schuster, 2006.

White, Walter F. *A Rising Wind*. Charleston, SC: Nabu Press, 2011 [1945].

"White House Tea Starts Senate Stir." *New York Times*, June 18, 1929, 38.

Whites, LeeAnn. "Love, Hate, Rape, Lynching: Rebecca Latimer Felton and the Gender Politics of Racial Violence." In *Democracy Betrayed: The Wilmington Race Riot of 1898*, edited by David S. Cecelski and Timothy B. Tyson, 143–62. Chapel Hill: University of North Carolina Press, 1998.

Whitfield, Stephen J. *A Death in the Delta: The Story of Emmett Till*. Baltimore: Johns Hopkins University Press, 1991.

Wilentz, Sean. "Jeffersonian Democracy and the Origins of Political Antislavery in the United States: The Missouri Crisis Revisited." *Journal of the Historical Society* 4, no. 3 (September 2004): 375–401.

Wilkerson, Isabel. *The Warmth of Other Suns: The Epic Story of America's Great Migration*. New York: Random House, 2010.

"Will Defense Put Character of Leo Frank before Jury?," *Atlanta Constitution*, August 8, 1913, 3.

Williams, Alfred B. *Hampton and His Red Shirts: South Carolina's Deliverance in 1876*. Whitefish, MT: Kessinger Publishing, 2007 [1970].

Williams, Chad L. *Torchbearers of Democracy: African American Soldiers in the World War I Era*. Chapel Hill: University of North Carolina Press, 2010.

Williams, George Washington. *A History of the Negro Troops in the War of the Rebellion*. New York: Harper and Brothers, Franklin Square, 1888.

———. *History of the Negro Race in America from 1619 to 1880*. 2 vols. New York: G. P. Putnam's Sons, the Knickerbocker Press, 1882.

Williams, Keira V. *Gendered Politics in the Modern South: The Susan Smith Case and the Rise of a New Sexism*. Baton Rouge: Louisiana State University Press, 2012.

Williams, Lou Falkner. *The Great South Carolina Ku Klux Klan Trials, 1871–1872*. Athens: University of Georgia Press, 1996.

Williams, Patrick G. *Beyond Redemption: Texas Democrats after Reconstruction*. College Station: Texas A&M University Press, 2007.

Williams, R. Hal. *Realigning America: McKinley, Bryan, and the Remarkable Election of 1896*. Lawrence: University Press of Kansas, 2001.

Williams, T. Harry. *Lincoln and the Radicals*. Madison: University of Wisconsin Press, 1965.

———. "Lincoln and the Radicals: An Essay in Civil War History and Historiography." In *The Selected Essays of T. Harry Williams*, with a biographical introduction by Estelle Williams, 43–62. Baton Rouge: Louisiana State University Press, 1983.

Williams v. Mississippi, 170 U.S. 213 (1898).

Williamson, Joel. *After Slavery: The Negro in South Carolina during Reconstruction, 1861–1877*. Chapel Hill: University of North Carolina Press, 1965.

"The Wilmington Riots." *New York Times*, November 15, 1898, 1.

Wilson, George, Jr. *The Greenbackers and Their Doctrines*. Lexington, MO: Intelligencer News, Book and Jobs Power Print, 1878.

Wilson, Ivy G. "Introduction: Reconstructing Albery Allson Whitman." In *At the Dusk of Dawn: Selected Poetry and Prose of Albery Allson Whitman*, edited by Ivy G. Wilson, 1–17. Lebanon, NH: Northeastern University Press, 2009.

Wilson, John F. "Harding's Rhetoric of Normalcy, 1920–1923." *Quarterly Journal of Speech* 48, no. 4 (December 1962): 406–11.

Wilson, Matthew. "Reading *The Human Stain* through Charles W. Chesnutt: The Genre of the Passing Novel." *Philip Roth Studies* 2, no. 2 (fall 2006): 138–50.

Winant, Howard. "The Dark Matter." *Ethnic and Racial Studies* 35, no. 4 (April 2012): 600–607.

Winik, Jay. *April 1865: The Month That Saved America*. New York: HarperCollins, 2001.

Winter, William F. "The Evolution of Politics in the Deep South." *Southern Quarterly* 51, nos. 1/2 (fall 2013/winter 2014): 93–105.

Wintz, Cary D., ed. *African American Political Thought, 1890–1930: Washington, Du Bois, Garvey, and Randolph*. Armonk, NY: M. E. Sharpe, 1996.

Wish, Harvey. "American Slave Insurrections before 1861." *Journal of Negro History* 22, no. 3 (July 1937): 299–320.

Witcover, Jules. *Party of the People: A History of the Democrats*. New York: Random House, 2003.

Wolffe, Richard. *Renegade: The Making of a President*. New York: Three Rivers Press, 2010.

Wolters, Raymond. *Du Bois and His Rivals*. Columbia: University of Missouri Press, 2002.

———. *The Negro and the New Deal Economic Recovery Program*. Berkeley: University of California Press, 1967.

———. *Negroes and the Great Depression: The Problem of Economic Recovery*. Westport, CT: Greenwood Press, 1970.

Woodman, Harold D. "Post–Civil War Southern Agriculture and the Law." *Agricultural History* 53, no. 1 (January 1979): 319–37.

Woodward, C. Vann. *Origins of the New South, 1877–1913*. Baton Rouge: Louisiana State University Press, 1951.

———. *The Strange Career of Jim Crow*. 2nd ed. Oxford: Oxford University Press, 1966.

———. *Tom Watson: Agrarian Rebel*. Oxford: Oxford University Press, 1963.

Worden, Daniel. "Birth in the Briar Patch: Charles W. Chesnutt and the Problem of Racial Identity." *Southern Literary Journal* 41, no. 2 (spring 2009): 1–20.

Wormser, Richard. *The Rise and Fall of Jim Crow*. New York: St. Martin's Griffin, 2004.

Wright, Gavin. "The Economic Revolution in the American South." *Journal of Economic Perspectives* 1, no. 1 (summer 1987): 161–78.

Wright, Joshua K. "Black Outlaws and the Struggle for Empowerment in Blaxploitation Cinema." *Spectrum: A Journal on Black Men* 2, no. 2 (2014): 63–86.

Wright, W. D. *Black History and Black Identity: A Call for a New Historiography*. Westport, CT: Praeger, 2002.

Wynn, Neil A. *The African American Experience during World War II*. Lanham, MD: Rowman & Littlefield, 2010.

ya Azibo, Daudi Ajani. "Teaching the Mulatto Hypothesis to Combat African-U.S. Colorism: Just Knowing Can Cure." *Race, Gender & Class* 21, nos. 3/4 (2014): 88–100.

Yarbrough, Tinsley E. *A Passion for Justice: J. Waties Waring and Civil Rights*. New York: Oxford University Press, 1987.

Yoo, John. *Crisis and Command*. New York: Kaplan Publishing, 2009.

Young, Rowland L. "The Year They Stole the White House." *ABA Journal* 62, no. 11 (November 1976): 1458–61.

Yuill, Phyllis. "Little Black Sambo: The Continuing Controversy." *School Library Journal* 22, no. 7 (March 1976): 71–75.

Zambelli, Anthony, JD. "Looking at History through an Economic Lens: A Short History of North American Slavery from an Economic Point of View." *Social Studies Review* 52, no. 1 (2013): 53–60.

Zinn, Howard. *A People's History of the United States*. New York: HarperPerennial, 1980.

Zuczek, Richard. *State of Rebellion: Reconstruction in South Carolina*. Columbia: University of South Carolina Press, 1996.

Index

abolitionism, 50
abolitionists, 162, 183, 247; differences
  with Abraham Lincoln, 27, 31;
  paternalism of, 30, 305; and Radical
  Republicans, 32; rise to prominence
  of, 1, 24, 25
Academy Award, Best Supporting
  Actress, 212
accommodationist approach to race
  relations, 159, 160, 167, 168. *See also*
  Washington, Booker T.
Adams, Henry, 183
Addams, Jane, 119
Adkins, W. A., 92
advertisements, 196; images of blacks
  in, 201–9, 239, 240
Aesop's fables, 199
Africa, 3, 172, 210; and deportation,
  143; and Marcus Garvey, 172, 252,
  254, 255, 256, 258, 259
Agricultural Adjustment Adminis-
  tration (AAA), 288–89, 290
Agricultural Wheel, 109
Agriculture, United States Department
  of, 287, 288
Akerman, Amos T., 77
Alabama, 157, 184, 226; and the Great
  Migration, 189; and representation
  in Congress, 151, 267; and the Scott-
  sboro case, 274–78, 280–85; and

segregation, 153; and slavery, 25;
  and white supremacy, 54, 56, 233.
  See also Scottsboro Boys
Alabama Board of Pardons and
  Paroles, 285
Alabama Supreme Court, 278, 282, 284
Alabama, University of, 159
Alexandria (Louisiana), 306
Ali, Muhammad, 6
Aluminum Ore Company, 88
American Community Party, 278, 279
*An American Dilemma: The Negro
  Problem and Modern Democracy*
  (book), 2, 303–5, 311
American Medical Association, 68
American Revolution. *See* Revolu-
  tionary War
"American Skin (41 Shots" (song), 10
Ames, Adelbert, 55
Amidon, Thomas, 202
Amos 'n' Andy (radio and television
  show), 210
Anderson (South Carolina), 145
Andrews, Charles O., 271–72
Angelou, Maya, 6
antilynching legislation, 121, 171,
  262–74, 313. *See also* lynching
Anti-saloon League, 228
anti-Semitism, 112, 223, 224–25, 229,
  232

An Appeal to the World: A Statement of Denial of Human Rights to Minorities in the Case of Citizens of Negro Descent in the United States of America and an Appeal to the United Nations for Redress (petition), 307–8
Appomattox Courthouse (Virginia), 21, 71, 132
Arkansas, 92, 94, 95, 96
Armstrong, Louis, 250
Armstrong, Samuel Chapman, 157
Army Air Corps, 295
Army Air Forces, 299
Army of Northern Virginia, 27
Army, United States, 250, 295, 299, 300
Army War College, 295
Article I, Section 3 (United States Constitution), 110
Article III (United States Constitution), 40
Articles of Confederation, 36
Associated Negro Press, 246
Athens (Georgia), 131, 158
Atlanta Compromise, 158–59, 163, 167, 262. *See also* Washington, Booker T.
Atlanta Constitution (newspaper), 84, 129, 132, 147, 166
Atlanta Daily World (newspaper), 246
Atlanta (Georgia), 166, 172, 246, 259; and the Ku Klux Klan (KKK), 226, 227, 228, 231, 235; and Leo Frank case, 222, 225; as the site of political speeches, 58, 68, 158; as a progressive city, 83, 133; and segregation, 165
Atlanta (Georgia) riot, 83–86, 170
Atlanta Georgian (newspaper), 84
Atlanta Journal (newspaper), 81, 84
Atlanta University, 39, 165, 244
Atlantic Ocean, 80
Auburn Avenue (Atlanta, Georgia), 85
Augusta (Georgia), 78
Aunt Jemima (character), 121, 204, 206–9, 211, 219
Aunt Jemima Mills Company, 206
The Autobiography of an Ex-Colored Man (book), 245

Bailey, H. G., 276
Baker and Farrell, 204
Baker, Vernon, 300
Baldwin, James, 6
Baltimore (Maryland), 12, 13, 241, 308
Banking Act of 1933. *See* Glass-Steagall Act
Banks, Nathaniel, 30
Bannerman, Helen, 199
Barkley, Alben W., 272
Barksdale, Ethelbert, 54
Bates, Ruby, 275, 277, 278, 279, 280
Battistone, Sam Sr., 200
Baum, L. Frank, 116, 118
Bay Area Rapid Transit (BART) Authority, 11
Beaumont (Texas), 306
Belafonte, Harry, 6
Belgium, 194, 299
Belgrave, Bernard (character), 242
Bell, Sean, 10–11
Belton, Roy, 97
Benefield, Trent, 11
Bentonville (North Carolina), 35
Berlin (Germany), 163
Berlin, University of, 164
Berry, Shawn Allen, 7
Bilbo, Theodore G., 143, 147, 271
bimetallism, 115
biracialism, 128, 133
Birmingham (Alabama), 226, 233, 261, 265
The Birth of a Nation (film), 212, 217–22, 225, 226, 228, 229
Black Belt, 157, 189
black buck (character), 209, 212
black brute (character), 201
Black Congress, 254
The Blacker the Berry: A Novel of Negro Life (book), 246
Black, Hugo, 233
Black Jumbo (character), 199
Black Magic (book), 247
Black Man's Verse (book), 246
Black Mumbo (character), 199
Black Nationalism, 250, 257, 258

Black No More: Being an Account of the Strange and Wonderful Workings of Science in the Land of the Free, AD 1933–1940 (book), 258

black soldiers: in the American Revolution, 250; in the Civil War, 27–28; in World War I, 90–91, 250, 251–52, 295–96; in World War II, 192, 295–301, 306–7

Black Star Line, 256, 258, 259

Blackstock, George W., 85

Blair, Henry W., 184

blaxploitation films, 212

Blease, Coleman Livingston, 138, 140–42, 144, 145, 147

blue discharge, 300–1

Boas, Franz, 67

Bohnett, Newell, 200

bolshevism, 91, 92

Bone (film), 212

Borah, William E., 266

Boston (Massachusetts), 5, 214, 222, 240, 248, 248

Bourbons. *See* Redeemers. *See also* Neo-Bourbons

Bowdoin College, 38

Bradley, Joseph P., 62

Bradley, Tom, 7

Brandeis, Louis, 120

Braun, Carol Moseley, 6

Brawley, Tawana, 14

Br'er Rabbit, 199

Brewer, Lawrence Russell, 7–8

Brooke, Edward, 6

Brooklyn Dodgers, 6

Brooklyn (New York), 9

Brough, Charles Hillman, 93, 94, 95

Brown, Henry Billings, 64

Brown, John, 183

Brown, Michael, 8, 12

Brown v. Board of Education of Topeka, 172, 193, 304. *See also* Separate but equal doctrine Bryan, William Jennings, 113–17, 118, 124, 128

buck. *See* black buck (character)

Buchanan v. Warley, 309–10

Buckwheat (character), 210

Bulge, Battle of the, 299

Bull, George, 202

Bunche, Ralph, 303

Bureau of Abandoned Refugees, Freedmen, and Abandoned Lands. *See* Freedmen's Bureau

Bureau of Investigation. *See* Federal Bureau of Investigation

Burton, Scott, 87

Bush, George W., 7

Buster Brown (cartoon), 198

Buster Brown (character), 198

Butler, Benjamin F., 30

Butler, Marion, 128

Butler, Matthew Calbraith, 78

Byrd, James Jr., 7

Caesar's Column (book), 109

Calhoun, John, 146

California, 267

Callahan, Daniel, 92

Callahan, William Washington, 281–82, 283

Calloway, Cab, 249

Cameron, Ben (character), 217–18, 219

Cameron, Flora (character), 217, 218, 219

Camp Logan (Texas), 251

Candler, Allen D., 165

Cane (book), 245–46

Cannon, Joe, 150

"Can't Help Lovin' Dat Man" (song), 206

Cape Fear River, 80

capitalism, 149, 292

Capitol Building, 112

Capitol Hill (Washington, DC), 92

Capone, Al, 195

carpetbaggers, 157, 305; and *The Birth of a Nation* (film), 216, 217, 218, 219; and the Dunning School, 67, 121; and the Mississippi Plan, 54, 55; and Reconstruction, 71, 75, 126, 136; and southern state redemption, 44, 45, 46, 57, 71, 77

Carnegie, Andrew, 158

Carnegie Foundation for the Advancement of Teaching, 303
Carrier, Aaron, 99
Carrier, Sarah, 99
Carrier, Sylvester, 99
Carter, Sam, 99
cartoons, 43; images of blacks in, 121, 196–201, 239, 240
Catholics, 229, 232, 233
Cedar Creek, Battle of, 111
Census Bureau of the United States, 189
Century Magazine, 245
Challenge (journal), 246
Chandler, Zachariah, 32
Charleston (South Carolina), 13, 134, 135
Chattanooga (Tennessee), 274, 276, 281
Chesapeake region, 23
Chesnutt, Charles W., 242, 243
Chester County (Pennsylvania), 247
Chicago (Illinois), 68, 113, 119, 185, 191, 197, 201, 202, 206, 208, 236, 246, 306
Chicago Daily News (newspaper), 94
Chicago Defender (newspaper), 95
Chicago (Illinois) riot, 91–92
Chisholm, Shirley, 6
Christianity, 84, 116, 155, 162, 214, 217, 218, 229, 230, 232, 244
Churchill, Winston, 301
Citizens' Committee of New Orleans, 63–64
Civil Aeronautics Act, 296
Civilian Pilot Training Program, 296
Civil Rights Act of 1875, 51, 56, 62
Civil Rights Act of 1964, 5, 193
Civil Rights Cases, 62
civil rights movement, 1, 118, 193, 207, 212, 238, 273, 305, 307, 313
civil service reform, 110
Civil War, American, 55, 91, 100, 134, 156, 157, 198, 217, 243, 247; and changing race relations, 16, 32, 41, 42, 47, 58, 102; consequences of, 21, 30, 71, 74, 77–78, 106, 214; in public memory, 83, 114, 121, 185, 221; and slavery, 25–26, 30, 125, 155, 195, 308

Civil War amendments, 50, 51, 59, 60, 62, 95, 195. *See also* Fifteenth Amendment; Fourteenth Amendment; Thirteenth Amendment
The Clansman (book), 215–16, 217, 226, 239
Clark, Bob, 269
Clarke, Edward Young, 228–29, 230, 231
Clay, Cassius. *See* Ali, Muhammad
Clemson University, 137
Cleveland (Ohio), 7, 185, 188, 242, 247
Cleveland, Grover, 84, 111, 124, 135
Clifford, George, 202
Clinton, Bill, 300
Clinton (Mississippi), 55
cloture, 272, 273
Clyburn, James, 7
Coca-Cola, 140
Colfax (Louisiana) Massacre, 61, 71–74, 77, 78, 79, 71–74, 77, 78, 79
collective bargaining, 292
Colombia, 252
colonization, 181
Colorado, 111, 183, 269
Colored Farmers' National Alliance and Cooperative Union, 110, 118
"Colored People's Day," 197
Columbia University, 247
commerce clause, 62, 308
Committee of Seven, 93, 94
communism, 92, 172
Coming for to Carry Me Home (book), 1
Coney Island (amusement park), 199
Confederate battle flag, 13
Confederate Memorial Day, 222
Confederate monuments, 13
Confederate Spy (film), 210
Confederate States of America. *See* Southern Confederacy
Confederate veterans, 21, 22, 37, 44, 53, 72, 78, 80, 111, 129, 213, 215, 216
Congress of the United States, 1, 6, 61, 109, 116, 151, 294; and antilynching legislation, 102, 121, 260, 262, 263, 264, 265, 267, 269, 270, 271, 272; and

the Civil War, 27, 33, 34–35, 37; and the Freedmen's Bureau, 36–37, 38–39, 40, 41; and the Great Depression, 288, 289–90, 291; and the Ku Klux Klan (KKK), 77, 229, 230; and racial policy, 5, 22, 34–35, 37, 28–39, 41, 56, 57, 61–62, 64, 162, 217, 260, 305; and World War II, 296, 297, 300

Congress of Industrial Organizations (CIO), 187

Congressional Black Caucus, 6

Congressional Record (publication), 265

Conley, Jim, 223

Connally, Thomas, 270–71, 272, 273

Conroy, Bryan, 10

Constitution of the United States, 36, 59, 110, 193, 252, 264, 271, 314; and Reconstruction, 31, 40, 41, 195; and slavery, 22, 25, 27, 32; and white supremacy, 60–61, 64–65, 214, 253, 282, 304, 311

conscription, 297

Contending Forces: A Romance Illustrative of Negro Life North and South (book), 241

contrabands, 26, 27

Coolidge, Calvin, 259, 261, 286

coon (character), 149, 197, 209, 210–11

"Coon Town" (fictional town), 198

Cooper, Henry Allen, 265–66

Cornell University, 223

Cosby, Bill, 6, 209

Cosmopolitan (magazine), 244

Costigan, Edward P., 269, 270

Costigan-Wagner bill, 270

cotton, 23, 25, 132, 135, 144, 146, 150, 181, 190, 288

Cotton Club, 249

Cotton States and International Exposition, 68, 158–59, 162

Cottonville, Georgia (fictional town), 198

counter-Reconstruction, 42

covenants, racial. *See* racial covenants

covenants, restrictive. *See* racial covenants

Coxey, Jacob S., 112

Coxey's Army, 112

Cream of Wheat, 202, 204, 205

Crisis (NAACP magazine), 95, 172, 245, 247, 258

"Cross of Gold" speech, 113–15. *See also* Bryan, William Jennings

Crow, Jim. *See* Jim Crow

Cuba, 256

Cuff, Jim, 51

Cullen, Countee, 172, 245, 247

Curley, James, 222

Currier and Ives, 197, 198

Daily Record (newspaper), 81, 82

Dallas (Texas), 231

Daniels, Josephus, 220

"Darkies' Day at the Fair" (cartoon), 197

Darktown Comics (cartoon), 121, 197, 198. *See also* cartoons

Darrow, Clarence, 357n21

Darwin, Charles, 66

Darwinism, 53

Davis, Benjamin O. Jr., 299

Davis, Benjamin O. Sr., 299

Davis, Frank Marshall, 246

Davis, Henry Winter, 32, 33

Davis, Jefferson, 43

Davis, R. T., 206

D-Day invasion, 299

de Blasio, Bill, 11

The Debt (film), 211

Decatur (Alabama), 280

Decatur Street (Atlanta, Georgia), 83–84, 85

Declaration of Independence, 41, 195, 255, 305, 314

Declaration of Rights of the Negro Peoples of the World, 255–56

The Deep South region. *See* The South (region)

Democratic donkey (symbol), 196

Democratic National Convention (1896), 113–15

Democratic National Convention (1924), 151

Democratic National Convention (1936), 146
Democratic National Convention (2004), 5
Democratic Party, 124, 126, 184, 233; and antilynching legislation, 264, 266, 267, 269; during the Civil War, 34, 35; and Franklin D. Roosevelt (FDR), 270, 294; and the Ku Klux Klan (KKK), 233; and the Mississippi Plan, 53, 54–55, 63; and Populism, 108, 109, 111, 112, 113, 116, 118, 128, 142; and Reconstruction, 39, 42; and Redemption, 44, 45, 46, 57, 58; and southern wing, 135, 142, 146, 149, 150, 151, 152, 153, 313; and white supremacy generally, 71–72, 76–77, 80–81, 82, 84, 126, 309
DePriest, Jessie, 142
DePriest, Oscar, 142
desegregation, 193, 296, 297, 299, 304, 313
Detroit (Michigan), 185, 189, 191, 311, 357n21
Detroit (Michigan) riots, 306
Detroit River, 306
Dewey, John, 120
Diallo, Amadou, 10
Diamond Milling Company, 202
Dieterich, William, 270
Disneyland, 206
District of Columbia. *See* Washington, DC
Dixiecrats. *See* States' Rights Democratic Party
Dixon, Thomas Jr., 214–17, 219–21, 222, 226, 227, 239, 242
Dolezal, Rachel, 15–16
Donnegan, William, 87
Donnelly, Ignatius L., 109
Dorismond, Patrick Moses, 10
"double consciousness," 167. *See also* Du Bois, W. E. B.
Double V initiative, 296
Douglas, Aaron, 247–48

Douglass, Frederick, 16–17, 47–51, 68, 158, 183, 184
Doyle, H. S., 127
Dred Scott v. Sandford, 65
Drew, George F., 45
Drexel Building, 97
Du Bois, W. E. B., 89, 120, 154, 168, 242, 251–52, 304; background of, 163–67; criticism of Booker T. Washington, 163, 167, 168, 169, 170, 172; and Sam Hose incident, 165–67; and Marcus Garvey, 253, 258; and National Association for the Advancement of Colored People (NAACP), 171–72, 262; and Niagara Movement, 167, 169–70; and United Nations, 307–8
due process of law, 37, 50, 60, 61, 95, 150, 161, 166, 167, 262, 279, 285
due process revolution, 95–96
Duke University, 14
Dunbar, Paul Laurence, 201, 243
Dunning, William Archibald, 67
Dunning School, 67, 121, 318n8
Durham (North Carolina), 14
"Dustie." *See* Gold Dust twins
Dyer, Leonidas Carstarphen, 264–67, 269
dynamic cubism, 249

8th US Colored Troops, 157
East Louisiana Railroad, 63
Eastman, George, 158
East St. Louis (Illinois) riot, 88–89, 264
Ecuador, 252
Edgefield County (South Carolina), 135, 136
Edison, Thomas, 210
Eisenhower, Dwight D., 301
Elaine (Arkansas), 93, 94, 95
Elberton (Georgia), 135
Electoral Commission of 1877, 62
Ellington, Duke, 249
Ellison, Ralph, 240
emancipation, 22, 155, 241; aftermath of, 38, 40, 47, 50, 72; as a goal of the Union in the Civil War, 26, 27, 31,

32, 33, 34, 37, 125, 131; and gradualism, 24, 33; and "re-enslavement" after the Civil War, 53, 54, 55, 182, 308
Emancipation Proclamation, 27, 30, 33, 195
Emanuel African Methodist Church, 13
Emerald City, 116
Emergency Relief Appropriation Act of 1935, 293
Enforcement Act of 1870, 61
England, 119, 301
English, James W., 85
The Enlightenment, 28
equal protection of the law(s), 50, 60, 61, 63, 64, 150, 279, 282, 283, 309, 310, 311
Europe, 90, 91, 150, 164, 184, 188, 194, 225, 247, 295, 299
Evans, Hiram Wesley, 231–33, 234, 235–36
Evans, John Gary, 145
Evansville (Indiana), 235, 306
Executive Order 8802, 298–99
Executive Order 9808, 312–13
Executive Order 9980, 313
Executive Order 9981, 301, 313
Exoduster movement, 183–84
Exodusters. *See* Exoduster movement

54th Massachusetts Volunteer Infantry Regiment, 28
47th Street (book), 246
477th Bombardment Group, 299
Fahy, Charles H., 313
Fair Employment Practices Committee (FEPC), 299, 313
Fair Housing Act of 1968, 193
Farina (character), 210
Farmers' Alliance Exchange, 107, 124, 142
Farm Security Administration (FSA), 289, 290
Fayetteville (North Carolina), 242
Federal Bureau of Investigation, 258–59

Federal Deposit Insurance Corporation, 151
Federal Elections Bill, 264
Federal Emergency Relief Administration (FERA), 293
Federal Reserve System, 145, 151
federalism, 22, 26, 51, 59, 60, 62, 143, 262–63
Felton, Rebecca, 81, 82
Ferguson (Missouri), 8–9, 12
Field, James G., 111
Fiery Cross (newspaper), 235
filibuster, 264, 266, 267, 272, 273. *See also* antilynching legislation; Senate of the United States
films, 209; images of blacks in, 209–13, 239, 240
Fire!! (magazine), 247
Fire-eaters, 44, 57
First Amendment, 61
Fifteenth Amendment, 50, 60–61, 150, 309
Fisk University, 39, 158, 163
Florida, 22, 35, 44, 45, 99, 226, 246, 271, 273
Florida bar examination, 245
Ford, Ezell, 12
For Massa's Sake (film), 210
Foreign Relations Committee of the United States Senate, 32
Forrest, Nathan Bedford, 75, 231
Fort Dix (New Jersey), 306
Fort Lauderdale (Florida), 269
Fort Wagner (South Carolina), 28
Forten, Charlotte, 30
Founders (American), 59, 143, 144, 305
Fourteenth Amendment: and due process of law, 50, 61, 95, 150, 279; and equal protection of the law(s), 50, 61, 63, 64, 150, 282, 283, 309, 310, 311; and Negro rights, 51, 59–60, 62, 64, 271, 308, 309, 311. *See also* due process of law; equal protection of the law(s); privileges and immunities clause
Foxx, Redd, 6

France, 194, 243, 299
Frank, Leo M., 90, 223–25, 227
Franklin, Aretha, 6
Frazier, E. Franklin, 304
Frederick Douglass (ship), 256
free silver. *See* silver standard
freedmen: and *The Birth of a Nation* (film), 217, 218, 219; and the Freedmen's Bureau, 36–41; during Reconstruction, 22, 26, 30–31, 41–42, 66, 156, 305; during Redemption generally, 44, 45, 46, 50, 53, 54, 56, 58, 70, 125, 126, 182; and the Mississippi Plan, 54, 56; and Special Field Order Number 15, 35–36; and US Supreme Court cases, 59, 62; violence against, 70–71, 75, 78, 79, 81, 83, 105, 136, 213
Freedmen's Bureau, 36–41, 157, 162
Freedom Rider, 7
freedpeople (also, freed people). *See* freedmen
Free Soil Party, 32
French Revolution, 44
Fruitvale Station (film), 11
Fugitive Slave Act, 27
Fulton County (Georgia), 85
fusion principle, 46, 82, 118, 128

Gainesville (Florida), 100
Gammage, Jonny, 9
Gardella, Therese "Tess," 206
Garner, Eric, 11–12
Garner, John Nance "Cactus Jack," 152–53
Garrison, William Lloyd, 24–25
Garvey, Marcus, 89, 172, 242, 252–59
Garveyites, 254, 256
"gator bait," 200, 219
Gavagan, Joseph A., 270
Gehrig, Lou, 195
General Electric Company, 313
George, James Z., 54
George, Walter F., 273
Georgia, 7, 39, 81, 123, 184, 189, 241, 272, 273; during the Civil War, 35; and the Leo Frank case, 222, 223,

224, 225; and lynching, 165, 166; and the Mississippi Plan, 56; and the New South, 132; and the People's Party, 124, 125; and the rebirth of the Ku Klux Klan (KKK), 227; and white supremacy, 128
Germany, 164, 299
gerrymandering, 56
GI Bill. *See* Servicemen's Readjustment Act of 1944
Gibson, Althea, 6
Giddings, Joshua, 32
Gillespie, John Birks "Dizzy," 249
Glass, Carter, 151–52
Glass-Owen Federal Reserve Act of 1913, 151
Glass-Steagall Act, 151
Gloucester County (Virginia), 308
God's Trombone (poetry collection), 247
Gold Dust twins, 201–2, 203
Gold Dust washing powder, 201–2, 203
"Golden Thirteen," 299–300
Goldenweiser, Alexander, 67
"Goldie." *See* Gold Dust twins
gold standard, 108
Goldsboro (North Carolina), 214
Gold Standard Act, 116
Gomer, Nina, 164
Gone with the Wind (film), 212
Gonzales, Narciso Gener, 140
Good Luck, Miss Wyckoff (film), 212
Gordon, George W., 75
Grady, Henry W., 129, 130–33
grandfather clauses, 51, 221
Grand Forks (North Dakota), 202
Grand Old Party (GOP). *See* Republican Party
"Grand Parade of the Sons of Ham" (cartoon), 197
The Grange, 46, 106
Granny Maumee (play), 244
Grant, Oscar III, 11
Grant, Ulysses S., 198: as general officer, 21, 132; as president, 32, 44, 57, 77, 136
Grant administration, 55

Grant Parish (Louisiana), 71, 72, 78
Gravely, Samuel L. Jr., 300
Graves, Bibb, 284
Graves, John Temple, 84
Gray, Freddie Jr., 12–13
Great Barrington (Massachusetts), 163
Great Barrington High School (Massachusetts), 163
Great Depression, 100, 149, 152, 172, 187, 192, 194, 273, 274, 294; origins of, 286–87; and New Deal programs, 289, 291, 293. *See also* New Deal
Great Migration, 173, 243, 249, 251, 252, 264, 306; causes of, 179–86; challenges associated with, 177–78; effects of, 186–89, 244, 271; long-term consequences, 190–93; and Second Great Migration, 192–93
Great Plains, 106
Great War. *See* World War I
Greeley, Horace, 27
Green, Nancy, 206, 208
Greenback Party, 46, 106, 110
The Green Pastures (film), 211
Greenwood (Tulsa, Oklahoma neighborhood), 96, 97, 98, 99
Griffin (Georgia), 166
Griffith, David Wark "D. W.," 212, 216–17, 219, 220, 221–22, 227
Griggs, John W., 263
Griggs, Sutton E., 242–43
Grow, Galusha A., 32
Guinn v. United States, 221
Gulf of Mexico, 71
Guntersville (Alabama), 276
Gurley, O. W., 97
Gus (character), 212, 217–18, 219
Guzman, Joseph, 10, 11

habeas corpus, 77, 95, 136
Hadnot, James, 72, 73
Haiti, 68, 181
Hale, John P., 32
Hale's Ford (Virginia), 155
Haley, Nikki, 13
Hall v. DeCuir, 61, 308

Ham, 66
Hamburg (South Carolina) Massacre, 78–79, 80, 136–37
Hamilton, Alexander, 128
Hammond (Indiana), 237
Hampton, Wade, 55
Hampton Institute. *See* Hampton Normal and Agricultural Institute
Hampton Normal and Agricultural Institute, 39, 156, 157, 158
Hansberry, Lorraine, 6
Harding, Warren G., 91, 194–95, 286; and Ku Klux Klan (KKK), 230–31, 262; and race relations, 260–62, 265, 266–67, 268
Harlan, John Marshall, 61–62, 64–65
Harlem, New York (neighborhood), 6, 247, 253, 271; as a center of black culture, 188, 192, 243, 249; as Marcus Garvey's headquarters, 254–55, 256; origins of, 243–44. *See also* Harlem Renaissance
Harlem (New York) riot, 306–7
Harlem Opera House, 243
Harlem Polo Grounds, 243
Harlem Renaissance, 172, 191, 243–50
Harper, Frances Ellen Watkins, 241
Harper's (magazine), 245
Harpersville (Alabama), 226
Harris, Joel Chandler, 166, 167, 199, 239
Harrison, Benjamin, 68, 111, 263, 264
Harrison, Hubert, 244
Harvard University, 159, 163, 164
Hastie, William H., 299, 308
Hawkins, Alfred E., 276, 277
Hayes, Rutherford B., 57–59, 62
Hayes administration, 58
Henderson, John B., 34
Henry V (play), 250
Here's the New Bully (cartoon), 197
The Hindered Hand (book), 242–43
Hirshhorn Museum and Sculpture Garden, 249
History of the Negro Race in America from 1619 to 1880 (book), 68, 304
A History of the Negro Troops in the War of the Rebellion (book), 68

Hoar bill, 264, 266, 272–73
Hoar, George Frisbee, 263–64, 265, 266
Hoar, Samuel, 263
Hogan's Alley (cartoon), 197, 198
Holiday, Billie, 6, 249–50
Hollywood (California), 209, 216, 217
Holmes, Oliver Wendell Jr., 95
Honduras, 252
Hoover, Herbert, 286
Hoover, Lou, 142
Hopkins, Harry, 293
Hopkins, Pauline E., 241–42
Hopkins Colored Troubadours, 241
Horne, Lena, 6
Horse Thief Detective Association
   (organization), 235
Horton, George Moses, 240–41
Horton, James Edward Jr., 280–81, 282
Hose, Sam, 165–67, 170, 263
Houdini, Harry, 195
House of Representatives Rules
   Committee, 230
House of Representatives of the United
   States, 6, 32, 34, 35, 44, 124, 150, 151,
   152, 232; and antilynching legis-
   lation, 264, 265, 266, 270
Houston, Charles Hamilton, 172
Houston (Texas), 233, 251
Howard, Oliver O., 38–39
Howard University, 39, 303
Howell, Clark, 84
How Rastus Got His Turkey (film), 210
"How Ya Gonna Keep 'em Down on
   the Farm After They've Seen
   Paree'?" 251
Hughes, Charles Evans, 282
Hughes, Langston, 172, 246–47, 248
Hull House, 119
Hunter, Jesse, 99
Huntsville (Alabama), 283
Hurston, Zora Neale, 246, 247

Iago (character), 43
I am the American Negro (book), 246
Ickes, Harold, 293
Idaho, 111, 266
"If We Must Die" (poem), 245

Illinois, 32, 270
*Imperium in Imperio: A Study of the Negro
   Race Problem* (book), 242
income tax, 110, 145
Indiana, 32, 55, 184, 233, 235, 236, 237,
   238, 270
indigo, 23
influenza outbreak of 1918 and 1919,
   194
In Humanity's Cause (film), 211
In Re Slaughterhouse Cases, 60–61
In Slavery Days (film), 211
integration, 252, 297, 308
International Labor Defense (ILD),
   278–79
interstate commerce, 61–62. *See also*
   commerce clause
Invisible Empire. *See* Ku Klux Klan
   (KKK)
Invisible Man (book), 240
Iola Leroy, or Shadows Uplifted (book),
   241
Iowa, 110
Irish immigrants, 189
Isnora, Gescard, 10, 11
Italy, 239, 301

Jackson, Andrew, 114
Jackson County (Alabama), 275, 282
Jackson, Edward, 236
Jackson, Mahalia, 6
Jackson, Michael, 6, 209
Jacksonville (Florida), 244–45
Jamaica, 252, 253, 257, 258, 259
Japan, 295, 299
jazz music, 249
Jefferson, Thomas, 29, 128
Jeffersonian (magazine), 224, 225
Jemima, Aunt. *See* Aunt Jemima
Jesus Christ, 115, 166, 215, 219, 229
Jim Crow, 1, 6, 7, 141, 207, 244, 263, 310;
   and Booker T. Washington, 86, 159,
   162; death of the Jim Crow regime,
   153, 273, 301, 311; and the estab-
   lishment of a color line, 68, 77, 196;
   in the federal government, 56, 59,
   308, 309, 311; and the Great

Migration, 173, 177, 178, 185, 188–89, 190, 191, 192; and the National Association for the Advancement of Colored People (NAACP), 171; and the New Deal, 294; origins of state laws, 51, 83; as a popular character, 51, 52; and Populism, 123–24, 128; and the US military, 251, 295, 296, 301, 307, 313; and W. E. B. Du Bois, 163, 252; and violence, 100, 285. *See also* segregation

Johns Hopkins University, 214, 219

Johns Hopkins University Medical School, 226

Johnson, Andrew, 26, 35, 40, 41

Johnson (Andrew) administration, 32

Johnson, Dorian, 8

Johnson, James Weldon, 91, 244, 247, 261, 266, 267

Johnson, Lyndon B., 5, 190

Johnson, Rosamond, 245

Jones, J. B., 166

Jones, J. L., 166

Jones, Loïs Mailou, 248–49

Jones, Marion, 269

Joplin (Missouri), 246

Joplin, Scott, 6

Jordan, Barbara, 6–7

Jordan, Michael, 6, 209

Judge Lynch. *See* lynching

Judiciary Committee of the United States Senate, 34, 264, 265, 266, 270

Judiciary Subcommittee of the United States Senate, 266

Julian, George W., 32

Justice, United States Department of, 313

Kaiser, Kevin, 10

Kansas, 107, 111, 182, 183, 184, 222, 241

Kembel, E. W., 201

Kentucky, 40, 60, 241, 243, 246

Kersands, Bill, 204

Key, V. O. Jr., 16

Keynes, John Maynard, 286

Keynesian economics, 287

King, John William, 7

King, Martin Luther Jr., 5

King, Rodney, 9

Knight, Thomas G. Jr., 281

Knights of Labor, 109

Knights of Mary Phagan, 225, 227

Kokomo (Indiana), 233

Kraemer, Louis, 311

Kroeber, Alfred L., 67

Ku Klux Klan (KKK), 51, 276; and *The Birth of a Nation* (film), 216–22; during Reconstruction, 54, 69, 75–77, 96, 136, 182, 213, 214, 226–27, 228, 231; during the twentieth century, 96, 99, 143, 151, 226–38, 262

Lady Sings the Blues (book and film), 250

LaFollette, Robert Sr., 119–20

Lake Michigan, 91

Lamar, Lucius Quintus Cincinnatus, 44, 57

LaMothe, Ferdinand Joseph. *See* Morton, Jelly Roll

Last of the Mobile Hot Shots (film), 212

The Last of the Scottsboro Boys (book), 285

Latham, Charlie, 275

Latimer, Asbury C., 145

Latin America, 199–200

Lawrence, Jacob, 179, 249

Lawrence (Kansas), 247

League of Nations, 120, 220

Lee, Robert E., 21, 132, 221

Leibowitz, Samuel S., 279, 280, 282, 283, 284

Lenin, V. I., 92

The Leopard's Spots: A Romance of the White Man's Burden, 1865–1900 (book), 215, 239, 242–43

The Liberator (newspaper), 25

Liberia, 181, 183, 256

Liberty Hall, 255

Liberty League (organization), 244

"Lift Ev'ry Voice and Sing" (poem), 245

Lilies of the Field (film), 6

Lincoln, Abraham, 1, 21, 37, 198, 217; and colonization of freed slaves, 181; and emancipation, 27, 30, 32, 35; and the Freedmen's Bureau, 36, 40; legacy of, 86, 108, 162, 171, 294; and the Radical Republicans, 31–33; and wartime reconstruction, 26, 31, 32

Lincoln administration, 32

Lincoln Memorial, 311, 312

Lincoln University, 247

Lindbergh, Charles, 195

Lindsay, Vachel, 247

literacy tests, 51, 56, 63, 152, 221, 273

little black Sambo. *See* Sambo

The Living is Easy (book), 246

Locke, Alain LeRoy, 247

Lodge, Henry Cabot, 267

London (England), 252

Long, Huey P., 147, 149–50

Long, Walter, 218

Long Island (New York), 149

Los Angeles (California), 7, 9, 13, 306

Lost Cause mythology, 47, 56, 239–40

Louima, Abner, 9–10

Louisiana, 221, 249; during the Civil War, 27, 30, 33; and Huey P. Long, 147, 149; and the migration of blacks to other states, 183, 184, 187, 189; and the Mississippi Plan, 56; during Reconstruction, 44, 53, 54; and Redemption, 57, 60, 61–62; and segregation, 62–64; and slavery, 22, 25; violence in, 54, 61, 71–74, 77, 79

Louisiana State Militia, 72

Louisiana Territory, 25

Louisville, New Orleans, and Texas Railway Company v. Mississippi, 61–62

Lowden, Frank, 88

Lowie, Robert H., 67

Lovejoy, Elijah, 32

Lovejoy, Owen, 32

Lynchburg (South Carolina), 144

Lynchburg (Virginia), 151

Lynch, Charles, 100

lynching, 94, 97, 128, 158, 185, 285; federal responses to, 260–67, 269–71; as a form of social control, 81, 120–21, 143, 161, 164, 170, 195, 207, 212, 278, 285; Harding's responses to, 231, 260–62, 266–67; and the Ku Klux Klan (KKK), 218, 232; and the Leo Frank case, 90, 224, 225; literature on, 240, 244, 245; National Association for the Advancement of Colored People (NAACP) investigations of, 120, 171, 261, 262, 266, 267; as part of a mass riot, 87, 89, 96, 99, 100, 101, 165–66, 170; political and popular support for, 137, 140, 143, 240; origins of, 100, 102; statistics on, 100, 274, 287; and Scottsboro Boys case, 274, 275, 276. *See also* antilynching legislation

Lynch, Silas (character), 218, 219

Macon (Georgia), 166

Macune, Charles, 107

Madison Avenue, 209

Madison Square Garden, 255

Maine, 128

mammy (character), 201, 204, 207, 208, 209, 211–12, 272. *See also* Aunt Jemima

Mangum, Crystal Gail, 14

Manhattan (New York), 243

Manly, Alex L., 81–82

Mapes, Emery, 202

Marietta (Georgia), 225

Marion (Indiana), 101

Marriner, William, 200

The Marrow of Tradition (book), 242

Marshall, Thurgood, 172, 308

Marshallville (Georgia), 166

Martin, Trayvon, 8

Maryland, 32

Mason-Dixon Line, 16, 24, 42, 54, 71, 83, 87, 120, 163, 272, 283

Massachusetts, 32, 56, 57, 263, 264

McClure, Samuel, 120

McDaniel, Hattie, 212

McDuffie County (Georgia), 124

McGhee v. Sipes, 311

McGill, Ralph, 147

McKay, Claude, 245
McKenna, Joseph, 63
McKinley, William, 115, 116, 128
McKinley Tariff, 108, 111
McLaurin, George W., 309, 310
McLaurin, John L., 138
McLaurin v. Oklahoma State Regents, 309, 310
Medal of Honor, 300
Meeropol, Abel, 101
Mehserle, Johannes Sebastian, 11
Memphis (Tennessee), 94, 150
Mercer University, 124
Merrill, Lewis, 76, 77
Merrimon, Augustus Summerfield, 42
Metropolitan A. M. E. Church, 47
Metropolitan Museum of Art, 249
Miami (Florida), 269
Michigan, 32, 285, 306
mid-Atlantic states, 24
Middle East, 254
Midwest, 96, 109, 182, 192, 233
Migration Series (paintings), 249
Milledgeville (Georgia), 225
Miller, Benjamin Meeks, 276
Miller, Doris "Dorie," 299
Minnesota, 184
minstrel shows, 51, 202, 204, 210, 244, 249
miscegenation, 81, 181, 211, 214
Mississippi, 151, 184, 187; and the Great Migration, 42; and Retrenchment, 45; and representation in Congress, 43, 44, 57, 143, 150, 265, 271; and slavery, 25; and violence against freedmen, 54–55, 93; and white supremacy, 53, 54, 56, 62, 63
Mississippi Plan, 53–56, 62–63, 80
Mississippi River, 71
Mississippi Valley, 30
Missouri, 34, 107, 184
Missouri Pacific Railroad, 92
Missouri, Supreme Court of, 311
Mobile (Alabama), 306
Montgomery County (Kentucky), 206

Montgomery, Olen, 275, 284
Moody, Milo C., 276, 277
Moody, William H., 264
Moore v. Dempsey, 95, 96
Morand, Paul, 247
Morgan, Irene, 308–9
Morgan, J. P., 111–12
Morgan v. Virginia, 308–9
Morrison, Toni, 6
Morton, Jelly Roll, 249
Morton, Oliver P., 55
Moskowitz, Henry, 171
mulatto, 3, 7, 157, 162, 181, 199, 209, 211, 307
Murphy, Eddie, 6
Myrdal, Gunnar, 2, 303–5, 311

99th Fighter Group, 299
99th Pursuit Squadron, 297
Nash, Christopher Columbus, 72, 73
Nashville (Tennessee), 163, 164
Nast, Thomas, 43, 196–97
Nation (newspaper), 95
National Association for the Advancement of Colored People (NAACP), 15, 86, 261, 307, 310; and *The Birth of a Nation* (film), 222; and the Great Depression, 287–88, 289, 290, 294; and the Great Migration, 187; and the Harlem Renaissance, 242, 244, 245, 247; and lynching and riot investigations, 88, 89, 91, 94–95, 100, 262, 266, 267, 270; origins of, 120, 171–72, 252; and the post-World War II era, 307, 310, 311, 312, 313; and President Harry S. Truman, 311–13; and Scottsboro Boys, 278; and World War II, 296, 297, 301
National Bank of the United States, 114
National Board of Censorship, 222
National Equal Rights League (NERL), 33
National Farmers' Alliance and Cooperative Union of America, 107
National Farmers' Alliance and Industrial Union, 106, 107

The National Grange of the Order of Patrons of Husbandry. *See* The Grange

National Guard, 88, 89, 97, 98, 276, 278

National Industrial Recovery Act, 291

National Medical Association, 68

National Portrait Gallery, 249

National Recovery Administration (NRA), 291, 292

National Urban League, 187, 245, 294, 296

National Weekly (magazine), 150

Native Son (book), 240

Navy Cross (award), 299

Navy, United States, 292, 299, 300

Nazi Germany, 295

Neal v. Delaware, 283

Nebraska, 107, 113

Nebraska, University of, 247

"The Negro Question in the South" (essay), 125–27, 134

Negro soldiers. *See* black soldiers

"The Negro Speaks of Rivers," 247

Negro World (newspaper), 254

Nelson, Levi, 73

Neo-Bourbons, 150–53

Nevada, 111

New Deal, 143, 146, 152, 286–95. *See also* Great Depression

New England, 22, 24, 39, 131, 132, 156

New England Society (organization), 129

New Hampshire, 32, 184

Newnan (Georgia), 166, 263

The New Negro (book), 247

New Negro Movement, 243. *See also* Harlem Renaissance

New Orleans (Louisiana), 30, 33, 60, 71, 221

News and Observer (newspaper), 266

New South, 129, 131–32, 133

New York, 101, 222, 223, 229, 270, 279, 285, 292

New York City (New York), 89, 129, 185, 188, 191, 199, 214, 269

New York Herald (newspaper), 198

New York University, 245

New York World (newspaper), 197, 229, 230

Niagara Movement, 167, 169, 170, 242. *See also* Du Bois, W. E. B.; Trotter, William Monroe

Nicaragua, 252

Niebuhr, Reinhold, 289

Nifong, Mike, 14

"Niggers in the White House" (poem), 142

N. K. Fairbank Company, 201, 203

Noah, 66

Norris, Clarence, 275, 276, 277, 278, 282, 284, 285

Norris v. Alabama, 282

North Africa, 301

North Carolina, 35, 42, 44, 56, 80, 81, 83, 128, 184, 214, 240, 263

North Carolina Central University, 14

North Carolina General Assembly, 214

North Charleston (South Carolina), 12

Not a Man, and Yet a Man (book), 241

Notes on the State of Virginia (book), 29

Oakland (California), 11, 306

Obama, Barack, 5

Oberholtzer, Madge, 236–37

octoroon, 7

The Octoroon (film), 211

Ohio, 32, 112, 164, 184, 197, 243

Oklahoma, 56, 96, 98, 183

Oklahoma State Regents, 309, 310

Oklahoma, University of, 309, 310

"Old Aunt Jemima" (song), 204

Omaha Beach, 299

one-drop rule, 211

Opper, Frederick, 197

Opportunity (National Urban League publication), 245, 247

Othello (character), 43

Our Gang (television series), 210

Outcault, Richard F., 197–99

Ovington, Mary White, 171

Pacific Ocean, 25
Page, Sarah, 96–97
Page, Thomas Nelson, 239–40
Pagones, Steven, 14
Paint Rock (Alabama), 275
Palmetto (Georgia), 165
Pan-Africanism, 257
Panic of 1873, 135
Panic of 1893, 112, 135
Pantaleo, Daniel, 11, 12
Patterson, Haywood, 275, 277, 280, 281, 282, 283, 285
Patterson, Robert P., 297
Patterson v. Alabama, 282
Patton, George S., 299
Peachtree Street (Atlanta, Georgia), 83, 84, 228
Pearl Harbor, 299
Pearl Milling Company, 204
peculiar institution. *See* slavery
Peculiar Sam; or, The Underground Railroad (play), 241
Pendleton, George H., 184
Pennsylvania, 32, 219
Pennsylvania, University of, 165
peonage, 278
People's Party: failures of, 118, 128, 134; origins of, 105–6, 108–12; and "Pitchfork Ben" Tillman, 137, 142; and the Progressives, 119; and Tom Watson, 124, 126, 127, 128; and William Jennings Bryan, 113–16, 118, 128. *See also* Bryan, William Jennings; Tillman, Benjamin Ryan "Pitchfork Ben"; Watson, Tom
People's Party Paper (newspaper), 128
Pepper, Claude, 273
Pepsi-Cola, 140
Perry, Lincoln Theodore Monroe Andrew, 210
Phagan, Mary, 222–23, 224, 225
Philadelphia (Pennsylvania), 30, 306
"Philadelphia Story" (story), 146
Phillips, Ulrich B., 318n8
Phillips, Wendell, 25

Phillips County (Arkansas) riot, 92–95
pickaninnies, 200, 201, 202, 203, 205, 210
Piedmont, Belton (character), 242
Piedmont Hotel (Atlanta, Georgia), 85, 227
Piedmont Park (Atlanta, Georgia), 158
Piedmont region (South Carolina), 77, 135
Pillsbury, Albert E., 264
Plessy, Homer Adolph, 63–64
Plessy v. Ferguson, 63–65, 161, 221, 308, 309. *See also* Separate but equal doctrine
Plymouth Rock, 131
pocket veto, 33
Poems of Miscellaneous Subjects (book), 241
Poetry (magazine), 245
Poitier, Sidney, 6
Polk, Leonidas L., 124
Poll taxes, 45, 51, 56, 63, 135, 152, 193, 273, 313
populism (generally): and biracialism, 111; and the development of a social movement, 106–7; and the fusion principle, 80; and Huey P. Long, 147, 149–50; and the Progressives, 118–19; and the Redeemers, 46; southern populism, 124, 128, 132, 134, 142–43, 144, 147, 149, 150, 152, 153. *See also* biracialism; fusion principle; Long, Huey P.; Populism (social movement); People's Party; Progressives; Redeemers
Populism (social movement): and biracialism, 111, 128; and the election of 1896, 113–16, 118; origins of, 105–12; and "Pitchfork Ben" Tillman, 142; and the Progressives, 119; southern Populism generally, 128, 133, 134, 142–43, 144; and Tom Watson, 123–25, 127, 128, 132, 224. *See also* People's Party; populism (generally); Progressives; Tillman,

Benjamin Ryan "Pitchfork Ben"; Watson, Tom
Populist Party. *See* People's Party
Pore Lil Mose (character), 198–99
Portland (Maine), 241
Postal Service of the United States, 95, 259
Powderly, Terence V., 109
Powell, Adam Clayton Jr., 6
Powell, Colin, 7
Powell, Lazarus, 40
Powell, Ozie, 275, 284
Powell v. Alabama, 279
Pratt, Charles, 92
President's Committee on Civil Rights (PCCR), 312–13
President's Committee on Equality of Treatment and Opportunity in the Armed Services, 313
Pressler, Mike, 14
Price, Victoria, 275, 276–77, 279, 280, 282
Prince, 6
privileges and immunities clause, 60
Progressive Farmers and Household Union of America, 92, 93
Progressives, 118–20, 121, 145, 147, 220, 265
Prohibition, 195
Provident Hospital, 68
Pryor, Richard, 6
Public Works Administration (PWA), 292–93
Puck (magazine), 197
Pullman railroad strike of 1994, 112
Punch (magazine), 201

quadroon, 7
Quaker Oats Company, 206, 207–8
Queenie. *See* Gardella, Therese "Tess"
Queens (New York), 10
Queens of the Golden Mask (organization), 235

"race first," 254
racial covenants, 188, 309–11

Radical Republicans, 44, 57; depicted in *The Birth of a Nation* (film), 218, 219; and disagreements with Abraham Lincoln, 1, 26, 31–32, 33; and the Freedmen's Bureau, 39, 40, 41; legacy of, 1, 162, 217, 305; and the transition from slavery to freedom, 22, 56
Raleigh (North Carolina), 266, 300
Ramitelli (Italy), 298
Randolph, A. Philip, 297
Randolph Truett Davis Milling Company, 206, 208
Rangel, Charlie, 6
The Rape of Florida (book), 241
Rastus, 121, 202, 204, 205, 210, 219
Rastus in Zululand (film), 210
Raymer, Abraham, 87
Readjuster Party, 46
Reagan, Ronald, 7
Reconstruction, 1, 49, 80, 123, 124, 127, 171, 185, 220, 245, 260, 263, 305; and Andrew Johnson's plans for, 41; failures of, 16, 42, 67, 162, 169, 182, 214, 215, 220; and the Freedmen's Bureau, 36–39, 41; postwar effects of, 31, 38, 42, 134, 179; and public memory of, 67, 121, 165, 215–16, 217, 219, 221, 239, 318n8; and Redemption, 44–45, 46, 47, 51, 53–54, 55, 56, 66, 71, 77, 91, 133, 180; and Rutherford B. Hayes, 58–59; and segregation, 193, 272, 306, 313; and the Thirteenth Amendment, 33–35; and the US Supreme Court, 60–62; wartime plans for, 26, 30–31, 32–33, 35; and white supremacy, 29, 30, 75, 78, 96, 129, 136, 196, 212, 213, 226, 227, 228, 231, 313
Red Ball Express, 299
Red Cross, 228
redlining, 188
Redeemers, 44–45, 46, 133–34, 135, 144
Redemption, 44–45, 53, 57–58, 71, 126, 213
Red Shirts (organization), 54–55, 80, 81

Red Summer (1919), 89–96, 245
Remus, Uncle. *See* Uncle Remus
reparations, 15, 99
Republican elephant (symbol), 196
Republican Party, 6, 126, 184; and
    Andrew Johnson, 40–41; and anti-
    lynching legislation, 264, 266, 267;
    and Black Republicans, 72, 73, 80,
    294; and efforts to protect the
    freedmen, 71, 73, 81, 82, 217; and the
    Ku Klux Klan (KKK), 233, 236; and
    Populism, 108, 109, 111, 112, 116,
    118, 142; and Redemption, 53, 54, 55,
    57, 63, 108; and Theodore Roosevelt,
    120; and the Thirteenth
    Amendment, 34, 35; and Warren G.
    Harding, 194, 266–67; and William
    McKinley, 115, 116. *See also* Radical
    Republicans
retrenchment, 45, 46
"Returning Soldiers" (essay), 251–52
Revels, Hiram Rhodes, 43
Revolutionary War, 100
rice, 23, 134, 190, 288
Rice, T. D. "Daddy," 51
The Rider of Dreams (play), 244
rifle clubs, 54, 136
Riis, Jacob, 120
A Rising Wind (book), 301
Roach, Hal, 210
Roaring Twenties, 238
Roberson, Willie, 275, 284
Robeson, Paul, 6
Robinson, Jackie, 6
Rockefeller, John D., 214
Roddy, Stephen, 276, 277
Roof, Dylann, 13
Roosevelt, Eleanor, 270, 294
Roosevelt (Franklin) administration,
    288, 289, 290–91, 296
Roosevelt, Franklin D. (FDR), 145–46,
    147, 149, 152, 153, 172, 294, 296; and
    antilynching legislation, 270; and
    race relations, 297–99; and the New
    Deal, 286, 287, 290, 291, 292, 293
Roosevelt, Theodore, 120; dinner with
    Booker T. Washington, 86, 137, 142,
    162

Rosewood (Florida) riot, 99–100
Ross, Diana, 6, 250
Rowland, Dick, 96–97
Royal Black Steamship Company, 258
Ruffner, Lewis, 156
Ruffner, Viola, 156
Rural Free Delivery, 124
Russell, Daniel Lindsay Jr., 80, 82
Russell, Richard B., 272, 273
Russian Revolution of 1917, 91
Ruth, Babe, 195
Rutt, Chris L., 204, 206

7th Cavalry, 76
761st Tank Battalion, 299
Salvation Army, 228
Sambo, 199–201
Sambo and His Funny Noises (cartoon),
    200
Sambo's (restaurant chain), 200–201
Sambo's on the Beach (restaurant), 201
San Diego (California), 306
Sands Point Bath Club, 149
Sanford (Florida), 8
Santa Barbara (California), 201
Santa Claus (image), 196
Santana, Feidin, 12
Santop Licorice, 258
Savannah River, 78
scalawags, 80, 121, 216, 218
School of the Museum of Fine Arts, 248
Schuyler, George Samuel, 258
Scopes Monkey Trial, 116
Scott, Robert K., 136
Scott, Walter, 12
Scottsboro (Alabama), 275, 276, 278,
    280
Scottsboro bar association, 276
The Scottsboro Boy (book), 285
Scottsboro Boys, 274–85
Sea Islands (South Carolina), 30
Seals, Ray, 9
Second Amendment, 61
Second Great Migration. *See* Great
    Migration
Secret Yearnings (film). *See Good Luck,
    Miss Wyckoff* (film)

segregation, 65, 154, 242, 243, 245, 246; black resistance to, 120; and Booker T. Washington, 170; and the color line, 158, 161, 162, 191; and the death of segregation, 61, 193, 272, 273, 301, 304, 308–14; and Ellison Durant "Cotton Ed" Smith, 145; and the federal government, 17, 60, 61, 63–64, 220, 221; as a form of social control, 66, 67, 68, 10, 120, 121, 158, 180, 201, 278; and the Great Migration, 177–79, 180–81, 187, 190, 192; in higher education, 309, 310; and Marcus Garvey, 253; origins of, 16, 51–52; and "Pitchfork Ben" Tillman, 137, 139; and populism, 110; in residential housing, 96, 293, 309–11; and southern state laws, 1, 16, 51, 83, 196, 201, 262; and Strom Thurmond, 153; in the US military, 250–51, 295, 296, 297, 299, 300, 301, 313; and Warren G. Harding, 261, 262; and W. E. B. Du Bois, 163, 164, 167, 172. *See also* Jim Crow
Selective Training and Service Act, 297
Senate of the United States, 6, 32, 34, 43, 57, 128, 138, 142, 145, 151, 153, 183, 184, 232, 236; and antilynching legislation, 264, 266, 267, 270, 271, 272, 273
Separate but equal doctrine, 64, 161, 172, 196, 309. *See also Brown v. Board of Education of Topeka*; *Plessy v. Ferguson*
Servicemen's Readjustment Act of 1944, 190, 300, 307
settlement house movement, 119
Seventh Amendment, 145
Sewall, Arthur, 128
Seward, William, 35
Shakespeare, William, 43, 250
sharecropping, 59, 186, 188, 190, 287, 288, 289
Share the Wealth, 147
Sharpton, Al, 14
Shaw University, 300

Shelby (North Carolina), 214
Shelley, J. D., 310–11
Shelley v. Kraemer, 311, 357n21
Sherman, William T., 35, 36, 37, 39
Sherman Silver Purchase Act, 111, 112
Shiloh, Battle of, 150
Shipp, Thomas, 101
Shortridge, Samuel, 267
Show Boat (musical), 206
silver standard, 110, 111, 113, 137
Simone, Nina, 6
Simon, the Cyrenian (play), 244
Simmons, William Joseph "Doc," 226–31, 232, 235
Simpson, O. J., 13
Sinclair, Upton, 120
Singleton, Benjamin, 183
Sisson, Thomas,, 265–66
Sixteenth Amendment, 145
Sixth Amendment, 278, 279
Slager, Michael, 12
Slaton, John, 224
Slaughterhouse Cases. See In Re Slaughterhouse Cases
slavery, 51, 68, 155, 163, 240, 246; and the Civil War, 25–36; and Frederick Douglass, 48, 50; in the nineteenth century, 16, 25, 129, 135, 165, 207; origins and evolution, 22–25; in public memory, 16, 81, 210, 211, 215, 241, 318n8; and Redemption, 44–45, 46, 59, 108, 134; and the transition to freedom, 36–42, 64, 70, 71, 74–75, 129, 131, 158, 179, 180, 195; vestiges of, 59, 62, 68, 182, 278, 307–8
'The Slave's Complaint" (poem), 241
Slavery by Another Name (book), 68
Slaves' Escape; or, The Underground Railroad (play), 241
Smith, Abram, 101
Smith, Alexander, 14
Smith, Bessie, 6
Smith, Ellison Durant "Cotton Ed," 144–47, 148, 271
Smith, M. Hoke, 84
Smith, Michael, 14

Smith, Susan, 14
Smith v. Allwright, 309
social gospel movement, 244
socialism, 108, 110, 149, 235, 244, 291
The Song of the South (film), 211
The Souls of Black Folk (book), 167
The South (region): in the antebellum
  era, 23; and antilynching legislation,
  264, 265, 271, 272; and Booker T.
  Washington, 157, 158, 159, 169, 253;
  and black political power, 80; and
  black soldiers, 295; and the Civil
  War, 21, 25, 26–27, 55, 126, 198;
  during the Great Depression, 287,
  292, 293, 294; and the Great
  Migration, 172–73, 177, 178–79, 182,
  183, 185, 188–89, 190, 192, 193, 243,
  274; and Gunnar Myrdal, 303, 305,
  318n8; and the Ku Klux Klan (KKK),
  75, 96, 151, 214, 215, 216, 218, 227,
  232; and the Leo Frank case, 222,
  224, 225; and the Lost Cause
  mythology, 239–40; and lynching,
  143, 244, 269; and the New South,
  129, 131, 132, 133, 149; and
  Populism, 105, 109, 110, 111, 116,
  118, 127, 133, 142; and race
  generally, 125, 131, 134, 153; and
  Reconstruction, 39, 41, 121, 179,
  318n8; and Redemption, 42, 44, 45,
  46, 48, 51, 58, 71, 123, 126, 128; and
  Scottsboro Boys case, 275, 277, 278,
  280, 281, 285; and slavery, 25; and
  Thomas Dixon's works, 215, 216,
  217, 218, 221; and violence against
  blacks generally, 74, 78, 79, 86, 88,
  138, 306; and Warren G. Harding,
  261; and W. E. B. Du Bois, 164, 169;
  and white supremacy, 42, 53, 56, 69,
  71, 75, 134, 135, 138, 144, 147, 196.
  See also New South
South Carolina, 7, 263; and Coleman
  Blease, 138, 140, 141, 142; and
  Ellison Durant "Cotton Ed" Smith,
  144–47, 148; and the Great
  Migration, 189; racially motivated
attacks in, 12, 13; and the Civil War,
  28, 30, 35; and "Pitchfork Ben"
  Tillman, 137–39, 140; and Reconstruction, 44; and Redemption,
  134–35; and Strom Thurmond, 153;
  and white supremacy, 54, 55, 56,
  76–77, 78, 79, 80, 136, 271
South Carolina Constitution, 135
South Carolina Negro Militia, 78
Southern Confederacy, 39, 41, 71, 78;
  and Alexander Stephens, 195; and
  Jefferson Davis, 43; values asso-
  ciated with, 21, 53, 56, 57, 80, 107,
  131, 132, 135, 165, 224, 305; and
  Reconstruction, 86; and the war, 80,
  144
Southern Cotton Association, 144–45
Southern Farmers' Alliance, 107, 109
Southern Publicity Association, 228–29
Southern Railway, 274
South Pacific, 301
Spanish-American War, 226
Special Field Order Number 15, 35, 37
Spokane (Washington), 15
Springfield (Illinois) riot, 86–88, 170
Springfield (Ohio), 241
Springsteen, Bruce, 10
Stacy, Rubin, 269–70
Starnes, Joseph, 276
Starr, Ellen Gates, 119
State (newspaper), 140
Staten Island (New York), 11
state rights, 60, 62, 137, 143, 146, 264,
  269, 271
States' Rights Democratic Party, 153
Steffens, Lincoln, 120
Stephens, Alexander, 195
Stephenson, David Curtis "Steve," 233,
  235–38
Stepin Fetchit (character), 210–11, 219
sterilization, 278
Stevens, Thaddeus, 32, 219
Stevenson (Alabama), 274
St. Ann's Bay (Jamaica), 252
St. Crispin's Day speech, 250
Stimson, Henry, 299

St. Joseph (Missouri), 204, 206
St. Joseph Gazette, 204
St. Louis (Missouri), 109, 183, 264, 310
Stockholm syndrome, 159
Stokes, Carl, 7
Stone, I. F., 120
Stone Mountain (Georgia), 227
The Story of Little Black Sambo (book), 199, 200
Stowe, Harriet Beecher, 199, 209, 215
"Strange Fruit" (poem), 101
Student Nonviolent Coordinating Committee, 7
"subtreasury plan, 137
Sumner, Charles, 32, 44, 56, 57, 62
Supreme Court, United States, 120, 172, 220, 233, 267; and the assault on segregation, 5–6, 193, 304, 308, 309, 310, 311, 312; and the Scottsboro Boys case, 278, 279, 282, 283, 285; and support for segregation, 17, 51, 56, 60, 62, 63, 64, 161, 221, 308; and twentieth century race cases, 95–96, 278–79
Sweatt, Heman Marion, 309
Sweatt v. Painter, 309
Sweet, Ossian, 357n21
Sweetwater Sabre Club, 136
Syracuse (New York), 33

332nd Fighter Group, 299
Taft, William Howard, 172
"talented tenth," 163, 169–70. *See also* Du Bois, W. E. B.
Tarbell, Ida, 120
Taylor, Fannie, 99
Tennessee, 27, 39, 183
Ten Pickaninnies (film), 210
Terrell, Mary Church, 171
Texas, 25, 107, 152, 184, 189, 241, 242, 270, 273, 309
Texas Law School, University of, 309
Thackeray, William Makepeace, 199
Thanksgiving, 227
Their Eyes Were Watching God (book), 246

Theodore Roosevelt Memorial Fund, 228
Third Army, 299
Thirteenth Amendment, 30, 35, 50, 62, 64, 179
Thurman, Wallace, 246, 247
Thurmond, J. Strom, 142, 153
Till, Emmett, 356n10
Tillman, Benjamin Ryan "Pitchfork Ben," 135–40, 143, 144, 145, 147, 149, 153
Tillman, Jim, 140
Tillman Act of 1907, 137
Time (magazine), 233, 246
Titanic, RMS (ship), 256
tobacco, 23, 132, 181, 190, 288
Tom (character), 209–10, 211
Toomer, Jean, 245–46
Topsy (character), 210
Topsy and Eva (film), 210
Torrence, Ridgely, 244
To Secure These Rights: The Report of the President's Committee on Civil Rights (report), 313
tragic mulatto. *See* mulatto
The Traitor (book), 239
Trenton (South Carolina), 135
Triangle Shirtwaist Factory fire, 119
Trotter, William Monroe, 167
Truman, Harry S., 301, 311–13
Tulsa (Oklahoma) riot, 96–99
Tulsa Fire Department, 97–98
Tulsa Race Riot Commission, 99
Tuskegee (Alabama), 297
Tuskegee Airmen, 298, 299
Tuskegee Army Air Field, 297
Tuskegee Institute, 68, 157–58, 159, 164, 170, 253, 297
Tuskegee Normal School for Colored Teachers. *See* Tuskegee Institute
Tuskegee Normal Industrial Institute. *See* Tuskegee Institute
Tuskegee University. *See* Tuskegee Institute
Twenty-Fourth Amendment, 6, 193
Tybee Island (Georgia), 81
Tyler, Mary Elizabeth, 228–29, 230, 231

Uncle Ben's Rice, 209
Uncle Remus (character), 166, 199, 211, 239
Uncle Sam (image), 197
Uncle Tom. *See* Tom (character)
Uncle Tom's Cabin (book), 199, 209
Uncle Tom's Cabin (film), 210
Uncle Tom's Cabin (play), 215, 216
Underwood, Charles G., 204, 206
Underwood, Oscar W., 151, 267
Union (South Carolina), 14
United States Military Academy at West Point, 38
United States v. Cruikshank, 60, 61
United States v. Reese, 60–61
Universal Negro Improvement Association (UNIA), 89, 253, 254. *See also* Garvey, Marcus
Up from Slavery (book), 155, 156, 253
Utah Beach, 299
Uvalde (Texas), 153

Valentino, Rudolph, 195
Valparaiso College, 235
Vance, Zebulon B., 184
Vanity Fair (book), 199
Van Nuys, Frederick, 270, 271
Vardaman, James K., 143, 144, 145, 147, 150
Vasquez, Anthony, 10
Vaudeville, 195, 206
Venezuela, 252
Viareggio (Italy), 300
Vicksburg (Mississippi), 30
Villard, Oswald Garrison, 171
Vinson, Frederick Moore, 309, 311, 312
Virginia, 23, 27, 39, 46, 56, 100, 111, 156, 220, 221, 239, 308
Virginia Union University. *See* Wayland Seminary
Virginia, University of, 150
Voice (newspaper), 244
Voorhees, Daniel W., 184
Voting Rights Act of 1965, 5, 193

Waco (Texas), 107
Waddell, Alfred Moore, 82

Wade, Benjamin, 32, 33
Wagner, Robert F., 269, 270, 271, 292
Wagner-Van Nuys bill, 270, 272
Waite, Morrison R., 60–61
Wake Forest College, 214
Walker, Alice, 6
Wall Street, 144
Wallace, George, 153, 285
Walling, William English, 171
Walton County (Georgia), 356n10
Wann, M. L., 275, 276
Wappingers Falls (New York), 14
War Department of the United States, 37, 297, 301
War on Poverty, 190
Ward, William, 72
Warren Court, 96
Warren, Earl, 304
Warwick, Dionne, 6
Washington, Booker T., 68, 86, 137, 142, 164, 252, 297; and accommodationist approach to race relations, 159–62, 167; and Atlanta Compromise, 158–59, 163, 262; background of, 154–58; Du Bois' criticism of, 163, 167, 168, 169, 170, 172; and Marcus Garvey, 253, 254 Washington County (Mississippi), 63
Washington, DC, 47, 64, 76, 112, 125, 144, 145, 233, 234, 297, 312
Washington, DC, riot, 92
Washington, George, 198
Watson, Tom, 123–29, 130, 131, 132, 134, 135, 137, 142; and the Leo Frank case, 224–25
Watson's Magazine, 224
Wayland Seminary, 156
Ways and Means Committee of the United States House of Representatives, 6, 32
The Weary Blues (book), 247
Weaver, James B., 110
Wellington (fictional town), 242
Wells-Barnett, Ida B., 171
Weems, Charley, 275, 278, 284, 285
West Africa, 240, 247

West Coast, 185
West, Dorothy, 246
West Virginia, 156
West Virginia militia, 156
West Virginia, USS (ship), 299
wheat, 288
Wheatley, Phillis, 240, 241
Whig Party, 44
White, Edward D., 220–21
White, George Henry, 263
White, Walter F., 86, 94–95, 270, 297, 301
White, William Allen, 120
White House, 86, 91, 137, 142, 162, 219, 220, 230, 236, 267, 286, 294
White League (organization), 54, 71
White Line (organization), 54, 69
White Man's Party (organization), 54
White Star Line, 256
white supremacy, 13, 66, 100, 180, 213, 259; decline of, 313–14; and the federal government, 58, 59, 60, 120; and Franklin D. Roosevelt (FDR), 294; and the Ku Klux Klan (KKK), 229, 231, 232; and the National Association for the Advancement of Colored People (NAACP), 95; and "Pitchfork Ben" Tillman, 135–36, 137, 138; and Populism, 110, 118; and Redemption, 44, 45–46, 54; and the Southern Confederacy, 21, 56; and southern politicians in general, 143–47, 152; and southern states, 17, 56, 59, 77, 83, 120, 123, 196, 261, 271, 273, 281; and Thomas Dixon, 216; and Tom Watson, 128–29, 135, 224; and the US Supreme Court, 63–64, 95; and violence against freedmen, 71–73, 120–21; and W. E. B. Du Bois, 169; and Woodrow Wilson, 220. *See also* Jim Crow; segregation
Whitman, Albery Allson, 241
Wilberforce University, 164, 241
Williams, Billy Dee, 6
Williams, Daniel Hale, 68
Williams, Eugene (Chicago youth), 92

Williams, Eugene (Scottsboro defendant), 275, 284
Williams, George Washington, 68, 304
Williams, G. Mennen, 285
Williams, John Sharp, 150–51
Williams v. Mississippi, 62–63
Wilmington (North Carolina) riot, 80–83, 84, 242
Wilson, Charles E., 313
Wilson, Darren, 8, 9, 12
Wilson, Henry, 32
Wilson, Woodrow, 90, 91, 116, 150, 151, 220, 239; and Thomas Dixon, 214, 219–20, 221
Wilson administration, 151, 267
Windom, William, 184
Winthrop College, 137
Wisconsin, 119, 265
Wizard of Oz, 116, 118
Wizard of Tuskegee. *See* Washington, Booker T.
The Wonderful World of Oz (book), 116, 118
Woodard, Isaac, 356n10
Woodmen of the World, 226
Woods, Tiger, 6, 209
Woodward, C. Vann, 111
Woodward, James G., 85
The Wooing and Wedding of a Coon (film), 210
Works Progress Administration (WPA, also Works Projects Administration), 293–94
World War I, 90, 91, 98, 120, 182, 184, 194, 235, 239, 243, 267; and Black Nationalism, 250, 254; and black soldiers, 295–96; and racial issues, 213, 220, 225, 228, 241, 260, 264, 306
World War II, 1, 190, 192, 294–301, 303, 306, 310
World's Columbian Exposition, 197, 206, 208
Wormley Agreements, 57
Worth, Thomas, 197
Wright, Andrew (Andy), 275, 284, 285
Wright, Leroy (Roy), 275, 278, 284

Wright, Richard, 181, 240
Wyeth, N. C., 208

xenophobia, 223

Yarmouth (ship), 256
Yazoo City (Mississippi), 55
Yazoo County (Mississippi), 150

yellow fever, 183
Yellow Kid (character), 197

zambo. *See* Sambo
Zimmerman, George, 8
Zongo, Ousmane, 10
Zoot-Suit riots of 1943, 306
Zululand, 210

About the Author

J. Michael Martinez works in Monroe, Georgia, as a government affairs representative and corporate counsel with a manufacturing company. He also teaches political science as a part-time faculty member at Kennesaw State University in Kennesaw, Georgia. Martinez is the author or co-author of nine previous books, including *Carpetbaggers, Cavalry, and the Ku Klux Klan: Exposing the Invisible Empire during Reconstruction* (2007) and *Coming for to Carry Me Home: Race in America from Abolitionism to Jim Crow* (2012), both available from Rowman & Littlefield. Visit him on the Internet at www.jmichaelmartinez.com.